JUNG, MY MOTHER AND I

EDITED AND NARRATED BY JANE CABOT REID

for Michael, Diana, Christopher, Christina and Henry

Jung, My Mother and I

The Analytic Diaries of Catharine Rush Cabot

Edited and Narrated
by Jane Cabot Reid

DAIMON
VERLAG

We are grateful to the various contributors (see "Acknowledgements") for permission to include photographs and excerpts from correspondence, in particular: the Erbengemeinschaft C.G. Jung, represented by Niedieck Linder AG; Eva Sarasin; Markus Fierz; and Dr. Paul Naeff

ISBN 3-85630-601-3

Cover design by Macnab Design Visual Communication, Albuquerque, NM

Cover photos from the Jane Cabot Reid Archive

Contents

Preface

The world of today is familiar with the considerable contributions of Carl Gustav (C.G.) Jung (1875-1961) of Switzerland, who, together with Sigmund Freud (1856-1939), pioneered our attitudes and possibilities for self-reflection and for understanding ourselves as never before. His scientific writings span some twenty volumes, and his 'autobiography' (*Memories, Dreams, Reflections*, compiled and edited by Aniela Jaffé) enjoys wide popularity to this day. Jungian Training Institutes and interest groups are to be found throughout the world, and many of his concepts describing phenomena once little recognized but now well-known have become a part of our everyday language: introvert/extravert, complex, animus/anima, collective unconscious, synchronicity, projection, or shadow.

Jung's students and admirers – as well as his detractors – have been prolific in putting their observations and reflections into print or onto film. There have been numerous textbooks, biographies, public lectures and television documentaries about him and his work, each from another perspective, each demonstrating how this remarkable Swiss pioneer contributed to our culture and knowledge.

The present volume approaches C.G. Jung and his contributions from a different point of view – one that has scarcely been represented previously. Catharine ('Katy') Rush Cabot (born in Germantown, Pennsylvania, in 1894) was a young American woman living in Zürich in the late 1920's when she first sought the help of C.G. Jung. From her initial consultation until Jung's death in 1961, she kept careful diaries recording the details of her analytic sessions with him as well as vivid recountings of many other events in her life. These included

her trips with Jung and his associates to the annual Eranos Confer-
ences in Ascona, visits to Jung's Bollingen Tower in Küsnacht, her
participation in the events of the Psychological Club of Zürich, as well
as events from the social scene of Zürich life, with particular refer-
ence to Jung and his circle, to which she came to belong. It was not
only Jung himself who was to have such a powerful influence upon
her: Mrs. (Emma) Jung, Toni Wolff, Barbara Hannah, Linda Fierz,
Dr. Carl Alfred (C.A.) Meier, Dr. Marie-Louise von Franz and other
leading figures from the early Zürich days came to play integral roles
in the life of Catharine Rush Cabot in the ensuing decades.

The diary entries themselves are augmented with photographs
from the period, many taken by the diarist herself and never before
published. There are also numerous private letters from Jung and
some of the others who were key figures in Katy's life story. With the
authoress' inclusion not only of personal family material but also of
these illustrative documents, it transforms from being 'merely' her
own story, of interest in its own right, to a more timeless, impersonal
documentation of indisputable historical value to practitioners and
scholars of Jung's work.

Katy's daughter, Jane Cabot Reid (born in Bern, Switzerland, in
1923), grew up in this same milieu during the years covered by the
diaries (ca. 1929 – 1960) and thus experienced many of the same
events and relationships as her mother, albeit from the perspective of
a child and then as a young woman. 'Janey' herself was unaware of
the existence of the secretly kept diaries until after her mother's death
in 1976. She married, raised five children and later returned to Zürich
to become a Jungian analyst, which she remains to this day. She
recognized the unique perspective and value of the diaries – not only
as an unprecedented personal record, but also as an invaluable
historical document, offering a view of Jung and his psychology that
has never before been revealed.

In the present narrative, we are granted the privilege of observing
and experiencing – from the perspective of the 'patient' herself – just
how intimately, and even humoristically, Jung responded and
worked. We know of his passion and his empathy, and his occasional
outbursts of anger are legend, along with his brilliant intuitions and
his uncompromising confrontations in the depths of the unconscious.
But in the chronicling of Catharine Rush Cabot, we find for the first
time an undiluted and powerful recording of Jung conducting an
analysis with a highly charismatic and unusual woman, extending

over three decades. It directly illustrates not only how he worked 'clinically,' but also evokes, at times, poignantly, who he himself was. We see how Jung was inclined to proceed using his powerful intuition and natural instincts, with often dramatic results, and we also see that – in contrast with today's great attention to 'boundaries' and 'limits' – the phenomena of transference and counter-transference were not preeminent concerns of Jung and his circle.

I feel strongly that the material of which *Jung, My Mother and I* consists should first and foremost be allowed to speak for itself, without undue interference; consequently, these introductory remarks shall remain brief. And yet, there are still some issues to be addressed. The question will inevitably be raised – as, in fact, it already was at the outset both by the authoress and myself – as to whether or not such 'personal' and 'private' material should be made accessible to a public readership. After all, what transpires behind the closed doors of a therapist's consulting room is to be treated with the utmost confidentiality and discretion. Certainly, any publication of these private diaries at the time of the actual events described would *not* have been appropriate. However, we now have entered the Twenty-First Century, and even those individuals merely referred to in passing – not to mention the protagonists themselves – are no longer of this world. With that, the material of Katy's diaries belongs ever less to the personal or private realm and ever more to an objective, impersonal one with an undeniable collective interest and value. The diaries reveal typical examples of projection, envy, shadow issues, compensation and many other phenomena of our daily lives providing potential for change, and we see how analyst and analysand, doctor and patient, proceed in their work through the labyrinth. The invaluable educational contribution it provides and the conviction of Katy's next-of-kin that publication is appropriate were the primary factors behind the decision to now make this material publicly available.

Whether in agreement or not with what transpired in the course of the analysis and how it was understood at the time, we are in any case provided with fascinating biographical material that can help us to reflect on our own stories and our own approaches to life. For much of what transpires in the course of these pages is not merely 'Catharine's story,' but rather a timeless and nameless one that can be found anywhere and at any time – wherever there is human life. In this sense, it can be very relevant for us, here and now.

Finally, historically, we can also observe how C.G. Jung, while never ceasing to develop and revise his analytical theories, here experienced a highly personal, surprisingly warm and intimate contact with a remarkable, charming and vivacious woman, who, again and again in the course of their relationship, never failed to elicit the most unsuspected qualities within Jung himself. It makes this story both a touching and unexpectedly revealing one.

We owe a debt of gratitude to Catharine Rush Cabot for having recorded her experiences in these precious and timeless diaries and also for having entrusted them, at the end of her life, to her only daughter, Jane. As well, we owe much to Jane Cabot Reid herself for having the courage, the insight and the magnanimity to bring the diaries forth, to gather additional illustrative material and to share this fascinating story with us all.

Robert Hinshaw
Boulder, Colorado
October, 2000

Acknowledgements

My thanks are due to a number of people, whom I would like to mention in chronological order. First, Rhoda Isaac, who, over twenty years ago, when we were training together at the Jungian Klinik am Zürichberg, read my mother's analytical hours with Jung, and said the diaries should be published. Her enthusiasm gave me much encouragement, and motivated me to seek a second opinion.

Shortly thereafter, Professor C.A. Meier read the diaries. He made some suggestions and corrections. He was also of the opinion that the diaries were worth publishing. Some years later, in 1992, I visited him to obtain some extra information. Again he generously gave me of his time, and I am sad that, because of his death in 1995, he was unable to see this book in print.

I also mentioned the diaries to the Jungian analyst, Sonia Marjasch. She suggested I send them to a younger Danish colleague of hers to read, who had not known Jung personally. Kirsten Rasmussen read them, and sent me useful suggestions and advice both on paper and on tape. She too thought the diaries should be published. To Kirsten I would like to express warm thanks for her considered advice.

The above opinions were valuable and removed any doubts I had about publishing such personal material.

Sonia Marjasch also gave me the name of the publisher and Jungian analyst, Robert Hinshaw of Daimon Verlag. He thought the diaries could be expanded to include biographical information about my mother, the story of our life together and some family background. He also advised me to learn to use a computer! I am grateful for his suggestions and also for the editing which he and John Peck provided in preparing the material for publication.

Thanks are due to my daughter Diana Macleod, for carefully reading the ms. and making corrections and suggestions; her approval of it was important to me. My thanks also go to my son Christopher, my daughter Christina Vuillin and my daughter-in-law Lucy Blackburn Reid, all of whom read parts of the manuscript and provided feedback, and to Mr. Alberto Braconi of Lausanne for his 'technical support.'

I would like to express my gratitude to the Jung family for allowing me to print many letters my mother received from C.G. Jung and Emma Jung. My thanks also go to Joan Meier and her daughter Eva Sarasin, for allowing publication of Fredy's letters; to Professor Markus Fierz for permission to include his mother's letters in the ms., and to Paul Naeff, a nephew of Toni Wolff, for giving me permission to publish some of her letters. All of these letters have been a valuable addition to the manuscript.

Family letters, many sent to me by John and Jane Bradley from Boston, have been crucial in giving family background to the book. I would like to thank them particularly for sending the correspondence between my father and his parents.

Last but not least, thanks go to Jim Kelly, the official historian of the *U.S.S. William R. Rush*, for sending me information which I lacked on my grandfather's years of service in the U.S. Navy.

Jane Cabot Reid

Introduction

My mother was living in her Villa on the *Corso degli Inglesi* in San Remo, Italy, when she was taken ill with a heart attack and stroke early in April 1976. Though ailing all winter she had remained socially active, and once stricken she expected to be nursed at home. Much to her annoyance the doctor insisted she must go to a clinic. Being very independent, Catharine notified no one in her family, but simply packed her bag, called a taxi, and settled in at the clinic. The doctor, knowing that she was seriously ill yet noticing that no relatives were turning up, tactfully asked her if she had any family. She admitted that she had.

My youngest daughter Christina and her husband, who lived in Trieste, were the first to reach her bedside. My youngest son Henry came directly from the end of term at his school in the Engadine. Eventually I was contacted in a mountain hut in the Bernese Oberland, where I was leading an alpine ski course. When I arrived three days later, my mother showed no signs of having had a stroke or a heart attack, so I assumed both had been slight. She was not her vigorous self, but then she had not been for several months. In fact, she appeared more energetic than before; she was not allowed much time in bed, the nurses having her sit in a chair in her room and walk up and down stairs several times a day. She seemed to enjoy these excursions, and seemed to all of us to be on the road to recovery. For three weeks, over Easter, we visited her twice a day. Not only did she say she enjoyed our visits and their regularity, but also one day, out of the blue, she suddenly turned to us and declared that she *now* realized how important it was to have a family – for her a profound statement, as she had always disparaged family ties.

After Easter my daughter and her husband returned home, and my son also had to leave. One of my other three children was in Brazil, the other two in the United Kingdom. I stayed on in San Remo, and one day when my mother and I were alone in the clinic bedroom, she rose from her chair by the window and, without saying a word, crossed to the Wardrobe and took from its shelf a thick brown-paper parcel tied with string, which she handed to me saying in a casual tone of voice, "Take this home and let me know what you think of the contents."

She volunteered no further information. Back at her Villa I laid it aside unopened, as I suspected it might contain a problem which I would be unable to deal with before leaving next morning for Switzerland. The doctor, seeing my mother's improvement, had let me go off to attend to matters left undone because of my hasty departure nearly a month earlier. When I told my mother I was driving to Switzerland for a couple of days, she instantly asked me to go via Ascona, off my route, to collect an inscribed photograph of Jung which she had in her flat. Though I noticed her disappointment, I told her that I had no time for the detour and that the photo could be fetched later. Awaiting me at home in Lucerne was a large pile of mail among which I found a volume of the *C.G. Jung Letters*,[1] with a photo of Jung as its frontispiece. I took it with me back to San Remo, hoping it would make up for my failure to produce the picture, and it did: my mother was thrilled and kept the book by her bedside like a Bible.

Before visiting my mother, I stopped at the Villa to fetch my eldest daughter Diana and her baby daughter, just arrived from Scotland. When we entered my mother's bedroom she was in her chair by the window wearing her blue house robe, looking exactly as when I had left two days before. But an uncanny feeling came over me and I said to myself, "She is no longer of this world." Though her body was present I sensed that she had gone. This feeling evaporated when she spoke, but after we left I asked my daughter how she had found her grandmother. "Much better than I had expected." Her words comforted me. The following day my mother told us how thrilled she was to have the new Jung book, that she kept it by her bedside and

---

[1] *C.G. Jung Letters*. Routledge & Kegan Paul, London, 1976, Vol. 2

Last photo of Katy on Clinic balcony, April 1976,
with daughter Jane and granddaughter Christina

frequently browsed in it. We also walked the clinic stairs together. Everything seemed normal, so I forgot my premonition.

The day after that my daughter and I went to the hairdresser early before visiting the clinic. The clinic reached us by telephone to come quickly. We found my mother propped up on pillows receiving an intravenous infusion, appearing calm. After greeting us in a firm voice, she announced that her kidneys had stopped functioning and that apparently there was no way to make them work again. Before I really took in what this meant, she cracked a joke which made us laugh. I vowed to remember the witty remark, but promptly forgot it. She gradually fell asleep from a sedative in the infusion; while my granddaughter Catharine toddled blissfully around the room, the doctor told us the end would come in a matter of hours. We hastily returned to the Villa to make some important international calls (the clinic's exchange was being rewired) which took a long time to put through. Just as we were leaving to return, a message came that my mother had died peacefully in her sleep. Though she had not wakened, I was sad that I was not with her when she died. During the next few busy weeks, I forgot all about the brown-paper parcel. When I finally opened it and discovered all kinds of notebooks in longhand and typescript recording in detail her sessions with Jung over twenty-five years, I regretted the delay, as it was impossible to give her an opinion. But remembering the way in which she handed me the parcel (she did not insist that I attend to it immediately), and knowing she would have said so had she wanted me to read them promptly, I concluded that she was leaving it to me to decide what to do with the diaries.

Strangely, it never occurred to me to wonder *why* my mother had taken them with her to the clinic. But hindsight instructed me. The following winter I learned that she had often discussed Jung with her doctor and that he was fascinated by what she told him of her analytical hours. He told Christina, who hinted he would like to acquire the notebooks, but she was evasive. After my mother's death this same doctor approached me through a middleman who phoned me at the Villa to persuade me to part with them, saying it had been my mother's wish for her doctor to have them. Knowing how *mafioso* certain people in San Remo were, I whisked the parcel off to Switzerland as soon as possible.

While I knew only too well that my mother would never wish her documents to fall into a stranger's hands, the fact that she had discussed them with a stranger made me realize that she might not be averse to having them reach a wider audience. Among her papers I found a longhand letter addressed to her son-in-law in November 1972 which says, "I must 'get down' to my Jung memoires, after November 15th in Ascona, as here [San Remo] it's impossible to get down to *anything*." My mother never found the energy to write her "Jung Mémoires" in Ascona or anywhere else, but they might have been superfluous as her memories of Jung are lodged directly in the record of her analysis, where she vividly portrays both him and the Jungian group he led in Zürich from the 1930s through the 1950s. As she had no axe to grind, she portrayed the Jung we knew at the time. Toni Wolff, in a letter to my mother in August 1945, wrote, *"I really do think that you understand Dr. Jung's teaching far better and deeper than almost anyone else."*

Neither during my childhood nor later did my mother mention that she was writing up her sessions with Jung. When I finally read the notebooks, it became obvious, from her spontaneous rendering, that much she had taught me about analytical psychology in my early years arose straight from her hours with Jung rather than from the books she had read.[1] Not only do the notebooks confirm what she had taught me *viva voce*, but they portray Jung as I remember him, faithfully recording many of the turns of phrase he used when speaking English. How she did this was a mystery to me, so I asked Professor C. A. Meier, with whom she had analyzed, how she did it, and he replied that during her hours with him she wrote constantly. Eventually I found a set of notes from her last recorded session with Jung, in a mixture of longhand and shorthand. Though not written out in full, I have included it nonetheless. I have rendered all of her session notes as she wrote them with only minimal editing. I have also included a great deal of other primary material that came to light as I went through my mother's papers: letters from Jung, Mrs. Jung, Toni Wolff and other members of the psychological group in Zürich written in the 1930s and 1940s.

Katy began analysis with Jung late in 1929, but did not begin recording her sessions on a regular basis until 1934. Much of her analysis deals with her psychological problems and involves her family background and personal history. Catharine's childhood, adolescence and marriage were all pertinent to her seeking out Jung, so I acquaint the reader with her family and personal background before the record of the analysis begins. Once that record opens, the analysis also revolves around members of the Zürich psychological group from the 1930s through the 1950s, and so Zürich Jungians of this period figure prominently in the narrative alongside the many facets of Catharine's private life.

The likelihood that my mother's diaries sooner or later would have fallen into irresponsible hands, and have seen the light of day in a manner inappropriate both to her memory and to Jung's, is reinforced by further details in the "Epilogue." While my own role in my mother's life naturally grows as the sequence unfolds, making me an involved witness, Catharine safely speaks for herself in these pages.

---

[1] Though the *Collected Works* had not yet been published in English, there were a number of books by Jung in English translated by H. G. Baynes, C. F. Baynes, Beatrice Hinkle, Stanley Dell and others.

Beyond that, the memoir which I have woven around her diaries comes to include the story of my own childhood, youth, and marriage, and my disentanglement from my mother's influence, which parallels the separation, through her analysis, from background influences in her own life.

Chapter One

Early History

Catharine Rush Cabot (1894-1976) had ancestors on her father's side who were among the first Quaker immigrants to Pennsylvania in 1683. Captain John Rush (1620-1699), a cavalry troop commander under Cromwell and a friend of the Lord Protector, brought his wife Susanna, their eight children, and several grandchildren to Byberry, a farming colony twelve miles from Philadelphia. Descendants soon joined various Protestant denominations, and the Rushes became part of what was known as the "Quaker-Episcopal" upper class[1]. Among the fifth generation of these descendants was a signer of the Declaration of Independence, Dr. Benjamin Rush, whose eldest son Richard served as Ambassador to the Court of St. James and later as Treasury Secretary under John Quincy Adams. Benjamin Rush, who inherited Captain Rush's watch and sword, became America's first psychiatrist. William Rush, America's first notable sculptor, portrayed George Washington from life in bronze and was best known for his carved figureheads for ships.

Catharine's father William Rees Rush, named after this sculptor and coming in the ninth generation, was born in Philadelphia on 18 September 1857. His father Joseph Rush, killed in the Civil War, was

---

[1] Captain Rush, the fifth child among seven sons and three daughters born to John Rush and Eliza Johnson (m. 1648) of Chipping Norton, Oxfordshire, with his wife became a "Christian" or baptized Quaker soon after coming to Pennsylvania. When that movement died out, the Rushes with other such families joined various Protestant denominations. See Digby Baltzell, *Puritan Boston and Quaker Philadelphia* (Free Press, New York, 1979).

KAMEHAMEHA V.,

King of the Hawaiian Islands.

To All Who Shall See These Presents, Greeting:

Know Ye, *That*

We Have Appointed and Commissioned, and By These Presents We Appoint and Commission

Lieutenant William Rees Rush, U.S. Navy,

a Knight Commander with Star

of Our Royal Order of **KAMEHAMEHA I.** to Exercise and Enjoy all the Rights, Pre-Eminences and Privileges to the same of right appertaining, and to wear the Insignia as by Decree created.

In Testimony Whereof, We have caused these Letters to be made Patent, and the Seal of Our Kingdom to be hereunto affixed.

Given under Our Hand, at Our Palace in Honolulu, this *18th day of February A.D. 1873*

By the King.

The Chancellor of the Order of Kamehameha I.

By the King and Chancellor of the Order

Charles C. Harris

Minister for Foreign Affairs

a landowner who farmed at Byberry, but his mother Ardelia lived until 1914, and an uncle Samuel survived to 110 years. At fourteen William joined the Navy, graduated as Midshipman four years later, at twenty served on an extended world cruise for two years, and by 1893, when he was thirty-five and Lieutenant, served on the *S.S. Boston* in 1893, in the Hawaiian Islands. Jockeyings between the Japanese, British, and Americans for influence in Hawaii, which had been under American protection since 1851, led a cabal of American citizens placed highly in administrative circles there to overthrow the native monarchy by having the *Boston*'s officers, in the person of Lieutenant Rush, declare American "protection" while raising our flag over the capitol and ushering in a Provisional Government. U. S Minister John L. Stevens issued the proclamation but had left both Washington and the officers of the *Boston* in the dark. Washington revoked the action two months later, although annexation did eventually come five years later. Although the resident Americans behind this devious move to gain complete control of the Islands aimed at overthrowing the Hawaiian monarchy, the Royal Family realized that resistance would be futile and made the best of the situation. They considered the U.S. officers *persona grata*, entertaining them lavishly and appointing William Rush, in spite of his flag-raising role, Knight Commander of the Star by King Kamehameda in February 1893. He was decorated by the Queen. (The U.S. had taken on Hawaii as a Protectorate in 1851, but moved to depose the monarchy, which proved weak in the face of reactionary forces, preparatory to eventual annexation.)[1]

It was during these turbulent months that William met my grandmother, Jane Pomroy Hare, whose Virginia-born father John, a man possessed by *Wanderlust*, had become an adviser to the Hawaiian Queen and perhaps also her lover. Jane was then in her early twenties and William was thirty-six. She sometimes issued her own invitations on Palace stationery, but the forceful Lieutenant, the opposite to Jane's rather ineffectual father, his face ruddy from exposure to the elements, married her in Honolulu in January of 1894.

After their honeymoon trip Jane went to Philadelphia to live with William's mother Ardelia, known as "Grandma Precious," and a

---

[1] For background, see *The Betrayal of Liliuokalani, Last Queen of* Hawaii 1838-1917, by Helena G. Allen (Mutual Publishing, Honolulu, 1982) and *Hawaii's Story by Hawaii's Queen* (Charles Tuttle, Rutland & Tokyo, 1964).

sister, Elizabeth Rush Bosler or "Aunt Bessie," who was a difficult character, my mother said, while William joined the staff of the Naval War College. She was already pregnant with Catharine, who was born on 2 November 1894, in Germantown. Mother and daughter stayed in Philadelphia until Catharine was nearly six, escaping the Rush household whenever they could on trips, while William served at sea in Europe and the Spanish-American War. A move to Newport and the War College proved brief, since William was posted again to sea duty in a few months. Rather than return to Philadelphia, Jane Rush took her daughter to Paris, then very cheap to live in. Wealthy Americans traveled extensively at this time, imbibing the culture of Europe, and although Jane Rush could count on only a junior officer's salary, she had courage and a spirit of independence (which her daughter inherited). She installed Catharine in a convent school on the Avenue d'Iena and maintained inexpensive quarters at a *pension de famille* near the Étoile. There she met another American family, the Greens from the South, whose son Julien Green became the well-known writer and later member of the *Academie Française*, rare for a foreigner. Catharine and her mother rejoined William only in 1904, when he was posted to the Boston Navy Yard. There Catharine attended Miss May's School, where she made lifelong friendships but also ran into some nasty experiences. My mother told me several times about the bitterly cold winter afternoon when some classmates tied her to a tree during a snow storm and departed. She was terrified of freezing to death, but with great exertion eventually she was able to wriggle free. Such episodes tainted her view of America. In 1906 William was posted to the Philippines, and so Jane took Catharine back to Paris, the same pension, and the school on the Avenue d'Iena. A few months later Jane traveled to China, where her husband had just been posted, and placed Catharine as a boarder at the convent school.

    This time Catharine, no longer a day pupil, discovered that as a *protestante* she had certain advantages denied to the Catholic girl students. For instance, she could actually bathe in the nude, dispensing with the long nightdress which was compulsory in the bath, an exception which made the other girls envious; and she was also permitted to open her window at night – an important exception, since many of the Catholic girls, sleeping with their windows closed, developed TB. Otherwise she kept to the same routine as the French pupils, spending many hours a day, especially on Sunday, in the school chapel. She was not drawn to religion, but she liked the Catholic ritual, the music, incense, and colorful vestments. Protestant services seemed dull in comparison. However, despite the attractions of Catholic ritual, my mother remained Protestant until her late seventies, when, for worldly reasons, it suited her to join the Catholic Church.

Over the next several years, when Catharine was a teenager, her mother spent more time in the Far East while her husband was posted to China, traveling with her friends the Singers of sewing-machine fame. Because of his seniority (he was commissioned Commander in 1905), Jane Rush could now spend more time with her husband (by 1907 he was fifty and she a vigorous thirty-seven). Catharine was therefore left to her own devices during several school holidays. And so early in this period, in 1907 when Catharine was thirteen, her mother engaged a German governess for her, having decided that she should learn German. Although she herself loathed the language, saying that it sounded like chickens picking up corn, she maintained nevertheless that one must learn it. Catharine wrote of that period, "I was a lazy devil, and hated to work, but got right down to it with Fräulein Speck and learnt an astonishing amount of German, in a short time." They spent the summer in Obladis, a *Kurort* village in the Tyrol, where they climbed the surrounding mountains, and during the rest of the year took sightseeing trips through Germany. Catharine had her *certificat d'études* when her mother returned in 1908. Jane decided that her daughter should change to a school in Berlin, one that served the *Junker* families of the Prussian nobility. These girls were an austere lot; the buildings were grim and the food atrocious. When Catharine informed her mother, who was an epicure, that she was served lung regularly for lunch, she was immediately moved to a school in Dresden, for daughters of upper-middle class families. The headmistress was most sympathetic and the girls much friendlier. Catharine enjoyed her Dresden years, and was invited to the homes of her classmates during vacations, which was convenient for Mrs. Rush, who continued to travel whenever possible, both with her husband and an "Uncle Francis" otherwise unknown to me. Knowing my grandmother, I assume that the relationship was platonic.

In my mother's view, German education was superior to the French. In mid-life she wrote that while French education had value, "the volume of work one had to put in so as to be able to pass one's exams every semester, was not only very hard on the health and the constitution, but a certain spiritual drain as well. On the other hand, education in Germany was less severe and much less traditional. The Germans gave way to more modern principles, which seemed at the time perfectly sound and obvious. One was given a much more general education and allowed to use one's imagination." Further on she writes,

> Germans in those days were not at all conservative. They readily adapted to new ideas and were keen about "fads" such as *Reformkleider, Reformschuhe* and any other *"Reforms"* that struck their fancy. When the whole world was encased in iron stays, our teachers forced us to take ours off, by first showing us a statue of the Venus de Milo and going into great detail, as to how much more healthy and esthetic it was to allow nature to go unconfined! … The German girl had a very definite and straightforward personality and much independence … until she married!

My mother spent two years at the Dresden school, seeing her father again for the first time in four years during Christmas of 1910, in Paris. During most of this time her parents traveled in the Far East. In January 1911 Catharine made a short visit to St. Moritz where, in an ankle-length dress, she attempted to ski for the first time. Then during her summer vacation she traveled with other school girls to Venice and Megeve; her parents had disappeared again. While in Germany Catharine visited one family frequently, the Weiersmüllers, who owned a *Lebkuchen* factory in Nürnberg. They had two daughters and two sons, and she kept in touch with them all her life. They were not aristocratic, she told me almost apologetically, but were natural and good fun, as I discovered for myself when we spent Christmas with them in 1935. During these years in Dresden my mother began a collection of postcards, mostly the European royal families, of every age: baby princes, teenage princesses, the Kaiser, the Russian imperial family. Friends often sent her other such cards. After the First World War, when many crowned heads had fallen, she added the Pope, Mussolini and Hitler.

In the autumn of 1911 my grandmother, who realized how useful it would be later for her daughter to be proficient in languages, transferred Catharine to a finishing school in Florence for older girls *de bonne famille*, run by an unmarried Englishwoman, Berta Penrose, at the Villa Laletta. By her exposure to so many European cultures,

Katy and her mother

my mother would later find it impossible to live in provincial America where her husband's work would take him. Among several lifelong friends she made at this school was Daria Hesse, whose father was the Tsar's aide-de-camp; Daria was a friend of the Tsar's daughters. The Tsar's family invited Catharine to visit them, but my grandmother, despite the social advantage of accepting such an invitation, considered the journey too dangerous. Even in those days, before the Revolution, Russia had a sinister reputation.

A studious girl but no blue-stocking, Catharine liked having fun too much, being extraverted and enjoying companionship, to become lost in her studies. She worked at her Italian, however, and learnt to write and speak it well. She learned languages quickly and fluently, and spoke each without an accent. Her first real schooling was in

French, with a switch to English during the two Boston years; after that it was French again for two more years, then three years of German, and finally Italian. She appeared to take all these changes in her stride. Spending her childhood on two continents, however, in those days much farther apart than now, made it impossible for her to put down roots anywhere. As Jung eventually would discover, she remained ungrounded.

Her first love, however, a one-sided *grande passion*, came to Catharine during this year in Italy, when she was seventeen. She wore her long brown hair on top of her head, as was the fashion at the time. Of medium height and slim, with freckled fair skin, blue eyes and the aquiline Rush nose, she looked both cheerful and attractive. She acted Doctor Scanarelle in Molière's *Le Médecin malgré lui*, and was thrilled to meet both Leoncavallo and Puccini. The object of her love was a Finnish opera singer, Jean Theslof. Catharine met him with a group of other girls from the school. He played tennis with them, and being at least ten years older than they, and a well-known opera singer, was interesting to be with. Of medium height, still slim, he was obviously attractive in spite of already receding hair, and Catharine fell for him – why so heavily it is hard to guess, but he may well have awakened in her a latent father complex. A few years later in New York she happened to see Theslof emerging from a subway accompanied by a woman, which gave her a terrible shock. Her attachment to him made that seem like treachery. According to her diary, which she kept in Italian, she eventually forgave Jean, who remained an ideal against which she repeatedly compared the men whom she met in America.

In June 1913, Catharine sailed alone for New York from Genoa, after her second year of school in Florence. She would be nineteen in November, and she had not been back to America since 1906, seven years. On arrival she joined her parents on the *Hancock* in Brooklyn Navy Yard. Her father was soon given command of the cruiser *Washington*, on which her mother gave Catharine a coming-out party. There were other parties, appreciation of art and nature, and cycling and swimming, and a great deal of reading. Though my mother always told me what a cultural shock returning to America was for her, her diary, written over fifteen months (and in four languages, though mostly in Italian), belies those words. Only once, during a short dull period, does she report that she became depressed; otherwise her account is full of meetings, parties, and trips, and gives the impression that she was entertained without let-up.

She was thrilled by her mother's proposal that they spend the winter months of 1914 in Paris, but Aunt Bessie put a spoke in that wheel, proposing Bermuda, *à trois*, instead. Oddly, or perhaps not so oddly, my grandmother threatened to stay in Bermuda alone (a port of call for her husband's ship) if not enough rooms could be found at the Palace Hotel, and to park Catharine in the custody of her aunt in New York. After a bit of sarcasm in her diary my mother admits that the discipline would do her good because she wants "to become a big-hearted, strong woman; a woman who can make a husband happy *for life*." For that reason, she adds, "it is good to work on oneself and to learn to be without egotism." Luckily, rooms enough were found and the test was not made. Before sailing to Bermuda, Catharine visited Philadelphia, discovering that the Rush mansion was now part of a hotel. She would have liked to live in it, she writes in her diary – an interesting remark from a girl who had never had a home, and later would never really want one. During the long winter stay in Bermuda, Catharine had her first bout of real boredom which manifested itself as a depression. As her original acquaintances departed, the lack of stimulation brought her exuberant personality down. The depression was brief, however, for the British *H.M.S. Suffolk* arrived, and Catharine befriended three of the officers, with one of whom she corresponded for a time afterwards – Caradoc Prinsep, whom she told me, she might have married had he not been killed on the last day of the War.

The depression at Bermuda was a warning that something was not in order. Parties were stimulating while they lasted, but made a too one-sided way of life for Catharine. Since her return to America her intellect had been neglected, in spite of her attempts at serious reading. Her great interest in art while in Florence – an interest already sharpened in Paris, Berlin, and Dresden – was frustrated in America where, though she had a social whirl, she felt a palpable lack of "culture." Even the eating habits were different, and the way Americans greeted each other. A friend of the family remembered Catharine as a cultured but timid young girl who, when she met her childhood friends again at seventeen, to their consternation *hugged* them. Catharine also ate enormous amounts of bread in restaurants, he recalled, and wondered why you always had to ask for more. Had she been born a generation later, Catharine might have gone to a university and had a career. At that period, however, the only career her mother had in mind for her was a good marriage. And the best way to find a suitable husband was to live an intense social life.

During the Bermuda interval, Catharine's father, on the *U.S.S. Florida* with the Atlantic Fleet in the West Indies, was ordered to Veracruz to intercept a German arms shipment destined for rebel forces under the dictator Huerta, and to prevent these forces from seizing the port of Veracruz. The first to sail, his ship was ordered peaceably to seize the Customs and Cable station, but when Commander Rush landed with his force of 787 seamen and marines, the Mexicans opened fire. Rush received a flesh wound in his leg, which he bandaged with a scarf, carrying on the fight. They were under fire for two days before Veracruz was finally occupied.[1] For this operation Rush was awarded the Congressional Medal of Honor; later a destroyer was named after him. Catharine received, on her return to New York, a detailed account of the action in a long letter from a young officer serving on her father's ship. Because the *Washington* was being refitted, she and her mother stayed at the Hotel Astor, and a round of parties followed, with visits to friends at Boston, Philadelphia, and Rhode Island. Depression was a thing of the past, for the moment anyhow.

Because Commander Rush had been celebrated for valor at Veracruz, his friends thought he should be considered for promotion to Admiral. A recommendation for this step also reached the Secretary of the Navy, Josephus Daniels, from a family friend and prominent member of New York society, Mrs. Paschael A. Carter. She was assured by Secretary Daniels that her good word would play its part. The preliminary review by a Board of Examination, however, heard testimony from junior officers about "lapses from sobriety" running back fifteen and twenty years, incidents never before cited in Rush's reviews for promotion and never recalled by senior officers. This testimony was extraordinary, as junior officers were not normally asked for their opinion. Furthermore, it was not correct to take testimony about events twenty or more years back; seven years earlier Rush's promotion to Captain had shown his record to be clean. No senior officers remembered what the junior officers were referring to. Secretary Daniels denied Rush his promotion to Admiral. Because

---

[1] See John D. Eisenhower, *Intervention! The United States and the Mexican Revolution, 1913-1917* (W. W. Norton, New York & London, 1993).

Rush was known as a hard taskmaster, severe with subordinates he did not think were pulling their weight, most likely these junior officers took their revenge, "testifying out of pique of 'getting even,'" as Rush said. He was next given command of the Boston Navy Yard, which he exercised for two years until his fortieth service year in 1916, when he asked for early retirement. But his retirement was countermanded after one day, the War in Europe then being in its third year and participation by the United States an imminent possibility. He became the First District Commandant and "Chief of Industry," staying until July 1919; the then-Assistant Secretary of the Navy, Franklin Roosevelt, praised his work highly and awarded him a distinguished service medal. In recommending Captain Rush for the decoration, Mr. Roosevelt said (according to the *Boston Globe* of 27 September 1940, after my grandfather's death): "The Boston Navy Yard, under Capt. Rush, has given the office of Assistant Secretary of the Navy less worry and less cause for dissatisfaction than any other Navy Yard in the country." His duties included hosting foreign naval and military dignitaries and U.S. politicians; among these were Josephus Daniels, Secretary of the Navy, and the Prince of Udine, a cousin of the Italian king (who years later, as the aged Duke of Genoa, visited the destroyer *William R. Rush* at anchor off San Remo). During the War, Jane Rush shelved purely social events to entertain V.I.P.s – as well as the Hawaiian sailors drafted into the U.S. Navy – and to write a cook book whose proceeds benefitted the Navy Relief Fund.

Catharine's life during the period after September 1914 is less distinct, since her diary ends at that time. Parties continued, though mostly official functions; she learned typing and shorthand, and joined the French Players, touring with them. But she also fell into depression again, in 1915 or 1916, developing claustrophobia and staying briefly in a clinic. The illness might well have been avoided had she had meaningful activity, but obviously she was bored with the restricted life she lived at home with her parents. Her mother's expectation also suffocated any initiative, and Catharine herself seems to have been unconscious of what she wanted from life. The life of leisure offered by her parents was most seductive, sheltering her from responsibilities or serious commitments. It was an ideal climate for regression. "Daughts" (as she was sometimes called) remained her parents' "little girl." An inferiority complex blossomed, which clouded her vision of herself so successfully that she was unable to see where her talents lay. Since she had no idea what she wanted from life, even her modest intellectual ambitions came to nothing.

Catharine saw herself as very French, not remembering that her ancestry was sturdy English pioneer stock, and realizing that she had copious American energy. She was physically strong, far more so than her European counterparts, but she played the role she thought people would approve of. Instead of being directed outwards towards study or a job, her energy turned inwards, consumed by depressions, illnesses and operations – the latter beginning at this period of her life and serving her as a means with which to hoodwink both herself and others, that she was delicate. Thus the neurosis began during the War, the period of youth and its distractions, and developed gradually; it would be many years before she would feel the need for analysis.

In 1917, Catharine met her future husband, James Jackson Cabot, the eldest son of Godfrey Lowell Cabot. Godfrey went to Harward, graduating at a very young age, and after learning German and studying at the Polytechnique in Zürich, returned to America and made a fortune in oil and gas in West Virginia. Carbon black became his chief business, which after 1912 was used in tires to darken them and make them resistant to punctures. James Cabot, after graduating from Harvard in 1913 and training at MIT, was often away working for his father in the oil and gas fields, so Catharine knew his sister Eleanor before meeting him. Theirs was a chance encounter, although my daughter Diana has told me that her grandmother said that this encounter was contrived. Catharine, who had just learnt to drive, had taken her Model-T Ford out for a spin when, to her dismay, she had a flat tire. She was wondering what to do next when a handsome young man dressed in black leather from head to foot rode up on a motorcycle and asked if he could help. To his astonishment, he discovered that the attractive young motorist in distress knew his sister well. Nonetheless, he saw little of Catharine thereafter because he joined the Army as a flier. Before training at Forth Worth, Texas, in a camp run by Canadians where a large number of trainees died in crashes, Jim and his younger brother Tom were given private instruction at Curtis Field near Buffalo. They became not only good fliers but skilled mechanics as well, and early in 1918 James was posted to England, where he excelled in marksmanship, learning to dive his plane (which stabilized it) nearer to the target than anybody else. He ferried planes between bases in England and across the Channel to the front. He saw only two days' combat duty, near Verdun, and received a bullet through his fuselage the day before the Armistice was signed, which upset his navigator but exhilarated him. Returning to Boston in January 1919, he met Catharine again, and within one month they were engaged. It had been four and one-half years since Catharine had returned to Boston, missing Europe, bored by the older Boston ladies whom she found to be stiff, more so than her relaxed mother, who had been partly brought up in Hawaii. Yet she grumbled about her mother's authoritarian ways, and later made her out to be a monster to Jung. (Neither her diary nor letters from the period imply that her mother was bad-tempered or terribly bossy.) During those years she had not been as morose as she later claimed. Life at the Navy Yard, even, had not been so monotonous. She christened ships and presented colors, enjoying the attention she received on those occasions. Her last such ceremony involved the oil tanker *U.S.S. Brazos*, named for the Rio de los Brazos in Texas, linking her to her future husband's business. She was now twenty-four, and it was time for Catharine to leave the nest. Marriage was a means to that end.

Chapter Two

Marriage and Motherhood

James and Catharine were married on May 10, 1919, at St. Paul's Cathedral in Boston. A soloist sang *O Perfect Love*. A sit-down breakfast for close family members at the Commandant's residence, a Bullfinch house, was followed by a large reception. Though of modest means compared to the Cabots, the Rushes made their daughter's wedding one of the important social events of Boston. The bride wore a magnificent gown of ivory satin and old point lace "with a court train which fell from the shoulders." Only shortly before, my mother had been ill with the terrible postwar influenza, followed by pneumonia, but in the photographs she looks radiant. After the wedding trip, *Salvo* [a newssheet published by the Navy] states that Mr. Cabot and his bride would live on Bay State Road in Boston, adding ominously that they also had another home in West Virginia.

Jim Cabot had joined his father's carbon black business as an executive after leaving military service early in 1919. His father Godfrey, with his independent spirit and frugal habits, left a partnership with his eldest brother Samuel Cabot in the paint business and set up making carbon black for dyes and inks. As carbon black is made from burning natural gas on metal plates, my grandfather went to West Virginia and walked for miles prospecting for gas wells, building a large business which really took off during the First World War, when carbon black began to be used to strengthen rubber tires. While Godfrey was away for long stretches, his wife Minnie[1] saw to

---

[1] Maria Buckminster Moors descended from Thomas Dudley, several times Governor of Massachusetts between 1634 and 1651, when governors were chosen annually. (Godfrey also had Thomas Dudley in his family tree.)

the children's education in Boston. He also sold gas to local utilities. This was the business whose operation he turned over to his eldest son Jim, retaining control while Jim went to West Virginia.

My mother never mentioned to me that she had lived on Bay State Road for several months. I always understood that she had gone directly to Charleston, West Virginia, after her wedding trip. Catharine found the move to backwoods Charleston unbearable. It felt like a life sentence. She had never absorbed the Puritan ethic of selflessly doing one's duty, for neither her mother nor her frequently absent father had drummed it into her. Indeed, her father expressed boredom about the official functions and entertainment he was forced to endure. "Are frozen-faces coming to dinner?" he often asked his wife. Catharine relished the limelight on these occasions, but otherwise had little home life. With the abrupt move to Charleston, she felt lost to the public eye forever and had few interests to fall back on. She often quoted to me the young Boston couple who, as they drove away from the church, said in unison, "Now that we are married, life is over." Catharine was newly married and in love with her husband, which for awhile made the pill less bitter. But being forced to live for years in West Virginia ultimately doomed the marriage – though not through divorce.

My parents rented a house on Kanawha Street, which Catharine set about making as comfortable as possible, furnishing it with pieces found at auctions and also donated by her in-laws, which included a Duncan Phyfe table with two matching chairs and a very fine four-poster bed. She put her silver wedding presents on display. Her talent for all of this became rapidly apparent. Soon, however, she was at loose ends. A black woman did the cleaning and a Japanese man-servant was their cook. And a child was slow in coming. In a letter of September 1919, she told her mother-in-law that "of course … one does not mind anything that will help one's husband in his career," but then drops the bomb that she has developed a hernia and will soon travel to Boston for an operation. This hernia was the first of many, and other kinds of operations would follow throughout her life.

After setting up house and meeting new friends began to pall, Catharine looked for her pastimes further afield. She discovered a sophisticated resort three hours from Charleston over rough roads, White Sulphur Springs, where President Wilson had gone during the War. On high ground and therefore cooler than Charleston in the summer, it made an habitue of my mother by the time I was born four years later. At the Greenbriar Hotel she met friends her own age who encouraged her to take up golf. During her husband's visits on alternate weekends, she led him to do the same. She was very demanding. Not only did she leave him alone in Charleston to spend long periods at the resort, but she also traveled as often as possible. Being much in love with his young and attractive wife, Jim tried to satisfy her expensive tastes. Luckily, his mother sent him the occasional cheque. His loyalty to his family and its business of course led to an insoluble conflict for him. He tried to combine business with the travel on which his wife insisted, but on a Caribbean cruise that was out of the question. In the second summer of their marriage, they traveled out west for two months, consuming time he needed to devote to business, and using money from the meager salary his father allotted him. Catharine groused about both the salary and his parents' stinginess, being thoroughly unaware of the ways of the real world. She had been used to living like a rich girl at home when in fact she had not been. Now that she had married into a family that in fact was rich, the spoiled only child suddenly found herself tight for money. While her parents-in-law gave gifts to the young couple, what Catharine wanted, though she did not say it, was money as it gave independence.

The rented house did not satisfy her for long, and so she prevailed on Jim to get his father to buy a house for the company's use. In 1921 she was thoroughly occupied doing up the new house, and then, between October 1921 and June of the next year, my father became vice president and ran the Boston office while his parents went on a world tour. With no trip in view, the young couple found excitement in Boston in another direction. They decided to have operations. Jim had his appendix out, and Catharine her gallbladder and appendix. Gall bladder surgery was no joke before saline drips were invented; my mother suffered excruciating thirst for two days after the operation. Jim wrote to his mother, "Personally I don't think my father is having simple indigestion; I think he must have either a gall bladder or an appendix cutting-up. Both Catharine and I are feeling much better since our operations."

My mother had wanted a baby for some time, but pregnancy had eluded her. There was no hormone treatment in those days for infertile women. She had to make do with a primitive treatment which included warm baths and douches. Finally, with the baby a few months on the way in early spring 1923, Catharine decided that a baby should not be born to an unbaptized father, so persuaded her Unitarian husband to be baptized Episcopalian. I arrived three weeks late, on 1 July 1923, at Philips House in Massachusetts General Hospital. A fall my mother had taken disengaged the head and made it easier for her to insist on traveling to Boston. I was named for my grandmother, Jane Rush, then in London, who wrote about "the first Jane being born right here in London – a beautiful woman, who had eight children and was dead at forty-two." When I was four, my mother became pregnant again, which did not suit her at all. So she began practicing her golf swing more vigorously. A miscarriage followed in February 1928 – a boy, she later told me. When I was older, she told me that she was glad she had never had him. It was strange how neither my grandmother nor my mother could handle more than one child. The former had experienced a difficult birth, and so had some excuse for not wanting another, but my mother's Caesarian had not been particularly unpleasant, so she should not have feared physical discomfort. The reason must have been psychological. She identified with her little daughter, and that was enough. With her youthful psychology, a second child would have been *de trop*. How often as a child did I long for that brother who never saw the light of day. I fantasized about having both a helpful ally and a different life. I particularly wished my mother had never divulged its sex as it made the baby more real and its loss greater.

Restless once more when I was a few months old, Catharine got all of us in November 1924 on board the *S.S. Duilio* to San Remo, Italy. With my parents and me went a nurse and a large supply of frozen cow's milk. Catharine's parents were staying in a tiny house that had been the library of a larger villa, situated in a large historic garden planted by a German botanist in about 1850. We occupied a hotel full of British spinsters, as my father wrote in a letter. Among the photographs taken then, one on the rocky beach with my parents is the only I possess in which we are *all three together*. After Christmas, my mother took my father off on a tour to Venice, Ravenna, Siena, Florence, Rome, and Naples, and then off again to Genoa, Milan, Germany, and Austria. Her reason was that my father desperately needed a cultural education which could not be found on the Riviera. My father's youngest brother Jack, more sophisticated than Jim, joined them. Of my long-suffering father, Catharine wrote to her mother-in-law, "Jim has derived such *tremendous pleasure* out of this

Catharine, James (Jim) and Jane, San Remo, January 1925

trip. Jack and I have been his instructors in art and we have found him a very apt pupil." Around the same time Jim wrote to his sister, "I am having a little trouble with friend wife, she is all for churches and 'modern' stuff, I am for the glories of ancient Rome and for ancient sculptors." Once again, Minnie Cabot came through with a cheque to cover their return fare to America in March. My mother was profuse in her thanks.

Back in Charleston, my father plunged back into his work, but my mother had nothing to occupy her tremendous energy, what with a nurse, cook, and maid to see to everything. No longer did she hold the ideals of age eighteen, "to become a big-hearted, strong woman, a woman who can make a husband happy for life." Less idealistic now and more preoccupied with herself, she fled during the summer months to White Sulphur Springs, where she could play golf during the day and dance at night. My father was left to join us at weekends. I was a plausible excuse for leaving the heat of Charleston. I remember little of my time there, except the spittoons dotted about down-

Catharine, ca. 1935

stairs in the hotel, and the indoor swimming pool. I thought the spittoons disgusting, seeing old men clearing their throats and noisily spitting into them, but curiosity compelled me to inspect their contents. I enjoyed the pool, wearing white inflatable water wings under my arm pits, which looked to me rather like bosoms. The fat lady swimmers puzzled me for using the same devices; I asked my nanny why they could not just tuck their own enormous breasts under their arms and use them for keeping afloat.

Unlike other women of her class without a profession, Catharine did not take up charity work, which she despised, believing that most of the money raised was consumed by operating costs. She preferred occasionally to give directly to needy persons. Deep inside, Catharine hid a stingy streak, but on the surface she appeared extremely generous, so much so that it was all the more astonishing to suddenly come up against her miserliness. Luckily, it did not surface often. She also avoided charity work because her European upbringing had rendered her unfamiliar with it, leaving her exposed to the feeling of inferiority here which she had never experienced in Europe. America confused her, and she felt herself to be different from her American contemporaries. She avoided competitive situations with American women her own age, and dubbed the Puritan ethic of her Boston milieu hypocritical. Her own in-laws, who provided presents and cheques, she felt to be stingy, preferring more than the periodic largesse which left her feeling dependent on them. She had a permanent Cinderella complex.

The result went against her tendency to extraversion, gradually turning her into a rebel and a loner. She could play in the company of others, but not join them in serious activities, where competition might arise. Whenever this kind of play was denied her, energy went inward and fed a depression. To counteract this, she traveled. If it was not White Sulphur Springs, it was Newport, Rhode Island, in the summers, and Washington or Baltimore in the cooler seasons. My father was left not only with his hard work but also with minding the baby. Or else the nurse and I went along as well. Washington had become the home of Jim's father, who for two years was head of the National Aeronautical Association. During the War, he had patrolled Boston Harbor for submarines, and had patented an invention for picking up loads in flight, a device used for a long time afterwards. Traveling with a three-or-four-year-old child to visit grandparents made my mother's escapades look respectable. In Washington, she saw many friends and went out a great deal. Only the odd memory of our visits comes back to me. I often walked with my nurse along the broad pavements, noting the many road works in progress, which upset my sense of order. Hardly was one hole filled than another appeared! This was my first experience of the fact that order (which meant perfection for me) was an unobtainable condition, and it was terribly frustrating. I briefly developed an obsessional compulsive tendency, avoiding walking on blades of grass between the paving stones, in case I "hurt" them. I also remember a discussion of blackmail among the adults while I rode squashed in the back seat of the car, seeing in my mind's eye people receiving letters from the postman in black envelopes, and feeling terribly disappointed when one of the passengers threw my fantasy to the dogs. My memories of

Charleston are few and dim, although two of them convince me of
Freud's view that small children *are* sexy and that a latency period
follows. I played "doctors" with children of both sexes in a woodshed
– very interesting – and also twisted my legs together like a corkscrew
when falling asleep, which led my nurse to untwist them and wake
me. I wondered why, since the position was most comforting.

In 1926, my mother shortened her skirts and cut her hair. This new
freedom produced a new personality. She decided to call herself
"Katy": "Catharine" was suddenly too tame. The change was resisted
by both families, but gradually was allowed. Katy was addicted to
dancing the new "Charleston," which enlivened her and slimmed her
thighs. The shorter hair also liberated her from the enormous chi-
gnon which she had worn from her teens, and soon she adopted
artificial side curls suspended from combs that were sometimes
hidden by a turban. In this way, she never had to waste time having
permanent waves, which then could take as much as eight hours. She
kept the same hairdo for twenty years! I preferred the marcel wave
that I saw on other mothers, and longed for my mother to be
conventional. When she added the side curls later, I loathed them
from the beginning. But it would be only much later that I realized
that she was just not like other women. At the time, I could never
reconcile myself to the fact that she did not belong to the normal run
of mothers. Her clothes were relatively normal during the twenties,
but in Switzerland she stressed that she had dressed abominably until
she met Jung, and had also lacked an interest in alcohol. Analysis had
made her like both, she told me proudly. Though I was young, I
thought this was a pity, because her clothes seemed too chic, and her
social drinking made her even more irascible.

The years from 1927 to 1929, when I was just shy of four and until
I was five, saw much traveling. My mother cruised in the Caribbean,
and for two summers camped and she and her husband learned to
fish in Canada on trips organized by an older British naval attaché,
whom she had met in Washington and seen in Newport and White
Sulphur Springs, Captain the Hon. Arthur Stopford, the son of an
Irish peer, the sixth Earl of Courtown. Though not tall and handsome,
this man attracted Katy, who may have been searching for a benign
father figure. But two camping trips were enough. She began yearn-
ing for the sun and beaches of Hawaii, where her parents had met.
She talked my father into taking the trip; alas, it was to be their last
together.

Catharine in San Remo, ca. 1932

Before they left, I had my fifth birthday party in Charleston. We wore fancy dress, and for some reason, I intensely disliked my Gypsy outfit, with dark skirt and light green apron and head-scarf. The whole occasion made me unhappy; my parents' imminent departure may have upset me, but I cannot remember being worried about that. A huge rocking horse arrived from Boston from Grandmother Cabot, with real horse hair not just on the mane and tail but all over it. When I was hoisted into the saddle I burst into tears, which developed into howls of fear. The other children climbed onto the undercarriage platform and sat under the horse's belly. To this day I do not understand my fright, unless it was from the unfamiliar rocking motion, for I had been riding ponies since I was three. I screamed until I was lifted off, and a bolder child took my place in the saddle.

While my parents were away, joined by my Grandmother Rush, I stayed with my Cabot grandparents at Beverley Farms on the North Shore, their summer residence. There I would meet several cousins of my own age with whom I played every day, among whom were Johnny, Betsy, and Hannah Bradley. We rolled down slopes in large Chinese baskets, and saw a chicken fly past minus its head. The farmer said it was dead all right, because he had beheaded it, but I believed he was lying. This summer idyll of 1928 was interrupted first by an operation for the removal of my tonsils, and then later by a spell of constipation. It was the fashion then to have children's tonsils out for no particular reason, and a letter from my father in July 1928, from Hawaii, may have unwittingly condemned me to the operation: "Dr. Ladd did not think she was very well when we arrived [at Beverly Farms] and thinks she should have her adenoids and tonsils removed." After my parents returned from Hawaii and we returned to Charleston, I ran a temperature with what was first diagnosed as "indigestion." But this was soon changed to a diagnosis of heart trouble, and I was whisked off to Johns Hopkins hospital, a horrible experience, where the verdict was TB of the chest glands. Just as I had been condemned to indefinite bed rest when thought to have heart disease, the new diagnosis condemned me to the very same fate. Grandmother Rush suggested San Remo rather than Arizona for recuperation, and my mother needed little persuasion. The tragedy for my father was that once his wife left for Europe, she had no desire to return to the United States. While the Italian Riviera indeed offered a healthy climate, my illness offered an excellent excuse for a six-month-or-so stay in Europe. Even when I was pronounced well at

Zürich's Kinderspital in the late summer of 1929, my mother used me
as her excuse for delaying our return. As we shall see, my health was
used as a means to control me, and to keep me away from my
American family throughout my childhood.

It was sad to leave the only home I knew, especially as I had a
feeling I was leaving Charleston forever. As I remember, it was early
morning and dark. Descending the front porch steps, I heard a rustle
in the undergrowth. Out slid my pet grass snake! I had kept him a
secret from the grown-ups, and had not seen him since my illness.
"Oh! he has come to say good-bye," I cried, no longer worried about
hiding our association. My spirits rose; he had remembered me and
had come to see me off.

We sailed early in 1929 from New York to Genoa on the *Conte
Biancamano*, without my father, as he had to stay home and work. On
10 January I "dictate" to my mother a letter for Grandma Cabot,
thanking her for the sweaters, leggings, and even a hot plate and tray,
then I ask after my Bradley cousins twice, obviously pining for my
summer vacation with them, then report that sitting in my steamer
chair I ate "a nice big dish of spaghetti," and had gone through a
storm, and had been sick.

In San Remo, we stayed at the Royal Hotel, as my grandparents
had not yet built any extra bedrooms at their villa. I spent my days in
bed or, when the sun shone on the balcony, lying in a deck chair. The
nurse from Charleston, Mrs. Minsker, began to teach me to read and
write, as well as a number of card games. One of these, "Old
Bachelor," I invented myself, referring to it in another letter to my
grandfather which I supposedly dictated to my mother. I wanted to
write my own letters, according to a postcard I dictated to my father
on 4 June, "Cos I like to learn how to write." The card was posted from
Villa Serbeloni, Bellagio, on Lake Como, for San Remo was warming
up. The heat persuaded my mother to move north to Switzerland, and
so my next dictated letter to my Grandfather Cabot comes from the
Altein Sanatorium in Arosa: "I have a little white bed where I sit out
on the porch in. ..." After describing the snow-capped mountains, I
say, "Grandpa, I drink lots of nice milk – its fine milk here and I love
it. I have five meals here a day, and two of them is milk and zwieback
– 4 p.m. and 10 a.m." I may have spoken of the hours myself, as I had
received a wristwatch for my sixth birthday and was a keen learner
then, with no inferiority complex vis-à-vis other children thanks to
my spasmodic schooling. Later, because of long gaps in schooling not

Capt. W. R. Rush and Katy Cabot, Lake Como, Italy, 1929

due to illness, I lost interest in acquiring knowledge until I grew up. At five and six, however, I was still completely natural and never questioned my strange fate. Only the absence of my cousins bothered me; I continued to ask about them and promised to bring them presents from San Remo.

But there was to be no permanent return. From Arosa we would soon go on to Zürich. By the summer my mother had been in touch with Ernest Jones, Freud's pupil who lived in London, and knew that Jung existed. We may already have moved to Zürich when my mother received the following letter from Mrs. Jung dated 25 September 1929:

Dr. Jung is actually absent and will come back on Sunday or Monday to resume work. I am not quite sure if he will be able to see you on Tuesday, as I don't quite know what appointments he has made already. The best thing would be to ring up on Monday in order to fix an appointment. However it could only be a single one as Dr. Jung can take no new patients for the next term.

I expect my mother wrote from Arosa, where I was still languishing in the little bed on the veranda. My father arrived for a short visit then, and he and I played two-handed bridge. Much to my annoyance, I always lost, but when my father saw I was getting worked up, he teasingly confessed that he had rigged the cards. It snowed that July in Arosa. "How can it snow in the summer?" I asked, and I expect my scientifically minded father explained. All too soon, it seemed, he disappeared again, and I have no idea where my mother spent her time. Probably she played golf. When she moved to the Pension Neptune on the Seefeldstrasse in Zürich, I was immediately placed in another "little white bed" in the Kinderspital under Professor Fanconi, a well-known children's specialist from Poshciavo in the Graubünden. Tall and slim, with greying brown hair parted in the middle and combed back, he wore glasses, I believe, and was reputed to be no psychologist, as I would soon discover. Not one to beat about the bush, he had me out of bed when the x-rays showed me to be cured. I could have left the hospital immediately, but for the continuing constipation and bilious attacks, some of which had been very sharp ever since November 1928, according to my mother, the latter returned from time to time through my early teens. Professor Fanconi did not tolerate either the attacks or chronic constipation alleviated by enemas, and vowed to cure both conditions. He cut the enemas and prescribed a diet of roughage (Birchermüsli, raw and cooked vegetables and fruit); during my sixth day on the pot the miracle finally took place, and from that day on, I never had any more problems with constipation.

But the Professor also decided that I could not have a local anesthetic administered while he sewed up a gash on my wrist from an accident with a glass door at the clinic, because I was such a badly behaved American child. So I was strapped down in the operating theatre, with thick, wide brown leather straps, under an ominous and powerful electric lamp overhead. It was a terrifying experience. I squirmed and struggled, and the suffocating mask was foul-smelling.

When I awoke, I vomited several times, and the details of that experience have never left me. I would hide under my bed when a nurse arrived with the trolley for making tests, and the bilious attacks increased. Professor Fanconi, impatient, threatened the stomach pump, describing the procedure in lurid detail, but the very next night I had another attack. Next morning, six young men crowded into my small room, announcing that they would hold me down while one of them made me swallow a stomach pump. Determined not to be held down again, I told them, in as dignified a tone as I could muster, that they need only hand me the pump and I would swallow it! After some consultation, one of them reluctantly handed me the pump, which I swallowed at first go. I savored their expressions of astonishment and the discomfort of those hanging around with nothing to do. This incident made me feel good for a change and helped raise my declining self-esteem.

My mother saw Jung for the first time while I was at the Kinderspital. She also began her analysis with Toni Wolff that same autumn. What else she did with her time I do not know, but being extraverted she probably began meeting members of the Psychological Club in Zürich. I do know that she became friendly with one of Jung's patients from New York, Dr. Draper, and probably came to visit me off and on, but she remains a shadowy figure at that period. The events of 1929 were mostly unpleasant in my memory, with the exception of one interesting occurrence: The *Graf Zeppelin* passed over the Kinderspital one afternoon, and many of the nurses, and the children who were not bedridden, rushed to the flat roof to wave and watch it go by. This unusual, new experience opened a window for me which stayed open; when older, I continued to seek unusual experiences which would add to my knowledge of the world. During my stay at the Kinderspital, my American nurse returned home and was replaced by a Swiss-French trained nurse, Elsa Pradervand, who entertained me with gory hospital stories which I lapped up – I became very fond of her.

After I left the hospital, we spent Christmas 1929 at the Winter Palace in Gstaad, where I first learned to ski and skate. The skis and poles were wooden, and the bindings were flimsy leather toe and heel straps with clips behind the heel to fasten them to the boot. Novices were taught to stand very straight with one foot ahead of the other, then glide down short slopes. My mother and I posed immediately for photographs, then learned to stem and eventually to turn doing

Stemmbogen. We also skated on the Palace rink, on equipment much like that used now. Katy had little balance on skates but made the effort to do a few rounds occasionally, as skating was still fashionable then. I met a number of children my age, some in Gstaad for the Christmas vacation and others attending a private school there in the winter. We played together on the rink, and tobogganed down to the village, which my mother loved.

In those days, the mountain resorts were not plagued with cars; people arrived by train, and either walked or hired sleighs. It was great to be up and about, and I enjoyed my time in Gstaad, but we stayed there far too long. It was my mother's habit to keep me in one place longer than normal while she went off somewhere else. Hotels were not like home, and long stays in them did not make me feel more secure. The Gstaad visit fell flat for me as all my friends departed and the resort emptied. The hotel season ended on 15 March and my nanny and I moved to the Pension Oldenhorn, and my school, the *Montesano* – we wore uniforms of navy-blue knitted jerseys and berets adorned with light blue stars – closed for the Easter recess. There was no more skating or skiing, and in the strong spring sun the streets were oozing horse manure. I was bored, and disgusted at having to walk through the dark yellow brew in the village, but fortunately we moved to San Remo for Easter. When we did so, my mother had long since disappeared from Gstaad. After her first interview with Jung in the autumn of 1929, she was now analyzing regularly with Toni Wolff, as it was Jung's habit to send a new patient to his assistant for weekly analysis, occasionally seeing the patient himself.

In San Remo, again we stayed at the Royal Hotel, and I played in both the hotel gardens and in my grandparents' jungle-like garden at their villa, inventing many exciting games. On Sundays and feast days, my grandfather hung the Italian flag, the Stars and Stripes, and the Union Jack from iron flagpoles on the terrace, flags which disappeared during the War. My nurse and I often went down to the beach to collect stones. Elsa Pradervand, or Ziquette, wore wide-legged beach pyjamas made of thin but not diaphanous material, getting away with this costume for several seasons. My mother never came to the beach at Easter, but finally, when word of the costume reached her ears, Ziquette lost her job.

Chapter Three

Back to Boston, On to Zürich

My mother vanished pretty quickly in the Spring of 1930, if she went to San Remo at all. She joined a party of British friends on a motoring trip to Spain, although she was unable to obtain a visa (being American, therefore *persona non grata* because of the Spanish American War of 1898); taking the chance that heads, and passports proffered through the window would not be counted, Katy slipped through. While she was away, a telegram came to my grandparents in San Remo saying that my father had become paralyzed after a riding accident on March 11, in which his horse had rolled over him. The paralysis had developed gradually down his left side; he was taken to Boston by train on a stretcher. A letter that my father never sent, after the accident but prior to the paralysis, indicates how lonely he was. It must have been grim for him to have my mother constantly putting off her return, a very unnerving treatment which I experienced myself later. Realizing that I was no longer the excuse for her staying away, he wrote, "Jane is getting hard and strong – no more mollycoddling – and she ought to be in good health for a long time." We had been in Europe for fourteen months.

Though my father was a stoic Puritan who did not show his feelings, he must have become apprehensive that my mother did not plan to return to him. Of course, forcing her to come back by becoming ill was far from his conscious mind. The accident was not serious, and he did not mention it to her for two weeks. Only the subsequent paralysis forced her hand. Whether the accident triggered a terminal illness caused by an abscess already growing in the brain, or whether the abscess was caused by the fall, the doctors never determined. (His brother, Tom Cabot, suffered a nearly fatal abscess in the kidney region shortly after Jim was taken ill.) His sister, Eleanor Cabot Bradley, wrote in her memoir, *Stories from My Life* (Beverley, 1988), that my father's assistant reported that my father sometimes sat with head in hands at his desk "as if it hurt him. He didn't seem to be with it. Then he would snap out of it and be his usual executive self." While this may have been due to an abscess, it could also have expressed the mental pain and preoccupation during my mother's long absence. Mother chose to think the abscess was tubercular. The autopsy, however, revealed, besides the right-hemisphere abscess, a series of infections throughout the body: "a basilar meningitis, a bronchitis and tracheitis, an infection of the right kidney, pelvis and the right ureter, and a strep abscess at first thought to be a tumor." Though only thirty-eight, my father must have had a weak immune system, which broke under the double stresses of his father's pressure – Jim's brother Tom wrote that Jim "was so ridden by my father that he couldn't call his soul his own" (see John Bradley's memoir, *Everything was an Adventure*, Beverley, 1992) – and of the desertion by his wife.

We sailed from Cherbourg to New York and went straight to Boston, to my grandparents' house at 242 Beacon Street. I have no memory of visiting my father in hospital. I do remember that my Swiss nurse came along, and that I played on the Common with children of my age, who to my astonishment asked what job my father did and how much he earned. When I replied that he did not work, they were contemptuous, so I hastily explained that it was because he was very ill. The world's foremost brain surgeon, Harvey Cushing, operated on my father four times, each time under local anesthetic. The abscess was too deeply seated and could not be reached. My father knew that his case was hopeless, but to protect his family he put on a brave face and was jolly rather than morose. He spent his last weeks in his brother Tom's house at Cohasset, in the cool sea air, at first sitting in his wheelchair in the garden but finally confined to bed. While still in his wheelchair he was entertained by Merrill Griswold's[1] first wife, who danced for him in the garden. Photographs show me standing there by my father, but I remember

---

[1] Merrill Griswold, who served under my Grandfather Rush at the Boston Navy Yard during the War, was keen on my mother and would have liked to marry her. He remained her friend and later became her lawyer.

little besides breaking a front tooth with a stone one afternoon. Instead of sleeping, I threw stones with my upturned feet, one of which missed the circle of cloth wrapped round them and struck my mouth.

It was also a period when I began to plan my future while lying in bed at night. In my fantasy, I was going to do great things when I grew up. All this came to an abrupt end when my father's condition suddenly deteriorated. He preferred to stay in bed; every day he became more drowsy, and his speech became slurred. I remember very well visiting my father shortly before he sank into a coma. I was told he was dying and felt very unhappy, yet also was curious about death. He lay on his side under the sheets, addressed a few cheerful words to me, and then I was whisked away. The next day I was allowed to gaze at him briefly, but he did not speak. Late the following evening, on 24 July 1930, my father died, in his thirty-ninth year. I cried. My mother decided that I was too young to attend the funeral at Walnut Hill Cemetery in Cambridge. A formation of military planes flew over the cortège, and Jim Cabot was buried on high ground, alone, in a clearing surrounded by pine trees, where the graves of his parents and his brother, William Putnam Cabot, later joined him.

I thought of my father quite often after his death, but back in Europe, his memory gradually faded. My mother did little to keep it alive, being determined to cut ties with the Cabots, whom she had never liked but who also now stopped Jim's salary, leaving my mother without financial support. Occasionally during our travels she had economized by staying at a Pension in Zürich, but those periods had been short-lived. Now they would have to be permanent.

On the same day that my father had his riding accident, 11 March 1930, she was writing to her father-in-law from Zürich. After criticizing as outmoded *Zig-Zags*, a popular critique of Freud's work, which Mrs. Cabot had mentioned, she writes:

> It might be of interest to you to know that Doctor Jung, with whom I am working, was originally a friend and co-worker with Freud, but he soon broke away from him for various reasons, which are too complicated to write you in a short letter. … He is one of the most deeply religious men, in the true sense of the word, whom it has been my privilege to meet. All of intellectual Europe is beginning to recognize that he is one of the most, if not the most powerful intellectual force which has appeared since Schopenhau-

er. Keyserling told a friend of mine the other day that he considered Jung the most superior mind that he'd ever encountered. It is
a liberal education to sit at his feet and it is a most inspiring
experience to attend in the new great lecture hall of the University
his special lectures in German before the Philosophical Society,
and to hear the tremendous applause with which they receive the
man whom previously the University had forced out because of
their inability to understand his high and advanced thinking. ...
Analysis is Work, hard, tedious and at times discouraging but I am
sure the results justify all the work and energy one puts into it. It
is of course just as lonely for me as it is for Jim but the extraordinary reestablishment of Janey's health has justified the long stay in
Switzerland.

Analyzing at this time with Toni Wolff, Katy wore her intellectual
personality in this letter, but her interest in things of the mind usually
yielded to the pursuit of pleasure after a few weeks, due to her
inferiority complex. So it was that soon after writing this letter, in
which Katy professes her loneliness, she went on the trip to Spain
with her English friends, not lonely in the least.

My truly lonely father, no philanderer, most likely remained
faithful during the long months of my mother's absence. Because he
was both ethical and very much in love with his wife, his puritanical,
stiff-upper-lip nature most likely destroyed him. He might well have
survived had he been able to live a more hedonistic life. For a family
man, raised in a constant environment unlike my mother's and trying
to maintain a regular routine, living in an empty home must have
been an ordeal. What my mother's thoughts were as she sailed for
Europe again after his death, I do not know. Most likely she felt more
relief than sadness. In 1973, she wrote to a cousin whose husband was
divorcing her: "Neither you nor I were prepared for a Cabot marriage,
which means dealing with the Puritan soul. It would need a life[time]
of preparation which, as young girls, we did not have!... I found
myself stuck with a man I really cared for, but who was browbeaten
by a brilliant but feelingless father until he hardly dared breathe. ... I
tried by every means then in my power to take him by the hand &
carry him along with me; it was useless, the years of browbeating
were against me, & so he was lost." Luckily, she did not realize, as she
embarked with me in the autumn of 1930, that she would never be
entirely rid of the Cabot genes, which were in me and would survive

even the most radical change of environment. My mother could not mold me to her image, however strong the pressure. I often caused her disappointment and frustration by my rather stiff nature and frugal habits.

After returning to Europe on the *Bremen*, we traveled via Paris to Zürich and then on to Gstaad again for Christmas. But we did not return to the Winter Palace for the 1930-1931 winter season, instead staying at the small Hotel Rössli in Gstaad. There we met an English couple, the Oswald de Traffords. He was tall, with a military bearing, a florid but handsome face, and grey hair. The Ski Club of Great Britain representative in Gstaad, he looked older than his mid-forties, probably because he had lived many years in India. His wife was also tall, slim and had fair, permanently waved hair cut in a bob. I immediately took to Major de Trafford, who played with me, telling me that he had a mouse in his breast pocket, which I half believed as he adroitly made the pocket move about. His rather colorless wife Mary had been a barmaid whom the Major met after many years of celibate Army life in India. She showed little interest in me. The de Traffords joined us daily for coffee after lunch, and suggested my mother go to Château d'Oex the following winter. It was our last stay in Gstaad for many years. While I stayed there in the winter months, my mother would periodically return to Zürich for analysis with Toni Wolff.

In 1931, my mother sailed to Boston to straighten out her finances. She had inherited a third of my father's estate, and I two-thirds, which was the law in cases where the deceased had not made a will. These were shares in my grandfather's company, without dividend payments; but then my grandfather had a change of heart and paid out a small dividend to family shareholders. It was insufficient for my mother, who had no profession. She had once translated an Italian book but a translator's salary would have been inadequate. The Cabots offered to bring me up, but Katy preferred to keep me with her and find her own way out of her financial difficulties. At this crucial moment, Pond's Cream offered her $2000 if she would advertise their products in a society magazine. She consulted her father-in-law before accepting to 'sell her face.' He replied immediately, saying:

Dear Catharine,
Answering yours of September 3, I see no harm in your accepting the offer if you really think the product in question is good. I

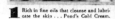

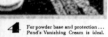

think it is chiefly a question of merit of the commodity and the character of the people that are interested in it, whether, in short, they are people who will not ask you to say anything that you don't think is so.

Ever affectionately yours,

Godfrey L. Cabot

This bailed her out of her difficulties for a while, two thousand dollars being a handsome sum in 1931. During these months, I stayed with my French-Swiss nurse in Avenches on the Lac de Morat or Murtensee. Her fourteen-year-old brother, Jackie, taught me to row and to ride a bicycle, and I attended the local primary school, where we wrote on slates rather than copy books. I loved being in the country, and the weeks sped by.

I met my mother in Paris in the autumn, where for the first day I could not speak a word of English. It was tough being plucked out of my school in Avenches. I missed my friends. But I did not languish for long, becoming adept at winning sticks of barley sugar, the *sucre d'orge*, by snaring metal rings on a stick on the *Champs Élysées* merry-go-rounds. I collected a pile and became unpopular with the operator. While my mother visited the dressmakers, I also played golf at an indoor school. Soon I was bored, but was told I had a natural swing, which pleased Katy, who had planned years before that her child would begin golf lessons at the age of eight.

Katy began her analysis in 1929 with Toni Wolff, after that single hour with Jung to which Mrs. Jung's letter from that autumn alludes. While we were on our second visit to Paris, a letter dated 1st October 1932 reached my mother, which said:

It is true that I shall have my seminar already on October 12th. I enjoyed your picture postcards very much. It is exceedingly nice of you that you gave me a sign of your existence from time to time.

Hoping to see you soon, I am,

Yours sincerely,

C.G. Jung

As I said earlier, two things that Jung taught my mother early in analysis were to appreciate good clothes and to enjoy alcohol. Unfortunately, my mother was not moderate in what she took up, so she bought more clothes than she could afford, and she drank more than was good for her, though she was certainly no alcoholic. My mother ordered her winter clothes in October, and went again to Paris in the Spring for the summer collection, leaving me in San Remo with my grandparents. She brought back two or three models each season and had them copied in different colors by *"la Sarta,"* an inexpensive seamstress in San Remo. She did the same for me with models from the *Enfant Chic* in Milan, so that I would have enough dresses to wear a clean one every day. I must say, however, after having later read the record of her analysis, that the liking for alcohol and the need for smart clothes were *dormant* facets of my mother's personality, which surfaced during the work. What Jung actually "taught" Katy was to use her mind better.

I liked Milan not only for the clothes, but also for the Panetone, huge chunks of which I ate at breakfast, and for the Duomo. The stained-glass windows letting in their dim colored light, and the multitude of small candles burning in the side chapels, especially appealed to me. In contrast to these was the climb about on the roof among flying buttresses and gargoyles, exhilarating but frightening, from which people in the piazza below seemed the size of ants.

The fittings in Paris kept us for two weeks, so I doubt that Katy made it for the October seminar in Zürich. She did attend the autumn and winter seminars, but traveled in spring and summer. After Jung's morning seminars in German at the University, or the English seminars at the Psychological Club, he would lunch with a few of his patients and pupils at the nearby Pfauen Restaurant. Among them was Barbara Hannah, an artist and the daughter of the Dean of Chichester. When from time to time my mother overcame her fear of not measuring up to the other members of the "intellectual" group, she would join in, but on one occasion, Barbara Hannah criticized her red varnished fingernails in front of the group, hinting that my mother was frivolous! Katy was crushed. She took the seminars seriously and wrote notes, in the form of letters, to recall them. I quote an undated example:

Thursday

As I told you, yesterday's seminar was most interesting, Jung spoke about people who love to be compassionate to others; they are the great helpers and eternal saviors! It is such a nice feeling for them and quenches for them their unquestionable thirst to be on top! He said it would be very much better if such people were compassionate with themselves – with the ugliest man in themselves! But it is nicer to forget him in oneself, and instead go to one's neighbor and weed out his garden! Let all the weeds grow in your garden, don't bother about them, just go and help your neighbor weed out his. Naturally, if you give your compassion to yourself, to the imperfect man in yourself, you bring up a monster, and run into that terrific cataclysm man carries within him, that eternal skeleton in the cupboard of which he is afraid. It just boils down to the question of whether man will accept the ugliest man in himself, or not?

Jung went on to say later that it was only a metaphysical truth that every man was equal to every other man. Everyone must realize that the 'mob' consists of inferior beings, inferior types of the human species. Jung says, he thinks that animals are as dignified as a lowly developed man. We must deal with such men in their own way. It is idiotic and cruel to treat inferior man as we would superior man. There is a fundamental mistake in our democratic ideas. We owe it to Christianity that all men are considered equal and that God looks at everyone the same way.

He went back to say again that if you have the missionary in you which tells everyone what is good for him, you will certainly arouse a thundercloud … and if you preach to yourself only, you won't be able to accept the socially inferior individual which is to be found within everyone, as he is a nuisance and naturally not acceptable. But to bring up that being, the shadow side in oneself, one must quietly look within and bring up one's inferior man in an acceptable form by being genuinely sorry for *yourself*. But if you bring up your inferior man by telling people how awful *they* are (with a brass band) then he will never be acceptable to you.

Then Jung went on to say that people often say, "No one loves me." But we have to create that thing which loves us, and which we love. We are inclined to take love like a tree or a gold mine. We simply can't go on taking for granted that love is something that we get from 'somewhere.' It has to be *created because it does not exist, it must be made first.*

Again Jung returned to the fact that one *has* to accept the inferior sides in oneself first, if one hopes to build up the superior sides. It is like building a house, one doesn't begin with the roof. One must dig the foundations first and go into the dirt. One must swallow one's inferiority before one can create something new and better.

Then Jung went on to say that, in the course of man's history, man has elaborated certain forms to deal with the collective danger. The powerful means to deal with it is the Church. The priests busy themselves taking care of the laws, morality and culture, in order to keep man ensconced in a 'form.' He said the Church was the most important, for what can you put in its place? Inferior man doesn't believe in the individual, he believes in great gatherings and in huge and fine buildings to house them. If someone says, "So and so many millions believe in this or that," then he, too, will believe. Inferior man thinks a thing is good because millions do it or believe it. Naturally, in the Church, thousands believe the same thing. What to do with inferior man is a problem. People are inclined to think that their Church is all right but that all other churches are wrong. Jung said he was once speaking to a clergyman about religions and the clergyman insisted that the protestant religion was the only true one. Jung hazarded that Buddhism was also a good religion, and had millions of followers. Whereupon the curate said, "I am not concerned with that!" That is just it, Jung said, and went on that clergymen are not concerned with the spiritual strivings of man.

Jung continued, saying that life is truth and a doubt of truth – a question. If something is *finished*, a definite truth, then it is dead, as it cannot develop further. Best is a half-truth, for a living truth emerges. If truth is static, it is dead. But primitive man must *know* that things are true. He wants to go to sleep in the [bosom] of the Church. If he can't sleep in it, he can't rest. The Church is made for the inferior man. And for that reason we need it, because we are all inferior. A wise man would never want to disturb the Church. It is a spiritual stable for spiritual lambs – and for wolves! With a good shepherd who will show the sheep the way to good pastures (inferior man demands good pastures) the Church is a most desirable thing and the more Catholic the better.

What is good for inferior man, is bad for superior and creative man: Church is a prison for him, belief is hell to him, because he must create. And if he is fettered by eternal truths, then he suffocates and says, "The Church is wrong," forgetting the Church is right in about ninety percent of himself! The superior man can't stand the sheep in himself and the smell of the stable.

The priests are in the same enclosure as the sheep. They are two different aspects of the same thing. A priest who isn't fettered and doesn't believe in the dogma of his church, has no value … we suspect him of hypocrisy. He is a cheat. In the Catholic Church, the priests have to have a wider viewpoint – otherwise they could not deal with the more educated members of the Church. A famous Catholic priest once said to Jung that with more educated people one can protest against certain church dogmas, but one mustn't talk about them in public as that might disturb the masses. (Just as you wouldn't upset the minds of your own children with doubts, so you must be careful what you say.) The above standpoint is valid immediately as soon as the Church deals with the more educated part of human society. There is a story, that at a dinner party a cardinal was sitting next to a certain lady, and he spoke of something in Zola's book called *Rome*. The lady asked if the book wasn't *à l'index*. The cardinal answered: "Yes, but not for you or me."

Jung went on to say that a herd of sheep left alone has no life and is eaten up by wolves. So it is with certain people, they must be prisoners. They are happier that way. It is what inferior man wants. The Catholic Church is a great psychotherapeutic institute which feeds people. The Church has a catching power; one lives in peace within those walls, and people are fed within them. Truly, Catholic nations have fewer problems than we have. One can't talk about psychology in France, Italy and Spain: they think it is mysticism. Those people cannot understand what psychology is talking about, because the whole world of problems and symbols is all within the walls of the Church, for no society can provide the human being with the same help that he can expect from the Church. No human relationship can provide the miracle of transubstantiation. If you realize that then you can have your spiritual food every day. That is the side that people don't reckon with when they leave the Church and expect to live off others. Even an Atheist, if he is a member of an atheist club, still has the Church within his reach. He can confess and repent, and with one leap he is back again in the fold.

We are convinced that people who live in other countries are not all devils, but primitive man believes that they are. They have in that way security in their tribe. Nothing welds people together more than collective misdeeds. Communities will often commit crimes so as to bond themselves together. When the Church was falling asunder, they burnt the heretics, started the Inquisition. They committed a common crime, and that apparently creates unity. A great part of the European Church blew up, as more enlightened people, disgusted with such methods, brought on the Reformation, which is still a festering wound in the side of the Church.

If we say, "This church is false ..." then we have expelled ourselves from our own home – we have uprooted ourselves. If you deny the Church, it is as if you had appendicitis, yet you are convinced you have no appendix. You can't cut out an appendix you don't have, so you are lost. The devils we have within us make us believe they don't exist so they are able to work on in the dark.

When someone is devoting himself to a cause, people think he is doing it for ambition. They think an abbot lives his miserable life in his own interest. These priests are to be taken seriously, for they live their miserable lives for a cause. They accept their miserable lot for the cause. If you have ever looked into such a life you will be deeply impressed by the misery of it. It is tolerated and borne for a cause, and it works.

When one leaves the Church, one must *realize* that one goes out into the wilderness, and one mustn't say, "This is the wilderness, let's go home again."

There was a medieval poet, Angelus Silesius, a German who wrote poetry reaching far beyond the Christianity of his day. He became frightened [of what he had written] and went back into the Church as a monk, and who developed a neurosis. The inferior man in him began to howl, and he ran home. He died in a monastery – a terrible fate.

Protestantism is a long stretch on which people can wander. They can develop through all the different stages of the different Protestant churches until they arrive on the last summit, where they are confronted with God alone. Others die without covering half the stretch. Some people, with more speed, get through it all, and fall outside the church/temple and land in the wilderness. That is a collective problem nowadays. Today there is a collective misunderstanding that doesn't give credit to those things that have been lived for years and have meaning.

The winter of 1931-1932 saw us at Château d'Oex, in an old chalet apartment on a street that was situated above the railway station and had a sunny prospect. Katy brightened the rather somber furnishings with bits of yellow crockery and wooden table lamps painted orange. She began skiing seriously, going on tours with a guide and climbing on seal-skins, on one occasion for seven hours. I did only short climbs – it was considered a strain on children's hearts – and skated a lot, began the piano, and went to a local private school. One hot sunny February morning, my mother had us both photographed on skis wearing bathing suits. There was a cold wind, so we wore our fur coats to the last minute and then whisked them off, grinning broadly. From time to time, my mother disappeared for analysis with Toni Wolff or occasionally Jung, leaving me unworried as I was quite contented with my life. After three months, we did the same round as the previous year: San Remo for Easter, then Avenches for me in the summer and autumn.

In mid 1932, my mother spent some time in Biarritz with friends, and at least March and April in Zürich, as two letters from Jung confirm. He writes on 31 March:

> I tried my best to fit you in somehow. But there has been such a flood of consultations that together with an abominable cold, I was quite unable to live up to all my obligations. I am extremely sorry that I could not squeeze you in any more. If there should be any particular trouble I wish you would whisper into my ear at the occasion of the April Fool's dinner. Thousand regrets.

No letters from my mother to Jung were kept by him before 1937. But she must have been persistent about seeing him, as he writes one week later, saying:

Küsnacht-Zürich
Seestrasse 228
April 6th, 1932

Mrs. C. Cabot
Hotel Royal
San Remo

Dear Mrs. Cabot,
Thank you for your kind letter. This is just to confirm that I am looking forward to your appointments in May. I am fully conscious of the necessity to catch the lump this time. Did you ever suspect

that this lump has something to do with the lack of what you call *Weltanschauung?*

Mr. *[1] told me marvels about your cook,[2] not to speak of the amiable hostess.

His tale was so good that I began to envy Mr. * quite seriously.

With best wishes,

I remain yours sincerely,

C.G. Jung

In 1932, Katy had not yet started to record her analytical sessions regularly in a notebook, but one session is represented on a sheet of notebook paper, dated 9 May 1932, with a letter from Jung pasted on its reverse side.

May 9th, 1932

Back again in Zürich & seeing Jung more often, so as to get at the "lump" that is causing my panics. I told him today about X, & he said that X was a great fantasy artist & could sometimes tell the most astonishing lies! Also that X *"hat sich eingebildet"* [X had imagined] that he could ski & wanted to be *le "Tartarin des Alpes" le protector* got himself into that role. He roared with laughter over X. I'm in a particularly depressed mood now over Dan [Dr. George Draper] & told him again how I couldn't seem to get over it. He said Dan's letter was thoroughly superficial, like himself – that he was a featherweight, and that is why, though brilliant, he couldn't become famous because he *couldn't stick* to a thing long enough – had to go on always to something new and exciting. He is like a cork just floating; if he had had a little lead in him, he could sink into something & remain anchored. Jung said he heard ... [The page ends there. On the following page, in different ink, is written:] "... his cage. No man could help Dan, only a woman."

This was the man in my mother's life after my father's death, if not before. Dr. George Draper of New York was also in analysis with Jung and Toni Wolff. In 1932, he was in his early fifties, slim and handsome with thick grey hair above a thin angular face. Catharine

---

[1] In cases of very personal references, the names have been deleted.

[2] The cook Jung mentions in his letter was Jenny Tibaud, whom we had engaged for the two winters we spent in Château d'Oex, and one winter in Arosa.

preserved part of one of his letters, which describes his analysis with Jung:

> ... truths about myself which I fancy I needed to hear. The main point seems to be that I haven't a fundamental philosophy of my own which I hold to sincerely amid the storms & stress of life. It strikes me as being very true the more I think about it. I've always been trying to please everybody, be on everybody's side & cut my cloth, as it were, so that it will always be accepted & acceptable to the herd. Then he [Jung] pointed out that I make too much fuss about my affairs and experiences – as though mine were the only & original ones & no other man even had the like. He counseled me just to get a *Weltanschauung* – something I believed in – & then quietly go about working inconspicuously. Then, when I had something to say with ample proof & data, to say it. He talked about what he called 'living double.' If a man has a philosophy of life which differs from that of the group he works and plays with, he must do what is expected of him in the expected way insofar as his routine group responsibilities are concerned. But he can go on thinking, working & living his own ideas quietly & unostentatiously. It is all getting very much clearer to me & I think the implication is that I must return to my clinic & not try to force my new ideas into that great medical machine – but do my job there & quietly, inconspicuously work out my thoughts. So much for the work side of life. Whether or not I can carry out the same technique in the 'family circle' is not so clear to me. In respect of that situation, Jung kept emphasizing that many men were in trouble of that sort – that my case was not unique. "If you get a Divorce," he said, "the skyscrapers won't fall down on your head."
>
> I can see much more clearly now that I've taken everything in life far too hard, put myself in the wrong unnecessarily most of the time & supposed that my life experiences were unique. Much more terrible than anyone else's. Absurd of course. Now having perceived it, can I overcome the habit of years & cease reacting to life that way? When I think of you ... [Katy destroyed the rest of the letter.]

The Draper relationship lasted at most two years with numerous painful intervals. He was sixteen years older than Katy, and thirteen years older than her late husband. Fortunately for Katy, Tommy de Trafford came into the picture in a serious way soon after the break with Draper. All the same, the break upset Katy very much, as a letter from Toni Wolff of 15 July 1931 indicates: "Mary Sweetzer [unknown] is absolutely right in saying that your husband, as well as Draper, were two exceptionally bad and difficult experiences." Toni Wolff commiserates with my mother about Dr. Draper's cruelty; in veiled language, she indicates that he had decided to break off the relationship quite suddenly before it became too serious. Married, he could not face the divorce that Jung had reassured him about. The breakup, however, cleared the road for Tommy de Trafford.

The relationship began slowly. He was nine years older than Katy, and found it difficult to part with his wife even though he soon admitted to Katy that he was unhappily married. He had lived many years in India on military service with the British Army, having little experience of women while on duty and therefore remaining a bachelor. Officially I knew nothing, but suspected something was up when we returned to Château d'Oex a second time in the winter of 1932-1933, knowing that my mother preferred Gstaad. For me every-thing was the same – school, piano lessons, skiing and skating. The de Traffords were again in a village pension somewhere below the M.O.B. railway line. One morning this sameness ended abruptly when Tommy arrived unusually early looking distraught and announcing that his wife had tried to kill herself with sleeping tablets. He didn't seem to mind my listening, and told us that he had immediately called a doctor, who had injected caffeine into the soles of his wife's feet, and that she had eventually come round. The mental picture of the long needle jabbed into the soles of one's feet horrified me, and remains with me still. At the same time, I secretly thought that many problems would have been solved had the doctor not arrived so promptly. My mother appeared quite shocked by the news, which astonished me as she had made no secret of her dislike for Mrs. de Trafford. Tommy and his wife quickly vanished from the scene, while we stayed on at Château d'Oex.

My mother had been gradually getting jealous of my Swiss nurse, Elsa Pradervand, of whom I was very fond – she being a sort of second mother to me since the autumn of 1929. Mother said that she put on airs, once she learned that Ziquette had pretended to be my mother by wearing beach pyjamas instead of a uniform! When I was older, I discovered that Katy thought people were marvelous at first, but then, when they did not conform entirely to how she thought they should behave, they were out. There was no compromise. It was clear that Katy was becoming jealous. Though we had no fixed abode during the three and one-half years that Elsa was with me, she gave me security, thanks to her affection and continuous presence. She also stimulated my mind, telling my mother that I should do *des grandes études* (higher studies). By the time my mother told me this years later, I was numbed by a bumper inferiority complex and thought the remark absurd. When we left Château d'Oex, my nurse just vanished! I have no memory of saying good-bye to her, or of being particularly sad. I was hardened to disagreeable happenings in my life by then. Shortly after this, I began having the stomach upsets that I had not had since being in hospital. The first bout coincided with the onset of measles, from which I recovered in San Remo. My mother must have arrived then, as the following letter indicates:

Küsnacht-Zürich
Seestrasse 228
June 24th, 1933

Mrs. C. Cabot
Villa Aloha
San Remo

Dear Mrs. Cabot,
Thank you for your nice letter and all the good news. Of course it is so much more important that you get right with your child than to spend your time in Zürich analysing. There was something lacking, I must admit. I chiefly realized it at the Wednesday-lunch in the Pfauen [Restaurant].

It is too bad that I'm not at home on July 27th, as I shall be up in Bollingen already. If you did go up to St. Moritz with the diligence, that is, the mail coach, you would pass my place and we could shake hands, but I assume you are living in the twentieth century and you are flying up to the Engadine by means of electricity.

I don't think the Zürich atmosphere is particularly peaceful. It is true, however, that all my patients are of different opinion in this respect.

I sincerely hope that you have outlived your parents' historical atmosphere and that your health has not been injured by such a predicament.

I am just leaving for Berlin, where I have to give a seminar.
My best wishes and au revoir.

Cordially yours,
C.G. Jung

My mother then decided that I should spend the summer in the mountains, and chose St. Moritz. Horror of horrors for me, a German governess named Fräulein Rable arrived unexpectedly. She was quite nice during the two days my mother was present, but when my mother did her usual disappearing trick, the governess turned nasty. I was left at the mercy of this unattractive middle-aged female who told me she had worked in the houses of the German aristocracy. After being told a few times that the daughters of German nobility were well-behaved but that I was an impossibly spoiled American child, I began to loathe her heartily, and longed for the return of Elsa Pradervand. My mother phoned from somewhere every two days to see how I was. The governess reassured her, and I said nothing, because my mother kept saying she would be back in a couple of days. But after being told this a number of times, I eventually became desperate and locked myself in my hotel bedroom one morning. The governess used dulcet coaxing terms at first, hoping that the hotel staff would not notice her dilemma. But when she got angry, I remained firm in my resolve not to open the door until my mother arrived. She was actually close by, playing golf with Tommy at Bad Ragaz, and turned up the same day. Tommy moved to St. Moritz as well, to another hotel because Katy liked to keep up appearances, and motored us about the area in his Chrysler with the governess in tow, who again was reasonable in my mother's presence. (It was then I noticed that Tommy's forearms were heavily tattooed.) I golfed, swam in the icy lake, and sometimes we had picnics.

Then I was packed off to San Remo with the governess, to stay with my grandparents. By this time my Grandfather Rush had built a small guest house in the garden for us. The following letter to my mother was addressed to her there:

Küsnacht-Zürich
Seestrasse 228
October 13th, 1933

Mrs. C. Cabot
Villa Aloha
San Remo
Italy

Dear Mrs. Cabot,
I shall be very busy in the beginning of November. In the second half of November it would be better because up to then one or the

other of my cases will leave. There is moreover a new complication in my life and that is that I have to deliver a course of lectures at the technical university, which of course takes up a good deal of my time.

I have seen the "Flying Draper" too. He was as flimsy and unsubstantial as ever. Of course perfectly delightful as far as it goes.

Hoping you had a splendid summer and a correspondingly beautiful autumn, I remain,

Yours sincerely,

C.G. Jung

In San Remo that autumn I attended a convent school run by French nuns, whose order had emigrated there during the French Revolution. They were excellent teachers and would not take any nonsense. When it sank in with me that I could not play the fool with them, I learned more French grammar in three months than I was ever to learn afterwards. But I was under great strain when not at school, which showed in frequent bilious attacks and traumatic bouts of hay fever. The governess coped expertly with the latter by placing my nose under a cold tap for ten minutes. The astringent effect was miraculous. My grandmother coped with the vomiting by giving me bowls of chicken broth when it ceased. By the third day I had fully recovered. Fräulein Rable seemed to me just as loathsome in San Remo as in St. Moritz, and my grandmother, although old-fashioned and strict, independently noticed her browbeating, and wrote to her daughter saying that she should be given notice. But my mother was in no hurry to have her go, for this woman was no rival for my affection. She remained until the following spring. But there were good moments in San Remo too. I often visited the cook and maids in their cellar redoubt, next to the kitchen where I learned to speak Italian quickly in order to converse with them.

It was during my stay with my grandparents that Katy began to keep a regular record of her sessions with Jung. From 1933 to 1939, they are in longhand, and after that, mostly typed.

November 20, 1933

Have seen Dr. Jung again today for the first time since last winter – almost a year! I had a long talk about the past year and told him that my rapport with Janey was getting much better but I

myself felt that I was of flimsy stuff and like "our friend feathers."
In fact I could actually see myself talking insincerely to people, and
felt I appeared and was *oberflächlich* [superficial]. He said that that
was so and laughed! He said that, way in the background, there
was some good in me, but it was far hidden and would have to be
got at. As things were now, I was very unstable and unsound – but
he added, "You have learnt something." We spoke of Draper, and
he said he had seen him and that Draper was 'thin' as ever. I said,
"Oh thin?" He said, "I mean spiritually thin!"

Only on reading her diary after my mother's death did I discover
that she felt like "our friend feathers." About three years later than
this entry, in my early teens, I began drawing crayon cartoons of her
as a bird, which I called *Oison* [gosling]. Neither of us bothered to
check the meaning, which can also indicate "ninny." My mother
accepted and even liked the cartoons. My bird had a large oval yellow
head with a long orange pointed beak, poised on a narrow blue neck
with a larger oval pink body. It had long spindly orange legs,
rudimentary wings of pale green, and a blue topknot tied with a
bright orange ribbon. A large observing eye in profile completed the
picture, and sometimes the bird wore clothes. Accompanying this
figure in many albums was a cartoon of Tommy wearing shirt tails
only and carrying a *chaise percée* [commode] strapped to his back,
representing his shadow. He was called *Cochon* [pig], a name I gave
him when I was ten; I probably picked it up from his frequent use of
the word "swine." I portrayed myself as a child with a trumpet-shaped
nose. The series of cartoons described our daily lives and began
spontaneously. For one thing, they got me attention – my mother and
Tommy enjoyed them – and then, too, they were a vehicle for acting
out on paper frustration and anger after childish rages were outgrown. My teasing, funny at the time, was thinly disguised aggression. Also, I had excess energy. One day, I stuffed two maids into tall
wicker clothes baskets in the hotel laundry room! Luckily, they were
young and glad for a bit of diversion.

My mother's bird-like quality was difficult for me to live with. I felt
so dependent on her, yet in spite of her rudimentary wings she was
always flying from the nest. There was no stability. I was constantly
on tenterhooks and very often disappointed. While my mother was
conscious of the need for physical health, and though she studied
with Jung and Toni Wolff, it never seemed to occur to her that mental

health was also necessary. Perhaps in this she was a child of her time. Her psychotherapists never seemed to give her much advice where I was concerned, about the adverse effects of changes of scene and her disappearances, perhaps assuming that her developing work would eventually benefit me. But such work is slow, and childhood passes quickly. My mother retained her bird-like quality into my teens, with only the War curtailing her travels, so that my last years living with her were less harrowing.

A physical manifestation of her lack of solid footing, or *Bodenständigkeit*, was her foot problem. Her feet were small and well-shaped, but also flat and troublesome. Not only did she need arch supports, but she always had to have her shoes made to order. Being a chip off the old block, I too had a foot problem as a child, and to some extent later. I regularly twisted my ankle as I walked along the street, and stumbled. It was terribly painful, but only for a moment, and never became swollen. When in middle age it occurred to me that I stumbled because I was not properly grounded, the habit began to fade, though not entirely. I became conscious of all this only in a "wilderness situation," hiking through the Lairig Ghru, a long and rough trail through the Cairngorms, from Coylum Bridge near Aviemore to Braemar. My friend, a Welsh woman from Paris, was out of training, so I put her in the lead (an old Swiss guides' trick to keep a tired client moving). At our furthest point from civilization, I twisted my ankle on a loose stone, experiencing such agony that this time I thought the ankle was surely broken. I stumbled on, gritting my teeth behind my unsuspecting friend, remembering the other, less painful occasions. After fifteen minutes, the pain faded and the ankle supported me, and I reflected that it was about time that I become more bound to *terra firma* and give up my ankle nonsense. Later, when working at the Jung Klinik am Zürichberg, I was faced with two extreme cases of ungrounded women, one who felt that she floated inches above the ground and the other who said she was suspended from balloons, frantically trying to touch the ground. Both loathed the sensation.

Catharine continues the diary on another subject:

> Then I told him Oswald and I were still fond of each other. He asked me if O. had got a divorce and I told him that it was not possible because his wife would not give him one. I told him that being with O. was like married life, and sometimes not easy as I did

not have a minute to myself. He said I must take time – take two hours a day – and arrange my affairs with method.

It was not in my mother's nature to arrange two-hour absences from Tommy. Her method of showing independence was constantly to be late for appointments with him. She kept him, and me, waiting for what seemed hours, and then arrived apologizing profusely.

He [Dr. Jung] then asked me if I had any special dream of late. I said that the night before I had dreamt that I had a big swelling on my right thumb, and a man suggested cutting it open with a huge knife, a yard long, and putting disinfectant in it. He explained that the long knife was really a sword – a sword is used in one's right hand to kill – if one's right thumb is incapacitated one can't use a sword. (The Romans used to cut off their enemies' thumbs to incapacitate them.) The right hand denotes the wisdom and understanding one has, so that it is most important to keep one's wisdom and not have it go off in an abscess. Therefore, I have been living wrong and allowed myself to be *infected* – otherwise there wouldn't be an operation with a sword. Now, I want him (Dr. Jung) to cleanse my thumb and perform an operation with a sword. He said I had become infected by the atmosphere of St. Moritz, and that one is all wrong inside to go to such a place. The atmosphere of St. Moritz is the worst possible one. It shows my *conscious* is wrong to wish to go there and to look at or be with such people. At any rate I want Dr. Jung to cut out the abscess on my right hand. The right hand, as I said before, shows one's understanding and conscious conduct of life – all that must be wrong for me and I wish to cut the abscess out. I am too easily swayed. I should not put myself in St. Moritz positions and expect not to be swayed. I said to Jung, "What about putting oneself in such positions and being able to stand firm, wouldn't that be the ideal?" "Yes," said Dr. Jung, "but that is very difficult, for if you went there, you would perhaps be swayed." Jung said he would only go to St. Moritz if he had to, but if he stayed on and said to himself, "Let's stay and look at these people," then he would probably begin to say, "Why has that terrible person got the Rolls and that terrible one such lovely clothes, etc." He went on to say, "If I had the mentality to go and look at them, then I'd probably be jealous. If you go into a situation which is wrong then you are wrong. If you have contracted a wrong situation then you must purify yourself – you can't put a whole crowd right! Try to understand yourself and clarify your motives so as to recuperate your former right attitude. You can clear out of the place! Leave things to themselves if an unparalleled wrongness is in place. Certain places are wrong just as certain places are right and have a beneficent effect in style and atmosphere." He went on to say that the Rainmaker of Cracow came to an arid province where he was asked to induce rain. He promised to do so if he were allowed to stay three days by himself in a lonely house. At the end of three days, it snowed! When asked why it snowed at that time of year, he said that he had gone wrong because he had got into the atmosphere of such wrong people!

Katy was attracted from time to time to what Jung calls "a place of unparalleled wrongness." And in fact she suffered from finger infections, which she blamed on the dirty instruments of manicurists. When the psychological atmosphere in Zürich began to stifle her, she went off to play for a while, indulging the taste for society which she had nurtured in America. In Europe she had less opportunity to meet the so-called smart set. But though the style of life among such people impressed her, she never really attempted to join their ranks. After she had begun analysis in earnest, yet was still drawn to that way of life, she became ill with a sinus infection which put her to bed. My mother must have had a weak immune system, and she was also a very anxious person:

I told Dr. Jung that I occasionally had the 'fears.' He said that evidently the 'Lump' still got loose and rolled around. Certain people have a lump when they get into the swell. A lump is an inherited, and not assimilated piece that is like an Imp who keeps civil until you get into rough waters. It causes instability and in the important moments of your life comes up and plays you a trick and ruins things. A person will say, "I'm O.K. but it is always circumstances which ruin things for me!" You can always say it is circumstance or the other fellow who is wrong, when it is you who always gets into trouble. Facts can heap themselves up to such an extent that it is as if you were always accompanied by an Imp who spoils everything.

Dr. Jung said he stayed with Dr. Curtius[1] in Duisberg, Dr. Curtius would never have come to analysis if it had not been for the War [First World War] and the German economic situation. He

hankers after the Baur-au-Lac [Hotel] life, as he is always saying
that he is through with it.

One also talks about bettering oneself because one isn't doing it.
Jung advised me to live amongst decent people and not a St. Moritz
crowd.

My mother's serious side would not allow her to play indefinitely.
The Imp would also come in the form of an illness which required an
operation, which like the infections grounded her for a while. Or else
fate stepped in if she was being too extraverted and self-indulgent, as
it did with my father's illness or when I forced her return by locking
myself in my hotel bedroom. Unfortunately, bedrock situations like
these, or even regular attendance at analytical sessions with Jung or
Toni Wolff, soon came to seem too onerous, and the urge to fly off
gripped her again. She fluctuated between the serious and playful
poles of her nature in part because she felt inferior to the Zürich
intellectuals, even though Mrs. Jung, Barbara Hannah, and several
other bright women in the circle had not been to any university.
Moved in this way to switch off the serious side of her nature, she
repeatedly let the urge to play gain ascendancy.

Though Katy lacked a higher education, and therefore the mental
discipline which is acquired by serious study, her intellect remained
impressive. She read serious books on various subjects, had an
extensive library, and kept herself well-informed on politics and other
world events. In 1931, shortly after my father's death, she toyed with
the idea of studying at Oxford, which Toni Wolff, educated at Bern
University, also advocated. But as this narrative will show, she lacked
staying power. She would take up something, such as Latin, enthusi-
astically, only to become discouraged and give it up. Her itchy feet
also made it impossible for her to stay long in one place. That is why
she would never rent a flat in Zürich, even though they were cheap in
pre-war days, nor did she want to be tied down even during the War.
In a resort, with short-term rents, it was different. To save expensive
hotel bills when we were locked in Switzerland during the War, she
usually took a flat in Ascona during the summer.

Catharine's next session with Jung came ten days later. She writes:

---

[1] Dr. Curtius was a *Statuarischer Gast* of the Psychological Club, Zürich,
between the World Wars, and was forced to resign (*ausgeschlossen*) in
1945.

December 1st, 1933

First I spoke of the panics which I had in the Dolderbahn the other day, so that I finally had to speak to the *Schaffner* [ticket collector]. He said that it showed I was not enough with people in spirit – not near enough to them – that I hold myself too much aloof. The unconscious is trying to drive me to people. He said that my speaking to the *Schaffner* was an interesting experience. Also, he went on to say that a 'thirst for liberty,' an insatiable thirst for liberty, came from being held in too much in childhood. However, I explained to him that it didn't come from that but from too much liberty. I had been allowed to choose my own schools and gover-nesses, and had had freedom of spirit and of pocket while my parents were in China. Dr. Jung said that was an unusual situation, and one rarely ever heard of such a bringing-up, so now he could see that what I craved was a *'settled situation,'* though my *conscious* was afraid of it and thirsted for liberty. My conscious was afraid boxed up in the Dolderbahn, but my unconscious was delighted as it was looking for a frame. He then gave me an example of such a conflict: A young girl who is afraid of men, runs away from them, is shy and blushes etc. ... it is all because in her unconscious she longs for a man – which is the right thing. One's conscious usually behaves strangely when in conflict with the unconscious because the conscious attitude is wrong and the unconscious is usually after the best thing for one. He said that I had no roots, have lived a precarious existence and my uncon-scious craves a *box* – a *frame* to be fixed in – something stable and permanent. That is one reason I like Oswald [Tommy]. He is absolutely the antithesis to Draper: stable, dependable, rational and with real substance, and that appeals to me.[1] On the other hand, I am afraid of losing my liberty so that is why I want Oswald to go to Africa for six months. But, as Jung says, I must neither suggest the trip to him nor deter him from it. It is his own concern and must be his choice. Maybe he prefers being near me! My unconscious likes the way Oswald holds me in bounds and anchors me. He goes after women outside of his conventional circle be-cause his unconscious feels that to compensate him he must get a woman who is 'different.' If he didn't get such a woman *nothing*

---

[1] My father was such a person, but it did not seem to appeal much to my mother when she was married to him.

would happen and that would be too dreadfully dull for him to be alone with nothing happening. He can afford to go out after such a woman as me because he has so much stability that he can hold me down. Dr. Jung told me again the story of a man who was afraid, a Trappist missionary, who was finally killed in Africa. He said that he too had always been afraid of tropical diseases, so he went out to Africa and into wild dangerous regions where the tsetse fly was etc. [to overcome his fear]. [H. G.] Baynes was very difficult out there and went into moods, and sometimes did not speak for three weeks. One day Bevers (the other American with them) heard a shot, looked out of the tent and said, "I hope it's Baynes blowing out his brains!" I had an unconscious desire for a mold. We spoke of Roosevelt, and Jung said that is what comes of electing a man with no legs – only brains and surrounded by a bunch of scientists. He said that Roosevelt must be a terrific optimist if he could accomplish all he has [in mind] in face of his infirmity.

As we have seen, my mother had a thoroughly unsettled childhood. Most of the time her father was not present to give her a framework and keep her in bounds. He himself, sailing the high seas since early youth, must have had little stability. To some extent Tommy's stability replaced what she had missed. Living abroad without parents or other family members must have been trying, and even back in America she lived on ships and in hotels. She was spoiled with continual parties and frequent trips, all with a destabilizing effect. Nor did she have a serious occupation. She liked acting, but touring with the French Players was not fulfilling, and she became depressed and developed claustrophobia. Her intellect was in cold storage during those years, and she became so one-sided that the suppressed urge to do something more worthwhile eventually forced her to Zürich and Jung. With his help, intellectual pursuits began to interest her again, but the butterfly habit was hard to shake off. Instead of concentrating her attention intellectually, she invested her tremendous energy in various hobby horses. She entertained, studied, collected, learned to cook, redecorated, and later was always in correspondence with lawyers to improve her finances. Only at moments after starting analysis did she achieve some of her aspirations. Her obsession to throw all her energies into controlling a man gave her no time for the long-term mental growth that she really wanted.

Katy had few invitations to parties when she came to live in Switzerland. Tommy was an introvert and not keen on society. I often wondered if my mother were truly an extravert, as she did not appear to find it difficult to spend time on her own. She loved her bed, spending hours there reading or doing a diet, or taking two days' bed rest when she had her periods. Even in bed she was busy reading or writing long letters. I believe she tanked up her energy in bed, then was fit to sally forth again ready for action. Bed rest for my periods was enforced on me at puberty, and unlike my mother I loathed being in bed. I was even forced to have supper in bed until I was past thirteen! With my father's character, I complied, rarely asking myself why I was doomed to live such an unconventional life. Even after my marriage, when I was in my mother's company, I tried to conform to her expectations, until one day in my forties I finally blurted out that I was thoroughly bored by society. She was shocked. My reason for making the revelation was that whenever I visited San Remo, where she then lived part of each year, I became allergic to champagne at her parties, and so suspected that my sneezing and wheezing was an allergic reaction to party-going. When this truth dawned, the reaction cleared for good.

As Jung says, Tommy gave my mother stability and dependability. Katy, he said, sought these qualities in men. My father had them but was too young to be a surrogate father, and Katy felt that his powerful family hobbled him. (Tommy's family was mostly gone, his parents being long dead as were some of his siblings, while those still alive did not interfere with his life.) It was only after meeting Jung that Katy began to appreciate stable qualities. Not only did Jung exude stability himself, but he also made her aware that stability should be aimed for and did not equate it with a dull, boring life. As for the Africa project, I never heard of it. It is difficult to imagine Tommy leaving Katy for six months, or for her allowing him to go, though a temporary break in the relationship might have been good for both. As the years passed, Tommy grew more and more dependent on my mother, both emotionally and financially, becoming moody and drinking more. He lost self-respect; my mother spoke of his "anima moods." Although his pension as a Major was a meager £ 350 per annum, he left my mother a small inheritance when he died.

December 7ᵗʰ, 1933

    This is the last session this term. At first, I spoke of coming out to Küsnacht in the train, how easy it was and much cheaper [than a taxi!]. We spoke of my trying to be franker with regard to people. In other words, I must be *conscious* that I want to say something rude, then either not say it, or make it milder. For instance, when I said to Mrs. Strong, after her remark, "We shall miss you so much in Château d'Oex this winter," "But you never saw me last winter," I should have thought out and let out a platitude which could not possibly have offended her.

Katy would sometimes make me cringe with her *enfant terrible* remarks. She and Tommy were leaving Château d'Oex for good because of his wife's attempted suicide the year before. Mrs. Strong may well have touched a complex.

    We then spoke of Hannah [Barbara]. He said she was like a bad dog, some days so nice and other days so snappy. He said it was a pity she did not have a lump as it might hold her in check. When I mentioned the fact that she wanted to share a studio with me, he said, "So that she can have someone on whom to vent her nasty remarks." He went on to say that Hannah was jealous and tried to get me fussed about nails the other day at the Pfauen when she announced to the whole table that she did not like them. He then said that I still have the Lump, it was still rolling about, and I should know, for instance, that the Dolderbahn frightened me *because* my conscious didn't want to get into a fixed mold (whereas my unconscious does!).

Barbara Hannah was the daughter of an English clergyman who had been the Dean of Chichester Cathedral. She was a few years older than my mother and had been in analysis longer. Among the books she came to write was an early biography of Jung. She was living at the Hotel Alpenrose when she made the suggestion, but the proposal would have been a disaster; Katy would not have lasted two minutes with Barbara. They were poles apart temperamentally, and my mother never could have shared an apartment, let alone a studio, with another woman. Eventually Barbara shared a flat with Marie-Louise von Franz, successfully, until Barbara's death at ninety-five.

    As a girl, Katy had no difficulty relating to female friends. While they matured, however, she retained a girlish mentality, so that new acquaintances became unconscious mother figures. This complex put Katy on the defensive with women her own age. Concurrently, she passed from fondness for her mother during her teens to a thoroughly negative view of her by her early thirties. She spoke to Jung about her in unflattering terms. I, too, became her unwitting confidante on the subject. But she never spoke ill of her father to me. Rather, she portrayed him as a saint who had put up with a difficult wife – whereas to Jung on one occasion she confessed that her father was irascible. When she entered analysis at thirty-five, burdened with the parent problem and unable to form satisfactory adult relationships, personalities were commonly discussed in analysis. The Jungian community at that time was very small, with Jung in the role of village elder with his analysands. With my mother it was unavoidable that she discuss her Zürich contacts, whether they were Jung's analysands or not. What looks like idle gossip was a necessary part of the therapy. Discussions of personalities between therapist and patient may seem inappropriate today, but in the pre-war days of analysis they were the usual thing and may well have been helpful.

The German governess was due to leave after the winter season in Arosa. My mother decided that she could look after me in the winter when she was not traveling, but required a boarding school for the summer months. Chilgrove Manor, which Barbara Hannah recommended, was near Chichester and catered mainly for children whose parents served overseas in the colonies. The headmistress, Gladys Aspinall, kept children for the holidays when parents or relatives were unable to take them. She was unusually flexible, and so accepted me from May to mid November. My health was the reason my mother gave for my spending winters in Switzerland, but I suspect the real reason was that she did not want to lose her influence over me as she had done with the Swiss nanny. Also, she then had an excuse to spend more time in the mountains, where there was a thriving social life, and less time in Zürich. The snag for me about this arrangement was that I loved the school and loathed leaving it in November. Its routine gave me the experience of stability for the first time in my life. I was dubbed "colonial" and therefore inferior, and came in for my share of teasing. But that did not upset me too much. I began to show leadership qualities and led some of my contemporaries on daring escapades. I was nicknamed "the Swallow." Unfortunately, any ambition I had for studies was killed by missing the winter term. Feeling inferior there, I compensated in other ways.

Katy's diary continues:

We spoke of a dream I had recently of a lion carved in stone in a sculptor's *atelier*. Afterwards the sculptor and I went to a Gothic Catholic church. There a monk showed us round and we saw *bidets* of all kinds and colors, in front of one altar, left there by grateful mothers, and over another altar rail we saw large, voluminous skirts of 1850 – Crinolines – which the priest said were called 'Roxanas.'

Dr. Jung said that the man who chiseled the lion in stone (with the Medici emblem around it in the form of three pills) was an animus figure. He asked what the lion meant. I said it meant him perhaps, as I always thought of him as a lion. So the lion could easily be Dr. Jung's picture in the rock, with pills as a garland *autour*, which could mean healing. Dr. Jung said skirts and *bidets* emphasized the lower part of the body, belly and buttocks. The mothers have left their sexuality behind as they don't need *bidets* and skirts – skirts suggest enormous importance to the lower regions. I then told him I had lost my sexuality, and he said that it was stored in church then! Paradoxically, I have lost touch with the basic facts of life, the profound things, and Dr. Jung, in trying to speak to me of them, touches on my sexuality. I said T. was shy in such matters. And said that was what I didn't like evidently, and that one could be obvious without being coarse. Unconsciously, I am very sensitive, and maybe I 'got' Tommy's Catholic attitude [to sex]. Nothing one can notice, yet his unconscious attitude might have entered my unconscious.

All my signs are in the same Zodiacal sign and that is what forms the Lump. I am in Scorpio, which is a sexual sign, but my sun, which stands in Scorpio, is a cold sun as it is late November.

Dr. Jung then said it was strange that I thought of him as a lion, as he stood in Leo, and was born on July 26 [1875]. It was a warm sun! He then asked me when T. was born. I said, "July 26, 1885!" He was surprised, and said, "He also has the Warm sun, but his Venus is not strong."

Then we spoke of Frau Volkhardt, and he said she was pathological, was depressed and 'down' and wanted others to carry her burden for her. She was jealous of a pretty young American woman whom she thought was trying to attract Dr. Jung. He said everyone thought it strange that she kept on *insisting* in the face of no argument whatsoever that Miss de Caro was so nice. He said

Mrs. Volkhardt doesn't know what she wants and might easily fall for Ali Baba, who looks beautiful lying on a sofa and wiggling only his manicured big toe, gazing at one with languid eyes – that is why she tried so hard to tear down the girl's belief in Ali Baba because she was afraid herself of being attracted. Dr. Jung said that the *'Lump' was Mrs. Volkhardt!* I was aghast!! Then he went on to say that I had grown my coating of ice again, and that I have become identified with my persona and can't use my persona as a cloak to take off or put on according to the situation. He takes his off and puts it on at will, and as circumstances demand. It must be a cloak to wear when needed, but one must not become identified with it.

At the end of the hour, Dr. Jung seemed very undecided as to whether the lion meant himself or T. The pills (Medici crest) made him think it might be himself.

I remember that my mother was fascinated by the fact that Jung and Tommy were born on the same day ten years apart. She liked the fact that they were both Leos. It is difficult to believe that Jung was so much older, for to me they looked about the same age. Identifying with her persona was child's play for Katy, who had liked to play roles from girlhood on, both at fancy-dress parties and in real life. In 1932 she put on a play for her in-laws that involved bidets, though only as an aside. My mother was a keen bidet user, probably because bathrooms were scarce in France before the First World War. Her friend Roxana van Rensselaer, from a wealthy New York family, was also a bidet fan when most Americans thought them shocking. Despite her love for bidets, however, my mother was old-fashioned about sex, disapproving of sex before marriage and thinking that married couples should have separate bedrooms. Menstruation she made into an illness requiring two days' bed rest, and invented her own aristocratic pseudonym for it, *le duc d'Alençon*. I could not stand it. Katy pretended to be liberal yet was really conservative in matters pertaining to sex.

My Grandparents Cabot visited Europe in the spring of 1932, and wrote saying that they would stay in Nice for a few days at the Hotel Negresco (Edwardian style, with turrets and white stucco). When Katy received the news in nearby San Remo, where we were staying with her parents, she immediately conceived a plot and rapidly put it into execution. She announced our arrival, at a *pension de famille* with no running water in the rooms or bathrooms. Each room,

Katy and Jane on the "Promenade des Anglais" in Nice, 1932

however, was provided with a porcelain basin and jug, and an enamelled bidet. "What a lovely doll's bath," I thought as I poured water from the jug into it and began undressing my doll. I had just placed my doll in her "bath" and was beginning to wash her when my mother and nurse returned from collecting the luggage. With horrified expressions on their faces, they whisked my doll out of her bath. Before I could burst into tears or ask what I had done wrong, they both informed me in a rush of words about the facts of "French" life and the danger of diseases. We took our baths at a clean, well-run public establishment, where the tub in each cubicle was lined with Hessian cloth that was changed after each use. We were also given little bags of bran to soften the water. The reason for our staying at the pension was to bring home to my grandparents how poor we were, in the hopes that grandfather would be more generous with dividends. They arrived bearing gifts for me just as the *pensionaires* sat down to lunch at a long narrow table covered with a paper tablecloth. My grandparents appeared undisturbed by the congestion, sat down at their allotted places at the *table d'hôte*, and remained perfectly at ease, appearing to accept their visit to the pension (including the public baths, which I told them about in detail) as perfectly normal. The next day the Cabots had us as guests in the large, ornate dining room of the Hotel Negresco. We then collected our luggage at the pension and returned to San Remo, where my mother waited hopefully for a letter announcing higher dividends. But her whole scheme to shock my grandparents had fallen flat. Grandmother Cabot wrote offering once again to raise me during the winters in Boston. "I love the child so dearly. I wish that I could have you, too, but grown-ups in the house tire me, while children do not; and I have got to be very very careful from now on." Aunt Eleanor Bradley offered to bring me up, too, after her youngest child died, but my mother's brainwashing had been effective, and I had no desire to be involved with such monsters! My grandmother died in November 1934.

Even when other members of the family visited Europe, my mother never made it easy for them to see me. When my uncle was *en poste* in Holland, and later Ambassador to Sweden, my mother turned down their invitations, saying that we were too poor to make the journey. Aunt Eleanor visited me at Avenches and also at school in England several times with her children, but as they had become complete strangers over the years, I projected my mother's negativism

about the family onto them. When I returned to Boston in 1950 for a
visit after twenty years, I was able to form my own opinions about my
relatives, or so I thought. Actually, it took another twenty years to
elude my mother's influence and really to form my own opinion.
When Grandfather Cabot visited me in St. Moritz after his wife's
death in 1934, I felt hostile towards him, even disliking the icicles on
his moustache when he kissed me. One day he said he wished to give
me a present, and asked what I wanted. I instantly replied that I
would like to have a microscope. Thinking that I was too young for
such an expensive instrument, he bought me a small, strong magnify-
ing glass instead, confirming all my mother had said about Cabot
stinginess. In the diary entries below Katy speaks of being more
conscious, but with her Cabot in-laws her powerful projections
prevented her from seeing them clearly.

The diary entry for 7 December 1933 ends with the following note:

In the seminar: Dr. Jung told us that Jesus said to a man working
in a field on the Sabbath, "If thou knowest what thou doest, thou
art blessed; if thou knowest not what thou doest, thou art cursed."
The highest accomplishment of man is to be conscious of himself.
The whole thing is to know what one is doing. All the moral and
ethical valuations of things are a mere interlude, a step in the
development of consciousness.

Two days later comes the testimonial to my mother's progress.

Hotel Waldhaus-Dolder
December 9th, 1933

Dear Doctor Jung: –
Only a few lines to tell you that despite the fact that I have only
seen you three times this term, I have been able to catch the
heretofore intangible thing which you have been trying to make
me see for so long – viz., my icy covering and the contents of the
"Lump." I speak of "catching" your meaning because it has just
begun to permeate very slowly – a glimmer, as it were – and I am
so afraid that maybe I won't be able to "hold" it. I went away from
our last interview feeling at last released from a burden because for
the first time I had begun to understand what you have tried for so
long to make clear to me. You know how one "suddenly" experiences a thing, whereas before then, you could talk and talk, and
one would never grasp it.

It was your last Seminar combined with my last hour that brought home to me all that you have been trying to tell me. I was deeply touched by some of the things you said in the last Seminar, and the heart that was behind, or *in* the things you said to us that day made me realize what I was lacking. I am going up to the mountains as usual for the winter, this time Arosa. The good cook will be with me so if you come up there please let me know.

Financial complications may prevent my coming back for a while but I am going to do my best to "stick to it" until I see you again.

I can never express to you my gratitude for all that you have done for me.

With all good wishes to yourself and Mrs. Jung for a very merry Xmas and a happy New Year,

    I am, sincerely yours,

            Catharine R. Cabot

Chapter Four

Further Travels and Katy's Illness, 1934-1936

Our next winter we spent at Arosa in Eastern Switzerland. With us came the German governess, the cook from Château d'Oex, and a lady's maid, Amélie Lallé. Tommy stayed in a hotel with his two brothers and his sister Agnes, who were Arosa habitués. His wife had disappeared. I skated and skied, enjoying both. When the weather did not favor these, I built igloos in the pines near our flat, pretending to be an explorer, especially during blizzards. One day I was wrenched from this fantasy by a man who appeared from nowhere, opened his fly, and exposed himself. It did not bother me much, since in the apartment below us was a German couple who liked to sunbathe on their balcony in the nude. I also did ski tours with the de Traffords, climbing on seal-skins, and learned a good deal of snow lore.

My mother and Tommy moved to Arosa because they were keen on a change of scenery. Katy spoke to me about ski touring, but the fact that Arosa was at the other end of Switzerland from Château d'Oex was not mentioned. She also mentions "financial complications" at that period, which kept her from analysis with Jung. But his fees were modest – about SFr 20 per hour – and she could afford a staff of three. It was nearly a year before she saw Jung again. The Tommy relationship had taken first place.

I went to boarding school in England in June 1934, staying until November. My mother never visited, but sent postcards from all over the British Isles, and kept in touch with the headmistress.

She had no fixed abode at this time, but only a bank address in London. When she wrote to Jung again in the autumn, he replied:

Küsnacht-Zürich
Seestrasse 228
October 11, 1934

Mrs. C. R. Cabot
c/o Guaranty Trust Co.
50 Pall Mall
London S.W. 1

Dear Mrs. Cabot,

Thank you for your letter. I am very busy this autumn, but I will do my best to fit you in somehow.

With best wishes,

Sincerely yours,

C.G. Jung

He writes again six weeks later:

Küsnacht-Zürich
Seestrasse 228
November 27th, 1934

Dear Mrs. Cabot,

I'm sorry but you were not forgotten. I only was unable to find time for you because a great deal of my time was taken by an expert's testimony for the court in a murder case. The fact that you are free in the afternoon only makes things still more difficult. The first possibility therefore is Tuesday next (4 Dec.) at 4 p.m.

Sincerely yours,

C.G. Jung

Her journal that winter notes:

December 4, 1934

I saw Dr. Jung this afternoon after a year's absence. I first talked of Janey and the skating problem. He said by all means, if I can, I should let her develop her talent, as one talent can lead to another; therefore, one should never refuse to let a child develop its talents and follow its bent. He said that I would be wrong if I did and one might regret it later all one's life. A person who has the knowledge that he does something well has a big advantage over other people and never gets those feelings of inferiority.

All that Dr. Jung says is perfectly correct, but the snag was that he took my mother's words at face value. Male analysts can forget how devious female analysands can be. My mother found Arosa a bore, needed an excuse to go to St. Moritz (heartily disapproved of by Jung), and used my foolish suggestion to go there. (A kindly skating teacher in Zürich, Frau Frenzen, noticing my loneliness, suggested St. Moritz because I would meet children on the rink there, some of whom I knew from Zürich.) I was useful for my mother's plans, and was forced by her, not my teacher, into the role of talented skater, so that I might shine later in Boston. Developing my skating was also a handy excuse for moving to the resort Jung so disapproved of. I had neither talent nor desire, but simply the wish to meet other children on the rinks, for in Switzerland, I met them nowhere else.

We took rooms at the Privat Hotel in the center of St. Moritz, used by "chic" parents staying at the Palace Hotel for billeting their nannies and children. My mother stayed with me, having eliminated the governess, and everyday I took the bus to the Suvretta ice rink where I met many children, just as Frau Frenzen had promised. I passed tests, competed, but failed to win a prize. By now my mother, both for convenience and because she was bent on making a skater out of me, transferred me to the Palace Hotel rink and a Swedish teacher, Bror Meyer. There were few children and I was horribly disappointed. I befriended Maedi Neubauer from Magdeburg, a girl my age who was a far better skater than I was. Next to her I was a gangling colt with a higher center of gravity, but there was no point in telling my mother that I had no vocation for skating, which I had tried to do at first. She told me firmly that *when you had chosen to do something you had to see it through.* So I concluded there was no escape from skating until I had taken my Swiss gold medal, and somehow the heretical thought kept me going. For a girl who lacked ambition, the training was heavy punishment: five hours a day of solitary practice, monotonous and unstimulating to the mind. Any mental potential I had was put on ice for the next six winters.

My mother's report on the session with Jung has some bearing on my ordeal:

> I then read him the fantasy of the cruel old woman and child. He quite rightly said that the old woman was my dark and shadow side, and the child was me at times, too. I said I had lost my sex and my digestion. He said that sex might be in the Lump and some

other strange things as well, for after hearing about the old woman he could bet that the Lump contained every old thing imaginable! He said he thought the Lump must be something rather ghastly! I told him that O. [Oswald, or Tommy] was here and my sex was gone. He was just opening his mouth to say something when the lights went out and we were in utter darkness. We roared with laughter! He said that O. being here and my having no sex made the whole thing ridiculous, which of course it does. There was so much to tell him and the time so short, that I could hardly catch up on it all. Jung went on to say that by writing [fantasies] one slowly gets out what is in the Lump, and then gets to know oneself. A person must know himself; otherwise, he becomes self-conscious. You can always tell that people are self-conscious inasmuch as they know not themselves – it is a sure sign they don't know themselves!

One must let a child gain all the knowledge that it wants to get.

The senator story was my animus flying around – superficial and unstable.

Katy was humble enough to acknowledge her dark side, but her inferiority complex enlarged it greatly. I feel that within the lump was a strong personality that failed to blossom, save for bossing me about. I would like to think that "the cruel old woman" was her undifferentiated attitude towards my skating. Since Jung, as a father figure, had approved of her plans for me (because he did not have the full story), she did not have to think further for herself. The father complex kept her childish, blotting out her ego judgment, while all those loops on the ice with *no double lines* failed to build up my ego at all. Much of what children my age picked up at school passed me by. When I finally emerged from the skating cocoon at seventeen, I had developed an enormous inferiority complex instead of avoiding one. Always different, I had not been allowed to be a member of the herd! I became self-conscious, because I could not measure myself against others and learn what I was capable of. Miss Aspinall, the headmistress, noticed the self-consciousness and wrote to my mother about it ("Yes, I wish one could alter that funny little brusque manner. ... Janey is intensely self-conscious") – but Katy did not take note. For all the psychology that she was imbibing in Zürich, my mother never used it to help me. My own needs did not count; I had to satisfy her own. Among these was her ambition that I shine as a skater when I became a débutante in Boston, justifying her decision to take me to live in Europe. The War, however, would alter that fantasy.[1]

The next session, two days later, moves to a subject which touched her in a special way – Catholicism:

December 6, 1934

I started talking at first of the Ten Commandments, and told Dr. Jung of Tommy's friend who left church before the benediction, and said, "I obey all God-made laws, but I do not feel bound to obey all man-made laws." Dr. Jung said that inasmuch as the Ten Commandments are near to a natural morality, they represent the will of God. If a person is not obedient to his parents, and does not honor them, he does not honor himself either. So if you violate and trespass against those Commandments, you do a thing against life.

He went on to say that the symbols of the Catholic Church have a peculiar validity and can function as if they were a truth despite the fact that they are so absurd. If the Catholic Church did not administer magic, so to speak, it would lose its hold over the people. The only place you can get this 'magic' is in a Catholic Church, administered by priests with apostolic succession. It is wonderful for people to have a place where actual magic is happening, for then the unconscious is caught. Dr. Jung said, "If I imagined that a priest could perform a rite of *real* magic value which could not be repeated or bought anywhere else, I would gladly turn Catholic." He went on to say that the Catholic Church insisted on these things because they express the unconscious as well as the sacrifice of the intellect demanded by the Catholic Church, and are in keeping with a church. Dr. Jung continued, "Suppose there are two kinds of people: some who know that elephants exist and others who don't believe it and they say, 'How absurd to invent such an animal with a trunk and such a thick skin,' as they don't know it really exists. One can hardly believe in the duckbill platypus, which is a warm-blooded animal which lays eggs. Those who have seen it know that it exists; those who have not seen it, say, 'How absurd!' But those who have seen it and know it is true, are like the Catholics – for to them, the Virgin birth has

---

[1] Much later, in the 1960's, my mother decided to bring out my eldest daughter Diana in Boston, so her ambition to bring out someone in Boston was finally satisfied.

happened: it is to them like the elephants and platypuses. Others say how absurd to invent such a story of elephants and platypuses. They are the Protestants, who have forgotten that the Virgin Birth is a fact – of course the Virgin Birth and the Trinity are *psychological facts* and not historical facts."

At the beginning of the 19th century, there was a man who collected meteor specimens, and the testimony from eye witnesses who saw the meteors fall. He wrote a paper and handed it in to his academy of science, who read the paper and refused to publish it 'since there are no stones in heaven, no stones can fall from the air'! The man was called an inventor. In other words, the teachings of the Catholics are similar: for them, the Virgin Birth and the Trinity are facts. Jung said that people often confused reality with psychological reality. When Nietzsche did not grasp the psychological reality of Zarathustra, then he *is* Zarathustra and is mad. If Dr. Jung did not realize the Wise Old Man psychologically, he would *become* the Wise Old Man with spectacles, a long beard, and then, by identifying himself with the Wise Old Man, he would become crazy.

As my mother had been brought up in a convent, Catholicism interested her, touching her emotionally but leaving her intellectually resistant. It was only some years after Jung's death, when Katy married an Italian, that she actually became Catholic, mainly so that she could ensure that she would be buried next to her husband in the family vault. After his death, the understanding Bishop of Ventimiglia received her into the Church. On her death, in 1976, he conducted the burial service at the Pro Cathedral in San Remo.

The record for the session continues:

O. has finished his life – it's over as far as he is concerned – if he did something and was interested in something else outside of me, I would feel a tension, and that is what I should feel. O. is exaggeratedly interested in nothing but me, whereas one wants a happy medium in such things.

I mentioned the fact that O.'s War experiences had been pretty terrific, and that he had never been the same since. [Tommy had been taken prisoner by the Germans in World War One]. Dr. Jung said that people, who had been through the War, had seen so much that it had completely altered their outlook; he had seen so much human suffering and had had such stirring experiences with people. He said that O. had made those society people see what they have never felt; that they are awful and impossible, so they take it out on him and say, "He's dull." O. gets out of it all that he puts into it with me. If he'd say, "I'll make money" and go about making it, then there would be tension, and for passion, there must be that tension.

Dr. Jung said [Barbara] Hannah admired me very much and would like to do as I do, but doesn't know how. [Mary] Foote is afraid I am a very bad person and suspects I might have a beau.

The relationship was still young, but Jung's analysis of Tommy was correct; in less than eight years, he would be dead. I could see that Tommy smoked and drank too much, but right up to his final illness my mother remained oblivious to his excesses. As for "making money," it was a strange example for Jung to use for a pre-war upper-class Englishman. A gentleman did not go into business. Only vulgar people did that! If you were an eldest son, you inherited lands which brought in rents, or if you were not, you either married a rich wife or joined the army or the church. As a younger son who had not married money, Tommy was resigned to being poor. He had never lived in the real world; the army was just a continuation of boarding school. His path was that of the officer and gentleman. His first major mistake was his marriage; retirement brought him his first experience outside an institution. Eventually Tommy did turn to something outside the relationship, increasing the tension, but the venture would be frustrated. As for Barbara Hannah and Mary Foote, they had arrived in Zürich at about the same time, a few years before Katy. Both were artists, and in analysis with Jung, and both lived at the Pension Sonne in Küsnacht before eventually taking apartments. As noted earlier, Barbara Hannah was the daughter of the Anglican Dean of Chichester, while Mary Foote's father, from New York, had built an Anglican church in the grand manner on his six-hundred-acre estate in Connecticut. Petite Mary was a well-known portraitist, twenty-two years older than Katy, who looked the typical elderly spinster, while Barbara, bigger-boned and with a strong chin, was more energetic and was Katy's elder by only three years. Jung's impromptu comments were meant to bolster Katy.

The next entry concerns something I knew at first-hand, Katy's infrequent but violent rages, probably on a par with her father's. She would shake me by the shoulders like a jelly, when I took pleasure in provoking her:

December 10, 1934

One builds up one's external persona not knowing that one is compensating. Nurses are frequently sadists. That is why they make themselves so understanding and devoted. I have something like sadism in me when I am in a mood of rage. If I put myself on the level of a stupid person, I will understand wanting to marry Dr. Jung. Dr. Jung has an extraordinary understanding for women's unconscious. Every woman is:

> Cave woman
> Primitive
> Medieval woman

In my dream of Dr. Jung, in which I belittle him by saying, "He's sleeping with his cook," I am an enraged woman in a love plot which has been thwarted. I felt Dr. J. was unable to take me seriously because 'that old swine' was sleeping with his cook. If he were a decent chap, he would love me and not that elephant of a cook – a low down eros and not living up to a wonderful height! Disappointed love. One can bring down everyone to a lower level where they give up their mind and get into an emotional condition.

My pa-in-law must be sensitive as he acts so hard – maybe to disguise his tender side. Dr. Jung went on to say that in analysis first lovely feelings are exchanged, but after that one can go lower to affectionate gestures and a kiss, then on the ground floor is bed.

My mother could not see her father-in-law's sentimental side, and so could never relate to him or control him as she did Tommy and other men. She called Jung *Onkel* eventually but was never in love with him; he was a *bona fide* father figure. The dream shows a child wanting to marry daddy. The entry ends:

Dr. Jung said that if I talk psychological jargon these Zürich spinsters would like me, but of course it would be *précieux*.

The Vaudois man [Professor Vodoz] is a distinguished lecturer [who spoke at the Psychological Club].

I get along with society people because I put myself out to please.

The last remark points to Katy's being ill at ease. The people she felt comfortable with were waiters, maids, concierges, and hotel managers, who had the common touch and who responded to her by liking her.

The summer of the following year brought Katy to the work of the dark side:

June 11, 1935

I spoke first of his front door, which is utterly charming swathed in green trees and is the only thing visible in the vista of his house from the street. "Almost symbolical," I said, and he said, "Yes."

He spoke of the Lump and asked me how it was getting on. I told him that I had digested the horrible old woman and realized that she was me, or *in* me. He said there was much else to come out in me and that I must find *my shadow side* before I find out my other side. I said I had felt depressed when I got back to Zürich, and that Mrs. Fierz saying, *"Prozit caviar,"* had made me realize there was nothing in me. He said that depressed meant a depression. One must go down before one can come up. One has a black and a white side. One must get to know both sides within, and when one knows them one can conciliate them, so to speak, and sit astride of them. He then went on to say things I couldn't grasp. He said that one had to experience all that to grasp it, so I sat dumbly by while he spoke as I did not understand a word! Maybe he meant that by finding out my two sides, one gained a spiritual freedom? At any rate he pointed out to me vigorously that by having got to know myself inasmuch as the cruel woman is part of the Lump, I have not harmed myself. On the contrary, I have done myself lots of good! Panics in the funiculaire show that all the contents of the Lump are still unknown, and that *I must get the shadow out.*

My mother's attention to her shadow was so thorough that she sometimes became discouraged. The Lump was an enigma that puzzled both her and Jung. My view in hindsight is that it consisted mainly of her father complex, the Old Sea Captain whose anima may have been the cruel old woman.

I told him I was miserable as I felt there was nothing in me. He said, "You take the panics *seriously*, don't you?" I said, "Yes." "Well," he said, "if you take the panics seriously then there is seriousness within you." If a person stands in front of a picture and raves over it, and feels inferior because he cannot create such a lovely thing, then it shows there is *beauty* in him for otherwise he could not feel that way.

My mother had many good sides she was unaware of and did not develop. Her sense of humor made the dullest people laugh and helped her past difficult moments. She had intelligence, good taste, charm, kindness, generosity, and a great deal of energy, alas often expended on useless causes. Obsessed with her shadow in this early period of her analysis, she projected it onto others:

I spoke of the emptiness of certain older American and English women who are like harpies sitting around in a circle or like wolves in front of the fire ready to pounce on their prey. Dr. Jung said that once he had had to wait for an hour and a half in the Crillon lobby [a Paris hotel]. There he saw the fashionable and beautiful, old and young, English and American women coming and going, and the emptiness of their faces and the vacant stare of their eyes was appalling. I said that nevertheless the opinion of such people carried more weight with me than the opinions of a person like B. Hannah or the other worthy flat-footed females of the seminar. "Oh, those," said Dr. Jung, "if you put Hannah in trousers she'd be a typical Scottish minister. She envies you and would like to be like you. She'd like to have your nails, but they wouldn't suit her, she'd be ridiculous!" I said, I thought the French women were wonderful, for though they were chic and well turned out they were not empty and vacant, but had substance. And the old French women were rare charmers with charm and wit of experience. Dr. Jung said they lived near the earth and in their own country.

I then told him about Minnie and Va [her mother and father]. He said that if one were brought up in such filth one naturally imbibed some of it, for as a child one did not *think*. It is just as if a child were brought up by criminals: naturally, their atmosphere would get into him even though, as he grew older, he would lead a decent life. He would have the criminal stuff in him even if it were canned, and like canned vegetables it would remain closed and untouched, yet the tin would be inside him full of that stuff, and so it is with me. If you are brought up by such people with such meanness in them even though you later discover that you are decent, and intend to lead a decent life, you have imbibed that mean stuff and put it in a can hermetically sealed where it will stay 'as is' for years!

I told Jung that I could not stay with Minnie the last night and had left, and had felt like shooting the bunch. He said, "Oh, were they as bad as that?" (Which showed he must have had a lot of confidence in my story.) I said, "Fancy having such parents." He replied that you are not only the child of your parents but the child of mankind. One does not necessarily take after one's parents; one can have some very decent ancestors to take after. He added that if one could go back far enough in the history of one's parents one could find out why they became that way.

I had always heard that her father was a saint and that it was her mother who was difficult, but Jung obviously heard the whole truth and got the full strength of her feeling. Unconscious people will quarrel a lot, but I am astonished about the "filth." I did hear later that William Rush used to browbeat his subordinates at the Boston Navy Yard – probably the real reason for his failure to be promoted to Admiral. His smaller pension must have provoked my grand-mother to let her husband know her thoughts on the subject. When I knew them, they seemed mild, and more in touch with *terra firma* than mother. My grandmother read to me and was kind; the only shadow side I noticed was her gossip, which bored me. I simply switched off, thinking my own thoughts while she talked but answer-ing appropriately when addressed. My grandmother had great energy, but was only fifty-two when her husband retired at sixty-five. I remember them sitting in their library wrapped in blankets against the cold, even though she wore seven petticoats and a woolen undershirt. She was still too young to lead a retired life. She enter-tained, but once in San Remo after her husband's sixty-fifth year, her only stimulus was reading, and her active consolation was vigorous gardening. She was very fond of sweet peas, and maintained that if you removed the tendrils, the blooms would be larger. That was my job, during the long season for sweet peas in the mild climate of San Remo. My grandparents never quarreled in front of me. They traveled little. My grandmother obtained some excitement by playing the stock-market in a modest way. She was astute, so made some tidy sums of money. But she was cautious about spending. She told me time and again that it was the *small foxes* who ate up the vines. Though my mother tells Jung how awful her parents were, she was very upset when her father became ill just before the War, arranging that he go to Zürich rather than remain in the hands of Riviera doctors. When he died in 1940, she moved heaven and earth to get her mother into Switzerland, which was difficult at the time. Jane Rush lived in Geneva and Lausanne until her death in 1947, infrequently seen by Katy because of her negative mother complex. Even the arduous trip my grandmother planned to take to Washington, D.C., in 1947 – which her final illness prevented – to bring her husband's ashes for military burial in Arlington National Cemetery when she had heart trouble and high blood pressure, led my mother to beg off as companion, again using me as the excuse when writing to her sister-in-law, Eleanor Bradley in Boston: "I am *so* disappointed not to be able to go, but I had promised Janey to go to Turkey, and she is counting on it and urges me to come in every letter." True, I had asked my mother to come out for the new baby, but had I known of her mother's needs, I would not have pressed my suit. Katy went neither to Turkey nor to the U.S. in 1947.

Though my mother often told me she was a feeling type, I was not so sure. She sometimes showed gross lack of feeling, and could not sense other people's needs. Of course, she thought that she did, enjoying the role of the great provider, for instance. One of her targets were the Jungs, to whom she was always sending flowers. (Mrs. Jung reciprocated with books at Christmas.) She also liked to give unsolicited advice, especially in matters of health, not only to her Boston father-in-law in his nineties but also to Jung. I was the main target or outlet for her authoritarian side. Like many older upper-class women in pre-war days who did not have to earn their living, Katy ran other people's lives for them.

June 17, 1935

I told Dr. Jung that a dream I had, and the stuff I wrote, showed me up to Miss Wolff as vulgar and commonplace, and yet I did not mind that very much and said to myself, *"Je m'en fiche* [I don't care] if I am vulgar or not." He said, "Let's hear the dream." And I told it to him: I was having an earache, and Mrs. Baumann[1] suggested I have an operation performed on my ear. I took the man

---

[1] Carol Baumann was an American pupil of Jung, married to a Swiss and living in Zürich. Née Fisher, her father was important in finance. Divorced from a Mr. Sawyer, she remarried, then later divorced her Swiss husband (information Prof. C. A. Meier).

she suggested – a valet – a vulgar man. He performed a bloodless painless operation. Later he performed an operation on the other ear. I asked how he sterilized his instruments. My night nurse, a Boston hairdresser, said that because he was sexually pure he sterilized his instruments with semen!

Dr. Jung went on to say that the ears had to do with 'hearing,' and that 'obedience' in German was *Gehorsam* – to hear is to obey. A *Hörig* [bondsman] belongs like a slave to a feudal lord, and also comes from hearing. A *Hörig* hears his master's voice: he takes it unto himself and follows it.

The trouble is in my ears for I don't 'get' the feeling understanding through my ears; there is trouble with my emotional understanding. I *see* more than I *hear*. I can't get the 'feeling' nuance in seeing, but due to my Pa's terrible avalanche of words, I am a bit deaf. My ears ought to be operated on, and it is done by a vulgar person – a magical operation with semen, impregnating me through the ear. An old idea that the Virgin conceived through the ear, *Suepem aurum conceptis*. (She conceived the word, and *hearing* the voice of the Lord, took it into her heart.) I try too much to think intellectually, and I do not allow the feeling to go with it. I do not link up the feeling with what I actually hear. I hear words and try to *think* them. A simple mind should come and operate on my ears so that it will reach my heart and not my brain. When I listen to what people say, I grasp it intellectually and not with my heart. Jung said it was as if he told a man that he was 'not thinking clearly,' or something similar, and the man then goes home and looks up a medical diagram of the head and wonders where the proboscis is on his brain which prevents him from thinking clearly.

I said that Mrs. Baumann was only a cold intellectual. He rather caught me up on that, and said, "Mrs. Baumann understands analysis better than anyone in an intellectual way." I felt snubbed as I had rather tried to belittle Mrs. Baumann. It is an intellectual conclusion that I ought to have a pure mind so as to hear the feeling part too. That is (the feeling) that I don't get correctly, for I have been badly poisoned in my hearing by my father's bad language, so I don't get the feeling side of things through my ears. My intellect is not a great or reliable function, but it is not so prejudiced, while my hearing is badly prejudiced. He repeated that I do not get the feeling aspect of things, I take in things intellectually. On the contrary, I thought, I took them in with feeling. He said that an idiot, who has no intellect, can be frightfully intellectual and can miss the feeling values just as much! A person can be prejudiced by an intellectual way of understanding. I take things in intellectually, for when a thing is *black* then it is *black* and that is that.

For instance, I say, "That must be difficult if Dr. Jung thinks so hard over it and how to explain it clearly to me." Someone who *hears* would say that I must be dull if I don't understand the effort Dr. Jung is making to get me to understand what he is driving at. He is putting into it great effort and kindness to help me, and if I don't *get that* with my feeling, then I have a 'feeling dullness.' I must *Hear* the feeling behind the words and get the *rhythm of it*, the *intensity of it*. Unfortunately, all that has been poisoned in me by Pa. If one is kind to me, I don't get the particular quality of feeling, or on the tympanum of the ear, so I don't hear properly anymore. It does not have to be *personal* stuff one gets feeling with, but can be what Jung, or other people, say on political events etc., which are interesting, apart from the personal. For instance, a person can give you a modest bunch of flowers, and they have personal value, and another can give you diamonds, but they have no value as there is no personal relationship there. Jung said that he could well understand that I could get the beauty and feelings in paintings, as that comes through the *eyes* and not through the *ears*. I asked Jung not to leave me hanging on the jibet [sic], so he said he would see me Friday at twelve. He was most sympathetic as I left and said, "If you hear the right way you will hear the unconscious and what it is trying to tell you."

Before I talked with him about the foregoing, I asked him what he meant when he said that Hindenburg was the symbol of the 'Old Wise Man' to the German people, without the wisdom. He said then that Hindenburg was a very simple soul and that once out of military affairs he did what he was told by the politicians. There is a story that a man went to see him and waited for hours; finally, he took his lunch out of a paper and ate it, leaving the paper lying on the table just as Hindenburg entered. Hindenburg took the paper and signed it!! Later his secretary said to this man, "You must never leave a paper lying around, for he signs all the papers he sees." Another time Hitler, Göbbels and Göring went to a restaurant and met Hindenburg, and he signed the menu!

I asked Jung how it was that Hitler had such power over the German people. He said it was because he spoke to the Unconscious – for instance he would say, "We need an army," ... "We are being oppressed by foreign powers ..." etc. and in their hearts was the answering cry: "He is right, we are oppressed – we do need an army" etc. I suggested that Hitler had been cruel – murdering and decapitating women etc. Once they told him he *must not* leave the League of Nations. He shut himself up for three days in his room, and at the end came out pale and shaken, and said: "We *shall* leave the League of Nations." Jung said he doubted whether Hitler was homosexual, but that friends of his who knew Hitler said that he was – or at least they strongly suspected he was.

My mother certainly had a problem with her ears. Listening to what people said was difficult for her; to gain and keep her attention was a monumental task. I excused this particularity by deciding that she had learned to switch off just as I did, but over the years I have concluded that "not hearing" might be a genetic trait, because several family members have the tendency. As for the bad language and temper in her father that she shows distaste for in the sessions with Jung, both her own bad temper and the way she laid down the law were masculine, a side which she never saw, hiding it from herself with the conviction that she was extremely feminine and with her interest in modish clothes. Katy not only identified with her father in this unconscious way, but also remained his meek little girl. This split, which she never grasped, generated her depressions and claustrophobia. Katy blamed it all on the adjustments forced upon her by her return to America, not sensing that her own unresolved polarity was at issue. Her shifts between the dual sides were difficult for me to understand as a child, but have grown clearer to me as I look back.

The idea of the animus was pivotal. Though much of the Lump's contents remained elusive, Katy had turned forty in 1935, and the little-girl side was retreating while the masculine side was in the ascendant – a normal process for women, according to Jung. The animus that had always floored me at home began to manifest in the outside world, even symbolically. At the fancy-dress parties of the Jungian group Katy went from a seductive Merry Widow's outfit in the early thirties to a Pierrot, a British Spinster with man's hat and flat shoes, and a Swiss Peasant with pipe and beard, a favorite of hers, which won first prize. She also showed male *bonhomie*, getting on

Carnival, Zürich, 1932

very well with men in a non-flirtatious way, enjoying risqué jokes, and enjoying jolly drinking companions. Katy had a deep voice and was often addressed on the telephone as *monsieur* when she phoned for breakfast in a hotel. This she liked! Katy told me that her voice had broken because her mother had forced her to take singing lessons as a young girl. In her middle years, she certainly felt more at ease with men than with women. (When in love, she had to dominate.) Though she could be enthusiastic about a new female acquaintance, after a while the woman, failing to live up to an ideal image, was dubbed totally evil. As Jung said, "Then it is black, and that is that."

Dr. Jung did not leave her hanging on a gibbet, seeing her again four days later.

June 21, 1935 (Longest day)

This interview was so astounding and so profound that I can hardly write about it for it has made the most tremendous impression on me, and I am 'afraid.' (I say 'afraid' because one is afraid of changes.) He has changed the whole course of my life. Dr. Jung first asked me if I had finally understood what he meant by not feeling through the ear. I told him it had permeated, and that Tommy had helped me understand it. Jung said, "De T. has a very good mind; even though he knows nothing of psychology, he is able to express a psychological problem to you in simple terms."

I then told him of my transference to Wolff and how I hated her saying she was not seeing me again, and how I finally asked her to dinner; that at first she was cold then said she would come. Jung said that Wolff had certainly released my feeling.

I then asked him why Mr. Crowley had an ANIMUS, and I went on to say that despite the fact that he might think me queer I was determined to hold to it that Mr. Crowley had an *animus*!! He said indeed it was true and that he had saddled himself with *Mrs.* Crowley's *animus*, so it was really Mrs. Crowley's animus speaking through Mr. Crowley. He said that when they first came to him they were the most extraordinary couple he'd ever seen and that he saw from the beginning that they would have to part. He laughed when I told him how Mr. Crowley's *animus* conversed viz: "Mrs. C. and I met up here [in the clouds]; now we are down on the mountain top and I'm dragging her down – it's an angel tied to a pig and the pig has left the angel up there and gone to wallow in mud." etc. etc.!! How Jung laughed!

Then I read Jung the Juanita fantasy:

Juanita lives for gaiety, marries and finally returns to gaiety then leaves and goes into a convent, saying good-bye to her husband and all the things of this world.

After I had finished reading it Jung looked pretty serious for he realized that I had touched on something pretty fundamental in myself. He said that, as a child, I had been so fed up with my parents' language, I had made myself deaf so as not to hear, so it could not reach my heart, otherwise I would have been too unhappy. He said that often a child can stand parents another child could not stand because he has learnt to live with them by growing defenses. I grew a rhinoceros hide over my heart so none of my parents' avalanches could reach me. It was a defense which grew thicker and thicker as the years went on. When my parents said things, it went in one ear and out the other. He said I was like *two sisters*, the one ran away into the desert. The other stayed as a mold of parents and had the panics. Something in me would not persuade me into life. He said that he long suspected that, as I returned year after year to Zürich, I was looking for the ascetic way of life. He knew I must be interested in the *subject* I was studying, not in *him* personally.

If I returned year after year to Zürich, I said, with tears, that it was because I had found a gold mine here, and once having seen it, I could never look away and I had to keep coming to Zürich. He said that my neurosis did not warrant my sticking on as I had done. I said that I did not *want* to go into a convent. He said, "Naturally not." I said I thought monks and nuns were not human, and he replied, "Are people very human after all?" He added that one may be looking for a plane that was not the futile society plane that one was pushed into. As a child I had covered my heart with rhino hide so that my parents could not hurt me. Jung said I must answer people back, like Hannah, when they are rude. As a child I did not dare answer back to my parents as that would have been unwise, and now I have adopted the same attitude with others. I was forced into a way of life completely foreign to my desires. Certain desires, like my desire for asceticism, were repressed in childhood and reappear in me as a neurosis; that is to say, the unconscious forces are attempting to achieve conscious expression! That is clear. All this is something I have vaguely felt, and suspected, but until now it has not been brought home to me, and I feel shattered and afraid of a new way of life.

I had once been puzzled by the "two sisters." My mother's frequent illnesses and long bed rests, and the operations which took her out of circulation, gave an advantage to the ascetic side, to the need for reading and reflection. Unfortunately, the social side imprinted by her parents always regained the upper hand, so new illnesses were required to force her to introvert. When Jung was older and my mother saw him infrequently, she was seldom reminded of the ascetic sister. The over-indulgence of her social pastimes began to affect her strong physique, bringing on "flus" at any time of the year, which I discovered later to be problems with her heart and circulation. Katy left Zürich in the early 'fifties and took over her parent's villa in San Remo, where she became a much-appreciated hostess, entertaining well. But she could never entirely banish the ascetic side, even then. It would manifest itself in San Remo with long reading sessions late at night. (Because the Italian upper classes expected books to be kept out of sight, she said, she kept hers in bookcases in her bedroom.) From time to time, Katy had to get completely away from the Riviera, fleeing San Remo's oppressive small talk, gossip and intrigues, by taking trips to Ascona or Paris. When it was inconvenient for her to leave San Remo, she would take a day's excursion to the mountains behind the resort. Her chauffeur, Semeria, a confirmed bachelor who had served in a tank regiment during World War II, took her to the stone hut he had fitted out in his terraced vineyard, cooking simple meals over a charcoal fire and serving them with his excellent homemade wines. He had even constructed a W.C. with running water for my mother. When Katy was on one of these excursions, she would announce that she felt like giving up society for good. Yet back in San Remo she would be shocked if I mentioned that society bored me. She seemed programmed to live out the urge to play the social part that both parents, even her father, had implanted. The memorable hour with Jung did not lead Catharine to become sufficiently conscious to hear correctly what a new way of life would ask of her, for the idea shattered her.

June 24, 1935

This interview simply blew up the foregoing one because I let my animus (as Dr. Jung said) whisper utter nonsense to me such as the idea that I ought to go into a convent. Of course, Dr. Jung never meant such tosh as that. He only meant that my fantasy showed that I wanted a way of life which was between the utter frivolousness I had led, and the ridiculously poisonous existence of say, my grandparents (Rush). He said he was surprised that I took what he had said in the way I did, for there was a big distance between the café and the monastery! It was a 'joke' of my animus to make me think I must choose between either – a café or a monastery/nunnery! It was just what my Pa would say, "Either you enjoy Vichy or Deauville or you go to a nunnery." I should no longer be under the spell of my *Eltern* [parents]. I seem to have taken what Dr. Jung said as a reproach. If I had heard through my heart, I could not possibly have reacted in such a way. Evidently, I don't hear right yet. My ear must still have a scar over the tympanum for me to have reacted that way. I took it as if a father had reproached me, and told me to begin a better life! I took that opportunity to release a flood of opinions. It was what a person without an education would think: namely, that a decent pursuit of mental activities is unworldly. I told him how I thought perhaps I was becoming an ascetic because I took no more pleasure in cafés, and going about to places of amusement. He said quite casually that I had just got blasé about cafés. Finally, after loving that kind of thing, I got bored stiff. When I said, I thought I wanted a higher walk of life, Jung answered, "The nunnery is another kind of curiosity, not a higher walk of life." Instead of *conscious thinking* my animus was weaving threads – a powerful animus like a Methodist parson who knows but vice and sins of the flesh. My sex is in the unconscious. It's amazing how I don't follow my feeling, and how the animus spins its awful web. It's as if I were a very old lady without sex. It must be my identity with the mother because I am not old. It is in order to escape the youthful person in myself, who is a youngish woman who has fantasies she can't subscribe to, so I need an identification with an old woman because then I renunciate, but my sex still exists though only under certain conditions! My sex is associated with a different sort of treatment (than the *kind* and *considerate* treatment given me by O.) on account of my Pa. My personal relationship to O. is *too good*. My sex would accept manhandling, or at least be connected with rough things such as fights, tiffs etc. My animus puts me up against terrible dilemmas: either the life I now live or a nunnery! A florid animus! My sex seems to have gone into that animus and he seems to be 'my man,' and has eaten up my sexuality and also prevents me hearing through the ears. I must realize that when my animus comes out, it comes out red hot and wants to get to the point without thinking, and the thought about the thing – it's red hot.

I seem to grasp the animus for the first time in my life. I really 'feel' and 'realize' that animus man whispering and telling me things and pushing me into idiotic actions and sayings. It is a wonderful relief to REALIZE the animus at last. I saw last evening at B. Hannah's lecture how the animus prevented my speaking to Dr. Jung in a nice human way. I was cold and aloof when he accosted me in French, and as my animus was saying, "The thundering Jove is talking to you." I just did not listen to what he said. I have also seen B. Hannah as she is, for I had the nerve to be rude in return, as Dr. Jung said I should be ... I saw her as a *little girl* and she just as suddenly ceased to interest me, and lost her power over me. And then I began to feel sorry for her.

The snag was that my mother would see her situation pretty clearly for a while but then fall back into her old ways of thinking and behaving. The café society that she thought she had outgrown would attract her again. And Barbara Hannah would turn ogre once more, and my mother a little girl. She forgot what Jung told her about her animus, instead seeing a negative animus only in other women. It might have helped her to understand her animus better by giving it a name. (Though the Lump rolling about was an impediment, its contents, roughly derived from her father's rougher sides, were unknown, so unnamed.) Her animus was caught in her father complex, so that she identified with an old man rather than an old woman; no wonder she had problems with her sex. Obviously, as a child Catharine had been unable to form an emotional bond with her difficult father. A not infrequent occurrence between fathers and daughters ensued: as no *relationship* was possible between them, she *identified* with him instead. At the clinic where I worked, the small private Jungian Psychiatric Klinik am Zürichberg, several women had a similar problem. Two of them astonished me by mirroring their fathers physically as well as mentally, one of them posturing as her father did, the other, though anorexic, displaying the arm and leg muscles of a man. From my work with women patients, I learned how important an emotional marriage with the father, or with his substitute (the first man in a woman's life), is vital for feminine development.[1]

My mother's visual function was very well developed; maybe it was for that reason she loved art so much, and was forever dragging me around museums. Her love of Nature was less intense, though she was fond of dogs. She liked gardens, and often spoke of Jung's garden at Küsnacht and particularly of the approach to his front door, which she describes in her interview with Jung of 11 June 1935. She must have suggested to Jung that Barbara Hannah paint the vista of his house, because he writes:

Küsnacht-Zürich
Seestrasse 228
July 10th, 1935

Mrs. C. Cabot
Waldhaus Dolder
Zürich

Dear Mrs. Cabot,

Miss Hannah has indeed asked me concerning the picture you propose to her. I told her that I have no objection against that plan. I even think it is a very good idea because it is a nice vista down the path.

Hoping you will have a nice summer, I remain,

Yours sincerely,

C.G. Jung

Katy spent part of the summer of 1935 traveling with Tommy in Germany, visiting places to which Fräulein Speck had taken her as a girl. I spent the holidays with the school in both Sussex and Somerset, where Miss Aspinall had rented a country house for a month. These summer holidays over four years running were the most pleasant moments of my childhood. We swam, visited abbeys and cathedrals, and went on evening picnics. Most exciting, when I was fourteen, was our discovery at Haccombe House, near Taunton, of a "secret passage" (a tunnel) leading to a "secret" wine cellar with shelves from ceiling to floor. The old, oddly shaped bottles were enveloped in a thick, spongy grey mold about an inch thick. Only my impersonation

[1] See Jane C. Reid, "Der Lebenswichtige Vater," *Analytische Psychologie* 17: 38-56 (1986), and S. Levenkron, *Treating and Overcoming Anorexia Nervosa* (Scribners, New York, 1982).

of the Scarlet Pimpernel, which required a certain *noblesse oblige*, prevented me from tasting one of these to show my knowledge of wines to the other children.

By September, still without a fixed abode, Katy wrote to Jung for an appointment. He replied to her Paris bank address:

Küsnacht-Zürich
Seestrasse 228
September 16th, 1935

Mrs. C. Cabot
c/o Guaranty Trust Co.
4 Place de la Concorde
Paris

Dear Mrs. Cabot,

Thank you for your kind letter. I take notice of your intention to come back at the beginning of November, and I hope I will be able to do something for you, which, however, is a mere hope for the time being.

Well, I don't wonder that you had some intimations from your uncanny friend. One could suspect as much.

Yes, the situation of the world is terrible. I only hope that the fire can be isolated.

My best wishes,
Cordially yours,

C.G. Jung

Both Katy and Tommy had been shocked by Nazi Germany during their extensive visit there in 1935. Tommy was "uncanny" because, having been a prisoner of war in Germany for most of the First World War, when he saw the Nazis rearming, he predicted that a second world conflict was imminent. Katy and Tommy had also visited her old school friends, who were anti-Nazi and who found it a relief to speak openly. There followed two Christmas visits, which I made alone with my mother, in 1935 and 1936. She may have sensed that the Germany she knew was rapidly coming to an end, and that she might never see her friends there again. Though I was young then, I remember very well how grim the atmosphere was. Frugality and a depressed atmosphere prevailed in those homes. The Weiersmüllers, owners of a *Lebkuchen* factory in Nürnberg, and Mucki and Daria Holenstein, impoverished aristocrats who lived in a run-down country Château, had in common a lack of food, an intense dislike of Hitler and his regime, and fears of the worst for their country. At Christmas of 1935, when I was twelve, we arrived at the Weiersmüllers'. Full of her 1909 school spirit, my mother came laden with rubber buns, fake sugar lumps embedded with flies, a chocolate bar made of soap, and other delights from the Franz Carl Weber toy shop in Zürich. I felt a little apprehensive, but kept my mouth shut. The first gift my mother produced was the bar of chocolate. Her hostess thanked her profusely, saying that chocolate was difficult to find. The following day at lunch, she brought in a delicious looking chocolate pudding, saying proudly that she had made it with the *Swiss* chocolate. Katy went pale as a sheet, and then with a rush of words confessed. I squirmed. Frau Weiersmüller, grinning broadly, placed the dish before my mother and, after a long pause, said that she had discovered the joke when she sliced bananas with the same knife she had used on the chocolate. A reserve bar of chocolate from her storeroom had repaired the breach. My mother's relief was palpable, and repeatedly we were full of praises for the pudding. This close shave did not deter my mother from producing more of her jokes. During Christmas 1936 at the Holensteins' she produced a luscious looking rubber bun covered in fake sugar which she placed surreptitiously atop a pile of grey sliced bread. At lunch the Holensteins' rather plump daughter of fifteen, Marie-Thérèse, seeing the bun lost her party manner and stretched across the table, took it and bit into it greedily to the horror of her parents. A loud squeak emanated from the bun and, blushing and confused, Marie-Thérèse dropped it like a hot brick. The thin soups and meatless stews at the Château, grey and dismal, prompted my mother to leave without a word and comb the countryside. The best she could do was an emaciated chicken, which I looked at with contempt but which thrilled our hosts, who served it stewed with boiled rice.

Katy's jokes lasted well into the mid nineteen-forties, either at her own dinner parties or at other people's. I remember one dinner at the Jungs' house in Küsnacht in the winter of 1941, where the other guests were the Princess Hohenzollern and Toni Wolff. My mother deftly sprinkled some cold fluid onto Jung's seat cushion when he rose to carve a goose (a rare treat during the War). When he sat down again, the fluid went into action, and he shifted on his seat for a bit, but as the cold penetrated, he was forced to stand. Guessing what was up, he burst into great guffaws of laughter, astonishing the others but relieving me. When Katy explained, Mrs. Jung laughed, but Toni was not amused.

November 25, 1935

I came to Dr. Jung today with all my material of the ghastly animus who beats, kills, decapitates babies and is generally a scoundrel, rascal and murderer. I read him all my animus stuff, which ended with the animus's mother finally leaving and going off to America and getting ten years younger while the animus went down into the underworld (or into a mine in the story to liberate entombed miners) – to liberate people down there; which means that the miners are a bit of my *mind* in darkness, and the animus goes to give it life, like *les eaux nouvelles* or milk after birth which comes to keep the infant alive. This condition of the animus is a preparatory condition, Dr. Jung said. The time in the analysis which precedes the birth of the animus is terribly trying, or has been for me until I bore that son. Up until then the son was identical with myself, a bad shadow. The animus will now be helpful, Dr. Jung added. I asked how. He said that he would light up the unconscious and bring back valuable thoughts. "How will I know it?" I asked. "You will know it all right," answered Jung. I did not quite see it at the time, but in the last few days, I have seen it, or glimpsed it at intervals. As the Animus is now divorced from me, I am not one with it anymore. The baleful shadow of its ghastly personality has lifted and allowed me to glimpse unconscious contents which may be stuff to rejuvenate and embellish my life, as in the story I wrote, when the mother left the son and she became younger and unrecognizable. I gave birth to my animus as I did to a child, and at the time suffered as in childbirth, but it was worth it.

Then Dr. Jung got up and went out and brought back a typewritten manuscript, a translation from the Greek into French, copied by Mrs. [Cary] Baynes. It was wonderfully well written. At first Dr. Jung said I would not understand it, so couldn't have it. But as he read, and I seemed to comprehend, he said I could take it to copy the passage I wanted. (I noticed that he had seen where I was going, and the road I was taking after the birth of the animus.) This is what I copied:

Lorsque l'esprit ténébreux et fétide est rejeté au point de ne laisser ni odeur ni couleur sombre, alors que le corps devient lumineux et l'âme se réjouit ainsi que l'esprit. Alors l'ombre s'est échappée au corps. L'âme appelle le corps devenu lumineux, et lui dit: "Éveille-toi du fond de Hadès et lève-toi du tombeau, réveille-toi en sortant des ténèbres. En effet tu as revêtu le caractère spirituel et divin." La voix de la résurrection a parlé. La préparation de vie s'est introduite en toi. Car l'esprit se rejoint à son tour dans le corps, ainsi que l'âme dans le corps en elle réside. Il court avec une joyeuse précipitation pour l'embrasser, il l'embrasse et l'ombre ne le domine plus depuis qu'il a atteint la lumière: le corps ne supporte pas d'être séparé de l'esprit à tout jamais, et il se réjouit dans l'ombre, il l'a trouve remplit de lumière. Et l'âme s'est uni à lui, depuis qu'il est devenu divin par rapport à elle, et il habite en elle. Car il a revêtu la lumière de la divinité (et ils ont été unis) et l'ombre s'est échappée de lui, et tous ont été unis dans la tendresse: le corps, l'âme en l'esprit. Ils sont devenus un. C'est dans cette unité qu'a été caché le mystère. Par le fait de leur réunion le mystère s'est accomplie. La demeure a été scellé et alors s'est dressé une statue pleine de lumière et divinité. Car le feu les a unis et transmutés et ils sont sortis de son sein.

Jung also said that it is a very difficult enterprise to go to yourself. Often even the Catholic Church is in doubt whether a person has a vocation or not to become a priest. The way to the self, if you have the power to take it, is a difficult way – *if* you have the power to do it. Most people indulge themselves but they don't work on themselves. Dr. Jung said, "I sometimes have to show them how they indulge in their fantasy. It is different to read a book in order to work with it or just to indulge in it. People think that when they are going to the self they can *dodge* something. They go to the self as if to cheat the world, as an indulgence. In whatever situation you find yourself, you have to accept it, and if you do not take up your job in this world and do what your situation demands then you have lost your last value – your *servitude.*"

He continued, the difficult entanglements, in which one finds oneself, are one's roots. If you don't touch the soil, and instead lead an artificial, cut-off existence, then the self has no real feet – it is a ghost and should never have been born. It is a futile indulgence to neglect a job to indulge in self. People who think they can escape the servitude to which they are called through fate and life, by indulging in their own ego, are cast out on the shore of life and are of no account. If you accept the servitude [to the self] then you have the right to your own way. But that way can only be trodden if you accept the fact that you are your own law. Can you take such a stand against the collective? There is no judge nor law book as severe as oneself. It is better not to continue on the path to the self, if one cannot stand against the collective conscious opinion. Jung added that if you can stand the sight of yourself as a murderer, or an offender, then you might be strong enough to continue on the right path.

Though Catharine was full of enthusiasm to reform after a good hour with Jung, her fine intentions soon evaporated. I never noticed the development of a new animus. The old one remained overpowering through my childhood, though it somewhat mellowed with age. Katy may have appeared mild, even timid, to outsiders, but with those at home she was quite different. Freed from the anxiety of having to make a good impression, she would assert her forceful personality, laying down the law with Tommy and me, and with anybody else she knew particularly well. Sometimes I could do nothing right, while at others I was told how beautiful I was and smothered in kisses. I loathed both as well as the frequent criticism. I know now that my mother was genuinely fond of me, but as a child I felt that her sudden expressions of affection were insincere, and that like a doll, I would be cast aside – an assessment which, at the time, was quite fair. As Jung had told her, she did not "hear with her feeling," which meant that she heard only what suited her. She never analyzed the reasons for my sometimes aggressive behavior in childhood, which was my way of fighting to preserve individuality. In my teens, I was able to abandon frontal attacks and express aggression unconsciously in the caricatures I drew of my mother and Tommy, which she enjoyed. I also teased *viva voce*. Nonetheless, I mostly adapted to what my mother expected of me. Still, this compliance did not prevent her from considering me brusque, puritanical, and lazy, a Cabot soul inside a body she had produced. It never occurred to her that she might be responsible for some of my disagreeable ways. Like her mother, my mother was trying to mold me into the person she wished me to be. I was not aware of it at the time, and so, among other silly reasons, married early in 1943 and went to Turkey a little over three years later to become free of her – followed nonetheless by a continuing stream of advice.

The following entry includes two dreams, which it would be difficult to interpret without a true sense of their details. I suspect that Dr. Jung had heard a censored version of the reasons for Katy's departure from Charleston in 1928, and for her not returning immediately to Charleston when I was cured:

December 2, 1935

We started speaking of my arm and finger. Dr. Jung said I was wise to have the Wart cut off. He was amused at *le petit veau* [little calf] drawing in Dr. Paul Meyer's[1] office and said he was of course perfectly unconscious of it, and ought to take it down. We laughed about that. I then told Dr. Jung with emotion what I felt about him and his teachings, and what an extraordinary deep person I felt him to be. I read him the paper I carry around with me about "going to the self," which I wrote about [see above]. He seemed rather glad, I thought, that I understood it all, or at least that I seemed to understand it, and that it had made an impression. I spoke of the Pfauen lunches, and I said, I thought that the bunch [who attended them] were just as bad as the society people – only psychological snobs instead of social ones. He asked me if it ever occurred to me that the Pfauen bunch could be jealous, too? "Whenever you feel that people are contemptuous of you," he said, "you know you have value."

Then he went on to say that one must do one's job, even if it is a small one. A pear tree is bigger than a hazel-nut tree, but nuts are good too. Some of us are pear, apple, peach trees, and as such, we have our unique values. If you are a good dog, you have just as much value as a human being in your own way. There is a lot [of value] in doing one's job and making those happy who love you. There is no need to be ambitious, and, as Nietzsche says, "Go beyond yourself," for one has enough to do just being oneself. To go beyond oneself is tiring. If one has accomplished "the being oneself" then one can *think* of going beyond, but not before. He said that if he tried to be a politician, he would be a bad one, a total failure. A person must not try to be what he cannot be.

---

[1] Dr. Paul Meyer must have been the surgeon who cut the growth out of her arm. It was much larger than a normal wart and red, but not malignant.

Jung went on to say that the foolish interest you have in *judging* people is a loss of time. He asked me what was in myself that I was running away from when I mind superficiality in other people. I must be too superficial myself. He said, "You must apply the same criticism to yourself that you apply to others, and thus see where you are lacking. Christ said, 'Do not judge so as not to be judged.'"

Then I told Dr. Jung of my dream about going back to West Virginia. No one seemed pleased to see me in Charleston, which was followed by a second dream of the same nature the next night:

I was lunching with Dot Smith and Nan [Grosscup], and they said that Dr. Jung laid the table and had insisted that I should sit on a certain side of the table with an empty chair beside me. The empty chair annoyed me as it took up room. Later, I saw two magazines on the table; one contained, "The Story of the Cathedral," which told of a cathedral being slowly and systematically emptied of its contents, sarcophagi, statues, holy relics, and even the bells in the belfry rolled out onto the portico. The other magazine contained an article by Dr. Jung on how it all took place – explaining the phenomena.

Dr. Jung said this dream contained a hint that I should not imagine my values as my own for I am not alone at the table in Charleston, as there is an invisible guest there, viz., the empty chair. Usually the empty chair is removed so that a ghost won't sit on it. Jung said he seemed to be in the position of a waiter, and if he were anywhere, he would be at my side. It looks as if I thought I was the whole show, and it shows that I have a tendency to put things down to myself alone on my own account. Jung says while he is in the game there is the empty chair where he belongs. I exclude him for some reason, it may be jealousy. (I told him I was jealous of his personality and his character, for it is rare to meet the two together. He laughed and admitted it.) I try to put him out completely in the eyes of the girls, so that I can play alone. There is the possibility of my getting an inflation and saying things I only got through Dr. Jung. I have been much too rational and seen him only as a doctor, but he is also something *inside* me, something which is mysterious in me. Statues, sarcophagi, pictures and relics etc. are the living things of the church, the bells the voice of the Church. Evidently, for me, the values leave the Church; we are speaking of the Catholic Church as naturally Protestant churches don't have statues, relics etc. (Dr. Jung so often speaks of why the values are leaving the church.) To me even, the Catholic Church is evidently depleting itself, though aesthetical values of the Catholic Church are still living, but the dogma does not seem to convey anything. It must have to do with Jung being in me: his spirit seems to be around me in the dream, even though I am in America. Like a ghost, it accompanies me, and a chair should be ready for it. I must find out what the connection is in all that.

I mentioned to him that there were certain things I could not tell Miss Wolff. He looked surprised, and said, "Why not? She might have some values! You may also be jealous of her. Try the cathedral dream on her." Then I said that I could not have read "The Way to the Self" to her, and he said, "No, I understand that as it is very personal."

In the last interview, Jung mentioned the persona as being a terrible task master, and I thought how true this was, *hélas*.

I expect, indeed, that Jung had heard a censored version of the reasons for Katy's departure from Charleston in 1928, and for her not returning immediately to Charleston when I was cured. Without the true details of those events, the dream would be difficult to interpret. That nobody felt pleased to see Katy in Charleston, in the sketchy first dream, could have been so in actuality had they known the facts behind her absence in Europe. The details of the second dream suggest that Jung sets the scene for Katy to confront her past. As Jung puts it in his interpretation, the empty chair, if it remains, awaits a ghost. Katy's annoyance in the dream is therefore understandable if the ghost who might appear would be her dead husband. Dead men can tell no tales, but a ghost might undermine her version of the last months of their marriage.

Two similar dreams on the same subject, following each other so closely, indicate that an unconscious content was attempting to become conscious. Katy had never faced up to her husband's death, and to any indirect responsibility she might have had for it by staying away so long. Instead, she blamed her father-in-law for insisting they live so many years in West Virginia. (Tom Cabot also attributed Jim's death to Godfrey Cabot's rough treatment of him.) Be that as it may, had Jim been supported by his wife, he might have withstood the paternal onslaught. My mother never discussed the matter with me – even after I had grown up – continuing to blame her in-laws for everything disagreeable in the marriage. The diary never mentions that Katy discussed Jim's death with Jung, but in the dream, Jung's spiritual presence around her even in America suggests that he well could have probed the event. Occasionally Jim appeared in dreams, in spite of Katy's repression, but Jung may have judged the subject too hot to handle unless she brought it up herself. Katy did bring it up with Toni Wolff, but only because she could hoodwink this otherwise sometimes sharply critical woman. My mother often praised her to me for driving Red Cross ambulances during the 1939-1945 War despite her age and rheumatics. The several long letters which Toni wrote to my mother in 1937, analyzing her dreams, reveal that she never saw beyond Katy's meek-maiden side.

The question of my mother's ability to gain a deeper perspective on the overall evasiveness of her attitude comes into sharper focus, though indirectly, through her interest in the genuineness of the woman in the next entry:

December 5, 1935

I spoke to Dr. Jung of the revelation Princess Hohenzollern was to me. (She is Alix, daughter of the last King of Saxony.) She is so simple and has such a marvelous rapport to him, calling him, "Onkel." *"Wo ist der Onkel?"* she asks. Besides her exquisite simplicity, the comfort and ease that one feels in her society is extraordinary. Jung said that in some ways she was childish and irrational but that her simplicity was her greatest value. He said that he never had the difficulty of making her conscious as he did with others – she has a visible ancestry – a conscious ancestry. Jung said that when I come to something dark I am immediately confronted with insecurity, not so she, for she knows what is going to happen. She knows what figures enter the play. Her animus has gone through life consciously, and while my panics are black and dense, her panics are black with a translucid cloud with distinguishable figures. She comes from the Wettin Family, that goes back a thousand years. He said he had always treated her as a princess, and as a number of her ancestors had had a court astrologer, and had placed their trust in that man, she immediately put her trust in him. Jung said he was playing the historical role of physician to the King. He said that when *I* enter certain strange situations, I have no models, and my feeling of uncertainty is likely – whereas with her, it is different: she is quite certain and completely at ease with the situation. For instance, when she comes to the Pfauen lunch in this little town of Zürich, one would expect her to be awkward and have feelings of superiority, but not at all; she is most easy and puts everyone else at their ease, for it is understood that Dr. Jung is a loyal subject and a man of competence who has the ear of the King – an old and experienced man to whom the King turns in trouble. Queen Victoria had a confidential valet. Jung is the court physician, but as the court physician, he is also the administrator of poison. It is a dangerous position but she has great confidence. Jung said that we ought to have kings and queens, that England was wise to keep hers. These people have such tradition and were conscious of their past. No situations were new or difficult for them. When the aristocracy of England is taxed out of its existence, then England is doomed. Germany would be better off if it again became little kingdoms. These people are made for ruling, and they deserve to have the confidence of the people. A person who can give confidence, as Princess Hohenzollern seems to give me, shows that one *can* have confidence in such a person. My sense of uncertainty has all the primitive factors in it, as I can only go back a short time – then there is darkness – whereas she goes back a thousand years. Jung said, "She knows all about the kind of fellow I am. For such a fellow has happened a thousand times in the history of the world; so she has met such a fellow before, as these men have often been in the vicinity of the court. People who have no history behind them, have never met such a thing as me! I am an unheard of novelty, a dangerous man, a sorcerer only to be found in fairy tales."

He told me that a woman, whose ancestors came from the hills, found out after a short time that she liked him and got awfully insecure. Whereas with Princess Hohenzollern, liking him is taken as a matter of course. Some women think it would be awful to have a transference to Jung, but she accepts it as a matter of course, for to her when you have an alchemist he is a rare fellow to be taken care of. When she discovered that she liked Jung, she said, "I came across a rare bird; the fellow we needed." There is no trouble with the transference for she feels she is in good hands. It is the lack of education which makes the mountain woman afraid. She is filled with primitive terrors of strange men. He added, that unlike Princess Hohenzollern, I have no form in which to appreciate Dr. Jung.

C.G. Jung and Princess Marie-Alix Hohenzollern, Eranos, 1936

He then told me that men of no experience, who have resistances against him, think of him as a dangerous magician. He told me the story of a professor, whose ancestors also came from the mountains pretty recently, who had an antagonism to Jung. He was ill and said that he saw serpents in the room which were sent by Dr. Jung!

One man, whose wife Jung had cured, came to Jung and asked him what magic he had used! Another man said to Jung, "Excuse me if I ask you an indiscrete question, but what do you do?" Jung

said, "I see patients all day." "Yes, I know that," replied the man,
"but what do you *do*?" "Well, I am writing a book," said Jung. "Oh
yes, I know all that, but what do you really *do*?" In the village when
the extraordinary Man produces an effect which cannot be explained by plough, shovel or hoe, then something is the matter. I
told Dr. Jung of Rennet's[1] rage – his fist banging down on the table,
and his saying, "I hate Dr. Jung." "Rennet is afraid of unknown
things," Jung said.

Many people cannot place Jung. Some think he is homosexual,
or either a devil or a saviour. People from old families have the
right form. They may be decadent, but their great asset is that they
have history behind them, which gives them a marvelous certainty
about people and their behaviour. He said that was why the Bishop
of Salisbury had placed him so easily. He could meet him more or
less correctly, not being shocked by Jung's liberal ideas, because he
understands that such a man must have such ideas.

Princess Hohenzollern was a very natural person, one of the few
women in the Zürich group with whom my mother got on well. Their
friendship lasted even after both were mostly away from Zürich. She
never put on airs, and was nice to children, which, of course, I
appreciated. She attended my mother's marriage to Vincenzo Visconti in 1963 in London, and her seventy-fifth birthday party in 1969
in a Lugano hotel. After the aperitif, when everyone rose from the
initial seating to get hors d'oeuvres, the Princess was the swiftest to
collect her plateful and return to her place. Alone and without
preamble, she began tucking into her food. The sight was so unusual
that I suggested taking a photo, to which she was agreeable, the result
of which in fact delighted her.

Katy's way of differentiating her femininity by comparing herself
to other women continues into the next entry:

December 11, 1935

I told Dr. Jung about my three-hour session with Mrs. Fierz[2] at
tea. He roared with laughter over my description of Mrs. Fierz and
myself sitting together and feeling the hypnotic atmosphere, and

---

[1] Rennet Dieter, an American friend of Katy.

[2] Linda Fierz-David had been a patient of Jung's. Katy probably met her
either at Jung's seminars or at the Psychological Club, where she was on
the Committee.

Linda Fierz with an unidentified woman, Eranos, 1939

she saying it came from us being two women together – like the old women who speak by the well, or the old women who crouch down over the fire. And then I was hazy about what she said about the lesbian connection with it. I think she said there wasn't that.

Dr. Jung said, I had the effect on Mrs. Fierz of taking her out of herself, and she addressed herself to my inferior function which is intuition. When people talk to me of fires, old women and wells, I don't get it because I have seen no fires, old women nor wells as I am a sensation type, and only see things as they are. That is why I have had such difficulty seeing Dr. Jung other than as a physician. It is as if Dr. Jung said to me, "Do you remember the chalice overflowing with gold which we saw together at the last session?" I wouldn't understand what he is driving at. Mrs. Fierz was not affected by the hypnotic feeling I had. But if I was affected by her, then she was affected by me. I told Dr. Jung, she had said she was through with love. He said, "Does she look as though she were through with it?" I said I didn't think so in the least, and was dumbfounded and incredulous when she had tried to make me draw such conclusions. He said, "Look at her hands, so thin and nervous – not like mine or yours," and he spread out his solid hand for inspection. She looks nervous and can easily be stirred by men, and must have been pretty unconscious not to have known she was pretty when she was thirty-eight."

I then told him of de Caro and Maertens. He said that Maertens was a relative of his wife and entered The Psychological Club years ago and had had a few talks with him, but never an analysis. I said, I felt less unworthy in having asked to enter a club where there were such members as Maertens. He said there were a few other early members like that, and one rather nursed them along and let it go at that. It seems Ali Baba tells his followers that he is the eightieth incarnation of Christ, and Maertens actually takes it seriously and announced the fact during a Club evening. Jung said that if he [Jung] announced the fact that he was the eighty-first incarnation of Christ, Maertens would drop Ali Baba and follow him. I gathered it served Maertens right to have a girl like de Caro living with him. He takes her in for nothing as it is good for his soul – or so he was told by Ali Baba.

Katy's main function, according to the analysts who knew her well, was sensation, with thinking as the auxiliary. She told me, however, that she was the feeling type. She also had flashes of intuition, generally negative. She reported how once or twice she dreamed of a relative dying (one was her Grandmother Rush) then heard shortly afterwards that her premonitions were correct. When a relative of ours married a woman whom my mother had never met, Katy dreamed that the bride was an ominous grey figure standing atop a mountain. The dream very soon proved to be correct. In spite of these intuitive gifts, I noticed when I was old enough to begin understanding her that her attention leaned towards tangible objects; the color and style of clothes and furnishings had to be just right, and she collected paintings, antique furniture, and *objets d'art*. She certainly perceived people first by their looks: a man was judged handsome if he were six feet tall and had other good physical qualities, and a woman did not have to be beautiful as long as her clothes were chic. She sought visual perfection everywhere, which could be irritating to a non-sensation type. Perhaps because of her strong sensation she could visualize the Lump's shape and color in her mind's eye, but could not intuit its contents. Maybe to prove she was not "sensation," she told me she could not draw a single stroke; nevertheless, she did a number of sketches in the margins of her Jung diaries.

December 13, 1935

I went into Jung's study and immediately remarked the *Stimmung* [mood] there and the beautiful modern glass plaque which hangs in his window. He told me that glass was Switzerland's oldest industry, and is still flourishing today, though no one knows it, as it is not often mentioned. He said that his lovely plaque (given to him as a Literature prize by the town of Zürich) represented the deposition of Christ, in a Swiss landscape: here is a big mountain, and on its lee side is Mary with Christ's head resting in her lap. Christ's tortured white body, lying with the last rays from a big yellow setting sun, shining through clouds. It is beautiful, dark, mysterious.

I admired his three windows in the study. They are stained glass, one representing the flagellation, one the crucifixion, and one the deposition (burying Christ in the tomb). Jung said that he had sent one of these glass artists to a little church near Brugg to copy the panes. Then I asked him what was behind the curtain which was over a small picture. At first, I thought he hesitated; then, as if it were something very precious, he pulled back the curtain, and a face of indescribable beauty hit me. It seemed blurred and indistinct, at first, but appeared more distinct as I looked at it. I thought at first it was an old mural, but Jung explained to me that it was a photograph of the head of the *Linceuil du Christ* [shroud of Christ], which was preserved in a metal casket in a church in Turin, and only taken out on fête days, which were the Royal marriages – and then only! He afterwards showed me the book written on the *Linceuil du Christ* by a Frenchman. There were illustrations in it which showed the whole imprint of Christ's figure on the winding sheet. It seems the *Linceuil* looks like a worn, faded cloth with dark brown spots, which could be blood, and no one realized there was the imprint of Christ on it until the *Linceuil* was photographed and the whole face and figure of Christ ap-

peared on the shroud. The theory was that the shroud was damp
with essences of myrrh etc., and Christ was wrapped while still
moist from the sweat of the agony, and so his form imprinted on
it. It was most moving to see, and it was brought home to me what
agony Christ had suffered. We do not realize this enough.

The above illustrates how developed my mother's visual function
was. It is not surprising that art, in its many manifestations, attracted
her. While I was at school in England in the 'thirties, she spent much
time with Tommy visiting cathedrals, abbeys, and other such old,
venerable structures. I would receive many postcards, all written in
French, with photos of these edifices. She was trying to pump culture
into me. I dutifully admired the cards, but much preferred cards with
photos of the Loch Ness Monster, which she inscribed as if she had
taken them herself. Still, she persisted in writing these in French also.
I loathed this because it made me feel alien at school, where the other
pupils received *letters*, which I envied, written in *English*. Her fear
that I would forget my French also moved her to have me miss the
winter term in England. *Toujours le meilleur!* [always the best]

After my father's death, Tommy and I were the people whose good
taste needed cultivating. Unfortunately, when it came to culture, I
was rather like my father; I wearied of it. During the Easter holidays
in Italy, I was given long sessions in museums and developed what I
called "museum pains." Luckily, when I was thirteen and fourteen,
Katy found that she needed a nap after the long morning's sightseeing
and a heavy lunch, and sent me off every afternoon alone in a hired
gondola. The gondolier steered from the rear platform while I rowed
standing at the center. We did most of the interesting canals and went
out to several of the surrounding islands. The gondolier was a
respectable fatherly man whom I enjoyed and who taught me much
Italian. When not sightseeing or gondoliering, I sat with mother and
Tommy at Harry's Bar for a lunchtime aperitif on the waterfront. On
one occasion Harry Cipriani and his wife invited us to Sunday lunch
at their old-fashioned, somewhat shabby apartment, a contrast to the
bar – Victorian and filled with bric-à-brac, whose parlor chairs were
upright with very hard backs and plush seats. Harry's cocktails were
famous, but we saw no sign of a party after climbing the narrow
winding stairs to the fourth floor. Harry disappeared for a moment,
then reappeared carrying a tray with a decanter and glasses. Without
offering us a choice, he served us a red Port! I found it sickly sweet

and knew only too well what Katy and Tommy were thinking. But the enormous luncheon and rough purple wine were very enjoyable, and my mother, uninhibited, talked and translated for Tommy. Our hosts were thoroughly at ease with us, so the luncheon party stretched on into mid-afternoon.

The diary resumes with the issue of transference:

June 10, 1936

I told Jung of my financial betterment, but he did not seem impressed. He said $7000 was not so much to have in the bank at one time – nothing to get excited about.

I read him my desert fantasy: of seeing and going after him. He said the desert was the extraordinary extension of the unconscious. He said because in the fantasy I went traveling with him, lost him in the desert, then went north to Zürich to find him, shows that I seem to have lost the connection with him. I had a connection with him but it was not strong enough. The rapport isn't yet right. A certain amount of libido came up, went the wrong way – did not find the way to Jung. I am expected to make some progress in my rapport. The fact that I hate being 'shut in' in funiculaires shows that a piece of the unconscious is loose. The Lump gets loose in the funiculaire, for the Lump is a thing that can't live in me, so it wants to kill us both by doing such a fool thing as jumping out of the funiculaire while it is in motion. I am caught in enclosed things. The Lump is locked in too much. I want to get out from there. Something in me wants a liberation. ... My mind evidently does not provide enough width. I am too much caught within a small frame. I should have a greater extension of my feeling experience. I am too fastened down by certain conventional things. I have too narrow a scope. I have boards before my eyes for I don't see what I ought to do. I don't see what the unconscious is after and what my tendencies are. I have mental and spiritual needs that I don't realize. I must realize, if I should meet Jung again, what I am really after. He said that if he had time, he would go with me on a trip and see what developed. I must make believe that I and he are on intimate terms and write, and see where it leads to. I told him that it was perhaps why I had offered Miss Wolff to accompany her to the U.S. For aboard the ship, I would be near him. He says to write and see to where it leads.

I remember no particular event which led to our "financial betterment" in 1936, but I did notice that we had become less hard-pressed
than we were on our return to Europe in 1930. We acquired a lady's
maid, however, a fashionable thing prewar but a ridiculous expense
when living in a hotel. My mother's society persona needed such
trappings. She was extravagant and, like a child, demanding, which *à
la longue* might have impeded her rapport with Jung, who as a no-
nonsense Swiss was thoroughly natural. When the War began and we
were confined to Switzerland, she matured, gradually becoming
more natural and modest in her requirements, although her libido
still shifted its direction, leading her into enthusiasm for the work
with Jung but then into boredom and off, in another direction, on her
high-society horse. I remained the excuse that I had always been for
her doing what Jung disapproved of, spending long periods in the
mountains at Palace Hotels that I was supposed to love!

June 15, 1936

I had to wait for Dr. Jung by the lake as he was taking us [his
patients] today at his summer house. When he appeared, I told him
how lovely and peaceful and beautiful I thought it all was, and how
wonderful it must be for someone straight from New York to sit in
such a spot. He said that people coming straight from New York
do not realize beauty or peace. Their feelings and perceptions are
dulled: otherwise they could not exist in New York. They are
absolutely deaf and blind to all beauty. I told him of Tom Cabot's
whirlwind trip through Europe. He said, he did not think anyone
could get much out of such a trip.[1] I spoke of his own ghastly
forthcoming trip to the U.S. He said it would be pretty bad. He was
going to see a few people while in Cambridge, but on the island off
of Maine, he would see nobody and just enjoy Nature. He said that
if it were not for Mrs. Jung, he would take a tramp steamer across
the Atlantic, which he would really enjoy.

As my mother loathed living in America, anybody else's trip there
seemed "ghastly." Since she had a perfectly good life there both
before and during her marriage, why she was so complexed seems at
first sight astonishing. She hated Charleston, she told me, yet she

[1] Tom Cabot, her brother-in-law, brought his wife, three sons and daughter
to Europe in June 1936. As they visited only the Continent, I missed seeing
them while at school in England.

made friends there. Her dislike of America was general; not only her in-laws but also other Boston people were stiff, stingy, boring, though at the same time she told me she had plenty of amusing young friends. The Roaring 'Twenties and the social changes after the First World War must have posed a difficult adjustment for older people; young women had rapidly become emancipated while their elders, maintaining an Edwardian mind-set, grew bewildered. The generation gap then must have been a chasm! As a young married woman, Katy was constantly moving between the fast set and her husband's conservative relatives, thereby living a painfully split life. Knowing her in-laws' disapproval, she felt guilty, a fact intensified by her sensitivity as well as by redoubled disapproval of her occasional "ascetic" side. In America, "Catharine" and "Katy" were in perpetual conflict. Only back in Europe was life somewhat more even for my mother, thanks to analysis and also to her restricted finances, still more limiting during World War II, though the contents of the Lump remained an enigma.

My mother would often wax sentimental to me about Jung, using endearing names for him. She was very attached to him, as a daughter to a father. Thanks to Princess Marie-Alix Hohenzollern, she found a name for Jung which reflected this affection. The remainder of the entry for 15 June, and the next entry, both feature this disclosure to Jung himself:

> Then he went on to explain to me that all the feeling I had for him (seeing him as a woolly lamb unprotected) might be a projection of my own inner feelings on him. I told him that he seemed so at the mercy of wolves, and I felt people took his time and did not appreciate what he was doing for them, and how he tried to help us all. He said that *in a sense* that was true; he was imposed upon and people did not always appreciate him. But I must remember also that feelings change the world for someone. The world is painted by one's feelings, and this is *half* projected.
>
> I told him I had great difficulty seeing things as they were, and usually when I finally saw something, there was some truth in it. He said that I did have great difficulty to get through to my feeling and when I do get through, it's intense and *half* projected. He said a person who did not know me, and who did not have very nice feeling, might say, "What a worldly woman!" A person with better feeling, or the same person with their feeling improved, would say,

perhaps, "What a lovely woman." People can see one in the most extraordinary aspects according to their feeling. The world changes its face completely according to one's feeling.

He said I was right to hang on to my persona with Fierz, that all she wanted for the moment from me was a persona to dine with. I then talked of Ascona. Dr. Jung said there was a big international gathering of scientists who gave lectures and was the one meeting place of his school of psychology. He was going there, he said, even if it were difficult for him, so as to keep it going. He thought I would like it.[1]

June 22, 1936

When I went in, Mrs. Crowley was leaving. Then, halfway up the garden path, she ran back to ask Dr. Jung when she was to see him again. It showed her up as such an egoist. Dr. Jung, or Onkel, then talked to me about Crowley. He said Mrs. Crowley was so harassed by his [Mr. Crowley's] letters, as he was writing her that it was Miss Wolff who wanted to stop me from writing to him. Crowley apparently has a transference on me. Onkel asked me if I disliked him or what? I said that he bored me with the stuff he wrote – just like Dr. Baynes! Onkel then said Baynes comes out with adolescent psychology stuff – college boy mentality, like Crowley – that is their degree of maturity. But Baynes has to handle Miss Wolff as an adult being. Such men as Baynes and Crowley can only deal with or relate to women whom they treat as if being on an inferior level, or who *are* on an inferior level. No one understands Crowley, he's just a mess. Men like him are funny 'originals.' Onkel said he tried to put him in a village where he would be the original of the village, the funny man. People would say, "Old Crowley, the funny old chap. ..." He would be the funny man to invite to the Squire's etc. but Crowley wouldn't stay. That is why he didn't stay with Frau [Olga Froebe] Kapteyn for she put him in his place. I told Onkel how Crowley hated Miss Wolff, and I said I wondered why I had, and others did. He said that people misunderstand Miss Wolff because she had to talk as if through a thick wall with people because they won't *hear!* Jung said that people think he is out to violate and suppress them, "So now I say what I have to say in an

---

[1] The Eranos Tagungen were held at Frau Froebe-Kapteyn's Casa Gabriella near Ascona, and took place annually in August.

ordinary voice." If people think you want to influence them, then you must not influence them at all. The Master speaks only once!

I then read Onkel the nice part of my fantasy about him, then wept and told him what a darling soul he was. He was simply sweet and gave out little noises – sort of kindly little grunts – and he was just like a furry, white Persian kitten purring by the fire – it was delightful, and he just one big darling. I was happy he had accepted so kindly my transference for him. I told him how I had wept one morning because no one loved him, and how de T. had come in and asked why I was weeping, and I answered, "Because no one loves Dr. Jung." He roared with laughter, for he has much humor in all things. (He said de T. would be nice about my weeps as he is such a gentleman.)

I told him one heard people saying, "Dr. Jung and Miss Wolff are wonderful psychologists, just marvelous, the best you know, a magnificent team!" "Yes," he retorted full of humor, "a good pair of horses to drag people uphill." We both simply roared with laughter.

Then I read him my horrible and revolting fantasy, the black mass. He said he understood and sympathized about it all, as he himself had had such awful fantasies; it was human nature to have such fantasies and one must realise one is not alone in having them.

I told him that I just hated people, suddenly, could not abide them, and said that the famous revolutionary, General Carnot, had remarked about Talleyrand: "He hates men for he knows himself too well." Onkel said I was not at one with myself to so hate my fellow beings. If I know certain things in myself then I can stand them in mankind. Talleyrand was certainly not at one with himself. I have also not yet made peace with myself about them. It is important to have these fantasies, otherwise we could not stand mankind.

I told Jung, or Onkel, how much I thought of Miss Wolff now. He said that she analysed dreams for him and was wonderful, that she was rather reserved and one did not see her coming forward much, but there was much behind the veil – pure gold – but she emphasized things too much at times and got people's backs up.

I remember my mother weeping over Jung from time to time. Unlike Tommy, I was too immature to be kind, loathing what I judged to be sentimental nonsense. I could not be objective because we were caught in a symbiosis. In retrospect, I can see that both the feeling function and femininity were in need of catching up within my mother, as the following entry also indicates:

June 29, 1936

I saw Jung for the last time this term. I asked him if it were true that he would see no one next autumn. He answered, "I am not quite inhuman," so I felt relieved.

Then I told him my dream of skiing on the slopes of Mount Everest with Ras Tafari (Haile Selassie's other name). He said: that I was on a high place and I take sides with the Abyssinians, who have recently been overcome by the Italians. What I have read in the papers about the Italo-Abyssinian conflict has been taken by my unconscious as a symbol of the conflict in myself. I have a primitive side, half-Negro,[1] and a sort of dago in me that does not represent the best of European culture! It looks as if I had escaped the danger of being overcome by the dago element, for I am with the primitive animus high up, and safe from Italian attack. The Italian also represents an animus. I have many thoughts in my unconscious, and part of my thoughts are primitive, like the Abyssinians, and part of the thoughts are like the Italians, and each set of thoughts will explain in a different way a sort of fight of opinions, a two-thirds civilized kind of thinking, and a primitive understanding which probably applies to my feeling problem. There are certain primitive and bad opinions in me interfering with the sincerity of my feelings. Feelings of a woman can be subject to many different viewpoints. It is a conflict between naive primitivity and a sort of Italian interpretation.

There is a general problem of my feeling. We have brought about a much better rapport. Inasmuch as you build up a better rapport to the world, you feel better about it. But there is still more to it; we are not at the end of the problem as I have the Lump. We can suppose that there are more feelings that want to come up to the surface ... that want to be integrated in my personality. When such feelings come up they can be submitted to all sorts of standpoints. I then spoke to him of what Wolff had said about looking into myself and seeing if I was honest about my feelings

---

[1] Jung said that white Americans had absorbed much of the Negro culture.

towards him [Jung]. For instance instead of the 'Onkel [lit. Uncle] feeling,' I might have a love feeling. I told him I did not think that was the case, that I felt as if he were just 'Onkel.'

He said that I being a woman and he a man, and that we sit discussing personal problems ... – to a primitive, he'd make no bones about it, for a man with a woman in a hut – everyone knows what that means ... he would take it as *that*, and never give it another thought. The Italians would laugh and make jocose remarks about it, and never for a moment believe that it was platonic. But they would joke about it, whereas the primitive would not even discuss it, or make remarks about it [to him] in such an obvious situation! He went on to say that I was not out to produce a particular flirt with him, but if I were, I'd be foolish not to admit it, whereupon he would say, "My time is too precious to waste over such a flirt." In order that I can make progress in my conception of things, we have to realize all the points of view, so that we can be sure we don't fail to admit something. If it were

Mary Briner, T. Wolff, Emma Jung, C.G. Jung, Tommy at Eranos, 1939

nothing but a flirt we would be fools to waste time. We must know what we could think about the situation and then appreciate correctly the feelings we are concerned with. Miss Wolff's tendency is to force one to a realization so that you see what you are at, and can concentrate on that side of the problem, for when you look closely you discover something you have not seen before. Jung said, "She stresses the point, as I did, when I said the important thing is the rapport." Wolff wants me to put my searchlight on it so that I can discover what I am about. It is not quite obvious what I mean when I say I feel warm and have confidence, and then all the things unanswered in me come up and want to see the light too. A living woman, and being, is interested in more than a warm feeling; other things are mixing themselves up in it. ... The better the rapport, the more you have a legitimate need to know the truth about the situation. It is natural to want to discover what it is ... for instance, he said, "You might be curious about me." I looked sheepishly at him, then said, I was a bit, but it was rude. He told me to ask him what I wanted to know. I asked him why Mrs. Jung had become an analyst. She was much too much of a mother woman etc. He said that she is not an analyst and that only certain people wanted to talk with her etc. – they asked to. I said that de T. had said that Mrs. Jung and Mrs. Sigg talked exactly alike, and that I did not like it myself and agreed with de T. Jung said Mrs. Jung came back [from Mrs. Sigg's?] and said she had asked a stupid question. He said she was interested in Latin and Greek and was studying this and that. I said "What a pity," and he said, "Not at all, her children are grown up and are gone and she'd have nothing to do. It is good that these things interest her." He then went on to say that with a good rapport one can ask the type of question I have asked.

"What a pity!" is a good example of Katy's *enfant terrible* remarks, which made me cringe when I was a child – though I was unaware of why they did. Later the insight came that such spontaneous remarks dogmatically excluded other points of view. Jung says to her that a living woman is interested in more than a warm feeling. Katy's affection, as I said, was that of a little girl who wants to marry daddy. My mother had been complaining for a while to Jung that she had lost her sex, even with Tommy! She was still emotionally a child with undeveloped femininity, with the consequence that her feeling remained weak. She was Sleeping Beauty without the Prince to wake her up, a role that her father should have taken on, but which he had failed her through long absences, bad moods, and rough language. Of course, my mother was not unique; even today some women have problems with their sexuality because of poor fathering, remaining immature while "falling in love" (usually with a father figure), marrying, and having children. Though unfeminine herself, my mother was allergic to women who did not live up to her conception of femininity. Not only was Mrs. Jung's interest in Greek and Latin suspect to Katy; she also was jealous of Mrs. Jung's intellectual abilities. That jealousy was the real motive then; later she admired Mrs. Jung's studies and recommended I follow her example.

C.G. Jung at Eranos, 1936

Katy's illness in the autumn of 1936 was preceded by much travel. She visited friends with Tommy and went to the Eranos Tagungen in Ascona. Then came an extensive tour of Germany, touring cities and castles as well as visiting old school friends. Somewhere in Germany she met her newest sister-in-law, Jack Cabot's wife Elizabeth, for the first time. (Jack, Jim and Katy had toured Europe in the winter of 1924.) Now she was touring with Tommy, and in the 1930s, traveling with a lover was not yet socially correct, yet for all her pretence at being modern, my mother was fundamentally old-fashioned. So it is not astonishing that after all the extraversion and strain, she returned to Zürich and took to her bed. Katy had not been seriously ill since the 1919 flu, so the 1936 episode must have come as a surprise. She uncharacteristically told many people of her illness and received many messages of concern:

December 14, 1936 (At the Waldhaus Dolder)

This is the first time I have seen Dr. Jung this term as I have been ill all autumn with two flus and an exhaustion caused by overdoing, so the doctor said. In other words, I must learn to husband my strength and not use it up in useless ways.

Great Dream

I told Dr. Jung of my strange dream on October 25, 1936, during the worst part of my illness – how I dreamt that:

I had an appointment with him and found him in the Parthenon, and asked him if I could equal his spiritual development. He said it was painful, but I was to lie down naked in the pool in the middle of the interior of the Parthenon, and die for a thousand years. Could I do that? I did do it and heard a rushing noise: the whole place filled with wind like the wind that descended on the Apostles' heads. A great blackness, then I was rushing upwards. It was terribly painful and I suffered acutely until I became unconscious and then I found myself a thousand years later lying on a sunny beach with a peaceful ocean in the background. On a hill, the Parthenon stood supreme, and I wondered if Dr. Jung would be there.

Dr. Jung asked me what gods the Parthenon housed, and I said 'Athene.' He said that Athene was the anima of Zeus – she represented the wisdom of Zeus. She was his thought that took form. The Parthenon was an apt place in which to meet him. It was an invitation to wisdom represented by the woman Athene. The descent into water is a baptism; such a pool is often the symbol of the mother. You are put back into the womb – the pool is a place of rebirth when one enters it in a naked condition. The meaning of the baptismal rite is called 'going into the womb of the Church.' The *piscina* is the old name for baptismal font. In order to be reborn again as a spiritual being, the *pneuma* [wind] lifts me out of it.

I asked Uncle, "How can I attain to spiritual development?" He replied that I must die and be born again and go back a thousand years until I reach the state of the child in the mother's womb where I have no persona at all, where I am a living thing moved by the unconscious; then the spirit would seize me and I'd be lifted up and that would cause me unbearable pain and then I'd be lifted up onto the earth again. That is all terribly symbolic.

Jung's response to Katy's question, "How can I obtain spiritual development?" confirms that he felt Katy was due for a serious regression. But what Jung advocated is difficult to implement among the distractions of modern life. At the Klinik am Zürichberg, one of my patients went through such a long and painful process, worthwhile in her case because it was followed by a gradual return from the depths and a complete cure from a serious and long-term mental illness. Her rebirth came about only because the Jungian clinic shielded her from regimentation and distractions, allowing her the solitude to regress.[1]

Then I told Onkel the following dream, which I had the next night:

I met a man who was a marvelous connoisseur of art. He had written especially fine criticisms of certain very beautiful Greek statues. I decided I would prefer to love that sort of man than all the other men pressing around me. I told him so and he told me he would teach me art. Then he lifted me up and carried me off – to the surprise of my other friends.

This dream refers to the man who knows Greek art and is going to teach me the art of the Greek mind, which transformed the human being and made him beautiful like the statues of the gods.

I told Jung also a dream which took place in Countess [Margarita] Lüttichau's garden:

An oak tree was all lit up at a garden party, and someone put a dagger between my shoulder blades, and I slashed their face crosswise with a knife, and some guests at the party finally killed the person who had put the dagger between my shoulder blades.

Onkel said that old oak all lit up is pretty flamboyant!!

In some way we got onto Princess H. and the Countess Lüttichau whom Uncle said was a devilish woman. I told him the gigolo tale. He said that such a woman exuded poisonous fumes; these women leave a bitter taste; they put the wrong light on things. Speaking of Mrs. McCormick, he said when you are treating rich people they think you are treating them for money. As a matter of fact he said he'd talked with Countess Lüttichau, for one

---

[1] See Jane C. Reid, "Der Gang zum Brunnen des Lebens: Geschichte einer Regression," *Analytische Psychologie* 1990, 21: 81-97.

must try and see if one can help such people, but that was the way she rewarded him. When he was treating Mrs. McC., everybody had fantasies, people can't understand that certain beings have a soul. Countess Lüttichau exhales nasty fumes and she repaid him with nasty talk. For instance, I am in a delicate situation with him and nobody would assume that the whole thing is a spiritual performance, for people know of dirty mysteries and don't know of anything pure. Lüttichau would poison everyone, a dirty devil, she is pestilential – she should confess to him. She will be utterly cursed and she is full of dirt. Princess Hohenzollern is frightfully decent and suffers herself to be poisoned by that woman. I asked if P. Hohenz. was really *so* decent, and he said no: she is torn to pieces by the pig in her. The fact that she likes to eat poison shows there is something vulgar in her, and that is why she cultivates that poisonous Lüttichau.

I had the following dream of the Parthenon, which is pure white marble and gives me the pure white vista. The man in the second dream carries me away.

I said I felt that there was something awfully nice in P. H., and he said that there was something awfully nice and decent in her, otherwise he would have given her up long ago. Then Onkel asked me for another dream.

I told him of being with friends – Mrs. Jennings worldly, and her daughter a hermit, in a hotel. We drove in a car down some stairs and met great women of granite clumping up the stairs. And the Jennings said they were the dead who changed into that form. And then I suddenly discovered I had on Janey's beret and blue dress!

Uncle said that the foregoing dream of statues, Greek, and then living granite statues appear. Those are the people made into stone. The fashionable people, my worldly aspect. And then I make the descent into the unconscious and meet the woman of granite – that woman who has been changed into stone. If I am made of granite I am unchangeable – a sort of mother. I come out of the form of my own child. I am rejuvenated with the psychology of a young girl in curious contrast to the dead person of granite. Through the descent, it is as if I had been transformed into the granite form: on the surface, simple like a child – but inside, stiff like granite. Outside, I am now hard society; inside, infantile and in a hard shell like a crab! Now my *inside* must become like granite and the *outside* like a child. Then if someone sticks a dagger into me the dagger won't enter because the inside is granite: the dagger will break itself against the granite. I cannot change from within only. These things are on the way, potentialities, possibilities, when I become more simple; that is why my dreams are making progress my [way] of becoming more simple. Taking off my own clothes is taking off the persona and just being what one is, just what one feels, just moved by the Unconscious, then things are on the move.

Then Uncle tried to show me things as they are: natural and simple. I have all the hardness outside. I am like a child lost in a huge ice box! That must be turned around and the child in me must come out and must be replaced by granite. Inside I am still too liquid.

My mother was impressed by Jung's remarks about being soft outside and granite inside, often repeating them to me, and even drawing the granite woman (extraordinary, given her distaste for drawing). With age, she became tougher (as the Sea Captain personality emerged), but she was never able entirely to transform her sensitivity into granite. Yet she was never a hard society person either, remaining a curious mixture, impressed by society people but also keeping the common touch. She knew the style of the social elite too well, telling me that New York society women were the hardest women on earth!

I told Onkel that I still had the panics in the funiculaire. He said that *granite* would not mind the funiculaire – that fear of the funiculaire is childish. Often such a panic will remain as barometer to show you when at times you are not right. The panics might easily return at times when you are not quite right. Then I mentioned that I saw extraordinary things in people such as Mrs. F[ierz], as Queen of Hades, and that I only recognized her as such as I had been there. He said that when you see the demerits of people you also see their light. Naturally, he went on, I want to see the real substance in people and am thankful I have the vision. It was always there and is in everybody. But the more you live in the persona the more you see people the way you want to see them. When you can stand your own nakedness then you can see other people's nakedness as well. I told him that I had a tendency to get inflated when I suddenly see all these things. Then Uncle reminded me that I was the person who saw the dirt, and dirt can only be

the man in the second dream carries me
away - I said I felt there was something
really nice in P. H. + he said that there was
something awfully nice & decent in her,
otherwise he'd given her up long ago,
then Uncle asked me for another dream
and I told him of being with friends, Mrs. Jennings
worldly + her daughter a hermit, in a hotel
and we drove in a car down some stairs and
we met great women of granite clumping up
the stairs and the Jennings said they were
the dead who changed into that form - and
then I suddenly discovered I had on Janey's
blue dress! Uncle said the foregoing dream
of statues, Greek, and then the granite living
statue appear - those are people made into
stone - the fashionable people, my worldly
aspect and then I make the descent into
the world of the unconscious and meet the
woman of granite - that woman who has
been changed into stone - If I'm made of
granite, I am unchangeable - a sort
of mother, therefore I come out of

granite
woman!

seen through dirt in oneself. And for everything bad I see I must ask myself, "Where am I bad?" You do not think you possess that evil, but you must revert to yourself [to see it].

Then it was lunchtime and Uncle stayed on to lunch [at the Waldhaus Dolder with Tommy and myself]. As we went down-stairs, he put his arm affectionately on my shoulders and said, "It is so nice to be lunching with you." During lunch he talked of his American trip and his stay in London etc. It was all very interest-ing, and a jolly atmosphere pervaded! He said he thought Roosevelt had dictator stuff in him and told the story of two men who came to see R. The door was ajar and Mrs. R. was listening. The first man put a proposition to R. He apparently seemed to be listening, and said, "I agree with you." Mrs. Roosevelt then came in and said, "I don't see how you can agree with the first man and tell him so, then you listen to the second man and you agree with him." "I agree with you!" Uncle also said one could not fathom his, Roosevelt's, mind. He listens to the speeches written for him. Sometimes he won't accept them and sometimes he will take them up. He has an extraordinary changeable type of mind, and you don't know what the devil he will do. Sometimes he will damn a sane advisor from whom he has taken good advice in the past. He is so changeable that one can't get at his mind and find out what it is. He is a dictator. In comparison, Hoover was easy to see through.

Uncle said that Boston had changed so. All the decent people had gone to live in the suburbs. The old quaint part, the Hub etc., … all invaded by Irish. All the decent people have moved away and it has been completely taken over by such people – of course the Irish are utterly irresponsible!

We then touched on Edward VIII and Mrs. Simpson. He said Mrs. S. had taken a heavy burden on her shoulders; for she is the cause of all the excitement, of the British Government, towards the King. Nevertheless, Uncle thinks the King would have given up his throne for another reason anyway if the 'Simpson reason' had not come along at that moment. He went on to say that the English refused to believe that problems existed – absolutely refused. Tommy said they were hypocrites, but Uncle said No, that they were *repressed*. He said that when he spoke to an English husband or wife, he would ask, "Did you discuss that with your husband/ wife?" They, horrified, would reply, "Of course not!"

He sneezed, and I laughed, and he said it wasn't a cold, but that there was a change in the weather. He said that when people make a loud noise or sneeze, or blow their noses violently, it was a sign they wanted to be heard – probably they did not feel important enough! But he said repeated sneezes often went with a change in the weather.

He and I then spoke of transferences – for when I offered him more wine, he refused, saying that he would have to see three ladies in the p.m. and that he would be too witty! Then the next time, when sober, he would be quite different and they would be at sea! I said that really some of those people's transferences were a bit thick – they thought him an ethereal being. He said, "They think I fly around on butterfly wings, from flower to flower, nibbling nectar from the petals and drinking dew!"

Chapter Five

Regression and the Last Months of Peace, 1937-1939

We returned to St. Moritz in the winter of 1937 and stayed again at the Privat Hotel, where I took up skating with Bror Meyer as usual. In January, Katy received a long "analytical letter" from Toni Wolff (4.01.37) which mentions Katy's need to become a "woman of granite" and less fluid. Toni also analyses Katy's dream that "second-rate" women have let the dukes of Windsor and Kent make them pregnant. Identifying them as shadow figures, Toni says optimistically:

> You see, your personality has changed a great deal: formerly it was *yourself* instigated by your mother partly – who fabricated such plans and ideas more or less. You wanted to be on top of society, as every woman would. And now you don't want this anymore; you have seen better values. ... The socially ambitious person has drifted into the background and is now your alter ego, that is, your shadow. ...

Another dream, about an abscess on Katy's left thumb (also analyzed by Jung, who took the abscess to be on the right thumb: see previous discussion on this subject), denoted for Toni something wrong in the unconscious (the left side). "The abscess could refer to the shadow problem which I explained above, and which you may overlook a bit, or not see for what it is." Elsewhere in the letter, Toni touches on Jung's luncheon-visit at the Waldhaus Dolder Hotel before Christmas, with Katy, Tommy and myself. Of Katy's relationship to Jung there she writes:

Apparently Dr. Jung has been accepted by your whole background; your mother is charmed by him, and he sits in your father's cabin, more or less in your father's place – but only the nice side of your father is important. Naturally, because your father has these fits of temper, you felt him to be emotionally unreliable, and part of your lack of security comes from that reason, also your mistrust of people. Therefore, if you feel towards Dr. Jung as towards a fatherly figure whom you can trust absolutely, and if you express this to him in one way or another, you would have gained a lot of ground. So don't hesitate to do it.

It was not long before my mother took to her bed once more with the "flu," which she had had in the autumn, now complicated by sinus trouble. Writing to Jung from her bed, she seems to have taken Toni's advice:

> Privat Hotel
> St. Moritz-Dorf
> February 2, 1937

Dear Doctor Jung: –
In a few days, the Club "Fastnacht" will take place, and it is a real blow to me that I won't be able to come down, for I was so looking forward to the party and seeing you there informally. Those parties are such fun and I have always loved them. Now that I know you so much better, the party would give me even more pleasure than the past ones did. Do you remember a few years ago when we all had our photos taken with you in gay *"Stimmung"*? I really would have given anything to come to this one, but another 'flu,' the third one since last October, is keeping me bedridden. I have had enough introversion now and hope these 'flus' will stop.

I'll be thinking of you all the night of the 6th, with sorrow that I can't be there, and envy in my heart for those who are able to attend and have a good time with you! One always has *such* fun with you at those parties, but to be with you anywhere is always so nice and comforting and agreeable. I shall not forget that lunch at the Waldhaus shortly before Xmas, it was so nice. But there was a curious thing about that lunch: I seemed to see a light, like sunlight, around you and de Trafford, and I sat in the shade with Janey and looked on. What was taking place was hard for me to understand, but it was of a benign nature, in the nature of a miracle, as when the flames descended on the Apostles' heads at

Pentecôte, only this was just a light that enveloped you both. It was very vivid and blinding to a *"Zuschauer"*[onlooker].

I hope you are well. Before I went to bed with flu I met Prince Boncompagni here, who asked after you. He goes to Ascona and is a fervent admirer of Buonaiuti. Buonaiuti was his tutor – or so he tells me. He is very fond of Ascona, but thinks that Frau Froebe has changed a lot since a Miss somebody or other has left her, who used to be with her. Not knowing Frau Froebe before last summer, I didn't quite understand that part of it.

Princess Hohenzollern is now in Zürich to see you, as you know!! She was to have come here first, but decided to spend her time in Zürich. She has much real affection for you, and was the first person who ever spoke to me of you as a human being, calling you "Onkel." Ever since then we have both called you that to each other and when writing; somehow it just seemed to fit, and now I can never even *think* of you except as Onkel. At times, when I have spoken to others of you as Onkel, I've raised a black cloud, but it has just been *impossible* for me to speak of you as anything but that. I had been meaning to get you in a corner, a moment, at the party, and "call" you that, and you would have thought I was drunk, and wouldn't have realized that, to me, you are just that – Onkel! It makes me feel rather sad as I write it to you, for it brings you so vividly before me, and then I realized how nice you are and what you mean to me, and how much I would give for just a sight of you.

I can't help but think, as I write, of the years you have toiled with me, dense as I was, and yet you were so patient and always kind. No one but you would have taken all that trouble, but it was just like you to do it. Maybe someday I'll become part of your spiritual world, though at the moment it looks pretty hopeless, as I'm still so "fluid." Nevertheless, I have learned something, but there is still so much to learn. I don't have panics in funiculaires or anywhere else anymore, and yet there is still so much to learn!

Much love, I will close now, and tell me someday, if you mind very much my calling you "Onkel."

Affectionately yours,

Catharine Cabot

Jung replied swiftly on 8 February 1937:

Dear Mrs. Cabot,

Thank you very much for your nice letter. I'm indeed sorry to hear that you suffer again from flu. Just lately I had a touch of it too.

It is too bad that you can't come to the carnival evening. I remember delightful sights of former days.

Hoping that you are not too long chained to your bed.

I remain yours cordially,

C.G. Jung

P.S. There is no objection against the "Onkel."

Women particularly seem to have been frequently ill in the 'thirties, as Toni Wolff, Linda Fierz, and Mary Foote often complained of being unwell. Since antibiotics were not yet available, infections took a long time to cure. But boredom may have been a factor. Rest was frequently prescribed, yet instead of being a tonic, it may well have increased boredom. Illness was a favorite topic of conversation. As for "flu," the word was used rather loosely to cover a number of respiratory disorders. By the time I was conscious of my mother, her immune system seemed very weak; she was always ill or due for an operation, many of these for hernias (a tendency inherited from her father, she said) and others for the removal of various organs. She must have had a very strong constitution to have survived so many surgical interventions. As for the more routine illnesses, nobody felt it was strange that Katy was so often laid up in bed; even her analysts accepted it as normal.

Her bout with infected sinuses had begun already in October, letting me stay on at school past November to act in the school play for the first time. After a good spell over Christmas, with a round of extraversion with Prince Boncompagni, Katy sat in bed for weeks with antiphlogistine, a stiff white paste, smeared thick on her forehead and cheeks, swathed in bandages. Reducing inflammation by this method was a slow process. My mother may also have taken so easily to her bed because Tommy was repping for the Ski Club of Great Britain at Gstaad. Toni says in her letter, "I am sure you are right in saying that you enclosed yourself in a paradise alone with de T., and therefore it is all the harder to have to contact the world, and quite by yourself without him. But it is necessary, and you can practise now."

At the time of my mother's long bouts with illness, my education remained pretty sparse, due not to those illnesses but because, while staying in the mountains, I was there first of all to learn skating. While there I received daily language lessons with a Frau Berry, but these I found boring, as I was the only pupil. My headmistress in England, Miss Aspinall, had written about me in November 1936: "She is a lazy little monkey, but no doubt we do not see so much of this, as it is more interesting for her working with other children, and she is anxious to get good marks, etc., for her section!" I must agree with her: I was extremely lazy. Frau Berry, in turn, must have found me difficult because she was often in a bad mood. I was into psychology rather than into learning, so I drew Frau Berry's shadow as a big fierce black dog named *Hermexes* who followed her everywhere, wearing a gold collar and leash and belching fire like a dragon. My mother must have been sensitive to my meager program, because she decided, while in bed, to give me a course in French literature. She obtained paperback *Tauchnitz* editions of plays by Molière, whom I liked, and Stendhal, whom I found heavy, and most mornings would read part of a play with me before I went skating. When I was not on the ice rink or having language lessons, I drew cartoons to amuse my mother. Years later, she would repeat, *"Tu m'as tellement égailé pendant ma maladie."* [You cheered me so much during my illness].

Though we had a ladies' maid, a nurse also ministered to my mother's daily needs, an extra measure that was strange even in those days. My mother's needs included enemas, which I gave when the nurse was not available, and heat treatments beyond the electric pad constantly in her bed. Three types of heat lamps were used, which my drawings at the time rendered; one was called a *Blaulichtbad*, an ultraviolet lamp directed towards her nude back as she sat on the side of the bed, and the other two were different sizes of *Glühlichtbogen*, a wooden box shaped like an upside-down U. The smaller one covered her back as she lay on her stomach; it had electric bulbs on its ceiling and walls. This machine was obviously too weak as it was soon exchanged for a far larger model, which covered her almost from head to foot.[1]

---

[1] I would never have remembered these machines had I not found drawings of my mother using them, which I had made at the time.

Toni Wolff wrote her analysand a second long letter on 22 January 1937:

Dear Katy,

I am so sorry that you are ill again and will try to write an analytical letter to give you a little comfort. Though I don't think you need much explanation, as you do see everything well for yourself and analysed your dreams very clearly. I am sorry you got punished for having been too nice to the Fräulein by getting the flu in having to enter her room. But on the other hand, to be a hermit for a while is what you desired and probably needed too after all these 'revelations.' And too after a dose of St. Moritz life, which must have been a bit too much, coming right after your very quiet life in Zürich.

Of course you are right too when you say it is better to go out once in a while so people can't say you don't care a damn when de T. is not with you. But now the flu has solved that problem for the time being. But on the other hand, you can't act the very jolly person who cares nothing whether de T. is with you or not when his absence makes all the difference. Such are the complications of life and real feeling – that is probably the reason why you tried to keep the feelings at bay and made *reason* the basis of your attitude – as of course lots of people do. Feelings mean more complication, but also more fullness and depths – I mean of course your own individual feelings, and not those social ones where one is just "nice" to people. …

A. in your dream must represent your former society person side, which has grown apart from you. Her having to have a baby might mean that the social side is coming up in a new way – which it has done already, for your insight into people makes you relate to them again, only in a very new and individual way. That would refer to the mandalas in the room also.

You must not expect "loving" feelings to people to come through again. Your insight into their unconscious would prevent that. But you have a much fuller realization of their whole personality as you have into your own – when you can see the good *and* the bad in them. …

I think, I thought you were a sensation type because you repressed your intuition so much, as it made you vulnerable. And also because up to now you really had the attitude of a French woman with very much common sense and being almost too reasonable. (The money situation, your feelings for de T. and the social side.)

I only hope D.'s visit will not interfere with your coming down to Zürich to the carnival party, it would be an awful pity. As for D. coming too I am rather uncertain whether she would fit into our group, you know she is so easily shocked, and of course at such a party no one can be expected to treat her specially, she would have to be just like any other person. ...

The dream of B. shows you a girl who hasn't given a damn about her birth and went all along on the individual way – probably rather a bit too much. But in association with her you discover these men's pyjamas which you try first to give away, but finally remain with you, for your *own* use if made smaller. That means a more masculine attitude, firmer and more self-dependent, as a man has to have in regard to the world. ...

I think you are right about C. in the dream and all it involves. Though I wonder if in reality you would decline a party which is given by C. That is to say, if you analyse the dream by taking C. *subjectively* your analysis is perfectly correct. But as C. is a person whom you meet in reality and who belongs very much to the Analytical group I think you have to take her *also objectively*, and then the meaning might be a bit different. I should say that then one is led to different conclusions, the sum of which would be that you ought to get somehow in contact with C. socially, not analytically. The party would be a chance to do that, for instance. By the way I don't think C. likes parties and gatherings more than mildly; in a way she does, but in a very introverted sensation type way. She enjoys herself being in a group, but does not make much effort to do something about people. This attitude of an introverted sensation type might be quite useful to study. And don't forget too that as C. she is always somebody – perhaps too much only the wife of her husband, she likes to be taken on her own values, but on the other hand, it is of course much simpler and easier than it is for a person who like you has no husband along upon whom one can rely and who does create the social situation. This may be a difficulty you *undervalue*, probably because in the USA it is the women who make the social situation. But in Europe it is very much the men. A married woman is always getting her persona by the social position and profession of her husband.

I do hope you can come to the party, you just belong to it and we would feel decidedly that something were missing if you were still not well to come down. But I do hope rather that D. is not coming, I don't think she could get into our atmosphere.

Do take care of yourself and enjoy the days in bed in your room. I am quite well and we don't have much flu here. I am trying to get my dancing a bit refreshed – took a course before Christmas. E. really encouraged me. F. and G. were also coming. Our teacher is going to St. Moritz next week to lead the international dancing competition she had organized.

Love and good wishes,

Toni

The social position which Catharine had enjoyed in America she forfeited when she decided to live permanently in Europe. Whether she was conscious of that consequence when she took her fatal decision is not known, as she never spoke about it, but she may well not have foreseen its long-term effects on her social ambitions. Already before becoming seriously involved with Tommy, she had no plans to return to the USA. Though Katy had no position in Europe and no real hopes of a husband to give her one, she seemed strangely indifferent to her nomad status. This makes me think that the unconscious side of her personality did not care for position, a side that became more visible as Katy grew older.

The slow-to-cure sinus infection left Katy far too sick, unfortunately, for her to join Toni and other psychological people for the Carnival. For her to miss a party was unusual, even with the psychological crowd. She was forced to spend many weeks in bed but never appeared bored, reading a great deal and writing letters when not doing treatments. On the way to Bad Ragaz in the spring with Tommy and a private trained nurse – not a common provision in those days – she arranged a visit in Küsnacht to see Jung:

May 14, 1937

On our way to Ragaz, I went to see Uncle. We had the hour in the little summer house by the lake. It was lovely. Uncle was so simple and nice when he came forward to greet me. I told him how unnatural I was, and how I had been unnatural with certain English people I had dined with. He said I might well have had feelings of inferiority with rather natural people. The mere fact of *trying* to be simple and natural is a sign of not being natural, for the mere fact of trying is in itself not natural! Natural people don't try. Not being natural, or simple, is a game one plays inside. Instead of just *being* something, one *thinks* it, and reacts to it – then one is not natural.

He told the story of a toad who asked a centipede how he managed to know which foot to put first and where he put his feet? The centipede began to think and fell into a ditch! You cannot force yourself to be natural. If you get rid of your feeling of inferiority you will be natural. With Americans this unnaturalness has to do with something primitive. Minnie [her mother] is afraid to let her primitive side come out. These colonials cannot be natural because they would be like natives. I would not be that way, because I have more the European style. But Minnie has had always to be self-conscious, for if she had been natural she would have done things which were not correct. That is the primitive in her! I told Uncle how they liked her in the U.S. but not me! He said that in America they can deal with such people as everyone has something of it. I have more of the European style ... Americans all have the [primitive side] and forgive it. I told him of Janion [Aubrey Janion, known as 'Jane,' was a skiing friend of Tommy's] and his primitivity, his Venezuelan mother, which means colored or Indian blood, and his living so long in Hawaii etc. He whistled, then said that Janion, having passed through an English school and having got the 'Form,' could afford to be vulgar. Terribly well-bred people can do things that others, less well-bred, cannot do – they can do something really shocking, and say, "I am terribly vulgar," and you can say nothing about it. Uncle said he would be afraid that he might make a mistake in form, but form is ingrained in these people so they can afford to be vulgar. English people can afford to wear dirty clothes. That perfect form of the British is something that cannot be imitated. Other people have to be careful – try to relax and trust the good form will hold out as one is accustomed, and one can try to let the temperament manifest itself so that the form doesn't break.

Uncle said that I do not need to be stilted, but I have to be more careful than if I had been brought up in an English school. He continued, "We Swiss have to be more careful than the English as our education does not contain much form." Uncle said that he could not allow himself the 'leeway' of an Englishman of noble family. "We Swiss have a more modest kind of family. We don't possess these forms they have developed in England which gives these people their extraordinary certainty," he said.

"Form" in the sense used here by Jung is a word that seems to have gone out of usage, but before the War, when Britain still had an empire and the pound was a strong currency, the general run of upper-class British who traveled on the continent were the type described by Jung. They despised foreigners, including their Anglo-Saxon "cousins." We were called "colonials" even in England, as I learned at first hand in school, although by that time "form" was yielding at my own school to a more liberal teaching and attitude. The British were slowly evolving as if in anticipation of the War which would soon, to a large extent, disrupt the pre-war order of society. But the adults whom we knew in the 'thirties had been to school before 1914, educated to serve the empire and thus cast in a stiff mold to withstand the trauma of leaving England and living in the colonies. These British with their superior airs were capable of making even a child like myself feel inferior. Though I loved school, I was so put off by the British adults I met in the 'thirties that I hoped my mother would never make good on her threat to bring me out both in Boston and London.

It does not astonish me that my mother behaved "unnaturally" with her English dining companions, for I am not so sure they were very "natural." Tommy was about the only natural English person I met then, and he had lived for years in India. The pre-war breed of English were apt to regard anybody not born in the British Isles as inferior – "natives," in fact. My mother's account continues:

> I then told Uncle of my worrying about and being incensed over Anna and her gossip. He said an English lady would not care or notice it – it just does not matter what such people think. They are foreigners and have funny ways. It is beyond and beneath one's dignity to worry or care what people say. These people are like a special kind of monkey that plays pranks, and you would never dream of putting yourself on their level. "You think that English people are naive, but it is not that: they are just *above* the queer foreigner," he added.
>
> I told him that I talked to maids and sometimes confided in them. He said that was a 'native' streak; it was an identification

with the rabble. The typical English person of breeding would never do a thing like that.

That may have been so, but when she talked to maids my mother became human. With maids, waiters, or workmen she felt no inferiority, and so could drop the persona and be herself. I too was on pretty good terms with the Waldhaus Dolder maids (the washing basket incident). I think Jung was speaking tongue-in-cheek about the "English" (which at that period stood for all British) as he did, in order to stiffen my mother's backbone and reduce her inferiority complex. In the diary entry, he continues:

> Even an ordinary Englishman has a natural contempt for anything foreign. They say, that one may not like them, but they are what they are. These English can be benevolent and kind to a foreigner but he is always a 'foreigner.'
>
> This form the British have is the education of the court, the exquisite form of French politeness.
>
> I had a feeling of vulgarity at dinner. There must have been something in her attitude to make me feel like that. He said that she had the typically English attitude, and if one could acquire it, it would be nice, but that acquiring it was not so easy, and reminded him of Andrew Carnegie who, when he went to Oxford, remarked on the beautiful grass courtyards of the colleges. Carnegie asked how it was rolled and kept so beautifully and how it grew so well and was such wonderful turf. The guardian told Carnegie that it was a matter of a couple of hundred years' care! "Roll it for a couple of centuries!"
>
> I told him my famous Hannah dream:

Preceding Barbara were two white Russian wolfhounds being carried by lackeys on red velvet cushions, wherever she went.

He said it was a most perfect dream of Hannah's attitude. I told him Toni would not let me accept the dream that way and turned it to myself. He said that Wolff was a great friend of Hannah's and loyal to her. I said I didn't think Toni would be loyal to her for no reason, and that Toni was primarily honest. He said I was right.

He said the dog dream was roused by Hannah. Those dogs were highly differentiated beings. Hannah, he said was a lady on the outside, and on the other side, had an identification with a valet. I said that de T. found her coarse. He replied that women of the aristocracy were often coarse. I then told him of the hateful tea when Hannah and de T. talked, and I felt a horrid atmosphere and resistances in the air. He said that English people usually had resistances to each other, and she especially, being an artist on one side has definite resistances against family traditions, and she often burst out into flames! "One can't tell really whether it is inferiority or resistance at tea. The different sets in England have hellish resistances against each other. In Switzerland also the man from Bâle[1] looks askance at the Zürichois. When English people get together, they get snappy as local things come up."

Both my mother and Tommy loathed tea parties, and so they already must have had resistances when they met Barbara. Katy's resistances would have multiplied whenever Tommy and Barbara began a conversation without her, because she was used to being the center. When occasionally a conversation did leave her excluded, she did not attempt to join in. At first she remained strangely silent, then fiddled with things in her handbag, and after awhile made for the ladies' room, where she powdered her nose and fixed her hair-do. When she returned, she made sure that she was not overlooked.

I then thanked Onkel for all he had done for me and said that he had borne me as difficult as I was! He said that I must have had most extraordinary men around me, and had to protect myself. When one man had failed with a woman, another man had to expiate it. He said that had made him so patient.

I then told him that de T. did not seem to be interested in changing and didn't like going into 'bad sides' etc. Onkel said that my attitude brings out dreams in de T. and he becomes changed. He said that often he analysed a woman and the man changes with what the woman *is!* He added, "The effect of what I say depends on what I am." (These were not the actual words used.)

Men failed Katy because she chose weak men whom she could control, gravitating to the type opposite to her father. They may have been gentler, but they were not resolute enough to stand up to her. She may have wanted that in the short term, but *à la longue* it was not stimulating enough. With all her talk of being "a weak woman," she was in fact too strong for these men, carrying beneath her timid

---

[1] Basel. Before World War II, Swiss towns bore French appellations (Chur, for instance, was Coire).

exterior the commanding personality of her sea-captain father. Toni
Wolff may have been shocked by the behavior shown by Dr. Draper
to Katy which I mentioned earlier, but he may have realized that
nothing else would serve his purposes, since he could not stand up to
her. Some of these men were addicted to smoking, which eventually
provoked a fatal illness in Tommy and later in her second husband. It
could be costly not to measure up to Katy's veiled challenge. As for
sizing up my mother in this regard, almost no one could do it. She
could hoodwink even intelligent people like Toni, for her persona,
well-developed in public, was that of an actress. Burdened with an
inferiority complex, she could be rather artificial, though not unskill-
ful, when trying to hide it. But not so at home! There her most
disagreeable, even cutting, self came out. Failing to see another
person's point of view, she was astonished if they reacted negatively
to what she said. This side she showed only to those she was close to,
for with them she did not feel inferior. Yet she remained always very
sensitive to people's behavior towards *her*. The following entry shows
Jung bringing the issue home to her:

June 1, 1937

I came in and told Onkel I felt absolutely as if I could not go on!
I was up against a wall, exhausted, discouraged. He asked me when
I felt this. I said that it was after having tea with Miss Foote!![1] He
said, "Ah!" then went on to say that the fact that I see the shadow
in people is questionable. I am too little concentrated on the black
side in myself, so that I see the others as monsters, but I do no see
my own monster! The worldly woman I saw in Miss Foote is
written all over me. She is all the time stuck in something. She
suspects other people have *the good things* and feels that someone
should bring them all to her. ... "*Only the good things in oneself are
to be had*!!" Uncle said.

I told Uncle that I had made a list of my bad sides, but it did not
seem to help me. He said that the fact that I recognize, and make
a list of bad sides, won't get them out of me. I shall just have to
learn to *accept* and *live* with them. One has inside a mixture of

---

[1] Mary Foote, a well-known New York portrait painter, was the typical old
lady of that period: her face was pale and wrinkled, she wore a little hat
perched on her head, a black velvet band around her neck and drab,
unfashionable clothes. She was petite, appearing very prim and proper and
spoke in a quiet voice. I liked her!

good and evil. The thing is to get the good and bad sides to work. We must learn to stand on our own. We are all monsters – a mixture of good and bad qualities.

I told him of Foote's ambition to be a 'Duchess.' He said that was a servant's mentality to wish to be a duchess. But he said, "You have had just such ambitions to play the role or duchess," and went on that if one is impressed by the shadow of other people one must say, "Why have I been so shocked by that?" It touches one on the raw. If one is shocked by a nasty joke one must ask, "Why am I so innocent and naive and shocked by such a joke?" If you find you are particularly shocked, then it has touched you on the raw, and it is something that is in yourself, no matter how evil it is. You cannot wipe out fundamental traits in character. *Instincts* are those basic tendencies in character which enable us to live our particular individuality.

For example: if you have a very delicate nervous system, you must avoid coffee and such stimulants, things other people do not have to avoid. People with delicate lungs might have an 'instinct' to seek fresh air. A certain instinct teaches people, who get a chill easily, to keep warm.

For instance, an unaccountable 'feeling' warns you not to talk about a certain topic if you feel that someone in the room will react badly to it. That 'feeling' that warns you is an instinct. Instinct warns you and prompts you to certain actions.

As I said above, in her home Katy displayed no such "instinct," whereas with outsiders she let it lead her to be more careful, although on occasion even then she blurted out an *enfant terrible* remark which made her audience shudder. Jung, for one, did not seem to be very impressed by Katy's dramatic words at the beginning of that hour. Not only could she put on an act, she could also exaggerate. When I was ten or eleven, I drew a picture of her in which *Oison* is dressed in regal robes and crowned Queen of exaggeration! Below it I wrote as her motto, *"J'exagère toujours."* Jung shrewdly suggested to her that she wanted to play the duchess, like Miss Foote. Miss Foote, however, never became one, whereas many years later, Katy managed to become a countess. Because Miss Foote appeared friendly and harmless to me, I never understood why my mother got so worked up about her. My mother did try to understand, at Jung's prodding, and got a little surprise, although she then gave one to him in return:

Foote stirred up a lot of stuff in me – it was the Lump and it began to roll, that is why I felt so badly after tea with her. She has a way of stirring up peoples' unconsciouses. Foote could also make a long list of her bad sides, but it does not help her to know those. I am terribly worldly like Foote. When we see something in someone which irritates us, especially, we can be sure we have the same characteristic in us. Uncle said that he could not read about people being cruel to dogs or animals; he just could not *stand* to read about such things because he had it in him. I was not surprised because I suspected it.

Then I suddenly told Onkel that I had the most awful fantasy of wanting to take his revolver out of his drawer and shoot us both! He laughed, and looked highly entertained and pleased, and said, "What a plot the unconscious weaves!" Then he went on to ask me what it reminded me of. I said, "The tragedy of Meyerling." He laughed and said that of course it would be a wonderful sensation: "Noted psychologist and Mrs. Cabot found shot – love tragedy etc. etc." Just a sensation to suit me! He said that I must realize what the unconscious is planning when I had those 'love dreams' about him. When you do not acknowledge a thing to yourself you usually dream about it. He said that he dreamt of certain erotic situations with patients, then he realized that he had not taken them consciously into account! He said there was 1) the higher level which takes Mrs. Cabot as she is, 2) the level which is less lofty, and, 3) the animal level where all thoughts take place. We ought to be conscious of what is present in us – the whole thing – then one is no longer astonished. If one *does not realize* one's erotic fantasies then one dreams them. He said that he himself had to take notice of his unconscious when he treats an interesting woman. "I argue to myself, 'She isn't bad; she's got nice legs,' isn't that an erotic fantasy?" He went on to say that his lower layers were always ready for any kind of woman. "If we don't realize how we look to each other and take into account any fantasy we might have, then we are dead pillars of salt," he said. One cannot sit there and analyse people in a cold-blooded way. Sometimes, he said, he had such terribly boring people that he had to make a tremendous effort with himself to bring out his unconscious fantasies, so as to help them. "One feels as if one would like to sit there and make no effort, they are so boring, but in such cases one has to make the effort with my unconscious. I must get into contact with my patients, and I can't if I hold myself aloof. I must think and realize my fantasies about them as about anyone I meet in daily life. I have to make an effort of the heart."

Then he said that, in my dreams, I live an unconscious love affair with Onkel, and now we come to the tragic conclusion where I want to shoot him and myself so as to make a sensational affair out of it.

When I told him of the dream I had of all his pupils coming to seminars clothed as animals, he laughed, and said how true it was that people manifest themselves as animals. He asked me how I came. I said that I was sitting on a camel. He asked me what sits on a camel, and I said, "A monkey." He said that was right, and it was most probable that I would manifest my instinctive being as a monkey. My restlessness is a monkey. The monkey instinct in man is pretty strong and also shows itself in the attention monkeys give to each other. That picture we all had taken bunched up together at the psychological ball, back in 1931, was typical of human beings acting as monkeys. We are all warming each other – practically delousing each other!

I have the great American failing of being too far away from my instincts: there is a great distance between me and my instinct. My shadow is the monkey – playful and treacherous. I asked him what I can do about it. He said that instinctive action and reaction is the true working of instincts. He said that when his instinct woke up and prompted him, he was a bear: it was his way if he did not suppress it. If I am aware of my monkey instinct, I will be prompted to do something ... that was his reply to my question, "What can I do?" "But what *can* I do?" I reiterated. He answered, "No one knows what an animal thinks. You can never say what it's going to do next as it is moved by unconscious instincts."

He then went on to say that when a woman weeps (I had just wept) it was a cry for sympathy. Unconscious women are astounded when men fall into the trap.

I must keep track of my dreams of my instinctive being, Uncle said. My separation from my instincts is too great. If I were a foreign [Latin?] woman I would know what was wrong with me – know that I loved Onkel. But that is the great U.S. failing: they are too far from their instincts.

I am so restless – that is the monkey in me.

Fastnacht, 1932
From above: Carol & Hans Baumann – Toni Wolff –
Katy Cabot, C.G. Jung & an unknown woman (de Caro?)

Then, as I left, I said to Onkel that I did not know how to proceed. He was very nice and sympathetic, and said I must follow my dreams. I said that I hoped to see him soon, and, as he bent down to catch my words, I kissed him on the back of the neck. He was a bit taken aback, I thought. Bless him.

The shooting fantasy bespoke more than my mother's love for playing a central dramatic role. Its purpose most likely was not to stage a sensation but rather to lead her to the realization that her love for Jung was infantile. Jung had Teddy-Bear qualities which her father had lacked. Psychologically, Jung was standing in for him; Katy's unrequited love for her father had much to do with her failure to grow up emotionally. Though Tommy was Katy's lover officially, it was Jung's figure which helped her to grow beyond a focus on the parents, whom she had already fantasized shooting also (see the entry for 11 June 1935).

What Jung may not have realized, as he had not seen his patient since December, was that in the past months Catharine had been in the throes of a partial regression. A total regression requires almost continuous sleep, medication, and a more quiet atmosphere than a hotel can afford. Katy may already have been in her partial one before December 14 when Jung went to visit her at the Waldhaus Dolder. She had asked him then how to attain spiritual development; he had replied that she must die and be reborn again, go back a thousand years until she reached the state of a child in the mother's womb (see entry for 14 December 1936, Chapter Four). She seems to have tried to take his advice, but unconsciously, and assisted by an illness. My extraverted mother, who had often had the fantasy of entering a convent, was able to "leave the world" only by falling ill. This time she had been off and on in bed since the autumn, and the course of the regression was to run for eight months. In her *Privat Hotel* bedroom she lay bundled up in bed, with a bed-jacket and often a woollen cap or scarf, although the hotel was well-heated. Surely Katy's need for so much warmth – this clothing plus the "warming machines" – symbolized a return to the womb. Even in May she continued to seek this warmth, in the Warm spring waters of Bad Ragaz. June still found her there, with a trained private nurse in attendance (the same one, I presume, that I depicted in drawings of us leaving St. Moritz in March). Both my picture of the nurse, and Toni Wolff's mention of her in the P.S. of her letter of 25 June 1937, made me realize with astonishment the nature of Katy's need just then. (At the time, I was at school in England, and so never knew that the trained-nurse episode had lasted so long.) Toni wrote, "It is fine about the *Schwester*. I did not know that you took her to Ragaz. I don't suppose you need her there really." Even in those days, to employ a private nurse when you were up and about would have been most unusual, especially so for a woman of forty-two. Seen in the context of a regression, however, having a nanny in tow makes sense!

The regression must have been concluded in Ragaz, because the next place Katy chose to visit that summer was the Lido in Venice. Certainly she took no nurse with her there. She gave up the Eranos Tagungen in favor of the society resort! Judging from Toni's letter of 25 June 1937, it is hard to believe that Katy had fully confided her summer plans to her analyst, for Toni writes:

> I think it was very fine and courageous of you to have made this decision to [to give up Eranos]. I realise how difficult it must have been for you. But I am absolutely convinced that it was the only course to take not to come, as your health matters far more than anything else. And you can be sure to make a great moral and spiritual gain by this most wise decision. One always gets something in another direction after having made a sensible sacrifice. You will somehow get far more than you would have got at the lectures. I am sure that you are progressing psychologically, this very decision is proof of it. And in the acceptance also of your own nature *as you really are*, the more you will feel that your nature and character are really a nice thing, and nothing at all to be despised. To despise one's self simply shows that one has not yet made friends with one's self.

Toni here sees Ascona from only her own point of view. It was certainly no sacrifice for Katy to give up Eranos and the mass of psychological people she would have encountered there, who made her feel less at ease – to put it mildly – than society people did. The Lido was the easy choice.

Toni continues to misperceive her analysand in the following paragraph:

> And I am glad too that you have accepted your dependence upon de T. If you think this over carefully you will have to admit that he is a man of sense and judgement and good taste. So, if he loves you as he does, you simply cannot be such an utterly impossible person. Have you never thought of this? I do hope that de T.'s divorce will come off in the near future. I think you deserve a more quiet and settled sort of life. And, to tell you the truth, I really do believe that when you have reached a certain inner attitude of complete acceptance of yourself, this can work miracles

Tommy de Trafford, Toni Wolff, C.G. Jung,
Bad Ragaz, 1937

and that outer things begin to happen, such as for instance a way
opening to the divorce.

The last thing that Katy wanted was a quiet life. Either a settled life
with Tommy, or some other kind of dependence on him, would have
been terribly boring for her. That Toni imagined Katy depending on
anybody indicates how little she understood her analysand. With the
regression behind and the nurse gone, Katy was her own master – as
probably she had been potentially all along. Giving up Ascona was not

really *accepting herself as she really was*. Such a thing she never really knew, and so constantly fluctuated in her needs. At this moment for Katy, just emerging from her regression, the playful rich at the Venice Lido were right up her street! And what Katy and Tommy got at the Lido was a good look at the Duke and Duchess of Windsor, a sighting about which Katy wrote to Toni.

In the same letter to my mother, Toni says, "I am so glad that you begin to feel that you are liked, and that it is Swiss people where you begin to feel it." Unlike many foreigners, Catharine began to appreciate the Swiss very soon after her arrival in Switzerland. She liked their honesty and stability, and the fact that they did not put on airs. Eventually she had a large number of Swiss friends; her Old-Sea-Captain side, when positive and full of bonhomie, was a great asset at Swiss parties. After the War, she wrote articles on the Swiss, including an excellent lecture, and collaborated on a book about them. Therefore, it was a shame that she was unable to settle down and enjoy living in Switzerland; her anxiety rarely let her feel comfortable about herself, instead making her strive for something which eluded her. Not an international society position, but some sort of recognition was what she wanted, at least in her conscious mind. In that direction Tommy could be of no use, since he was married. Social position was important to Katy mainly as a palliative for feelings of inferiority, which worked on her authentic inclination to intellectual interests, rarely allowing that side to surface. When it did, generally it was due to Jung's encouragement. Yet even he could not keep it alive for very long, so strong were the inferior feelings which undermined it. Always she went on to something else, usually a social fling, bearing out the solution which her upbringing had driven home. As her mother had made it plain in pre-First-World-War America, a good marriage could not be made without a place in society. Katy made the good marriage but strangely had little interest in maintaining it – another instance of her fluctuating needs and the lack of self-acceptance behind them.

So in the summer of 1937, after such a severe illness, Katy was in no mood to face the intellectuals gathered at Casa Eranos. Reluctant to admit her actual holiday destination to Toni, my mother eventually did so, and Toni replied from Ascona on 3 August 1937:

> Before I leave Ascona to-morrow I want you to have a few lines, particularly to thank you for your letter which I enjoyed tremen-

dously. I am so glad you can settle the "American complex" at
Venice, and I can't say what fun I had in reading your description
of those Americans. I really do think you write awfully well and I
wonder if you could not write for a magazine, but of course not for
an American one, as they would probably feel offended.[1] The
"clou" of your description was of course about the Duke and
Duchess of W[indsor]. I read that part to G., and she was simply
transfixed with amazement. ... You don't say if they stay in your
hotel; at any rate, you are bound to see something of them and I
would even venture a bet that you are going to meet them. So
please give me all your impressions, they are prizeless the way you
find words for it all ...

   ... If I would feel like going home via Venice I would let you
know, but it would probably have to be with Barbara, and also I
am afraid we would not have the clothes for the place, and anyhow
your hotel is probably pretty expensive. Maybe we simply will not
be able to resist the temptation to have a close look at Mrs. S.!!!

   I shall think of you in Ascona, so you don't have to do any
thinking about it, and I shall miss you very much, as you belong to
our crowd, with de T[rafford] of course.

The Windsors were the topic of conversation that summer in
Zürich, as Toni reports, even in intellectual circles, but Katy did not
meet them. And Toni and Barbara's curiosity to see the Windsors
faded at Eranos, so they took the direct route back to Zürich. Before
they left Ascona, the whole crowd – Toni, Barbara, Marie-Alix Hohenzollern, Emma Jung, C.G. Jung, Liliane Frey, and Cornelia Brunner –
sent Katy a postcard on 8 August saying how much they had missed
her. Receiving it must have made Katy feel very guilty about shirking
Eranos, despite Toni's encouragement to go to Venice instead. The
preceding month she had avoided still another gathering, which Dr.
C.A. Meier says was a favorite excursion of the Psychological Club.
Her diary reports:

---

[1] Ten years later, in 1947, she wrote an article for *Annabelle*, the Swiss
women's monthly.

2 July 1937

I first told Onkel how I hated missing the Club gathering at Rafz. He said not to miss it, but to come, and so persuaded me to do so. Then I went on to talk to him about more important things.

In spite of Jung's urging, my mother did not go to Rafz, a small town approximately thirty-five kilometers north of Zürich in a Swiss enclave north of the Rhine. Obviously she produced one of her excuses, but the real reason was the usual capitulation to inferiority feeling around intellectuals. The entry prior to the Club excursion continues:

I told him that I realized suddenly that I was [worldly] and *liked* worldly things. That I was just a *Oison-Pinson*[1] (at which he roared

---

[1] The imaginary bird invented by her daughter.

with laughter). I said this new discovery was a pretty bitter pill to
swallow, or at least I hated swallowing it, as I felt I was after
'higher' things, but realized now that I had been after the worldly
side all along.

He said it depended on what I felt about being *Oison-Pinson*. My
long illness was a stumbling block because one did not know *why*
I should be so ill. Maybe too much serious work did not agree with
me, but all the same there was no reason to force oneself to be
quite so empty. My illness denotes that I don't like the style of life
I lead. He said he understood that Toni tried to get me into shape.
If I feel O.K. leading the life I lead now, and am satisfied with that
fact, then it is O.K., but if I don't feel right about it, then that is
something else. If I enjoy myself, and feel good about it, why
shouldn't I live that style? Some live in one way and others in
another way. And which is my style? Onkel said he had to teach
people to be lazy. It is an art to be lazy. When you live a certain
kind of life and you are all the time ill, one says, "Is that style of life
the one you should live? Is that satisfactory?" The conclusion is
that it is not. I am, he said, very sensitive, a *most* sensitive
disposition.

I said I thought the O. affair a burden that I carried, and I had
too much work as *femme de chambre* to Janey. (I forgot to mention
skiing, which I also think has a lot to do with it.) All this has made
me so tired.

He said that the O. affair was a burden. I then returned in an
animus way to *Oison-Pinson*, and started in the face of no opposi-
tion from him whatsoever to defend myself, and show my square
hands and say that I did not seem to be built like a *Oison-Pinson*.
He seemed annoyed and caught me up pretty sharply, and I got
calm and out of the animus mood.

For some reason, Jung does not suggest that her many months of
illness had been caused by a need to regress (see his earlier comment
in the entry for 14 December 1936, Chapter Four). Forcing her to be
"empty" was surely a part of the regression. Jung often said that, for
extraverts, illness was the only way to make them turn inwards;
through forced introversion they learned to know themselves better.
In spite of the long regression, however, with her bed as the only thing
that gave her distance from society, Katy still did not know of the Sea-
Captain's powerful personality contained in the Lump, and was

therefore unsure about what type of life suited her. Since arriving in
Zürich she had been swinging between two poles: the one advocating
play as a way of life, the other insisting on mental development as far
more vital. The regression might have dissolved Katy's illusion that
she had to choose one or the other, but it did not, and so of course she
could never choose, her serious and fun-loving moods being exclusive
or split. In her words, if you lived only a serious life you became a
nun. Her either/or mentality kept her vacillating between nun and
deb. The fact that Jung and the others around him worked hard but
also made time to play was lost on her.

Katy also never realized that she had a strong constitution and a
great deal of energy, which sometimes turned inwards and fueled a
depression. When she felt tired, she thought she was weak; she was
unaware that it might be due to a psychological problem. Katy
learned some introspection through analysis with Jung, but certain
helpful insights continued to escape her. Whenever her analysis with
Jung was about to bring her to such an important insight, she would
switch to another topic. The following dream from the same entry
addresses this tendency:

> I then spoke of Princess Hohenzollern, and he said I was right,
> she was awfully nice. He did not seem to mind those letters she
> wrote this spring, at all. I felt happy and vindicated, because I had
> always stood up for her and found her nice.
>
> I told him that I still had a sort of vendetta towards Barbara
> [Hannah]. He said that I was jealous of her friendship with Toni,
> and that she *wasn't* a fine character (Barbara wasn't). He laughed
> when I said I did not envy Toni having Barbara as a friend.
>
> I then told Onkel of a dream I had had of going to see him a lot,
> and there was a death in the in-law family in Boston. All in black,
> I went to Boston. People in Boston asked me about this work with
> Onkel, and I showed them a diagram, like a light, that threw a light
> on part of one's soul, and I told these people in Boston that there
> were people in Zürich ready, at a moment's notice, to give up all
> and leave Zürich, even after what they had experienced with Uncle.
> At that moment Onkel appeared himself with large books under
> his arm and walked around amongst these people. I hated to have
> him there, for I felt he was wasting time unnecessarily on unappre-
> ciative people who were not taking him seriously. Some of the
> Zürich crowd was there and was talking of not returning to Onkel.

went to Boston — People in Boston asked me
about this work with Unkel & I showed them a
diagram — like a light, that their a light
on a part of one soul —

and I ask that people in Boston, that they were
people in Zurich ready, at a moments notice,
to give it all up and leave Zurich even
after what they had experienced, with Uncle.
At that moment Unkel appeared himself with
large books under his arm and walked around
amongst these people. I hated to have him
there, for I felt he was wasting himself
unnecessarily on unappreciating people, who
were not taking him seriously — Some
of the Zurich crowd was there and was
talking of not returning to Unkel.

    Interpretation of above dream,

A normal woman would have a certain longing

Interpretation of the above dream:

A normal woman has a certain longing for family ties and likes to be in a clan. I have too little of that in my life and I try to establish a family tie with Onkel. Ascona is where the family comes together. I have a desire to belong to the family. He went on to say that I depend on impressions I get, and am easily influenced. That influence is in me and is represented by people who are in the dream. I am very sensitive and am ready to take up things and to catch 'infections.' The difficulty is how to explain Onkel to the imaginary surroundings. What am I seeking here? I have the difficult task of sticking to my feeling – a family need – the need of having people one can trust, an infantile trusting, it is difficult to explain to other people. Princess Hohenzollern knows millions of people, but with Onkel she can let herself go; he is a father she can trust. She can be simple with Onkel and exactly what she is. She knows Onkel is not blindfolded by certain exaggerations.

As I said earlier, in the Introduction, it was only during her last illness that my mother realized how important it was to have family. The sensitivity which Jung rightly underlines kept her from this realization earlier. She was so fearful of being rebuffed, or of receiving criticism from people near to her, that she kept her distance from her close relatives and sought a surrogate family. But even in this "Zürich Family," she could accept only the head, Jung, while remaining wary of "the crowd" (Toni Wolff's word). Most of her negative projections onto members of the Zürich group were caused by feeling inadequate. Psychological women in particular left her feeling ill at ease, notably Barbara Hannah, because they were so forthright. Her problematic relation to women began with her return to America in 1913. At school in Europe, she made many girlfriends, who remained friends all her life, but in America, only a few. In Zürich, the only new woman friend she made was Princess Hohenzollern.

Jung continues interpreting the dream, and my mother adds his reflections on Tommy:

I look at Onkel through the eyes of other people. How can I expect others to see Onkel as I do? I have never talked to any man as intimately as I have with Onkel, with whom I didn't have a love affair. It is a unique situation, this analysis. It is natural that I should ask what it is all about and how could I explain to my friends or relatives, such a unique situation? I could say, "I am going to the doctor for treatment." And they would say, "What sort of a doctor is it who doesn't cure you?" Or I could say, "I go to a learned man to study." And then they would say, "Why ask his advice, are you a scientist?" I would again be in trouble. Then I would say, "He is my uncle!" And everyone would say, "What? We did not know you had a Swiss uncle!" I share so much other people's atmospheres that I wonder how I can explain to the hoi polloi who Onkel is? Analysis creates an entirely new level of human relationship, which is not to be found in our civilization. If I were a Catholic and Onkel a priest, then it would be understood.

Onkel went on to say that people give him the name that best expresses his role to them, in the most dramatic form. Some men have called him Mother or Ma, others Father Confessor! This relationship to Onkel is unique, and has not existed before in the social structure. The family doctor was the figure who replaced the priest.

People are neurotic on account of lacking the chance to be themselves, anywhere, not even when they are married.

> I don't need a doctor,
> I'm not religious so I don't need a priest,
> I have no Swiss uncle,
> I do not need an analyst.

A hundred years hence, Onkel said, people would speak quite naturally of 'going to their analyst.'

Being influenced by my surroundings makes me unconscious, but I must remember that the people who criticize will never help me, or do anything for me. It is a question of the fable of the donkey, the old man and the little boy. I must say to myself that I like these two fellows [Jung and Tommy] and to hell with the world. I stick to these fellows. I live my style and to hell with it, if they don't understand it they can PERISH!! I am independent and I must do what I think to be right. My relationship to Onkel and de T. is my concern, and that is enough. If I want a special diet and I know it pleases me, then I must have it. It is my way of living, and when you have your way of living you feel all right. It is a lack of inner independence to worry about what people think. Certain ways of living and doing have to do with the *best* in a human being.

People cannot understand that. They always think what is the best is the worst. The TRUTH for them is a Lie and a Lie the TRUTH.

November 16, 1937

I had not seen Onkel since last July when I was living in Ragaz taking the cure, and drove over to Küsnacht twice with Tommy. Uncle looked so well, and was so nice as always. I told him how lovely I found his garden – the red bushes full of berries etc. and I quoted what Tommy had said, that they were the sign of a cold winter and would give food to the birds. He seemed surprised and interested.

Then we mentioned de Trafford, and I said I wondered if de T. was neurotic as he seemed so *renfermé* [enclosed] in himself. Onkel said that de T. had made up his mind that there is nothing for him in life anymore, so he represses his feeling about it, and puts on a good façade. A man will never talk of things he can't do. Women will go on at great length about things they never expect to do really, but a man says, "Why in the hell talk about things one isn't going to do?" De T. has a certain definite circle or horizon, and I am within it. He finds it is no use talking about things that are beyond that circle and in the realm of (to him at present) the impossible. If a man excludes too many real possibilities then he gets neurotic. One must not exclude a real or vital possibility. It is like a woman, who, when she gets married, excludes the possibility of anything ever happening to her in the love line again! She will then become neurotic. If a man is getting old and he can't climb mountains as he used to because his doctor thinks it unwise, then he excludes any possibility of ever climbing again, or doing less difficult tours, and he also becomes neurotic.

I then told Onkel that de T. had seen the doctor who said that he was suffering from nicotine poisoning. Whereupon Onkel laughed, and said that de T. smoked too much, so as to narcotize himself – a diluted suicide.

Because I was fond of Tommy, even when I was quite young, I worried about his excesses. His chain smoking was matched by a kind of chain drinking, and I knew instinctively that they were dangerous. But they seemed not to worry my mother, who never, to my knowledge, discouraged them. Both before and during the War, people smoked and drank much more than they do now; but even so, Tommy exceeded the norm. He drank two cocktails before lunch, followed by half a liter of wine with the meal; with coffee he would have a double *Kirsch* or *Pflumli*. As he was a good customer in many of the restaurants he frequented, the waiter or waitress gave him an extra-large measure, poured well above the statutory white line for double portions. As the level rose to the brim, my heart sank into my boots. I kept secretly praying that Tommy would decline to order a second lethal drink, but my prayers went unanswered; I tried to distract him from reordering, but was rarely successful. Tommy never appeared to be tipsy, but after lunch, he would generally have a long snooze. In the evening, the drinking ritual began anew, but I was having supper in bed and so escaped a second worrying session. Possibly my mother was not bothered about Tommy's drinking because she thought it was sophisticated to drink and smoke. Also, she may have looked benignly on drinking because it had been frowned on in her late husband's family. (Her father-in-law, Godfrey L. Cabot, who never smoked or drank, lived to be nearly 102.) I bothered less about the smoking – in those days it was not considered dangerous – but I remember his terrible "smoker's cough" in the morning. His cigarettes, having no filters, left his index and middle fingers permanently yellow. The diagnosis I mentioned earlier, when Tommy's doctor pronounced him "poisoned by nicotine," did not appear to worry either him or my mother. He did not cut back; they shelved the problem, even though both smoking and drinking were discussed in Katy's hour.

Though impervious to Tommy's smoking at the time, my mother became frantic five years later when he was taken seriously ill. Her apparent indifference may have covered a motive which would have been active already at the time of the November 1937 journal entry, and which Jung brought into the light:

> I then told Onkel of the night at the Palace Hotel in Lausanne, when I felt a strong impulse to thrust a dagger between A.'s shoulder blades [Aubrey Janion, Tommy's friend]. He said that A. had a suicidal tendency, which he does not realize and that my unconscious realized it, so I wanted to help it along! When you are dealing with a person whose unconscious wants to make an end of his life, you have a tendency to want to kill him. Smokers and drinkers to excess are committing a mitigated suicide.

Katy's unconscious may have been keen to help Tommy's suicide along by condoning his addictions, in a situation that was hopeless for both of them. Neither took well, in the long run, to the type of life forced upon them by the refusal of Tommy's wife to give him a divorce. Of course, when eventually he became ill her conscious mind came to the fore, and she did everything to save him. The following long portion of the same entry splices one of Tommy's dreams with attention to another couple, one of whose problems was also expressed in drinking:

> Then I told Onkel of de T.'s dream of owning two cars: his old one on tractor wheels and the new one. The old one can naturally go anywhere as it is a sort of tank. (The two cars are his relationship to me and his wife.) Then in de T.'s dream appeared a monk, whom he had gone out to fetch for me, as I said I wished for one to sleep with. Then his rage knew no bounds and he yanked the monk out of bed when he saw me cuddling up to him, and tied his beard to his sexual organs. Onkel said that the monk was the man de T. is and that makes me a nun! He said that de T. had no spiritual life, no creed, no nothing to fill his life, like a real monk who has a spiritual life. De T. still lives a worldly life, he has no spiritual life or life that would work and produce, and have a content. He is half worldly and half monk; the two lives are checking him. If he were a monk, I would be interested in seducing him. He would not be so neurotic or 'dead' if he did not assume that his life had no issue. He and I are both in a sort of impasse, and he does not know what to do in such an impasse, so prefers to deny it. People in such predicaments prefer to say that there is no impasse at all. You then have a breathing space, but it is all done without the realization of where you really are. You cut off part of yourself. You are like a bird with a string attached to its leg, for you can only go so far. The situation is like a person in love who won't admit it! It is an imaginary freedom. You would go beyond it, if you would allow yourself to suffer. De T. tries to narcotisize himself. In order to find a way out one must allow oneself to suffer over the situation. As de T. believes there is no way out, he behaves as if nothing were the matter. Onkel illustrated it in this way, "It's just as if in the middle of an analysis I told the patient we had come to an obstacle which puzzled me, and that I couldn't explain it, or go into it, so we would just leave it out and go on – jump over it!" He said that, nevertheless, the obstacle was still there, and there was no use side-stepping it, for after that the analysis can't

progress satisfactorily, as we have refused to go into the problem and have left it unsolved. We behave from now on as if it did not matter that the blocked issue is between us – a dead issue! Something worries me so I drown it in drink or suffocate it with smoke. De T. has shut the door. A monk can shut the door if he has a living religion. A monk lives vertically for he finds the devil or aspires to heaven; he doesn't live horizontally like de T. If you have nothing but the worldly side, or half worldly side, you get blocked and neurotic. I then asked Onkel if I could help de T. He said "Yes" through my analysis. Such men would take it from women, but will not take it from men as it injures their prestige: it is as if the other man had won out, and they had suffered a defeat. With a woman, you can 'grunt' against it, but a man makes you feel he is one point better.

I then asked Onkel about the H. affair, and told him I had had lunch with her and there had been trouble, for she had asked me question after question, and then got mad when I answered them. I then said that I finally took a fiendish pleasure in answering *truthfully* and that she was half hysterical and almost 'blowing up'; and her atmosphere was tense. He said, "Well, evidently you did not get on together and got on each other's nerves." Then he went on to say that Toni did not know the situation when she said that Mrs. H. could relieve herself by a divorce. He, Onkel, said that he had told me that Mrs. H. was getting a divorce two years ago. I had written this to her (out of meanness) and, as I thought she would be, she was furious. I told him all that and that I was a mean person and not 'sweet' at all.

Onkel then said Mrs. H. had a terrible burden to bear. First, her husband's drinking, then her daughter's mental illness, then her loss of money, and living with a ghastly mother-in-law! Onkel said a divorce would not help, and that he has to back her up so that she can deal with all the awfulness. He said it would be utterly wrong to analyse her. One can't analyse a drowning man. He has to tell her she is doing well and carrying on nobly. It comforts her in her awful situation. He has to keep her courage up, to prevent a breakdown. When people are in such situations, one has to get them out of their material difficulties first, for they have no mind and cannot concentrate. He is treating her under the assumption that 'we are not doing analysis.' First her external condition must be normal, or she would get into an awful mess and have nothing to fall back on except a kettle of boiling water.

He then told me of a man, whom he had analysed for a year, who then compared notes with a friend and found that while his friend had his dreams analysed, he did not. Uncle said that there was no use analysing dreams of a person if he does not know the A.B.C. of the world and living. This man had to have everything explained to him first. Such people have only a fair understanding of their surroundings – they are blind and deaf. He went on to say that in the H. case, I did not see behind the screen, and if such a person hurts you, it is because she herself is hurt. An animal does not bite if he is not wounded. I said, "How sad, poor thing." Onkel went on to say that she could say nasty things to him too! She is hard up and life has been unkind to her, and she is carrying a heavy load. He again said: "Don't just look at the surface, but see below!" He said that his wife had said after the dinner, "What a charming woman."

I can remember Mrs. H. only dimly. An uncomfortable experience of my own is linked to the H's, however. I went over to Nice from San Remo to spend a night with their daughter, who was about my age (eleven or twelve) and who seemed perfectly normal. We walked to the very pebbly beach, unaccompanied, to bathe. The beach sloped gradually at first into the water, then suddenly fell away steeply. I lost my footing, and the current began to drag me under and out to sea. Luckily, I knew how to swim, so I did not panic, but with great effort, in spite of the strong tug of the current, managed to regain a foothold and walk ashore. I had never experienced such a strong current at San Remo, so was quite unprepared. I never told my mother about my nasty experience, not because I thought she might interpret the event psychologically, but because I did not want her to forbid further excursions to visit children. Back at the house, the H. girl and I talked most of the night, a great treat for both of us as we were much on our own. I never met Mr. H. My mother had warned me that he was an alcoholic, so I presumed him to be away in a clinic.

When my mother's journal resumed in early November 1937, one of Jung's commitments, to travel for an extended period in India, briefly accelerated the pace of her analysis. Toni wrote on 8 November:

It is so nice to know that you will be here soon. You simply
belong to our group and there is a real vacancy when you absence
is too prolonged. I do hope de T. is better and has not taken serious
damage by his rather astonishing carelessness ...

... There will be no seminar this winter, because Dr. Jung will
not be here. Quite soon after I had written you he formed a plan to
go to India, that is, he is invited with a number of European
scientists, mostly English, to attend the 25th anniversary of Calcutta University. So, having just got back from the USA the other day,
he will be off again in the very beginning of December and not
come back again until well into February. You see Dr. Jung will
have his hands full for the few weeks he is home, and I wanted to
tell you so that you could ask for a few appointments with him
right away. ... I shall await your telephone call and fit in your time
with me to your appointments with Dr. Jung.

Au revoir and much love,

Toni

The notes for the next session eventually return to the issues of my
mother's grounding in her neglected side, the splitting and incoher-
ence in both her and her friend the Princess, and Tommy's avoidance
of his own life. Given the tenor of the discussion around the Princess,
I would say that when I met Marie-Alix Hohenzollern after the War, I
thought she was charming, not at all snobbish, and very natural. By
then, my mother and she were on first-name terms.

November 26, 1937

I first told Uncle about my father's condition. He said that often
in such cases (hardening of the arteries of the brain) the pressure
at sea level was too great, and the air being lighter here [in Zürich]
it was far easier for people to get along. Down there [San Remo]
there is four hundred meters pressure.

Then I spoke to Onkel of his trip to India, and said that I hated
to see him go there and that I hoped he would take good care of
himself and take all the precaution for such a trip in the tropics:
warm clothing etc. He said that he had a chest of tropical medicines and would take quinine and put chlorine in the washing
water and drink only bottled waters and eat no uncooked foods etc.
He said that in Africa they boiled all the water which was full of
Hartebeest or Buffalo dung, and often in the glass there would be

a couple of inches of dirt which one would let settle, then drink the water lukewarm. Just once did they come to a crystal clear pool in the woods, and the party was going to drink the water as it was because it looked so clean, but he would not allow it, so they had put chlorine tablets in it, but at least they had the advantage of having it fresh and cool – the only time in their African stay.

He said he was not going off the beaten path and would be in a private train with every luxury and that J. was going with him – the son of K. This J. looks upon him as a father as he had such strange parents. A Guru, the spiritual adviser to the Maharaja of Mysore, is going to conduct them through India. They go to Bombay, Calcutta, Agra and other places, and finally he goes to Ceylon with Fowler.

This Guru is well known in India, and has lectured a great deal about Onkel's philosophy. He said that in the East he is a philosopher and in the West a scientist. There is a difference, and in the Indian sense, Onkel is a philosopher. But Harvard gave him a degree of Doctor of Science. I told him he was a really a 'Wise Man' – and the word 'psychologist,' as it was used in the West, and understood by us, did not suit him at all. I also told him how Freud had said in his book, '... since Jung had ceased to be a psychologist. ...' He said that he had left Freud's theory as he could go on no longer with that kind of stuff – it is a creed with Freud. He then said that India was interested in his philosophy, and that he was invited by Hindus, not the English. I told him how the Kundalini Yoga penetrated into me though I had never read it. He then showed me a picture in a book of old German *Hermetisch* philosophy, where a pole rose up in the air topped by a crown and clouds above it, with the lamb of God lying across the cloud. The bottom of the pole was in water and mud – Muladhara! Then it went up through the fire and had the snakes of wisdom coiling around it until it reached the clouds. The pole represents the backbone.

He said that the whole Kundalini Yoga was a psychological system. It tries to formulate how things that are in the unconscious, reach consciousness with all the symbols. He said it was unknown, but he discovered it in the West too, though it is specifically Hindu. I asked him about the hermetic philosophy. He said it all hung together, in a way, with the Cabbalistic philosophy and the Gnostics, but the Hermetic philosophy was older than the Cabbalistic philosophy. Cabbala was the mystic philosophy of the

where a pole rose up in the air, topped
by a crown & clouds above it, with
the lamb lamb of God lying across
the cloud – the bottom of the pole,
was in the water & mud – Muladara;
then it went up through the fire and
had the snake of wisdom, coiling around
it, until it reached the clouds. the
pole, represents the backbone

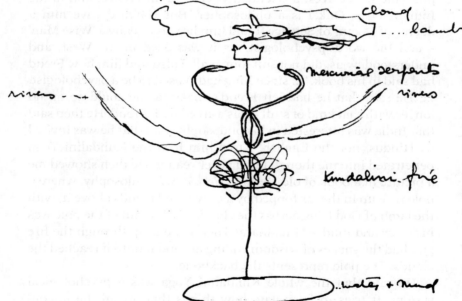

Jews, a contemporary of hermetic philosophy. Cabbala is a Greek philosophy and is the 'Gnosis' of the Jews, and still going in Galicia, and in Poland in the Jewish sector.

I then asked Uncle if he had read *La Rôtisserie de la Reine Pédauque* by Anatole France. He said he had not, but had it, and suggested I read the following: *La Tentation de St. Antoine* by Flaubert, *La Pierre Blanche* by Anatole France, *Îles des Pingouins* by Anatole France, *Les Romans et les Contes Philosophiques* by Voltaire (*L'Ingénu* et *Candide*), *Hypathia, Life of a Woman Philosopher* by Kingsley, *Salambo* by Flaubert. One must have *finesse d'esprit* in order to enjoy the subtleties of the allusions in these books.

I said my father had *de l'esprit*, but was so under Minnie's [his wife's] rule that he had hidden it. He said that it was difficult for me to acquire *de l'esprit*, as my father, though he had it, gave me no interest. I told him that, as a young girl, I had an interest in books and things, but that America 'finished' me. He said he saw that when I first came to him, and that many 'such people' came to him. I bristled inwardly at the expression 'such people,' for, I suppose, I hated to think that I had been 'one of those people.' He told me that now I was seeing what I was missing and what I was not missing. I feel the gaps all the more. I can do a lot by reading, and it will give me matter to think about, and I will get a more flexible mind. It is just like doing gymnastics to get a more flexible body – as if I were exercising my brain muscles. When people have no decent education, they have a brain that is useless as it is not supple enough.

We then spoke of Marie-Alix and said I felt something lacking in me when she dined with me the other night. He said her 'Wall' was her snobbism – she was a terrific snob. I said I was too. He said he knew that. He said that she is such a snob that one mustn't forget [when with her] that one is an underdog. She would have liked to have treated Onkel like a dog, if he had let her. He said that he found all royal persons were snobs, and none were great enough to rise above it. He said those German princesses were brought up as goddesses before the War [First World War] and they could not get over it. He said that the day she came to see him, after meeting her cousin, King Boris of Bulgaria, there was no holding her down. (She even told Jung's secretary how glad she was to have met him.) She is a charming little woman, but not big enough not to be a snob. She is a bit of everything: no snob, a snob; simple, pretentious; tactful, tactless; truthful and a liar; decent, indecent. All that is alive in her, and she does not know who she is. She believes in the Catholic Church, and she doesn't, and she believes everything and she doesn't. She is loyal and she is disloyal. She likes you and she dislikes you. She admires Onkel; and she doesn't. I then told Onkel that she told me she had schizophrenia and I asked him what that was. He then said, "She has not got that, at least only in a very slight way," and he went on to say that for instance, he knew I have a snob in me, and I am *it* and I don't criticize it. I am a snob and I am a child, and a ridiculous bird, and I am good, bad, reliable, unreliable and in turmoil. A snob in one compartment, a nice woman in another compartment. These things do not hurt each other and touch each other, and one does not ask: "Am I all that?" If you are everything and nothing, and don't criticize, you can fall asunder. One is like a great plate of ice, that is already split in many, many pieces, still floating together. One can jump from one piece to the other. Then in schizophrenia a storm blows it asunder, and that square mile blows to pieces. But with Marie-Alix, it freezes over and forms one lump – the things hang together. She does not stand on the 'whole' and say, "I am this." One moment she is in one ice compartment and is the snob with all the simplicity gone. Another moment she is in another ice compartment and is all simple again. She can hop from one ice compartment to the other and often changes three times in one hour! She is five or six different things: a box full of tricks and a box full of good things.

I told him she called me 'Catharine,' *but I had to call her by her title*. He said never fail to do it, and keep at a safe distance, and then she will be simple and you will have a warm feeling. She cheats herself in human relationships – she is not a friend to herself. How can you form a loyal attachment if you change all the time? You cannot be the friend of the King of Bulgaria, then something quite different! The more you forget you could be a snob, the more you are capable of causing a 'split' by repression. She has a compartment psychology.

I then said to Onkel that I had a tendency in that direction myself, but he said my own picture was far less complicated and that I am more synthetic. I said, 'Synthetic? That means a fake, a *Nachmachung*.' He laughed, and said that was the chemical sense of the word synthetic, but the psychological sense meant 'put together.' I hang together more, except when the Lump has me. I asked him why Wolff insisted so much I marry de Trafford. He said it was to give me a definite goal, a definite aim, for it is very important to have a goal ahead as it keeps me liquid. You easily lose yourself when you have no goal, you get distracted. Wolff keeps it in mind as it is a goal. She thinks it might flow asunder, as I have a tendency to fritter away. I was so dissolute in my mind and had so little concentration. She has to *insist* on a purpose, especially to insist, as I do not take a woman so seriously. With a man there is a sex appeal that helps me along. A man can be casual with another man, but he takes a woman seriously. I am now far more concentrated, he tells me, and I read, with intelligence, books that I could never have enjoyed before.[1]

I then spoke about O. [de Trafford] and said there was no sex between us, and he was not good at it, hence my cooling down, but that I still had plenty of sex in me. Onkel said that O. must have something between his mind and his sex for it not to function properly. I asked him how one could find out. He said by watching our dreams.

My Grandfather Rush lived another three years after the Zürich diagnosis to which Catharine refers at the beginning of this entry. He had developed diabetes. Both he and my grandmother ate a rich diet, copious with butter and cream, taking no proper exercise. When my grandfather first realized that he was losing his mind, he attempted to shoot himself; later, when he no longer noticed his senility, he became peaceful. After their return to San Remo, we visited them for Christmas in 1939, during the "phoney war." But by late spring of 1940, with Italy entering the War, San Remo was bombarded by French warships, their villa was badly damaged, and they were forced to flee. My grandmother hired a car and took her very sick husband to Pallanza on the Italian side of the Lago Maggiore. The Swiss having closed their borders, they were unable to join us. My grandfather died at Pallanza on 2 August 1940. When my mother and I tried to go over the border for the funeral, the Italian authorities firmly denied us entrance, and my grandmother had to organize the funeral and cremation alone. His ashes remained at Pallanza until the end of the War; after a week or so of string-pulling, my grandmother was allowed to enter Switzerland.

[1] Catharine's diary reports that she still enjoyed serious books when she first returned to America in 1913.

Katy's slowly growing self-confidence is evident in this session with Jung, concerning her most touchy complex around her intellect. That she was neurotic about her mind is not astonishing, because the inferiority complex made her sometimes say silly things, which then made her appear stupid. One analyst even told me that she was, in fact, stupid. Actually, my mother read a great deal, mostly serious books, prided herself on her fine library, and took an interest in many things including politics. She had attended excellent schools, and spoke and wrote fluently in four languages, having mastered them in a short time. Despite these accomplishments, she was unable to hold her head high. She felt inferior to the intellectual Zürich women, but many of them had not had a university education,[1] just as she had not. Nonetheless, the analysis with Jung gradually gave her some self-confidence. In this particular hour, she dares to ask Jung if he has read such-and-such a book. When he admits he has not, he reacts quite normally, countering with a list of books that *she* should read. Knowing Katy, my guess is that she may well have felt squashed by his deluge of titles, losing the gain that she had just ventured. These few sessions had another constructive effect on her, however. Jung's 1937 trip, of which she often spoke, inspired her some thirty years later to make an extended trip to the Far East. India fascinated her; she took many photographs and colored slides. One photo in particular, of which she was justifiably proud, shows the Taj Mahal: family members received framed copies of it at Christmas. The effort she made to catch this monumental structure in a certain aspect shows her to have been aiming at the middle-way which had been so difficult for her to achieve within her oscillating temperament. In a letter of December 1939, she writes to the captain of her father's ship, "You will soon get a calendar from me & my Xmas card, a picture I took at 6 a.m. at Agra, India, of the Taj Mahal in the early morning mist. It is such a wonderful monument, floating between heaven & earth, as it were, hardly of this world, & I hated not having it in a 'mysterious' light, for it is always pictured in a bright sun & very white."

July 13, 1938

I had not seen Uncle since his trip to India. He left end of November at about the time my Pa had his 'accident' at the Baur

---

[1] Toni Wolff had attended Bern University. Emma Jung and Barbara Hannah had no higher education.

au Lac. He had been suffering mental tortures before, and he felt he was losing his mind – going insane. On November 30th, he had his last vital moment, and though he suffered afterwards much depression, he finally snapped out of it and has become pleasantly senile. I told all that to Uncle; he said that was usually the case. When such people felt insanity or senility coming on they were still in possession of their powers and could not face the truth, though, in some way, they sensed it. Because it was too much for them to face they tried to end it all. If such people pull through they go into a psychosis or senility and can live on for years.

I told him that Minnie & Co. meant nothing to me anymore. It is as if my father had never been a relation of mine. I feel completely like a stranger with both of them. He said that I had slowly got detached from the past and the *participation mystique* was cut. If one gets detached, naturally, one feels nothing. It is as if a pin pricked you and you screamed, and another person asked you what the matter was. But if you had been attached to that person by the flesh then they would not have to ask you as they too would feel the prick. To become an individual, a person must be liberated from his origins. The sapling transplanted does not know its mother. Animals grow up and never know their parents or brothers and sisters. It is perfectly normal. The primitives bring about the separation in the initiation rites. They are told their parents are no longer theirs. Returning from the initiation, they must live alone, or, at least, no longer with their parents – for they are severed.

Telling Jung that she is detached from her parents is more bravado than truth. Letters in my possession written at the time her father first become ill in 1936, and before her mother's death in 1947, belie her words. Her attachment to them was constant and usually negative; when their health was in danger, she did her utmost to keep them alive, and even after they died she was unable to detach herself from them, mentioning them frequently in conversation, usually in a negative way. But not always: Katy spoke with pride that her father had a destroyer named after him which went into service in 1945. When the ship paid a visit to San Remo for several days, my mother gave parties for both officers and crew in her garden and of course was invited to lunch on board. The *U.S.S. William R. Rush* was recommissioned in 1952 as a specialized destroyer and continued in

Sea Captain at the helm of her ship, the U.S.S. Rush,
1971, San Remo

service until two years after my mother's death, when it was sold to
the South Korean Navy.

Katy's oscillations in temperament, described above, made it
difficult for me to decide whether she was an extravert or an introvert.
At times she loved large gatherings, while at other times she took to
her bed even when not ill. The social, deb side was extraverted, but
the Sea-Captain side introverted and more inclined towards intellectual pursuits. During her sessions in bed, Katy never read cheap
novels or even detective stories.

I then told Onkel that I could not stand huge gatherings anymore, that I had a fluttering feeling in my breast, when I had to attend large teas, seminars or anything big. He said that my consciousness was more profound, and I can realize better. I possessed nothing before, but now I have consciousness and cannot stand huge gatherings – they wipe me out completely. That is why people went into monasteries; they had such a developed consciousness and wanted to have solitude so as to enjoy the precious jewel they had found. People in the East develop this power of realization and they must get away. It is as if you were listening to beautiful music: you must be in solitude to enjoy its strains. Onkel said that he, like myself, used to enjoy big gatherings, but now he only wants to get away and work and enjoy his solitude. You realize a peculiar beauty, then in come all these damn people and disturb you. When you 'possess' and only risk to lose, then you do not like big gatherings. You want to be left undisturbed so that your realization can work. Then you become aware of the beauty of things and the atmosphere. By not going to large gatherings I rescue what I possess and guard myself. Formerly, I had no jewel, but *now* can be robbed. People nag at you and try to take it away from you – not to be mean, but because they envy you as they are looking for the same jewel. The whole world is looking for just that – which is liberation, and for being able to stand for oneself. One must look out, for robbers are about.

Then I read Onkel my long dream, where he is standing in the Pitti Palace, which is connected with the Uffizi Galleries. And later, giving big garden parties at Küsnacht. He said it was a very difficult and complicated dream. (He was standing in that gallery to control the people who were passing.) The dream is concerned with a question on my mind about him. That increased faculty of realization in me is not yet very conscious. People are always to us that which we conceive them to be. If I realize only to a certain extent, then I cannot take in a personality anymore than that. You discover new levels and new forms of relationship. This dream is an attempt to call my attention to Onkel, so that I have a chance to realize more about myself. The more you realize about yourself, the more I understand and realize about others. This dream leads me to it. Uncle finished by repeating, "The more I realize about myself, the more I realize about you." I wanted to get it clearer, but with that he got up and said our half hour was up. I had a feeling that there had been no time wasted beating about the bush, and that the salient points had been tackled. In other words, if your self-knowledge, and therefore your horizons are limited then your knowledge of other people is likewise limited.

July 20, 1938

I did not come back and write this hour down right after seeing Onkel, but I am doing it three months later from notes taken at the time. The salient point of the interview stands out that: *I am Toni at eighteen!*

Onkel started by telling me of a professor who became a pupil of his as he needed the opening of the inner eye. He went on to say that to see things you had to go through the narrow pass – then you will open your eyes and ears, and things will sink in. He said the wife of his host in New Haven [Connecticut], when he gave the Terry Lectures [at Yale], was a simple woman, an elderly lady. She said to him after his lectures, "I didn't understand what you said, but it was wonderful." His words had reached her unconsciously, though she had not known by what means.

He said that I was *so* far away when I came to him that it was a *miracle* that I had covered all that distance, especially coming from a milieu, as I did, which was lacking in mental and spiritual development. People, who have been influenced in their early youth in matters of the spirit, have a natural ear. I was tough material to get through – not plastic material! [not pliable]. If my father had been an academical man, it would have been easier to reach me. (If you know more about people, you know more about yourself.)

I then read him some of my dreams about his giving social functions. Jung appears in social situations – is an unusual sight to me. It looks as if my dreams were presenting him under this social aspect, it is how a person reacts and how they are. I was trying to form a picture of Onkel in order to learn more about myself. I chiefly see Onkel under conditions where we talk together, but that does not give the complete picture of him. I may also need Onkel's collective appearance.

I said that, in the old days, I had loved big gatherings, but now, I did not anymore. He said that – as an *individual* – I was unconscious, and had no attitude with which to meet another individual, having only an organ to meet crowds. I had a terrible feeling of uncertainty and sheepishness. I said, I hated going into drawing rooms where there were very big gatherings. It was sheepishness as my feeling about such gatherings had changed. I am at a loss to know what to talk about. Onkel said that as soon as you begin to see behind the farce, your feeling is different and you cannot show the same creativeness as you did before. You do not put out your strength as you no longer believe in it! He said, "If I lost all my interest in patients, I wouldn't know what to say!" Then he said that it would be valuable if I could find something that interested me particularly, that one gets so much out of such things; it is a fascinating voyage of discovery. But it must be something I can follow without him. Mrs. Baumann did not need Onkel to go into the caves of the Dordogne. Something is attractive and fascinating to a person, and one does not know why!

When one is young, one learns things in a different kind of spirit, but later it is otherwise. Onkel said that when he was young, Plato's philosophy did not interest him in the least. I told him that architecture interested me a lot. He said it was a fascinating study and very pleasant and interesting, and one got into the history of old places. There is a lot of symbolism in it, and in Italy, you have a marvelous chance of studying it.

My mother, however, was no Mrs. Baumann. As Jung said earlier, she was "a restless monkey," not grounded enough to be interested in one thing for any length of time. In her summary of the session she mentions that Jung saw her as being *Toni at eighteen*. Her more conscious personality remained that age all her life, the same age at which she had returned to America from Europe after finishing school. She said the "cultural shock" she experienced on her return to the United States as a teenager had blocked her development, and indeed her lifelong lack of self-confidence stemmed from the American and parental emphasis on having a good time and having no responsibilities. This emphasis had an obstructing effect. Catharine was not only easily influenced by her surroundings, but she also had a father complex that kept her childish, along with this predisposition to be easily influenced by her surroundings. With the double hindrance, she could not prevent herself from being swept along by the current into which she was tossed. Like most teenagers, she enjoyed parties and so was the willing victim of the social whirl. And for a while all her schoolgirl ideals and interests (her love for art, music and architecture) were thrown aside. But she could not adjust to this one-sided existence. The first signs that all was not well began in Bermuda with her first depression, and then the claustrophobia which she lived with for ten years, until fate brought her to Zürich and to Jung.

Jung did much for her over the three decades she worked with him. She was eventually rid of most of the panics and claustrophobia, and her desire to shine in society lessened. But the father complex in the Lump, a factor in her failure to grow up, continued to prove elusive, leaving her in the dark about the neurosis which stopped her development at eighteen. Despite Jung's help, she remained a teenager, pleased all her life with a youthfulness that kept her physically and mentally less stiff than her contemporaries. To Katy this attribute was positive; the awful truth that her youth had gone forever hit her only after her eightieth birthday party in Winterthur at the club *Zur Geduld*, when she said to me in a sad, bewildered voice, "Janey, I'm no longer *eighteen*, I'm no longer *eighteen*." This shattering realization left her inconsolable; none of my words had any effect, and from this moment forward, her health, which until then had been fairly robust, began rapidly to deteriorate. Within eighteen months, she was dead.

Then I told Onkel a dream I had:

> *Toni was giving a sort of class lecture in Charleston, West Virginia. She stood behind a curtain which was only half pulled back, so that only half of the audience could see her, and with a rod she pointed to a big tree, in the trunk of which was a hole, and first [words missing] came out and crawled all over the tree. Then a baby came out – as in the picture by Luini, in the Brera in Milano, called the 'Birth of Adonis.' I stood where I could see Toni, but others sat behind the closed part of the curtain. I wondered why they sat there seeing nothing, and being bored to death. Toni was dressed in a pale, pink frilly dress. She was many years younger than she is today. In fact she looked quite a young girl. She seemed also shy and awkward as she gave the lecture.*

Those images of Toni are things that are going on – a perception of the happenings in the unconscious. That tree trunk is a human being – all that is symbolism; it depicts something which happens in me – to bring one so far, so that I perceive what is going on. She is young in me, shy and awkward. Toni has no knowledge of the things within – in me, the same figure would be quite a young girl who is shy and awkward, because I haven't acquired any certainty about these matters going on in me.

I then told him I was so self-conscious and striving for effect, and did not dare speak out in the seminar like Mrs. Baynes, who made an idiotic remark and did not seem to mind it. He said that the person in Mrs. Baynes quietly risks it; it is a thought as any other thought and she talks of it even if it is idiotic. That corresponding person in me would be shy, and whisper to me that whatever I say must be stupid. Mrs. Baynes does not mind as that being in her is adult. Mrs. Baynes *thinks* without *feeling* and is apt to make mistakes. She has an animus that disregards feeling altogether, so she gets out of tune and sings the wrong note. It is intellectual talk, absolutely without feeling. She has no sense of consideration, and feelings do not disturb her. Considerations do not exist in her, so she brings out an intellectual statement which is beside the point. Intellectual people bring out such things and feeling types never open their mouths for they are too concerned with *themselves*. They waste so much time thinking of themselves and how they appear, and what impression they are making. Mrs. Baynes is just the opposite: she never thinks of how she appears, and she is then apt to make certain stupid remarks. If we could be *one* person, her mind and my feeling, then we could say the appropriate thing and be a perfect being![1]

Then we went back to the Toni Wolff dream. I am (in the dream) Toni Wolff as a young girl, the one who has knowledge, who is at the beginning of her intellectual interests and studies. Toni Wolff is the expressive symbol of the state of my unconscious development; looked at from a certain angle it is indeed Miss Wolff at seventeen or eighteen.

Onkel went on to say that he and Toni would not become intimate friends of their pupils because if people are with them continually they do not feel the need to develop; for when you are with someone who understands things better than you, you don't lift a finger. Onkel said he traveled with a friend once, who got lazy

---

[1] In this hour, Jung concludes that my mother is the feeling type. Elsewhere, he considers her to be "sensation." C.A. Meier also told me that she was "sensation," and I would agree.

and had a dream, and was utterly helpless in trying to solve it. He had not seen that his presence was hindering the man. "My friendship for a patient is not good as it deprives him of his own development." He then said that Barbara got stuck [in her development] with Toni. Never try to make a friendship, unless there is one. Take things as they are. Toni was not aware that I was building a little Miss Wolff in me, which is killed and suffocated when I have the real Miss Wolff. He said that people like himself, or Toni, suffocate developments. I asked how they both developed so far. He said they were forced, by their patients, and by circumstances, to get on. "The water of the great flood forced me up to a Jungfrau or an Everest. I had to get up there. I had to be up to my task and the understanding of difficult cases. My patients forced me by their neuroses, otherwise I would never have lifted a finger. Some doctors hang behind and are below their patients. A doctor who doesn't allow himself to be forced along will be a damn fool after a while." He said that, as a young man, when he knew very little about the work, he asked Freud how many people stayed in order to go through a real analysis. Freud answered that half of them break away. "At that time I was working in the Klinik [Burghölzli] and wondered why, for it is very rare when they break away from me here." I then suggested Anne M., who came here a lot and then finally left in a huff and rage against him and Toni. Onkel said that she was a half crazy person, who did not listen, and who really was *convinced* that she was Siegfried and that he was a woman Brunhilde. I was astounded, and asked if she was really crazy, and Onkel said she was absolutely! She is careful not to say these things to other people, but only to him. That sort of case does not need to go to an insane asylum. When she was shown that these ideas were morbid, she learnt that much was scared [sacred?] and doesn't mention these ideas. Her love for him turned to hatred as it leads her into her insanity. Then I asked him about a certain woman in the Seminar, who, when I waved a fly off her nose, said, "Don't do that. I love animals!" He said the woman was a Frau Doktor who was born in the East, and had Buddhist ideas, and a fraction of Hindu blood. Her grandmother was half-caste. He went back to Anne M. again, and said that he tried to save her from the meanness of her psychosis, but because she could not have her way, he (Onkel) must be the devil. To come to Küsnacht is a tremendous lure for crazy people. All the time you have such cases. They are on the border line and so destructive, for the devil is strong and crazy.

The next hour took place after Katy's summer visit to England.

November 12, 1938

Onkel looked so well, so charming and so gay. I think I have never seen such a delightful Onkel, *'alone,'* and yet in the seminars he has a *barbe* growing. I told him I had been in England all summer in the provinces! He laughed and agreed it was awful, that there was no shifting those people, that the English provinces were so boring. Nothing to do whatsoever, nowhere to walk, only golf or games, and they take the golf so seriously – make a work out of it. I told him the same was happening in Switzerland with skiing. He said he makes climbs in the autumn, before people came up to the *Jungfrau Gletscher* where it was so beautiful.

I told him about the school tea and everybody leaving as I arrived. He said that was probably their time to leave and so they did, to go and play their absurd games. (I *did not* tell him that I have a power complex, like a queen, and want to be treated as such! It was because I did not think of it at the time.) He said there was no place to walk in England, and a stout German cook of Dr. Baynes had said to him that in England there was no place to go on a Sunday. I told him that I saw 'Barbaras' everywhere I went in England. She was to be found everywhere. He said she had never got over dressing like a British spinster. I told him that I had written to Barbara, telling her, that she was right after all about England, and the English being so boring. She was not pleased! He said that Barbara can say and know these things but that I must not.

My mother was always late for appointments. I loathed that habit, particularly when she visited me at school. It was just not done to arrive late for tea with the headmistress. When she failed to arrive on time, I had the disagreeable feeling that she might have forgotten all about coming, and not turn up at all. Then when she did arrive, instead of looking like a "Barbara Hannah," which I would have welcomed, she appeared all dressed up in a chic Parisian outfit that made me cringe. I felt thoroughly ashamed having a mother who came to the country dressed in a chic town outfit instead of in country tweeds like the other mothers. I am pretty certain she knew my feelings in the matter, but for her it was important "to stand out" not "blend in."

My mother also seems to have forgotten to tell Jung of my accident at Malvern, where she had insisted that I take a *double* riding course. I was just fifteen. Even adults did only one week and found the course strenuous. Midway through the second week my horse stopped dead while jumping, I was told – I remember nothing of the accident – and threw me over its head. I was not wearing a hard hat so was severely concussed and broke my left wrist. My mother was contacted when returning from sightseeing. At the nursing home she engaged a private nurse to read to me (I was bedridden and not permitted to read for several weeks though I was allowed to listen to the radio.) I could not concentrate, so missed most of *The Witch of Endor*, which I had always wanted to read! My mother and Tommy, bored stiff in Malvern, left again and returned only three weeks later, when I was released. Tommy drove us to Bath, where I reacted to being reunited with my mother by having a terrible bilious attack. Tommy's expedient, a bag of barley sugar which I sucked as we drove along, worked, and I recovered by the time we arrived in Folkeston. Just then the Czechoslovakian crisis began, and war seemed imminent. People were urged to be fitted for gas masks, so we joined a queue waiting to be fitted at a shoe shop. I found trying on gas masks more fun than accompanying my mother to Elizabeth Arden's for a facial; I was just fifteen, and had secretly purchased my first lipstick and nail varnish at Woolworth's only shortly before. It was at Folkeston that I began to take an interest in reading the newspapers. We had already listened to Hitler's speeches in 1937; his ranting at rallies sounded awful yet comic, so we did not take him seriously at first, nor did my mother's German friends. They and we failed to understand his appeal to Germans and certain foreigners such as the Mitford sisters. With Chamberlain's second mission to Germany, at Munich, we finally realized that Hitler was dangerous. Complacency returned, however, to many people when Chamberlain waved his famous umbrella while stepping off the airplane and assured us all that we would have peace in our time. The tension broke and I returned to school for the Michelmas term.

Then I asked him why he had a *barbe* at the seminar, and at his lectures now. Was it because he had found that we had not made progress? He said it was difficult to get people of such diverse character together; it was a heavy task to get people together so that they can follow. "It's as if you are talking to a flock of geese, that all scatter as soon as you begin to talk," he said. "One feels they can't stand each other. In a collectivity, people get like that. There are jealousies and foolishnesses going on, and you have to talk into a chaos of personal feelings and get all this personal stuff out of the way so that they will become interested, and settle down and really listen. It only flows smoothly when you can lift people out of their personal concerns, for they are thinking all sorts of things about each other, such as, 'What a hideous hat,' or 'What a stupid face' etc. It's a criss-cross of emotions going around in the room. It is difficult to get them to an actual interest, and make them give up their distractions. As soon as you finish making the effort to get them out of themselves, then again they instantly drop to a lower level and become self-conscious, and stare at each other. The same happens in theaters and at concerts, but to a lesser degree. At the seminars people are so occupied with themselves and so aware of their personal things, and trying to sniff out other people and try to find out what neurosis this one or that one has. Of course when you are in analysis you have an interest in others. I could just smash their heads when I come in, it's disgusting. You feel all that going on, also with new people."

Then I asked him how he felt with no one to carry on [his work]. He said it was not necessary; he was leaving behind a wealth of literature, and the ones to come would glean from it. "After all," he said, "Nature does not produce a *series* of me, and after Goethe or Schopenhauer, there was no one – after all, notes etc. are kept, and I put my thoughts into them, and leave behind a great deal of literature." We then spoke of *Zarathustra*. He said that no one had quite understood it; it was read because it was beautiful, and also there were many quotations from Nietzsche in German literature. Nietzsche did not realize what he was doing, and he produced, like Nature, a lot of things which he did not understand or know about. Onkel said that he first read Nietzsche in the Canton du Valais, and was first impressed with its beauty; then he saw it was an amazing tragedy: that it was a slow approach to the world of the shadow. It is like a patient who defends himself against the growing shadows: he grows more and more afraid of the blackness. Nietzsche thought he was writing a gospel to the world in order to make the way for the Lord. The German soldiers read *Zarathustra* in the trenches: it spoke to their unconscious. I asked him why people read *Zarathustra*. Was it because it was so beautiful? He said that was it, and repeated that also there was a lot of it quoted in German literature. He went on to say that nobody has sounded the depths of it, and shown the real tragedy. Forty years ago, people would have thought it crazy stuff.

I then asked again whether he disliked not leaving someone behind him to carry on his work, and he repeated that he was leaving so many books behind him, full of his thoughts for future people to read and study. He said that people like himself did not appear *en série*, they only happen here and there. Who was there to follow after Goethe, Schopenhauer and Schiller? He said that people, not understanding his teachings, thought sometimes that he was a charlatan, or were very nebulous about him, and when they think like that they are asses. "After all, the Archbishop of York would not have consulted me on matters of dogma were I a charlatan."

Onkel said that Nietzsche was not always crazy. People call somebody crazy when they themselves are crazy and stupid. ... When you say something more intelligent than they are able to understand, then they just say the person is crazy. When Galileo Galillei said the world moved, and then demonstrated this with his telescope, people said he was crazy; then they put him in prison and put the thumb screws on him. Nevertheless, on coming out of gaol, he said, *"Eppur si muove"* [But it does move].

Onkel said that he was ahead of his time, but some day everyone will learn what he now teaches. When at school he was punished for a thesis which he wrote. His teacher told him that he must have copied it somewhere, which he denied vigorously, saying that he had written it himself. Nevertheless, he was even punished a second time for 'copying' another thesis. People were astonished that he knew something! When he was in New England, he discussed certain psychological problems with some learned professors, and they kept repeating, "But that is *research* work, *research*." "Yes," said Onkel, "it is research." People have an idea, when one talks psychology, that it is 'mere talk,' and these professors could not believe that psychology is not 'just talk.' The Freudian idea goes back to sex. You dream of a door and have no key – quite obvious what it means. It helps a lot of people just to be able to talk over everything that is on their mind.

Then he told me not to talk so much, as I did in the Miss Welsh business, when she said how nice it was that Uncle could talk about his dysentery so openly. ... First, I never talked enough, and now I talk too much! When I told Onkel that I seem to antagonize people, and wondered why, he said, "Go your way and don't care. You don't antagonize me!"

The first half of 1939 commenced with the same theme of circumspection in speech:

January 17, 1939

I told Onkel of my Klinik [Hirslanden] experience after he had asked me about my operation. I said, I had a row with the nurse and also those feelings [of claustrophobia] about the two people on each side of me [in the recovery room]. He said that I was naturally irritated by such worthless carcasses and wanted to see them put out of the way. He said when one is weak, devils catch hold of one. He said it was stupid to tell the surgeon about claustrophobia (pronouncing it in a humorous way). One must not hand oneself over to a doctor with a diagnosis, and especially not speak of *him*, as Onkel is incomprehensible – and deals with 'bad cases.' I can mention Onkel when I feel normal, if I wish, but never in connection with my own symptoms, otherwise I get identified with queerness etc. Doctor [Max] Fingerhuth understands, as he is a practical doctor, and also has taken care of some of Onkel's patients, but surgeons are only supposed to know their surgical work – and specialists the same. Fingerhuth is favorably prejudiced in favor of analysis.

As I have mentioned already, my mother was "operation-prone." She had her first major operation at twenty-four and continued with them all her life. This one was probably for a hernia, of which she had a good half dozen. The last occurred in her seventies, when the surgeon obligingly (though unsolicited) cut out a thick layer of fat. The shock nearly killed her.

Then I told Onkel that I had, at last, rid myself of those old women and old maids by whom I had been 'ridden' for so many years, and I felt like a person out of gaol. Onkel said that to get rid of them completely, the more I take it naturally, that I don't have to be polite to them, the more easily I rid myself of them and can be more natural – I shall be, without offending them or their noticing it – like Lüttichau[1] who stands and observes and yet offends no one. When I still feel that I should be nice, I am uncertain. Lüttichau doesn't need to be unkind, he just withdraws and shows his indifference. I am under no obligation to be particularly forthcoming.

Katy could not stand old maids, of which there were many in Europe in the thirties because the First World War had killed so many men. Strangely, despite her loathing of spinsters, Katy liked to dress up as one at fancy-dress parties. Her British spinster outfit was most unbecoming!

I then mentioned to Onkel how touched I was when at the *Technische Hochschule* I had seen him drawing so hard on the blackboard, working like a young professor at his first lectures trying to make a reputation. He said that he would not have got his reputation if he had not always given quality. He went on to say that I had never thought about such aspects and now I am beginning to discover such things. It widens my horizon and I become more human and less auto-erotic. It shows that I am at one with myself if I can see things that are happening around me. Being auto-erotic shows that one is looking for effects: the effect one makes when coming into a room – not seeing or even thinking of the other people, only thinking of oneself and the effect one makes. One must retain a certain amount of 'thinking of oneself' because otherwise it is just as bad, when you forget yourself as when you forget other people.

Katy never overcame her autoerotic side. She loved to be noticed when she entered a room, and the people in San Remo, terrific flatterers, played up to her. The incident which stands out in my memory came when she was in her seventies, during a party in a villa in Taggia, near San Remo. Wearing a gold lamé dress, Katy swept into the room where everyone stood drinking aperitifs, like a female version of *Le Roi Soleil*. Everybody looked at her, and the men dashed to her to pay homage, calling, "Katy, Katy!" while I, relegated to a page's role, received a mere nod. Her way of securing attention, when

[1] Count Viktor Lüttichau, whose wife was in analysis with Toni Wolff. He was not in analysis, but lived in Zürich with his wife while choosing not to work.

the conversation veered away from her, was by noisily fumbling in her handbag then going to the ladies' room to return only after a long delay. For my mother, other people were there to be impressed. At eighteen, when she managed to hold center-picture in group photographs, such an attitude is normal, but later less so. Luckily, she reserved her *Roi Soleil* manifestation for Italian society, after she became a *contessa*; in Switzerland, the Old Sea Captain came to the fore, and went down well because he was more *gemütlich*. This side, favoring male fancy dress and a beard, came out already in her teens and again in middle age. Jung's comment, as the entry continues, underscores the personal cost of such attention-loving attitudes, in anyone:

> It is pleasant for other people when a woman is carefully groomed. If I have less egocentricity, then I get much more out of life. It is a question of having too much or too little. A woman with none is unpleasant, but a woman who only sees herself is a nuisance, and one who can only talk of herself and her family is insupportable. We should be ready to realize values and see things. People should be awake, and aware of what is going on: they will not then say unkind things and will watch themselves. *Auto-erotic* means not conscious of the presence of other people – they are people who play up to everyone to see what effect they make. One is in a dark world when too concerned with oneself, a sort of mirror labyrinth, and you get into a panic. Auto-erotic people only see themselves, and that is why they have panics.

He told the story of a man who said he did not know women. When Onkel asked him if he was married, he admitted that he was, and finally confessed to having thirty-two women in his life. Nevertheless, he stoutly maintained, he knew nothing about women. In his vanity, he only experienced himself and never saw the women. He was in a dark world and only saw himself. Those thirty-two women were not his choice. He performed sexual intercourse with them to prove he had seen 'someone.' He only saw himself in that experience; to him a woman was merely an instrument for his vanity. He was a fine fellow, who made an impression on women, but the women did not exist for him. There was no personal relation because the mirror only mirrored him. It is like Roosevelt, with his stereotype smile which he puts on for everyone. He does not mean it for the people he smiles at, it is *his* smile. Onkel said he saw him listening to the Harvard lectures with a stone-like, impenetrable face, but when someone spoke to him, instantly, a 'smile' sprung on his face. Despite the fact that the person he was smiling at, was to him, less than a fly! He just screws up that smile. I told Onkel of having seen President Roosevelt's mother, Mrs. Delano, at the [Venice] Lido, and that she was a terrible old hag, a monster beyond description, horrible. A sort of wart-hog-like creature, not a woman but just *un être*![1]

Onkel went on to say that President R. had no human connections with anyone. He would not take the trouble to say, "I don't agree with you!" Onkel said that other people with such mothers had an 'infantile paralysis' too. Women like that have an unconscious desire to keep children dependent. Onkel told the story of a man who dreamt that a wasp came from his mother and stung him. He got infantile paralysis. The wasp is the symbol of an exteriorized poisonous libido. Valerie [Greene, an American at school with Catharine in Florence] had that effect on her child. I told him of Valerie's illegitimate son. He said that a woman like that is capable of killing her own child. Onkel said he had analysed a woman who had killed her child. She allowed two of her children to drink dirty Seine bath water while in their tubs. One child died of typhoid. She then went crazy. Onkel decided when called in, and after making tests, to confront her with the murder. He said it would either make her permanently crazy or cure her. So he announced the fact to her [that she had killed her child]. At first he thought she would die, but she 'took it' and was cured.

While the instance that Jung dealt with is drastic, my personal experience of motherly domination was quite real. Women of Valerie and my mother's generation wanted to keep their children dependent, for just as men dominated their wives, so did mothers their offspring. These well-fed middle-class women had lots of energy but no regular occupation to consume it. Bored and infantile personalities, they felt "adult" only when bossing their children about. Fortunately, most women now work and so are less obsessed with their children. While

---

[1] This must be a subjective judgment – presumably colored by her mother complex. In photographs, Mrs. Delano is very presentable – a typically conventional looking old lady of her period. But Mrs. Roosevelt, as Jung says, certainly dominated her only son. See Doris Kearns Goodwin, *No Ordinary Time* (Simon & Schuster, New York, 1994).

my mother had interests, she never had to deal with problems at work. Never having been subjected to difficult bosses and colleagues, Katy was used to having her own way, and apt to find anybody who did not entirely agree with her difficult. Though Tommy could be moody at times, he was easy meat for her, and so she dominated him, as she did me.

Then I asked him about Cuthbert [another name for Tommy]. He said Cuthbert was under a secret, like a murder, or something, in the family. And he repeated the example of the woman who let her child get typhoid. In other words Cuthbert could be cured if he knew the secret of the skeleton in his closet.

If Tommy knew of a family secret, he never divulged it.

Toni Wolff writes from Zürich on 7 February 1939:

My dear Katy,

Many thanks for your letter, which interested me greatly. I am so glad that at last you can enjoy St. Moritz. It must be glorious now with the sun. I wish we had some of it. It is not the dangerous kind, I understand.

Your description of the Palace Hotel sounds most vivid and very apt. I think it is awful and a very bad sign for our epoch, and one understands why people like Hitler and Mussolini think that everything has to be changed. I think it is particularly awful, that is, pathological, that the women and young girls are so completely devoid of instinct to lead such a kind of "life." You must feel calm and thankful for real companionship when you sit there with de T. watching that awful circus. It sounds like the late days of old Rome.

I am so glad that you discovered why the spinster and so-called worldly women are jealous of you. It is of course a very rare thing indeed to find real companionship, and not only to find it, but to be able to work for it for years. And yet it is the thing which every woman has a longing for, and really is born to get, if only she knew and were willing to work for and to sacrifice artificial values.

Janey's drawings are most awfully good and funny, but don't need an analytical letter to understand them. They seem to be very plainly that which they show. Incidentally, they are a marvelous commentary on the way she sees you in regard to de T.'s moods, quite helpless in your attempts to calm him down; for after all, what can you do if a man is seized by such anima moods? The Poliphile scene, Nr. 1, is most funny, only one would have to know what Janey knew of Poliphile in order to understand what she wanted to express. They are probably all the beautiful nymphs who always come to Poliphile and lead him to the places of his quest. But it is clear that de T. does neither see nor want them, being preoccupied by his mood. (Could it be a tender and, of course, to Janey, quite unconscious allusion to the things de T. misses in his rotten attitude to sex? I wonder, and would think it not improbable, particularly as it would coincide with the problems of Poliphile who also had to learn that a woman, or rather, the woman he loves, is not just to be taken as if she were a nymph and he a satyr.)

But the really interesting thing, it seems to me, is de T.'s queer mood, before he got the news which, alas, meant an anticlimax. He must have been absorbed by something going on outside of him, probably in Mrs. de T. It must have been an awful shock to her. Why did the friend commit suicide? She was not an emigrant in trouble, I suppose. I wonder, too, because such things do happen, if the whole incident could have been something like an anticipation of further events. Otherwise why would de T. have been drawn in so much? You know it happens that people just dead, draw after them another person into death, or try to and naturally if possible a person near to them, such as a best friend. By the way, why is the password Z – Passug, does it come from "She has passed away?"

Mrs. L. ran up today to say she was feeling queer and is going to bed and taking antigrippin, so we only hope she can have her last lecture on Thursday. I enclose the drawings with best compliments to Janey. I hope of course de T. has seen them: it is a very apt picture of his bad moods, which he ought to see.

With kind regards to de T. and Janey,

and love to yourself,

Affectionately,

Toni

Unfortunately, no answer to Toni's letter is available, if one was written, so I will address some of Toni's points. First of all, Katy's good health in the winter of 1939 may have been at least partly due to Tommy's presence with her; he was not "repping" for the Ski Club of

Great Britain in Gstaad. It also seems that she had emerged from the regressive period which had lasted from October 1937 until June 1938, and so had enjoyed much better health for awhile. As for Tommy's "anima moods," which became more frequent as the years passed, I was forced into participating in them as my mother constantly discussed them with me. I am not sure what I was trying to express with my drawings of "Poliphile," but Toni's analysis is probably correct. I always imagined Tommy to be rather asexual, and my mother often hinted that their relationship was platonic. Certain passages of the diary imply that it was so over long periods. Nonetheless I was sensitive, as an idealistic fourteen-year-old, to any hint of sexuality. One afternoon, when I knocked on Tommy's door and walked into his bedroom, I was horrified to find them in bed together. Nothing indecent was going on, they were just reclining side by side, but this was enough to dash my fantasy of my mother's purity, and, horrified, I beat a hasty, angry retreat. To show my disapproval, I put my mother in Coventry – I refused to speak to her for three days – but she cleverly pretended not to notice, and so on the fourth day, I stopped the punishment. I can only guess at de T.'s "queer mood" which perplexes Toni, the one that preoccupied him before he received news of his wife's friend's suicide. Toni may never have heard of Mrs. de T.'s attempted suicide at Château d'Oex, so it would have been impossible for her to place Tommy's acute sensitivity before the fact. As for his reaction after the news, he may have been asking how different his own life could have been had he not called the doctor so quickly when his *wife* took an overdose of sleeping pills. What Toni is getting at with "an anticipation of further events" seems to imply that Tommy might have been hoping that his wife might follow suit. Tommy would not have permitted himself to have such a thought, but the scenario that night in the hotel bedroom at Château d'Oex may have come back to him, with his rescue and his missed chance at freedom. Possibly, in her letter Mary de Trafford may also have hinted that she might repeat *her* suicide attempt if he continued to press for a divorce. Unfortunately for Tommy, nothing of the kind happened, and Mary outlived Tommy by many years. As for "Z-Passug," it was the password for my mother's bank safe in Zürich; it seems to me that Toni's imagination ran away with her when she suggests that it might mean: "She has passed away."

June 23, 1939

I told Onkel of the Weidmann dream, which was:

I had been living in the same house as the Lüttichaus. They left and I remained on, and a young man came to stay there who looked like Weidmann, and was very strong, and a killer. I entrusted myself to him until I found the awful man was a killer. I stuck close to Tommy. It was an awful feeling living in the same house with such a man.

Onkel said that the analysis of the Weidmann dream shows a dangerous enterprise which might have murderous consequences. An old animus means opinions, and a young animus means an enterprise. It is a parallel with the Lüttichau situation. 'Maisie' [another pseudonym for Tommy] is in the same position as Viktor [Lüttichau] doing nothing, no money and that is why Margerita is leaving him. In our unconscious we are animals somewhere, and Viktor's lack of money is causing the divorce. I was surprised. Onkel said a man's egoism is so great that he can smear his boots with the fat of his murdered brother. Such a dream where a young criminal animus reveals itself, means a dangerous enterprise is afoot. My unconscious says that I could kill Maisie when he is in such a mood. Then Onkel told me of his African experience with Baynes. They were all in a tent, and Baynes was outside. Suddenly, they heard a shot, and one man said, "Let's hope that's Baynes blowing out his brains!" It seems Baynes was in terrible humors all the time. Onkel said such moods bring out a murderous feeling in one. I could kill Maisie, and if I run away from Maisie, it is as if I had killed him. One must make use of every instance of a bad mood, by saying the next day, when the mood has worn off, "Yesterday, you behaved in such and such a way, no reproach meant! Were you in a bad mood, yes or no?" Then ask purely for *a statement of facts*. Ask the person for a reason why he was in a bad mood. The cause and why. Maisie, of course, hates like hell to be in such a mood, for a gentleman has no moods. He dislikes it himself and he feels defeated, and angry and irritable with himself for it shows that he is not master of himself. In analysis, one has fewer moods because one has an emotional outlet. In a personal relationship, resentments store up. "I" am the apparent reason for Maisie's moods; he has resistances against me, and I am quite likely to arouse resistances. I am a 'very nice person' and such 'nice' persons have nasty feelings. I have a spark in my eyes, from which one can conclude that in me there are hidden nasty reactions. Maisie is too tactful, and too much a gentleman, to talk of his resistances. There are millions of opportunities in a life together for having bad feelings which ought to be talked over, so as to create an atmosphere of understanding and compassion. Maisie's unconscious is chuck-full of resistances and resentments.

I told Onkel I had repeated to Toni what Maisie has said about himself, which was that, if he were analysed, he would be found quite empty, and not full of horrid things. Onkel said that his moods show there is lots in him, and he added that he had a lot of sympathy with a gentleman, for he had always wanted to be a gentleman, and suddenly saw how difficult it was, so gave it up. He went on to say that Maisie would fall into his anima because he cannot be decent twenty-four hours a day; it is impossible. You cannot be flawless. Maisie suffers from the fact that he tries to be decent, but he has an indecent anima, that is why he married such a woman.

I told Onkel that Toni said that I was ahead of him. Onkel replied that if I go out walking with a person and walk faster than my companion, I am ahead of him. Then I go back to find where the other fellow is, and I have to make an effort to walk more slowly. One must try and keep pace with Maisie and give him a chance to talk. He imagines nothing is the matter with *him*, but everything is the matter with *me*. When I run and leave him, he says to himself that *he* is normal, but *I* need analysis, as I have no contact with him and therefore can't be normal. But he is normal at the expense of his *terrible* anima. That's his wife! If he could acknowledge his own anima it would have an influence on his wife. It is a *cercle vicieux*. He tries to be decent, his anima gets indecent and possesses him, and he tries to be decent all the more. When the moods get very bad, one has to do something about it. I must try and tap the reservoir of his resentments. One must wait until he has had his day out with his anima, then [afterwards] he is softer and he renews his attempt to be decent. I must ask the next day, "No reproach meant, but you didn't feel well, you were so peculiar, is there something on your heart?" He will try to make me irritable. It is a question of relationship, and one must try to bring these things to the surface – otherwise they rankle in the unconscious.

Naturally, he is not satisfied with himself – the woman is the reason. When I get him to say something that to me is disagreeable, I must just swallow it. *I must be hurt.* The mere fact that people are close to each other arouses resistances. I am not the cause, it just happens this way. His conscious is perfectly empty, but behind it, not at all. Someday I must support him, for as a soldier, he has feelings of intellectual inferiority. He has a straight and simple mind. One could have a serious talk with him because he thinks logically and in a straight and simple manner. Onkel added that he could explain to him complicated things if he talked simply enough. He has some punch in his mental makeup; he is quite a man. Try patiently, and if you feel it does not work try again, and he is sure to come around, in a nice way, to understand what it is about. If I can establish such an understanding with him, and give him a chance to come out with his negative stuff, what he might say might hurt. There is no positive relation to people if you don't swallow their negative qualities. There is nothing positive without a negative side. A gentleman tries to be nice and then he develops 'such moods'! He realizes the negative feelings he has against me are unjust and it is all d... nonsense. And he says to himself, "I shan't talk about it."

If I have negative feelings against you, I have nothing against you, but bad moods are thrust on me from the unconscious by certain resentments, and these resentments come against me. I must tell Maisie, to tell me what the contents are of such a bad mood, for he *must* have certain resentments, it's natural and also ask how he appears to himself when in such a mood, and does he appreciate himself when in such a mood, or does he say, "I am a d... ass," or "I think the same of you." He thinks his moods come from the fact that B. [another name for his wife] won't give him a divorce, but that is only apparently so. The fact is he has them. The anima first tries to bring about the separation, secondly, tries to call forth the murderer in me – "Kill that fellow!" The anima is also out to destroy our relationship, creating the illusion that happiness and fulfillment are somewhere else. We both are running after illusory fulfillment. My devil animus is an answer to his anima.

Tommy never mentioned skeletons in his closet or black sheep in his family – *à propos* Jung's query about Tommy's being "under a secret," January 17 – but he did say that because of the family's ancient lineage and its current lack of wealth, that its members displayed a certain arrogance while being, as he implied, benighted people. While the eldest son had retained the family seat, Haselour Hall, and lived off income from the estate, the younger siblings had little money. The parents had been typical Victorians; Tommy rarely spoke of them except to tell us that his mother had been cold and unloving but very religious, going to daily mass in the family chapel but taking little interest in her many children – eleven or twelve. His father Tommy called, rather bitterly, "a begetter of children." The younger sons in pre-war Britain had to enter either the Army, the colonial services, politics, or the Church. Daughters who did not marry became governesses or looked after their parents, because for them university education, training for a profession, or going into business was frowned upon. Either the sons or daughters who failed to contract a good marriage lived on minute incomes from savings, military pay, and pensions. Even Tommy's eldest brother lived frugally, the estate bringing in little, and Tommy's major's pension of about £ 350 per annum was difficult to live on even in the 'thirties. Living as he did in a Zürich hotel, he depended on my mother for financial support and, as he was honorable, this weighed upon him. Though he did not say so, it was obvious that Tommy's financial dependence was the main reason for his moodiness. From what Katy writes, it appears that she did not mention Tommy's precarious finances to Jung. This spared her as well as Tommy from certain scrutinies in the analysis. As my mother had no intention of living like a pauper, she could not alter the financial imbalance between them, and Tommy's anima moods on the whole grew stronger as the years passed. Katy's feeling side with regard to Tommy was not strong. Impervious to his predicament, she remained in charge, not only because she held the purse strings but also because she was the stronger character. She decided how they would live – each in a separate hotel for convention's sake, save during the War when, to economize, they both lived at the Waldhaus Dolder. Katy also decided where they would travel and even chose Tommy's clothes! Despite her running the show, however, Tommy was very fond of Katy, for she brought life to his humdrum existence. When he died, he left half of his small estate to my mother and half to his estranged wife.

July 1, 1939

    I asked Onkel what he had said about the wine the evening he had dined with Toni and me at the Exposition's[1] Hotel Suisse. He laughed, and said, "I said it had reached its summit!" He went on to say that "summit" was not a correct word and quite a homely term. I suggested *apogee*. He said that using such a word denoted that one had read a lot of good novels and was a person of culture.

    Then I told him of my adventure with Mrs. Fierz, how I went in all innocence to talk about the Club etc.[2] Then the *ouragan a éclaté* (hurricane burst)! I said I was annoyed, suffered, was exhilarated, and went through a bit of everything, while getting Linda's dressing-down. But it all ended well. I held myself in and we parted the best of friends, she inviting me to dinner. I told him that Toni wanted me to see Mrs. Fierz, and also tell her of my successes and friends so as to show her that, after all, I was not the complete failure in relationships which she supposed me to be, because I could not make a relationship with some of these very difficult and neurotic people in Zürich. Onkel said that Mrs. Fierz's attitude puzzles Toni, and that I must leave it to her to talk to Mrs. Fierz. I must do nothing for I am under no obligation to Mrs. Fierz to prove that I am not a failure. It was right that Toni made me realize that I had a long list of friends, so that I shouldn't fall into feelings of inferiority. But that list need not be talked over with Mrs. Fierz, otherwise I would start her up again. Mrs. Fierz must smell it (that I am not a complete failure). She smelt the wrong thing, now she must smell the right things. No one has the right to say awful things to anyone, and Mrs. Fierz has no right to talk to me like that. I said she was so clever. He said that indeed she was, but her feeling was thin! He warned me not to repeat the *séance* [session], and if I presented such a list, I should lose all my points. He went on to say that she had already applied her success with another applicant for the Club, the next day. The person was 'trapped' (a big row) and something very valuable was discovered, so it did not matter. He added that when you trap someone, you trap yourself – and worse. If your scheme succeeds, you suffer a defeat. You should not set traps. I told him that Mrs. Fierz had something

---

[1] The Swiss *Landesausstellung*, Zürich, 1939.
[2] Catharine had been a *Statuarischer Gast* for some years. She became a member of the Psychological Club in May 1940.

hypnotic about her, that I had felt it in the past when with her, but couldn't put my finger on just what she was. He looked at me, with a really humorous expression, and murmured, "Witch!" I told him that I had had a dream in which Mrs. Fierz had put a black fur robe over the foot of my bed. "Ah, the black cat," he said with a laugh.

Then leaving the Fierz topic, we launched into the de T. one. I told him that he had been right about my looking at myself and seeing how, when and where I irritated de T. I told him that I was always late and suddenly realized that de T. must have a resistance against it. He said that was very impolite towards de T.'s feeling, and reckless too towards a man who believes in time, and to be careful! Naturally de T. has an anima which reacts! (Also he is touched by my good will.) He is human and resents any kind of brusqueness, but he is a man who can be talked to, and very sensitive. I then said that I had asked de T. if he didn't have resentments or resistances. Onkel said, "I never say, 'You must have a resentment,' but instead, I say, 'But *it* resents, and if you are not conscious of it, it's your handicap for you are too little conscious of your own resentments.'" Then people can *realize* their resentments, but as long as a person is identical with the role of gentleman, he doesn't resent. Of course a person can say, "I am not vain" but somewhere we are all vain and touchy, and if one says something derogatory we are wounded. If you are shot at, and a bullet passes through your skin, you are hurt. We can't be hit without receiving a wound, and if we are unconscious of that wound we must seek it. That's why de T. must not identify with his role as gentleman otherwise he refuses to see where and how he is hurt.

Then we went back to Mrs. Fierz. I said that the next morning I was really angry and had written her a letter which I tore up. But I said the feeling of exhilaration was uppermost, as there was so much 'life' in the whole thing. He said that the most dangerous thing is when one is exhilarated by a thing like that. It means I am waiting to get back at her – like a *ressentiment* it is there. It is lingering on and I am far more dangerous just because I am exhilarated. I want something with pepper – nothing small! My revenge will be something big which I don't yet know. When somebody gets exhilarated, the fighting spirit is coming up and is waiting. ...

The Psychological Club in Zürich, 1971

Miss Wolff and Mrs. Fierz were on the executive committee of the Psychological Club, the former as President and the latter as Secretary. Both played important roles in vetting prospective members. I expect my mother was exhilarated because she 'passed' the grueling interview and was soon to become a member of the club. (She had felt intellectually inferior to the other members and had imagined her application would be turned down.)

Then I spoke of my *échec* [failure] with Miss Foote. I told him it was positively painful to have her around – so abject, so groveling, and apologizing for herself. He said that Miss Foote had an abysmal feeling of inferiority. Such people, he said, have a terrific power complex, and Miss Foote can spoil everything with her feelings of inferiority. People like her are sadists, and they act in a melancholy way. It is only wise to reckon with the possibility that Miss Foote will react badly if, after asking her to come home with me, I say I don't want her to. She naturally takes this as an affront to herself.

I told Onkel that I still had the panics in the Dolderbahn, but not in the *Schwebebahn*![1] He said indeed it was crazy! I was horrified and explained to him that in the *Schwebebahn* I could speak to someone and say I feel ill; that would be considered by those present as quite natural. The very fact that I could say I felt badly would prevent me from having the panics. But in the Dolderbahn, one could not say one was ill: it looked too absurd to be scared in such a thing. That very fact would make a panic start. He then said that he understood and that it was not crazy (at which I felt immensely relieved!). He went on to say how he felt utterly suffocated and panic-stricken when he went up to the Jungfrau-joch the first time.[2] He then said that it was of course only wise that I reckon with the possibility [of being panicky] and where I can say such a thing. The animus is converted into a natural mind. If I were cornered in a place I could not leave, I would resort to violence. My Lump and panics are my violence. In the mental form, my natural mind is masculine, direct, brutal and reckless. If I don't say I feel badly I get into a panic or a violent mood. He said he was scared of such panics, having seen two awful cases. There is a good deal of the unconscious that I have not tackled yet, and I haven't got down to the rock bottom of it yet, but through dreams I will find a clue. I must pierce the Lump to find consciousness.

On 25 July 1939, Toni Wolff wrote from Zürich:

> ... I have not forgotten about having you to dinner at Bollingen, but unfortunately we simply couldn't manage. We had to go to Zürich again for two days, and I got a bad intestinal cold. ...
>
> I saw Mrs. L. just for a minute at Bollingen just before leaving myself ... I was amused at her letter to you, it was so elaborate and *umständlich*. She, like a good deal of the people here, seems to be under the impression that you are a person of the 'big world,' and that it is quite a condescension on your part to dine with the L's and other "Zürich Bürger." It is queer how so many of them misjudge you. I believe it comes partly from the fact that you are almost the only one here who has kept up (if they ever had it!) a real social form and who does not talk shop (i.e. analysis). It is of

---

[1] The cable car which spanned the Lake of Zürich, linking the two sections of the 1939 *Landesausstellung*. It was removed after the exhibition was closed.

[2] Almost the entire journey is spent in a tunnel through the Eiger.

course the only thing to do, but nobody will understand this, as so very many of them make analysis a surrogate for real life. So don't get disoriented by what they say. But try to see why they can't understand your attitude. ...

I am so sorry for Janey that the weather is bad, she does not get the nicest impression of the Exposition in this way.

I hope you have a nice celebration of de T.'s birthday, with no bad humours to interfere.

With Love,

Affectionately,

Kind regards to Janey,

Toni

I had just returned for the summer holidays from my English boarding school. The great event in Switzerland in the summer of 1939 was the *Landesausstellung*, a national exposition with many associated festivities which took place every twenty-five years.

Toni Wolff wrote again on 31 July:

Dear Katy,

I suppose you have moved to Ascona. It is a great pity you were not in Zürich these days. We are going from one festivity to another, and all in glorious weather. Saturday I stayed at Hügenins [a Bahnhofstrasse tearoom] all from 10:30 a.m. to 4 p.m. with Dr. and Mrs. C. We saw the procession of the Schaffhausen people, and then the state procession for the Lord Mayor of the City of London. It was very fine, all for being simple and democratic. And yesterday was the finest thing of all, a real demonstration of our arms. Pity de T. could not see it, he would have been pleased. The firing was real, mostly infantry and artillery cannons and machine guns. We feel quite secure now against our various neighbours. ...

After mentioning her travel arrangements to Ascona, Toni continued on a more analytical line:

I am sure you are right that people [Psychological Club members] may get your reaction of being bored underneath. So if you try and cover it up that will help a lot, at least as far as you are concerned. I am afraid the other side will remain what it is though – hopeless. The way they all snubbed the Exposition was incredible, and all under the pretense of analytical work!! But I do think that in spite of your not *being able* to talk about analysis, you *do* deserve merit, as it would be so easy to ingratiate those people in a cheap way by talking shop. Well, you can't change mules into horses, so they must be treated as mules. ...

... I am so very glad de T. feels so much freer. That will mean of course he needs no surrogate outlets in furies.

Do you dream again that I am writing you, I wonder. But please don't answer, it is really my answer to your letter.

Affectionate regards to Janey and de T.,

and love to you,

Toni

We had indeed moved to Ascona for the Eranos Tagungen, but not before visiting the Exposition several times. Since I was far less sophisticated than the psychological people whom Toni mentions, I really enjoyed the visits. We often ate in the "Dörfli" (small village) restaurants in chalets built for the exhibition in the style of a particular canton, and offering cantonal specialties. I began a collection of wine labels at this time which I pasted in an album. One of our favorite white wines was *Clos des Murailles* from Aigle in the Canton of Vaud. (Its label many years later, to my astonishment, was identical except for one word: *Aigle des Murailles*.) These restaurants were situated on the right bank of the lake; one, the Fischerstube, still exists. On the left rested the industrial exhibits, the two banks being joined by the *Schwebebahn* cable car. For those not keen to walk through the many exhibits, there was the *Schifflibach*, a narrow, artificial stream on which wooden boats carrying six passengers traveled at preset intervals. It flowed both outdoors and also through the exhibition halls. The *Schifflibach* was a huge success with young and old; the Jungs loved it, as did Toni Wolff. In the article she wrote for *Annabelle* in 1945, my mother mentions that when traveling through the Aluminum Hall (partly open to the sky), "a Swiss gentleman" banged a kettle hanging overhead with his walking stick. As there had just been a thunderstorm, a lot of water fell down onto his "lady companion's" hat. "She took it in good part," my mother wrote. The "gentleman" and the "lady" were apparently Dr. Jung and Miss Wolff.

C.G. Jung, Ascona, 1936

Chapter Six

The Eve of War and Winter 1939-1940

Tommy, my mother and I left Zürich for Ascona on 29 July, and stayed at the Hotel Monte Verità. On 6 August the Zürich people, as well as others from around Europe, began to arrive, and on the following day the Eranos lectures began. They ran for ten days, and my mother attended them while Tommy played golf. The psychologists also held meetings, one of which was headed by the Paris Jungian group who were keen to found a world-wide federation of Jungian psychological clubs. Several parties took place both at Frau Froebe's Casa Gabriella and at the Hotel Monte Verità. I went to the parties, played golf with Tommy and even a couple of times with Dr. Baynes (the only golfer among the Jung group), and attended some of the lectures. It was warm and sunny, the group seemed relaxed, and for one moment, politics were relegated to the back of people's minds.

On 17 August the three of us drove to Orta, further down the Lago Maggiore into Italy, where we stayed the night on our way to San Remo. Tommy and Katy thought the village quaint, even romantic, but the poverty prevailing there, in such contrast to Ascona, shocked me so much that I took to my room until called to come for aperitifs before dinner. I cheered up briefly when Tommy handed me my first *Americano*, a mixture of Vermouth and Campari, but soon felt depressed when we walked through the streets after dinner. I was glad to move on. We stayed a few days with my grandfather at the San Remo villa; he was too ill to move to Grasse with his wife for their annual summer holiday, to escape the heat. My mother took us for the day for a rendezvous with my grandmother in Nice on the 25th. Being on holiday, and English and American newspapers being difficult to obtain in Italy, we were not *au courant* with the political situation, and so at Ventimiglia were astonished when both the French and Italian border guards warned us that war was imminent and that Italy soon would be no place for us. We hastily packed our bags and left San Remo the following afternoon. Because Tommy was British and our car had British number plates, we had to be cautious. Nobody could anticipate Mussolini's reaction if war were declared; he had been on the best of terms with Hitler since their meeting at the Villa Reale di Stra in 1936. We left Italy at Ventimigilia, on the shortest route into France, then spent three nights at Cap d'Antibes, hoping that we would be able to return. The usually busy resort was deserted, but I was not put off and soon was into my bathing suit. Swimming off the Cap, I noticed a large slick not of oil but of talcum powder. Through it spread a litter of mostly toilet articles; with teenager zeal I swam out to this flotsam and jetsam and fished out a wooden hanger bearing the name *Rosemary Kennedy*. At the hotel we learned that indeed the Kennedys had been on holiday at a nearby villa but had departed in haste for London, where Joseph Kennedy was American Ambassador. We also learned that the inhabitants of the Cap were disgusted by the Kennedys' dumping all their rubbish into the Mediterranean. My grandmother joined us a second time at Antibes, where all of us hoped the international situation would improve, as it usually did when Hitler exacted concessions; but this time, tension continued to grow, and we realized there was no hope of returning to San Remo. We packed again and from Cap d'Antibes drove north on the *Route Napoleon* to Grasse, leaving my grandmother to collect her effects and make her own way back to Italy. We spent one night in Grenoble as Tommy never liked driving long distances. There we found the streetlights were *en veilleuse*, and were told that dimming the lights was the first stage before a full blackout. After booking into a hotel, we went out into the darkened streets to seek a restaurant. En route a group of young soldiers accosted us and embraced us like long-lost friends. The lights in the restaurant were dim, but we had an excellent dinner by candlelight. On every table rested an enormous bowl of very yellow butter, locally made. As we helped ourselves liberally, we wondered how much longer such a *décor* would be possible. The following day Tommy drove us to Geneva, crossing at St Julien. My diary reports an unheard-of pre-war experience with customs: that they "were very nice and didn't even ask if we had anything to declare." During our second night in Geneva, where we stayed to visit the Prado Exhibition of Goya paintings, the Germans invaded Poland.

We spent the following night in Bern en route to Zürich, at the Hotel Schweizerhof opposite the station. That same night the Swiss *Generalmobilmachung* [general mobilization] began, and company after company of soldiers marched throughout the night below our windows, heading for trains to various strategic points on the frontier. I spent much of that night watching them march past, hardly believing that such a small country could suddenly produce so many soldiers. The next day, September 2, the roads to Zürich were empty except for horse transports of troops; gasoline had been rationed to 60 liters a month, but prudently we had filled our tank at St. Julien before crossing to Geneva. A few days after our return to Zürich, we again visited the *Landi* – which we had enjoyed so much only one month before –, but the Exposition was now a sad sight. Hardly anyone was there, and rain, strong winds, and prematurely falling leaves left the unswept pavements very slippery. Only the odd school party and a few soldiers in uniform silently wandered through the exhibition halls. We did go several more times, when the weather improved, but the *Landi* never recovered the *Stimmung* we had enjoyed in July and early August. We went to the restaurants, ate the cantonal specialities, and drank the native wines, but the War had thrown a pall over the whole place. It was like attending a wake.

When War was officially declared Tommy, a reserve officer, decided to return to England and to serve. My mother was not enthusiastic, but for once, Tommy was adamant. Before he was due to leave, my mother decided that she must be able to drive her Packard, the big car that Tommy usually drove for us (she had not driven for over ten years, and then only Fords). On our trial runs, however, her lack of confidence had her treading constantly on the brakes, bumping us down the hills and, as my diary puts it, moving us "rather like ... snails" and exhausting us. Tommy put the car in "mothballs" for the duration of the War – which was no great loss since soon gasoline would be unavailable to private citizens. We accompanied Tommy to Geneva, where we saw him off on the special train which evacuated British subjects from Switzerland. When Tommy had asked Barbara Hannah whether she, too, would be on that train, she answered emphatically, "No!" – rather shocking him. Back in Zürich, my mother must have felt very flat and anxious, but kept a stiff upper lip and showed no anxiety to me. No one then knew

Toni Wolff, C.G. Jung and Barbara Hannah at Eranos, 1939

that the "Phoney War" would last eight months, and that Tommy would be back in Switzerland long before Hitler attacked the Netherlands and Belgium.

The Waldhaus Dolder became our permanent address during the War even though, from time to time, we rented a flat in Ascona. With its gabled roof and wooden balconies, the hotel offered a pleasingly Swiss, homelike appearance which attracted displaced foreigners. It had a large garden and a fine view over the Lake of Zürich, along with a cable-car connection to the Zürich tramway network. Even before the War a variety of foreigners booked there. On one occasion, I heard someone talking loudly in the next room, and stepped onto my balcony to have a look. A teenage boy with cropped fair hair, wearing short trousers, earnestly addressed a mirror and made extravagant gestures – the first Hitler Youth I had ever seen, and whose fanatical behavior sent a chill down my fifteen-year-old spine. During the War, both German and American Jews took up residence at the hotel, including an American Jewish woman and her adult son from an internment camp in Germany. Even a few Swiss took up residence at the Waldhaus when they ran short of coal to heat their houses. It was large enough for everybody to keep to themselves.

There was no talk of returning to school in England. Nor did I change to a Swiss school: my mother decided to keep me near her, glad for my company, and my shyness made me dread starting in school anew. Besides, I already felt very grown-up. While my mother thought about what she should do with me, I lounged about lazily and had a fine time (I thought) listening to the War news on the radio, collecting clippings and photographs, and writing my diary. I also went with my mother to the Zürich dressmakers and modistes, and to the hairdresser; by contrast, we also invested in gas masks. Though only sixteen, I felt suddenly grown-up; all the young men I knew in Zürich were in uniform, guarding the frontiers, and the few girls I skated with appeared only when the Dolder rink opened in November. Being an introvert, having no one my age to be with, did not bother me too much. Suddenly, my mother came up with the idea that we ought to attend a cooking course. On 20 September, we had a preliminary lesson at Fräulein Fülscher's school on Plattenstrasse 86, lasting over two hours. "It was only theory," I noted in my diary, "except that we peeled a potato." By the 23rd, my mother had become so enthusiastic about cooking that we boiled potatoes and made scrambled eggs, all on a small Meta (solid fuel) stove in our hotel bedroom. She spent the next two days in bed – exhausted, because she had never had any experience of cooking – but we repeated the exercise four days later, and on 3 October, began the classes. These started at 8 a.m., and we were expected to be punctual, which strangely enough we were, as normally my mother liked to sleep late. The other pupils were mostly young girls about to be married. We read and discussed the menu for the day, and how to set about preparing the various foods; at 10:15 we began cooking in pairs, each pair being assigned a particular task; whenever something important came along, the teacher would call out in Swiss German, *"Alle ans Herd cho luege!"* [Everyone to the stove come to look!], and we would drop whatever we were doing and rush to the cooker for her demonstration. At 12:30 we ate what we had made – both plentiful and various, as rationing was not yet serious, and Fräulein Fülscher wanted us to learn as many dishes as possible. Then we washed up and left around 1:15. The course ran for six weeks, and the menus became progressively more complicated. One morning, my mother was given the job of gutting a chicken, which she did dexterously and without turning a hair, hauling out the bloody entrails with her bare hands; I would have been too squeamish to do it. We saw the course through, never missing a day, and this was astonishing, as Katy's enthusiasms often waned early. But with Tommy far off, she was able to focus her energies. Whenever a man was about, she spent much energy on him, drank too much, and went to bed late. Katy was quick to let people in Boston know that she was taking this cooking course, because she liked to make a good impression on her father-in-law, Godfrey Cabot. Already on 14 October, she received a long letter from him, which begins: "I was very much pleased to hear from Merrill Griswold[1] yesterday that you and Janey were studying cooking with a view to doing your bit, were opportunity to present itself in the present European War. ..."

Though occupied with cooking and analysis, Katy was missing Tommy very much, which she alludes to in her next session with Jung. Her touchiness may have led to some remarks in a letter which offended Toni, who replies in a tone that suggests distinct annoyance:

> Freiestrasse 9
> Zürich 7
> Oct. 4th, 1939

Dear Katy,

I don't think it is any use to go into a discussion by letter, and so we better postpone it until a time when you can bring yourself to speak about your feelings right away, the moment they come up. For only in this way there is a means to find out if your feeling gives a true picture of my attitude and to discover, if your reaction should happen not to correspond to what I really think or feel, why your reaction is what it is.

I have given you so much proof, by letter on Friday, of how well I understand and sympathise with all the decisions you made, that I feel grieved and shocked by the way you take it for granted that I should be "annoyed" and even "disgusted." It seems to me that it would help your contacts more if, instead of going on to explain your side, which has been fully understood, you were trying to understand the other person by taking in what she says or does,

---

[1] In 1939, Merrill Griswold was my mother's Boston lawyer. He had known Catharine as a young girl at the Boston Navy Yard, and had wished to marry her; he served under Captain Rush in the First World War.

C.G. Jung lecturing at Eranos, 1939

and by asking what you don't understand, and by finding out whether your reactions are justified.

It does not seem to me to help at all – in fact, just the contrary – when you allow yourself to discuss any questions or doubts with Janey, instead of with myself. Not to speak of the implication that this method will certainly not help Janey's rapport with you. It is evident, now that Tommy is away, that you feel the lack of a companion in immediate response, and that Janey ought not to be made a surrogate. All the more, anything to do with myself ought to be given to me directly and immediately.

It is quite possible, in fact I do believe, that your cooking course will teach you more than cooking: namely, immediate reactions in the right place and sizing up facts where they belong.

Affectionately yours,

Toni

The discussions which Toni mentions may well have been about the visit she had arranged for Katy to Bollingen, and which Katy had turned down, perhaps tactlessly. The following hour with Jung would seem to indicate this:

October 19, 1939

I went to see Onkel because I wanted to explain to him why I had not gone to Bollingen, at Toni's invitation, right after getting back from Geneva and seeing off the "English train." I found him not feeling too well – sinus trouble – and he was going to Dr. M. I begged him to ask Dr. M. if he should have calcium. He said that was a good idea and he would ask. Then I told him all about Bollingen, and that I had not gone, first and foremost, because I had felt, that feeling worried *and* frightened and unhappy, I had to work it out all by myself. If I had gone running to him instead, I would have gone down a lot in my own estimation. He had given me the strength to go on and to stand alone, and I had been able to. Therefore, from now on, I could go and see him in a 'difficult' time because I *knew* I had the 'stuff' in me. He replied: "You were considerate, too considerate." I said my consideration came from wanting to prove myself – my own worth. I realized also that he, too, had his own problems. He said that 'war' was not a 'problem,' but that it was just a 'fact' – like any catastrophe. Then, looking at me intently, he said, "I *know* you, and I knew if you didn't come, you had a good reason. Don't worry too much about the women,[1] they are always a bit difficult. Just don't mention it to anyone again." I wept and was deeply touched by his evident trust, and added that I had been supposed to spend the night with Mrs. Fierz, but did not, at such a time, wish my feelings to be trampled on. He looked astounded, and said he had no idea that I had to spend the night at Mrs. Fierz's and that he had many guest rooms, and that I could have spent it in his house. He said that if I had come and

---

[1] Toni Wolff and Linda Fierz.

played the *bella figura* (which I might have!) and not told him what was on my mind, I would have had a bad atmosphere, and he would have had to ask what was the matter with me. "There is nothing more bothersome than when people don't tell what troubles them; it makes a strained situation. It produces a strained atmosphere, if you don't say what is on your mind." He said it was quite natural to be apprehensive and worried about everything that was now taking place, as these were very difficult times.

Then we started on the War, and Onkel quoted his remark to the news correspondent, Knickerbocker. Knickerbocker had asked Jung: "What would happen if you were to lock Hitler, Mussolini and Stalin in a room together, and give one loaf of bread and one pitcher of water to last them a week? Who would get all the food and water?" Jung answered: "I doubt if they would divide it. Hitler, being a medicine-man would probably hold himself aloof and have nothing to do with the quarrel. He would be helpless because he would be without his German people. Mussolini and Stalin, both being chiefs, or strong men in their own right, would probably dispute possession of the food and drink, and Stalin, being the rougher and tougher, would probably get all of it!" He then went on to explain how Hitler had maneuvered the whole of Germany into a hole, like the man who kicks the football into the other fellow's goal! Hitler lost his reputation over Czechoslovakia. In order to get out of that disagreeable situation, he called the Russians, who then cut him off from Rumania and who now surround *Ostpreussen* [East Prussia], and who could easily control it if they wanted to. If the Russians take the Åland Islands, then they control the iron ore in Sweden; then it depends on Stalin whether or not the Germans get it. Stalin wants Hitler to weaken the French and English first; then, when Hitler has thoroughly weakened himself, Stalin will pounce on him. Hitler certainly handed himself over to the devil, *Er verkaufte sich dem Teufel mit Haut und Haar.* [He sold himself skin and hair to the devil.] He is convinced he will beat England and France, and cast out the Russians. Hitler is like a man who wants success and produces a swindle to make his gain; but there is the 'swindle' which he wants covered-up – he then gets another set of creditors, but he is in a new hole and produces another 'swindle,' and then gets in another hole ... until he finally finds himself at the bottom of a hole. This policy of his has cost him his Axis partnership. The Italians now hate the Germans. All the German [freight] cars coming up into Switzerland from Italy are smashed. A Swiss train, which came up, with one German carriage attached to it, had all the windows broken on the *German* car only! Hitler is in the claw of the Russians. *Il est roulé par les Russes!* I said that I thought, to save himself and his people, Hitler should go over penitently, to the Allies side, and give up all he has taken, and, together with the Allies, chase the Russians out of Poland. Onkel said that no one would believe Hitler if he tried to do, or suggest, such a thing, and besides, he is a very *small* man. Only a great man could do such a thing. Onkel said that it was the foolish German expectation of a 'German Messiah' which had been projected onto him.

Then I asked Onkel how to get out of irritating people. I said I always seemed to be nasty, suddenly, and I told him about de Neuville. He laughed and said such people needed nasty things said to them. He said people have a certain aggressivity when they suffer from panics and self-inflicted tortures, and now, at last, it has all come out. Whoever suffers from unnatural fear, suffers from aggressivity – a bad shadow.

When I told him of the remark I made to Mrs. Baumann about no one listening to his (Onkel's) seminars, he roared with laughter, and said again, *"Enfant terrible!"* He said the trouble with Mrs. Baumann was that she had no sense of humor. She was a horse. I said, "A young horse?" He laughed and said, "No, an old horse!" I ended up by saying I would like to be like him, nice to all, and not irritate anyone. He said it took him time to learn it – that it hadn't come in a day.

Katy certainly had the "stuff" in her to deal with her loneliness. Though she was unaware of her strong inner man, he would stand by her in the far more serious crises of the future. It was because she was unfamiliar with the Sea-Captain animus that Katy did not understand her sudden outbursts of nastiness. Jung attributes her aggressivity to fear, but to that we might add the fact that she was aware only of her weaknesses and not her strengths. Katy's powerful Sea-Captain animus also manifested itself in her keenness to cure illness. Yet while she was eager to minister to illness, she was not particularly interested in preventing it. She never tried to encourage Tommy to live a healthier life by curtailing his heavy drinking and smoking, but if anyone she liked got sick, she immediately began prescribing medicines – even to Jung. This practice continued throughout her life. In her later years, when she liked taking day trips with her chauffeur from San Remo into France, she found an old wine merchant in a village above Menton. Alas, she noticed that his health was failing, and brought medicines. Obligingly, he took them, while my mother collected his wines for her cellar, enjoying the excitement of crossing the frontier with "contraband." The doctoring trips grew more frequent, and the stocks in the cellar mounted. After only one year, however, the old man let her down by dying, and so my mother's wine buying ceased. The elder Katy sought excitement in other ways – for instance, by having her chauffeur, after a dinner with plenty of wine at a vineyard restaurant in the mountains above San Remo, drive her down the winding road at high speed, urging him on with, "Faster, faster!" He pretended to obey, replying *"Si, si, si,"* but never actually did drive faster, being too professional to take such foolish risks.

Tommy had been in England just over a month when the above interview with Jung took place. My mother was in touch with him by letter and telegram, but not on a daily basis, and still had no idea how long he would be away. She imagined it might be years; that he might have to go to the front, or soon be subjected to bombing. (The British had already raided Wilhelmshaven on 5 September, so she expected there might be retaliation.) In actual fact, Tommy, at age fifty-four, was considered too old to serve in any way, during the Phoney War period, even though he had been a Regular Officer in the British Army in India. After umpteen rejections over four months, he finally gave up; deeply disappointed, he returned to Switzerland and his old life with my mother. His pride and self-esteem suffered immensely now, though he refused to show it; the unpleasant experience aged him, probably shortening his life. My mother, of course, was delighted to have him back, but in October, she still had no idea if she would ever see Tommy again.

October 26, 1939

I started right in and told Onkel how I admired his way of not ever hurting people, and how he made himself nice even when telling a [psychological] truth. He answered so humorously, "One can't get right away into the proper shape; it takes experience with people, and learning. I didn't set out the first day in ship-shape. If you are a diamond at all you are a rough one. If a person saw his mistakes, and what he was doing, he could mend them, but he is heedless." I told him how I felt when being nasty, and that previously I only cared what *people* thought, but now I am ashamed in front of *myself*, how I was ashamed the other day escaping 'Plumpa' [unidentified]. He said that trying to escape 'Plumpa' was a sport! I said I had always cheated in life, in the past, and now I don't enjoy cheating. He said that when one cheats to a greater extent, one suffers from the fact. For instance, he said, people who are awful in a family suffer from a neurosis, and wonder why. The evil consequences of their behavior brings about that fact. He then told me the story of a brilliant man who came to him with a complete 'analysis,' made by himself, of his own neurosis. Onkel said it was a magnificent analysis, in which the man saw all his bad sides; in fact, everything was analysed and put down. Onkel read this brilliant analysis and could see no flaw. But he thought and thought, whereupon it dawned on him that the young man had not mentioned *how* he lived in all the spas and fashionable resorts, which he had mentioned in analysis. Onkel asked him if he had a big fortune. He then confessed that he lived off a school teacher's money; she was very much in love with him, and sent him every *centime* she earned, so as to keep him in luxury, and enable him to travel and live in expensive hotels. The man would not give up this life, so he could not rid himself of his neurosis. A girl, who was always playing two melodies at a time, and always giving her husband hell, and was *schlampig* [sloppy] also could not be cured. Onkel said that Mrs. Fierz had been told by him that crazy people got a tremendous kick out of being crazy. He said there was a man in an asylum always writing things down in a little book, and he often wondered what the man wrote. One day he looked over his shoulder, as the man had put down his broom to write a few words. He saw the following: "Disturbance through Madonna," then came the date and the hour. Onkel said it gave those people a tremendous self-importance, and a sort of happiness, to be disturbed by the Mother of God, or King George. If they think Christ sent them a wire, a hell of a wire, they consider themselves to be a wonderful and unique person, in direct connection with heaven, an extraordinary adventure. Onkel said he once treated a girl who was mad (a Polish girl) whom her brother said he would rather risk having treated than not [treated] as she was impossible as she was. Even though the treatment had a risk to it,

C.G. Jung in the Eranos garden, 1937

the brother told Onkel it would be better to have her dead than alive as she was. Onkel cured her. When she became normal, she told Onkel she hated him, as he had robbed her of all that was worthwhile. In her madness, she had been a Queen on the moon, adored by the moon folk, and on the top of a tower, she had nocturnal interviews with the devil, and was seduced by him. It was a terrible come-down for her to be brought back to normal.

I then told Onkel that I was so impressed by his lecture in Ascona, where he had spoken of El Kadir. He said he thought he had given an especially bad lecture that day. He went on to say that he had *lived* El Kadir, had *seen* him, and those things jump into the eyes of people, and their own experiences become alive, and that gets them. He went on to say that he was aware he talked of important things, and through his own feelings, he also had been particularly moved by that story of the Koran. He said, "I talk of something which I have experienced! Massignon hasn't seen *him* – he doesn't know what he *is*." The religion of Mitras was a religion of soldiers. Because Mitras, a learned man, said this and that, and the soldiers realized it was religion between those two gods. *"Ich hatte einen Kameraden, einen besseren findest Du nicht."* [Title of a German song about comradeship among soldiers]. But when an archaeologist shows you Mitras, you don't ask his feeling, you just stand in front like an ass. It is like standing in front of a crucifix and not feeling. People feel an emotional connection and I felt that with El Kadir. I then told Onkel that I had seen El Kadir in Florence at the age of seventeen, and later here, but it was fleeting and only twice. I could not tell what he thought.

Then we spoke of Cuthbert,[1] and he asked me what he was doing, and I said he was 'impossible.' Onkel said he was too *comme il faut* [proper], believed in respectability, and what the world said etc. He said his wife kept him over here, so she could be free to enjoy her lover in America, and she had no desire to have him return. Also he *refused* to see clearly and thought his marriage was ideal; he would not look the truth of his marriage and wife in the face. I then returned to El Kadir and asked Onkel how one could *see* El Kadir and still remain a swine. He laughed!

---

[1] Cuthbert was usually a pseudonym for Tommy, but in this context, it does not seem to fit. I never heard of the wife having a lover.

Katy often attempted to escape from people who bored her or who, seeming "impossible," made her feel uncomfortable. She did this with both Toni and Linda Fierz, and may have withheld herself from visiting Bollingen for the same reason. The people whom she eluded also included visitors from overseas, often relatives, who were keen to report home about her. She would tell them an elaborate story, saying that she was *so* sorry to miss them but she just *had* to be away, etc. Sometimes, to prove that she was miles away from Zürich, she had a friend in another town post a letter for her to the visitor. As far as I know, she was never caught doing this. The good intentions which she had voiced to Jung in the session were genuine, but unfortunately melted away, yielding to her lifelong habit of organizing elaborate fictions to secure an avoidance of others.

The next session came around to the animus issue once again, with a hint of support for Katy's individuality:

November 2, 1939

I went on my birthday to see Onkel and spoke immediately about his E.T.H. lectures, and said that I had not understood them last year. He looked 'bored' at that remark, and said that the lectures were more theoretical, and that people easily lose their bearings in such material. They are 'obnubilated' [over-clouded] (at which I laughed) – befuddled in a mist – the word 'obnubilation' means more or less that. He went on to say that I had never used my mind in such a way, and that you must have a certain amount of education in order to comprehend the terms at all. If you have sufficient preparation you can understand them to a certain extent.

Then I spoke of everyone being so alike in America, just as if they came out of the same box. He said that was the way they were, because to be yourself and original was not *bien vue* [well looked-upon] in a country like America, and such people are devoid of soul and interests; they learn their jobs, have good manners and no personality at all, like Dr. Hutz (U.S., son of Baronin Maltzau). You can die by mental starvation with such people. And then he went on to say that I was like them when I first came to him – completely extinguished – a little heap of misery. With a man like Hutz, it is his aunt or his mother-in-law who won't let him *live*. In America, it is expected of one to appear as if one had no education. One must not talk differently, or voice ideas that are different from the 'herd,' for that is what people don't like. I told him how Jim [Cabot, her late husband] found his [Jung's] books so difficult to read and understand, even though he had had a good education. Onkel answered that books such as his, to be understood, need psychological knowledge. People never *look in* – they always *look out*. They never realize they have a *'mind.'* They use their mind, when they *do* use it, to kill their own mental life. Psychology is the science of the *living mind*. And people use psychology to kill their own mental life. They make a philosophy out of it, and make everything dull. That is what the matter was with me, people, in America or at the Club, not liking me, was caused to a certain extent by my being 'different,' and trying to express my real self and not just remaining in the herd mentality. That is my Lump rolling about when I get an 'animus' with it together. I mean, when I express my personality 'with a vengeance,' the animus is there trying to irritate people.

Katy never connected the "Lump rolling about" and the "animus with it" to her inner father image. Being ashamed of the Lump, she imagined it contained only bad things, whereas the Sea Captain, though disagreeable and expressing himself "with a vengeance" well known to my mother's intimates, also had many good qualities: notably, strength and fearlessness. These qualities stood her in good stead throughout her life. Thus the Captain's figure explains much of the behavior that was quite the opposite of a meek maiden's, Katy's image of herself. The sad truth is that the Lump remained an enigma, never taking on a personality that could be confronted and analyzed, and so too elusive for my mother to understand.

He went on to say [presumably after Katy broached the subject] that Mrs. Fierz was after prestige, and wanted to play a role, and in consequence, she has a hole and a void which she does not see, and she overcompensates it with the role of the perfect mother. Onkel said she also played this role with him. One day, she asked him what he thought of her. He replied, "I see you sitting on a cart as the family mother, or as a Queen. The cart has four wheels, which are your four sons, and the ass in front who pulls the cart is your husband!" She is within the security of the four sons and the stupid husband, who does not see through her, and whom she rules. In fact, she rules the whole show, showing off the happy household! Onkel went on to say that when he went to their house,

Mary Foote, Klaus Fierz and Barbara Hannah
at Ponte Brolla, during the Eranos Tagung 1939

there was always an icy atmosphere. An icy blast greets you as you open the door. But he said he always thought they were poor things, empty, and that they bored each other. She is just all blown-up with the possession of four sons. But why does she try to make me believe that all is tip-top? When he went to dinner, like me, he had an *undrinkable* wine and nothing [good] to eat. Even Linda, herself, was ashamed for having done that. She gives herself an air of generosity and there is really nothing behind that air. Then he told me of the episode of Klaus' catching a fish on his [Onkel's] birthday, and bringing it, just a minnow, as if he had really brought something very fine. The Fierz's idea was that, if Klaus caught it, Dr. Jung would enjoy it!

The Fierz family thinks that, when they say something, one should be on one's knees, as they are very special people. "Klaus acted as if he were on equal terms with me when they sent me that absurd fish. They have that style. Everything they do is inflated and marvelous and wonderful." The oldest Fierz son once said to Onkel's daughter, "It's very difficult to be so beautiful as I am." The Fierz sons had a hell of a time while in the military service, and also in the rowing club. The Fierzes esteem it an honor for others to meet such rare people! They say, "I am the wonderful fellow!"

I first met Klaus at Eranos in August 1939, when I was just sixteen and he, twenty-three; he was the first young man I went out with, and I found him friendly and not stuck up at all. Klaus arranged for me to meet his elder brother, Heiner, who was on duty as a medical intern at the Burghölzli Klinik; I met Heiner later when I began training at the Klinik am Zürichberg, where he was *Chefarzt* or chief psychiatrist. Though less natural than Klaus, he was perfectly friendly.

Then I told Onkel that I was letting out too many 'truths,' and I felt I surprised and shocked people. Especially when tipsy, out comes a truth! I told him what I said to Mrs. [Carol] Baumann, and how shocked she was. (What I said was that it was a pity no one listened to Onkel's seminars!) He roared with laughter, and said that people like that deserve the truth. At any rate, I have said something substantial, and if they were simple and straight, they could stand it.

Then I gave him Griswold's letter to read, the one announcing to me his talk with Mr. Cabot and Mr. Cabot's intention to leave Janey a big sum of money *in his will*, and wanted her to start being a philanthropist *now!* (She hasn't the money now!!) Onkel had a good laugh, and said that she could not spend money now that she would receive in the future. If I teach her to spend money she hasn't got, I only teach her to make debts! I can only teach her in a general way how to take care of money, but I simply cannot teach her how to spend money when she has not go it. I must write to my lawyer, or to Mr. Cabot, that I have so much and not more, and we need that money for our existence. Then he went on to say that if Mr. Cabot planned to send us some more money, then we can do something about it; otherwise, if we give away what we have, we will starve! Such ideas, as Griswold writes, are thought out by a mind that has always had money. Then he told the story of a rich old lady who had a washerwoman who finally asked her for her wages, complaining that she was hard-up, and had to buy some meat for the family. The old lady asked her if she could not eat potatoes and cheese from time to time, whereupon the washer-woman replied that that was what she ate most of the time (!). "Then," said the old lady, "you should use some of your capital," and she [the old lady] was dumbfounded to learn that the washer-woman had no capital. Mr. Cabot just thinks in terms of people who have money. I must tell him that I am only too willing to collaborate, but I haven't a cent over what I normally earn. I am not extravagant in what I spend on myself and my daughter, and I can only spend the money I have, not the money I have not. Onkel said that Grandpa Cabot would really open his eyes if Janey started giving away large sums to charity. What he tells the lawyer is a mere promise.[1] If I had surplus money, I would naturally give it to deserving people more than to large institutions, because with their huge staffs, a great deal of the money is wasted, and just disappears no one knows where. Whereas if it is given to individu-als, or to small charities, which you can really investigate, and you know that the person who is running it is sincere and honest, then your money gets directly to the deserving people without passing through so many hands – as it does when given to large charities, like the Red Cross or Harvard and Yale Universities. Janey is happy and contented, I told Onkel, and she finds a simple life and place like the Waldhaus to her liking, and even considers it luxurious. A man like Mr. Cabot thinks of money being always there, and he can't conceive of an existence where there is no money!

Godfrey Cabot knew that my mother was inclined to spend money; his wife Minnie shared that tendency, though most of the other Cabots were frugal. My grandfather's message was really a veiled warning to Katy not to teach me her own bad habits with money. If we had any spare cash it should be given away rather than squan-dered on luxuries! My mother goes into detail in writing about this session because she knew perfectly well that she enjoyed spending money *when it was available.* She did not save, but neither did she accrue debts. I was very careful with money – out of an inborn tendency, I suppose; my mother gave me a generous allowance and encouraged me to use it, fearing I would become a stingy Cabot, but I hoarded most of it, buying only materials for my drawing, writing, and knitting. I was also, as my mother says, perfectly content with the

---

[1] Godfrey Cabot died at over 101 years of age, or twenty years later!

Waldhaus Dolder.[1] During the War, we rented a small back room which my mother converted into a *salon* which she partly furnished herself and where she entertained. This also gave us relief, as the bedrooms were pretty stark. I had urged my mother to rent an apartment, but although they were cheap, it was to no avail. She was full of excuses, and later foreigners were forbidden to rent. When I married in 1943, and we were eventually allowed a flat because of diplomatic status, it felt like a castle to me who had always lived in hotels.

   Onkel then told me the amusing story of a man in Basel, whom everyone avoided. When people asked, "Why is he avoided so?" the answer was, "Because he has been using up his wealth!" Mr. Cabot evidently enjoys the idea that Janey be brought up to be "the ideal lady" and spend a lot on poor people. He thinks that because he has money, everyone has money. He thinks that everyone must be satisfied because "I" have money!! He says to himself that no one needs money, though he never has enough himself, and he just won't believe there are people with no money. That letter of Griswold's, Onkel seemed to think, was a damn fool's letter. Just too ridiculous for words – and how a lawyer with any sense could write such an idiotic letter was just beyond him. He went on to say that when the money was there, I could look into it, but that it was immoral to bring up a child to *what might be*, instead of to *what is*. If I do that, I have spoilt the child. Had I a definite assurance of money in hand, I could do something about it, but it is ridiculous to talk of money you don't possess. He said it reminded him of vendors in Algiers, who yelled, "*I want to see your money, Sir!*"

As for my mother's ways with spending, Jung knew very well what the money complex in her could do, and so he makes it perfectly clear where he stands in the matter, even going on in a long-winded way to do so.

   At the time of this discussion with Jung concerning Merrill Griswold's letter, my mother may not yet have received a four-page letter on the same subject from her father-in-law, dated 14 October 1939:

---

[1] Later on Jung is told I love Palaces such as the Palace Hotel in Gstaad – in fact, I was not fussy and tried to make the most of where my mother chose to stay.

You of course appreciate that Janey is likely to have a large income under my Will, and it is very desirable that she should be encouraged to give away money to help necessities of the present, sad condition in Europe and thus train herself to use wisely for unselfish purposes the money that she will have at her disposal later on and she will save herself many mistakes and grief under your competent guidance in this matter. I feel, with the late Theodore Roosevelt, that the most important question with regard to any human being is does he or she pull his or her weight in the boat that carries us all in the human community?

My mother was never impressed by Godfrey Cabot's noble sentiments, nor did she bother to study his words carefully. It is obvious that my grandfather was merely advocating "token-giving," so that I should learn, during this time of War, to think of others and not just of myself. But the letter's meaning, not being well-phrased, was easy for my mother to twist. (It appears that Merrill Griswold had done the same.) In a postscript, my grandfather adds:

I feel that Janey, owing to her frank and candid nature, is particularly exposed to the dangers which always beset a girl who has enough property to attract selfish men – such as she is likely to meet in fashionable society and pleasure resorts.

With this dig at his daughter-in-law, whose taste for frequenting fashionable resorts he knew, Godfrey is trying from a distance to save me from taking the same road, using flattery to make the point more palatable. In an earlier letter from 20 June, it is apparent that more than my habits with money worried him, he expressed his concern that I might grow up to be a "playgirl." Good habits were imperative, as the postscript of the October letter drives home:

On the other hand, her income will make it possible for her to do an increasing amount of good, as her experience and your guidance improves her judgment. The principal under my Will that will come to her will be in trust, when she becomes of age. ...

Mrs. Cabot [his wife] received many diplomas for her participation in various kinds of work for this and other countries during the World War, and if I remember correctly, your mother, also, was the recipient of similar appreciations, and it is eminently fitting that their joint descendant should follow their excellent examples.

Wealth in itself is a neutral thing, which, very wisely and generously dispensed, together with devoted and unselfish and intelligent personal services, becomes a blessing, both to the donor and to the beneficiary. If selfishly applied, it becomes a curse to its possessor and often to others.

Though Katy may not have been impressed by the 'highfalutin' tone of the last paragraph, at least part of Godfrey's message reached her, for she decided, shortly after receiving this letter, to raise funds from her friends in America to help the British internees in Switzerland. She did not, however, contribute her own money to such charities, reserving it for individuals from time to time.

The misunderstanding between Toni and Katy seems to have been resolved by 3 November 1939, when Toni writes the following note in longhand:

> Dearest Katy,
>
> In anticipation of this evening I am sending ahead all my warmest wishes for the day and for the special date. In a way 45 is just a number like any other, and yet it feels a bit more important and probably is psychologically. The "second half" of life is nearer and more imperative. Perhaps the little book carries a meaning for you – provided you don't possess it already.
>
> I am looking forward to the evening and think the number 4 and the combination of persons just the right one for the occasion.
>
> I forgot to say that I am sure it's safe if you order dinner for 7.30 p.m. And as far as I know, Dr. C. does not like aperitifs.
>
> > With much love,
> >
> > Affectionately,
> >
> > Toni

My mother's birthday was on the 2nd [of November]; the party was postponed to the following day, and since Tommy was still in England, I may have been the "fourth person." (The party is not mentioned in my Diary). Toni herself becomes a subject for reflection in one of the next sessions, after the outset of the War's first winter, and the Cabot side of the family, has its chance for expression.

November 14, 1939

We spoke of Germany, and of how long the War would last. Onkel said that Germany has extraordinary fighting power, but had no sustenance. For one *coup,* they would be stronger than in 1914, but they could stand only one tremendous push, and that the first onslaught would be terrific, because they would be willing to sacrifice up to two million men. The Nazis have no regard for human life and would just pour men in. The Allies are more human and don't wish such a loss of life as in 1914. In Germany, they are really inhuman and will push their soldiers on, and these soldiers cannot turn back, for, if they do, they have to face their own *mitrailleuses* [machine guns]. The Germans are able, and willing, to sacrifice five hundred thousand men on the spot without turning a hair. Onkel said he thought the *Attentat* [attempt to assassinate] on Hitler, in the Bürgerbraukeller, in Munich, on November 8 [1939], was staged, and that a lot of old *Parteigenossen* [party members] were sacrificed. The Nazis just destroy, if it is necessary, for their aims, and so it would be with a *coup* on the Western Front. They would just pour in material and men with no regard for human life. He then cited an example of some Russians, in the Middle Ages, who tried to take a town which was surrounded by a moat. They poured in men until the moat was full of corpses, then the remaining men marched over the bodies of the fallen – to victory. The Germans drive the men over the mine-fields as the French drive the swine. If the Germans could make one hole somewhere [in the French defences] anything could be reached, for one can reach almost anything if one sacrifices the necessary amount of people. The terrible question is, could the French shoot fast enough to kill all? There would always be a few million who would get through. In 1917, the Germans forced regiment after regiment through in an endeavor to take a certain fort. They were mown down by British machine-gun fire. It was a horrible sight. War is sweet to those who have not experienced it. Keitel and Brauchitsch want to make their career. The spirits in Germany are low. A sort of apathy reigns over the country. – They needed an 'injection.' – That is why Hitler staged the Bürgerbraukeller *Attentat*, for it roused the people from their lethargy. Hitler had a meeting with the General Staff, who advised him not to attack. They have an *acute* fighting strength, but it won't last.

Then we switched to Mrs. Fierz, who had the hour previous to me. I laughingly told him how I had hung her coat outside the waiting room, when, on arriving, I found it inside, as I was hoping to escape seeing her. He laughed. Then I told him she was apprehensive of his not liking her book on Poliphile. She had jokingly said to me, "You may find a *barbe* [beard] on the floor!" He told me her work on Poliphile was really very fine and that he had advised her to publish it.[1]

Then I read him Mr. Cabot's letter, and laughed over the fact that Mr. Cabot thought Switzerland a 'good' country. With a twinkle in his eye, he said, "A small country – small vices." We were both amused at Mr. Cabot giving us news already so old. Onkel said that Mr. Cabot had to give a 'thoughtless little thing' like me, news, because I can't read the newspapers! One just *has* to elucidate the state of affairs to such a little bit of fluff as myself! We returned again to the War between sentences in Mr. Cabot's letter. Onkel said that most of the people in Germany were influenced by Hitler, but if they would think straight, they would say, "We are the real devils of Europe." But instead they say, "England is the evil spirit: we Germans are good people, and devils are attacking our dear *Vaterland*." I told Onkel that, in some way, Stalin did not irritate me, and that next to Hitler, he was *sympathique* [sympathetic, nice]. Onkel said that Stalin was frank in his dealings with people, did not put on hypocritical airs, just said what he wanted to say, stating his aims quite plainly. When Lady Astor[2] asked him how long he was going to keep on killing people, he answered her, "As long as it is necessary!" Stalin feels that certain elements are unhealthy so he wipes them out. Stalin does not presume and invent such stories and such lies [as Hitler]. He is a straightforward brute, a cunning brute, while, on the other hand, Hitler is just a rotten devil, and an hysterical, neurotic individual, always excited and believing what he says. Stalin is just an 'Oriental' – cynical, matter-of-fact and brutal.

---

[1] Linda's book was *Der Liebestraum des Poliphilo* (Rascher Verlag, Zürich, 1947), which has been translated by Mary Hottinger as *The Dream of Poliphilo: The Soul in Love* (Pantheon, New York, 1950; reprinted by Spring, Dallas, 1987).

[2] Lady Astor was American-born, married Lord Astor, and became the first British woman Member of Parliament.

Then I went on with Mr. Cabot's letter. Onkel said, when I had finished it, that wealth changes your psychology on the spot. I must tell Mr. Cabot that I will naturally look into it – that Janey will make the right use of her money, and that I have such a wonderful model in him and my mother-in-law.[1] I then told Onkel how I had refused to be a hypocrite, and had always said what I thought quite openly, and had thus shocked and antagonized many people, but now I had become a hypocrite. He said it was not hypocrisy but *adaptation*! When one lives among wolves, one must howl with the wolves. I told him that my animus had always hindered me from having the right kind of persona. Now, when I say an *énormité* [make an outrageous remark], I do it in the right place. Then he went on to say that I could also say to Mr. Cabot, "I gather from your letter that one should give Janey a chance to use her discretion already now, but I can't do it now, because we haven't got the necessary money for that purpose."

Then I told Onkel the dream I had had:

I was a guest in his house, and sitting with him and Mrs. Jung downstairs discussing the three roads which go by his house – one of which roads the town of Küsnacht wishes to appropriate as a right-of-way. Then I went upstairs to bed, and in the corner of my room was a safe, and Jim [Cabot] was asleep against it. To my horror, the door suddenly opened, and long claw-like yellow hands hauled him inside [the safe], then the door closed behind him. I woke screaming with horror!

Onkel said the 'Chinese hands' are the usual motif in a detective story. They come out of the safe where I keep the valuables. It is the money itself that pulls Jim into the safe. It is peculiar that it happens in Dr. Jung's house, and shows a particular degree of friendship. (I told Onkel that I have known him for such a long time that it is as if he were part of the family.) That is the general mood of the beginning of the dream. My memory is now reinforced by that money which his father writes about. Out of the safe, where you keep the money, the hands come. It is as if I were going to forget that I am "Mrs. Cabot" when the memory [of Jim?]

---

[1] Mrs. Cabot, I heard much later, liked spending money, but at the time I understood her to be stingy.

is taken away. The hour came to an end, and we will take it up in the next hour.

Although my mother distanced herself from the Cabots after my father's death, and hoped I would forget them, she was unlikely to forget that she was Mrs. Cabot. Just what the dream was getting at, therefore, remains uninterpreted, because they do not take this subject up again in the following hour. My mother resumes with an interjected note on one of Jung's lectures, and then continues with her session notes:

In his E.T.H. lectures, Onkel said some remarkable things. For instance, in a Buddhist temple, young girls were bringing flowers to place in front of Buddha: they were sweet smelling Jasmine flowers. When asked why they were bringing this flower-offering to Buddha, the young girls replied: "It is not to Buddha that we are offering these flowers, for he is long since gone and lives in the great spaces, but it is to show that life is fleeting and fades away, like these flowers."

Thursday November 23, 1939

When I saw Onkel, we spoke of the Mellons. We said how nice they were. He affirmed that they were sincere and honest people, and said that Mrs. Mellon[1] has size, and is a 'character' in a way, but is unfinished and a rough diamond. She is easy-going and bright, and has a remarkable American freshness, and is very direct and straight, also very natural, and just steps in and is on the spot. He, Paul Mellon, is a nice fellow, and has already picked up considerably. They are unusually nice people. I said I supposed they didn't really need analysis so much, and Onkel said that *indeed* they did need it. He said they had a blow-up with the van Waverens, a real row, as the van W.s were clinging to them. They each had an hour with Onkel and talked about their condition, and he told each about his case. Then 'they broke through the wall' and flung the van Waverens aside. The Mellons had no idea of psychology, and, because the van Waverens knew something about it, they were impressed by them. Mrs. Mellon had gone to the van W.s before she married, and afterwards, she took Mr. Mellon there.

[1] Mary Elizabeth Conover Brown Mellon (1904-1946), the first wife of Paul Mellon (1907-1999).

The van W.s spoke of, and quoted Onkel, and they, the Mellons, were very impressed, because they knew nothing of psychology. When they met Onkel the whole thing blew up. It suddenly came to them that the van W.s were nothing, but they had heard Jung's ideas expounded by the van W.s and that had interested them. Mrs. van Waveren overrates herself with the little she knows. She was put on the psychological scent by Seabury, but she has been left with a neurosis as big as a mountain. Onkel said that he and Toni had put her together, and she then thought she knew enough to 'swing it' – become an analyst. The van W.s prejudiced the Mellons against Toni, but Mrs. Mellon was charmed with Toni the other night at the Rüfenacht lecture and asked her to tea.

Paul Mellon recounts in his memoir that his wife Mary, before her marriage to him, had suffered from asthma and had been in analysis with Ann Moyer. After the marriage, Paul too briefly analyzed with her and then, when Ann married a young Dutchman named Erlo van Waveren, Mellon worked with him. Mellon writes, "Suffice it to say that although Mary suffered under Moyer's hazy and mystical advice for longer than I did under van Waveren's, we both ended up with a feeling of having been hoodwinked by this pair, whose understanding of Jung seemed to be warped by their own misinterpretations and wishful thinking. In the end, we parted from them on friendly terms."[1] After this Katy writes, "Then follows the rest of our interview typewritten." She shifts her style, casting things in the form of a letter to an unknown recipient:

I had an extraordinary interview with Uncle today and would like to write you about it, because it concerns an analysis of Toni and might help you with your own family problems, or give you insight into them. I asked Onkel why Toni was so hard and rough and gruff at times, and not at all understanding, sometimes. Uncle said that she had a remarkable mind, was a genius and a person of quality. Her animus is her hard and gruff side which comes through whenever the *unexpected* happens. I said that to me she seemed like a grouchy old man with the gout, and was at moments difficult. He said that side of her was absurd and grotesque and you often get such a side with people with a special gift. Those

[1] Paul Mellon, *Reflections in a Silver Spoon* (William Morrow, New York, 1992), 158-159.

sorts of people have something original and unmanageable. After all, everyone has a flaw and Toni has a remarkable natural mind. What Toni cannot stand is something unexpected! When something changes or something unforeseen happens, she resists it like hell!

She likes to be prepared. When she is not prepared for something different, it is as if she were toppling over. She expects no door, and there is one, so she loses her countenance, becomes unmanageable and vanishes out of the picture. Uncle went on to say that it was ridiculous, but that nothing he could say would help, 'If I wear a necktie she hasn't expected, it's all wrong with her! She likes everything to be the rule, and is frightened if something unexpected happens. It's far better if

Toni Wolff

one takes the trouble to get her accustomed to the unforeseen. He went on to say that she could not foresee that I would not come to Bollingen, when invited after Tommy's departure. If she has made up her mind that the devil is to come, woe unto him if he doesn't appear; he must appear as she expects to see him, so that she is not overcome by something *new* to face, for she will have no 'attitude' to it. She is an introvert, and like all introverts, she fears the unexpected; it is hostile! Extraverts, on the contrary, like to have things different from what they expected. They just love it when something unforeseen happens.

Toni is a very advanced person, but she comes from a most conservative family, who has lived in Zürich for centuries, and are like hard, old wood. Her mind is the only thing movable in her. If she had not that mind she would be stone-hard. She would live with the furniture of her great grandparents; she would not have a phone in the house, for the phone can ring to announce something unforeseen! Then Uncle went on to explain that with those old patrician families, you do not exist if you have a strange name, one which is not aristocratic, and one which they have not heard before, and know is all right. They must be able to invite the person on equal terms. Then Uncle went on to tell a story about his mother-in-law, who had lived in Schaffhausen for years; afterwards, coming to Basel, where she moved in the innermost circles. (Her ancestors had been famous in Schaffhausen as far back as 1430, an old patrician family.) This mother-in-law went to Ragaz for a cure, and met there another old lady like herself, also from Basel's most conservative set. Of course they saw quite a lot of each other. There was a girl in Ragaz who was alone, and seemed very sad. Uncle's mother-in-law, who was a kind-hearted woman, sat down next to her on a bench one day, and talked to her, for which the young girl seemed very grateful. The next day, Uncle's mother-in-law saw her friend from Basel, who looked horrified. She said to her, "How *could* you talk to that young person – one doesn't talk to people one doesn't know: she could be the daughter of an executioner!" Such sayings are a precious information regarding an instinctive resistance – a dark secret.

I asked Onkel if *he* couldn't analyse Toni and cure her of that absurdity, the rough side of her nature, as it was unworthy of her to keep it when she had the opportunity to get rid of it, through some work with him. He said one cannot touch that subject with her– one cannot 'get at it' – as when you approach her about it, the *same* revulsion takes place as when something unexpected happens. It is sort of wheels-within-wheels, and one cannot do anything about it. She refuses to let one broach the subject. Besides one can't, as the same process takes place and she gets gruff and annoyed. *It is stronger than herself.* She won't own up to it, and *it* pushes her away and won't allow anyone to approach it. It is like a mine: when you touch it, it goes off. You can't touch a mine: it is untouchable, he said. "So I dismissed it and have not tried to cure her, as she can't be tackled yet. Maybe in time she can approach it, her great problem. But those humors of hers, those grouches, are flimsy nonsense and don't make sense, so don't pay any attention to them."

I told Uncle that for a long time (since September) I had seen that her queerness and rudeness were absurd; that I had made up my mind to disregard them and just take her for her good sides, which were many. He said that was the thing to do. I then spoke of my operation last year and how she said good-bye to me and said she wouldn't have time to come and see me, and how he and I thought it was so queer of her, and *he* was in fact quite annoyed with her. He reiterated that he hoped she would get over it in time, that it was just nonsense, and not to be taken seriously; that I had good judgment and had evidently seen it was absurd and disregarded it, which I had. He went on to say that silly things put Toni in those moods, such as Janey's appearing unexpectedly – as though Janey's coming along on an errand, uninvited, means you underrate her [Toni]. That she should think you were being chaperoned by your daughter and protecting yourself against her (Toni) is again the executioner motif. Those old families, like Toni's, carry the extraordinary load of the centuries – of exclusive people who exclude. And it has piled up in the past centuries until now: a wall is built around her. Toni is adapted to a life where nothing happens – they lived that way through the centuries in Switzerland. It is similar to primitives: when a tribe which wears blue feathers comes upon a tribe which wears red feathers, then it is liable to kill the other tribe just because it is different! A missionary once put up a flagpole near the native crops. The tribesmen had never seen a flagpole, so when a thunderstorm came along and devastated their crops, they said that the missionary had aroused the storm through his flag. Toni's stuff is all nonsense, but like the primitives, she does not see it. They [the primitives] have lived their usual and regular lives for years without flagpoles! Toni is a typical Zürich lady of the 18th century. Then, life here was quiet, and you met the same people: they had names you knew and were old families you knew – but let one stranger appear, and they were all a-flutter. It seems, in the 18th century, a foreigner came and bathed in the Zürich Lake, and everyone was aghast! No one had ever thought of bathing in the lake, as it was considered most dangerous. Old families are immovable: they are rooted to the place they come from.

Onkel went on to say that if one restores old conditions, as he did when he built Bollingen, a medieval house (he always felt himself a medieval man and had the desire to return to his natural surroundings), you live the ancestral life, and you feel fundamentally *well*. If you put Toni back into the old walled city of Zürich of the 17th and 18th centuries, she will be right and feel right, because she can again just be *herself*, the Zürich *Bürger* woman – upright, severe and Protestant. With her, a new face is [automatically] a bad person! I asked him how she then carried on her work so success- fully, as she was always seeing new faces? He said that she had a beautiful mind, which out-grew her. But behind that mind, she loathes everything that is unforeseen. He said that if, on a Sunday, a stranger suddenly loomed up in Bollingen, when she was there, it was as if a catastrophe had happened – so ridiculous but true! He went on to say, to illustrate his point, that a new invention scares us. He himself did not like crossing the lake at the Exposition on the *téléphérique*. We are somewhere, within ourselves, 'historical man,' and are not adapted (like Toni) to new inventions. Our ancestors would have killed the man who invented that *téléphéri- que!* Toni is an historical person, peasant-like and coarse in parts of herself. It is hard for such people to adapt, for one is lost if one lives in the past. He said he saw Toni in an old-fashioned gown, in the 18th century, and he had a three-cornered hat and was bowing low in front of her. The more she is advanced on one side, the more she feels that rough side of herself – the untouchable flaw! She has been blamed by a lot of people for it. She has also had people very jealous of her mind. He finished by saying again that as soon as he tried to touch on that bad side of hers, she would get a defensive attitude, and there was just nothing he could do.

Toni indeed had a stiff side, which I noticed myself. But she compensated for it with a very friendly personality. Being an introvert myself, I felt sympathy for Toni's not liking the unexpected; though one can be conscious of this weakness, it is very difficult entirely to overcome it. I do not remember the episode of my turning up unexpectedly at Toni's flat, although on occasion, I did fetch my mother after her hour with Toni at Freiestrasse 9, and once Toni lent me a black dress to wear at a funeral. I never sensed any rivalry; in fact, I remember her as always being really nice to me, never once talking down to me. Unfortunately, her mental stiffness showed itself physically. Even in the early days of the War, when Toni drove an ambulance, my mother wondered how, with her rheumatism, she could take on such a job. In later years, she developed very severe arthritis.

Catharine's record of the next session reverts to longhand, which continues into the following hour's notes:

I then told Onkel about going to Paracelsus [?] and having a 'panic' as I stood waiting to be called to see Baronin Böcklin.[1] Onkel said it was an undigested part of myself which goes on producing fears, and ideas, which make me a coward. That is the yellow streak in me! One finds such things in almost all people. Not everything in our nature is up to the mark as it should be.

Then we talked of Toni, as the past typewritten pages show.[2] Onkel told me of Liselotte, Princess of Pfalz, who became Princess of Orléans, who came to the court of Louis XV. She took a bath every fourteen days, which people thought was wild and extravagant. Versailles stank, according to the English ambassador, and that is why perfumes were brought from Italy. The chamber pots were emptied into the courtyard, and are still emptied out of the windows in Marseille. A man in Marseille, upon receiving the contents of a chamber pot on his head, said, "*Ça sent l'arachide, ça doit venir du 5ème [étage].*" [That smells like peanut oil. It must come from the 5th floor.] The cheaper flats are high up in Marseille. [Cheap peanut cooking oil was used by people who could not afford olive oil.]

It was back in those old days, the 18th century and beginning of the 19th century (1830), that people had superstitions and feared things such as disease and epidemics. The fear of smallpox was a specter. There is an 'historic' fear of such things.

Onkel said he had built a medieval house [for himself] with thick walls and a barrel of wine in the cellar. Uncomfortably medieval, stone floors, cold – one has to wear fur coats! He said there was something in him which had to have that place. "In it, I felt my ancestral souls, and it was just like paradise. It was cold, uncomfortable and dark at night, yet something in me felt well beyond measure. I had finally seen what I was lacking, because when I was a boy, everything was cold – snow was drifting in the window, the water froze in the pitcher, ants were in the room, and the stove smoked. It was an 18th century house and never rebuilt." He said, he was so impressed by friends with warm houses. When you go to sleep, you return to your ancestors; you go back into the unconscious. When people slept in the past, it was cold. It had been

---

[1] Baron and Baroness Böcklin, an elderly German couple living in Zürich.

[2] Catharine had written her Diary in longhand until 14 November 1939. Thereafter for a while she alternates longhand with typewriting, and eventually goes over completely to typing her Diary.

cold for a hundred thousand years. We carry a man in us who is adapted to life a hundred years ago.

Onkel also said during the interview that it was not wise to help Lüttichau too much, as she's a bluff and a snob and has no charm. Princess Hohenzollern was a child in that respect, and easily deceived, and, of course, she had been unavoidably deceived by Mrs. Mellon, as Mrs. Mellon deceives herself!

I told him of my desire to become a Catholic. He said that Catholicism would be quite nice if there were no Catholics. I must get him to explain later the funny kind of psychology which he said they have.

December 1939

I did not write this hour down after I came home, as I left for San Remo, and had no time, so I am afraid it will be a very inadequate paper.

I think I started the hour by speaking of snobs. I seem to have met so many on my travels. Onkel, in speaking of them, said they all wished to move into very good society, because, instead of getting their values from within themselves, they get them from the society they move in. They say to themselves, "I am the chosen one who moves in such or such a set." These snobs exist at the expense of the society in which they move. If you are sure of your own value, and have the right *Weltanschauung*, it does not matter to you, or upset you, should you have to deal with people who are below your mark. When sure of yourself, you can say, "To hell with the whole bunch! I lose nothing of my [own] value by being with such people." Snobs are flattered by being with people highly placed, but if you have right values, which you can safely repre-sent, you are not exalted or lowered, even if you deal with people absolutely out of range. If you can discard the fact that a person is famous, or rich, then you can discard the fact that you are a swine! That is why you should be at one with yourself and know it. It is stupid to have feelings of inferiority. Snobs are unhappy and miserable people. It does not matter whether a person is Her Grace, or not, or what her family is. You cannot be a slave to that sort of thing: if you are, then you are not right with yourself. When you have the right relationship to yourself, that means freedom.

Then I asked him the question Princess Hohenzollern had asked me to ask him about: "What next?"

He said, "When you have an ugly thought about people, you usually dismiss it, as you hate to have ugly thoughts. *Don't dismiss it!* Say to yourself, here I have an ugly thought, and ask yourself whether you think something else about that person. Have you a grievance against that person? What next do I think about that person? What next? Then you go on having a lot of bad thoughts about that person, and finally you say to yourself, 'Do I hate, or envy, or am I afraid of that person?'"

When you are impressed enough by the fact that you think quite a lot of ugly things about the person, then you may have suddenly a disagreeable memory, or something else comes to mind. You find perhaps the cause of your dislike and bad thoughts about that person. Then the whole thing can swing around, and good things come to the front, and then you say, "Why do I like the person now?"

You never arrive at anything if you don't ask, "What next?" You may have a double attitude and not be one with yourself about that person. When you do not know how you feel – are on one side favorably impressed, on the other side not – then ask yourself, what next? If you have the hunch that the person may be disagreeable, it may refer back to yourself. Dismiss that person from your judgment and look into yourself, and see where you are decent or indecent. When you are in doubt, then there is something unconscious to get out into the light. You must ask yourself if the dual attitude is due to a split in your own character. Mrs. Mellon would not have suffered from neurotic troubles if she wasn't a dual personality. You, too, have that sort of personality. You must ask what is the truth about a person, and how does that person look from all sides? Then dismiss the case, or – if it seems important to *approfondir la chose* [to delve deeper] – then ask yourself where you are double.

One is unconscious that one has two faces! By your attitude, you can get people to put on their best face or their worst one. It all depends on your attitude and whether you have said, "What next?" Onkel went on to say that the way he was with people depended very much on how he was handled: "If a patient, or another person, is disagreeable or not, or polite or cheeky, I get pleasant or very ugly. You would be a complete saint if you did not react to a person's attitude and handling; you would not be human anymore.

To a certain extent, you must pay homage to people. If they put out their whole strength to please you, then you must accept it."

As we have already seen, Katy's inferiority complex repeatedly got in the way, spoiling her relationships by making her prefer the company of *chic* people because they had no intellectual ambitions. But in fact she was on the defensive with everybody. She did not attack people outright, but she avoided people she disliked and vigorously stated her reasons for doing so to people she felt she could confide in. As Tommy was away, I became her listening-post, yet I avoided discussing things with her because I did not want to encourage her protracted harangues. Often the persons she disliked had been friends – but being human, they had not lived up to the ideal against which Katy had measured them – so suddenly, they were dismissed. It was easy enough to break with friends but difficult to dismiss her own mother, whom she kept at a distance, with a kind of armed truce. She was much more charitable when speaking of her father with me, whom she now idealized, since he had been ill with diabetes for a couple of years. As with the French wine merchant, her nursing instincts had been awakened. The Zürich doctors could not cure her father, however, since his condition, compounded with arteriosclerosis, was too advanced. When we saw my grandparents at Christmas of 1939 in San Remo, his deterioration since the summer had become rapid.

As American citizens, my mother and I were still able to obtain Italian visas without difficulty in December 1939. This time, we went the easiest route, via Milan, rather than Turin, which meant going through French customs twice. When I was nine and we visited San Remo for Easter, my mother carried some Bustelli (Nymphenburg) figurines to ornament the "villetta," which her father had built for her in his garden under an enormous Eucalyptus tree.[1] These porcelain statuettes, copies of 18th-century museum pieces, Katy packed among her clothes in one of our many suitcases, to avoid the heavy duties. The French *douanier* [customs official], chalk in hand, intuitively homed in on the case carrying the contraband. I had been taught to keep my mouth shut, but even as a hardened frontier crosser, I was startled by his move. Just as my mother was reluctantly about to

---

[1] The largest tree on the Riviera, and possibly the largest in Italy. Yet – however magnificent, its roots had the tendency to enmesh themselves in the plumbing when we lived at the *villetta* [small villa].

comply, the official was called away. Our strong Swiss nanny, a country girl, speedily replaced one suitcase with another. When the *douanier* returned, he came to the exact place where the contraband case had been but did not question its new appearance. My mother was flabbergasted; the nanny explained that customs officers chalk the place but not the luggage itself. We sighed with relief as the lid of my overstuffed bag sprang open and toys tumbled out. Fortunately, at the early stage of the War the Milan trains were not too crowded, so I was not called on to deploy my usual tactic to prevent people entering our compartment by developing a terrible cold on the spot and sneezing and coughing violently. Another means that my mother and I used to this end was to speak the language of the *peuple Papalofsk*, which my mother had invented, using many Ks and guttural sounds, and which managed to suggest Eastern Europe and fleas: people would open and shut our compartment door and move on. My mother's proficiency in Papalofsk was such that from her mouth, accompanied by sweeping gestures, it sounded like a *bona fide* language. When the coast was clear and I sat up from my influenza act, she would often continue addressing me in Papalofsk, and I would have to remind her that she was speaking gibberish.

My mother wrote the following to Jung from San Remo:

> Villa Aloha
> San Remo
> Italia
> December 21, 1939

Dear Onkel,

Frau Dr. Jacobi appeared in Milan, the day before yesterday, and told us that you were ill, and we were most awfully sorry to hear it. Our cards must have appeared very *mal à propos* [inappropriate] indeed, as you were surely not interested, at the moment, in good food and wine! We hope that by the time you receive this, your indisposition will have passed. (Janey says one shouldn't use that word, but I was translating it from the French!) Mrs. Jacobi showed us her book, with your preface, of which she was very proud. Later, I went to the Brera [museum], and we found a very interesting picture of a "fauness," which she told me would interest you very much. It is the "Sacrifizio al Dio Pane" by Bernardo Luini. I got one for you, as she told me what you had explained to her, *à propos* of "faunesses."

The weather here is really lovely and the roses are in bloom in the garden. Would you believe it?? I couldn't, until I actually got here and saw them!

If only you and Mrs. Jung were here, it would be *much* more enjoyable. The archaic atmosphere, produced by my mother, has put me in the foulest humor imaginable! Christmas is going to be very peculiar here, due to the utter lack of *Stimmung* in Italy ... it's much more like Easter here, and even the windows have flowers and pigs and Santa Claus's in the shape of Easter Eggs.

At any rate, you won't be lacking the right *Stimmung,* and we shall think of you and Mrs. Jung on the *Heilige Abend* [Christmas Eve].

Affectionately yours,

Catharine Cabot

I wrote to "Onkel" on the same day, saying:

Dear Onkel,

I was so sorry to hear that you were ill, and I hope you will soon feel well again.

Tomorrow we are going out to the flower market to see if we can't find you a few flowers to cheer you up and to wish you and Mrs. Jung a very happy Christmas.

Affectionately yours,

Janey

(The flowers we sent would have been carnations, which grew in profusion in greenhouses on the hills behind San Remo.) We found my grandfather very sick, but my grandmother was in good form despite the "archaic atmosphere" that my mother felt coming from her. The weather was cold but sunny, although on 3 January, it snowed – for the first time in eleven years. My mother was always able to provide a Christmas *Stimmung* even under difficult circumstances; we bought a small tree and decorations locally, decorated the sitting room, and on Christmas Eve, after a Swiss-style supper, we opened presents – as do the Swiss. On Christmas Day, as no turkey was available, we had capons and my grandmother's home-made plum pudding. My mother liked to exaggerate, and so we celebrated Christmas twice, both *Heilige Abend* and an Anglo-Saxon Christmas. Christmas 1939 was to be my grandfather's last, and my diary notes that my grandparents "loved it, even he, poor man." The following June, as I mentioned earlier, the villa was bombarded from the sea by the French, and my grandmother was forced to flee with her ill husband north to Pallanza. New Year's Eve proved to be boring, and my mother was soon restless, just as she had been when I was a toddler. So we left for Genoa on 5 January, where we met Viktor Lüttichau from Zürich, on his way to Livorno. We spent a couple of days sightseeing *à trois* before returning to Switzerland. In Genoa, I developed a crush on Lüttichau, and he, evidently an intuitive, responded by surreptitiously holding my hand in a taxi. He was over fifty; this was the first of several crushes I would have on older men.

The next session with Jung, though undated in my mother's journal, comes from the winter of 1940 – after our return:

Undated

As soon as I went into Onkel's study, I gave him her [Princess Hohenzollern's] message, which I thought was beautiful, and I tried to remember her exact words: *"Dites à Onkel que je tiens à lui et que je l'aime ..."* [Tell Onkel that I value him and that I love him.] I told him that she wished me to bring it [the message] to him every time I went to him, *"comme un rite qui la protégerait dans la vie ..."* [like a rite that would protect her in life]. I felt *émue* [touched] as I gave him the message, and wept. He received it with great feeling, and said that he understood, and would do as she asked, and send his thoughts towards her. He seemed to feel that there was a great deal in such a rite, and I saw by the seriousness of his face that he was *attendri* [moved] and realized what it meant to her. He said she was brave, and realized everything. He was, as usual, most understanding.[1] He looked well and was having a cup of tea, though it was only 10.30 a.m. After delivering my message, I asked to see his paintings which had so impressed Janey. He first showed me a landscape, and then a beautiful little painting which he said was the *Puer Aeternus*, a figure on a blue background flecked with gold. Onkel remarked that there was no red in the picture. When I asked him why, he said it was a very long story which could not be told at that moment.

---

[1] Early in the War, Princess Hohenzollern did not expect to be allowed to travel to Zürich – though later on, she would be allowed to do so.

Then we talked of certain important things concerning me. The hour was almost over when I thought I had best tell him of the strange *contretemps* I had had with 'la Mellon' on Friday at the E.T.H. I explained that I saw so few of such Americans now – that the only ones I saw were the Europeanized and sophisticated ones – and la Mellon being a 'green' American, was the type I had forgotten. Would he explain her to me. After seeming so *épatante* [stunning], she was suddenly queer. I told him that the previous week she had told me most confidentially that she hated the gymnastic teacher, and had spoken to her as one might to a dog. The following week *I* had been her second victim!

Then Onkel said the following, and I am using his language:

"If anyone did that to me, or I saw anyone do that, I would know they had an awful shadow. With such people, one must keep polite – but at a safe distance: then they don't dare get near enough to you, and you just keep formal relations. When you heard what had happened the previous week with the gymnastic teacher, you should have realized that shadow and kept your distance. The Americans especially have that terrible black shadow behind them. It's as if they made a *Reinkultur* [pure culture] of all their good qualities, which they bring out into the open, and you think the person is a hundred percent pure gold. When I met Mrs. Mellon in Ascona, I was impressed, and thought what a charming person. But as soon as she entered the room for analytical treatment, I became indifferent to her, as I saw all her good qualities were frozen by that bad shadow. If – after a person has been with me for an hour and still has cold hands – it is caused by the presence of the shadow, for the shadow is very cold. When Mrs. Mellon leaves me after an hour, her hands are clammy and cold; that means she does not warm up, but gets colder and colder as the shadow approaches and falls on her. It is so impressive that you almost get the creeps! The shadow is constellated behind her and creeps up. Of such a shadow the American is totally unaware. A European is conscious of his shadow. If you say to a European, 'You have a black shadow too,' or 'Your motives aren't pure in this or that,' the European will say convincingly that he knows it to be true, but an American will be gravely offended, if you doubt his motive! An American expects you to call him your friend after only a few meetings, and he never doubts that he isn't one hundred percent pure gold. When she [Mrs. Mellon] comes to me, she sails in and is charming, and one is impressed and thinks all is as it ought to be. I told her that the fact that she was neurotic, was evidence that she was wrong on the other side. She admitted that I was right, but it was an 'academical' admission, just like everyone admits he is mortal, but will people admit of their death? One always thinks of the other fellow dying, not oneself. And so, in such a way she admitted the other side of her nature. Mrs. Mellon projects her shadow on to other women because of that. All her good qualities are shining, but then the shadow is all the blacker. She had a dream which showed a shadow, but I saw she was unaware of that bad personality in her. One can't stand one's own perfection all the time, for then you will fall over your own top. When naive people go to America, they are terribly impressed by the straightforwardness and frankness, and they say to themselves, 'I am a very bad character compared with these nice people.' Underneath all that outward niceness is meanness, vulgarity – that horse-like stable vulgarity. An American doesn't impress me anymore. Isn't it a clever bluff? And how they can put it over! When I saw her [casually] in Ascona, I did not know she was neurotic. But when she came to me here, I felt a million miles away and cold and unimpressed, and I began to peep behind her. I am sure if Princess Hohenzollern asked Mrs. Mellon to help her friend in America, she never got a cent. One would not get a cent out of that woman. It is typically American to make an *étalage* [display] of one's good qualities, but the shadow looks on. It is just such a demonstration of qualities that accounts for her neurosis."

I then asked him why it upset me so, and that I presumed it was caused by the inordinate vanity in me which did not enjoy being treated in that way. He said that it 'got me' by the *same thing* in me! I asked how that was possible, as I had for ten years been discovering my shadows, and was pretty well aware of them now! He said he knew that, but that I handle my shadow as my particular affliction, and *refuse* to see it as a general phenomenon. I must be more objective; then I can see other people's shadows better. He said that we are afraid of our feelings and then think *we* only have a shadow. One must become more objective, see through the whole thing and say, "Yes, this is a nasty thought which I have had about this person, but it is not my particular affliction, and what about this next person?" If you think something nasty about someone you must say, "What next?" By doing that you are enabled to see more through you own shadow. "I expect something every time Mrs. Mellon comes to me." He went on to say that if we only knew that we are *our own worst disappointments,* if we are more intimate with our own shadow, we would understand other people's.

Onkel went on to say that when he was in America, he saw a lot of a certain Rabbi Wise, who was supposed to be a sort of saint. Onkel said that he was most impressed by this man, and finally fell into an inferiority feeling and said to himself, "Isn't he wonderful, this man, and I am just an awful swine in comparison." Later, it seems the Rabbi's wife consulted Onkel; he was astounded and had an awful shock at what she told him. "You see," Onkel said, "I have now seen the fellow from the other side. His *épatant* side was just an artificial structure." If one gets such a shock, one deserves it. One should not be too nice to people like these Americans because it pleases them, tickles their shadows and spoils them. One must treat them politely and in a distant way, so as not to allow such people to bring out their shadow. If treated distantly, they will want a success, and put forth their strength to please, and one will see nothing of the shadow.

I then asked Onkel if Mrs. Mellon was not *tiers-état* [third estate]. I was sure she was not from a good American family. He said, he thought she was from the Middle-West, and her father a doctor. I very nastily, and snobbishly said that I thought so, and in that case, didn't mind a snub from a person like that; such people could not snub one. I realized that Onkel thought I was pretty nasty, and before he could say so, I told him myself. I added, that as he saw, I had my feet still firmly in the mud! He said to leave them there, for as long as we live in this body, they are usually to be found there. "But we can go on trying to achieve something, and not worrying about the feet – then one might succeed in lifting them out of the mire someday. Just take your feet, for being in the mud, for granted, and look for better things."

Et cela était la fin de l'analyse, et j'ai senti tout d'un coup, que j'avais appris beaucoup de choses. Il [Jung] m'a dit qu'après tant d'années en Europe, j'avais jugé les Américains comme une Européenne naïve! [This was the end of the analysis, and I suddenly felt that I had learnt many things. He [Jung] told me that after so many years in Europe, I had judged Americans as a naive European would!]

Though secure in her adaptation to Europe in this way, my mother also remained ungrounded when it came to the *chic* world of European society. Another undated entry records a pointed challenge to her in this regard:

Undated

I went straight to Onkel from the tea at which Mrs. Jung had also been, and where I had been so impressed by the 'magnificent society *Gestalten*.' I was especially fascinated by Frau Andrea, who was the sister of Rathenau[1] and who had a very fine house in Berlin, and entertained extensively and lavishly in her day. I told Uncle about her, and how she looked like a monkey, and was so ghastly that she was fascinating! I told him that in a way I had seen into her, but all the same I got into a sort of *tourbillon* [whirlwind] and had to keep a good hold on myself not to feel inferior with that most extraordinary woman. Onkel said that evidently, in those social situations, I get into a mood, and my feet are no longer on the ground. I get too impressed by social atmosphere. It matters still too much to me. I told him that he was right, that I liked to go out and meet people, and be 'someone' in society, – that in the old days, it meant a lot to me and I had taken great pains in society; but to my disappointment, I had never been very good at it. I had always wanted to be a society *Gestalt* [figure]. I told him how impressed I was by Mrs. Jung, who was not 'caught' by it. Onkel said that Mrs. Jung knows there is *nothing in it* and is therefore not at all impressed. But with me, it matters too much and I get caught. Onkel went on to say that Frau André (or Andrea?) *is* clever, and seems to have *de l'esprit* [wit], but it is of a terribly superficial kind. She was once a great figure in Berlin society, and was very closely affiliated with the von Schleichers.[2] Frau Andrea's great stunt is

---

[1] Walther Rathenau (1867-1922) was the German industrialist and statesman assassinated on 24 June 1922, whom Gitta Sereny calls a "great Jewish organizer of the German economy in the First World War" (*Albert Speer: His Battle with Truth* [Macmillan, London, 1995], 295).

[2] Major General Kurt von Schleicher was the Secretary of State at the Ministry of Defense under Hindenburg, then for less than two months in 1932, was Chancellor of the Reich. He was against Hitler. Both he and his wife, Elizabeth von Schleicher, were murdered by Hitler in the bloodbath of 30 June 1934 (see John Guenther, *Inside Europe* [Hamish Hamilton, London, 1938]).

that she quotes from what great people like Goethe have said, but she says nothing original. Far better quote something original, even if it is bad, than to quote an author and his *Sprichwörter* [proverbs]. He said that when he was in Berlin, she invited him to dinner in her marble palace. He sat next to her, and for one hour and a half she talked to him without interruption using the most tremendous words! Finally, she asked Onkel what he thought of her. He did not wish to say, but she insisted on an answer, so Onkel said, "You are an intelligent person, but you don't *think*: you just rattle things out which you get from books and encyclopedias, and you talk the stuff others have written in their books. You just don't *think!*" Upon receiving that answer, Frau A. blew up and was very annoyed, but finally calmed down, and said, "I *must* think." A few days later, she called Onkel for an appointment.

Onkel went on to say that she is a woman in hell. When someone is so bright and glibly quotes all the classics, what then is she covering up? Why does she need to produce such a shining surface? It is so that you won't see *behind*, the dirt which is there. Just look at her face – it is *ravagé* [devastated], and you can see the history: the terrible conflicts and the passions and the disappoint-ments, and in her eyes is the fire of hellish torture. She was sold out to the world. She now thinks only of famous people she has known; her whole life consists of those memories – the past and what she has done and what she has been. She is a heap of ashes! He said, "When in her days of splendor I was invited to her house once alone to dinner, I felt, as I entered those doors, that here was the entrance to hell. If her brother was like her, he deserved his fate – it had to come to him." They had nothing but ignoble ambitions, sheer torture for the soul. He *was* doomed, and she *is* doomed. She is hopelessly infatuated with 'shining' and knowing so-and-so. It all means nothing, and she is just a heap of misery. I told him she had said she disliked the Swiss. He said that of course she did, as no one in Switzerland pays any attention to her, or cares whether she is acquainted with ambassadors etc. Swiss people do not care for people who live on the surface. I said that, in a way, I found her *sympathique*, that she had found me so also. He said that she has an extraordinary sense for people who have social ambitions, and spotted them in me; therefore, she found me 'sympathetic.' She saw some of herself in me. Onkel said *I* must have false values, and when one has them, one is lost! "We in Switzerland are not interested in knowing the great of this world," he said, then continued that I had evidently had a particular ambition to be a social star – whereas, now, the main thing is that I learn something *real*. No wonder I had panics and uncertainty, as I had nothing under my feet and was hollow inside. He said it was all wrong, horrible and pathetic. I said that Frau Jacobi[1] (our hostess) had a different attitude to that of her guests. He said that she had a better nose for essential things. He went on to say, now that I was beginning to have something inside myself, that I can deal better with such situations – which are a real temptation and poisoning me. It is all rotten, idiotic and poor. He added that, when he first met Frau A., he thought, "Poor thing down from the throne," and saw a skeleton, a person spiritually dead and gone, and out of place, and thought how pathetic and terrible it was. She was decorated with feathers of birds she had stolen somewhere, and he was impressed by the futility of that person. He said, "I had invited her to dinner at Küsnacht, as she had been so very nice to me in Berlin. When she was with us, even my daughter was impressed because she seemed so utterly wrong and out of tune. She can only be where there are glittering toys, and say brilliant things. She is like a poor thing who has saved some of the family jewels and puts them on for a solemn occasion to show she is a lady. She is like *parvenus* who have lost their money – great shining figures who are selling matches!" Onkel went on to say that he could not be sure he would not be impressed if he were invited to Buckingham Palace, and as a matter of fact, when he was once driving along in a coach, belonging to one of the Indian Maharajahs, he suddenly started to laugh to himself and said, "Isn't this grotesque and comical for me to be in this gilded thing!" Then he told me how people can be impressed by their own position. He said that one day the phone rang, and a voice said, "This is Prince Boncompagni: I wish to come over right now to see you." Onkel answered that he had no hour free and that he would have to come tomorrow; whereupon Boncompagni said, "But I am Prince Boncompagni, and I wish to come now." Onkel explained patiently that this day was booked up, and that an appointment would have to be made for the following day. Again B. said, "But you don't realize that I am Prince Boncompagni and I must see you." Onkel asked him, "Are you

---

[1] Dr. Jolande Jacobi, a Zürich analyst originally from Hungary.

feeling very badly?" "No, not at all," answered Boncompagni, "but I must see you." Whereupon Onkel answered, as he hung up the receiver, "But you must not!" He said that the next day Boncompagni called up very politely and modestly, and asked for an hour.

Then I spoke of "her" [Princess Hohenzollern] again, and said that I wished to say again, as I had promised her, how much she cared for him and needed his protective thoughts. He replied that I had forgotten to say it the last time. I indignantly flared up and said that I had only seen him *once* since "her" departure and that I had immediately begun the hour with it. He then said he remembered it now, but had thought I had seen him once in between, which I denied, indignantly. He said that he had written to her, and he said that she had a very great sense of reality; a sense for things which are essential, and that is why she likes him because she knows that he too has that sense of values. He said that when you had been the child of a king, it is hard to get away from the fact. If he had been the son of a king, he would surely look back on it with regret, and say, "Wasn't it fine when I was the center of everything, the whole show!"

I then told him of Janey's regard for him, and how she is now reading his books and seminars. He was very surprised. I told him that Janey wanted to know the exact meaning of the word "mana." He said that mana was the primitive conception of a magic atmosphere, the prestige of the chief and the medicine man. It is a Polynesian word. In Swahili, it means, "significance." The significance of dreams is, *"mana Yota"* – the fascination, the spell, the dream conveys. The Totem and the Amulet have *mana* – magic power. They have power you can charge up and refresh. I said to him, "But Onkel, *you* have *mana*." He said he knew it, and when he is quiet, with himself alone and not doing much, it would work.

I then asked him about WOMEN, for I had recently seen a movie with no women in the cast and found it rather refreshing and delightful. I told him I found women difficult and thought the world without women would be very delightful. He said, not at all, but that women were twisted and men don't know how to deal with them properly. Women have a twisted influence and *talk* instead of being charming and nice. Women themselves would prefer to be charming but, for some reason, they are afraid to be so. He said that women become too greedy for sexuality, power and personal prestige. If only they would just be charming, nice and kind, then they would be better and feel better. A woman talks the house down because she misses the opportunity of being human and kissing the man. I then told him about meeting Maedi Schwarzenbach at a cocktail party, and how she had announced to the assembly that I was a patient of Dr. Jung. I said it was rather embarrassing. He said she was a horse, one of the big women of Zürich, and that it adds to your personality if you are known to be a patient of his. You are then *interesting*, as Dr. Jung is supposed to be dangerous, mysterious and unknown. But he said, the next time la Schwarzenbach says that to people, I can turn around and say to her, "And you know him too, don't you?" It seems she is *also* a patient of his – though she does not want it known! I had a laugh when he told me that.

I then asked him about growing old and told him I wished to talk about that in the next hour. He said that as you get old, you come down to *reality*, and then all the bad qualities come out. He said that Mrs. Jung was fifty-eight, and yet was not like that. I said, I thought she looked, and seemed, much younger. He said she had a remarkable personality and extraordinary qualities, and was a great student. He added that the most comforting thing on earth was a really nice old woman.

I told him I realized that I should study more. He said it would come in time, and then I would be less empty-headed! That last remark has certainly given me food for thought.

When Linda Fierz asked Onkel why he went on with analysis when it tired him so much, he replied, *"Man darf nicht versuchen sich etwas zu ersparen. Man muß alles leben, bis es zu Ende gelebt ist. Erst dann kann es sich ändern."* [One must not try to spare oneself. One must live everything until it is lived to the end. Only then can it change.]

Chapter Seven

Tommy's Return and the First Year of the War

Tommy sent a telegram while we were in San Remo saying that he was soon to leave England and that he had found a Scottish Terrier for me. After a tedious journey by boat and train to Gstaad via Montreux, he met us after the New Year carrying Tippler. I was delighted to have a dog. With Tommy's return, my mother's life settled back into its pre-war routine, except for travel outside Switzerland. She hoped to return to Italy in the spring, but by April 1940, the War had turned hot in Norway, then in the rest of western Europe by May. For the next five years, my mother's excursions would take her to Ascona and occasionally Bern, Basel, Lausanne and Geneva. She took an apartment for the summers in Ascona, and spent part of most winters at Gstaad. My skating career continued in Zürich only, because Bror Meyer did not return to St. Moritz. Both my mother and I were delighted to see Tommy again. Strangely, for me he was more of a brother figure than a father figure. He seemed the same outwardly, but his frustrating search for a military posting in England had affected him profoundly. Because he was very repressed, it did not show immediately, but it still was a major personal defeat.

The next session with Jung takes up the relationships among the three of us:

February 1940

Onkel told me about himself, when I asked him how he felt. He said he had an exhaustion of the heart muscle, caused by too much fat, and he must now diet and lose weight. He said, he got very tired because so many doctors were away and he had to see many patients whom ordinarily he would not see. [Many doctors were serving in the Army.] He said he also had to attend to the pesty old furnace despite heartbeats, temperature and sweat. It had started with a grippe [flu]. Finally, he had to give up everything and rest. He said the one ray of light, in these black times in which we live, was a wedding breakfast at the *Verenahof* in Baden. It has a famous kitchen. They served Champagne nature 1915. The buffet was a wonderful sight. He said he overate and drank, and was ill afterwards, but loved it, and was going to Baden for a cure during his holidays! I said my mouth watered, and he laughed and laughed.

I spoke of Tommy and how he was working on himself and really taking himself in hand with his humors. That being in London so long alone had given him time to think, and that he was really now doing something about it; no longer just sitting around and letting his humors take place. I told him of Janey's nasty attitude to Tommy, how she did her best to get him in a bad humor because she was mean and did not want him to improve. She finally succeeded, and in consequence, he hurt his leg going down the mountain in a rage. I also asked him if he thought Tommy could cure himself alone, without analysis of those humors.

Onkel said that he thought it splendid of Tommy to be trying, and that such men pick up analysis through a woman. I told Onkel that Tommy liked him. He said, "He likes me because I don't go for him." He went on to say that men like Tommy won't let a man tell them truths because it gives them feelings of inferiority; it would not be a good idea, feeling as they do, to be analysed. He said, they can get it better through a woman, as it gets under their skin.

Onkel said that if I go ahead with my work and impart what I know to him, that is enough, as it makes him *think*. It is as if a man couldn't take [things] in through his *mind*. It gets into his unconscious and 'works.'

I spoke of Tommy's difficulties in getting out here again, and how nasty they were at the French consulate, where he went for a visa. Onkel said that French officials can be nasty and disagreeable, worse than any others and anyhow, in war time, all sorts of nasty people come to the foreground.

I said I felt sheepish about being in a hotel with Tommy, where we were known, and not married to him. He said that my psychology must be very young. If it were not for the child, he would have told me to go ahead and not care about others who criticize. The serious thing in it is the daughter. Quite understandably, I should maintain my affection and a good relation with de T. It is a problem. Janey's attitude is a bit exaggerated, but being the only daughter, she is a bit inflated. I must just cheat her, and say I am going out with someone else, if it upsets her that I see so much of de T., for I am not responsible to her for a true *reportage* of what I do. It is all too much for her, and one must not burden her too much with it. Between her and me there is a sort of marriage, and she assumes she has rights, and is tyrannical. One must not upset her righteous ideas about marriage, but I must have my own life, too – otherwise, her life would be made unbearable should I not lead my own life, in a sense. I told Onkel how Janey thought Tommy was trying to take her little dog away from her, spiritually. Onkel said she *projects* her jealousy onto de T.

I remember nothing of discord between Tommy and myself after his return in January 1940, nor jealousy over the dog, who was in my exclusive care. For four months, however, I had been my mother's *ersatz* companion and confidante, a position which undoubtedly flattered me and left me inflated. I was glad that Tommy was back in Switzerland because my mother could be quite a handful to deal with solo, but obviously I was jealous when it became clear that she would leave me to vegetate in the hotel while they went out together. I plunged from the heights of an inflated grown-up at sixteen back to the nursery. No longer did I have to eat supper in bed, but it was not much fun either to eat alone in the Waldhaus Dolder restaurant among *Jass* players puffing on *Stumpen* [small evil-smelling cigars]. I felt embarrassed sitting there in splendid solitude at our large *Stammtisch* [permanently reserved table]. I had no companions my own age during this period. Other young people my age lived lives structured by school and homework, so I saw them only in the evenings on the ice rink. My skating friend, Köbi Biedermann, a few years older, was posted at the Swiss frontier. (Later in the War, he took me out, and invited my mother and me to meals at his mother's apartment on the Dufourstrasse.) I was too introverted to seek out friends, although by the time I was seventeen, I began going to dances with groups of young people.

Then I told Onkel that Janey refused to come out and wanted to study her art. He said, "Something is creeping out of the shell, a peculiar kind of butterfly," and he went on to say that she evidently had some right ideas and was beginning to see straight. I told him how much she likes him, and wished she could see him more often. He said that he was afraid that if he did see her more, it would help along her inflation. Only daughters, with no father, were a difficult proposition. He said that he foresaw that she would have difficulties with herself in life; therefore, when he met her, he tried to give her a *certain attitude* – how to understand her difficulties. By seeing him is how an 'image' would get into her unconscious. The immediate effect of that image would come out in the form of an inflation, which might last for a while, but not to worry about it as, eventually from the 'inflation' will come an 'inner measure' with which to judge herself and her behavior. At the moment, she seems rather formidable, but in not wanting to go to America and come out [become a débutante], she already shows there is something in her.

That "something" in me liked parties but did not think them important. The main reason for my reluctance to 'come out' in Boston was my cowardliness as an introvert. I dreaded coming out among strangers, and had no desire to meet the relatives my mother had ranted against for years. Nor did the long and difficult war-time trip to America appeal to me, though I yearned for excitement. I worried that, once in the U.S., we would not return for a long time. The prospect of going back faced us unexpectedly, however, when we found that the U.S. Consulate was reluctant to renew our passports. My mother raised the issue with me, and separately suggested to Tommy that he might like to go along, too. I firmly said no, being thoroughly brainwashed against my relatives, but I believe that had I said yes, she would have felt obliged to take me. Luckily the problem was solved by my Grandmother Rush's arrival in Switzerland in the late summer of 1940. Because the Geneva consulate gave her permission to stay, my mother could persuade the rigid Consul-General in Zürich to relent and issue new passports to us.

The entry continues:

> I then asked Onkel what he meant when he had said to me that 'Catholicism would be quite nice if there were no Catholics,' and that 'Catholics had a funny kind of psychology.'[1]

---

[1] See Katy's entry of 23 November 1939.

Onkel laughed and replied that a famous cardinal had said that to a man he converted. He meant that Catholicism is a splendid religion in itself, but it is what *people* make of it which harms it. A splendid institution – except for the people who make the wrong use of it and derive the wrong conclusions from it; just as Christianity would be a splendid thing, were it not for the Christians!

You find nowhere such narrow-minded or mentally dull people as in Catholic circles. A parson from Zürich told Onkel that every year he confirmed a child from a family he had never seen in church. He asked the man why he sent a child every year to be confirmed, but never came to church himself. The man was a shoemaker. He said that he and his wife were Catholics, but they had always kept their eyes open, and had said to each other that Protestants were nice people, nicer to each other than Catholics, so they decided to have their children brought up as Protestants, but he told the parson that he and his wife were remaining Catholics.

Onkel went on to say that he had bought land from a peasant, and while waiting for formalities to be concluded, they went to a neighbouring canton for a glass of wine. The man, who was a Catholic, was very curious as he had never been outside his canton. He looked around at the neat peasant houses and the manure heaps, and asked if they belonged to Catholics. Onkel said no, they belonged to Protestants. The man said it was very interesting to see such neatness and such fine manure heaps, and everything in such perfect order: that one would never see that in a Catholic village; and he finished by saying that there must be something wrong with Catholics.

In Switzerland, Onkel said, you can tell a Catholic community from a Protestant one: the Protestant one has nicer people, is more orderly, whereas the Catholic one is more primitive and less orderly. In a Protestant country, the people have better relations with one another.

The 'Church' in Catholic countries takes the place of the 'relation to people.' With Protestants, the church amounts to nothing, so a Protestant has to take his feeling of relatedness out of the church, and cultivate it in human relations. Whereas with the Catholic, his church is a mother, and every time he goes to church, he is in the lap of an all-enveloping mother. Naturally, he does not have the need to make relationships with people as he has such a perfect relation to his church.

The Protestants have no absolution, but the Catholics have, and they can get away with a lot and remain more or less primitive. In a Protestant country, if a man falsifies the milk, it rankles and smoulders, and is a moral reproach. In a Catholic country, a man who does that confesses and receives absolution. The case is then settled, and since everybody is alike, no one cares as they don't care so much for each other.

I asked why there were so few neurotic *practicing* Catholics. He said the Catholics were nearer to the original instincts, and nearer to primitivity. They were ugly, just as primitives are, and have no relation with each other. In the Catholic Church, men and women are not married to each other: they are married to Christ. In primitive communities, the sexes don't talk to each other. The only relation is their tribe. The Catholic Church is a tribe, and they are somewhat fanatical as to creed.

If one looks at the people leaving church on a Sunday, one sees the men, in Catholic countries, standing together and talking, and the women are a little way off, also together. Of course, with educated people, one hardly notices the difference, but it is like that in the lower part of the population.

Catholics are more easygoing, less moralistic. The Protestants, on the other hand, are more rigid, moral and law-abiding (like the Jews). The Catholic Church has little to do with morality, so it avoids moral conflicts. The law of the Church means very little to the Catholics as one always gets absolution: there is no sin that cannot be forgiven.

Onkel knew of a Protestant [Catholic?] who had a fight with a man, and thought he had killed him, though it was proved later that he hadn't. This man went to a Catholic priest and confessed his sin, saying that *once* he had committed a murder. The priest asked, "Only once, are you sure?" To us, a murder is an unspeakable thing, but to a priest, it can be forgiven by the grace of God. And to the Catholic, once he has confessed, it is a closed episode, for the Church has forgiven. The awful thing for a Catholic is to get on the wrong side of the Church. But with Protestants, a man who has committed a murder is wiped out, or will wipe himself out. The case is *morally* settled for the man, if he is a Catholic.

I suggested that the Church did not begin that way, but Onkel said that it did, and that was original Christianity, that one can see traces of it at the beginning of the second century. Callixtos, the first Pope, took all sorts of doubtful people into the Church, and raised no fuss about sinners provided they were in the Church. The Catholic Church says that everyone is unclean, so why in hell not give absolution *provided* they are good Catholics. It gives Catholics a fine feeling to come into the Church and be in the mother's lap.

In the Protestant Church, there is only a parson who says what a damned thing you are. Why go to a parson, then? – he will just tell you what you know already, for what else can he say?

I told Onkel that I thought *he* took the place of a confessor because you could go to him, tell him everything and get some good sound sense to boot, which a confessor might not always give. Onkel said that, in a way, I was right because one could tell him the most awful story and he would look at it from a human point of *vue* [view]. He said, "I teach people to agree and get along with themselves, and not to make too much fuss."

Then I spoke of my trip with Janey to Teufen, and of the American girl we went to see there, who told us she was rooming with a girl from the Tessin, who was a Catholic, and had recently come from a convent. She had now shocked the Buser Institute because she was so interested in men. I told him the American girl had been put in charge of her. Four other girls had apparently told the convent girl how silly and ghastly she was.

Onkel said the girl was evidently 'full of men' and was a Catholic, primitive; whereas the Protestant girls 'keep it under' and are neurotic. The girl should be taught not to talk so openly with Protestant girls, who are less outspoken on such subjects. But all girls are interested in men: that is not unusual and is so everywhere. It has always been like that – otherwise, the world would have come to an end long ago. If one could look into the mind of a young Negro girl, one would be shocked out of one's wits!

Onkel brought up the subject of "Cuthbert"[1] and asked me about him. I told him all I knew: that he was really a nasty bit of work. Onkel said that perhaps he should have come up here to see him, but they [?] hadn't asked for him, and he himself was so busy that he had not had time to do anything about it. I said they had the B.C., and he said they ought to be able to deal with that. He said he had only seen Cuthbert once, when he arrived and had sent him

---

[1] As once before, so too here, "Cuthbert" refers to someone other than Tommy, for whom the same name sometimes served as a pseudonym.

Katy and C.G. Jung

to M[eier?]. Once Cuthbert got out of analysis, and **M.** asked Onkel whether he should open his eyes to further possibilities, Onkel replied, "No, you can thank your lucky stars, he doesn't want to go on: just leave him alone."

Indeed, in the nineteen-forties, Catholic cantons were still much poorer than Protestant ones. The poverty was noticeable when crossing from Zürich or Bern into the Cantons of Lucerne or Zug. The Canton Valais, except in resorts like Zermatt, was abysmally poor and the people very primitive. Villages in the Protestant cantons were visibly cleaner, the buildings in a better state of repair, the gardens neater, and the people themselves cleaner and better dressed.

March 5, 1940

I told Onkel about Janey, and showed him pictures of Hermexes[1] in various stages. He laughed and laughed as if he really

---

[1] Hermexes was supposed to be my German teacher's dog. He was blue and looked like a dragon. I interpreted Hermexes as my teacher's shadow. My mother thought it was more likely mine!

enjoyed those pictures and thought them very funny. He then told me to ask Janey what was going to be done with the cotton fluff coming out, and the skin. When Janey has some work to do, I have more freedom. He said he hoped she would stick to her work, for she had a terrific drive, and she has to work or she will 'put her teeth in' all over the place. The difficulty will be to find a suitable occupation so she can do something worthwhile. She has tremendous energy with no outlet. He said he noticed at the [Psychological] Club that she had vast stores of energy and was tremendously pent up. I told him that I noticed at the Club that *he* and Janey seemed the only really dynamic and energetic people there, and that all the others seemed half-dead. He laughed, and said it was so, that he had tremendous energy, but tried not to show it too much, and to check himself. I went on to tell him that I hoped Janey would get into the art school, as I felt she would like to do this type of work. He said I had better be prepared for many different things, for she is *such a flame*, that she will burn through many things, if she chooses to. He said that, naturally, such a *dynamic* personality could not suit a Victorian like de T., and no wonder he found her difficult. All that dynamism, and energy, must be diverted into the right channels if she is to make something of herself.

I asked him if she should see Toni occasionally. He said, "NO," not to make her complicated, but let her apply herself and get into *life*. She must learn to branch out into life, seize possibilities and mix with other people; then she may learn something about life. She may discover this and that to keep her interest alive, and fix on something *definite*. All depends on how she applies herself to her job, and whether she produces something satisfactory to herself. She should go on cultivating her mental interests as long as she seems to enjoy reading the Jung books – he gave a sort of grunt, and said that he did not understand how a girl of that age took pleasure in reading his books and seminars. But he said that as long as she did, evidently she enjoyed mental interests. The best thing for her would be to take Latin lessons, as Latin was the base of all mental things, and would help her general education, and even make her accurate in her spelling.

He said he was reading a lot of Latin books: it was so interesting as one got so much out of them one could not get elsewhere and as lots of these Latin books had not been translated. If Janey takes up

Latin, she has a chance later to take up certain studies. She should also have a chance to become acquainted with things of good taste, and things to widen her horizon, so that she can choose those interests which are vital to herself. She will learn to concentrate.

I then told him that I thought I ought to take up Latin myself, as I was simply longing to get an education. He said that Latin was the foundation of all education. I told him how once I had taken philosophy lessons with Dr. Medtner[1] for a whole year and never understood a thing he said. Onkel said that it was absurd to begin at the top – one must begin at the bottom with Latin. Latin is a very basic language from which one can learn a lot, and it helps towards a basic education. I said I had terrible trouble concentrating. Onkel said one can do nothing, or accomplish nothing, if one has never learnt to concentrate or discipline oneself. One must *practice* concentration. If you have to learn something, then concentrate on it. When one can't concentrate, one is the victim of all sorts of moods and wrong ideas. It is like living in a house where there is no boss. One has an outer shell which one can keep together, but inside, a barbarous condition prevails. Mr. X, for instance, is the victim of a complete lack of discipline. He has ideas, but he doesn't stick to them. He plows a field, puts in a seed, then goes away and gives it up, so that he can never reap. One can excuse it on the grounds that he has an artistic temperament, but when one sees that nothing comes from his art, then "To hell with it," Onkel said. Concentration is the key to success. One can be ever so talented, but one will never amount to anything with one's talent unless one concentrates – and so it will be with Janey, unless she is taught to concentrate and stick to one thing.

Then he said, "As for you, you can't go on being so empty-headed. If you study Latin, you will find that it will teach you to concentrate: then you can apply yourself to learning something. There are literally thousands of middle-aged people like yourself, who do nothing with their minds, and just amble aimlessly and bored through the second half of their lives. I can't understand how such people live and do nothing with their minds. When one is

[1] Emili Karlovich Medtner (1872-1936), writer and publisher, was born in Moscow. Both his parents were of German descent. After the outbreak of World War I, he lived in Switzerland, where he became a patient and friend of Jung's, and a member of the Psychological Club. (See Magnus Ljunggren, *The Russian Mephisto* [Stockholm, 1994].)

older, one has a quiet conversation with one's books. I can't do what I did before as a young man. Now, my whole passion is in research. If I had to live, as I see a lot of middle-aged people doing, just going about, never reading or studying or thinking, I'd have committed suicide long ago! I am never bored as my day is full of interesting things connected with my work, or my books. Only people bore me sometimes, but I with myself am never bored. I don't know what boredom is. If I had no discipline, then I'd be the victim of my moods. Every minute I know what to do and do it with pleasure – I enjoy doing it. With many people it's a serious problem to know what to do with their time. It is very sad to see these people approaching old age with no interests. Thousands of people, exactly like you, have nothing to ask, to look into, and their whole lives and world are just dead."

I then asked Onkel why so many English ladies here, who are intellectual, and are working intellectually, were so dead; just as dead as the people he spoke of who had nothing to do. He said that these ladies were not working out of sincere interest, but just an *Ersatz* [substitute]. It is to be near him, and to please him, but not to please *themselves*. They do not link up their minds with the whole of their personality. They have no *genuine* interest in a thing. This intellectual life is a form. They are people with a store of knowledge they never apply. It gives them an excuse to live here and an obvious reason.

He went on to say that he never would have thought of studying the exercises of Ignatius of Loyola, for the idea bored him, but he said he saw that people should know about such things – so he studied them and found them most interesting. He said, "These *Exercitia* were a means to explain to my public, so I studied them for my people. You can use your knowledge for such a purpose, and then it makes sense, because you *apply* it. There is no use studying things in order only to heap up knowledge without purpose." He said that he knew people who had read a lot and could not put it into practical use. For instance, Mrs. Flower[1] has read everything, but does not apply it to herself as she is far behind what she is reading.

[1] An American living in Zürich, who used to take notes (for publication) at Jung's seminars.

He spoke of a Professor, who said to him one day, "I finally got an idea of what I was reading when I heard one of your lectures." This professor was a very learned man and had read many Eastern texts, but only to translate them, never knowing what they really meant. Onkel said he knew certain experts on Greek mythology, who do not know what it is all about, or what it means. Like people who live in a diamond valley; they know there are such stones, and they are called diamonds, but what a diamond really means, they have no idea. It is like a community where the commonest metal is gold, so it means nothing to them: it is like tin! Then someone tells these people that it is precious, and they realize they possess an enormous fortune. I then said to Onkel that perhaps I was like that. But he said, "What you know about psychology, you have learnt through yourself and your personal experience. It's all knowledge that is practical, and it works, and it is living, and you can talk of it sensibly. But people who know more than you do of psychology, often don't handle it intelligently."

"You can't grasp a thing unless you have experienced it – acquired it through practical experience. It's like a surgeon who knows the textbook of surgery by heart, but has never performed an operation. He knows a lot, yet it's no use to him at all, and it's as if he knew nothing. It's like a theologian who knows all about Christian healing of the soul, yet he knows nothing, and can't heal. Where is his method of healing? The theologian is as helpless as a sheep."

I mentioned Dr. Binswanger[1] as being a perfect example of a man who had studied, had a degree, and yet knew nothing, and could not help one, was flat, and had nothing to say. Onkel looked at me surprised and laughed a bit. Then he said that Binswanger had had the Freudian education, where the analyst says nothing and lets his patient do all the talking, and that is why patients get disgusted. He said doctors, when they had to do with someone who had been to him [Jung], act as if they had all been hit on the head, and seem afraid to say anything. A person is flat inasmuch as he does not apply his knowledge. One part of the brain *knows* it and the other part does not apply it! He said that sometimes he visits a colleague who has a large library all piled up with books, and he

---

[1] Dr. Kurt Binswanger, a feeling type (according to C. A. Meier), was a Jungian analyst who lived into his nineties.

says to himself that the fellow is amazing, then he finds out that he has never looked into the books!

Then I asked Onkel how to start to learn something. He said that I had first to get out my personal stuff before I could settle down to learning something. Also I had been pretty impossible when I first came, and he could not tell me to learn. He says, I cannot begin at the top but must begin at the bottom. When Mrs. Jung began to understand the need to learn, she got a professor of chemistry, of physics and of natural science, and learnt Latin and Greek between the ages of forty and fifty-eight. I told him, I would learn Latin and art as 'starters.' He said it was fabulously interesting to choose what one wanted to learn, and when you begin studying and seeing into things, it is as if a new world were opening up. He said there really should be a school for grown-ups, and that it would be good for me to have some schooling as an exercise in concentration. He said that he had treated a woman with a bad neurosis who did not know what a book looked like, and in a few years, she got a degree and got rid of her neurosis.

I do not recall attending lectures at the Psychological Club, and since shyness, especially among older people, was difficult for me to overcome, I am astonished at having been characterized as "dynamic." My only clear memory of the Club from that period was illustrating menus for a Christmas dinner; for my pains, Mrs. Fierz gave me Richard Wilhelm's *The Secret of the Golden Flower*.

Katy had the talent of deflecting Jung's suggestions when they were indigestible, sometimes even with flattery. For instance, instead of facing squarely the awkward point he made about my energy, which he hinted was not being used as it should have been, she instantly turns to *his* energy. And when the subject of my studying something serious came up, she said she, too, would like to study, and would like to do so with me! Though Jung addresses her as a responsible parent, she cannot be left out of anything and responds like a child. Her identification with me made it imperative for her that we do things together. The cooking school was all right, but Latin was a disaster. My mother's desire to learn was mostly wishful thinking; easily distracted, she could not stick to studying. When Jung tried to make her aware of the importance of intellectual pursuits, she quickly turned the subject to the "intellectual ladies" – deprecating them. By insisting on studying Latin with me in her butterfly way, she completely ruined my climate for learning. Looking back at this stage of my life, I realize that we were not two separate people, but lived in symbiosis. At that period, I was the same age as Katy had been when she was living with her parents in America; it was then, moreover, that she had become blocked in her emotional development. The symbiosis substituted for a relationship for a while, but when I entered my twenties, I was gradually forced into the role of severe parent – yet at the same time was being bossed about! A true relationship proved impossible. During Katy's lifetime, I could not understand why that was so. It was only years later that I began to understand the reason. From her side, my mother often said that she was astonished that I had a good relationship with my own daughters. I was fifty-two at her death, and felt frustrated and sad that despite the many years we had known each other, I had never felt close to my mother – and that now, it was too late.

My supposed excess of energy vanished when it came to boring lessons with the German teacher. Though I portrayed the teacher's shadow as Hermexes, that animal may well have symbolized my own shadow, which was bent on destroying all interest in learning – or at least with that particular teacher. Unfortunately, my mother collaborated with that shadow side in a subtle way. Her hopes that I would get into art school, "as I felt Janey would like to do this kind of work," were as blinkered as her earlier insistence that I take skating lessons from a first-class teacher. Unlived life also played its part in her feeling; my mother loved art but said she could neither draw nor paint, encouraging me to draw my cartoons of our daily lives, and praising my caricatures even when they flattered neither Tommy nor herself. I had fun and enjoyed the attention the drawings brought me, but knew well enough that my talents were not exceptional (as my mother made them out to be). When Maria Munch, the directress of my small art school, suggested I take the entrance examination for the *Kunstgewerbeschule Zürich* [the cantonal art school], I dutifully complied because it pleased my mother. The examination took two full days; already on the first day it was apparent to me that my co-examinees were far more talented. I warned my mother that I might fail, which I did. Friends consoled me that Swiss citizens were given preference over foreigners. I continued at Frau Maria Munch's art school, where she sometimes invited pupils to paint at her house in Zollikon, and where I learned engraving, bookbinding, lino cutting and block printing, stenciling, and printing in color on cloth. My mother's library suddenly filled with bound books, cushions stenciled with Ticinese scenes, lamp shades and other objects. She was proud of my productions. While the work interested me as a pastime, I never thought of it as a career. Despite Jung's warning that she should be prepared for many things with me, and his urging that I should apply myself to my job, cultivate my mental interests, and get into life, my mother was completely blind to any other field for me but art. Her genuine love for it, and her symbiotic relation with me, made her believe that I must share it, too, and led her also to construe "getting into life" as introducing me to her very active social set in Ascona. So my unnatural life became even more so: my untrained mind remained fallow, while I mixed with people twice my age who had nothing positive to offer. Maybe I was "pent up," as Jung called me, because I was always with older people, yet dependent on my mother, so there was little chance for development.

In spite of its rebellious streak, my ego was undeveloped. Incapable of knowing what I wanted or how to take important decisions, I accepted my mother's goal for me – dabbling in art until a suitable husband appeared. Just as with her own mother, my mother's sole ambition for me was to make a good marriage. Hence her preoccupation with "coming out." As for reading Jung's books, I did so because they interested me, but I never saw myself as intellectual – in fact, quite the contrary. I was certain that I was stupid, because my intermittent schooling made it impossible for me ever to shine, and lazy, because my mother drummed that into me constantly. She was right, but she never asked herself *why*, not sensing that apathy might signal boredom. My lessons came and went without either examinations or competition; my teachers were far too easy-going, insisting neither on good work nor on my learning to concentrate. It was all drudgery with no future. Latin, however, did interest me, because I saw that it would enable me to understand the quotations which I met up with in Jung's books. And unlike the six-week cooking course, the course in Latin would have to last years if I were to become proficient. My mother was keen to learn Latin with me at first, but with Tommy back in Switzerland, she lost the single-mindedness that she had brought to the cooking lessons. In an early burst of enthusiasm, she engaged Marie-Louise von Franz to teach us (most likely suggested by Jung). We had already met her parents, the Baron and Baronin, at a luncheon party at Frau Biedermann's flat. We went out to purchase enormous Latin-French and French-Latin Dictionaries and exercise books, and began lessons at the Waldhaus Dolder on 4 December 1940, across the street from Fräulein von Franz's parental home (later the Jungian psychiatric Klinik am Zürichberg). But there was a dual snag: Frl. von Franz was busy teaching and writing, and my mother's energy was directed towards Tommy. Lessons either came late in the evening, after my skating sessions, or were set for other times – only to be frequently canceled. There was no continuity, and my mother's interest in Latin was short-lived. She tried to encourage me, but my own interest waned, too, since our few lessons were spread over many months. The long summer holidays in Ascona dampened our ardor, though my diary reports that occasionally I studied Latin on my own. It is clear to me now that Katy's "longing to get an education" was genuine only during her hour with Jung; our time in Ascona, which lasted until the third week in October, was fertile terrain for regression. My mother stayed in Ascona not simply because life there was cheaper but chiefly because she liked the atmosphere. The apartment in the old Ticinese stone house, belonging to the German composer, Vladimir Vogel,[1] had great charm: it had the physical simplicity of a "Bollingen," but rather than considering the house as a retreat, she treated it as the starting-point for a parties – entertaining friends on the partly covered terrace with its large, wrought-iron sundial on one wall and creepers growing up the wooden posts and railing.

In Ascona, the main pastimes were golf and the social life that went with it. But cycling was mostly an agreeable necessity brought on by the War. We cycled everywhere – to the golf course, to Locarno to shop, even to Brissago to look across the frontier – a round-trip of twenty-six kilometers, which my mother gladly made to catch a glimpse of her beloved Italy. We also cycled up into the valleys behind Locarno, where we cooked our lunch over wood fires, and bathed in pools in the icy and swift, shallow river. We sometimes rose at 4:30 a.m. to be on our way before the heat of the day. My Scottie dog went, too, in an oblong straw basket made to fit the back of my bicycle. When my mother did a fruit day or otherwise kept to her room, I cycled or golfed with Tommy, whom she was glad to have off her hands from time to time while she recuperated in bed for the next bout of extraversion. Once, as my diary for 5 January 1941 records, she "took the Aga Khan's taxi man and drove to Crassy/Crassier" (a

---

[1] Vladimir Vogel (1896-1984) born in Moscow of German parents, died in Witikon by Zürich.

village straddling the Franco-Swiss border). There, looking into France, Katy saw "two German soldiers, well-equipped in great coats with fur collars." (Later, she bought a picture of a similar frontier scene.)

The outdoor life in Ascona was not our only one. Social life became more vigorous as we met more people, and strangely, my mother did not keep Onkel in the dark about the intensity of it all, though she must have realized that he would be astonished. (See the 5 November 1940 entry.) Although our hedonistic existence in Ascona now seems strange, with much drinking and staying out nearly every night until all hours, it probably arose from wartime uncertainty. As I turned seventeen, I was given far too much freedom for my age. My companions were twice my age or older and the life was rather dissipated, but my rigid, Puritanical side held me in control, leaving my mother confident that I could be "trusted" (which, in those days, meant that you would not allow yourself to be seduced). Luckily, the men around me, being of a certain standing, were reluctant to seduce virgins *de bonne famille*. Even so, it was a strain, since chaperons no longer existed and I had to keep myself out of mischief. In retrospect, I believe that my mother was so involved with her own life that she found little time to keep an eye on me. Most likely she prolonged the Ascona holidays, not to save money but for the uninhibited social life, where the absence of Zürich "intellectuals" spared her uncomfortable feelings of inferiority. She may also have hoped, by letting me loose in this prolonged interval of senseless pursuits, that she could counteract my Puritanical genes. Certainly she did not follow Jung's advice about my energy and drive; she let them go to waste in an existence without routine. During this crucial period of my development, my energy was consumed mainly in senseless pursuits. Cycling, golf, and a moderate social life were fine for a holiday of normal length, but for a girl of seventeen, going out until all hours of the night, for weeks on end, was not a good idea. My mother always exaggerated everything – *elle tirait tout en longueur* [she drew everything out] – just as she had at Malvern when she made me take *two* intensive riding courses. In Ascona, her motives may have had nothing to do with me, as the Zürich "intellectuals" were on the scene for the one Eranos week and, there being otherwise no competition, she was spared those feelings of inferiority which plagued her in Zürich.

During the next months, the War began in earnest, with the German invasion of the Benelux countries and France. On the eve of this period, and in spite of the War, my mother still hoped to holiday in Italy – her official excuse being to visit her parents in San Remo. She had no wish to join the Zürich crowd in Ascona for the Easter sessions of Eranos, and conveniently came down with one of her bouts of flu. Before that, Toni writes on 10 April from Freiestrasse 9:

> My dear Katy,
> Many thanks for your messages. [She then mentions her mother's illness and continues:] I am awfully sorry you can't come to the Ascona hotel. It is rather small (36 rooms), and all the lecturers are staying there. I did tell Mrs. N. to reserve rooms there – I don't know how many she needs – and one relief to you may be that G. will be there – of course! That's one reason why I should have liked you there – so that B. would vanish in the background. Well, it's fated otherwise. The [Hotel] Tamaro, Dr. C. wrote after seeing it, it is very nice. ...
> Maybe Mrs. L. did not yet write you. She was awfully busy with the wedding and all [her eldest son Markus was married in 1940], and having to go to Basel.
> I think your letter to her is very good and covers up the fact that you were ill – at least it would to most people.
> ... I do hope, Katy, that you consider 2 weeks in the Tessin. I am sure a change of air would be good. And Janey could begin her [art] school a bit later. The weather seems fine – only occasionally a bit of wind.
>
> I do hope you feel better every day.
> Love and good wishes,
> Toni

Having bowed out from Eranos with a convenient flu, she wrote to Jung on 28 April (with her other plans in mind):

> Dear Onkel,
> As I was unfortunate to miss my last appointment, due to the *Grippe* [cold], I am writing to ask if I could have it now, as soon as you begin to see people again [after Easter]?
> I am leaving Zürich for a change of air on May 10th, and hope very much that you will see me once, before I go on this holiday to Italy.
> I enclose this list of a certain number of works concerning St. Ignatius of Loyola, which came from a Jesuit source.

These [Easter] holidays were spent by me, getting rid of a second flu, which I got after my first "Cold": it's been most depressing, and seeing you would be a great help.

Affectionately yours,

Catharine Cabot

The Germans had already invaded Denmark and Norway on 9 April – before these letters from Toni and Katy were written. On the day of her planned trip, 10 May, however, Hitler invaded Holland, Belgium and Luxemburg in his sweep towards France, and she had to cancel her plans.

I was never told of those plans. Probably I was to have been left in Zürich on my own, occupied not only with the art school which Toni mentions but also with courses in household management at a state *Haushaltsschule,* which was obligatory even for foreigners. (Only a doctor's certificate secured an exemption, and while I tried hard for one there was nothing doing.) Girls *de bonne famille* normally did the course in six weeks as boarders in the Graubünden, while others attended a course in Zürich twice weekly for a year. Hoping that the War would end quickly and that I would leave Switzerland, I opted for the course assigned to working girls: once weekly for *two* years. It began on 3 May 1940. Early that morning with a young kitchen maid from the Waldhaus Dolder, I walked downhill to the Römerhof to take the tram to Burgwiess. Teenager style, I forgot an apron, so had to buy one *en route*; I loathed the idea of this school, being desperately shy about meeting a whole bunch of Swiss girls. When we arrived, we joined about a dozen girls in aprons milling about in a large airy kitchen with white-tiled walls and a number of cookers, sinks, and tables in strategic positions. Everything was very modern, but the food we produced was a lot less tasty than at Frl. Fülscher's private school; not only was the state school stingier with ingredients, but now, eight months into the War, rationing was beginning to be felt. On 17 May, when we came for our third session, we found the school closed; it reopened the following week, but with only seven of the original sixteen pupils present. Feeling that the country was about to be invaded, the Zürich Swiss left for safer areas. Those who still ran cars packed their families and as many belongings as they could take and drove off, some with mattresses on the car roof-tops to protect themselves from machine-gun fire or shrapnel. (Pictures of dive bombers strafing refugees in Belgium and northern France had begun to appear in the Swiss newsreels.) Their goal was the *inner Schweiz* near Lucerne, or what was to become the *réduit* [retreat] *national*, the Bernese Oberland – surrounded by high mountains. Suddenly Zürich was empty – even of dogs – and so, for the first time, I could walk with my belligerent Scottie off the lead.

For some reason, however, my mother and Tommy decided that we would remain in Zürich. I was only too glad to stay as I was hoping for excitement. As a precaution, my mother packed several suitcases of clothes and sent them off *poste restante* to Gstaad, imagining, I suppose, that if we had to flee, we could do so more easily unencumbered. Tommy probably intended to take the car out of mothballs for our eventual flight, because he and I visited the garage where it had been laid up. But fuel was becoming more and more difficult to obtain. It was only after everyone returned at the end of May that my mother opted for a holiday in Engelberg, not with our car but driving up with a Mr. Ochs, "whose wife was English," as my Diary reports. As schools were closed and I was at loose ends, I frequently went to the cinema on my own or with a girlfriend. We used makeup and lipstick to look eighteen, but soon discovered, in the usually strict theaters, that nobody cared: the empty cinemas were grateful for all customers.

The exodus from Zürich had begun soon after the invasion of the Netherlands and Belgium; people feared that Germany, attempting a pincer movement against France, would circumvent the Maginot Line by coming through northern Switzerland. My dairy for 15 May reports:

> Went to drawing school. On the way down [the Dolder Hill] saw many people packing, and leaving in cars. Everybody was excited. Drawing teacher's daughter leaving for Arosa with baby. Hotel [Waldhaus Dolder] completely evacuated. Everybody gone to Lucerne. Uncle at Saanen. Barbara Hannah and Miss Welsh at Gstaad. Mrs. Fingerhuth left. In fact, everybody. ... Packed in evening.

A strong rumor began to circulate that the Germans would invade Switzerland the following morning at 5 a.m. Herr Obertüfer, the Waldhaus Dolder director, brought us this news as we were eating our supper in the restaurant. Normally, I dreaded his turning up, as he always occupied my mother in long, boring conversation. But this time, it was different. As I knew war only from black-and-white newsreels, where gore is less discernible, I imagined it to be glamorous, and the prospect of an invasion excited more than frightened me. I fantasized myself as being an heroic nurse treating handsome soldiers in a Zürich hospital as the bombs rained down. The next morning at 5, I was wide awake. The sun was rising over the horizon as I waited for the invasion. I felt very flat when the Germans failed to invade. Herr Obertüfer suggested that the Germans had let us off because they had encountered so little resistance both in the Benelux countries and from the so-called 'impregnable' Maginot Line, which had fallen with scarcely a fight. Though tension continued into the summer, it eased as the Germans made good progress to the west of us. We breathed a sigh of relief and thought we would be spared. We did not then know that in fact the Germans still had an eye on Switzerland. The 800,000 men under arms in Switzerland by May 1940 posed no great deterrent to the German High Command. The greatest danger came in June and July; had French units attempted to take refuge in Switzerland in large numbers, they would have been pursued. Although France's capitulation eased tensions somewhat, the danger persisted until November 1940.

The Federal authorities discovered that Jung's name was on the Nazis' Blacklist,[1] so he was urged by senior officials in Bern to leave Zürich immediately. He drove the family car to Saanen with his wife, an eight-month pregnant daughter and some grandchildren. Lacking room for other family members in his car, he asked Barbara Hannah to drive two more grandchildren to Saanen. Miss Hannah also took a recent arrival from England, Miss Elizabeth Welsh, who stayed with her at a hotel in Gstaad for several weeks, where several more of Jung's analysands joined them. During their stay, Jung walked the three kilometers from Saanen to give the group analytical hours, and remained with them for lunch.[2] Toni Wolff, who had joined the *Frauenhilfsdienst* as an ambulance driver, stayed in Zürich. She lunched with us once during this difficult period, and we visited her at the Freiestrasse. Miss Taylor,[3] a "psychological lady" – according

---

[1] Both the Germans and the Allies had blacklists of Swiss citizens, who either traded with the opposite camp or were sympathetic to the other side during the War.

[2] See Barbara Hannah, *Jung: His Life and Work* (Putnam, New York, 1976, & Michael Joseph, London, 1977). New edition by Chiron, Wilmette, 1997.

[3] Ethel Taylor had been in Zürich since the 1920s. She took notes (together with Mary Foote and Anne Chapin) for Jung's seminars on dream analysis, she was not a member of the Psychological Club.

to my Diary – also stayed in Zürich, and gave us a good dinner (I note) at her pension with an excellent wine, as well as inviting me to her "cabin" for the day above Erlenbach. I remember nothing of these events.

Before the great exodus took place, Jung was able to give Katy the hour she had requested in her letter of 28 April, just before Hitler turned his attention to the Benelux countries and to France.

May 6, 1940

I told Uncle how annoyed I was over the whole episode I had with Toni, when having the flu this winter. It was about Linda [Fierz]. Toni seemed to think Linda should know that I had had the grippe, "as she is such a dear, good person, trying to arrange things for me in Ascona!" The irony made me boil. That Toni should take up the cudgels for her enraged me especially – for by now, she ought to know that one cannot tell Linda about illnesses.

Onkel said that one cannot always tell Linda the truth, that her annoyance with people who are ill is a revenge she takes because she had tuberculosis once, and had had to spend years in Davos. Only since analysing has she been cured and not had to go to the mountains anymore. I asked how 'analysis' had cured her. He said because she began to take things more calmly, and breathe more deeply – whereas before, it was just shallow breathing. Also she became more natural, less artificial and is now a peasant woman in comparison to what she used to be. Mrs. Jung also had 'experiences' with her. Once, when Mrs. Jung had the grippe, she had to call Linda up to tell her she couldn't come. Linda got annoyed and tried to persuade Mrs. Jung to come. She gets a *ressentiment* [feels resentful] when someone is ill. She was so sickly herself that now she has a satisfaction that those healthy devils are on their noses, and she just rubs it into them good and plenty.

As for Toni behaving curiously in the Linda affair, Onkel said that Toni hates to think of people who have a certain value being sometimes wrong. She is too fair: if she is in sympathy with a person, then nothing can be wrong and all is white; if she does not like a person, then all is black.

I then told Onkel that I heard I had had quite a difficult time getting into the [Psychological] Club. He laughed and said there were some dissenting voices [Barbara Hannah's and Carol Baumann's] among the people who felt disturbed in their own games, and were full of jealousy on account of personal shortcomings they suffered from (such as not knowing how to dress, having bad manners etc.): such people said I was not a suitable candidate for the Club. They criticized the fact that I was not intellectual enough and thought that [criticism] would cut ice with Onkel. Onkel said that he told them that I was naturally a 'child of the world,' and that I did not understand a word of what psychology and analysis were all about, but took trouble to learn something, and apply it. The Club should be glad to have members who were not intellectual, as they were always complaining that members were *too* intellectual. He said he always tried to right an injustice.

He then went back to Linda and said that sometimes she does not tell the truth at all. And she is sly and clever and knows Toni inside-out – therefore, she knows how to play on that instrument! Onkel added that I could be sure that Toni would not think anything nasty about me as she likes me. He finished the Linda topic by saying that of course one did not like Linda's "ill-wishing pity" when one was sick.

I then told Onkel a dream I had:

… *of him and Mrs. Jung being with me in a huge and beautiful hotel, on the sea, called "French Town." There came over from America to see him teachers, writers, philosophers etc. – all people of great talent. The Ralph Bradleys[1] came to see Janey and found us in this marvelous place. Tommy was also there. Onkel and Dr. and Mrs. Baynes came downstairs and saw all these people who had congregated to see him. Tommy waved his hand at Onkel, but did not rise to speak to him, and I was surprised. I went over to speak to Onkel. He told me he was leaving all these famous people to go home to Küsnacht, as their pet dog had died. He and Mrs. Jung were so upset that they decided to leave immediately to bury him in their garden. I wept a bit, and when Onkel asked me if I wanted to see the dog, I said, no, that I preferred to remember the sweet little fellow as I had always seen him. I asked if they really intended to leave all these world-famous people who had come to see them. They said yes, that the death of their dog had taken all the heart out of them – so I said good-bye. Then I saw that the Bradleys were astonished that it was so attractive in Europe, and were overcome by the beauty of the place they found us in. I then went to dinner and found Toni sitting*

---

[1] My aunt and uncle (Mr. Bradley was my father's sister).

next to Linda, and I squeezed Toni's knee, and she smiled, and all seemed well.

Onkel said that, in the dream, the death of the dog was a 'feeling' shared with him that would give me a connection with my feeling. I seem to be in a peculiar position with him, for he would not tell all those famous people that he is sad on account of the loss of the dog. But he informs me of the reason for his leaving. We have a feeling in common about the dog, or he would not have informed me. Squeezing Toni's knee is an intimate little sign that I am on good terms with her, and the dream shows my kind of approach to her. I am on better terms than anyone else, and trying to be on an intimate footing, which is compensating a conventional distance and uncertainty. What you dream is always a compensation, and it is difficult to produce a human feeling. He said it was of particular concern to me (and something I value highly) to a have a personal connection. The main gist of the dream is to fortify the feeling rapport, that liberates me from my unconscious. It gives me *a certainty, a foothold*.

He said that many people who are of the thinking type don't care for *feeling*. I said, I thought people without any feeling must be very unhappy in this life. He said that they were not at all unhappy. Not having feelings for some people is the same as when certain people enjoy traveling by sea. They just travel all the time on the sea. And so it is with people who have no feelings: they enjoy themselves as they are and do not miss what they do not have and have not known.

Some people enjoy themselves when alone; others prefer social intercourse and the admiration of other people. Onkel said he did not enjoy people and society very much. Whereas many Americans have to live a social life: parties and parties and people always dropping in. There are people who feel best when unloved, and, he added, most people won't make the effort to be loved.

Then we went on to politics. He said the English were not ready [for war], that was obvious. One cannot put up an army in five minutes. The English seem to be asleep. The French are behind in their aviation and their *"Front Popu"* [Popular Front] experiments. England had no army and no air fleet: they are not up to the Germans in planes. He said that Italy might go to war, and, with the Germans, they might take Switzerland so as to have a common front. He said he wondered why the English were playing around with Narvik [Northern Norway]. Why didn't they land twenty-thousand men there and take Narvik? They are obviously not ready, and have no army worth having. Mussolini is waiting to see what success [German] aviation over the [British] fleet will be. The English are too optimistic, as it has always gone right in the past, but it might just as well now go wrong. America has to look out for peace in the Far East. Germany may hurt Great Britain badly and force her to surrender her fleet; then Germany will take a trip to America, together with Japan.

America is coming into the War as much as she can at present. She's really in it already. Roosevelt had foreseen all this; therefore, he is building up his huge fleet to protect both coasts. Germany's plan probably is to threaten England to force her to give it her fleet. Germany relies on its aviation. Aviation has changed the aspect of war, and the English have no show unless they can be on parity with Germany. They need a thousand [airplanes] a month to keep up with German production. Together with Italy, Germany has two large airfleets – which is more than France and England can produce at the moment. They want to destroy England so that *they* can have the power. *Power* is a curse, and eventually they will cut each other's throats. Italy will be at the mercy of Germany, and Germany will take Trieste for certain. It will come to very critical times.

I said that I loved Italy and liked living there. Onkel said that, for a foreigner, it was very nice, but for the Italians not so nice as they can't travel and can't have an opinion. He said that 99% of the industrialists in Italy are against the War.

It is not surprising that personal problems in the analytic hour made way for general ones, particularly speculation about the probability of a catastrophe hitting Europe. An escalation of the War westward seemed likely after the invasion of Norway [April 1940]. Katy read the *Gazette de Lausanne* and the *Tribune de Genève* daily, cutting out articles, mainly about France, and pasting them into copy books. English-language papers arrived only irregularly, if they came at all, but like most people, Katy listened to the B.B.C. Radio [Wartime transmissions, broadcasting to the Allies from London]. The war was a universal topic of discussion, and Jung's view on how it would develop was of great interest to her.

May 23, 1940

Onkel came back from Saanen today. When I first arrived he gave me a long talk on why he had gone away precipitately. He said it was because his daughter-in-law was expecting (she was eight months along), and they had taken her and all the children to a safe place: he drove the whole brood up [to the mountains].[1]

Then we spoke of the War. I said I thought Lindbergh's [Charles Lindbergh, the aviator] speech was awful. Onkel said that Lindbergh was probably pro-German, and hated America ever since his child had been kidnapped. He probably says to himself, "What a hell of a country without a decent police. In Germany, that would never have happened."

Then Onkel said that the Italians are jackals, who are ready to pounce on the kill when the lion has done his duty. He said that the English may be forced now to pay dearly for having been asleep for so long.

The explanation offered by Jung was not the only reason for his hasty departure, of course; the other (see footnote) he could not divulge to my mother at the time. Saanen was in a mountainous part of Switzerland, which the Swiss intended to defend even if the *plateau* with all its cities was occupied. Already before the outbreak of the War, we knew of large quantities of food and ammunition having been stored in the mountain regions. It was said that wheat was sealed into drums and sunk into the lakes. Mountains were excavated and transformed into fortresses; secret cable-cars unmarked on civilian maps were eventually installed to transport troops and materiel. This fortified area, which stretched across the Swiss Alps, would eventually be called the *réduit national*. General Henri Guisan introduced this concept for Switzerland's defense to his army commanders in a moving speech on the Rütli above Lake Lucerne on 25 July 1940. This meadow was the site of the original Confederation in 1291 of the three forest cantons – Uri, Schwyz, and Unterwalden – [forming the original basis of what has now become present-day Switzerland, with twenty-six cantons]; the Oath sworn there, pledging resistance to any authority imposed from without [at the time, Austria had been attempting to invade and conquer this mountainous territory on the Western flank of its borders], came to define 'Helvetia' or the indepen-

---

[1] Only much later did we learn that Jung had been blacklisted by the Nazis.

dence and sovereignty of the Federal Republic of Switzerland. To General Guisan, the symbolic value of the Rütli thus far outweighed the danger of concentrating his entire general staff at the open site, ferrying them there in a single boatload. Secret preparations for a *réduit* [strategic retreat; refuge] had been underway for some time. The Achilles' Heel attached to this concept of a secret stronghold was that the *réduit* had insufficient room for the entire population. The question then became: would the soldiers still fight if their families were in German hands?[1] Later, it was thought that they would not have, but in 1940, nobody ventured such speculations; Guisan maintained that Switzerland had to be defended at all costs. This rigid attitude of the Army, personified by a French-Swiss General, was known to the German High Command, but they also knew that several members of the government were pro-German – thus at loggerheads with Guisan – and so might be easy to win over. Despite this internal division at the top in Switzerland, Germany hesitated to invade, not once but several times during the five years of hostilities. The Germans staged a number of frontier "incidents" to test the morale of the Swiss Army, and sent saboteurs, disguised as tourists, to blow up airplanes on the ground. The spirit which the people demonstrated, however, quickly informed Germany that morale was strong in the Swiss population – so they finally abandoned any idea of invasion during the last years of the War. Godfrey Cabot must have sensed the danger to us early on, because in 1940, he sent us the addresses of two prominent Swiss nationals, who could help us to leave Switzerland by air.[2] In a P.S. to a typed letter of 12 June 1940, he wrote in longhand: "I feel proud to think you and Janey are so near the firing-line & working to help the good cause." We realized the danger at that time, but we knew that the Germans found Switzerland a useful listening post, and that Swiss factories supplied them with arms and that some of these factory owners were on a Swiss Blacklist.

---

[1] The Swiss had two lines of defense in the *Mittelland*, one facing northeast along the river Limmat and the other, facing to the northwest – although the Swiss knew these lines would not hold up the Germans for long. The German High Command had reckoned that the occupation of Zürich, Bern and Lucerne, which they had code-named *Fall Tannenbaum*, would take forty-eight hours.

[2] Colonel E. Messner and Colonel Gerber were both friends of Godfrey Cabot. Colonel Messner was the President of the Aero Club of Switzerland, and Colonel Gerber was Vice President.

Though we knew that most of the Swiss were 'pro-Ally,' we did not know that the Swiss also supplied the Allies with precision instruments smuggled through France into England. The role of the Swiss banks towards the end of the War was unknown to us, though we had heard that secret bank accounts were introduced to stop the Nazis from appropriating Jewish accounts.

The same hour with Jung continues:

> He went on to speak of Janey. I said she was a 'mother-in-law' still. He said that when she gets to doing something reasonable, she will be more interested. [In leading her own life instead of bossing her mother about.]
>
> Onkel said one has an unreal feeling in Zürich during these days of tension, and one feels the vibrations of all that is going on near us. He said he preferred to be in Saanen, as he could think better there and could look at events from a certain distance. Here [in Zürich], one is too much in it. Then, beaming with pride, he said that Toni was classified in the Sanitary Corps and would drive an ambulance in case of war. He added that Toni enjoyed staying in Zürich – that all the excitement, etc., did not upset her.
>
> I then spoke to Onkel about the way people talked to me, as if I were a sort of lower being whom they condescended to and that I wondered why as I didn't feel that way at all! He said that I may 'invite' people to be that way. When people have a tendency to get you in a state [upset], it is because you invite them to try and get a rise out of you. Maybe it's done to me because of a certain apparent helplessness, which I cultivate – it must have to do with something in the way in which I talk, for a certain way of talking suggests a certain helplessness, which is not in my real character. It is a manner I have learned so as not to irritate people. It is a trap into which they fall. "If you change your manner," he said to me, "you will see that they will stop. You probably show a willingness to enter into their propositions."
>
> We then spoke of Mrs. Fierz, and I said I was getting fed up with her. I told him of sending the plant to Viznau by mistake, and she being annoyed, and never even thanking me for it. He said that, of course, Linda thought it was done by me in order to give her a kick. "She is a box full of tricks herself and thinks everybody else is." He said, I still minded too much when people were nasty, and I shouldn't mind so much – especially her particular foolishness, for

one sees how foolish she is. There must be with me the remnant of an inferiority feeling, for me to feel so much affected. He said *he* never was offended by what Linda did. "You must not mind, for [some] people *must* play such tricks." He said he knew people were foolish and stupid, but that he derives a reasonable amount of amusement from them. With new people one must say, "Here is a new proposition, let us watch and see what next." He went on, "You must always say to yourself that *you* are not the inferior person who has made the mistake. You must not expect too much from people, and must not be taken by surprise. People don't behave as reasonably as you expect them to. If anything unreasonable happens *you* are not the one in the inferior position. You should have asked yourself what was going to happen after that plant went to Viznau. It is now foolish to dread going to tea with Linda. If she tries to be nasty you must *withdraw*. If you approach her in a way as one approaches a cat about to jump on one, she will show herself in that light."

He said he was on good terms with Linda, but carefully avoided any topic which might injure. He warned me about talking about things of importance – things that *mean* something. You must be careful not to 'hand yourself out,' then you are reasonably protected. Linda has to be 'handled' and is a good practice piece. *I must talk as I wish her to talk*, and must not make the mistake of putting my *ressentiment* against her. Have less resentment and realize it is a mistake she makes. *You must be afraid only of your own emotion.*

To have *ressentiments* against people is an inferiority and one easily gets into trouble. One must not fall prey to one's resentment, one must try not to give in; one must be very conscious of one's resentment and the fact that one is not giving into it. Then one can hope and *expect* that something will happen to those people who are being nasty to one.

Someone else will take revenge for you: you, don't you take a revenge, as you will get into trouble. Don't interfere with your own resentment. If you are hurt by a person who really doesn't mean much to you, keep it within yourself, then it comes back to that person. The murderer will kill himself. (If you kill the murderer you have killed.) Someone else will do it, put their foot into it, that works in an extraordinary way.

Onkel continued, "When someone is doing something against you, and tries to knock you out, that knock comes back [to him] –

but you are away!" He said that, in Africa, the primitive medicine man sends his icicle. He sends it out against a man in order to kill him. First, he puts a rug and hat over his stick to give the impression that it is himself; then, he hides in the bushes. For when the icicle comes back from its killing, it will go right back to the medicine man and try to kill him, as it comes back hot and murderous ready to kill! The medicine man, hidden in the bushes, waits for it to come. When it does come back, it goes straight for the stick, over which is draped his poncho and hat, and [the dummy] is killed. The medicine man then grabs his poncho and 'worries' the icicle until it is harmless. If the medicine man was not aware of what was coming back, and didn't resort to that ruse, he would be killed."

Onkel added further: "If a man tries to knock me out and I avoid him, he comes to a fall. He is knocked out by his own emotion. If Linda does not reach you by a reaction, her *coup n'a pas porté* [her blow to you didn't attain its mark], and it is as if she were knocked out. That has an incredible effect and it is very dangerous to people." Onkel said there was a rumor that he was a Nazi. Someone called him up and said incredible things to him over the phone. Instead of getting angry, he just said, "You are mistaken," and hung up the receiver. Onkel said that he was amazed, and also suffered, as this person's tone had wounded him – but he held himself in, and a week later, the person died!

Onkel said that it would have given the man much satisfaction to have provoked his anger, but all he must have received was the feeling that he had not reached Onkel. Onkel said he was very angry and would have liked to have killed that man.

There is no greater revenge on a person than when their blow directed towards you does not 'arrive.' The person is hurt very badly when you have succeeded in giving him the feeling that you are not really hit. Sooner or later, such people are badly hit themselves.

"Keep your anger to yourself," Onkel said, "and *suffer* it, and if it hurts and smarts, then you know this is the hurt and pain you are causing the other."

My mother loved giving flowers and plants. In later life, the Jungs received them from her frequently, and I, too, was their recipient. Like Linda, I was annoyed, and in retrospect, I think I can understand why. For one thing, my typology was very different from my mother's. My view was that there were more important things to think about, and so these gifts often seemed to come at an inappropriate moment or to seem superfluous, a waste of money. But more deeply, I was also suspicious of the reason for these gifts, sensing that my mother wanted to draw attention to herself. I could understand why Linda was "annoyed" for it seemed strange to me that my mother was sending flowers at such a time. From Katy's side, flowers and plants were most likely her way of expressing feelings towards people, which she could show only by giving tangibles.

By the summer of 1940, the danger of invasion appeared to us to have passed. This was not the case, but seeing how successful the Germans were in France, we basked in blissful ignorance for a while – until the next alert. Italy had just entered the War against Britain and France on 10 June, but Mussolini did not seem to have his eye on us. The emergency had receded, but we were now surrounded by belligerent nations, and the possibility of a German attack was always in people's minds. No one was in the mood for parties. But my seventeenth birthday was celebrated on 30 June, for a birthday was an exception. (As was my own date of birth: since I had arrived at midnight on the 30th, there was some uncertainty about it; my passport reads 1st July, but at that age I enjoyed anticipating the event.) My mother liked to give small dinner parties, so she invited Onkel, Toni Wolff and Klaus Fierz to dinner with Tommy and us at the Waldhaus Dolder. It began quietly, but eventually became quite jolly. After the tension of the past weeks, everybody was disposed to relax before the next build-up. After a fine meal of trout, soup, *poussain* and a *Bowle* (fruit cup with wine, in this case pretty strong), I remember Klaus lying on the carpet in our sitting-room gurgling like a drain while Onkel attempted to pour *Bowle* into his mouth with a ladle. Toni, sometimes inclined to be disapproving, was also in good form. Throughout the War there was a: "Make merry now, for tomorrow, you may die" atmosphere, and people were inclined to drink more than usual, being more prone to inhibitions than nowadays and not yet considering social drinking a risk to health. Tommy, brought up in a rigid Victorian setting, was an example; he could relax only after a few drinks. My main birthday present was a bicycle, which would stand me in good stead throughout the War. Pretty soon, I was whizzing down the steep Dolder Hill, a prominent sledding hill in the winter; my dangerous exercise on wheels has since been long forbidden.

July 1, 1940

We started to speak of Janey's birthday party, and what a nice evening it had been. Onkel said what a change had taken place in Tommy, that he was astonished how Tommy talked about the [War] situation absolutely calmly, like an analyzed person. He said he did not dare say too much because once he had said to Barbara Hannah, "I hope the whole thing will not be a horrible catastrophe for England." Whereupon Barbara stopped the car they were driving in, looked at him angrily and said, "How can you say such a thing?! Don't you know that England has never been defeated?!!" He said that Barbara flew off the handle, so he said to himself, in the future, he must be especially careful, as some people might be particularly sensitive.

We then went back to Tommy's 'change,' and Onkel repeated that it was astonishing. I said that I had always talked and communicated parts of my analysis to Tommy, and that evidently he had taken it in, and it had opened his eyes and driven away the Victorian blindness which is so prevalent among the English. Onkel said that what I had learned with him were *general truths for everyone,* and it could only do a person good to hear them. Onkel went on to say that Tommy had become decidedly *un*cloudy. Formerly, he had been in a cloud, or as if he were looking through blinds, or opaque glass. "Now," Onkel went on to say, "one feels that the light comes in him and shines out of him. His *face* looks different, and very much more enlightened, much clearer, and he seems to have less feeling of inferiority. His trip back to England in September showed him how benighted those [English] people were, and he saw how he differed from those fellows."

Onkel added that it was very difficult to get men to come to analysis, that only women seemed interested. He said the [Psychological] Club was open to any man who wished to join, but that outside of doctors, only women joined. He said it was very hard for a man, who was not crazy, nor very neurotic, to make up his mind to come to him, so men got their enlightenment through their wives. In psychological matters, men are particularly prejudiced, but when they hear him through their wives, they go in. But when a man tells another man such truths, he resists them in a blind way. So Onkel said that he had come to the conclusion that analysis is handed on by women.

Then we got back to the War again. He said that the saddest thing was the tragic *insouciance* [lack of concern] of England. He said he liked England so much, and always enjoyed going there. But that *insouciance* and that extreme snobbism were dangerous, and should never have been cultivated to that extent.

He went on to say that up until two weeks ago Barbara had no idea that England was threatened. She was living completely in the past and had no idea that England was unprepared. She should have gone back to England when Tommy telephoned her [in September 1939]; then she could have seen for herself. Barbara is shocked out of her wits by the French catastrophe. Just two weeks ago she said to Onkel, "Now, for the first time, I realize that England is vitally threatened." It came home to her with a terrific bang. Onkel said that he had said nothing as he did not want to wound her national pride. He went on to say that one is very sorry for England, but England does need a blow over the head for her lack of *reality*. She must realize where she stands.

I asked Onkel if he thought Stalin was worried about Germany taking the whole of Europe. He said he thought Stalin's game was to play the two halves of Europe against each other. If Stalin penetrates too far into Rumania, Germany would have to send an army. But one can't see yet what Stalin's game is. It may be to attack Rumania when Germany and Italy are busy with England. Anyhow he is now on the new Rumanian border, waiting. He may want to go into the Mediterranean. And neither Italy nor England desires any strange power in that sea. The Italians have the Dodecanese Islands in order to stay the Russian invasion of the Mediterranean. Stalin might play in such a way that Italy has to join England to defend the Dardenelles. Stalin is trying to play the same role as England: always the two-power standard [tactic of 'Divide and conquer' or separate-and-rule].

He said he thought that if the Germans defeat England, they may wish to take Brazil; then they could take the U.S.A., from two sides, with the help of Japan. Nothing has been said about Japan, but he thinks there must be a pact between the two countries.

He thinks the French government should have left for North Africa. He says the French are rotten. He said that the British statesman should have read his interview with the newspaper correspondent, H. R. Knickerbocker – then they would have allowed Germany to expand to the east to Poland and Russia. They could have, then armed in the meantime. Chamberlain was a fool to give a guarantee to Poland when he had no army! Onkel had said to himself that either England was ready to an unexpected extent, or it was the damndest bluff one could imagine. I asked him if he thought the Germans could take England. He said they had a great superiority in the air and could bomb a part of the British coast until not a leaf was left, then could land on that part, as the British had built no fortifications nor shelters for the troops in the rocks.[1] He went on to say that even if Germany does not completely overcome England, she will be maimed. As for Switzerland, he thinks there will be a big German Embassy in Bern, which will tell the Bundesrat what to do. The Germans won't need to fire one shot to take Switzerland.[2]

Then I told Onkel of a strange dream I had, which is the following:

I got a bill from Onkel which I paid, but I was sad he had not written me a few words. Then I went to a large ball given for the soldiers. There I was reading a book of verse written by Onkel. It was a profound book, and suddenly my teacher (I was still young and studying) came along and said that she would be happy to have me study my grammar instead of reading such profound verses. I felt sheepish. I was then handed some letters, while still at the charity ball, for the soldiers. One was from Onkel, and this time there was an account in it for a ham (Schinken). The letter contained words of deep wisdom. Just as I was reading it, Onkel came up and stood next to me. I told him I had received his account for the Schinken he sold me, but had also appreciated the words he had written me. I

---

[1] This is incorrect, at least near Dover. In the 1950's, I took a wrong turning and drove into some extensive fortifications among the rocks above the town. Some helpful soldiers appeared and showed me where to reverse.

[2] Most likely Jung is referring to the defeatist element in the *Bundeshaus* [Swiss Parliament]. Marcel Pilet-Golaz, the President of the Swiss Confederation, would deliver a radio address a few weeks later (25 June 1940), suggesting that Switzerland might have to adjust to the new European order. General Guisan's famous speech, with the message that *Wiederstand* [resistance] – and not *Anpassung* [accommodation; adaptation] – was the order of the day, was still to come (on 25 July 1940), so the attitude of the Swiss Army was not yet fully known by the general public.

was glad he had not just sent me the account alone, for I would have felt lost if he had not shown me something of his soul. Onkel answered that he would never have sent me an account for the Schinken alone. I went on to tell him I was glad to see him at the ball. He said he came because it was for the soldiers, and also because Switzerland was at war, and besieged. He said that his soldiers meant everything to him, and on their way to Heaven and to their God, they stopped to see him in Küsnacht, and talked with him before going on. I was very much impressed, and said, "No wonder one sees you so little these days when such things are taking place at your house, and I wonder how you can tolerate 'us' when confronted with such a thing." It seemed to me that a world I had not known was opening to me. And Onkel pointed upwards, and I saw 'his' soldiers, as he called them, all going past, as on a cloud, a sort of apocalypse. They were all dressed alike in white silk shirts and velvet knee breeches, which looked rather like the 18th century. It suddenly came over me, that even Onkel could not save our souls unless we had the desire ourselves to be saved.

After I had told Onkel the dream, he said it showed I had better study the elemental things before the finished product. It is like people who build a roof before they build the foundations. Evidently, I think our relationship is an impersonal one. He builds up my mind and I pay him. It is as if I was learning something and being at school. Instead of discussing big ideas, I study grammar. The *Schinken* represents the personal touch outside analysis. (Having parties with him and eating, where I have a better chance of feeling a personal rapport.) But even when we are eating outside, I get a piece of Onkel's soul – and a personal touch – which I could not get in analysis alone. The third part of the dream is a cure of souls. It looks as if Onkel were busy with the souls of the soldiers, and had little time for other things, yet I assimilate a big part of Onkel's soul. The dream is in three parts:

1st Part – The teacher

2nd Part – The personal relation, fun besides analysis.

3rd Part – I see Onkel as a figure who plays an important role in the spiritual problem of our times.

Those souls were really spirits. That was an aspect I did not see before. I had an intuition about the general meaning of Onkel's ideas for our time, but I had not quite taken it in, as it were. This dream denotes that I share the big extension of Onkel's ideas. It is as if my unconscious says, "There is a whole world of thought and activity which I hadn't known heretofore." This denotes a more complete contact with Onkel than if we only had a gay evening and good food together. It is an increasing volume of understanding or contact. Onkel went on to say that a person who just 'enjoyed' himself with him, and only knew him on a 'good time' basis, hadn't got the whole message from him, only part of it. I should come to the realization myself, for my mind is reaching out for a more comprehensive understanding [of what he teaches].

This dream is a sort of program for the goal I would eventually reach: to that more comprehensive understanding of what Onkel means to our time. Onkel added, that 'on the surface' he meant far too little, but in the future he might mean more, and that one must see a personality *in its time and setting* in order to understand it completely. One becomes acquainted with a man, one knows his name and one can talk to him, but, one would also like to know *who* that man is: to what town he belongs, his position in the world, his beliefs, opinions etc., then a new light is put on the whole thing, and it gives a more distinct picture of the person you

Emma & C.G. Jung, Ascona, 1940

are inquiring about; you may hear that he is a Pope or King, then you visualize the man in his setting and get a complete idea of him.

Onkel said that up until now, I had not realized what Onkel *meant* for our time. This dream implies that I have a lot of thoughts which are in me but are not realized yet. I must see him (Onkel) against the background of our time. He said that he largely *belongs to the world,* and to the great psychical and religious currents of our time. He then told me how the Archbishop of York had asked him to come to England to discuss the devil and the further development of Christianity.

The dream shows that my unconscious is trying to fit Onkel into a larger frame which will widen my horizon. I have not the width yet which I could have. I am capable of realizing a greater horizon. I could widen out! Intuitions and thoughts come up out of the unconscious and will come into my hand. I must trust the unconscious.

Then Onkel told me of the time he was traveling in a train. Sitting in the restaurant car was a Swiss colonel in mufti [civilian clothes]. He asked Onkel the meaning of a dream he had just had. He asked Onkel though he didn't know who he [Onkel] was nor anything about him. He got angry when Onkel told him the meaning of his dream. (The colonel had just turned to Onkel and spoke to him as if he knew him and had been in conversation with him before.) It was the old colonel's unconscious which prompted him to speak. It seems this colonel gave up his general interests and became interested in every soldier's haversack! There is not much to a colonel who narrows his interests down to looking into every pot in the kitchen: that is the job of the sergeant. A colonel must not degenerate to that when once he has had such a wide interest. Of course the colonel did not like it when Onkel told him what his dream meant.

Onkel said that I must put something into myself, and the quality depends on what stuff I put in. But if one only has a *certain horizon* nothing will be changed, one will not grow.

He ended by saying that even if a fellow seemed a bore, one could find out more about him, go into the thing, and then perhaps the 'bore' might prove to be more interesting than one thought. With certain people, one has to hand out certain things. With other people, one should interfere in order to prevent them from saying stupid things, so that one won't have to correct their blunders later.

Two weeks later we were in Ascona for the summer holiday, arriving a few days before the Eranos meeting and staying well into October. A letter from Jung to my mother alludes to an unrecorded kindness, which could not have been the offer of hospitality, since our house on the piazza was tiny:

17ᵗʰ of July 1940

My dear Mrs. Cabot,

Thank you very much for your kindness! We shall spend one or two nights with Frau Froebe. I hope to be able to see you and your family while we are in Ascona. This year it will be a short Eranos-meeting. Thank you also for your picture postcard of Hospenthal.

Please give my love to Janey, and my best regards to Major de Trafford!

Yours cordially,

C.G. Jung

Jane, Onkel, Emma, Tommy (Ascona 1940)

Tommy's loathing for long-distance driving forced us to spend a night at Hospenthal before tackling the Gotthard's many cobbled hairpin bends, still visible from the Gotthard Road built after the War. We traveled by car as gas coupons were still available in 1940. Shortly after our arrival, Frau Froebe showed us her collection of early Christian symbols. Thereafter we regularly played golf, swam, and cycled. Our bicycles were handy in Ascona, and the road to Brissago without traffic was very agreeable. As I have said, my mother liked to cycle the twenty-six-kilometer round trip to the frontier to "look" at Italy. Shortly after the Eranos meeting, we had word of my grandfather's death at Pallanza, but could not attend the funeral. My mother, worried about what would happen to her parents' villa in San Remo if the U.S. entered the War, must have written to Jung on the subject, because she received two letters from him dated 16 October – the first, a typed one about the villa, and the second one, a letter of condolence in longhand.

Küsnacht-Zürich
Seestrasse 228
October 16th, 1940

My dear Mrs. Cabot,

Please let me know whether you agree that my son-in-law, Mr. Walther Niehus, take over the job of buying your house. I had a talk with him, and he had a talk with your lawyer and, being an architect, he agrees that he could do it much more easily than, for instance, myself, who could get into trouble with taxes.

The business could be settled at once, if you let me or your lawyer know that you agree with the choice of my son-in-law. As an *homme de confiance*, he is O.K.

Sincerely yours,

C.G. Jung

Küsnacht-Zürich
Seestrasse 228
16 X 1940

My dear Mrs. Cabot,

It is chiefly on account of my somewhat one-sided concentration upon my work, that I altogether forgot to tell you how sorry I was when I heard of the death of your father. I thought of it several times, and then something happened and it took my thoughts elsewhere. It is therefore with many apologies that I send you my

Jane and C.G. Jung, Main Street, Ascona, 1940

belated expression of sympathy. The death of one's parent is a painful experience under all circumstances, because it is a cruel amputation of one of the roots of our human existence. It means an increased isolation and an uneasy feeling of being left behind.

In order to lose no time, I have sent my answer to your request as quickly as possible. I think the arrangement I proposed to you is satisfactory in every way.

My best greetings to your daughter!

Hoping for a speedy end of the War,

I remain yours,

Cordially,

C.G. Jung

Dr. Jung's generous offer to arrange the sale of my grandmother's house to his son-in-law, a neutral Swiss, never took place. Obviously, the proposed transaction would have had to be kept secret, so I never heard of its prospect. Possibly the sale became unnecessary because my grandmother had made other arrangements. Swiss friends took in many of her possessions, and her cook hid some furniture in the country. Nevertheless, the houses were occupied in turn by both the Gestapo and the Italian Secret Police. Most of my grandmother's antique furniture was lost and never recovered after the War.

Our return to Zürich brought, in the next session with Jung, a review of events from the Summer of 1940. Life was comparatively calm in Ascona until Henry Clews came into our lives on 29 September 1940. My diary reports that during the summer I read a number of Jung's books, and other erudite ones besides, and studied Latin, and that on one occasion, we even spoke Latin at dinner – which, I noted, was "most amusing with such a small vocabulary!"

November 5, 1940

It was nice seeing Onkel again after so long. I told him about Clews & Co. down in Ascona. He was very interested, and when I told him about Quatrini falling for Janey, he laughed, and said, "Being from the Tessin, he *would*!" He said that Janey, being young, wanted to see the world and people, and that all we had done in the Tessin had been too much for me, as I now needed far less in that line than Janey, who was still young. He said he thought perhaps I should make a certain effort, to a certain extent [to be social], though of course Swiss people were not so extravagant as Americans in their going out.

We met Clews for the first time over drinks at the Ascona Golf Club. Babu, as he was also called, loved an audience, so immediately invited us to dinner. Before meals he would drink tumbler-sized glasses of Sidecars, Mint Juleps, or Planter's Punches, and begin declaiming. Through dinner and into the evening, with plenty of wine, his talk degenerated into repetitive nonsense, funny at times but usually pretty tedious. He had never had a job and continued his hedonism even in wartime, going to bed at mid-morning, yet would stand unsteadily at the first tee at 2 p.m., driving a perfect shot down the fairway. Henry Clews was in his late thirties but seemed older to me. He was the typical American playboy. His parents owned a house on the French Riviera near Monte Carlo, and his sister had married the Duke of Argyll. An extravert who had haunted the golf courses at Zumikon and Lausanne, he picked up acquaintances quickly and, like a monarch, formed a coterie who paid lip-service to his whims. His girlfriend, Leni Aichele, the Swiss golf champion, brought him to Ascona. Plenio Quattrini was a lesser golfer who formed part of Babu's retinue there. Plenio, a Ticinese silk merchant in his mid-forties based in London before the War, was married to an English-woman who did not join him until 1941; ignored by Clews and Leni as a golfing partner, he deigned to play golf with me, and serenaded me under my window. I fell for his voice. It never occurred to me that he could have been my father! As for my mother's needing to "make a certain effort" to enjoy going out as much as I did, of course my mother loved going out much more than I. For her, it was no effort at all, and she never grew tired, whereas I, though I enjoyed dancing with people my own age, was bored with all these people who just talked. My mother misled Jung about my enthusiasm, but he rightly sensed that Katy was overdoing it herself, and seems to hint that she should be more restrained about going out so much at her age (she was just 46!). Her summary ends rather abruptly, so most likely she felt the discussion was becoming unpalatable. All through my youth, my mother used me as an excuse for doing what she wanted to do, but did not like to admit to doing. According to her, she traveled to Europe because of my illness, partied because I liked parties, and went to Palace Hotels because I loved them. I became an extreme extravert in my teens, which must have perplexed anyone who really knew me.

The same session continues with the matter of my grandmother's house:

> Then we spoke of selling the San Remo house. He said that as his son-in-law was an architect, he could buy it as speculation and it would be 'swallowed.' He seemed to think that it ought to be 'sold' to his son-in-law, as very likely the U.S. would go into the War in the spring, or even before that, for Japan was behaving in a ridiculous way and getting cheeky. As America won't deliver fuel to Japan, she is up a tree and wants Dutch India. I said, I thought it would be a shame if America went in, yet he seemed to think it imperative that she come in – sooner or later. It was vital, he thought, that she be as long as possible in coming in, so as to be

ready. If Japan takes the Dutch East Indies, then America is deprived of rubber. Since the treaty with the Axis, it has been impossible to negotiate with Japan[1]. He added that the Axis want South America.

I told him how grateful my mother was to him for his kindness in lending himself and family to this *arrangement* for the sale of the house, and wanted to write to him, but thought that a great man like himself would not want a letter from her. He roared with laughter over that. The interview ended then and there, as it was just short of half an hour.

The bombardment and flight which I have described earlier brought my grandparents to Pallanza, only a short way from Ascona, where my grandfather died on 2 August. After my mother succeeded in getting my grandmother into Switzerland in early August, she stayed with us for a few weeks before going on to friends in Geneva, wearing white instead of black for mourning because it was summer, and getting onto a bicycle at our bidding, which she called her "wheel" and on which she wobbled all over the place. We also taught her bridge, and according to my diary, she was a good pupil.

The next session's notes give evidence of my mother's growing confidence in herself and her judgment:

November 7, 1940

I told Onkel more about the last weeks we spent in the Tessin as he asked me about them. I added that I thought Quatrini was just a child of his own soil, and very much imbedded in it, despite the fact that he had lived so many years in England. It has made no difference with him. He was very real and just one with his country. Onkel said that it was particularly so in the Tessin, though all Swiss are like that to a certain extent. They are really of the earth.

I then told him of Tommy's life down there and how he was trying to do a job with Clews, but that it was a pretty ungrateful job, and how it was tiring for Tommy to have to deal with such an undisciplined man. Onkel said that he understood all that but, nevertheless, de Trafford was enjoying it all in a way. I said that I

[1] Admiral Nomura, a senior member of the Japanese Government, visited Berlin in September 1940. He then came to Ascona, where he played Golf a couple of times with Tommy.

had not realized that, so I was sure it was just a bit too much for
de Trafford. Onkel said, "Nevertheless de Trafford's inferior extraversion enjoys it immensely!"

Then I told him a bit more about Clews, and how Toni had said
he ought to see a doctor; that a man like [Kurt] Binswanger would
be the person. But I had said I did not think so. It was the first time
Clews had known decent people, so he should first digest that and
get used to the phenomenon. Little by little, Tommy and Miss
Aichele would help him progress. I told Onkel how he came of the
'Robber Baron' stock in America – like the Vanderbilts, Goulds,
Morgans, Mellons etc. That these American robber barons were
not glamorous, as the name might denote, but that they were a
band of men who had appropriated a good part of the U.S. during
the forty years following the Civil War. These men grabbed property secretly and safely. (There is a difference between the man
who steals at the risk of having a writ issued against him by a judge
he knows he can buy, and one who steals at the risk of getting an
arrow through his throat.) These men had exhaustive greed and a
lack of scruples. The theme of physical cowardice runs through the
story of these robber barons. They were mostly young men during
the Civil War. They stayed in the background, selling their government leaky boats and worthless rifles. One of the Mellons, who
wished to enlist to fight for the Union, was deterred by his father,
who actually 'bought' a substitute for him; and the same with the
Goulds. Charles Francis Adams of Boston, a really cultured man,
wrote of the robber barons: "Not one of these great figures of
finance whom I have ever known would I care to meet again either
in this world or the next; nor is even *one* associated in my mind
with the idea of humor, thought or refinement." From such a
heritage and stock came Clews. Yet he had something in him that
would like to fight his robber baron side. He must be in continual
conflict. At least that is how I see it, and so told Onkel. Time and
publicity have begun to build these 'barons' into figures of heroic
size. But they were mean of spirit, timorous of body, small, greedy
and pusillanimous. One must remember, when analyzing Clews,
that his grandfather was one of the 'lesser' barons. His grandmother of eighty-seven is living still. There is in him none of that
[mentally] hardy stock of the early 'empire builders' like Washington, Jefferson, the Adamses, Benjamin Franklin etc. Those men's
dream was for an agricultural United States, where every man had

his land, his vote and his dignity. Unfortunately, Alexander Hamilton, who was one of these early figures, insisted on the British economic system being aped, and in the end, this brought the factory with its piecework, and sweatshops, and its big towns, which produced just the right conditions for the 'barons.' I told Onkel that and more – how you could see 'baron' characteristics in Clews. His drunkenness, his pride over his sister marrying the penniless Duke of Argyll, and a hundred other things.

Onkel said that he saw no reason why Clews should be considered crazy and needing a doctor, as Toni had suggested. He is just spoilt and likes to play around – as rich men are prone to do – with such ideas as going into a monastery or turning night into day. Onkel went on to say that Clews was an excellent job for de Trafford.

I then told Onkel how I had asked Toni the reason why the children of Americans and the English do not like their parents. She replied that Americans, in a country where only youth counts, had constituted themselves as rivals of their children. He said that was so, but also Anglo-Saxons educate their children by sending them away to 'Public [private boarding] Schools.'

These [upper-class] parents have an elaborate system of how to get rid of their children. In America, the parents are meeting 'other people' and never take time to see much of their children, so the children never really know their parents, for also the radio is going, or somebody drops in.

He said that Janey has so much of me that she doesn't know what it would mean if I were not there. It is not that she has too much of me, but she is young and likes the 'noise' elsewhere, as well.

Jung's closing remarks were true enough for this period in my life. But there were several things he may not have known. As the reader may remember, when I was small, my mother went away for long stretches, leaving me with a nanny, and when at home spent little time with me. She had been unable to nurse me, so that vital bonding never took place. Before my tenth birthday, there was little contact between us, and then much of the time we were at war. Most of my affection went to my two nurses, Minsker and Pradervand. Before my eleventh birthday, I began my career in an English boarding school, returning to Switzerland in the winters. (At school, I was called "the swallow.") I dreaded these returns to Switzerland, where I felt thoroughly insecure and lonely in spite of my mother's presence. Boarding school provided me with much-needed stability; there was no feeling of stability with a *Oison* mother! Adults, blind to my strange existence, repeatedly remarked how *lucky* I was to live that sort of life; though I disagreed, I was too cowardly to say so.

My English schooling lasted five years. When the War came, my mother kept me in Switzerland; therefore, suddenly, at sixteen, I was being "bonded" to my mother by circumstance – at the very age when young people begin to detach themselves from parents (!). Also, as I have already said, my mother then wanted to be my sister, doing things with me constantly– but only when we were teenagers together did we get on well, Katy dubbing me disagreeable and assertive whenever I showed any independence. Because she remained my mother, her opinion was always the 'correct' one; as a result, I became frightened to join in adult conversation or venture an opinion. Though I had been allowed to stop curtsying to adults in my early teens (still the prewar custom in Europe), I learned that the way to please people was to say what they wanted to hear. I became an expert at suppressing my own opinion. My mother was still treating me like a little girl when I was fifty.

Our tragedy was that – though she loved me very much– I found it difficult to return her affection. Moreover, her love took unlovable forms: she slobbered over me saying how beautiful I was and that I should become an actress or a film star, but also told me what a foul character I had, calling me *"ignoble"* in a joking way, and complaining that my mouth turned down, saying, *"Ne fais pas une bouche de truite!"* [Don't make a trout's mouth!] I was also told to keep my hands away from my mouth, as if I were a small child. (I could stand having a vile character, but I hated personal remarks about my mouth or hands.) These jibes at me, typical of Katy's strongly opinionated manner, were matched by less personal dicta that stay with me still: women must never pour wine, must never let men carry parcels, and must change out of their good clothes when coming home. Therefore it was of course enjoyable for me to be with other people who did not judge me all the time or make personal remarks; as Jung says, I liked "the noise elsewhere." Nonetheless, this healthy tendency was checked by a strong attachment that lasted my mother's lifetime, and that persisted through her presence in dreams for some months after her death. I am inclined to agree with my analyst, C. A. Meier, who felt that I had been held in check by her all my life, and only began to become my own master after her death.

Jung warning Katy not to smother her daughter:

Then I talked very seriously to Onkel, and told him that I was really ghastly when I first came to him. He had given me a good 'bringing up,' as it were, and now that I was at last brought up, I wanted really to amount to something in the character line.

He said that I wasn't really ghastly when I first came to him, only terribly bewildered. I was 'nowhere.' He said I must stick to something so I won't decay. I must not fall asunder. Naturally, I have to keep a contact with the world, so that Janey can keep a relationship to the world. But I must also have a 'retreat' and, at times, do something for myself. I must not make Janey my goal, or my oneness would produce a mother complex in her. If I make her my exclusive job, I would imagine I was still needed by her when she is married and gone. I must start now preparing something for myself so I won't cling to her.

Jung could not have been more correct, but by that time I already had a flourishing mother complex, one which through the years prevented me from having a proper and comfortable relationship with my mother. Tension was always there. Though my mother paid lip service to Jung's advice, talking a lot about mothers not being needed or wanted when a girl married, her constant advice continued after my marriage. She enlisted my husband in this project in her later years, the two of them ganging up on me as parents! Our only respite as a couple came when we left for Turkey in 1946. In this smothering behavior my mother was not unique; my theory is that mothers of her generation were so childish themselves that only by imposing parental authority in a way that did not allow their children to grow up could they feel adult.

Then I told Onkel of a dream I had. It was as follows:

Onkel was sitting in the clouds in the place of the Lord, in the midst of a large assembly, up on a dais. The whole picture looked like Raphael's "Last Judgment," with Onkel on the throne instead of the Lord. (How Onkel laughed when I said that!) Everyone was going up to speak to Onkel. Mrs. Mellon was there. I felt terribly because there were so many people, and one could only go up and shake hands, which I did. Then I went back and stood alone and felt

sad, and said to someone next to me that I hated leaving Onkel for-
ever – which I had to do. This person I spoke to said to me they
understood that as they had had to do it when they studied nursing.

Onkel said that the dream denoted that I should not make it an
exclusive goal to have hours with him, for I should see that there
are other people in the world beside himself. I must look around
and I will soon see people I can be useful to in various ways. I told
him I was trying to be useful in collecting money for the British
internees. He went on to say that I did not have to do *material*
things for people, that one can help people so much in quite
indefinable ways. Analysis and psychology make those who study
it more conscious, then they live more consciously and see what is
around them more clearly than before they went to the self. They
develop and see lots of things that others do not see. Then people
unconsciously trust them. ... And then Onkel said, when that
happens, his patients become aware that they have a place in the
world, too. He went on to say that he who *receives* will be called
upon also to *give*. You cannot get something from someone
eternally and not give in return. He then said, "You have got
something of me, something of myself. You will develop my
attitude to people. You will see things and think in a similar way.
When you are with people you will say things which puts a certain
light on them, and in that way, you can spread consciousness. One
does not have to do it in a professional way." Onkel went on to say
that one finds the occasion and the motive to make certain
remarks which prove helpful to people to whom one makes them.
One never has to mention the actual word 'psychology,' but when
one sees the necessity, one can talk – and you never know, your
word could fall on fertile soil.

Onkel said that a man like Quattrini was buried in his soil. Such
people are Catholics, and in a way children, and should be taken as
mere phenomena. Onkel went on to say that for Anglo-Saxons it
was impossible to get near southerners. You can't talk to an Italian
for he wouldn't know what you meant. They are quite childish and
have the 'experience' of instinct – it is their sort of wisdom – but
they do not bother about a thousand things which we bother
about. They are Catholic and cannot be anything else. Their blind
faith keeps them unconscious, for that is what religion does for
them. They could never understand what Onkel is after.

I then asked Onkel about the excommunicated priest [Professor Ernesto] Buonaiuti, and said that Buonaiuti had made very profound remarks in a lecture. Onkel said that he was well-educated, and naturally could give a profound sounding lecture without himself understanding the depth or the meaning. Onkel said that Buonaiuti is still a baby, and sits at home with his mother, and is a good boy. But he has no experience of women, and the hell of life! A man like Buonaiuti has a lot of book knowledge, but no knowledge of life! He is bright boy, and well educated, but has never 'died' or broken away from his mother, and does not know *what* he talks about. These southerners marry mamma; there is no problem, life is governed by the unconscious process, and remains so forever! The underlying motif in the life of these southerners is the 'mother.'

I told Onkel that I still got panics coming down in the Dolderbahn, or in a *Bahn* where I could not get out. He said the fact that I get the panics coming down means that I still have something to *realize*. When I come down to the basic facts then things happen. I can learn things.

I told Onkel that I felt as if something in me was ready to bud, like a bush with buds on it, but I added that I was not so sweet and nice. Onkel said *"Nulla rosa sensa spinis!"* – [No rose is without thorns] – which made me feel good. Onkel said to let the buds open. I said they could with warm, furry people like himself and de Trafford. With Toni it was difficult because there were so many icicles hanging around. Onkel then said that evidently I needed warmth, and I must seek warmth so that the buds can grow and open up.

He said I would get to the Lump when I imagine I am diving down. When I go into myself, then I will come to the basic facts. *I have a tendency to keep above these facts.* He wondered what the Lump would be. He said that, evidently, I want to approach the Warm countries for the 'sprouting.' I must go a bit deeper to things that are hidden: there, it will "get warmer" – as children say when they are looking for a hidden object. I asked Onkel how to get down to the hidden things. He said follow the heat like a lizard who creeps out of the shadow into the Warmth of the sun. (All this isn't easy.) He added that I must not be so self-conscious, and inasmuch as I am not self-conscious, I am warm.

I told Onkel that I was still 'small' about certain people. He said that one must not be prejudiced. When one meets a new person, one must say, "God only knows what this person means to me." One cannot limit, beforehand, by wrong judgment, what people will turn out to be. One must give everyone free access and have an attitude that welcomes people. One must not give the impression that one already knows all about them and their possibilities. One must give a salute to a strange vessel that might contain *anything*. When I get 'small,' I am taken away from essential things. It is essential how *I develop*. *People* can't make me happy. I am seeking that condition in which I am O.K. One always does that.

I told Onkel how difficult his book, *Psychological Types*, was – a regular 'brain-twister'! He said it was awfully difficult, and was the continuation of the German philosophy of the 19th century, Kant etc. He said to read Chapter 5, to begin with, about the "Types in Poetry."

Several times during this particular session, Katy indicates that she wants to tackle the shadow, for the subject of the Lump is broached yet again. Jung suggests that a warming-up (feeling) would help discover the elusive contents of the Lump. He mentions that Katy seeks warmth and needs it to help the "buds" blossom. Though symbiotically attached to me, my mother never discussed the Lump; I discovered its existence and its frequent appearance in the discussions with Jung only in her diary. As I have observed already that – like many women – Katy, when young, had desperately needed the affectionate warmth of a father – who, however, had rarely been present, and who, when he had been, was frequently in rages. Because her normal wish to be "daddy's little girl" – and, like lots of little girls, to "marry" him – was never satisfied, she *identified* with her father instead, retaining undeveloped feeling and a stunted femininity. In short, when Katy was not being daddy's little girl, she was being daddy himself – slipping from one role to the other – though, as she grew older, preferring the role of Old Man of the Sea. Jung often asks throughout the sessions, "I wonder what the Lump will be." The answer remained elusive, for Katy at least. Jung may have unconsciously picked up the Sea Captain's resonance, as he frequently uses nautical metaphors when discussing the Lump: "Give a salute to a strange vessel," "dive down," "go a bit deeper," and "above the surface," to mention just a few. Katy was probably advanced enough psychologically by 1940 to have confronted her negative-father animus, had she been able to visualize the Lump's contents, but she could not go deep enough – so it remained an enigma for her, though Jung seems close to solving the riddle, so that she might break out of the identification with the father which hampered her relations with men, even with Tommy. Only the fatherly figure of Jung made her feel comfortable; her relationship with him through analysis replaced the unrealized one with her own father.

Katy was careful to keep her disagreeable sea-captain shadow-nature hidden, from both Jung and outsiders, which may have prevented the personality of the Captain surfacing in analysis. With people she was close to, of course, this shadow side flourished. The father – whom she experienced as unfeeling and uncaring (he had been sent to a naval college at fourteen and had himself been raised without warmth), was the complete opposite to the furry, teddy-bear figures which she says Jung and Tommy were for her. With some of my own female analysands, notably the very sick patients I worked with at the *Klinik am Zürichberg*, I discovered eventually that a father problem had triggered the illness, but that it was hidden so deeply that they remained unaware of it, and only after many months of therapy did they gain insight that father had not been the saint they had imagined. As his deficiencies of character were remembered and enumerated, the insight gained so slowly and painfully let them recognize that mother was not such a villain after all. Katy saw her father's faults clearly enough to tell Jung about them, but with others, including myself, he was always portrayed as a saint, a discrepancy which suggests that her insight was not deep and so could not lead her to realize how much of his character she had inherited.

Although my mother's feeling problem inhibited the development of her personality, she did come to use her feeling more in the postwar years, when she lived in San Remo. Prior to that, all that I could register was her inability to give of herself, with her reliance instead on frequent gifts of flowers, clothes, and meals. Unfortunately for me, I never analyzed the origin of my annoyance with this excessive giving of tangible things, never asking Jung's question, "What next?" and so was ungrateful. My mother's later development of feeling came after the death of her second husband. In her last decade, she gave her Italian "*puer*" friends more than jolly parties and delicious dinners, for she actually saw their psychological needs and "spread consciousness," as Jung had bid her to do. I was not aware of

it at the time – but after her death, these men told me how much they
had admired my mother – how enlightened she was, and how she had
helped them. Some of them had lost all their money gambling, so it
was obviously not financial help or free meals they were referring to.
They made it quite clear that they felt they had imbibed much of
Jung's psychology through her.

November 14, 1940

I told Onkel about Janey's being invited to *Burghölzli* [Zürich's
state mental hospital] by Dr. [Heinrich] Fierz, and how interesting
she found it. But she was so surprised to find in the 'violent wards'
that the women were so much more abusive and difficult than the
men. Onkel said that women are so very particular and careful, and
better informed than men (when normal), but that when one
breaks through a certain defense with women, they are formless.
When they become insane, the ordinary shields and deceptions
drop off from them, and so they are utterly formless. They become
awful and obscene. When you have a certain relationship with
them, which is no longer conventional, and nothing is in between,
they then go 'the whole hog.' Women are much more inclined to be
without form, while a man keeps his form – even an insane man
does. A woman hides behind all sorts of niceties, but when the
varnish is gone, then everything is in the soup! Women are inclined
to be too natural and so have to cover it up with forms and
conventions and think they are everything, but they are not. As
soon as women drop that pretence at form, they become formless.
There is no deceit anymore, and their true natures come to the
foreground. Older women are afraid that if they behaved naturally
it would mean undressing.

Then Onkel went on to tell the story of the time he was with a
crowd of artists. Everyone was very drunk. There was a woman in
the party who was from an old Zürich family, and very *comme il
faut* [lit. 'as one should be'] in every way. But on that particular
evening, she drank too much and suddenly undressed in front of
these men in her own house (where they had all gone after the
party). Onkel said that he had to save the situation. The men were
shocked! "I led her out of the room and told her to put on some
clothes. The next day she never knew what had happened."

Such things can happen, Onkel said, when people are very
drunk. Men never get undressed, however, even when drunk, and

always maintain a certain form. Women, however, can do terribly indecent things. Onkel said that he would never dream of making an obscene attack, but more than once, he had them made on him. He said that when a woman does that it cools him off immediately because it reminds him of the insane asylum. I said, I would hate to go to *Burghölzli*, as I would feel so miserable and frightened. He said that my Lump would rejoice and get infected, and frightened, for it would be afraid that it might be tempted into similar behavior – for the behavior of the insane is most enticing, and shows one what one could do. When the formless side of a woman comes up, she calls herself crazy, and she feels she can behave like any old lunatic! That is why women cling to conventions: the more a woman clings to form, the more she is inclined to be unconventional. A woman is either very formal, or not at all. The more she is formal, the more she can break through conventions. Certain women who look nice and conventional, and sweet and severe, are quite amusing on the other side. Many of those insane women have been well brought up as children.

Onkel then told me of a patient he had who was from a good Zürich family: a girl of twenty who went insane and used impossible language – unprintable filth. She had schizophrenia. Her sister said that it was not so bad having her insane, but the fact that she used awful language in her insanity was terrible. He said, "You see, when you become insane, you remember all the language you have heard from the first years of life, and though at the time you have not taken it in, it is nevertheless all stored up for insanity. So it was with this well brought-up Zürich girl." Her disease had begun with a little shock. She went to visit relatives on the Riviera who had a big garden. She liked to get up early and walk in the garden and admire the flowers. While doing this one morning, she met the handsome, young Italian gardener, who smilingly said, "*Buon giorno, Signorina.*" She blushed and ran away– feeling herself to be an awful culprit, and a very doubtful character. From then on, she went from bad to worse. When she came to Onkel, she said to him that he must think a lot of bad things about her – think her a whore and not a virgin! While saying these things, she pulled off her clothes – and her uninhibited side came out! You see, Onkel said, that on this other side, there was not a 'nice little thing,' but a bad thing just as real as her goodness. She finally became so bad that she jumped at the doctors and went straight for the penis! She was simply fiendish.

People unfamiliar with psychiatric hospitals (trainees, for instance), *can* become 'infected' by the formless behavior of the insane, and are warned of the dangers when they begin an apprentice-ship in such establishments. There was a *Praktikantin* [a woman trainee] who brought an enormous dog to the *Klinik am Zürichberg*. The dog accompanied her everywhere – even when she visited patients in their bedrooms. I admired her tremendous nerve, as I would never have dared to bring such an enormous hound with me, and march him up and down the stairs and even into the tiniest bedrooms. Then it dawned on me, that maybe what appeared to be nerve was really fear, and that the mastiff was being used for protection.[1]

The experience at the *Burghölzli* alluded to in Katy's session fell on 8 November 1940, when I took the Number 11 Tram to Burgwiess and called on Heiner Fierz for our 4:30 p.m. appointment. Like many young unmarried doctors, he lived at the hospital, and I met him at his flat, where he lent me a white hospital gown. Then we began our tour of the various buildings, going first to the milder wards, then progressing to the tougher ones. As neuroleptic drugs were not yet available, some patients were very wild and verbose – especially the women. The men were calmer, usually standing about and smoking, permitted to light their cigarettes and *Stumpen* [cigars] at an electri-cal outlet on the wall. (The women, however, were granted no such privilege.) In a ward of particularly agitated women, the worst I saw, they had been placed in beds with smooth white walls to prevent their climbing out. Nevertheless, this did not prevent some of them from trying to scale these "walls" and milling about half-dressed or naked, screaming aggressively. One woman tore off her clothes before my eyes. The nurses had their hands full: hardly had they chased one down and put her back to bed than another climbed out. Previously, in a calmer ward, the women had appeared to be involved in a political debate. When Heiner Fierz and I entered their rather large day-room, one woman stood on a table declaiming in a loud voice. When she spotted me far at the back of the room, she stopped her speech, then exclaimed loudly that she could see that I was an

[1] See Jane C. Reid, "Der lebenswichtige Vater," *Analytische Psychologie* 17:38-56 (1986).

imposter, repeating several times in Swiss-German: "She can see nothing through her glasses!" Uncannily, she was perfectly right: to make myself look older and more like one of the staff (or so I thought), I wore my reading glasses as well as the white hospital gown that Fierz had given me. We were both astonished at the perspicacity of this patient, who had spotted my disguise at such a distance. Several hours and several other wards later, Dr. Fierz said that he was not going to take me to the Epileptic House, where the patients were far more violent than those in the "bath tub" ward. Though keen to see everything, I relented. When I finally returned home on the tram, I had a strong urge to embrace all my fellow passengers; each one looked so incredibly sane! I had never experienced this feeling with anybody – let alone strangers.

Katy's Diary then mentions a dinner party that took place three days after the *Burghölzli* visit:

> I told Onkel about the evening with the Messner girl and the Fierz boys [Heiner and Klaus]. Onkel said that in such a case the girls give the note and I had better play the old-fashioned chaperone. He thinks the Messner girl must have started it for she likes older men, and so does Janey, as they teach her something about love. But it is formless, and going a bit too far to get heated up like that. Such behavior is rather Dionysian, and the tendency of the time is to give free rein to the 'mass movement' and the Dionysian orgy – it is in the air – a Fastnacht all the year around. If I give too much rope, it's a particular lure for a girl. It is not necessary that, at her age, she has parties up to 3 a.m. It is too much – better for her to go to bed.

My Diary reports that the Rüfenachts[1] were there as well as Heiner and Klaus Fierz and a Regula Messner, the daughter of Colonel and Mrs. Messner, who had a fine property on the Lake of Zürich at Feldbach, and who might have helped us to escape – as my Grandfather Cabot thought – if the Germans invaded Switzerland. The older people apparently left early. "We had a rough house with plenty of kisses!" my diary reports. We were actually quite restrained; my report was mostly teenager bravado, and Katy's dubbing the evening "Dionysian" was absurd. Mrs. Fierz, who apparently wrote a furious

---

[1] Mary Rüfenacht was a Bostonian married to a Swiss man, and in analysis with Jung.

letter to my mother, possibly exaggerated her boys' so-called "confessions." But even so, Jung's admonition was correct: my mother and Tommy should not have left us on our own. My impression is that the Old Sea Captain personality came to the fore after a few drinks, with its jolly aspect, and so undermined Katy's conventional side. That lapse contrasts with the trait taken up first in the next entry from her Diary:

November 21, 1940

When I went to see Onkel, he told me not to worry about Dr. Fingerhuth saying I was an '*Asthenische Typus*' in the clinical sense. But he said I must be careful so that I do not waste my energies, because when one has a certain temperament one over-reaches oneself. I am too sensitive and take things too seriously. Things have too much of an effect on me, and I have an imagination that works. I must not overdo. One must never ask a doctor too much or one gets a terrible diagnosis! Just stop overdoing, for with my temperament and vivid imagination, things take on proportions they shouldn't, and I risk wasting my energies too much. My kind of vivacity depends on the wrong values. I consider certain things as important when they are not. There is no point making *small* things important: one just wastes oneself. Certain people make an elephant out of a louse. I have much too much imagination; I am not expected to worry about what people may be thinking. If I feel right about a thing, then it's surely the right thing … .

I then told him that Toni was a difficult problem for me in a way, as she was demanding and I often had to placate her. It made it difficult for me and like a burden I had to bear. Onkel said that Toni has too much imagination and is sensitive too. Take things quietly and not too seriously. He said that if he took things too terribly gravely, he could send people into spasms. Toni is apt to make too much fuss. "She is very fussy, so I don't tell her things for I don't want her to get into a fuss." Her sensitivity is good but full of fuss! Then he told me that Toni was so upset that he didn't have a clock in his car that worked, and fussed and fussed about it, and finally gave him a new clock, and saw that it was installed. Then of course he had to remember to wind it before he saw her, though at other times, he just let it lag! "I don't worry if she fusses, for I know that Toni is meticulous and fussy about certain details. I just say to her, 'Yes, yes it's all right.' People who are worth a great deal in certain respects, have bad habits in others, and her bad habit is to be fussy. If one knows people as well as I know her, then one laughs a lot until they come round. I never know, when I go to see her, what she is going to be like. She might well be in a hell of a mood, or absent. She changes like the moon. With the moon, you can tell – but with her, you can't. She is sometimes in abysmal gloom. She is sometimes quite impossible."

I then spoke of my relationship to Toni and how I felt her "clinging" to me. He said that – when the chicken is hatched, breaks out of the shell and starts picking up grain quite independently from the mother hen – then the mother doesn't like it. I then spoke of how good Toni had been to me when I first came to Zürich, and had had such hard work with him, and how she always consoled me. He said that Toni works with her mother instinct, for it is sweet to be a mother to helpless adult beings. "Never mind what mood she is in. Disregard it – for it's all vapor." When Onkel goes to talk to her, he says, he disregards the mood. It means nothing: you only have to get her onto something that interests her, and the whole cloud disappears. One just must not worry, and one must take into account that she is in a bad mood. She is usually contrary to what one expects!

I then spoke of Mrs. Jung, and the smooth and agreeable atmosphere she gives out. He said that Mrs. Jung does not worry unnecessarily about detail. She has the right values and is *interested in the right things*, – which keeps her mind away from the wrong things. You must have a real interest in big things: – then you are not interested in the small things. When you see someone fussing about small things, then you know that a *big* point is lacking.

I asked Onkel about his book, *Psychological Types*, which I am trying to read, and which is such a 'brain-twister.' I told him that I had started it at Chapter Five (as he had told me to do), which is called, "Types in Poetry." I said that I was very interested in Carl Spitteler's poem called *Prometheus and Epimetheus*, which Onkel analyses in that chapter. He said that Carl Spitteler was a Swiss from Basel county, and lived at the time of Nietzsche. He went on to say that Spitteler made Prometheus an introvert, whereas Goethe made Prometheus an extravert.

I then told Onkel that I was at last learning to work a bit, and not to waste time on non-essentials; that I had, in the past, spent hours and days doing 'sweet nothings' – and damn all the rest of it! I would write a letter, for instance, then read it again and again. Onkel laughed heartily, and said, "Well I hope you had a good time doing that. You certainly must have a lot of time on your hands."

Then I told Onkel I had the following dream:

I was in Onkel's house for tea. There was such a nice young man there for tea – a fledgling, who had never yet been in love. We all spoke of it, and it suddenly seemed 'sweet' to me. I went into a closet looking for something – singing Parlez-moi d'Amour *[Speak to me of Love] – wondering if it were true that he had never been in love, and having a feeling that he was for the first time.*

Onkel said that the young man represented my 'young mind,' the masculine personality in me that had been educated and trained, a personality related to Onkel, as Onkel 'brought him up.' This young fellow develops a love problem. That young fellow would fall in love with my anima. He hasn't discovered her yet; he is too young. (I did not ask Onkel what he meant by that but I will tomorrow.)

We spoke of de Trafford's anima. Onkel said de Trafford's anima was a gruesome person – like his wife. I spoke of the unsolved sex problem between us. Onkel said it was de Trafford's anima which kept us sexually apart – his anima is in between. I asked how he could get at her (the anima). Onkel replied that, as things stood now, de Trafford has no access to her, which is a pity. He should have a bridge to his anima, – for if there is none, then he has no access to her. (I must ask him more about that, too, as it is important that de Trafford get in touch with his anima.)

Then we returned to Onkel's book, *Psychological Types*, and how devilishly difficult it was. He asked me what I found so awful. I said I read along all right until I came to *Nominalism and Realism*. He said those terms were misleading, and asked me if I knew what an idea was. I said I thought I did.

He went on to say the following, "*Realism* was a movement in medieval philosophy, and the idea is an ultimate reality. Plato was a realist; he said that 'an idea' was a reality behind things. For instance, the idea 'book' is the reality. The idea of 'the man' is the reality, and man himself is only the application of the 'idea,' which is itself the ultimate reality."

The world of ultimate reality consists of things such as:

the man
the chair
the house
the book

Nominalism, on the other hand, says that what you call an 'idea' is merely a word, *flatus voci* [break of the voice]. They say that when a Platonist holds that an idea is a reality, then Nominalists say "That's air. What you call an idea is nothing but a word, for the *ultimate reality* is the object (book) itself. Those are only words; there is no reality to an idea." The Platonists, the realists, insist on the 'idea' being the real thing. There are millions of real things, but the real thing is the *idea* of things. They say there is only one book really which is the 'image.' (Idea = *eidos* in Greek.) The image is in a heavenly place, for if that were not so, there would be no book in the world. All things in this world are little images of the one great image: the 'idea' of heaven. Only one great man is in heaven – the God-man. Christ calls himself the son of man.

Instead of sticking to one topic with Jung, Katy jumps to others, leaving many important questions open, notably Tommy's anima. My mother had Thanksgiving dinner with me and the Jungs that same evening at the American Womens' Club and may have delayed writing up her notes, so she could have forgotten the question she wishes to ask at her next hour. But more likely she did not want to know more about Tommy's "gruesome" anima and how to deal with it. My own hunch is that not only was Tommy's rather anemic and disagreeable anima against sex, but also that Katy's Sea-Captain animus was not keen on sex either with such a "gruesome" anima!

Our Thanksgiving dinner party keynotes the quite active social life we led that autumn and winter, in spite of the occasional air-raid alert. (Both Basel and Zürich were bombed that December.) There were luncheon parties in late November with Miss Foote and also with Mrs. Briner and "her precocious ten-year-old son, Robin – who would" later become a prominent international lawyer. December brought with it balls and Christmas parties, including one at the Psychological Club for which I made the tombola cards. These entertainments continued into January as did the air-raid alerts. A laconic entry in my diary for 10 January states: "At lunch had an air-raid alarm. German planes but no bombs." This social activity marked a new development for Katy – who for the first time during this winter of 1940/41 – did not flee to the mountains to get away from "psychological people." Several weeks after her interview with Jung, Katy writes the following letter:

Waldhaus Dolder

Zürich

Sunday the 8th of December 1940

Dear Onkel: –

When I heard that on December 21st there would be a Christmas dinner at the Club, I asked Toni if she thought it would be a good idea to get a few donations from certain members (who could afford it) and have, during the evening, a *lotterie* for the soldiers. As Toni and Mrs. Fierz were very busy with other important matters for that evening, I decided to call up Mrs. Baumann and ask her to help me secure donations.

She, being very tactful, managed to get them from certain members, such as donations of pictures from Miss Hannah and Miss Foote. A quick horoscope from Dr. Liliane Frey, a gym lesson from Frau Stutz etc.

She suggested that I write and ask you for a donation of an analytical "hour" as the big prize of the evening and one on which we would probably realize handsomely for the soldiers' fund.

You are the *only* person from whom we are asking an analytical "hour." From the others, it's small gifts and a gym lesson, graphology and a quick horoscope. We are having only ten donations in all, including your "hour" – if you will be so kind as to give it.

Would you ask Miss Schmid[1] to call me up, or I will call *her* up on Tuesday and ask for your answer.

With kindest regards,

Yours affectionately,

Catharine Cabot

Catharine had become a full member of the Club in May. As a new member and also a timid person (or according to her own view of herself), she certainly became quite an organizer, with her Sea-Captain side to the fore. Whether Jung donated an analytical hour is not recorded, but the Club managed to collect a tidy sum of money for the soldiers who were manning the frontiers. Knowing how keen

---

[1] Marie-Jeanne Schmid was Jung's secretary and the daughter of Dr. Schmid-Guisan, an old friend of Jung's.

Americans are on doing good works, Katy soon turned to her Boston connections for further donations. In a letter to Godfrey Cabot dated 9 December 1940, she thanks him for a donation and tells him how the funds benefitted both Swiss soldiers and the Allied soldiers who were interned in Switzerland. This was to impress him since he had studied in Zürich and knew the German classics. She also told him that she was also collecting German books to send to the German P.O.W.s. (America was not yet at war.) Changing the subject, she boasts a bit:

> Am taking three courses at the university this winter and also Latin, as I found it was impossible to go on studying unless one also has Latin up one's sleeve. I don't think I have ever had such a busy winter since I have been abroad, for the War work takes up so much time.

All this was meant to be music to Godfrey's ears. Catharine's aim was always to show herself in the light she imagined would be acceptable to the person she was addressing; with Godfrey, she wished to appear "worthy," and [both study and] political events helped that image. With bombs falling on both Basel and Zürich in December – and just as Godfrey had written six months earlier[1] – he could now really be proud that we were near the firing line!

Katy's next session resumes with the Waldhaus dinner party theme again:

December 12, 1940

> I was awfully annoyed by Mrs. Fierz's making such a row about the dinner to which I had invited her two sons with Miss Regula Messner and the Rüfenachts. She called me up on the phone and began by reading me a 'riot act' – telling me that I had behaved badly by allowing the young people to remain alone after I had retired. She went on to say that I should have stayed with them. I asked her if, in Switzerland, the parents always remained glued to the young people (?). She said no; so I replied: "Then why should I?" "Well," she said, "you should have." Then she went on to the food and drink, and how it was too good for these days, and how

---

[1] See Godfrey's letter of 12 June 1940. Basel was bombed on 16 December and Zürich on 22 December 1940.

one must be a Spartan, Spartan, Spartan! I told Onkel that I just talked back straight to her for an hour and a half on the phone!

Onkel said that her son, Dr. Fierz's, attitude was depicted by the extremely simple dinner which he dreamt about. For Dr. Fierz had a dream that he came to dinner with me, and was seated next to Janey; on the other side of Janey there was a wall. Dr. Fierz said that it meant that he was in a position to have to talk to Janey, and that meant match-making in the air when one puts a young man in such a position next to a girl. He also said he dreamt he only had coffee and Rösti [fried potatoes] at my party.

Onkel explained that the extremely simple dinner depicted Dr. Fierz's attitude, and that he was up against the wall because of his attitude! [Dr. F. had interpreted it otherwise. See above.] Rösti and coffee are what simple [Swiss] people eat every second day, and it is a custom in better families to eat them only from time to time – but not in the company of invited guests. Onkel went on to say that he acted as if he [Dr. Fierz] were the son of a shoemaker and had been invited to the type of house which gives coffee and Rösti. With a small bourgeois idea in his head, he is up against a wall. Only in a tram conductor's family would you get coffee and Rösti. Never in the Fierz set does one give guests Rösti and coffee. Linda has foolish ideas [about being Spartan at a dinner party?].

I then told Onkel that I wished I could be more like Mrs. Jung. He said to repose within myself and not give myself away. In the Dr. Fierz case, when he came to visit me, I should have seen through him – seen that he was impolite to demand things. I should have anticipated how the meeting would go. Onkel said that I am always afraid I won't come up to what people expect of me, so I always overdo a thing. During the Fierz visit, I could have got up after half an hour and very nicely ended the interview, instead of letting him go on talking indefinitely. He is filled with his own importance, and not very clever, and just babbles on and on, and never comes to an end. I treated Fierz too much like a gentleman, and why did it not occur to me that a gentleman would never have asked for coffee and whisky?! I told Onkel that I let him stay on because I saw through him and, for some reason, I enjoyed the feeling of being with an ass. But Onkel said that one sinks below one's level if one goes on talking with people who are beneath one, and it makes them think that they make wonderful conversation. If a fellow expects coffee and Rösti from me, he puts himself down to the level of a tram conductor, and then being nice to him, and not ending the interview after half an hour, I raise him to a higher social level to which he does not belong. I should have closed the session after half an hour. One must not be so *gemütlich* [agreeable], for such people then forget the purpose of their visit.

Dr. Fierz had something to say to me and I should have handled it like medicine and ended the interview after half an hour. Otherwise he would go on demanding – as he has no form and is a spoilt boy – and at home is badly treated and has no such chances as with me. (Mrs. Jung told me that Linda [Fierz] would not let him go home to dinner unless he gave her twenty-four hours' notice.)

Onkel went on to say that, occasionally, at Bollingen these boys came to babble and, "I don't even ask them to sit down. They think I am their personal friend and that they can come in to see me and loaf about and bore me. The Fierz boys have no sense of proportion. Dr. Fierz has partial intelligence like his mother, but he's a damned ass." Onkel went on to say that I loved my new role of sitting with an ass and feeling superior, but, in the end, it does not pay to play such a role and is not efficient. "That damned Fierz boy," he said, "is so auto-erotic and thought he had passed such a lovely evening and never saw through his own damned fool conversation." Onkel said that there are plenty of fools who 'like themselves as they are' – in a foolish role, and one must let them be that way.

Then I told Onkel that I was always putting my foot into things and saying what I really did not want to say. Onkel said I must get over that habit – as one falls into a trap of one's own making. Slowly, one must learn not to get involved – not to get 'tempted.' The Lump wants to rush forward and jump into the fray. People try to provoke me, and I waste my time trying to let the Lump out.

I said that I found Mrs. Baumann much better now, and Onkel said that her Lump was an intellectual animus. If one tries to correct one of her views, she hits out. My Lump, instead, is a thing that reacts to social conditions. I try to rise to certain conditions and make a certain impression, and my social prestige means a lot to me. If people say this or that to me, then they have me on a hook. It has to do with my past life in America, when I had to reckon with the kind of impression I made on people, and it was important that I make a good one. Now, Onkel said, I do not have to make an impression on people or try to find the right kind of entry anymore, *for now I am what I am.* Mrs. Jung, he said, sits back and looks at the Whole.

Then I read Onkel my fantasy of December 3, 1940 – the fantasy of the Lump coming into his office, and of his opening it up, and of the exit from the Lump of the Fairy Queen, who had been excluded from me soon after birth, and locked up in the Lump; which I personally think meant that I was endowed with qualities and gifts which the bringing up of my parents sent into a gray lump, and which never came to life again until Onkel opened the Lump up. The end of the fantasy was Onkel and myself beholding the Son of Man on the right hand of God the Father high up in the starlit sky.

Onkel then asked if I had been to his last lecture. I said I had not been able to go. He said it was curious that we were discussing this subject because he had come to the Lump in his last lecture and had read an old Greek text to give his audience the mystic philosophy contained in these old texts. The round element was called OMEGA. It was a round lump of matter which contains the spirit of God that must be *liberated* through the chemical artist or divided by the sword. This Lump contains the Spirit, the spirit of the Lord. The idea in these old Greek texts is to liberate the 'Soul of the World,' which is part of the deity fettered in matter. Onkel went on to say that he mentioned that this World Soul was included in matter and has to be liberated. He then said to me, looking at me intently, that *if I don't allow people to draw me out, then I am capable of realizing the things within.*

Onkel said that the fantasy of the Lump was an intuition about my soul. That the Lump won't roll anymore when my soul is liberated from it. When one has an intuition, it means it is a 'possibility.' One always takes a long time after such an intuition to fulfill it. I must not allow myself to be drawn into such talks and excitement. My soul no longer needs to be protected by that Lump. He said, "You can deal with the Lump as soon as you sit back and resist the temptation of rushing back into nonsense."

I spoke of Carl Spitteler's poem, *Prometheus and Epimetheus.* Onkel said that Spitteler *did not want to know what was in his poem.* It was less morbid than *Zarathustra.*

While I was not at the interview between Klaus Fierz and my mother, I can attest that drinking coffee with whisky was not as uncommon as it may sound. In those days, the Swiss – normally drinkers of wine – immediately chose whisky when offered a drink by a foreigner. It was expensive during the War, but the Swiss male continued to yearn for it long after the War's end. As for the Lump, Katy would never be liberated from it. It should be interpreted not as the Fairy Queen of her fantasy, but rather as "the spirit of her father." She continued to be lured into "nonsense" because feelings of inferiority kept holding her back; no wonder she yearned to be like Mrs. Jung, whose maturity she sensed. Later on in the War, Katy arranged to have hours with Mrs. Jung from time to time. When she was in an hour with Jung himself, even when older, she hid the ambitious and rather disagreeable Sea-Captain personality from him. Even when younger, she showed some of his mental traits, the competent as well as the fierce ones; she was no timid maiden in difficult situations, and met all types of challenges well, as we shall see later. Among these were bad-weather conditions at sea. Astonishingly, she was very much at ease on a ship even when it was rolling about in a storm. When other passengers lay prone in their cabins, Katy ministered to them with her favorite remedy, champagne. She insisted that it settled the stomach, but advocated taking only small sips. When not nursing the sick, she was either up on deck or eating a hearty meal in the deserted dining room. Back on land, Katy would revert to her hesitant personality. Glimpses of the other appeared, however, on occasion. She became "one of the boys" at parties as she grew older, drinking heartily, exchanging ribald jokes, and wearing unflattering attire to fancy-dress parties. Her favorite costume was that of a Swiss peasant wearing a black *Zipfelmütze* [a cap with a tassel], a blue embroidered blouse, black trousers, boots, and a cherry-wood pipe with a silver lid, which she actually smoked. A thick grey beard, carefully shaped and glued to her face by a hairdresser, would complete the disguise. Katy had a deep voice, which she was rather proud of – a voice that had been broken in her youth, she said, when her mother had forced her to take singing lessons. This whole masculine side of her nature she counteracted by showing an inordinate love of clothes, which had to be French and *haute couture*. Her trips twice each year to Paris had to go by the board during the War, which forced her to make do with the *couture* houses of Zürich and Geneva!

C.G. Jung in his garden, 1937

Chapter Eight

The Lowest Point of the War –
Winter 1941 to Spring 1942

Waldhaus Dolder
Zürich
Saturday January 18th, 1941

Dear Onkel:

Miss Schmid tells me that you are starting to see people again next week and I so hope that you will see me, as there is *so much* I want to talk to you about and tell you.

I have had news from my lawyer in America, at last, and he says he thinks he ought to leave the decision about the Villa Aloha in San Remo to a wiser head than his![1] He will cable me the money any day that I wish it, so that if you still think it "wise" to sell it to Mr. Niehus, we can do it, as soon as I get my mother's permission, who is in Geneva.

Hoping that you had a very happy Xmas and wishing you the best of everything for 1941,

Yours affectionately,

Catharine Cabot

P.S. I have been going to all your lectures and can't tell you how much they have meant to me. I had a tremendous panorama the

---

[1] The lawyer in America was Merrill Griswold. The offer to buy the Villa was made in Jung's letter of 16 October 1940 (and is also mentioned in the Diary on 5 November 1940).

last time, which I would like to talk to you about.

C.C.

Would you kindly give the enclosed note to Mrs. Jung.

Katy received her appointment, but in her account of the session, she does not mention the Villa.

January 22, 1941

I told Onkel of de Traffords's dream: of the weights being brought to his bed, and he being asked by a man in classical robes to take in his hand a hand grenade to see if it were heavy enough – this classical figure said it was heavy enough after de T. had adjusted it, and put it back on some scales. Onkel said the dream was an impersonal one, typical of a man like de T., who is so impersonal. It has much to do with the actual situation in England, and how he takes this actual situation. This classical figure who appeared to de Trafford in a dream, and looked like Pluto, is very interesting because, in astrology, the star [planet] which rules wars is Pluto. The Dictators are under the constellation of Pluto. The dream has to do with the actual suspended condition – the scale with nothing on it is the German side which de T. takes too lightly.[1] The side which holds the hand grenade, which needs adjustment, is the English side, which is not prepared for this War: the English are not sufficiently armed to hold the balance of power. Their armaments should be 'heavier.' De Trafford knows that side and is disappointed that the British defences are so thin.

Onkel went on to say that it was terrible that the British had not realized the German danger and had insufficient weapons – but added that it is typically English not to be willing to see a thing as it is: consequently, they refused to see that there was a German menace anywhere about. Just typically English never to make a fuss about a problem, and to act as if it did not exist! They simply ignored Hitler's strong position, and saw 'nothing'! Hore Belisha[2] saw the German threat, so he was kicked out! The British just put

[1] The Battle of Britain had been won by the Royal Air Force. In the winter of 1940-41, Hitler was already planning to attack Russia.

[2] Leslie Hore Belisha (1893-1957), later Sir Leslie, then Lord Hore Belisha, Secretary of State for War from 20 May 1937 to 5 January 1940, when he resigned. In Britain, "Belisha Beacons" now illuminate pedestrian crossings.

their heads in the sand – a damn foolish and dangerous thing to do, either politically or in one's personal life. It is typically English, even when they see a problem, to make believe that they have not seen it. The English think one must not make a fuss and that things will just take care of themselves. In many wars, they have first been shockingly beaten – then wake up and take notice!

Gammelin[1] climbed so high because he refused to tell the British the truth [about the French army's lack of preparedness], and they loved him as he only painted a rosy picture. He just refused to say disagreeable things to anyone so became 'Generalis-simo'! He was altogether passive, and though he foresaw what would happen, he could not tell the English because it would have disconcerted them, and he might have lost his job. Gammelin was hypnotized by the danger. But he did not want to shock people for fear of being brushed aside. The British were better prepared than the French, but were not up to the real size of the thing!

No Englishman is up to the size of a problem for the very reason that he refuses to admit that there is a problem. De Trafford is not up to his *own* problems, and in his personal life, he expresses himself in the collective style of his nation. That dream of his was a collective dream. His problem is: can the British hold the balance? The British have said all along that the Germans were bluffing, yet when it came to a showdown, they were in fact well-prepared.

Onkel went on to say that all Italians were against the War because they were losing business. He said that Mussolini garbled all their prospects, and that Milan and the whole north of Italy is in upheaval. Italy will suffer the fate of Rumania, for the Germans have rushed a lot of troops to Italy.

Then Onkel went back to de T., and said again that he had the same attitude to a personal problem as the whole British nation has. Englishmen who have had de T.'s type of education just have 'no problems.' They would rather die than talk about or admit to a personal problem. De Trafford ought to wake up – just as his country should have done! He should increase his personal arma-ments so as to deal with the unconscious. In England, there isn't any unconscious. The Germans are the 'unconscious' of the British

[1] Maurice Gustave Gammelin (1872-1958), Allied Commander-in-Chief in France, 1939. He was relieved of his post in May 1940.

which they refuse to admit. By refusing to see and admit to the unconscious, it just breaks loose and devastates the world.

Onkel said that the Germans were in league with the devil, and had a lust for power which is satanic. I told Onkel that I thought the English had a lust for power, too. He said that they did, but were more decent about it, and allowed others to live. Onkel then went on to say that the Germans were Faust in his pact with Satan.

He said that the English have an irrational attitude and that the main line of British policy is never rational. It looks to them, and to the outsider, as if it were rational because they rationalize it and are sure of themselves: they are able to put it across to themselves, and to the world, that they are right in all things. Everyone then says how marvelous the British are. But they are thoroughly irrational! It is marvelous how they come out on top! They have the extraordinary virtue that they can suddenly pick up again. He went on to say that the first time Mussolini met Hitler, he exclaimed, *"Ma che è un Signorino!"* [Why, he is but a boy!] Mussolini is all that he is on the surface, whereas Hitler, on the surface, is all that he is not. Hitler is sinister – like the mild little schoolmaster who has lived and taught all his life in a quiet village, and whom everyone presumes to be harmless. Then, suddenly, this mild little man ups and murders his whole family. Mussolini's life is a reality, and everything that he is is in the foreground: it is in his face and manner and in his every gesture. Hitler is just the contrary; he can only impress a German who is very intuitive, and who 'smells' what is behind Hitler. Hitler is infected by the Unconscious and only a person who is 'infected' can 'infect.'

When Mussolini first met Hitler, he thought: "Poor beggar; there is nothing to him – just a *Signorino*." But he never asked himself where was the *Signorina* (Anima) behind Hitler. Hitler's *Signorina* – the ambitious anima devil-woman – is not a 'human being.' A human being would have boundary lines somewhere, but Hitler's woman is without limits: she goes to the stars – reaches for the stars!

Then going back to de Trafford, Onkel then said that de T. deals with his problems as if they were too light, and like his nation, he underrates the *terrific onslaught* of the unconscious.

The British had to give in to Italy, in the Abyssinian War, because they were not armed and would not arm. At that time they had an ass as a Prime Minister. Chamberlain was terribly misled by the German women who kissed his hands when he flew to Germany. If he had had any intelligence at all, he ought to have concluded, from the German women's demonstrations, that Germany was very near to war – otherwise, why would the women be so upset?

Onkel said that de T. was no doubt suffering with this unconscious of his, which he will not admit exists, and to whose voice he refuses to listen. If de T. suffers enough with the knocking of his unconscious to be let out to live, he may talk about it, and valuable things may come to light. But de T. is like his own nation: asleep. As it is with the British nation, so it is with de T. *All his valuable and reasoning qualities are in the unconscious.*

The British are just about to be overcome, Onkel said – yet if they do get through, it will be by the skin of their teeth and with terrific losses.

Then we changed subjects, and I told Onkel how bored I got, at times, with certain people to whom I had to be nice. Onkel said that we are all concerned with people around us, and that he is terribly bored with people at times, but nevertheless tries to help them along. I told him about Mr. Fessler's[1] accident. Onkel said that obviously Mr. F. did not want to acknowledge a truth, and then the unconscious overcame him, and he slipped in his bathroom. I told Onkel that I was always saying something awful which I regretted later. He said that when one feels particularly frank then there is always an 'unconscious' in the company who wants [to hear] a truth.

Tommy unfortunately never "woke up" in the psychological sense, and was shortly to be overwhelmed by a horrible illness. His reckless side made him oblivious to the effects of heavy smoking and drinking on his body. My mother's Sea-Captain side, of which she was equally unconscious, in turn encouraged her to indulge in the excesses of good living, which eventually undermined her own health, too. At the time of this conversation, the War was at its lowest ebb for Britain, just before the news of the first British successes in North Africa against the Italians, notably at Tobruk on 20/21 January 1941.[2] In a

---

[1] Walter Fessler, Sr. was a senior Director of the Crédit Suisse Bank in Zürich.

[2] The Germans had sent Field Marshal Erwin Rommel's Army to reinforce the Italians. Tobruk was to change hands five times and was finally taken by the British in November 1942.

letter to her brother-in-law, Ralph Bradley, on 17 February, my mother wrote of these victories, that they "of course made people feel much better, but now one wonders what will happen in the spring. ..." The Swiss were much concerned with whether Hitler would invade and defeat England. With most of Western Europe in German hands, Switzerland's fate depended on Britain's ability to defend itself. The feeling was that, if Britain fell, a Gauleiter would soon be posted to Bern. Everybody hoped that Hitler would do something stupid, but nobody in the winter of 1940-1941 imagined that he would be so foolish as to attack Russia. They would nod their heads and murmur under their breath something that sounded like '*der deutsche Michel*,'[1] hoping for his downfall.

We spent the entire winter in Zürich, my supposed need for mountain air completely forgotten. I skated about five hours a day on the Dolder rink – three hours in the morning, and two in the evening, and studied German and French regularly. My mother and I had occasional Latin lessons with Frl. von Franz, but unfortunately they took place at 8 p.m. after a busy day, and we were not fresh; Frl. von Franz always gave "lots of homework," my diary notes. I took no drawing lessons in winter, as skating occupied much of my time, especially in the evenings; I was preparing for my Swiss Gold Test. But the evenings were not all work. I was invited to a number of balls, post-ball *Katerbummel* ["hangover strolls"], and *thés-dançants* [tea parties with dancing] on the weekends. I did not miss the mountains for one second! In fact, I was thoroughly sick of them because of the long pre-war years of constant skating at the sacrifice of skiing. Now my skating career was on its last lap; I had secretly vowed that once my Gold Test was behind me I would never put on skates again. What I had once enjoyed as a pastime I had grown to loathe, in spite of having a number of friends on the Dolder rink who made the long hours of obsessive figure-skating practice tolerable. I longed to skate on the Dutch canals and travel from town to town, but that was not to be. Several of these skating friends would later become champions. On 22 February, with other skaters from Zürich, I and Karli Enderlin (later, several times a Swiss champion) entrained for the Federal Gold Test at Basel that year. Rain had covered the outdoor rink with a film

---

[1] The straightforward sense of this phrase – "a plain honest German" – was adopted by the Swiss during the War to imply that Germans typically made oafish mistakes and that they hoped Hitler would prove to be no exception.

Dr. Marie-Louise von Franz

of water, but the sun came out when the test began at 9:30 a.m., and by 2 p.m., we had performed all the necessary figures and received our certificates. I came in 6th out of ten. I did skate on the Dolder rink the following winter, but only to see my friends. My mother was resigned to my giving up skating, and now began to suggest I should become an actress.

The next several sessions would lay the groundwork for a step in my mother's development at that time:

February 7, 1941

I told Onkel that it was pure joy to see him again because I had been through so much in the last ten days with Toni. Every time I went to her, I felt as if I were in a dark cave with bats and owls flying about, and with spiders, snakes and toads – and with occasional witches whizzing about on broomsticks, too.

He said that it showed that the DEVIL was abroad when one had such feelings about a person, and that it was best to gain distance between oneself and that person, or otherwise something very disagreeable would happen. I said that it was not going to be easy to 'leave' Toni, as it were, and I dreaded doing it, but realized it must be done. Whereupon he said that it certainly must be done.

He said to write Toni that there is an incompatibility – that there is 'something between us.' He said that the whole thing was certainly the devil, and that if I go on, I will 'tickle' the devil. These bats and toads are stirring, and if I take up such devils, I will start [activate, beget] more devils. I must tell Toni that there is a sort of incompatibility between us, and that I would like to be more impersonal. If I don't want to get nasty with her, then I must stop work with her – for one can't get too close to the devils. If I do the right thing as concerns myself, then it is the right thing for everybody.

Then Onkel went on to say that such a thing would necessarily become a problem for Toni – if it were going to become a problem at all. But perhaps she would not be destined to have it become a problem and would go on as she is, for not everyone is fated to see clearly.

I rather cut in and asked Onkel why it was that women grew so hard as they grew older – whereas men grew so mellow. Onkel said the following: "As a man grows older, he changes into softer matter. I'm becoming a sort of 'mother.' The feminine quality comes up in a man if he has any wisdom at all. It's the man's anima which he allows to rule with her wisdom – Sophia – the eternal mother of wisdom which is in a man. As a young man, he may have been a treacherous animal, or a damn fool, but in either case, unless he allows his feminine wisdom to rule in later life, he becomes just a grumbling and disagreeable old man, instead of being benign."

"In older women, all the masculine qualities, which always lie dormant in a woman – just as the feminine ones lie dormant in a man, come out and assert themselves, and the woman becomes hard of purpose and hard in outlook. And if she can't manage to turn it into spirituality, then it becomes hardness, coolness of spirit. Mrs. Jung turned her animus into spirit and now has that serenity of the evening sky in late autumn. That is why in the second half of life a woman must look to spirituality, and achieve it, if she wants to escape being hard. If a man can't turn his anima into Sophia, he remains a damn fool. He simply must allow that womanly wisdom to come out in him."

Then I read Onkel a long fantasy which I had had about seeing God. It was long, and when I had finished Onkel did not say much, but looked solemn. I asked Onkel how it was that he could write scientific books with such *heart*. One could give most people these scientific books to read and they would only say that the books were too difficult and that they did not understand them. But later, as one studied and understood them, one found out that they were not only works of great scientific value, but written with warmth and feeling as well.

He said first that the fantasy of seeing God that I had read him was what my standpoint ought to be. Then – as to his works – he said that one must be a *total* man to write such things. Most people do not write that way because they are afraid of criticism and have too little feeling – no passion – only selfishness. People who read his books only see something intellectual in them – along with their own feelings about them. They are not developed enough to appreciate the feeling quality which is in his books. He said that his works were not only scientific, but that there was also *wisdom* in them and they were *human*.

I told him that his lectures at the university were so full of feeling, and of such marvelous simplicity, that they had a sort of church atmosphere. (My way of expressing *his* atmosphere.)

Then he said, "If the devil gets into a thing, one must clear out [remove oneself] as well as one can. It is not agreeable to have to do so." He went on to say that I must tell Toni that I have a feeling that she is turning things back into the personal – that I have had enough of the personal and I propose to stop for a while – these are my thoughts about the situation. To protect myself against the confusing effect of emotion, I must not go on with my analysis with her.

Then he told me Toni's dream: It seems that she left her bag on a stone wall out in the open somewhere. It had a lot of money in it, also the keys to her house, to her safe and to her car, and it contained certain important papers. She rushed back to where she had left it, but in its stead, she found Katy Cabot's bag.

Onkel said the dream showed that there must be a projection somewhere: an unconscious identity with me. Now the devil is trying to get in, in order to explode that identity. The dream denotes that we are like Siamese twins in some unconscious part of ourselves. Toni is trying to kick away that identity. There are unconscious parts in me with which Toni identifies. We have something similar in the unconscious and we don't know it. Both of us have the same lump or aspect. When Toni is trying to get me back into the personal; it is because she herself is so personal that she doesn't want me to grow out of that personal stuff. Toni is very good at clearing up the personal unconscious of people, because she is interested in it. But she makes no headway with people who want to get out of the personal into the impersonal. I then told Onkel that it was just stupid for me to be sitting there, paying her twenty francs an hour, *to come down to her level* to please her. On the contrary, she ought to be paying me twenty francs an hour for doing it (!).

Onkel went on to say that he had asked Toni what she had in common with me, whereupon he felt himself encountering something dull and black in her mood, and he couldn't penetrate it. He said to her: "The fact is that you have something in common with Mrs. Cabot, and you are neglectful about it. If you leave your bag in a public place, then you deliver yourself over to the street."

He went on to say that Toni is open to criticism, *but won't [refuses to] see herself.* He said it was a very difficult thing for certain people to do, and for some quite impossible. An idiosyncracy which cannot be forced – otherwise, you ruin things and do no good. Here is something she can't see and *doesn't want to see.* It has to develop, and if he pointed out the truth to her, she would complain that he had forced her hand; but if she discovers it herself, then something has been done of real value to herself. She is very intuitive and intellectual, and only *facts* can put people wise, especially with intuitives. One can never just *tell* people: they must 'experience' the thing themselves. Then Onkel went on to say that having heard her dream, he was prepared for my story, and said to himself that something was going to happen. He also said that up until now I had been too personal, which is her fault, too – and naturally, I became identical with her. He added that I did not have the [same kind of] dream because I am not so personal anymore. By the fact that Toni is so personal, she loses people.

Then I said to Onkel that I knew Barbara had been through something difficult with Toni. He said that she had – as in the first place, Barbara had been in love with Toni – yet that during that period of Barbara's infatuation, all had gone well because Toni had handled it beautifully; but later, when Barbara outgrew it, the trouble started because Barbara was full of personal plots, and she was bound to get into trouble with Toni. As long as Toni is with people below her, she is marvelous, for she can only be a mother to the poor. She is like a mother who is only interested in the children while they are young, but has no use for them when they grow up. She is good for weak people, but no good when they have grown up. She has an extraordinary ability with the weak. What she needs is more of the spirit and less of the personal.

Since Toni and Katy appeared very different, what they had in common must have been deep-seated. If I were to guess, I would say it was a bumper father complex. As for Barbara being "in love with" Toni, that sounds too strong; but I can imagine Barbara might have had a school-girl crush on Toni. Katy took Jung's advice, and wrote Toni on the following day:

> Waldhaus-Dolder
> Zürich
> February 8th, 1941

Dearest Toni: –

I am bringing this letter to you Monday, and it will contain what I am going to try and tell you, but as I have difficulty in expressing myself clearly by word-of-mouth, I thought it best to write out my ideas on paper, so that you can see exactly what I mean, in case I don't make myself clear in talking to you.

The last two or three times I have been to see you, I have felt very definitely that something intangible, and which I can't quite put a finger on, has come between us – and it has upset me and made me feel very sad, but also it has made me feel that for the moment I must give up analyzing with you, because feeling as I do that there is a wall between us, I can't make any headway and the 'hours' have become very painful to me.

Don't think for one minute that this means that I don't appreciate and value most highly all you have done for me up until now, because I do and I realize only too well that it is due to you and your untiring efforts, that I was able to make headway in this work and that I have achieved a happiness and inward peace, which I would never have believed possible.

You have been largely responsible – with your patience, understanding and sympathy – in bringing this inward state of mind about, and for that reason, I can say honestly that I *really* care for you sincerely, but I do feel an incompatibility between us at the moment, and being fond of you as I am, I would rather not go on for a while.

I am utterly convinced that you have your own problems and that this wall has nothing to do with me; nevertheless, it is there and I feel that you are suffering, and I am so sorry, and wish so that I could help, and be a friend in such a moment, though I realize that it can't be, because you used to know me as I was, and therefore it would be hard for you to realize that I have changed, and to take me on a different basis.

In the last weeks, I have come very close to certain impersonal things, which have greatly changed me and my point of view and I have suffered in giving birth to them, but I could never tell you about them, as I felt this wall – and now I know that for the moment it's better to stop work with you temporarily.

I do hope that you will understand and not think it's for lack of affection because it isn't, for I feel just the same deep affection and regard for you that I have always felt. Can't we see each other out of analysis once, for I don't want to lose you, for after all these years, you mean a great deal.

Always your affectionate,

Katy

Two days after delivering the above letter, Katy saw Jung again:

February 12, 1941

I told Onkel that I had seen Toni and given her a letter in which I had expressed my feelings, and that she was very nice and seemed to understand completely and could not have taken it better.

Onkel said that she had had the right kind of dream and that was helping her. I asked what her dream was – as she had told me a dream of hers the week before – but I saw he did not want to tell me for some reason of his own. But he did say that what Toni dreams is a sort of 'quintessence' of what other people dream. He said that she did not see the problem of the shadow of her personal psychology. Certain things in her personal psychology are not get-at-able.

He went on to say that Toni is in a way a *genius*, and such people live half their lives or more *on their genius*. An artist is satisfied to live just on his art, and most creative people have a very undeveloped personal side. It is so with creative people in general. They don't consider they are personal beings and that they are beholden to their co-people. These people do not realize the defects on their *personal* side; the personal side hampers them, so they leave it out of the picture. Toni is nice when you get on the right side of her, but when the devil is on her, then she is a black devil. It is all because she is utterly unconscious of the personal side. Creative people won't look at themselves just because to everyone it is more valuable to receive their creative 'products' than their moods! People only care for an artist's pictures or a musician's compositions. With Toni, you had to look for a field of application for her genius. You could not go on with the dream of the bag she left on the wall, then finding yours in its place, because she could not produce anything from that dream – so he just left it alone.

He went on to say that the next dream she had was the problem of the shadow: it 'filled the bill,' and he could help her. Of course she can go back to the previous dream, but he added that I must have patience, just as she had had patience with my dissolute mind at the beginning. I asked about her former problems. He said they were much more the dreams of the creative person and were not so personal as the present one she had just had. Of course, in the past, she had had many dreams that pointed to that darkness on the personal side. She is like a respectable woman who has another side and doesn't like to pay any attention to her creative animus to whom she is married. An artist is afraid of any kind of psychology because it forces him to look at himself and his deficiencies. An artist, or genius, does not like to see that it is as necessary for himself, as it is for other people, to have human relationships. Human nature does not interest the artist. It is like Beethoven, who was deaf and lived by himself, or the great German philosopher, Kant, who did the same. It is more important for these artists and geniuses to live 'selfishly' – within themselves.

Barbara Hannah, who is also an artist, made the same mistake as Toni, and of course there could be no relationship between two such people with the same *Weltanschauung* [world view]. The shadow rose between them. They were just nagging each other with their shadows! They both had a tremendous lack of personal development – they became too conscious of their mutual shadows and projected them onto each other.

Onkel went on to say, "Suppose I have a fault I don't realize, but I have a friend who lies and steals, and finally commits a murder. Of course, that's my friend not me, so I feel greatly relieved. People," he said, "have a very bad conscience, and it is a relief for them if they read of a crime, for if no one would commit a crime for a long time, there would be a dull pressure on everybody, and then one would have to do something, but thank God the 'neighbor' does it; then one has a relief, as when a thunderstorm breaks. For instance, if you wanted to commit an adultery, then someone else does it: one thinks it is fine – that it has happened. It is why people like so much to go to the theatre, for on the stage, they see the villain perpetrating his awful deeds."

"Toni can blindfold people as to her shortcomings, and when she is in a bad humor, or queer mood, it is in disagreement with her obvious character, so people don't get on to [correctly perceive] her."

I told Onkel that I liked Toni and would like to see if I could make a friend of her. Onkel said that was a good idea, and suggested that I ask her out with de T., as she likes him so much, and also likes to go out and meet people outside of the psychological circle. That is why she has enjoyed her military service. She is interested in other people.

I told him that I thought Toni was stingy. He said it was not quite that, as she could be ridiculously generous and had given large sums to charity, but that she could not be generous in a human relationship. She is very conscientious in giving money to the poor at Christmas, but she does not realize the need for a human relationship because her idea is of a 'creative relation.' If I want to make a friend of her, I must be more certain of myself. She is not keen on people because people 'suck her dry'; so if I want to make a friend of her, I must be up to the mark in a personal way. She will always be ready to take her dose, if one has the courage to tell her a truth. She has, however, a certain stinginess in personal relations and a lack of initiative. A friend can do a lot for her. Onkel said he knew that her shows of generosity to charities were compensated by an unconscious stinginess. She has done so much for other people *in analysis*; but outside of analysis, one has to go out of one's way to meet her there. Regarding the personal question, no one has been able to stand up to her; nevertheless, she is now more inclined to take something than she was before – especially since her mother died. When her mother was alive she was the eternal child, as her mother was such a charming person and did all the receiving and being nice to people. Now Toni really has to do something about things.

I told Onkel that I thought that Toni's sister, Mrs. Naeff, was the dullest woman imaginable. He laughed and said that Frau Naeff makes the most desperate efforts to be interesting, and is trying to climb out of her shell, that glass wall behind which she is sitting.

February 16, 1941

I told Onkel that everything was going on as well as could be expected with Toni, and though her feeling is very deficient, I must not forget how very dissolute my own mind was when I first went to her, and how she helped me to come out from the undergrowth, as it were. He seemed pleased, and smiled, and then we went on to other things.

I told him that I was still very much of a swine, and people did bother me. He said that people must not bother me. One must look at other people as one looks at a peculiar type of monkey! I thought that was a really good one and agreed thoroughly that one should do that if possible.

He then asked me what was especially bothering me. I said that I still had to have nasty feelings about certain people, and that I had been upset over a friend of mine, Baronin Böcklin,[1] saying that she thought Mrs. Fingerhuth marvelous. I told Onkel that I had held myself in pretty well, and not said much against Mrs. F., only that she was very nasty when drunk one night. And as I was not yet 'master of myself,' I had been annoyed when Baronin Böcklin had stood up so vigorously for her, and had praised her so extravagantly. I then continued saying, that Baronin Böcklin started again at Hugenin's [a chic tea-room on the Bahnhofstrasse] to praise her. So again, I had to hold myself in very well, and said nothing, and only laughed. Then she turned to Janey and asked her if Mrs. F. was her *bête noir*. Janey had also only laughed, so she had got no rise out of us. I told Onkel that I was pleased that I had held myself in so well, and had only made the mistake once in telling Baronin Böcklin, when I was *alone* with her, that I found Mrs. F. difficult. Of course, what I resented was Baronin Böcklin's taking advantage of me – getting nasty, though she and her husband did not mind saying that they hated Dr. F. and could not bear him as either a

---

[1] Baron and Baroness Böcklin were an elderly German couple living in Zürich. See the earlier Diary entry (for 23 November 1939, Chapter Six).

doctor or a friend. Nevertheless, when *I* said that I found the wife difficult when drunk, Baronin Böcklin got mad.

I told Onkel this story – which had been troubling me all the week and making me very unhappy. I think the reason why I was unhappy was that I found Baronin Böcklin less nice than I thought her to be. She had also said to me out of a clear sky, "I *hate* psychology." I had made no answer. I think I have discovered Baronin Böcklin's shadow. In any event, I simply must get so that I won't either hate too much or cling too much to things of this world; then I wouldn't care if everyone came and lauded day and night people I don't like. The thing is not to get 'caught' by people like Baronin Böcklin. Fortunately, I did not get caught very much, only *once*. She did not catch me again! (She also tried to get Janey to say something.)

Onkel said that I probably like to send out a *bouc émissaire* [scape-goat], so that I can say, "That is the devil, I am not so. It is that or that person." I laughed, and told him that it was probably true. I also told Onkel that I had a 'social' complex – and when people touched me on that complex of mine, I got nasty. It has to do with society etc. I told him that I had not liked it when my Latin teacher, Frl. von Franz, had said that she was so brilliant, though she had never studied, and had intimated that I was a dunce. But that even so, I was more willing to acknowledge that I was a dunce than to admit being a social failure.

Onkel said that Frl. von Franz [Dr. Marie-Louise von Franz] had had to study a great deal, and that he kept her up to it, and she worked like a dog. He also said that she had written a brilliant thesis.

What Catharine later called her "society complex" was forced on her by her ambitious mother in New York and Boston during the six years after Katy's return from Europe. This inane life – not uncommon for American débutantes then – suffocated the finer sense of things she brought back with her from Europe at age eighteen. Because she was so foreign to America and still so naive, it seems not to have occurred to her that being a "débutante" was not the only occupation for a girl. As I wrote earlier, the lack of intellectual and cultural stimuli led her to a serious depression with claustrophobia. Katy sought the 'ideal mother' – even in friendships with women her own age – and was often disappointed when they showed a shadow side. The Baron and Baroness were a typical upper-class German couple many years older than Katy, but they, too, failed her as perfect parents.

I then told Onkel the queer dream I had had, which was the following:

I had a hole in my arm out of which poured caviar. I went into a chemist and the chemist said that she could not take care of a thing like that, and that I must call a a doctor. In the meantime, I fainted and said, "So this is dying?"

Onkel said that the fact that it was not pus coming out, but caviar, points to the fact that it is something vital in relation to my touchiness about social things – vital to my social complex. I must have somewhere the qualities to fill a place in society. For instance, he said, when Mrs. Mellon[1] came to him, she was suffering from a neurosis because she did find and fill her social position. She has now been giving large balls, and has been very successfully doing big charity events and social things. She has also had most of Onkel's books and seminars republished, and is riding a big white horse, and is in every way a success in America. She came to analysis to learn how to do all that, and she has found the way.

Evidently, my social instinct is not satisfied. My right arm points to action – the food (which is caviar) is a luxury – what I would serve at a big dinner – for I would hardly buy caviar for my private use at breakfast. I produce out of myself, for my guests, a lot of caviar. Evidently, I contain caviar – which is a symbol for substantial conversation: interesting and piquant – the sort of conversation that might come from a person of quality.

One does not eat caviar in great masses. I seem to suffer from the fact that I have to produce it in this way, and not in another way. People can develop skin diseases because they don't let the thing [malady] out. I have the best chance with people with whom I can be intelligent.[2] What I give here must be produced elsewhere,

---

[1] Mary Elizabeth Conover Brown Mellon, the first wife of Paul Mellon, who had consulted Jung for her asthma. The Mellons returned to America in May 1940, and she died during an asthma attack on 6 October 1946; see Paul Mellon, *Reflections in a Silver Spoon* (William Morrow, New York, 1992). See also the Journal entry for 23 November 1939 (Chapter Six, n. 8).

[2] This did indeed prove to be the case for Katy, as we shall see later, when she began to live in San Remo after the War.

or, if it goes through my skin, it seeks a way out which is not normal: it is a disease, and I suffer.

I then told Onkel that I liked his conversation so much that I found him the only really intelligent person in the psychological group. He said that I am conscious that I like his conversation, but I must also be conscious that I can produce intelligent conversation. A woman who can produce intelligent conversation has a real social value. I must realize my own natural thoughts, which showed themselves to me in the caviar dream. I am not expected to know a great deal, but I must realize what I think, and produce it. Otherwise, I 'let it out' in the way of the *enfant terrible*, and it causes a wound to others and to myself. An *enfant terrible* = a person who has not produced any interesting stuff intelligently. Such people either blurt out something, or else it comes out when they are drunk.

I told Onkel that he was right, that I had always wanted to carry on intelligent conversation, and that I could have enjoyed having a *salon*, if I had been clever enough and had had the opportunity. But before that, I would have to become more educated generally and learn much more. He said that was so, and that was why it was good for me to do a certain amount of studying.

I told him I had received almost a general education from reading his book, *Psychological Types*, and other works of his, and also from going to his lectures. I thanked him for the loan of his book, with the poem, *Prometheus and Epimetheus* by the Swiss Spitteler, and told him that I had found it extremely educational to have read such a work, but that I thought I liked Nietzsche's *Zarathustra* better. Onkel said that *Prometheus and Epimetheus* is very psychological but is not as mad as is *Zarathustra*.

I asked him what I should read in *Psychological Types*, his supposedly most difficult book, after having finished reading his chapter, "The Types in Poetry." [*The Type Problem in Poetry*]. He said that after I had finished that chapter, to read *General Remarks upon Jordan's Types*. He said in that chapter was to be found a practical knowledge of man, and that the whole chapter was very amusing! I laughed and said *he* might think so, but should one hand that chapter to the layman, he would find it anything but amusing, as he would hardly be able to understand what it was all about. Then I told him about my late husband's [James Jackson Cabot] having tried to read his books – saying that, despite his education, he had said it was just like gibberish to him. Onkel laughed, and said that it was often so when people were given one of his books for the first time.

I then told him that I had no 'conversation' with the psychological crowd, because I could never talk about the 'human being' in connection with psychology, and I was not otherwise very much up on things in general, my education having been bad. Onkel said that I must have a language in which I can express myself so that I can get at things in a roundabout way with them. He said that psychological people simply would not study his works in a human way: they just played around with the 'intellectual idea,' and were generally very badly informed. He then told me to read in Chapter Five of *Psychological Types* about *'The Shepherd of Hermas.'* It is an early Christian script from about 140 A.D. It is written in Greek and consists of a number of visions and revelations, which symbolically represent the consolidation of the new faith. Hermas has an erotic fantasy, which develops into the love of the Holy Mother, and thus channels Hermas's libido to the early church – such that then he was able to be a moving force in building up the church of his time. Onkel said that he had analyzed the *Shepherd of Hermas*, and by reading it, one broadened one's knowledge in psychological matters; one could then talk to these people under a cloak of knowledge, and thus decipher a lot about human nature without bringing it out directly *as* 'human nature.' One must talk in the terms of such material as it is the only way in which psychological people want to talk. One can express many things if one has a knowledge of human nature combined with a knowledge of mythology, symbolism etc. By studying, I heap up value, and I will not be boring. Just asking people if they will have another cup of tea bores me and them. I told Onkel there was so much to learn and so little time to learn it in. He said: *"Ars longa, vita brevis."* [Art is long; life is short.]

Then we talked of de Trafford. I told him that de T. had read the A.B.C. by Corrie two or three times, and had found it very interesting. I also told Onkel that de T. was reading Harding and Wickes, and that I thought it the limit the way they had stolen all his ideas and incorporated them in books of their own. Onkel replied that if one is famous one is sure to have one's ideas copied. These 'copyists' make a dilution of his ideas, then people can swallow all that stuff more easily. He said that if he had not concentrated it they could not produce it in its diluted form to the world. He said once he was complaining to a friend that no one read his books. The friend said, "Just wait until you are dead and then you will see something!" Onkel went on to say that his books were beyond the grasp of most people: they were too stupid – and besides, they had no training in psychological knowledge. He went on to say that even people who *ought* to read his books don't do it and they haven't much psychological knowledge, either; they just don't know enough. I told him that I thought his books were written with so much *heart*, feeling and understanding of human nature. And now, after reading his books, such books as Wickes and Harding just did not interest me, as they did not touch anything in me. Of course, I told him, most people would say that I was mad to say that he wrote with so much heart, as scientific books like that were not supposed to contain 'heart.' He suggested his *Two Essays on Analytical Psychology* – as being, perhaps, the next book which might interest de Trafford, if he were getting bored with Wickes and Harding.

I told Onkel that de T. was not sleeping at night but reading, and sleeping during the day. Onkel said that many people are more accessible to learning and study at night, especially when they have not developed their minds. It is a *reversal* of their normal type of living. A light comes to them in that part of their personality which was benighted before, where the house was uninhabited – when there was no one. The night is sympathetic to such people who have certain parts of their psyche which have remained in the dark. Having never lived, these parts have never come to light.

Then I spoke to Onkel about sex. I told him that I found myself singularly uninterested in such matters at present. Onkel said that was quite normal. For in the beginning [of adult life], sexuality is far more dominant in a woman, she is more *in it* with childbearing. Then as she grows older, and does not function biologically anymore, *she gets out of it*. In the case of the man, he does not get out of it as he grows older, for the very reason that he is never really so much in it. He likes it and all that, but he has a career and outside things that occupy him, and sex is really a secondary matter. While with woman, it is her whole world during her childbearing years. The man, having a career, has to keep his head above water, he can't let himself get in too deep, while a woman, on the other hand, can allow herself to be unreasonable in sex matters while she is still young. When a woman's biological function comes to an end, then usually the interest in the whole matter comes to an end. She becomes like the man was in his youth, which means that she is quite separate from sex, and leads, as a man does, two lives. There remains, of course, with her a remnant of sex, a local sensation, but not an absorbing interest – just a 'local' one! She works it off in masculine fashion, and it is done, and then she turns to other things.

The hour was one of the best I have had in years.

Katy's conversation could be interesting, even "piquant," if she avoided blurting things out. As the reader knows already, "intellectuals" made her nervous, and then she expressed what Jung calls "natural thoughts." She did produce "intelligent conversation of social value" when she was older and felt more at ease with people, but only part of her wanted to shine in society through "substantial and interesting conversation." As she matured, another side also emerged.

February 27, 1941

Onkel said, when I told him that I enjoyed society things, and that society was my big complex, that behind it was a 'role in society' which was not what I really wanted. On the one side, there was my social complex trying to make an impression on society people, and to be 'in' with them; and on the other side, I have feelings of inferiority – even with his secretary, Miss Schmid. (I had told him that, for years, when Miss Schmid opened the door, I felt that I was, in her eyes, a swine being ushered in!)

One one side, he said, I have projections on Miss Schmid. (Somehow, I did not feel that I had projections on Miss Schmid, as for years, I have felt she was antagonistic, but never mentioned it before as I had other things to talk about. But I did not say all this to Onkel.)

Onkel went on to say that, on one side, I was a social climber and on the other side, less than a worm with Miss Schmid. Onkel said that what I was playing was a power game, and where there is power, there is no love – a pair of opposites. This brought to my mind what Onkel says in his book, *Psychological Types*, Chapter Five. In Chinese philosophy, there is the idea of the 'middle path' that lies between the opposites. It is called Tao. Tao is usually associated with the name of the philosopher, Lao-Tze, born in 604 B.C. Tao expresses itself as, "Dwelling without desire, one perceiveth its essence; clinging to desire, one seeth only its outer form." – "Tao is an irrational, hence a wholly inconceivable fact. Tao is essence, but unseizable, incomprehensible."

Tao is an irrational *union of the opposites* (opposites – one's good and bad sides blended to make an acceptable whole) – therefore a symbol which is and is not. Tao is the creative essence, as father begetting and mother bringing forth. It is the beginning and end of all creatures.

He whose actions are in harmony with Tao becometh one with Tao. Therefore the complete person is freed from the opposites whose intimate connection, and alternating appearance, he is aware of. Therefore to withdraw oneself is the celestial way, and he is the complete one inaccessible to intimacy, inaccessible to estrangement, inaccessible to profit, inaccessible to injury, inaccessible to honor, inaccessible to disgrace! Being one with Tao resembles the spiritual condition of a child.

The Taoistic religion says that Tao is divided into a principal pair of opposites, *Yang & Yin.*

Yang is warmth, light, masculinity.

Yin is cold, darkness, femininity.

Yang is also heaven.

Yin is earth.

From yang force arises, *Schen,* the celestial portion of the human soul.

From Yin force arises, *Kwei,* the earthly part.

As a microcosm, man is also in some degree a reconciler of the pairs of opposites. Heaven, man and earth form the three chief elements of the world.

This imagery is a primordial idea we find elsewhere in similar forms, as, for instance, in West African myth, where Obatala and Odua, the first parents (heaven and earth) lie together in a calabash until a son, man, arises between them – hence a microcosm, uniting in himself the world opposites. Man corresponds with the irrational symbol which reconciles the opposites.

The Chinese Tao presentation is also suggested in the familiar passage in *Faust*:

> Two souls, alas! within my bosom dwell –
> One would from the other sever:
> The one in full delight of love
> Clings with clutching organs to the world:
> The other, mightily, from earthly dust
> Would mount on high to the ancestral fields.

The existence of two mutually contending tendencies, both striving to drag man into extreme attitudes and entangle him in the world – whether upon the spiritual or the material side (thereby setting him at variance with himself) – demands the existence of a counterweight, which is just this irrational fact: Tao. That is why the followers of the Taoistic philosophy make anxious efforts to live in harmony with Tao, lest they fall into a conflict of the opposites. Since Tao is an irrational fact, it cannot be deliberately achieved, a fact which Lao-Tze frequently emphasizes.

Thus the aim of the Taoistic ethic sets out to find deliverance from that tension of the opposites, which is an inherent property of the universe, by a return to Tao.

Now to go back to: "Where there is power, there is no love." I asked Onkel just what he meant; he said he meant love in the greater sense: love for one's fellow beings. He added that love has a bright and dark side, and consists of opposites. He said that I chiefly had come to him because I had had a fantasy about him. And by seeing his wife, I had put up the right façade for Miss Schmid, his secretary, and neither she nor anybody else could suspect me of bad designs. He asked me why I always had plots. I was a bit surprised at all this, and did not quite understand what he meant, but shall ask him next time.

In all events, I said that I knew that Miss Schmid had some French blood. He replied that her mother was French. Then I told him about her friend, Frau Doktor Gerwig, with whom I could make no headway (when she was Janey's French teacher), and I said that always, with French people, I felt ill at ease despite the fact that I was supposed to be so 'French,' and that people who were not French thought me to be so.

Onkel went on to say that, with the French, *form* [style, appearance, image], *common sense* and *rationalism* go several inches deeper under the skin than with us. He said he could make a diagram showing how that 'common-sense' layer goes much deeper with a Frenchman than with us. He said that one could be on good terms with a Frenchman, but that that was all, and that one never got 'near the bottom.' One is always on a footing of form. One cannot get into the interior of a French family. No matter what one says, it will be interpreted as common sense and rationalism. With French people, one is only accepted for what one *is* and what one *produces*.

For instance, a man can pay attention to a French woman; she will just weigh it in the light of common sense. A foreigner might pay a French person a compliment; he would never suspect that the foreigner meant more than he did. One can say to a French woman things which would make an English woman jump out of her skin. He said that once when he treated a French woman, he told her that she dressed well, and looked well; she was pleased, and was glad he felt as he did. A naive American woman would take it as empty talk, or it would go to her head, and it would mean something. But to a French woman, it would mean nothing serious; she would consider it as quite natural, and take it with a cool head. He said that with us Nordics, it is a sign of insincerity if we pay a compliment – with us, it goes too deep.

An American girl would be horrified if you said to her that you liked her frock and the way she did her hair. But one can say such things to a French girl, and she takes it quite naturally. One always says in French such things as *"J'étais désolé, ou enchanté"* [lit. I felt desolate, or was enchanted] etc. All that means too much in English and nothing in French. When one tries to translate all the French phrases of polite conversation into English and German, they are much too strong. With French such things are not to be taken seriously, and are not meant as lies as they are in English, but are just polite. In English it is overdone; in English, one must not talk of *feeling*. In English, one must be polite, but one must talk of nothing else.

Onkel told me how he had traveled with some English professors in India, to Darjeeling in the Himalayas, to see the sunset, which was of unforgettable beauty. All the English did was to grunt. Finally, one professor turned to Onkel and said, "Won't you quote us *Faust*, the part where Faust is out walking on Easter Sunday?"

Onkel quoted the following [from Goethe's *Faust*]:

Vom Eise befreit sind Strom und Bäche
Durch des Frühlings holden, belebenden Blick,
Im Tale grünet Hoffnungs-Glück;
Der Alte Winter, in seine Schwäche,
Zog sich in rauhe Berge zurück.
Von dorther sendet er, fliehend, nur
Ohnmächtige Schauer körnigen Eises
In Streifen über die grünende Flur;
Aber die Sonne duldet kein Weißes,
Überall regt sich Bildung und Streben,
Alles will sie mit Farben beleben;
Doch an Blumen fehlts im Revier,
Sie nimmt geputzte Menschen dafür.
Kehre Dich um, von diesen Höhen
Nach der Stadt zurück zu sehen.
Aus dem hohlen finstern Tor
Dringt ein buntes Gewimmel hervor.
Jeder sonnt sich heute gern.
Sie feiern die Auferstehung des Herrn,
Denn sie sind selber auferstanden,
Aus niedriger Häuser dumpfen Gemächern,
Aus Handwerks und Gewerbes-Banden,
Aus dem Druck von Giebeln und Dächern,
Aus der Straße quetschender Enge,
Aus Kirchen ehrwürdiger Nacht
Sind sie alle ans Licht gebracht.
Sieh nur, sieh! wie behend sich die Menge
Durch die Gärten und Felder zerschlägt,
Wie der Fluß, in Breit und Länge,
So manchen lustigen Nachen bewegt,
Und bis zum Sinken überladen
Entfernt sich dieser letzte Kahn.
Selbst von des Berges fernen Pfaden
Blinken uns farbige Kleider an.
Ich höre schon des Dorfs Getümmel,
Hier ist des Volkes wahrer Himmel,
Zufrieden jauchzet groß und klein,
Hier bin ich Mensch, hier darf ich sein!

Onkel said he quoted it for them. The English professor of history thought that, on such an occasion, something ought to be done – and so appealed to Onkel to do it! Onkel quoted it for him. This Professor was in a hopeless position when he found himself in a situation where adequate expression of feeling should be shown. He just couldn't talk properly. It is very hard for such people to talk to women as English is not a 'feeling language.'

Onkel went on to say that the French take certain life situations merely from the standpoint of 'suitability.' It is the same with most Latins.

He then said that once, as a young man, he had been alone on a trip to Italy. None of the people he was with realized that he was married. They thought he was a bachelor on holiday because he was so gay with all the girls. Then 'matchmaking' began. They placed him next to an intelligent girl. He decided he must 'bring it out,' that he was married and had two children. Immediately, they became very formal, polite and frozen. The bubble was pricked! Onkel said, "They had worked up a situation, and had thought that I appeared like an unmarried man, but as soon as they knew I was a married man, they treated me as (for them) a married man should be treated. They had created a 'feeling' atmosphere which was nice and alluring, as long as they thought that I was a bachelor playing around with all the girls, but as soon as they knew me to be a serious husband, it was over. They were very nice, well-educated people, versed in the Fine Arts."

I said to Onkel that I thought that the Latin husband was unfaithful to his wife. Onkel said yes, but that when they are being unfaithful, they are like escaped prisoners regaining their freedom for a short time – it is like an 'escapade'! He, on the other hand, felt free and had no bad conscience in such a harmless situation. That is why he could be so carefree and gay, so they got the idea that he was a bachelor. He said that in the United States they would have understood his style better, for there they understand a natural temperament. In Latin countries, the feeling life is submitted to a rational scheme, and you are not taken *for what you are* but *for what you appear to be.*

To a married French woman, you can say all sorts of things, but she keeps in mind that you don't mean them seriously, and she takes it for granted that you are saying such things *en passant* ['just like that' = lightly].

Onkel said, "When French women come to me, they realize that these are consultations, and, though they may realize as a scientific fact that a woman can have a certain feeling for me, nevertheless, I am a doctor, and it's a consultation. Even if the transference is nice and positive, I have always had the feeling that she is a *French woman*. One woman whom I treated went away, and when I met her again a year later, she said to me: 'Do you remember me?' The whole thing was a phantasmagoria, and she was puzzled how I could like her."

Common sense goes deep with the French. By temperament, they are Catholic; their unconscious gives its peculiar weight to what they do. When a Protestant turns against the Church, he becomes sectarian. When a Catholic turns against the Church, he becomes an atheist. A Frenchman is bound to be a Catholic; one can't get through to the French unless one is a Catholic. There is no other way to touch a French person, except by being a Catholic, for their unconscious is woven into the tissue of the Church. In England, America, in Switzerland everyone is concerned with the unconscious as it is not caught in a church. It reacts, so we are influenced by it.

Onkel then told me how once he was invited to a meeting of famous French scientists. At the meeting there was Halévy (a famous biographer of Nietzsche) and Lévy-Bruhl. He said that they inquired about my concept of the Collective Unconscious. Another man present, the Baron de Ségur, said that my concept of the Collective Unconscious was a mystical conception. I explained to the scientists that it produces the myths of the world, a part of the human mind which functions everywhere. No one understood except Halévy and Lévy-Bruhl, who were Jews. The others said, '*Mais cher Monsieur, c'est de la religion.*' I replied, "Do you call that 'religion' when I tell you that I am a professor of the research of myths?" But they couldn't understand, and then I saw that the corresponding thing to the concept of the Collective Unconscious was for a Frenchman the Church.

The French Protestants are just as much in the Church as the French Catholics, Onkel said. They can be the most convinced atheists in France, but they are Catholic in their temperament. They are in the clasp of the Church. I asked Onkel why I couldn't get along with them. He said I should have the right connection with the Unconscious, I am not crazy enough!

Jung's discourse to Katy on the characteristics of a French woman's mentality, and in general of the French relation to the unconscious, might have helped her to regain a sense of her American identity, which she had lost as a girl and young woman. The homeless life to which her father's career had doomed her left her perplexed about who she really was, even after years of analysis with Jung and Toni Wolff. She was still unable to perceive whom she really was, continuing to attach herself to the first culture she remembered. She was sure that she was French because – though she had had an interim unpleasant two years of schooling in Boston as a child – she had lived in Paris from a tender age, studied in a French school and passed her *certificat d'études* there. Moreover, she was not really sure that she wanted to be American, because once – when she had returned to America – the very positive impression made on her by Philadelphia (her diary shows her to have been enthusiastic about the city and the old Rush family house) could lead nowhere. Instead, her family's move to Boston confronted her with a Puritanical ethic that was still very strong, and which had proved to be quite incomprehensible to a girl from Philadelphia brought up in Europe. The Philadelphian way of life, marked by the Quakerism that was part of Katy's inheritance, was far more liberal than Boston's.[1] The double displacement she lived left Katy a foreigner on both continents. Evidence for her uncertain identity presented itself to me constantly. Whenever we were together in public, she insisted on speaking French to me, on no account wishing to be taken for an American tourist. She regularly reminded me how very "French" she was. As a child – I believed her – but later on noticed that she had few French friends and that she was much more vigorous than French women. Even in Paris, her friends were mostly Americans. Katy spoke to Jung of her difficulties with Frl. Schmid, whom she reluctantly admitted was *half* French; Katy was obviously uncomfortable with her, but at first I failed to connect it with my mother's 'French' problem – namely, her attempt to hide her American background, even from herself, because she felt it was crude compared to a French person's. She therefore played a role instead of being herself. That [American] self would have been more relaxed, and even "a chip off the old block," for her father was very much an American gentleman, who also liked France. Despite his

---

[1] See E. Digby Baltzell, *Puritan Boston and Quaker Philadelphia* (Transaction, New Brunswick & London, 1996).

temper, she need not have been ashamed of him. But the complexity ran both ways: Katy blamed her difficulties in America on her foreign upbringing. When she returned with relief to Europe after sixteen years in the United States, she took on her French role again, even toying with the idea of living in Paris or Nice. She found no roots in France, however; settling in Switzerland in fact suited her temperament better.

May 6, 1941

"In every heart, there dwelleth a Sejin [a Sage] – only man will not steadfastly believe it: therefore, hath the whole remained buried."

***

When I saw Onkel, I spoke about Chapter Five in *Psychological Types*, and told him how interested I was in it. I asked him what the 'service of woman' meant in the Middle Ages.

He said that, for instance, Dante is the spiritual knight of his lady, Beatrice, and he undertakes the adventure of the upper and nether worlds for her sake – thus, in this heroic labor, her image becomes exalted into that heavenly mystical figure of the Mother of God, a figure which, in its detachment from the object, has become a personification of a purely psychological entity: that unconscious content whose personification is termed the anima or soul. Canto Thirty-three of the *Paradiso* contains this crowning of Dante's spiritual development in the prayer of St. Bernard. The fact that Dante speaks here, through the mouth of St. Bernard, points to the transformation and exaltation of his own being.

The same successive transformation is also seen in *Faust*, who ascends from Margaret to Helen, and from Helen to the Mother of God. His nature is altered through repeated figurative deaths until he finally attains the highest goal as Doctor Marianus, and as such, utters his prayer to the virgin Mother:

Supreme and sovereign Mistress of the World!
In the azure outstretched dome of Heaven
Let me behold thy secret.
The strong and tender motions of a man's breast
That with holy passion of love ascend to thee
Graciously approve.

Unconquerable our courage burns,
Under thy celestial guidance
Suddenly our passions cool
In thy assuaging calm.
O Virgin, in the highest sense most pure,
O Mother, worthy of all worship,
Our chosen Queen, equal with the Gods.

***

Gaze upon her saving glance,
All ye frail and penitent,
With grace accept your holy Fate,
For when ye thank, ye prosper.
Better seemeth every wish
To her service given.
Virgin Mother, Sovereign Queen,
Goddess, ever gracious!

These attributes show the functional importance of the Virgin Mother, and demonstrate how the soul image affects the conscious attitude – namely, as vessel of devotion, as solid form, as source of wisdom and renewed life.

In a most concise and comprehensive form, we find this characteristic transition from the service of woman to the service of the soul, in an early Christian writing, *The Shepherd of Hermas*, 140 A.D.

Onkel went on to say that in the 11th, 12th, and 13th centuries, the knights had a peculiar worship, the *'cour d'amour,'* the service of the *dames*. René d'Anjou made the laws of how the knight had to behave with his lady. The knight's lady was not his wife, but his friend, and had precedence over his wife. The knight had to be loyal to his lady. She was the one to whom he dedicated his victories. In the 14th century, this cult waned, and the Virgin and the witches took the place of the 'Lady.'

This *Cour d'Amour* was the service to the anima. In these *cours d'amours*, love affairs progressed as follows:

1st – looking at each other and not talking
2nd – talking to each other and holding hands
3rd – sleeping with each other

When the feudal system ended and the towns with the Bourgeoisie began to flourish, the culture which considered the Knight as its highest representative ceased.

M. de Magdeburg wrote a book called *Flowing Light from the Godhead* on this subject, as did Hildegard von Bingen, also a mystic like de Magdeburg, who wrote *Die Nonne von Toss [The Nun from Toss]*.

Then I went ahead and told the General Reilly story – about how this really brilliant man had come over here as an observer, had asked me out to lunch, and had done nothing but make the most indecent proposals to me – suggestions which, in a way, were as humorous as they were absurd, especially one: to go and spend a weekend with him at the [Hotel] Sonne in Küsnacht.

Onkel laughed and murmured, "What a clumsy ox!" Onkel went on to say that evidently the man had a very undeveloped anima and was certainly no white knight with the education and culture of the *'Cour d'amour.'* When one wants to win a woman, one must serve her – use one's brains to that purpose. He should have shown brilliance and tried, through his brains, to fascinate me, for women are easily fascinated by a brilliant man who gives out his best in that line. Onkel said that evidently this General Reilly had no education in this direction or feeling, and certainly *did not* slave for the great god Eros. He went on to say that such brains were rare and therefore to be prized, but so often such people had no feeling and were dreadful egoists.

Then I told Onkel the dream I had of Mrs. Baumann balancing three cones on top of her nose at the University on the day of his Friday lecture. The cones were of different colors, and she was balancing them as a seal does in a circus.

Onkel said he saw the significance of the dream, but could not tell it to me because I was not ready to grasp it. He said that one could not just *tell* people things in analysis, for to have something sink in, one must first have experienced it. I told Onkel that I could not grasp the significance of that dream, and I begged him to give me a hint. He said that even if he did, I still would not grasp the meaning because evidently I was not ready to do so. He added (which, as he said, would be the case – I did not understand at the time, though I do now upon rewriting this) that a person who is not very stable is not much good at such balancing tricks. In fact, an unstable person could not balance such objects. Yet I dream that an unstable person like Mrs. Baumann is precisely doing the steadiest trick. In my dream, I seem to have projected a part of *my own shadow* onto Mrs. Baumann. What I have projected onto her is part of my shadow which is still in the unconscious. (Perhaps my instability? my guess, as Onkel never said that, and, at the time, I did not realize what he was saying, and only do so now as I am rewriting this!)[1]

Onkel went on to say that I seem to choose Mrs. Baumann on whom to project my shadow, as she is a woman who is doing a stunt with her head. All that intellectual stuff she is doing is a stunt. He added that it is only a stunt Mrs. Baumann is doing when she goes to his lectures. Mrs. Baumann has a natural mind about her, and I read her character because it has a natural bearing on myself. Mrs. Baumann gets at Onkel's teachings through the head, and I through the heart. The dream shows that I am not deeply enough in the soul and can be caught by something else. There is still a certain unconsciousness left if I still like flattery. If such things as flattery (I had told Onkel I liked it) can reach me, then there is a big piece of unconsciousness still in me. Eventually I will see the meaning of the dream, Onkel continued. He added, that if he tells me what the dream means he does not help me. There is a door open, and it is ridiculous to shut that door artificially as it would deprive me of an *experience*. If one is told a thing, it is dead knowledge.[2] One must *experience* a thing. He said that there were people who had read everything and yet had *experienced* nothing.

Then I talked to Onkel about Chapter Five in *Psychological Types*. I said what a marvelous piece of writing I thought it was. Simply beautiful because it is so deep, and carried so much meaning and feeling in it. He looked surprised, and said that no one in reviewing that book had ever mentioned Chapter Five. It is always left out of all reviews – as if it did not exist, yet there is much more in it than in the other chapters.

---

[1] Professor C.A. Meier told me that Katy took copious notes, partly in short-hand, during her sessions with him, and then wrote them out in full later. She did the same with Jung, as I discovered when, by chance, I found some pages of notes from her last session with Jung which had never been written out in full.

[2] "Dead knowledge" sometimes takes root! People can come out months later with some bit of knowledge they have unconsciously absorbed, as if it had originated with them.

I told Onkel that I was beginning to experience 'Tao,' that perfect peace of spirit which comes to people who are in inner harmony with themselves. The most subtle secret of Tao is *essence and life*. He said that the western mind has no concept of Tao. (See Onkel 27th February 1941.) [Richard] Wilhelm, the great German who lived in China for fifty years, and who learnt to understand the soul of the Chinese, translates 'Tao' as 'meaning.' Others translate it as 'The Way,' 'Providence' or even as 'God,' as the Jesuits do. It means 'to go the conscious way.'

> "If thou wouldst complete the diamond body without emanations,
> Diligently heat the roots of consciousness and Life.
> Kindle Light in the blessed country ever close at hand,
> And, there hidden, let thy true self eternally dwell."

These verses contain a sort of alchemistic instruction as to a method or way of creating the 'Diamond Body.' 'Heating' is necessary; that is, there must be a heightening of consciousness in order that the dwelling place of the spirit can be 'illuminated.' The ancient Chinese sages knew how to bridge that gap between 'consciousness and life.' They cultivated both. In this way the mortal body is melted out and the great Tao (peace) completed.

I went on to tell Onkel that this being in Tao, as it were, was a wonderful feeling, like being carried on the crest of a wave. It was such a relief not to have to be a monkey on a stick and dance to everyone's tune, and such a feeling of relief to feel harmony. Wonderful!

Onkel said that when the unconscious is predominant it is just as if one were carried on a wave by a strong wind, and there is no effort. It is like a child being carried in one's mother's arms. It is a state of paradise, a definite condition of blessedness. One is carried on a wave of bliss. Then Onkel asked me if I remembered when I was a child, and went out on a lovely summer's morning and was happy all day – at one with the whole of Nature and existence. At that moment, one is contained in the eternal flow of life. It is a state of blessedness. You are 'at One,' and it is paradise and a very definite religious experience. You are now in the stream, and God works from within, from the hidden treasure in the Self, conceived as God's treasure.

I told Onkel that I had had glimpses of all the foregoing and had almost grasped it, only to have it leave me as suddenly as it had come. I realized, therefore, that I was not firmly planted in Tao yet.

Then Onkel went on to the fact that Miss O., his secretary, had without his permission, told Mrs. A. that she could come out to him in the car with me. He apologized to me, and said that it was impossible of Miss O. to have done that – that she had a lack of feeling and does and says terrible things. Also, she lies when she has put her *pied dans le plat* [put her foot in the dish = made a mistake]!

Miss O. was not the only person who put her *pied dans le plat*. Katy herself did so a few weeks later vis à vis her Psychological Club sponsors, Toni Wolff and Linda Fierz. Toni writes:

Freiestrasse 9
Zürich 7
May 8th, 1941

Dearest Katy,
I put you down for next Monday at eleven a.m.

I was really rather disappointed and embarrassed – not so much that you did not come – but that you had not sent an apology to the *Vorstand*. Several members were unable to come – two for the same reason as yours. But they either wrote or telephoned or sent a telegram.

If you had read the Club notice carefully, you would have realised that it was a matter of the most important meeting of the year and that members were especially told to attend, if possible. (It only turned into a party afterwards at supper.) As it was the first annual meeting, you could have attended as a member: it was particularly shameful that you did not at least send an excuse – and it was rather embarrassing for your sponsors. I said to you on Friday in parting, I will see you tomorrow – but apparently you did not hear. But why did you not then at least give me your excuses?

Affectionately yours,

Toni

Just as she had disliked enclosed places, Katy hated being tied down to dates. But Toni's letter made an enormous impression on her; she told me at the time how angry Toni had been, and afterwards attended the meetings fairly regularly. Years later, when I was due to attend my first Club Annual meeting, I also remembered Toni's admonition.

May 13, 1941

I talked to Onkel about the Easter holidays in Ascona. I said that I worked and read, and for a while I was in Tao, but soon dropped down to my old level again. Onkel said that I had obviously done too much work – had got bored and dropped out of it. Later, I will feel better and will then get into it again. Eating is very much the same thing. One has a marvelous meal, and one just feels one can't eat again for a very long time, but finally one does get hungry again. I had overdone this studying – one must not forget that one has another side which does not want to study or read difficult books. One must give into the other side and also let it live.

Then I told Onkel that I was finding the Latin so hard, and such an effort to keep up with Janey, and that I was afraid I was holding her back. Onkel said that Janey was to go on alone, as it was much easier for her. He said, that as we get older, it is not easy to go so quickly anymore. Formerly, things leapt at one and stayed there, but that at my age, it is painstaking work to learn something as things do not register [easily] anymore. After forty, we lose our elasticity, and we realize those things which come through our emotions, but mere instrumental material won't register. Latin is an interesting exercise, but it is not a good thing when I compete with young people. It is too American to think I can leap along with the youngsters. I am no flapper anymore. One must live the style of one's age: to [try to] run along with the young is terrible.

We spoke then of society, and again I told Onkel that I still had one foot in the trough as to that! Onkel laughed, and said that probably I would not care so much for society once I realize how obviously advantageous it is to be out of it. It is very obvious that it is the right thing *not* to be [in] it. But, until I see the advantages of being out of it, I won't get away from that longing.

Then I spoke to Onkel about Mrs. Rüfenacht, and asked him why she so hated Mrs. Briner.[1] He said it is because she puts herself on a level with Mrs. Briner, and at that level she considers

---

[1] Mary Rüfenacht and Mary Briner were Americans both married to Swiss husbands and both in analysis with Jung. Mary Briner later became an analyst.

herself as good as Mrs. Briner. Mrs. Rüfenacht does not realize that she is lower than Mrs. Briner's level. She does not realize what an advantage it would be for her if she did not have to rub up against, what seems to her, a skunk.

Onkel said that when one goes on associating with people and being intimate with them, one feels identical with them, and then, one cannot get away. Suddenly, when one experiences the advantages of being away from such people, so one gets out of the relationship.

With me and the society people, it is (as it is with Mrs. Rüfenacht and Mrs. Briner), a partial identity. The thing is to find out how to get rid of that identity. My old values are still hanging over me. I must realize my age more and get into something different: to *grow* into something different is essential. He added that it was very difficult to get out of one's former milieu and prejudices!

My mother could not let me go it alone with the Latin, as Jung suggests, because her teenager side identified with me in the learning project. But he may have unwittingly helped dampen her enthusiasm. Lessons became irregular because of our travels, and neither of us got anywhere in the enterprise. Finally, Marie-Louise von Franz lost any enthusiasm she might once have had for teaching us – having probably taken us on in the first place as a favor to Jung.

Then we went on to Toni. I told Onkel that I had had a panorama about her and realized suddenly that I would not want to get to know her intimately, or become her friend, as it would mean getting behind in the dirt, and being a charwoman of sorts for her!

Onkel laughed, and said that indeed one would not want to get behind the veil, and that the Toni one sees [outwardly] is the best Toni. He said that one had to accept her as *that* thing, a sort of phenomenon. If she let down her veil, she wouldn't be herself. If she loses her form, she would be a mess all over the place, and her bad sides would come out too much. One must never hope to see the real Toni *because what you see is the real Toni.* That is she. *That is the real Toni!* To be intimate with her, he said, would mean emptying her *pot de chambre* [chamber pot]!

If you want to establish a relation to a person, you must not wish for more than there is. You can't say to yourself, "I wish that person would be more intelligent, or more beautiful, or nicer, for he or she are *not* what you want them to be, but what they *are!*" I cannot say to him, for instance, "Doctor Jung, I wish you were younger." Or he cannot say to me, "Mrs. Cabot, I wish you were more intelligent." Onkel added that I expect too much. He said that when we meet someone with lovely qualities which we appreciate, we want more – we think they *ought* to give us more! He said that people find more with him in the hours than they ever expected, but that after a time, they expect more. They expect all! They want him to be the son, the brother, the father, the lover, the uncle, the old wise lover and so it goes – every infantile wish of theirs must be fulfilled.

People will tear even God Himself to pieces! And why? – because He does not fulfill their expectations.

Toni must be taken for what she is. Everyone has faults. We must be grateful for people with some qualities for some people are without a trace of mind, and at least she has that. Other people are nothing but stupid, unkind or rude, and offer nothing as a restitution. We can't expect people to have only good qualities; we cannot expect them to be perfect. One must take people for what they are – accept them. One can't always expect something interesting from them. Even boring people can produce something of a certain interest. There are many profoundly boring women in the world, but at least they are perhaps erotic, which interests a man!

You must digest yourself, Onkel said, and accept yourself and say to yourself that you also have good and bad qualities, and this realization will help towards being more understanding of other people.

He went on to say that when you get behind that *paroi* [wall], you have missed the real Toni. Onkel said he was not keen to get behind *parois* [walls]; that professionally he had to do it, but that you don't often discover much, really, nothing more than when you take the person as a whole. He said, "Only people who can't look into a person are fascinated by a person. When you can see into a house without stepping into it, then it is better to sit outside and look at the whole." He continued, "When someone insists on veracity then I know he is a liar. If a person is distinguished and well-mannered, then I know there is something behind. I am never keen to get into that dung heap, so I stay on the surface. If I dislike a person, I don't want to get to their good qualities. If a person is on the whole a bad person, it doesn't matter if they have some good qualities, as far as I am concerned. When a person is trying to get to know you, then you know they don't know themselves. Good heavens, this getting to know people's inner selves is a bore! Take people as they are, stay on the surface with people. If a person is, on the whole like Toni, a good person, then you want to know them, and some bad sides don't matter."

We spoke of Linda Fierz for a moment, and Onkel said that Doctor Binswanger did not really love her, but that he needs the moral support which she gives him.

The long conversation about Toni must have come about because Katy was still smarting from the reproaches she received in Toni's letter of 8 May. As I have said before, my mother had difficulties with the faults and different standpoints of other people, often breaking off with those she admired after discovering flaws in them – growing disappointed, and projecting all sorts of iniquities upon them. While she knew herself to be imperfect, she still expected perfection from everyone else.

The friction with Toni did not put her off, however, from inviting Toni, Mrs. Biedermann, Tommy and the Jungs ten days later to a "meatless" dinner at Restaurant Cerutti. I remarked in my Diary, "Toni awful – dinner good." Toni thoroughly disapproved of eating anything good in wartime.) With the War now away from Switzerland's frontiers, and the British successes against the Italians in North Africa, the Swiss tried to live their lives as normally as possible. Meatless days were introduced on 16 May, but despite the rationing of food, my cooking classes continued until the end of the term in March. In April, our class switched to another building just off the *Bahnhofstrasse*, where we were to learn sewing and cleaning for a further year. Though ordinary life went on, the Swiss authorities were still mindful of the danger of invasion. One morning at the end of June, our class joined with other groups of young people in a lecture hall at the *Kunstgewerbemuseum* [*Museum für Gestaltung*], where we sang patriotic songs and listened to a lecture. Upon leaving, we were each given "a little Red Book full of patriotic writings," as my Diary reports, long before the days of Mao Tse-Tung.

May 28, 1941

When I went to see Onkel, he was so nice, and we both immediately laughed. I said to him that I hoped he was still feeling well after that huge dinner. He said that it was a wonderful dinner, and that it made one enthusiastic even to think of such a dinner. He added, that in the days to come when we might be tightening our belts, he would often think of that dinner, and always with pleasure, and would rejoice that once before the famine, he had had such a meal.

Then I told Onkel of a dream I had had, after the dinner, about tucking him up in a bed with a plate of grape seeds next to him. He did not seem to think the dream of much interest, but laughed about the grape seeds on a plate near his bed, and said that he hoped the grapes he was supposed to have eaten did not hang too high!

Then I continued telling Onkel what a really awful time I had with people imposing on me, as Daria, Hedwig, Madame Roche,[1] Toni, Linda. Everybody seemed to appoint themselves as a 'Mother' to me, and that I was fed up to the back teeth with such people. Onkel said that such people were tyrants and indecent people, and have no respect for one's personal freedom. They seem to think that I am at their disposition: – that they are the overlords and that I am their slave.

I told Onkel how I had not realized that a notice, which I received for a business meeting at the Club, meant anything special, this being my first year as member, and that Toni and Mrs. Fierz fell on me like a ton of bricks, and were furious. I then told him that I had written such a nice letter to Toni, and apologized for not being there etc. Onkel said that was just what I had done wrong, that I should not have apologized, but written her a strong note of protest that they, my Club sponsors, had not notified me the first year, of this most important meeting; they should have done so, as there was no R.S.V.P. on the notice, so I did not even know that the Club expected a reply if I were unable to attend it. Onkel said that both Toni and Mrs. Fierz should have apologized

---

[1] Daria Holenstein, a friend from her Florence school. Hedwig Haniel, also known under the name "von Branca Kent," was a German Jewish artist living in Switzerland. "Madame Roche" was a nickname we had given to Katy's mother, Mrs. Rush.

to me for forgetting to tell me, in a friendly way, that the most important meeting of the year was about to take place. He said that he would be ashamed not to have told me about the *Generalversammlung* [General Assembly] if he had been my sponsor.

Onkel went on to say that both Toni and Linda disliked seeing their mistake, so they just put it onto me instead. I should have said to them, "You knew the importance of this meeting, and I didn't, so why didn't you tell me about it?" He added that it means a moment of fight, but one has to stand up for oneself and knock them over.

He said, he was incensed with Toni for going out during the dinner party and talking to the waitress about the food [saying that the food was too good for wartime]. Toni just constitutes herself the 'mother' and I am far too lenient with her. Onkel said that Toni and Linda wanted to have introduced the perfect element into the Club, so that was another reason they were annoyed I did not come to the annual meeting. He said that I must realize that *other* people make mistakes which I must suffer. Mrs. Fierz identifies with Toni. I must go ahead and assert myself. It was Toni's ambition to introduce the perfect daughter, the paragon of social virtues, to the Club; one who is spotless in her social behavior. Toni has a hell of a mother complex, and Linda is an artificial person. As soon as I put up my own head, Toni will begin to knock me down.

I then went on to tell Onkel what I suffered with my own mother, who is so possessive and selfish, and wants to kill me by devouring me alive. Onkel said that I must deal with such a terrible mother firmly. He said that 'Individuation,' or the 'Way to the Self,' was a lonely way, and that one must 'agree with oneself,' and do what one knows to be right for oneself even if, in the process, one finds one is alone. He went on to say that I can be sure that those people who like me will stick to me. He said, "Those who want you to be a puppet will give you up, and it really does not matter at all if they do, as you will have lost nothing by losing such 'friends.'"

He said that when people criticize me for not living with my mother, I only have to say to them, "Go yourself and live with her: try it out, and see if it is easy." (I had to laugh, as I thought that 'a good one'!) He added, "Say to those people who reproach you, 'Live with her, stay with her. Try and do the same as I have tried to do and see if you can stick it out; perhaps then you will see why I have done as I have done.'"

Onkel went on, "Just fire it back at them." I then told him that my mother became hysterical when I tried to make her see a truth about her terrible ungratefulness and selfishness in not wanting me to have my liberty after all I do for her. Onkel said that when she became hysterical, and went on prating about, "Sharper than a serpent's tooth is an ungrateful child," I should say to her, "God has punished you because you behave as you do, and has given you a devil as a daughter." He said, "That will fix her!" He added that I was the victim of my mother, having been browbeaten by her all my life, and that having had to become submissive, I now go around creating 'mothers' everywhere. That is why people try to boss and mother me. He said that I was overwhelmed by the mother that I create. ...

Then I told Onkel about a dream I had had of a long and loathsome animal lying on the tram lines in the street – a long grey, soft horrid thing which made my skin crawl to look at it. It lay prone and in danger of being run over. It was a huge prehistoric animal, with a long pointed nose and whiskers, which just lay there and took up the whole street.

Onkel said this animal was the opposite to Mrs. Baumann's seal-like balancing stunt. [See May 6, 1941.] This animal was a low-down lazy one and inert. I have a way of being submissive, as if I were younger than I am. Being too submissive, I am run over. It is a sort of inertia of mine that I behave as if I were still with my mother behind me telling me what to do. He added that Toni herself is seduced by my fear of the mother. He told me that the next time such a situation arose, I should bring the letter to him and ask his advice.

I then asked Onkel about Fräulein [Ida] Bianchi, who was a member of the Psychological Club, and even on the Committee, and finally left it. I said that I wondered if she were really as black as she was painted by Linda. He said that Fräulein Bianchi was the same kind of swine as the others who constitute themselves a mother. She could not compete with Toni and Linda. It was a case of dog-eat-dog: The two strongest dogs kicked her out. She tried a lot of foolish tricks. Her idea was that she could get into a place of power by gaining Onkel's attention, so she went to bed and pretended that she was too ill to rise, and Onkel even had to go and see her. She wanted to create a circle of intimate friends to listen to what she would produce out of a somnambulistic condition. She told a lot of lies, and picked up with a queer man to get Onkel jealous. She was an hysterical individual. She was efficient, intelligent and had common sense, but had no character.

Then Onkel went on to say that by being firm it means that I have to get up from the tram lines, or that awful inert animal, which is me, must get up. If I always withdraw, then nothing happens. Of course, I can let things go, but that means that I will always go on as before. He went on to say that I must simply write to Toni and tell her that she committed a breach of form without my consent. I should protest to her that she should not have eaten what she termed a 'sinful dinner.' He went on to say that if he could stomach the dinner then she could also stomach it. I told him how she had called me up a whole week in advance about this that and the other. Onkel said that people like Toni and Linda want to have someone with whom they can be infantile, and yet they play the role of mother and *assure* me as their child.

Onkel said that he thought Toni's way of behaving was impertinent. If she did not agree with the style of the dinner, then she should leave what she considers a sinful dinner. He said that I would have to write her and protest. He said that it was imperative that I defend myself vigorously. I must be reckless in such matters. If I just make Toni bristle, then she will go on bristling, and that will be that. Of course, he added, I could leave the situation as it was, but that then the same thing would arise again – the same situation will repeat itself. I must take a risk – as nothing is gained without risk.

As I have already said about Catharine's youth, during her last years at school in Europe, Catharine saw little of her mother, who traveled frequently. On returning to the U.S. at eighteen, she found her mother's personality to be as strong as ever, and soon found herself trapped in dependency, for the reasons Jung suggests above. Jane Rush was intent on making a suitable match for her daughter, in spite of Catharine's lack of a dowry. Catharine was a good mixer and very pretty, so for a while, she enjoyed a vigorous social life, but gradually found it too much even for her. She began to yearn for intellectual pursuits, but only a shorthand and typing course occupied her while she lived with her parents. Her unconscious was not so accommodating, however, and she became seriously depressed. A brief stay in a clinic taught neither her nor her parents anything;

when she came out, she went on as before, and depression and claustrophobia returned. Just how much of all this was due to an overly strong mother? Through her marriage, Jane Rush had extricated herself from a society comprising second- or third-generation missionary stock who had turned to business. Even as a girl in that provincial setting, Jane had been socially ambitious. But by the time I was old enough to know my Grandmother Rush, she was not as vigorous as my mother had made her out to be. All her life, I believe, Catharine saw her mother as she had been in 1913, when forty-three. As Jung said to Katy directly, she was overwhelmed by the mother she herself created. I came across this problem at the clinic where I worked, in a woman who continued to create in her mind a very difficult husband, who, with age, had in fact become quite mild. Periodically, this woman stayed at the clinic for "holidays" – sometimes lasting for a year. She longed to leave her husband for good, she told me, but never found the courage to do so, although with each return home from the clinic, she took with her some optimism (once beginning to wear skirts instead of her customary trousers). But the last time she left the clinic, she showed none, knowing that the "holidays" were over because her insurance would no longer pay for them. The negative mood worried me. Shortly after she returned home, she suffered a severe stroke and could no longer speak or move, confined to hospital where her husband visited her daily. Likewise, Catharine longed to cut the self-created bonds to her mother, but never managed to. Because these bonds were what they were, for an outsider it was difficult to see where the problem lay. My grandmother never appeared bad-tempered or quarrelsome, and had many good points which I admired. In fact, I had more in common with my grandmother than with my mother, and our relationship was good. The only thing about her which I found irritating was her habit of talking too much about people I had never met. She was a woman of her period, not brilliant but thoroughly practical and intelligent. Having only a small pension, she was careful with money, and played the stock exchange with real skill, making substantial gains with her modest investments. But she was not too proud to accept help from her daughter, thereby keeping her capital intact. Katy was annoyed at supporting her mother while she amused herself investing, especially so because Katy, loving clothes, felt obliged to make her mother presentable in chic outfits. My grandmother wore them, although reluctantly – feeling guilty about their newness. Her habit was to keep her clothes in the closet a year before wearing them, probably a custom in her day and milieu. Meanwhile my mother could not bear to present her mother to her friends dressed like "a cook." As for cooks, my grandmother did not dress like one, but in fact she produced an excellent cookbook during World War I. While she was with us in Switzerland, she supplemented our calories with delicious cocktails – not the strong martinis popular at the time, but 'White Ladies' made from lemon juice, cointreau and gin, and 'Alexanders' made from a third each of cognac, crème de cacao and fresh cream. She also introduced us to useful wartime expedients – "wine jelly" requiring only sherry and gelatin, and corned beef hash from the Argentine (like sardines, not then rationed). These innovations were very welcome at a time when eventually there were three meatless days per week and two eggs per month, and when bread could be sold only after three days, bread whose taste led us to joke that it contained sawdust.

June 5, 1941

I told Onkel that I had done what he suggested I do, and had written Toni a letter about talking to the maid that night at [Restaurant] Cerutti. I held out her answer [not extant] but he said that he had seen both my letter, and her answer, and that he had told her she should not answer me in that way; she should not have written that letter.

I said I found Toni a rather small, frail and pathetic creature. He said she was that and that I could not see her in that way – which was the true way of seeing her – if I had not written that letter. He said that I took a stand which made it possible for me to see her clearly. If I had not taken the stand, I would have been full of vendetta. Onkel said that one takes Toni too seriously. I asked if she could not be cured of this disposition of hers. He said it would have to be done against her will, so that she did not notice it. She is gifted and helpless! I had to write that letter so that I would come to a normal realization of what she is.

Then I told Onkel that I was still getting the panics in the [Dolder] *Bahn*. I even had to ask de T. to ride down with me. The panics had gone for a while but now were back. I had them particularly coming down in the *Bahn* because one cannot get out on the way down. [Nowadays one can.] He said that I was nearing the *Lump*. I asked him what could be in the Lump, that we had analyzed the Lump for ten years now and we never seemed to get to the bottom of just what it was composed of.

Onkel said the Lump was an enigma, that one could not say what was inside it in specific terms. Probably it contains all the things I don't understand yet, all the things I am not yet conscious of. I said to him that I was sure he could see me as I was, and the Lump as it was. He said that was so; he only had to look at me to see the Lump rolling around inside me.

He said the Lump contained *prima materia* ('primary matter,' as the Alchemists called it). It is chaotic matter which rolls around in the ship in heavy weather and gets the ship loose. This materia prima has to be differentiated and turned into something tangible. It has to be shaped. In a way, it is a mental lump which should materialize. It should become visible, but it has not done so yet.

Onkel went on to say that I probably had the Panics when I was sitting talking to Mrs. Jung because I began to think that I would soon be having my hour with him and the Lump is an unanswered question. He said that I was still confronted with a certain amount of that panic because there is a certain hollowness inside for the Lump to roll in. The fact that I felt the panic with Mrs. Jung shows that, when I am in his house, I am confronted with having to face myself honestly. I evidently get into a panic when I approach the problem. The Lump is constellated when I am going downhill in the *Dolder Bahn* because, going down, I come to the collective level which leads to the Collective Unconscious. In the Collective Unconscious, I am like everybody else! I get into a panic because I do not sufficiently realize the fact that, in the collective, we are all alike. When I come down to the level of everyone, I am no longer Mrs. Cabot, but a female. There is another person in me which does not correspond to the one above. It is as if I were living on two floors. When I am living on the ground floor, I am the wife of the *concierge*. I must realize that one is quite low and vulgar at that level. One must not forget that fact and just live on a higher plane. One can live on a decent plane, but also realize that there is a lower side of nature which must be *recognized* – otherwise, one is unnatural and afraid of losing the persona.

He said that Mother Nature pushes us to be conscious of ourselves in every respect. He said that when I first came to analysis, I was terrifyingly superficial – a painted surface. I was a hollow mask with *death* inside. I was so unreal, as if in a mist, and inside me was panic. Slowly, I had to become somebody. If one drops one's persona, it is like losing a rope onto which one has been hanging. As long as there is panic, it is a sign that the Unconscious is overwhelming me. Onkel said that I am not *safe* and that one cannot trust me. One cannot take a guide on a difficult mountain who is liable to get into a panic. He continued that we (he and I) would have to go about the thing with caution. We must see how much of the Lump is still there. We can only chip off a little bit at a time so that we slowly decrease it. Evidently, the Lump is not entirely done with, or I would not have the claustrophobic panics (occasionally, in enclosed places). He said that many people who appear normal suddenly show a surprising weakness.

I live above my level, and must come down off my pedestal and be human, Onkel said. That with him, one has to be natural, or one would not get anywhere in this work of 'finding the self.' He added that if my nature were acceptable to myself, I would not have a Lump or a split-off part. "Suppose you are more or less normal," he went on to say, "but you get into a secret panic, then you constellate the bad side in yourself. Let us presume that you are a very natural person, *well aware of yourself* and you meet a person who isn't. The person you meet can get into a panic because he, in feeling your naturalness, realizes his own deficiencies. Then he hates you because he hates the naturalness which he does not possess. If you hate something in someone else, then you can be sure that you have the same bad thing in yourself. Otherwise you are just indifferent to a bad or good quality in the other person."

In spite of my mother's care in this entry in recording Jung's comments about her Lump, she never completed the work of chipping away at it to decrease its size. My mother's talent for acting let her invent herself on a "high plane" and play a role there – for a while, anyway. Possibly Katy did not want to know herself that well; the version of herself that she had fabricated was good enough in its "hollow" way, in spite of the cost. After ten years, Jung was pointing out that the claustrophobic panics were the price she was paying for not coming down to a lower level and accepting her down-to-earth side. That meant realizing she was not just a timid, delicate, well-brought-up *jeune fille* [young girl]. And that side meant accepting the animus. In the early days of the analysis, Katy had told Jung of her father's horrible temper. Jung replied, "If you hate something in someone else, then you can be sure that you have that same thing in yourself." She disregarded his words, at least where she was concerned, and so remained unaware of her vigorous and disagreeable side. With her talent for acting, she invented false selves to suit the occasion: either the polished society hostess, or, more often, the timid débutante. The consequence was that the contents of the Lump remained a long way from consciousness, and continued to plague her.

Jung's metaphor in this session – cargo at loose in a ship's hollow during heavy weather – points to the Lump's "chaotic matter" – but at least it was *matter*, it was substantial. Captain Rush, though he had spent years at sea, was far more grounded than his daughter. He was, therefore, at least partly a helpful animus. As far as Katy was concerned, an animus was mostly negative, something other women had! As for her, she was very feminine. Her interest in clothes proved that. Her enjoyment at playing masculine roles at fancy-dress parties was good fun, nothing more. As for her dominating nature, she ignored having it. From her point of view, she was timid and fragile (enjoying ill health frequently) and therefore female. It was quite amazing how Katy could deceive herself. That she had a masculine side, that it made her effective in difficult situations, that she could be decisive when necessary, and that she thought her point of view was the best one and usually vigorously upheld it – all this never seemed to occur to her. The naturalness in Mrs. Jung, a strong and balanced woman, may have induced "panics" in Katy before seeing her because she feared that Mrs. Jung would see into her "hollowness." She was such a mature personality, however, that she soon made Katy feel at ease. Katy soon was able to relate to Mrs. Jung and greatly profited over the years from contact with her. With Jung himself, however, the self-deception about who she actually was and what the Lump consisted of continued. During the long analysis with him, when insights might have surfaced, the topic became too hot, and she would then abandon it for another:

> I then told Onkel of how Frau Doktor Biedermann had told me that she had been pursued by a tiger all night in her dreams after the Cerutti dinner. Onkel said that when you dream of a wild animal which pursues you, it is an instinct which assails you. He said it was, of course, her 'cut-off' instincts – which she had not

allowed to live – which were pursuing her all night in her dreams. He said that he caught a look in her eye that evening which could suggest an intimacy. I then told him how she had said to me, "Doctor Jung hates me!" Onkel gave a great big laugh, and said, "Why, I haven't got time to hate people." He added that he simply could not make that effort. When she says, "I like him very much, but he loathes me," it really means that she is afraid that he does not love her! I told him I knew he was right, because de Trafford had noticed that she could be 'wooed and won,' so to speak. He laughed, and said it was very obvious that evening. He was very nice but formal – though of course her unconscious did not like the formality as it was looking for something more intimate; so she just said, "He loathes me!"

Onkel added that Frau Doktor B. has an onslaught of libido in her, and that had he been willing to flirt, she would have been 'on the spot.' He said that such girls as she were brought up so conventionally, and in such a repressed fashion, that all their natural instincts were suppressed and not allowed to live. The tiger represented her cattishness, her female side which is not allowed to live and yet is discovered by the male.

Onkel said that I was on too high a plane because I would not admit to certain instincts in myself; I would not admit to the possibility of having lower instincts. I replied that I would, of course, admit base instincts in myself and that I had had queer fantasies about the headwaiter, and others. That I was no saint at all, nor had I any illusions about myself in that respect.

Katy ends that 'hot topic' with a flippant remark and embarks upon a less feeling-toned one:

I told Onkel that de Trafford was pretty cold as to love in the sexual sense, that I did not think that sort of thing appealed to him very much, or otherwise he would be more enthusiastic about it when he had a chance. Onkel said that de T. was not enthusiastic about sex because he had been *cut off* from part of his nature throughout his life. First his mother, who was of course far from her instincts, then that wife completed the destruction of any sex feelings he could have had. Onkel said that in de T.'s case it was difficult to 'feel' as the world destroys feeling.

With a man, sexuality is a business and he has to get rid of the sex tension by having passing affairs. With a woman, it is different.

Early in life, she begins to love the whole man, and later sex comes as an attack by itself. When she is older, she just feels a local sex excitement, just as a man does when he was a young dog. These older women can take on any kind of man just to satisfy their 'local' feelings. But with a man when he is older, it is different. He begins to realize the whole complex of love and the big role love plays. Such an older man depends very much on the feeling side of love. If he loves a woman, he can have a relationship with her without sex. That is probably the reason de T. does not put so much emphasis on sex in our relationship. The feeling side is much more important to him now than when he was younger, and the sex, which was always repressed, had gone into the background.

Onkel went back to the woman whom he said becomes more and more masculine as she grows older, just taking the man for one night as the man did when he was a 'young-blood.' The older woman looks at a man as a young man looks at a girl.

I then told Onkel that I was going to visit my mother in Geneva, that she was a pretty tough proposition, very possessive and domineering, and mostly in bad humors, and a scold. He said that my Lump was identical with my mother! He said to be as kind as was advisable to her, but to remain firm and not get sentimental, and to be sure to get rid of her for the summer.

Onkel went on that the more I am aware of my fantasies of the lewd kind (the waiter, for instance), the more I am aware of myself in that less elegant aspect. Being aware of one's own nature acts as a counter-poison against lumps and panics. Onkel said that one must avoid repressing one's personal problems; that people who did got very excited, even hysterical, about the War. In fact, he said, it was impossible for such people to talk about the War at all. Those are the people who are not concerned with the personal side, yet should be. All one's sides should be looked at.

Onkel said that there was a great deal of my mother in me – especially my evil temper. If I don't realize what the headwaiter can do to me, I could fall back again into bad tempers.

Jung seems to have the Lump's gender wrong, possibly because he forgot about the evil temper in Katy's father, which she had mentioned early in the analysis. Like certain other women with negative father complexes, Katy often brought mother's iniquities to the fore and shielded father. Actually, Katy had little of her mother's ebullient temperament; if she had, she might have stood the American social round better. Though a scold and ambitious, her mother was not subject to rages. Katy's illness arose when she disregarded the side of her personality which did not care for society, and she later resisted acknowledging that she had her father's evil temper. During the session, Jung's comments pertain to the father complex. He says that, in early life, a woman begins to love the whole man, through the father, who in Katy's case was both physically and emotionally absent. Her repressed longing for her father prepared a seed-bed for a father complex; as a good *relationship* with "Dads" was not possible, Katy *identified* with him, and the "Old Sea Captain" was thereby relegated to the unconscious.[1] That identification had its influence. Tommy fell for strong women; he would have been better off with a more feminine one who did not control him. Since Katy kept her vigorous side veiled when she discussed Tommy, Jung was possibly unaware that she was the one who 'wore the pants' in that relationship.

Then I spoke to Onkel of my desire for the limelight. Onkel said it was a practical piece of wisdom to get *out* of the limelight, to get out of focus, as it is unpleasant to be in the limelight and I should be glad to be out of it. Otherwise, I may get a *Geltungsdrang* [vanity, exhibitionism], which means I love to be looked at and be noticed. You must learn the *disadvantages* of being the center – there are people who are incurable about being in the center.

I told Onkel that as he was world-famous, he did not have to be in the limelight, for he was just automatically there. He said that there was a time when he was not world-famous, but that even then, he had had no desire to be in the limelight. He said it was more important to be loved than to be in the limelight [famous]. No one who puts themselves in the limelight [at center stage] is loved. One has to choose between the two. He went on to say that, of course, there were people who always want to be on top of the show, who think they are martyrs when there is a second sun in the heavens!

I asked Onkel if it was a nice feeling to be famous. He said that being famous was very nice and satisfying, and that was that, and enough. But what he really enjoys – and what really gives him

---

[1] See Jane C. Reid, "Der lebenswichtige Vater," *Analytische Psychologie* 17 (1986), 38-56.

more satisfaction than fame – is that he leads the life he wants – (just as if he were not famous at all). He added, "I don't show my belly all over the place, and I try to be as simple as possible – because it is wiser. The more I want to be the center of attraction, the more I am exposed to disappointments, for I have to pay the tribute. A man who keeps himself apart, and who doesn't join in with the others ... [such a man] will be snubbed. People are offended that I'm not in their *Verein* [group, association], that I don't seek their companionship, but that is the price I have to pay for my liberty!"

Onkel said that one must decide what the life is that one *really* likes, and then live it. Naturally, one has to pay a price for one's liberty. It all boils down to a question of being *simple*. Simplicity is the greatest art. I must realize what I like – want most in life – what I prefer. But of course *it costs a certain price*, as one can get nothing for nothing in this life. These things are not gratuitous!

I laughed over that last phrase of Onkel's, and told him that I thought he always expressed himself so colorfully. He said that if you see things in a colorful way, you choose words which are colorful, for you see things colorfully, clearly, plastically.

Then Onkel went on about the distance I had come in this work. He said that getting to the self was a slow process, and one must always look back to where one started; then you get an idea of what you have done. It all depends from where one has started. He said that, when I started life, it was under conditions which made it extremely probable that *I would get stuck in that type of life and that social set forever!* I was born a thousand miles from any probability of coming into this work.

I told Onkel that I had always felt stirrings within me and that I was not happy with the life I led, and developed a neurosis. I went on to tell him that in Charleston, West Virginia, – where I had lived – there was a girl, Eleanor Chilton, who was a writer and very intelligent, whom everyone in the town detested, but whose society I preferred to anyone else's there. She analysed later in London, with the Freudian, Ernest Jones, and through him I had been recommended to Jung.

Onkel said that evidently it was in me, or it would not have worked after I started to work here, but that I had had to cover an *enormous* distance to get as far as I have.

I then said to Onkel, "You have brought me in sight of the Promised Land, and I see it, but the Red Sea is between it and me, and how do I get to it?"

Onkel replied very simply, but his words were measured, serious and had a penetrating quality, and a sincerity which comes only with great experience and insight into oneself: "If people wish to come with me, I will take them to the Promised Land, but they have to give up power. But if you come along, you will see it. I am going through a country which I like, and if you join in, you will see pretty much the same as I do, I guess."

Then Onkel said that it was chiefly false values which prevent one from getting there. Priests can't help one because they have a lot of second-hand knowledge only. 'Immediate experience' is the only thing that can give one the power to take people to the Promised Land. People must learn to be exceedingly simple. When you can see clearly what could happen with you and the headwaiter, then you have seen something and know something about yourself.

"Have a cheery weekend with the headwaiter," he called laughingly down to me over the banisters as I left his house.

If Catharine had been inclined to be social only like her mother, she would never have made it to Jung. It was the father in her who took that initiative. His side of her nature made her unhappy with her early life, and produced the "stirrings" which resulted in neurosis and which affected her also physically with the need for operations during her early years in America. (The hernias, based on abdominal weakness, had been inherited from her father.) As the French say: *Elle n'était pas bien dans sa peau* [she was ill at ease in her skin)], but only a neurosis was compelling enough to force her to take a new road. Gradually but systematically, it dismantled the life she had lived for seventeen years in America. Had she seen then that she need not blindly continue with her vacuous society role, she might have saved her marriage and made life happier for all concerned. But she persisted in her one-sidedness until circumstances gave her a valid reason (my illness) for leaving. Without virtually having made a *tabula rasa* of her earlier life, Katy would never have developed the frame of mind needed to work with Jung. But even so, during the many years of her analysis, she never entirely shook off her need for a role in society; she had been too deeply imprinted with the idea that only 'society' afforded a woman the chance to shine.

June 19, 1941

I spoke right away of the horrid atmosphere in the Psychological Club. Onkel said that he knew all that. However, such a Club should be kept running. Toni and Linda did most of the work for it. He said that 'in our time' civilization was going down and to have a Club like that, where ideas were exchanged, and which had a high intellectual standard, was a good thing.

He said that it meant for him a lot of work, in a way, because it had to run on a certain level. But he couldn't be impatient with things like 'atmospheres.' The Psychological Club meant progress of human thought, and if one wants to maintain such an institution, then one has to do something about it. He said that Frau Froebe was doing a fine work, too, but everyone complained about her power drive. But then, he said, they would also complain if she lacked it! Onkel went on to say that it was all very tiring for him, and, of course, he would like to retire and write, but if he did, it would all go to waste. It would be throwing up the whole thing, like Jonah and the whale. Without the Club there would be nothing, no patients, no students to exchange ideas. He had to hang onto it and keep it together. It would be a pity to let it go, he added.

Then I said that I hardly had time to learn all I wished to learn. He said to make good use of time as it passes swiftly, and he quoted a saying from Goethe:

> *Das Lebens Mai blüht einmal und nie wieder!*
> *Noch ist es Tag, da rühret sich der Mann*
> *Die Nacht bricht an, wo niemand wirken kann.*

> Life's May blooms once only!
> As long as there is daylight, man can see
> For night comes, and work is over.

Then I spoke of the Spitteler poem, *Prometheus and Epimetheus*, and of how much I had derived from reading this poem, and also from reading Chapter Five of *Psychological Types*. Onkel said that Spitteler had written a second *Prometheus and Epimetheus*, when he was a very old man, and that it was in verse [the first poem was written in prose], yet this poem was not half so good – for, as he grew older, the devil caught hold of him, and he changed.

Onkel went on to speak about my Lump, which he says is "an airless and spaceless room" – an interesting simile [metaphor], which gives an idea of the ghastliness of the Lump.

I then spoke about dying – which I said I did not like the idea of. He said that it was certainly not a particularly likeable idea, but that one has to settle down to it. He said that, when one fills every moment of one's life as well as one can, then, when death comes, it comes at the right time and is not minded so much. He said that Cicero had written a treatise on old age and death. He went on to say that when one has lived everything within one's reach, such a full life brings maturity and the time which is right for dying. A full life brings satiation, and the ripe time for death follows naturally. In fact, he said that in any kind of relation to matter, when you have done what you could, then you are through with it, and it drops off. It is the same with a human relationship: when it has been lived and *out*lived, one can then detach from it. Onkel went on to say that, as one goes on developing, one forgets the other, and one slowly gains a certain clearness in a relationship, and looks at things from a distance, no longer being involved. Lao-Tze, the famous Chinese sage, said:

Klar siehet wer von ferne siehet.
[He sees clearly who sees from a distance.]

We went on about the Lump, and my not liking to be 'enclosed' in a place I cannot get out of. He said that the trouble was that I cannot submit to the fact that I am *enclosed* in the body. The analogy is being enclosed in the Dolderbahn. I must learn to submit to the fact that I am enclosed in the body. So far, I can't! We disagree with the body; we have ideas about it, and we think that if we accept our bodies we are in trouble. I am trying to get out of my body. I am trying too quickly to get away from the body. I want to be master of the body and not be the one who has to pay tribute to the body. I suppose, in other words, I must accept my body and realize that I am just a human being like other human beings. It isn't the whole thing being conscious.

Then we spoke of being stuck in boring situations. Onkel said to get out of situations that are boring – that there is no obligation to stick in them even though they may be awkward to get out of.

He said that we do not consist of reasonable and good things only. Everyone has a lot of dark matter in themselves, and so do I. I must look and see what are the unconscious impulses of my nature. Everyone tries to keep just to the surface of things and not to 'go down.' I must not assume that I have got to the very bottom and it is very important to realize that fact.

The dream with the wasp flying in is a symbol of magic, a witch-like effect which belongs to the witch quality of every woman, that tail with the poisonous arrowhead. I said that I didn't think I was by nature witchlike or laid traps for people. He said, no, that I certainly was not like that, but that every woman has a little of it.

He then said that I think too much in my head about things instead of allowing that 'Thing' to come out of the unconscious. I can only make discoveries when the thing living in me comes up. Onkel said to stop thinking and say to myself, "Let's see what is going to happen," then I will be apt to make a discovery. He told me to sit somewhere and to just let fantasies come up, and in that way, I might get somewhere. So I just sat quietly for a minute, and then I said, '*Cochon!*' [pig!] He laughed and said indeed it was that, and that I must see what that *cochon* wants to convey; for there is a story to that *cochon*. I must see what the *cochon* wants to do, not what I want to do. I must watch the *cochon*, what it says and produces daily; then I will learn something. The *cochon* is also a marvelous animal, for it finds *truffes* [truffles]. The *cochon* is one of the aspects of the Lump – for I feel that, when I am locked in my body, I am in a pigsty. I should realize that one must accept the body, the *cochon* and the pigsty. In particular, I must not think that, after so many years' work I had arrived – because it was untrue.

***

Onkel said, "As long as one is in any way held by the domination of *cupiditas* [avarice, greed; strong desire, lust] the veil is not lifted and the heights of a consciousness, empty of content and free from illusion, are not reached, nor can any trick or deceit bring it about. It is an ideal that can only be realized in death. Until then, there are real, and relatively real, figures of the unconscious."

Katy was definitely not witchlike. Her powerful animus would not have sunk to laying traps for people. As for her blurting out "pig" in

French, it may not have been utterly spontaneous. In French, the term *cochon* is also an insult, so not a common slur in French. But in English, it was acceptable at that period and part of Tommy and Katy's verbal arsenal, though Tommy preferred "swine" to "pig." Katy's possibly unconscious response to Jung's suggestion to sit quietly for a minute and just let fantasies come up might have been linked to her father; not only was he rosy and rotund and loved food, but, as she told Jung years earlier, he had also been very disagreeable to her.

June 26, 1941

This 'hour' was pretty painful. I had just left Mrs. Jung's study. She had just said that she did not like the spirit of the Psychological Club group, as they were so like the Pharisees, and full of *Grössenwahn* [inflated with their own importance] and *Selbstgerechtigkeit* [self-righteousness]. I was quite overcome by her remark, as I had thought myself it was so. When I went in to see Onkel, I told him of our conversation. But he was evidently not going to let me get away with sitting in magnificent judgment on the Club group, for when I told him that I thought exactly as Mrs. Jung did on the subject, he said that it was because I was like that myself! It certainly was a bomb falling in my lap – and I looked up – astonished.

I said to him that I was so sweet and nice and cherubic and straight and fine, and I did not understand that he could compare me with such hypocritical people. He said that I *was* nice with such people as Frau Dr. Biedermann, who were totally unconscious people. But that naturally when I was with the Club group, who were 'conscious' and cultured, they saw through me, and treated me as they did: seeing with their *consciousness* just what sort of person I was.

I said that Toni and Linda, especially, were to me the black persons in that Club, and that there had been a much lighter atmosphere the evening of Frau Jacobi's lecture – when they had not come. Onkel said that Toni and Linda were relatively harmless, and I project all my nastiness when I say that they are nasty. I project all my snakes and all the witch-like stuff, that is in me, onto them.

Then I spoke of Mrs. Rüfenacht's[1] coming to lunch, and speaking so loudly about her affairs and her love for Professor Straumann – about how badly he was treating her and all the suffering she was going through while being married to Mr. Rüfenacht; how she would like to marry Professor Straumann, but that he had said she was too old (being only a year younger than he) – and besides, that he was in love with a Swiss girl whom he intended to propose to and marry. Also that she had had a big sex affair at *Pfingsten* [Whitsuntide/Pentecost] with him. She had left Onkel forever when he (Onkel) had said that she must carry a burden, and never live again, but instead climb up to the sacred city of Lhasa in Tibet! She intimated that she got into a perfect fury when Onkel and Toni said she was living below herself. I also added that she had said that she had not come to me to save money on them, Onkel and Toni, but because she had *left* them, as the task of mounting to Lhasa, which they had recommended to her, was too great. She had decided to enjoy life instead.

Onkel said that of course she had come to me as I was nearer her level, and she doesn't feel such distance from me as she does from them. He said that she would not dare to talk to him and Toni in such a vulgar tone as they are people of culture. Mrs. Rüfenacht feels a great distance from people like himself and Toni. "She wouldn't dare talk to us like that," he said. The fact that I could sit there and listen to that stuff being poured over the Waldhaus [Dolder] porch, for everyone to hear, shows that I lack Toni's and his culture. Mrs. Rüfenacht dared to come out to me with her whole stuff, with all the vulgarity she has in her, and which she does not dare tell to them. She can only talk to people such as I, who have the same vulgarity, and who are not snobbish about sex. It is all in terrible taste for her to talk and for me to listen! It is pigsty stuff. She had a need to pour out her filthy stuff, and it touched the same in me, my lust and my sex. Mrs. Rüfenacht feels very guilty; otherwise, she would not go around telling the world about her illicit love affairs.

Then he said she was really stupid. For instance, when he gave a series of lectures about the Mass, she thought he must surely be a Catholic. When he gave a lecture on Alchemy, she thought he

---

[1] Mary Rüfenacht, mentioned earlier as an American in analysis with Jung, worked for Allen Dulles, head of the O.S.S. (later C.I.A.) in Switzerland. Under her maiden name, Mary Bancroft, she wrote *Autobiography of a Spy* (William Morrow, New York, 1983). Her father was of Boston Brahmin stock, and her mother of Irish descent. She died in 1996, aged ninety-three.

must be an alchemist! When he told her that to carry a cross meant that she must deal with life, take up her responsibilities in a dignified way, she mistook what he said and thought that he had meant for her to go to Tibet and be a lama. He said that Mrs. Rüfenacht had no subtlety – that she is impossibly coarse, like a factory girl. A vulgar fate awaits her, and her life will be difficult. Onkel went on to say that he didn't want to tell her that she would have to reckon with a vulgar life, unless she 'deals' with life and takes up her responsibilities in a dignified way. He added that he told her almost nothing except that she must try and deal with life.

If she cannot stomach such mild remarks as that, then she will never get out of 'whoredom.' She is quite shapeless and the victim of her nature. Her marriage is unpleasant – a hell. Her husband's soul is a prostitute, so that is why he had to marry one! He sees a lot of nice and cultured French-Swiss because he wants to compensate.

Mrs. Rüfenacht would like to hear sexy things from me and wallow in my sex fantasy. But I must be careful never to mention a sex fantasy to her as she would tell it around and cover me with mud, he said. Mrs. Rüfenacht prefers to smear herself over the face of the earth. She can't stand it that she is so sexy, so she goes around telling everyone about her sex life as she feels it makes it less terrible if she confesses it publicly.

He said that Mrs. Rüfenacht is full of *inferiority*. She feels *abject*, so she has to confess around to everyone. She can't stand her own dirt, so she has to go around proclaiming it to the housetops. She can't hold her mouth and just blabs it to every newcomer. Now Mrs. Rüfenacht is handing it out to everyone about Professor Straumann. She is just 'handing Straumann' to the world!

Then I told Onkel that Janey and I always said that, after a Mrs. Rüfenacht visit, we had the props knocked from under us. Onkel said, "Mrs. Rüfenacht is your shadow. She couldn't knock the props out from under you unless she had a hand in your soul! There is Mrs. Rüfenacht stuff in you!"

Then Onkel went on to say that I project my extremes onto people. On one side – it is Mrs. Rüfenacht – on the other side, it is Toni. He said that – when I discover a thief *in myself* – I say, "Oh, Toni is a thief," or "Mrs. Rüfenacht is a thief." They are the thieves, but not for one moment do I say, "Perhaps *I* am the thief." It is the same in everything: if I discover vulgarity in myself, then I say right away, "It's those others who are vulgar, not myself, of course!" I go on to say, "Thank God, I am not like that!"

   1. Onkel went on to say that I consist of tricks, like Linda Fierz whom I condemn of playing *so many* tricks. I am terribly tricky!

   2. I lie beautifully.

   3. There is also something in me wanting to make an IMPRESSION!

   4. There is always something in me that wishes to be more distinguished than I really am!

   5. There is always something in me that wants to appear more honest than I am.

   6. I am a long chain of lies.

   7. I am a long chain of pretence.

   8. I am a long chain of deceit.

   9. I am intolerant.

   10. I am snobbish.

Onkel repeated that I am intolerant and also snobbish. If I find everyone terrible, then there is something wrong with *me*!

Onkel went on to say that I had come a great distance in the knowing of myself, since I first came to Zürich, and went to the Club seminars. One could see then that I felt thoroughly uncomfortable. I looked like a dream figure, a fish on dry earth, a figure all done up for a Riviera party.

He said that people felt I thought myself superior, when in fact I was feeling most inferior. He said that I behaved with people as if I were a precious jewel that had got into a dustbin. I was certainly not adaptable and not able to get out of my shell. I was hemmed in on all sides by a certain kind of persona which did not fit the occasion at all. He added that I must try to learn to be natural and return to the original condition.

I then told Onkel how indifferent and cold I had been to Barbara Hannah when I met her in Gübelin [a Bahnhofstrasse jeweler]. Onkel said that just because Barbara is nasty and does not know good form, there is no reason why I should be the same, and that incident shows that my form isn't very deep. He added that I probably vented my ill feelings about the Club to Barbara. Onkel said that when one is irritated by people, or by things they do, then one must turn the question *inward to oneself,* and ask, "How am *I* in that respect?"

Onkel said that Toni adopts ways that he doesn't care for. In the Club she is reckless and disturbing. But Linda is the opposite, she is false and unnatural with her put-on sweetness, and her mincing airs. He said that all the sweetness she puts on bores him to death.

He said that going to the Club to hear a good lecture was like going to a concert and hearing one violinist playing the wrong notes. Nevertheless, it does not profoundly irritate him to hear the wrong notes as it seems to irritate me. Evidently, he said, I could not deal with hearing a wrong note. When one is irritated by a person one must start dealing with oneself, and ask in what way one is like the person. Where am I like Toni and Fierz? Inasmuch as there is a Lump in me I am artificial. Inasmuch as I am separated from myself, I am artificial. I ought to look at myself in that line, for it is a serious matter if I am as artificial as Mrs. Fierz.

I then told Onkel a dream I had about being in a restaurant where a *grande dame* [lit. great lady] came up to me and scratched me on the thighs, and as she was doing it, she said: "Don't tell anyone that I am doing this to you, because I wouldn't want anyone to suspect that I wasn't all that was proper and *comme il faut*." [Katy had had a similar dream earlier where Toni instead of the *grande dame* was involved.]

Onkel said that dream figure was *me*! He added that it would be better if I did a thing like that consciously – then, I could not say I was *distinguished*! Otherwise, I will retain the 'being-the-grande-dame-in-society' attitude with all the prestige that goes with it.

Then I told Onkel a dream I had about Mrs. Fierz and Frau Jacobi.[1] He said that intellectually, I could not, of course, compete with them. Fierz and Jacobi are not natural and this 'intellectuality' with them is a compensation for their lack of naturalness. Fierz plays *intellectually* with *natural* thoughts.

I asked him if he thought Mrs. Fierz's lectures would be interesting. He said she would give her lecture in an intellectual way playing with natural thoughts. She will be trying to climb out of her problem of unnaturalness in an intellectual way. What she will say will be an attempt to deal with her difficulty in an intellectual way, in a substantial way.

---

[1] Frau Dr. Jolande Jacobi, the Zürich analyst mentioned earlier – who had escaped from Hungary to Switzerland during the War.

Onkel told me to try to be decent, honest, open and frank and real! Which, of course, is not so easy to achieve!

I asked Onkel how he observed that I was not natural. He said there were fringes of sophistication around my 'naturalness.' My naturalness is like a bad sausage made up to look like a pheasant! I have my ideas of being *comme il faut*, and I do not see how I could be if I were a child of Nature. I would be so different. Now, I simply imitate being natural just as Linda Fierz imitates the natural style. I am like a rococo lady dressed up trying to be natural, or like a sheep with blue ribbons.

"The whole art of living is living what you are!" Onkel said. (But how to realize what one is??)

Onkel said that, in Toni and Linda, I had found objects into which I can project my own unnaturalness. When I realize *my own* unnaturalness, then I can do something about becoming natural, and Toni's and Linda's unnaturalness won't bother me anymore.

Then Onkel told me again his Darjeeling story: the sunset in the Himalayas and the British Professor who could not express himself adequately about its beauty and had thus asked Onkel to quote *Faust*. I said that if I had been present at that sunset, I would have been off in *exstase* [a state of ecstasy] or have been quiet and dull and not have spoken. If I had spoken, I would have said what I thought was 'the right thing' at 'the right moment,' and have tried to play a role. Onkel said that that was just what I would do, and he would probably have wanted to spank me if I had been there!

I then went on to tell Onkel that if I followed my nature, I would be very quiet, not speak much and be a 'dullard.' Onkel replied that Mrs. Jung does not talk much, and yet when she does say something, it is the right remark, and her remarks have substance. He said that there was no use talking when there was nothing to say. I create an artificial naturalness. Onkel said, "Just be who you *are*: it's so simple, and easier than playing a role. If one is what one *is* and simple, one doesn't arouse projections from people. People can't project all their nasty stuff and damn nonsense onto one. If one isn't natural, people can project God-knows-what, and one then becomes – in their eyes – all the nasty things they are thinking." He went on to say that it is much more simple to be natural and real. By being that, one gains the sympathy of people. It is my idea that I must 'work' and 'slave' to be natural. He said, don't play up to people. "Don't try to impress: just be simple and yourself!"

Mrs. Fierz works like a dog to make the wrong impression! She takes *desperate* trouble to put herself in the wrong light. It is pathetic the trouble people go to make a bad impression!

Toni, on the other hand, is working hard to get the Club to be what she thinks is 'right.' She is slaving for that, and she damns herself and you if things don't go right. She almost kills herself to do things in a 'complete way,' in a 'conscientious way.' She sacrifices everything to that end and becomes stiff. However these two (Toni and Linda, do produce something. I should be more modest and realize that I don't accomplish what they do. I must not be supercilious. I must be myself.

Then I told Onkel Janey's dream of having an artificial leg. He said that, on one side, she has artificiality – she is not quite natural – she wouldn't be her mother's daughter if she were natural. She must be careful to have both legs really on the ground. For the time being she has an artificial standpoint and wrong values. Onkel ended by telling me to get natural and become one of God's children!

We then went back to Mrs. Rüfenacht. He said that he had been vulgar at Rafz,[1] but that he had been drunk, and just got that way. He told me to tell Mrs. Rüfenacht the following:

She must not make *the fatal mistake* of thinking that people are as stupid as she is! She should cultivate her own intelligence, for she has to see that if she goes on making such mistakes she will be at a terrible disadvantage, for it is terribly stupid to think that people are more stupid than oneself.

When one is with Mrs. Rüfenacht, one is talking to a 'whorehouse.' Onkel said that people who make such remarks, and hold such vulgar *propos* in his house, are no longer invited by him. It is like a blasphemy during Mass or making jokes to a mother about her child who has just died to behave that way. However one can do nothing about Mrs. R.: if she wants to have her nonsense, let her have it. If Professor S. gets a bad reputation, it is up to him: one cannot prevent people from having their experiences. If you talk

---

[1] Rafz is a town between Zürich and Schaffhausen – a place favored for excursions by members of the Psychological Club. The Hotel Kreuz still exists there.

about your lover, you make him a laughingstock! Onkel finished by saying that Mrs. Rüfenacht flooded him with all her stuff. "If she wants to have her experiences, let her have them," he said.

My mother often quoted Jung's remark that she was a sausage done up as a pheasant! She loved the remark. As she grew older, she became more natural, but never entirely gave up her role-playing when convenient. Deep down, I believe, she preferred a natural life, but felt compelled to keep up appearances, which must have been hard work. As I have mentioned earlier, she had a very earthy side, which included telling risqué jokes (the kind men might tell each other), yet which were certainly not fitting for a society hostess of her period. During my childhood and teens, I often wondered why my mother enjoyed ribald stories.

As for Jung's interpretation of my artificial leg dream, it is correct. Even though I had skated so much and had good balance and strong ankles, I was not properly grounded, mentally. This manifested itself physically from time to time, starting in my teens. When walking on a perfectly smooth pavement, I would twist an ankle and stumble. Sometimes it was painful, sometimes not, but strangely I never developed a swollen ankle. My later interpretation, before I read Jung's interpretation of my dream, was also that I did not have my feet on the ground!

Katy spent the summer in Ascona, but found it necessary to contact Jung in early September, before returning to Zürich:

Torre dei Carcani
Ascona, Ticino
September 7th, 1941

Dear Onkel,

I am very worried, because I may be facing deportation to America, early in November, due to the expiration of my passport and the unwillingness of the Zürich American Consul to renew it.

There is no point, really, in my going back to America, as neither Janey nor my mother wishes to go. My mother has been allowed to stay by the consul in Geneva, so that to return would be a sacrifice without a reason.

It seems that I must have a doctor's certificate, saying that I am unable to make such a trip. I have already written to Doctor Fingerhuth, asking him to give me one when the time comes, but it might not be enough, and so I am writing to you to ask you to give me one, should it be necessary. I don't mind being thought 'too nervous' to make the trip, which I am quite sure would be the case, if I had to leave all that I hold most dear in life.

I was most awfully disappointed not to have had you and Mrs. Jung here at the house, during your stay. It is a *real* house,[1] and Janey and I have been happy in it. It has a realness that I suppose only a house which has been lived in by people for four hundred years can have.

I have taken unto myself very seriously all that you said, in our last (for me) very painful interview, and I am trying hard to remedy things, because I know that you are right, but it is very hard for me to be honest, open, frank and real!

I did not take your advice, as to not doing 'missionary work,' and when Mrs. Rüfenacht appealed to me, I gave out, what I thought was my best effort. However, I have only landed in a quagmire. She came down here and gave me a good hard kick in the pants. Nevertheless, even though I got badly bruised by her powerful hoof, I don't regret what I did, because from that experience, I learned what a presumptuous ass I was.

To be absolutely honest with you, this whole letter has been caused by the awful kick she gave me, as I would probably have waited until I got back to Zürich on October 15th to ask you for the certificate, my passport not expiring until November 15th.

I got quite 'knocked out' by her and am running home crying to you.

I hope you and Mrs. Jung are having nice holidays and good weather; here, the weather is wonderful and has been so for the last ten days. Tomorrow we are going over to Muzzano (near Lugano) to spend a night with Mr. *'s bride. She takes in paying guests and * is there now and has been most anxious for us to come. He seems pretty real, compared to the people here in Ascona now.

With very best wishes to you and Mrs. Jung,

Very affectionately yours,

Catharine Cabot

---

[1] Torre dei Carcani is on the main Piazza at Ascona, facing the lake. It was owned by a famous German composer, Vladimir Vogel.

As far as I remember, the whole passport problem blew over without the need for doctors' certificates. The American Consul in Zürich, whose name I cannot recall, was rather severe, tall and thin with a long beaky nose. When we entered his office, he rose from his desk, motioned us to sit down, and remained standing, towering over us while he berated us like naughty children for *still* being in Europe! After his lecture, he reluctantly renewed our passports for another two years. We thought that maybe the Geneva Consul had influenced him because of my grandmother, who had refused to travel to America. As for Mrs. Rüfenacht, my mother never broke off her friendship with her in spite of the problems. After the War, Mrs. Rüfenacht edited a book on Switzerland for which she asked Katy to write three chapters.

Torre dei Carcani
Ascona, Ticino
September 23rd, 1941

Dear Onkel,

Yesterday, Frau Froebe told me that you had been quite ill this summer after leaving Ascona, and I am just sending you these few lines, to tell you how sorry I am – had I known that had been the case (your illness), I would certainly never have written you about my own problems. I hope, and so do Janey and de Trafford, that you are much better now and are enjoying this lovely autumn – it was beautiful here for the last three weeks – we have been out all day on our bicycles or playing golf and how we wish there was no winter ahead! We all three went to Lugano, to see Mr. * married, and he has certainly married a fine character – de Trafford says that she can pull him through, if anyone can. We all three send our love and wishes to you for a speedy recovery.

Katy Cabot

This letter must have crossed with Mrs. Jung's.

Küsnacht-Zürich
Seestrasse 228
Sept. 25th, 1941

Dear Mrs. Cabot!

It was a very nice thought of you to tell me of Mr. *'s marriage; of course we, my daughter and I were greatly interested to hear about it and about his new bride. How lucky he is in finding such a fine personality as she seems to be according to your description. I hope he realizes this! It might well be that she could make him find the right standing in life and a better relation to reality, which would really be his salvation! He seems unable to bring it about alone, and on the other hand, he has talents which it would be a pity not to bring to bear fruits. So let's hope for the best! I was glad to hear that you enjoyed the summer at Ascona; yet it was a pity we couldn't come to visit you at your "Tower" [Torre dei Carcani]. We went right to Bollingen afterwards, and it proved to have been a pretty great strain for Dr. Jung, as he felt not at all well afterwards, his heart being not quite in order. The doctor ordered him a good rest, which he is having now and not so much work in general, so that he is not going to lecture at the E.T.H. Now he is feeling quite well again. Fortunately, it was just due to overworking, the doctor said – nothing wrong with the heart itself, which is of course a great *Beruhigung* [comfort] to us. These lectures he had to write gave him so much to do, besides seeing patients, and when he is interested in a matter, as was the case here, he doesn't feel when he is tired! He is not taking up work again before the second week of October. On the 4th and 5th there is still this Paracelsus *Feier* [celebration] at Einsiedeln (where he also has to give a lecture), and he will not start before that. I enjoyed our holydays,[1] partly at Bollingen and partly in the mountains very much and feel quite rested now.

What a pity that the 'Rüfenacht' episode didn't come to a satisfactory end! She must be well under the Animus then! For I am sure you made it easy for her to become sensible! But the chief thing is, that it had a good result for you. I am looking forward to seeing you and hearing about it all.

How long are you going to stay down there? Do you know that on the 4th of October is Heiner Fierz's wedding?

With affectionate greetings,

Yours,

Emma Jung

Jung's reply to Katy's letter of 23.9.1941 came three weeks later:

---

[1] I have retained Mrs. Jung's spelling of "holyday" in all her letters as I believe it reflects her very special character.

October 13th, 1941

Dear Mrs. Cabot,

Thank you very much for your kind letter and all the news it contains. It is true, I have been badly overworked this summer and I have to be very careful now. I feel all right again, but I had to reduce my work considerably. There is, however, still enough of it.

I'm glad that you have a favourable judgement about Mr. *'s new marriage. I was afraid it would be another nonsense. But all competent people agree, that she is much better than the general expectation.

Please give my best regards to Janie and Major de Trafford.

Cordially yours,

C.G. Jung

The man in question had been previously married to one of Katy's American friends in the Psychological Club. He and his brother were both members, the brother being on the Committee and also later on the *Stiftungsrat* of the Jung Institute. As for the man himself, Professor C.A. Meier told me that he was a *Spinner* (which he translated as "a nobody").

His second wife was poles apart from the one my mother had known. Practical rather than intellectual, she had an uncomplicated and stable personality, and was close to Nature. The couple celebrated a country wedding at her house outside Lugano, where she also took in paying guests. The party, a *Festa campester*, was given in the evening, after a morning ceremony solemnized in Lugano, at which my mother was a witness. The simple *Festa* was set at a long table under a pergola in a rather wild garden hung with lanterns. There were about twenty guests and, after the first *boccalino*[1] or two of red wine, everybody became very merry. We drank the local wine, ate Ticinese dishes and played games until 11 p.m., driving back to Ascona the same evening. I had expected my mother to disapprove of such an unsophisticated affair, but to my astonishment, the society hostess in her did not prevail. She enjoyed it very much and later spoke of it often with appreciation. She could relax and let her unsophisticated side have its play, and as the years passed, I noticed that gradually she came to like the unsophisticated parties best.

---

[1] *Boccalini* are small ceramic pitcher-shaped tumblers used in the Ticino for drinking wine.

On her return to Zürich, towards the end of October, Katy must have sent Emma Jung a book, rather than her customary gift of flowers. Mrs. Jung writes:

Küsnacht-Zürich
Seestrasse 228
Nov. 8th, 1941

Dear Mrs. Cabot!

Thank you very much for sending me the book; it is indeed an interesting experience to read the New Testament in the language of our days: one gets a newer and more living impression, and many things strike you far more directly than in the traditional style. I have been wondering whether you were still in Ascona, and am very pleased to hear that you have come to your winter quarters again. I am looking forward to seeing you soon.

With kind regards,

Emma Jung

The next session begins with attention to world affairs:

December 13, 1941

America had just declared War when I went to see Onkel. I mean Japan had been forced by America to declare War. Onkel seemed to think that Roosevelt was a superhumanly sly man to have forced, by his uncompromising attitude, the Japs to declare War. Onkel said that the U.S. should have squashed the Japs long ago, but that England would not allow it as she wanted to appear tolerant. England underrates the Japs considerably. In fact, Onkel went on to say that England had underrated everyone and did not even have the right anti-tank guns to pierce the German tanks. Whereas even Switzerland had anti-tank guns which could master the German tanks.

Onkel went on to say that now the British swashbuckling superciliousness had made them risk their best ships, and they had even announced in the papers that the British fleet had left Singapore. The British have the mentality that thinks that when the British fleet appears, everyone, including their enemies, will fall on their knees and worship them! Onkel said that Roosevelt's plans were made because of the vulnerability of Hawaii, and because a war with Japan is far more popular than one with

Europe. He added that he thought it awfully clever of Roosevelt to have forced the Japs to declare war on big America, because if it had been the other way around everyone would have said how terrible for a large country like America to attack a small country like Japan. Now, Onkel went on, Roosevelt by his clever ruse, had got everyone to arm, and so has shown himself brilliant, because it has forced the nation together and to the realization that it must arm. By forcing the Japanese to declare war against America, Roosevelt has to stage something, he said, to make people sit up!

Then we spoke of the War in Russia, and the arctic winter which the German High Command was not prepared for. Jung said that he had met some of the doctors who had come back from Smolensk. They said that they had spent their time amputating the frozen limbs of German soldiers. He said that the German soldiers did not want to go to Russia. German troops stationed in Lille [Northern France] had revolted because they had been ordered to Russia.

Then he went back to the English and Americans and said that the stupidity, impotence and awful 'talk' of the British just made him sick. They come out with such stuff as, "Now we are going to launch a big offensive in Africa!" It is ridiculous to talk and write as they do. The whole world is upset because of British stupidities. If only they would be modest and keep their mouth shut and *act* instead, and let people see what they can do. This eternal talk with nothing accomplished is just nonsense. They ought to be more modest when they are inefficient and unprepared. They take a few kilometers and then brag about it. America, on the other hand, he said, had been plagued with strikes. She had not reconnoitred properly and therefore had not realized that the Japs were approaching [Pearl Harbor]. Onkel thinks now that Roosevelt can put through all the measures he wants.

Then we spoke of the Lump. Onkel said that I was not up to what the Lump contained yet. He said it was stupid to get panicky in the *funiculaire*. It is the fear of getting killed that gives me the panics. Every time I step into the *funiculaire*, I fear disaster and make my Will! Of course, one does not know now what the future holds, and with America coming into the War unprepared, anything could happen. I could be left without money and become so poor that I would have a sordid existence, which wouldn't be living anymore for me. If England and America keep on being unconscious, anything may happen. The English and Americans may be starving, yet if the Axis succeeds in taking over these two countries – which is in the realm of possibility, since both England and America are *still* too unconscious to realize the Axis menace – then … . He went on to say that the British had bluffed so often that one could not trust them any longer.

Then Onkel went on that I have at the moment in my unconscious some very real problems that I ought to realize, such as, if the Axis wins (which is in the realm of possibility) I shall have a sordid existence. If I were up to [facing] the fear of a sordid existence and the fear of death, I would not have fears in the *funiculaire*. But I have not faced these possibilities, so they lie partly in the unconscious. It does not really matter if one dies in a funiculaire accident or not as one has to die in some way. If I had passed through a mortal danger and then stepped into the Dolder *funiculaire*, then it would all seem as nothing. If I had crossed the sea in a terrible storm and the boat had almost gone to the bottom, the Waldhaus *funiculaire* would seem nothing at all – on the contrary, it would be a haven of refuge.

Onkel went on to say that I am spoiled and imagine that I am safe, then *the fear of death* and the *uncertainty of life* grip me. Wherever we are we are never safe, only we don't think of it. *Death is a supreme necessity.*

Then Onkel told me that I was not myself enough, that my psychology sinks down to the collective level. People have no idea what I am like – and could think I was anything. I have a collective psychology, which means that I think like the crowd thinks and have no personality or psychology of my own. As soon as I enter a theatre or lecture hall, or any big public place or gathering, I lose all realization of myself, and I just become a *bella figura*, and only think how I look or God knows what stupid thing. As soon as I am in a crowd, Onkel tells me, I am no more myself, but am only concerned with things about me, which are outside of me. If one is mature, and a grown person, Onkel went on, then one is free from such things, and one is still oneself in a large assembly. But to be mature, one must be familiar with the idea of death. In respect to *mortis*, a *funiculaire* or a crowded room is nothing. He said that when I handle my everyday life in every phase and aspect in relation to *mortis*, then I will no longer be foolish and will become detached.

Onkel said that 'hating to die' with me is a secret, unrealized fear, and can be compared to a very young person who is inclined against sexual life. Such a young person is afraid of life, as sex is the skeleton in the cupboard, and life would call her to sex, so she just tries to escape anything that could make her live and bring her to sex. I feel about death in that same way – hence my fears of the *funiculaire* etc., so like the young girl who feels safe in a state of paradise (but in the background has a fear that she might fall in love). I try to escape anything that seems dangerous and might bring death.

Onkel said that people develop morbid fears of all kinds of things. He once had a patient who was afraid of a clock or a woman in black. One patient had a tic which forced him, after buying an object in a shop, to go back to the shop and return the object without demanding the money back. ... He simply had to make his purchase invalid. I then asked Onkel if he was able to cure this man of such an inconvenient tic. He said no because the man did not wish to be cured. Onkel had said to him, "The moment will come when you will not wish to be cured, and you will see why." The man did not believe him at first, but after six months, the man said to him, "You are right, I don't want to be cured. I can't afford to be cured. My neurosis began when I was twenty, and now I am forty-five. In the meantime, I have lived in a happy neurosis island, and should I get cured, I'd have to realize that I have lost the best years of my life – and I can't face up to that." So the man left Onkel.

Onkel said the man would have had to go through hell in the years to come in order to make up for the useless life he had led for twenty-five years. But as he was very rich, and could afford to live an artificial life, he just went on living it. He did not know that a Jew cannot live such a life without becoming neurotic. He thought his problem was only religious; he did not know it was racial. He had a British upbringing and had gone to an English university, and just never realized that Jews cannot have that kind of bringing-up. He also treated his sexuality in a way that a Jew cannot afford to treat it – by being promiscuous. He never married because he never considered it a necessity, not realizing the strong family instinct in Jews. Onkel went on to say that the Jews are especially devoted to the family because they are nomads and not connected to the soil in any way. It is because the Jews are without country that they cling to the family, to the clan. Onkel said that Jews had offered him houses in America, and promised him fabulous sums if he would take over important clinics. But he said that he could not accept the offers because he is so bound to his native soil of Switzerland, and for him, no country but his own would do to live in.

Jews do not have this connection with the soil, so they have an exaggerated connection with the family. Jews have no connection with other people; they have a complete lack of connection with Aryans, who are rooted to their country. In Jewish families, there is intense love, hatred and fighting. With a Jew, everything takes place in the family circle, as Jews really do not participate with people outside their family circle.

Onkel went on to ask what the Lump could do to me if I die. One of the strongest points of the Lump is my fear of death, he said. I cling too much to the world. I have the Lump inasmuch as I can't adapt to the fear that existence might come to an end.

My fear of death is kept repressed and locked in a closet. I do nothing which could endanger my life. If I think anything is especially dangerous, or might be, I keep my fear secret. My fear of death is just as secret as sexuality is to young people: their secret love or their secret fear.

Katy would be faced with death in the coming year, though not her own. I doubt that Katy feared death more than other people, as Jung suggests, though she was fearful in some respects, of cows, horses, and enclosed places. Yet she flew in commercial airplanes, and even flew with her father-in-law in his small two-seater just after World War One. (He had learned to fly at fifty-six, and patrolled Boston Harbor for German submarines during the War.)[1] Her fears were usually irrational: the Dolderbahn was perfectly safe, whereas the animals she feared were passively grazing.[2] When a really serious occurrence took place, Katy was calm and resolute, her Sea-Captain side taking control and handling the crisis. As Katy grew older, she tended more to that side, though she herself never recognized it.

---

[1] His age and the small plane were considered less dangerous than her father-in-law's low blood pressure. The fact that no company would insure him came to be a family joke, as he lived to be nearly 102 years of age.

[2] A childhood experience may have put Katy off horses: a carriage she was riding in turned over after the horses had bolted.

Because she did not, she relied for her sense of identity, as I have said before, on the society-hostess persona – which she dropped at home, however, normally relaxing into good fun, but occasionally erupting disagreeably. Although during the course of the analysis Jung develops new ideas about the contents of the Lump, its dominant content, I believe, was the father figure with whom she unknowingly identified herself. Her masculine characteristics showed this, notably the deep voice of which she was proud, liking to tell that when phoning for breakfast in a hotel she was frequently addressed as *"Monsieur."* Because Katy was fearless in difficult situations, I am certain that she would not have gone under if Jung's forebodings, about an Axis victory had come true and she had faced a "sordid existence." Placed in difficulties, she became fearless; it was her so-called easy life that let her down, not giving her the challenges she needed. Her strengths, unused, remained unappreciated; her abundant energies were often wasted on ventures which frustrated her and brought little reward. In a scant few months, Katy would be faced with a difficult challenge indeed.

Katy had already been ensconced with me at the Palace Hotel in Gstaad for over a month when she contacted Jung's secretary, Miss Schmid. We had spent Christmas in Geneva with my grandmother and Tommy, taking the train to Gstaad on 27 December, with Tommy staying at the Hotel Rössli (where he and my mother had first met in the winter of 1930-1931). My grandmother, who disliked Palaces and anyhow could not afford them, joined him there after the New Year, while my mother, wanting to maintain appearances of respectability by not being under the same roof as Tommy, went to the Winter Palace, whose chic ambiance she preferred, and where she and I had spent our first Gstaad winter in 1929-1930. She received the following note from Jung's secretary:[1]

February 7th, 1942

Mrs. C. Cabot
Royal Hotel Winter-Palace
Gstaad

Dear Mrs. Cabot,

[1] Marie-Jeanne Schmid was the daughter of Jung's old friend "Boller" who died in 1932. Swiss French on her mother's side, she had trained as a secretary and was gifted for languages. She worked as secretary for Jung during the War.

Dr. Jung asked me to let you know that he could see you on Monday, Feb. 16th at 10 a.m. Unfortunately this is the first possible hour.

Yours sincerely,

Marie-Jeanne Schmid

February 17, 1942

I really was so glad to see Onkel after my five weeks and six days in a whirl of extraversion with what seemed to me uninteresting people. I almost fell on his neck and told him what hellish suffering I had gone through during the last three weeks of my stay in the Palace Hotel of Gstaad.

Onkel said that evidently my unconscious has a terrible resistance to people, as I seem to have adapted myself too much to people in the past. I said that was surely it, but also I did not think I got on with anybody very well, and that on my first day in the Waldhaus, I saw Frau Doktor [Eugen] Schlegel, who is the Club librarian, and she just looked right through me, as do society people. Onkel said that the Schlegels have had to come and live in the Waldhaus because they have no coal; they are also having a disagreeable altercation with the Club and are at loggerheads with everyone. He said they were the most difficult people at the Club.

Then Onkel went back to the life and people of such big 'Palaces.' He said it was a sinfully empty kind of life, so superficial, and he never went to such places. He said that after a few days in such a place, he got sick; that such silly and superficial people were like bad dreams, and though they may be thirty and forty and even fifty or seventy, they are mentally Janey's age, which is an age still full of illusions. Janey's infantile puberty atmosphere is their age. So, of course, it is a terrible bore for me to be shut up in a hotel with such undeveloped, unconscious people. There are not many people in that smart society set who ever grow up. It would be better, when it gets too much for me, to have a companion for Janey. I told Onkel I was not too keen on that, as it would take Janey right out of any kind of decent influence if she lived that life all the year – that I preferred to tackle the job myself and have time allocated for everything (if I could manage that), then I could have my free moments, too.

I wonder what story my mother had told Jung for him to suggest a companion for me. Catharine would certainly not have liked a companion to take her place, because it was when *she* was in *her* "infantile puberty personality" that she booked into Palace Hotels. When she had an urge for Palaces, she was as infantile as myself and all the other Palace guests. It did not bore her at all to be in a "Palace." But her mood would swing, and she would feel guilty, especially if she were not having a ball all the time. After those seven weeks, she probably had grown bored because the roles were slowly reversing: I was no longer the child she put to bed for supper until thirteen, but was now the more socially active one, whereas Tommy had suddenly aged, no longer keen on late evenings and wanting to dance. After dinner with my mother and Tommy most evenings, I met a younger group for dancing, and it may have been difficult for my mother to accept that her daughter was growing up. And Tommy was growing duller that winter, as unbeknownst to us he was very ill.

Onkel said that one can't preach: one must *do*. That is far better! I then told him that I envied Mrs. Baumann just shoving her daughter back to America, and thus being able to sit and study her white mice or lice, or whatever it was.[1] He said that it had cost Mrs. Baumann a lot to do that. She had finally sacrificed herself and sent the girl home as she decided that the girl needed the American milieu to develop in. He said that he only mentioned the companion because Janey was a huge task, which at moments I would like to be released from. He said that one should wish for Janey some work; she should get accustomed to a more serious type of life with duties, and when I had a home, she could help a bit with this or that. I said she had her drawing, but that she seemed to wish to give it up for just frivolous people she met in hotels. I told Onkel that was very popular with certain people. But he asked what was the good of that 'popularity' when she only gets an inflation and gets disagreeable. She seems to like the atmosphere of the international crowd. Onkel said that I must be firm and say, so much time for pleasure and so much for work. I must have my time for myself, too, or the devil will explode. Onkel said that was why he never

[1] Mrs. Carol Baumann's lecture with slides (9 November 1940) was "Tierpsyche und menschliche Psyche. Referat und Kommentar und Vergleichsmaterial über die *Seele der weissen Ameisen [Soul of the White Ants]*, von Eugene Marais."

went to such places – if he did, he would become a perfect fiend in a few days, would probably stay mostly in his room. And when he did go out into the public rooms, would probably glare at the people and be most awfully rude, generally. He said that he would easily become a devil in such an atmosphere as such places did not suit him at all. He said that of course I had become nasty, and the devil will explode if I have to live that life continually, and do not get enough time for myself, for I will become overwrought if pushed too much by Janey in that life.

What my mother said to Jung about envying Mrs. Baumann was bravado. She never wanted to hand me over to anybody in America; on the contrary, she fought my family's influence tooth and nail. As the reader will recall, Katy 'ran them down' to me, and made it impossible for me to get to know them, stalling them during their visits to Europe and never once taking me to America before the War. As for staying at the Palace, my mother makes me the scapegoat, for it was all *her* idea, underscored by the fact that both Tommy and my grandmother were at the cheaper hotel. Jung was not entirely right either about Katy's reasons for loathing "Palaces." When the teenager personality in her which chose such places was predominant, she would have "exploded" had she *failed* to have a good time! But possibly during the last three weeks of her stay, which she found difficult, the teenager personality may have waned, as her panics then in the *funis* suggest. The more adult Sea-Captain side, in the ascendant, would have had her view "Palaces" quite differently – more as Jung viewed them. Along with the panics came claustrophobia again, as it had when she overdid partying in her teens. One-sidedness led her to float off terra firma, and, as is frequent with puella personalities, the restriction of enclosures, such as a *funi*, led to panics.

Jung was correct about my need for a sober milieu in which to develop, the kind which my mother's teenage mentality was incapable of providing. Though I would have loathed it, it would have been better for me had my mother packed me off to America as Mrs. Baumann had done with her daughter. Luckily for her I did not want to go, being afraid of a place largely unknown to me, which I had not seen since I was seven. As for my life in Switzerland, I certainly never voiced a desire to give up my drawing for "frivolous people"; perhaps by then my mother may have sensed that drawing was not my vocation, as she had hoped. The "serious life" that indeed would have suited me my teenage mother could not foster, and my own mentality was too infantile to seize the initiative. I simply fitted in with her programs and made the best of them. After a few days at the Palace, my new acquaintances and I skied a lot together and occasionally skated, and in the evenings met in the bar and danced. Some of these were Greeks in exile who stayed the summer in the Lausanne Palace.

He [Jung] went on to say that young people have no proportion or measure. They see no end to life, nor even consider growing old. They see no end, just an eternity. It is due to their vitality of which they have so much to waste. Older people must keep together and not try to leap along with the youngsters. Naturally young people must have their outlet, but not all the time, however. The situation must be so that I can stand it. I cannot let myself be devoured, for then I get horrid and develop too many bad qualities, and it takes too much out of me. Then I react and take it out on 'that damned crowd.'

Whether my mother was being the Sea Captain or the *jeune fille* of seventeen, she always had an abundance of energy – at times much more than I had. The checks on her energy at Gstaad, if I may borrow Jung's terms, were that she both adopted the role of the chic "international crowd," which was an exhausting role for her, and also, probably, felt that she was being treated by my friends as an "older person," which she would have loathed. While not old, she had learned to ski late, and so could not keep up with my group, although according to my diary, I skied with her quite often, and dined with her in the evenings. I believe it was difficult for my mother to see me growing up and away from her. Although shy and introverted, I was in fact finding my feet in this easy-to-know group, having a wonderful time and being treated with respect. The older men were jolly father figures, and their wives surrogate mothers; the younger men liked to dance but never overstepped conventional good manners. In those days, a well-brought-up young man did not jeopardize a girl's marriage prospects by trying to sleep with her unless he was a cad; he looked for sex elsewhere. (A Swiss friend told me that after balls at Fribourg, the young men took their girlfriends home, then went off to the local brothel.) I met a very nice Greek girl, Annie Louloudis, a year older than myself, who was also treated with the respect due to a *jeune fille de bonne famille*. We became great friends, and she began teaching me modern Greek, which she continued to do after the holiday through correspondence.

I said that Janey seemed to have difficulty making friends in Zürich. She was always telling me what snobs Zürich young people were. He said that was not so and that Janey was the snob!

I asked him what he did when his children were young, whether he had to give up a lot of time to them. He said hat he did nothing at all for them except that they went bathing and sailing together, and lived in the country together. But they all had their young friends and did not call unduly upon his time. Besides, he said, he was terribly busy with his work and could not have given up the time to them to take them to nonsense hotels. I told him that of course for his children it was easier, because they had their place and position in Zürich. For Janey, a foreigner living in a strange country, without being properly introduced in Zürich, it was very difficult, and that, of course, in such a hotel she met people, and had the good time it was so difficult for her to have here.

He said that of course all that was true, that Janey must be allowed certain amusements, but that I must be sure to be able to have time to myself so as to build up strength for the time when I need to be in 'Palaces.' He repeated that he becomes a 'roaring devil' when things become too much for him, and begin to pile up. He said that one can make anybody into a devil if you give him impossible conditions. Given certain conditions, he would degenerate into something awful and get terribly nervous. He went on to say that living in such a place as the Palace Hotel, Gstaad, you get into the atmosphere of perfect strangers, who have God-knows-what psychology; you do not know who these people are. They may be awful – which is often the case! He added, that if you live in a pig-sty, or in a stable or in a monkey cage, the atmosphere permeates you psychically and makes you wrong. Atmospheres can do that: simply change a person and get him all wrong and mixed-up within himself.

Onkel said that the people I described living in the Palace Hotel in Gstaad can make you all wrong unless you are very conscious of just what they are. They give out a bad atmosphere *just like the inmates of a prison!* If a person lives for any time in a prison, he soon gets the terrible atmosphere which emanates from the prisoners. In an insane asylum, you get the atmosphere of crazy people. The reason people get all these different atmospheres is due to the fact that the psyche is not wholly in the body. It is *around one*. We *breathe* the psyche. It is as if one were *smelling* it! That, of course, only holds good for very conscious people who have worked and studied to make themselves so. The average person, who is quite unconscious, naturally does not breathe or smell the psyche.

I wonder how my mother had described my new friends to Jung for him to compare them with "prison inmates"! What I liked about my Greek acquaintances was their naturalness, in contrast to the stuffed-shirt British of that period. The husbands had been hardworking businessmen (mostly in shipping) until forced by the War to flee Greece with their families and become refugees. They knew Europe already and, having plenty of money, could afford to take refuge in Palaces. Nevertheless, none of them gave the impression of being spoiled. They may not have been very conscious, but at eighteen, I did not bother about that. What pleased me was that they were reasonably good skiers who were lots of fun to be with, making many jokes, some just risqué enough to make me feel sophisticated. But they never overstepped the line of good manners. As for my snobbishness, that may really have been my shyness. During the winter of 1941 in Zürich, not only did I see my skating friends socially but I also went to a number of balls, and I fell in love with a very nice young Swiss fellow. Unfortunately, though, his parents whisked him off to New York to do a two-year *stage* [apprenticeship] at the Crédit Suisse. I pined for him for eighteen months and then, as can happen at such a tender age (I was seventeen when he left), I fell for someone else – who was thoroughly unsuitable. Even I realized it, so I never got involved with the new boyfriend as much as my mother feared I might.

Onkel said that often before a patient comes to him, he dreams a dream about the patient's psychology. It is as if the patient were surrounded by an atmosphere which envelopes Onkel as well. The psyche is like a gas that fills the room. As soon as the person gets within the 'orbit' of that psychic bubble, he is permeated by it. The worst things can be caught from people unless one realizes what atmospheres can do.

Sometimes one gets something from people one does not even see. That is of course rare. Then Onkel told me of his adventure in a cinema. Once, after seeing patients at the Club, he decided to go to the cinema. While sitting there, he had a queer hot feeling in his back and began to wonder what was behind him. He finally looked around during the intermission, and saw a man, a patient of his, who waved to him. This man was accompanied by a lady. Later, on leaving, he met them going out. The man introduced him to his wife. She looked at Onkel in a queer way, which had 'invitation' in her eyes, so he understood the 'hot' feeling in his back as being certain feelings of transference which this lady had for him and which she sent out to him.

Onkel went back to 'Palaces' and reiterated that you are permeated by the atmosphere of such places. He said it was that criss-cross of psychologies which did it. He said that was why he always loathed those big steamers when he went to America with his passage paid for him. The last time he went, he told his sponsors, he preferred a small boat, which took ten days, on which he would meet only simple people. He said those old-fashioned steamers were hell. He felt all wrong on those huge elegant ones and simply dreaded his meals, as when he was alone, he had to have his meals [at a ship's dining table] with other people.

He went on to say that when he was in India, he tried to get off by himself, because at times with the people he was with (American and Maharajahs) he got 'permeated.' He could not stand it any longer and had to seek a few days of solitude, which was always hard to find on such a trip.

Onkel said that in Palaces, big steamers etc., he always had the desire to 'push away' such people as he did not like them because they filled him with their childish psychology, which is eighteen-year-old psychology, like Janey's. To be with such people is like eating bad food.

I then told Onkel how I really suffered in Gstaad, and had, whatever the weather, taken my [packed] lunch and fled down to de Trafford, who lived in a nice simple place with good food. I said that I often used to think of him [Onkel] ensconced in Küsnacht, leading the ideal life. He said it was not as ideal as that, and that his work was really very hard because he was not always up to it – it was often over his head. When he applied himself really diligently, he sometimes managed to keep level with it, but just as often not. It was mostly a horse-length ahead of him. He said that really his work was above him and it was no child's play trying to keep up with it. He said that he could find easy work but that *his* work was just too difficult for him.

I said I had always thought the contrary, and that he just sat and gave people advice with ease. He replied that it was not so. I said that I often thought he might be lonely because he once said the word *'einsam'* [lonely] in a game we played at the Club. He replied that he was, that he was quite isolated, and that it was a difficult thing to be related – to have adequate relationships. He said I must not imagine that his life is all honey and easy-going.

Then Onkel went on to say that evidently, after a few weeks in Gstaad, I was in need of something else, and the Palace situation did not suit me anymore. The 'panics' are the manifestation of the unconscious, and it is very clear the way the unconscious is manifesting itself, and says, "Away from that crowd!" The symptom has been reduced to a perfect meteorological system; my panics are a sort of barometer going up and down. Of course, he said, it was inconvenient to have this condition, but nevertheless it is a sign that I am in the wrong atmosphere for me, when I am with such people. So I am 'punished.' He continued that being with such Palace people was like a series of official dinners he once had to attend: the first dinner spoils the stomach; thus, one just cannot eat anything any longer at the subsequent dinners.

So now, he said, that when I know I am doing something which does not suit my nature, my 'barometer' – the panics – starts working so as to call a halt for a while. I told him, I remember that at first I was able to go up in the Gstaad *funis* [chairlift]; it was only later, when I got fed up with those empty Palace people, that the panics got so bad that I had to choose the lunch hour to go up in the [empty] *funis* and then I had no panic.

I told Onkel that I had read such an interesting book on Tibet by Alexandra David-Neel, *Mystiques et Magiciens du Tibet*. He said that she was quite a person, that he knew her because she came once to the Club to lecture. He said her books were excellent and well worth reading. One book, he liked especially, was written by her adopted son, Lama Yongden. He said it was both interesting and entertaining. I asked if her 'adopted son' was really adopted or just a convenient way of camouflaging a beau? He said he was in two minds about it, but thought it quite probable that Lama Yongden was a beau.

Then, before leaving, I asked if I should pursue my reading of *Psychological Types* with Toni, as I found it difficult to remain on the *Types* with her as she always wanted to branch off on the personal stuff. He said I was to continue with her so as to learn to *put through my point* and hold her down to the *im*personal.

I told him that I found Mrs. Jung knew everything, but that I didn't think that Toni did. Onkel said that Mrs. Jung possessed very solid knowledge, which Toni did not have. She did not like to study much and relied on her brilliant brains.

I said that I thought Toni's advice for me to introduce my mother around when the occasion arose, and not to hide her too much, had proved right. I had done so to a couple of people in Lausanne, and felt better about doing it in the future.

The hour ended with my telling Onkel that it had been wonderful to be able to see him again after Gstaad, and that I really appreciated him, and that it was like getting back into the Promised Land after having been in hell.

Catharine certainly could be dramatic! Instead of returning from Gstaad directly to the "Promised Land" she went first in the opposite direction to Lausanne, where we spent a week at the Lausanne Palace, officially to visit my grandmother at her pension. Jung knew only too well the part of Katy that loved "Palaces," the seventeen-year-old in her that was twin to myself. The actress, who produced the society persona, loved them also. But the side least known to her, symbolized by the Sea Captain, did *not*, and eventually, after too long a stay, got fed up. The Lump began to roll, and the panics made their point. In my Diary for January 1942, I report two instances of Katy's claustrophobia on the *funi* ten days apart. Jung was able, for a short while, to dissolve the chic persona and bring the genuine side to the fore, letting Katy abhor what she had previously thought she had enjoyed. When a fancy dress party occurred at a Palace and she could costume herself as a Swiss peasant, she was absolutely at ease and enjoyed herself enormously. My Diary reports that we won first prize at the Gstaad Palace as a peasant couple. Why Katy felt that she had to hide her mother is strange, unless her society persona was intervening once again. Her mother was perfectly presentable and could be excellent company.

March 2, 1942

We spoke of people putting on airs. Onkel said they had to in order to make up for their defects. Putting on airs and graces is a sort of compensation.

I said that I thought I had undergone a great change. Onkel said that I had undergone it long before this winter, but that I may not have noticed it, and it only came home to me in the Palace Hotel in Gstaad. It was there that I had realized it. One can be changed without knowing it: it just hits one and seems like a discovery, while really one has been that way for a while. Onkel also said that for years a person can take on, little by little, airs and graces and all that artificial nonsense and not realize he is doing it, going to such infinite trouble and pains to be artificial just because it is the thing in a certain milieu to be so. He said that people just take on foolish airs without knowing it: it is a sort of *'possession,'* just as if a peculiar kind of evil gets into them – but all the while, they do not know that they are possessed. People imitate this or that person and think themselves to be chic.

He said that, for years, I had lived in the clouds amidst all that falseness, and then the Lump brought me down with a crash, and I had to sit up and see what was wrong when the panics got really bad. ... The panics had brought me to him and to another life. It was the panics which 'told' me that I was leading an artificial existence. Evidently, any kind of artificial life is menaced with the panics. He added that: "Anyone who has illusions about himself has the panics. He can't help realizing that he is walking on air!"

He went on to say that a very distinguished man is frightfully keen that people respect his dignity, and beware if they don't! He is petrified that people might take him for something less fine (which he is, of course) and so he has to keep up [a façade of] terrific dignity. He is afraid his dignity will be injured, and for him, this amounts to a panic. I could not help thinking, as Onkel was telling me this, of that poor man, Schneeli, at the Lausanne Palace who had become so injured in his dignity when Tommy and Babu [Henry Clews] had not fallen on his neck the evening I had asked him over to our table. In fact, he felt himself slighted and left hurriedly in a sort of panic. His 'dignity' had been attacked!

I also told Onkel that I had had a panic just before I went down

to General Blacque's[1] dinner in the Palace at Gstaad. I felt awfully.
At the time, I attributed this to the fact that I had to dine with such
impossible people! But Onkel said that was not it at all: the reason
I had a panic that night was because I was afraid someone would
see *through* me and not take me for what *I would like to [appear to]
be!* I want to make an impression of being a *grande dame* or
marquise at such a dinner, and I am afraid I won't be taken for
such! And it brings on a panic because I am afraid I won't be taken
for an equal. Onkel went on to say that of course I wouldn't be
taken for an equal, as the people at the dinner think themselves far
superior to just an American, and in order not to injure themselves,
they simply wouldn't allow me to be taken for an equal – think of
what a blow that would be to their prestige! He said that I should
not go to such affairs with the idea of wishing to play the *grande
dame* etc., but should go quite modestly as the *quiet American
mother that I am*, and just sit back and look at the whole damn
show!

Onkel went on to say that the *marquises* and countesses are all
susceptible and their only value is their name, and of course, they
are terrible snobs, and are afraid they may not be considered
important enough, knowing they only have a name – so of course,
they look down on 'just an American' like myself, who is a 'nobody'
with, to their way of thinking, no name of importance. He said that
no American name, however good in America, cuts any ice with
Europeans. Of course, he went on to say, that if one is an American
with real merits, and possesses something real and natural, one
does not mind that attitude in the European aristocracy. But of
course, if like me, who is trying to play the role of *marquise*, one
fights it, then one gets the panics.

Then I told Onkel about the Sulger-Vischers,[2] – what a sorry and
inappropriate figure they cut at the Palace, and how nasty they got.
He said that he had heard that Mr. Sulger had a bad tongue. Then
he said it was foolish for such people to go to such a hotel and try
to make a *bella figura*. They would have been far better off in a

---

[1] General Blacque was a First-World-War Turkish General. Though he had
never mentioned it, we presumed he had been living as an exile in Switzerland after Kemal Attaturk had come to power in Turkey. His son, Charlie,
who was about three years older than myself, I had first known at the Palace Ice Rink in 1929.

[2] A Swiss couple from Basel.

smaller hotel, just a modest place, if not a *Wirtschaft* [an inn], or a quiet mountain hotel.[1]

He went on to say that the Swiss were peasants and in their lower layers, the peasant was ever present. There never was a court [royalty] in Switzerland, and it bores the right kind of Swiss people to be stiff and elegant and to put on *chi-chi* [false airs]. He said it would bore him to tears to have to go to such a hotel and be chic, and be with such people. The Sulgers just don't belong in such a place, for Swiss manners are not made for a salon, as is the case with French manners, which are derived from the Court of *Louis Quatorze* [King Louis the XIVth]. In the French salon, there is the utmost formality. It is a small Versailles. He went on, "We Swiss are not like that, such ceremonial is strange to us. We are like peasants and have no court ceremonial. For us, all that Versailles stuff is empty talk, the talk of the *ante-chambres*."

Then he went on to say that I had been imitating it by making myself into a *marquise* and that naturally I was miserable having to play that awful role and associate with such people, when, as the daughter of old pioneer stock, I would feel much better with *natural* people. No one is natural is such a hotel.

He said that in Basel the people are exquisitely simple, that the taste and culture of Basel is remarkable. Even the rich people live simply except for a few rich ones who like to imitate certain foreigners and go wrong, just as the Sulgers did in Gstaad. Probably Mr. Sulger thinks that if he does not play the *homme du monde* [man of the world)], he won't be considered.

Onkel said that, evidently, I am sensitive to falsified simplicity, if I did not like the Sulgers' nonsense. But, he added, that I too try to live *above* what I really am, above my level as the descendant of pioneers. I must remember that I am an American and that an American can never be a *marquise*.

We then spoke of the 'rough-and-ready' American. I said that after I had gone to live in America, I had adopted the 'rough style,' as I saw it was the fashion, but that it was not really my style, and that when I came over here, I saw it wasn't me. I told Onkel that I did not want to become a Mrs. Rüfenacht, as that was formless and wild. He said that Mrs. Rüfenacht was a woman who had flown

[1] Before the War, many Swiss went abroad to ski because they felt unwelcome in Swiss hotels.

asunder long ago. She had become too 'sophisticated' and had fallen to the bottom. Whereas I had risen from the bottom. (Mrs. Briner is a Middle-West *marquise*.)

He said that, when Americans come to Europe, they do not fit in because over here there are historical conditions. If one lives over here one knows the history and what people are. He said that no American, however 'mincing', or with marquise airs, could ever put it over on him, for Americans have no history behind them. No American is ever a "lady": a nice woman, yes – but not a lady. He said that the nicest Americans he ever met were *simple* people.

Then he spoke of de Trafford and said that if an American man had the same manners as de T., he would be affected; whereas de T.'s manners are perfectly in keeping with his birth and breeding. If de T. affected Swiss or American manners he would be ridiculous for he cannot jump out of his skin and imitate another style. He said that de Trafford was a real man and a true man and a simple man, and that his manner was natural to him.

I said to Onkel that I had had a French education and some French Canadian ancestry, and that I just could not affect the American style completely. He said that the French showed up in me to a certain extent, and that enough of the French education clung to me. But that it was a pity that I try to be always something more than I am. He suggested that I try to give that up and come down to brass tacks, down to my real style. He said that I would be forever a certain mixture as a certain French style had gotten under my skin.

He said that he had a certain French style himself, as he had been born on the frontier not far from Bâle [Basel], the son of a clergyman. I asked if his father had lived to see his success. He said no, but that his mother had seen it. He said his father had been a great scholar in Oriental languages. He said that he had one sister, and one brother, who had died young.

Then I told Onkel that I wanted to be absolutely honest with him: I wondered if I had submitted to all this grueling analysis because my [real, underlying] ambition was to be 'on top' and successful. He replied that one really doesn't come to him to try to be made a 'success,' and after all, what does the outer thing mean (?). I told him that I was afraid I was a sort of *postiche* [fake] person who was using him as a means to ambition. Onkel said that one worked because it pleased one to do so and not for ambition or to be on top.

I then told Onkel that I did not know what I was. That after ten years of work, I was not advanced in that, and was at sea, completely, as to what I was, or where I was going. Onkel said that as far as he was concerned, that went for most people. He was what he was, functioned as he was, and lived what he was. But that I must not be worried when I did not know what I was because he, too, did not know what he was. Nietzsche had said:

"Nie erhebt sich ein Mensch höher, wenn er nicht weiss, wohin sein Schicksal noch führen wird."

Which means:

"Never does man rise higher, than when he does not know where his fate will lead him."

Onkel went on to say about himself, "I know what I have *done*, but not what I *am*." He then went on to say that once in Africa, he had come upon an African tribe and had tried to find out its name, but the tribe just could not tell him what it was called, and finally just said, "We are the people who are here." Onkel said that to understand yourself you just say to yourself the following: "I have a feeling this is on my line."

There is no use playing the role of a French *marquise*, or of the rough American, as I am neither one nor the other. He said that I must see the picture of myself as I can be. He said that he could not see himself as a Catholic nor as a Protestant, nor many other things. But he felt better living in the country. He liked that type of life, so lived it as it suited him. Evidently, I felt that I was not in my/ the right place in that big hotel.

He said 'seeking oneself' is like trying to find a suitable place to stay in. One must find a place and a life that suits one. And as one looks around, one says to oneself, this is bad taste and this is good taste, then, finally, one comes to the place which suits one. Some people live more happily in a Gothic house, others in a Baroque house, and still others in a modern house. One must find out all that and live the style which is most suitable to one's taste.

Onkel said that you can judge people by the people they like. He said that I could judge myself by the people I was really fond of. If one lives in a God-forsaken crowd, then one is one of them; or if

one lives with respectable people, then one is one of them. He said
the fact that I liked de T. cast a light on me, for de T. is a simple
man with very natural good form. He said that he did not think I
was adapted to a sophisticated place with sophisticated people,
and so have the panics.

I asked Onkel why no one took me seriously when I said I had
work to do. He said that no one assumes that I have mental
interests as I was so much in the society of God-forsaken people
that one takes me to be the same sort. Also I have taken on so many
airs that people say it must be a 'new air.'

He said that Mrs. Rüfenacht exploded under the impact of
European ideas, for she had first lived in New York, and in New
York America collides with Europe. He said that it was very hard
for these young Americans, who had no historical consciousness
yet, to find their place in a European society. The American is not
sure of his base. He said I must remember I am an American and
am not historically differentiated. The European is shaped according to his history, and is made into something peculiarly one-sided.
That is why the Swiss, the Germans, the French, the English all
have a peculiar national character. The American character is too
young to be recognizable. A 'typical American' way has not yet
been established, for in America there is a bit of everything:
Negroes, Italians, etc. and a large contingent of Irish, not a
distinguished tribe, but a wild tribe of Irishmen, with manners that
are by no means English.

He said that the British are shaped in a particular way by the
fact that they are a dominating race. For centuries they have
dominated other races. I said I thought the English put on a lot of
airs. He replied that they didn't because *'they were airs.'* A Frenchman of noble birth *'is airs.'* He is born with them. I said that I
thought the English could be rude: he agreed, saying that distinguished English people talk to each other terribly. I said that it was
the same in Boston, where people of the same class talk awfully
rudely to each other. He said that the English call each other
names, which here in Switzerland, we would not dare call each
other: such as, "You greedy swine!" He went to say that, in
Switzerland, you do not talk *down* to people as the English do,
because the Swiss are not a dominating race. The English 'talk
down [condescend]' – that is their style.

The French, on the contrary, have great politeness. When a
Frenchman is rude, you know he *intentionally* wants to insult you.
A Frenchman says, "*Enchanté de vous voir, quelle joie* [enchanted/
delighted to see you – what a joy] etc." and the Germans say it is all
bunkum. However, it is the Frenchman's way – just as the Swiss
are *grob* [rough]. He said that the Swiss can sometimes be very
grob just like a peasant who is not ready to give an answer. I told
him that de T. always said that the Swiss were a peasant race.
Onkel then told me that when Keyserling came to Küsnacht once
on a visit to see him, he had said that he thought the Swiss were
just peasants. Onkel told him he was right, and that they never
dreamt they were anything else! They were not counts or dukes or
Lords, and had never dominated other races nor talked down to
them like the British.

Onkel said the British must talk down. The British consider
Americans as colonials. In fact they consider even their own people
colonials, even people of the aristocracy, if they have had the
misfortune to be born in a colony. He had had a patient who was
an Earl, born in Australia, and all through his years at Eton, and
later at Oxford, this man was considered to be 'below the mark,'
even though his family was a perfectly good one, and he just
happened to have been born by chance in Australia. Onkel said
that this man later became a hellish snob.

Onkel said that if an American is not effusive he thinks there is
something wrong with him. In France, one can never get near the
people – never know a Frenchman – for even they themselves do
not know each other.

Before I left, I told Onkel that I thought he was so humorous,
that everything he said was so amusingly put. He said that humor
is the only divine quality of man.

Notwithstanding her parting remark of appreciation, this must
have been a tough hour for my mother, as Jung emphasizes her
American side – which she liked to forget.

The dinner on 24 January was not the first we had had with
General Blacque, but it was a "Gala dinner"; we were twelve in all,
including General Blacque's son, Charlie. It was not especially chic,
nor terrifying, nor were the guests "impossible people." Old General
Blacque, a portly person in his mid-sixties, was friendly and welcom-
ing, and certainly "old school." Rumor had it that he had served as an

officer prior to the War, under the Ottoman Empire. We had known
him since 1929, and saw him frequently during our stay at the hotel.
It is strange that the anticipation of this particular party brought on
an attack of claustrophobia. Whatever Katy may have expected, the
party was actually for the General's Swiss relatives, the Benois, who
were charming and completely natural. Apart from them, everybody
was an exile of sort, temporary or permanent; he had invited some
Greeks and an Armenian as well as ourselves, and they too were quite
natural, which was why I liked them. In wartime, everyone, however
rich, was living a precarious existence; while Switzerland appeared to
be a safe haven, nobody in 1942 could be sure that it would remain
so,[1] and this uncertainty tended to make even the Palace Hotel people
human! The Greeks at the hotel were a companionable group, having
no time for people playing the *grande dame*. I was reasonably natural
because I was young, so they accepted me. The problem lay with
Katy, who projected a false image onto General Blacque's guests. And
she avoided the Greeks because she *felt* she had to play a role with
them. When she thought she *'had* to' look chic, she was uncomfortable, but when she could dress [freely, as she wished] for a fancy dress
party, she would have a wonderful time, wherever she was.

---

[1] There was a saying in Switzerland during the War that the Swiss worked
for the Germans during the week and prayed for the Allies on Sunday. But
as there was censorship of the press, we never knew to what extent the
Swiss "worked" for the Germans – so we felt throughout the War that Switzerland could be invaded at any time.

Chapter Nine

Tommy's Illness and Death; My Wedding, 1942-1943

The first signs that something was not right with Tommy manifested early in 1942. His enthusiasm for skiing diminished; he preferred to potter in the village. When he did ski he was slower, and his balance was poor. Also his skin, usually a healthy pink, acquired a grey tinge. I often skied alone with my mother as Tommy was apt to find excuses not to come with us. I noticed these changes but did not mention them to my mother, as I simply imagined he was aging. Indeed he was, but it was *accelerated* aging.

Some weeks after my mother's session with Jung about the Palace Hotel in early March, Tommy lost his voice overnight. At first he imagined that he had caught a cold, but as his disability persisted he could not speak above a whisper, and my mother insisted that he see a doctor. This he eventually did, in Zürich. Meanwhile we spent some time at the Kleine Scheidegg before the close of the ski season. During the War, Switzerland was a village; wherever you went you met people you knew, not just in resorts but in the larger towns, and even on trains. The Greeks too were at Kleine Scheidegg, which, at 2,000 meters [ca. 6,000 feet], had a much longer skiing season than Gstaad, a thousand meters lower. Bundled up against the cold and minus his voice, Tommy went with us for the two-week stay. Then I went on to our flat in Ascona while my mother and Tommy finally returned to Zürich. They came down to Ascona, however, for Easter on 5 April; my Diary notes that I received a bag of chocolate Easter eggs from my mother, but "nothing from T. too ill to buy presents." Nevertheless they stayed on in Ascona, going out with the same crowd, which included Henry Clews, his girlfriend, Leni Aichele, and Franco Franzoni, a blind pianist whom Clews had in tow as a drinking companion. For some reason, we christened him *Le Poupon* [large baby]. Tommy and my mother returned to Zürich only on 21 April to consult more doctors, and Tommy returned alone to Ascona on 3 May; I fetched him at the Locarno *Bahnhof* [train station], and took him out to dinner. A drunken Henry Clews joined us and followed Tommy to his bedroom, refusing to leave. On 5 May, I returned to Zürich with Tommy, and the following evening my mother and I took him to the *Roteskreuzspital* [Red Cross Hospital]. He was due for an exploratory operation early in the morning. At 10:30 a.m., my mother visited him; the news she gave me from the doctors, while we were at the hairdresser's, was ominous, and I found Tommy "shaky" during my visit that evening.

After that sad interval, I took up my life again and went off to Bern for a party at the *Grande Societé* to celebrate Robert von Muralt's forthcoming marriage to Madeleine von Muralt of the Bern von Muralt clan. To my astonishment, my Latin teacher, Marie-Louise von Franz – whom I had never imagined would go to a party – was also there. At the wedding on the next day, I noted, among other details in my Diary, that nine carriages and three taxis had taken the wedding party away. On 21 May, the Diary observes that Tommy, now at the Klinik Hirslanden, was looking much better. But the improvement would only be temporary. Poor Tommy had been diagnosed as having advanced cancer of the esophagus, so no operation could help him. My mother, ever desperate to find a cure, enquired about other treatments, and eventually the cancer specialist agreed to try to burn the cancer with radium therapy. This type of treatment was then in its infancy, so the rays could not be aimed exclusively at the growth, but also spread over neighboring tissue. Tommy's throat was terribly burnt, and he suffered a great deal of pain, but being a stoical individual, he did not complain.

I was packed off to Ascona to occupy our flat at Casa Eranos, as my mother wanted me away from the dreariness of hospitals, and also wished both to save the cost of a hotel bedroom and have me keep an eye on our maid. From there, I wrote my mother a number of letters about the difficulties of housekeeping under more and more severe rationing, and kept her abreast of the post we received, with an anxious eye out for the renewal of our three-month permits to remain in Switzerland. Katy stayed in Zürich to visit Tommy daily at the clinic.

Apart from playing golf, I took some drawing and painting lessons with a local artist named Kohler, and went out evenings. Through golfing I gradually got involved with a Ticinese [a man from the southern Swiss canton of the Ticino] many years older than myself, while my Zürich boyfriend, in New York now, and although we corresponded regularly, slowly took a back seat in my mind. Though I had held firm over months, the Ticinese was quite skillful in wooing me; being broke and hoping to make a match, he did not try to seduce me, and I, obviously sexually unripe, was content with good-night kisses after we left the group we had been out with. Nevertheless, as we regularly played golf together, we were soon called "fiancés," which I did not like a bit. I phoned my mother about the upsetting gossip, but she was too busy with Tommy to chaperone me, so I continued to play golf and cycle with this boyfriend. From time to time, he lay low – I suspect he was still seeing his so-called "ex-girlfriend" in case it did not work out with me – but I had plenty of friends, sometimes rowing with Henry Clews when Leni Aichele was recovering from a hangover, or rowing *à trois* with them. I had no desire for marriage, so I made a joke of the "fiancé" talk, but my mother was finally becoming worried.

After a month alone in Ascona, I returned to watch a golf tournament at Zumikon on 28 June, the Ascona group in tow. At dinner, I sat next to the Aga Kahn, who had presented me with a ski racing prize at the Gstaad Palace Hotel earlier in the year. But this time, though he generously poured wine for the lady on his left, he snubbed me. (He kept enormously fat, receiving his weight in gold every year from his subjects.) From then until the end of July, I was back and forth between Ascona and Zürich, with no celebration of my birthday on 30 June, and my mother's immediate return to Zürich after a brief trip to Ascona. On 25 July, Tommy celebrated his fifty-seventh birthday in Klinik Hirslanden. My mother had lost hope that he would recover; late in July my so-called fiancé showed me his family vault in Locarno where he suggested Tommy could be placed! On the 31st I returned to Zürich, visited him several times, and was about to return to the Ticino when my mother rang saying that Tommy was much worse, so I stayed on, his condition changing for the next few days, then went back to our flat in Ascona. During this unsettled time I received in Ascona a letter from my boyfriend in New York asking

me to marry him. He had completed fifteen months of a two-year
stay, learning banking with the Crédit Suisse; I had known him for
only three months, and was not ready to marry, being just nineteen.
His offer came when I was occupied with my mother's problems with
Tommy, traveling frequently and keeping house for her at Casa
Eranos. My own affairs were not at the center of my concern, as the
letters to my mother showed. They were full of housekeeping problems: the Wartime cost of food, the skimpy meat ration, the impend-
ing rationing of milk with cards available for us only in Zürich, the
piercing of our valuable (unrationed) supply of sardine tins (with
nails, I pondered), and the expiration of our living permits, without
which we could receive no ration cards for the following month.[1] I
also had to confess to her that I had been fined ten francs for cycling
during the blackout with my lights on. About the marriage offer, my
mother advised me to wait until he came back, so I wrote to him
accordingly. Early in August, after returning from another crisis-visit
to Tommy, I received the following from my mother, dated 6 August
1942:

> Janey dear,
> How I *envy* you being in that delicious Tessin! Sometimes I get
> jittery and so tired, after so many months of such *severe* illness, and
> as for the last ten days of 'deathbed scenes' well, I am just 'all in.'
> But now, today I feel better, *because* after all I think Tommy is
> going to pull through the treatment – the part that only 4 out of
> 1000 get through! Dr. Fingerhuth is still muttering in his beard,
> that he can't understand it, that it is the 'Miracle' and that by every
> rule, Tommy should be dead. However, Tommy evidently has
> *willpower* and has decided he is going to get well. Now today,
> *wonder of wonders* he has got down a bit of lime juice and gin, just
> a little, but it 'went down.' He did not have the 'aigue' after his
> infusion of 'Holofusin' and is generally better, talks more, asked
> me to rub his head with violet lotion to prevent his locks getting
> yellow. I suggested to Dr. Fingerhuth two things: one, feeding by
> rectum & the other a throat specialist, to see what can be done for
> the inflammation of all those mucous membranes. Dr. F. thought

---

[1] It should be noted that conditions in Switzerland during the War were
more difficult than the popular notion would have it. The ration of eggs, for
example, was two per month. Our rationing in general was more severe
than in Great Britain.

both suggestions good & so tonight Tommy is having a camomile enema to clean out what there is (?) & then he's going to have milk & eggs *per rectum* – as he is better now, he will *maybe* be able to 'hold it in' so that it gets into his system. Dr. F. says that is a very good way of getting food into a person & that it *does* go through the wall of the intestine & gets into the system somehow. Then in a day or two he is going to have Dr. Ruedi, who comes from Bern, look into Tommy's throat. One certainly has to hand Dr. F. the palm, for his handling of this case & his 50 injections (more than they ever give!!) of Cibazol, certainly have done wonders!

Of course it will be a long pull up & then one has the actual *cancer* to face – but maybe that has been destroyed by the so vigorous six weeks' treatment, which almost killed Tommy. When he is better, photos will have to be taken to see if the cancer was arrested *enough*, to make life possible for him – but that's later, as now it will be *weeks & weeks* before he is on his feet again, or even well enough to take X-ray pictures. It all looks like a long uphill pull, but *if he gets well*, then my job is done & I retire to a mountain for a *complete* rest as I am just exhausted now. I am glad you saw those 'deathbed' scenes & so *you* realize how *awful* it's all been.

Today I had my hair curled & combed by Ziegler[1] & there is a big fashion show from Milano, in a day or so at the Baur-au-Lac [Hotel]. An artist was making drawings of the head dresses, made by 'Hans.' After Ziegler had finished my head, he made one [drawing] of mine & really I had no idea how chic the headdress was, until I saw it on paper. Ziegler & I decided (he did really) that *'obsi Frisur'* suits you best, because you are so young & he said, *"mit der Frisur unten ist sie süss, aber mit obsi ist sie piquant!!"* [with her hair down she is sweet but with it up she is spicy] & I think he is quite right, it really is very nice.

I have talked with Madame Roche [her mother] in Crans & as yet, she has seen no view, frightfully cold with mist & cloud – too cold for Clews and Leni [also in Crans] to play golf today, as the wind was terrific. Clews told Mme. Roche that the 'Casino Greeks' were impossible people & that he could not understand that I so *neglected* my duty as a mother, as to allow you to associate with

[1] The Zieglers ran the Baur-au-Lac's hairdressing establishment, Mrs. Ziegler making her own face creams. The chiropodist there had the following visiting card: *"Wenn es zuckt und zieht bis zur Ekstase, gehen Sie schnell zu Dr. Hase."* [If it twitches and pulls like a snare, then go quickly to Dr. Hare.]

such people! Well, a fat chance I'd have to forbid it. I knew they
were ordinary people. From the way the Greek Minister's wife in
Bern maintained a dead silence, when I spoke of them, I saw they
weren't well thought of. But the Lagonicos are nice & after all, one
has to know & meet all kinds of people before one can be a judge
of people. I don't think your knowing them has hurt you.

    I enclose a letter from '*each suitor*': the Zürich and the Tessiner
one. I know the telegram[1] is *right* and *honest* & you can send it to
him in a day or so – When you see him again, you can see [decide
if you want to marry him]. He's a dear person [but] so is the other.
You are still so young: you may meet yet another one you like
better than both – *chi lo sa*? [who knows?] I think it best sometimes
to remain inactive & then the problem solves itself, usually.

        Love & a hug,

           Ma

Though my mother's hopeful letter about Tommy and the energetic program she planned for him made me think he might pull
through, his regained grip on life proved short. He had endured the
terrible burns of the treatment only to rally briefly and then sink into
a coma. Late on 9 August, I received a telephone call from my mother
telling me that Tommy had died at 8:30 p.m. I returned to Zürich the
next day, traveling 3rd-class with Dr. Jung, Barbara Hannah, Toni
Wolff and others coming back from the Eranos *Tagung*.

    I saw Tommy laid out among a beautiful array of flowers and
escorted friends to see him that afternoon, among whom was Toni,
who next day lent me a black dress for the funeral. On the 12th, with
my grandmother, we attended Tommy's funeral at the St. Antonius
Church, a grey stone pile near the Römerhof, then the interment at
the Enzenbühl Cemetery. Among the many who attended were Dr.
Jung, Mary Briner and Toni Wolff. Tommy's death must have been a
terrible blow for my mother, who had been game for trying every sort
of treatment. All her life she held to the belief that doctors could keep
death at bay. In 1940, when her father died just over the Swiss frontier
(she was not allowed to attend the funeral), she had been very upset
at not being able to do anything. But in Tommy's case, she had been
in charge. His English relatives could not travel in wartime, and she

---

[1] I had sent the letters from both men for my mother to read, along with a
  draft of the telegram for her approval.

had faith to the end that a competent doctor could somehow pull him through.

After Tommy's funeral, my mother and I were invited to tea with the Jungs at Bollingen, traveling by train to Rapperswil and on from there by taxi. In my Diary I wrote: "Toni was there, too. Bathed and had Nice Tea." (The capital letters testify to food's importance in those days; though we had just lunched at the Hotel Baur-au-Lac, the plentiful tea made its impression.) I left for Ascona on 15 August; my mother settled Tommy's affairs as far as she could in Zürich and then joined me on the 20th. She was drained by the harrowing weeks of Tommy's illness, and was very unhappy without him, but she kept her sorrow to herself and began going out and seeing people as before. Her cousin, Gardner Richardson, First Secretary at the American Legation, came to visit, as did several other people from Bern and Zürich, so she was not immediately exposed to Clews and his hangers-on. We did not escape for long, however. On discovering that we were back, he was at us, still drinking and full of pranks, as he had been with Tommy months earlier when he trailed him to his bedroom and refused to leave. A note in my Diary says that at 6 a.m. Clews climbed through our window, "unlocked my door and woke me up – pulled oropax out of my ears. I was furious." Katy had not the heart to return to Zürich that autumn, so we remained in Ascona until December. We played golf and saw friends. Along with Clews were his girlfriend Leni and *Le Poupon*, the blind pianist. As I was frequently at the same dinner parties my mother could keep an eye on me.

A week after the funeral, the first message Katy received from Zürich was a handwritten note from Jung about an offer she had made:

> Küsnacht-Zürich
> Seestrasse 228
> 19th of August 1942
>
> My dear Mrs. Cabot,
> It is very kind of you to call my attention to Major de Trafford's bicycle. It is very tempting, I admit – but after some consideration, I reached the conclusion that I am too old for a new bicycle. I can really do without one.
> Hoping you have fine weather down in Ascona.

I remain yours

    cordially,

        C.G. Jung

A letter from Mrs. Jung followed:

Undated [1942]
Küsnacht-Zürich
Seestrasse 228

My dear Mrs. Cabot!

Thank you very much for your letter; I was so sorry that I was not at home during those days and could be of no help to you. You have gone through it all very bravely indeed; I can feel so well what it all meant for you, outwardly and inwardly. It will still be hard on you to get accustomed to the void left by your friend's death, one who was near you during so many years! As I heard from Dr. Jung and Toni, the funeral was very beautiful; I was glad about that, as it seems to me that it needs something impressive and beautiful to form the final point in a man's life.

Somehow it helps to accept fate and build like a bridge to the spiritual realm, in which our beloved-ones live on for ever. I also hope that the demands of life will help you and that you will find new forces after this exceedingly strenuous time, which must have been rather exhausting!

In the lovely Ascona surrounding you will have an ideal place for resting.

I also want to thank you, for having left us your apartment, and provided us with tea-things, and cigarettes which we were very glad to use. We always made tea for ourselves, which was very nice and restful and helped Dr. Jung not get too tired. I also have to confess, that we ate some of the biscuits in the box in the kitchen – please excuse. For telephone calls I owe you 20 Fr. which I am sending you by post.

With warmest greetings also from Uncle.

    Yours very sincerely,

        Emma Jung

A few weeks later Katy received the following card from Mrs. Jung:

Bollingen, 24 Sept. 1942

Dear Mrs. Cabot! Thank you for your letter; I had no idea you were in Zürich and at the *Kinderhilfe* bazaar; it is a pity I didn't see you in the Poly. Now we are in Bollingen again until the end of next week; Dr. Jung is starting work again on Monday Oct. 5th.

I just rang up the Waldhaus to ask you, whether you would like to come to see us here in Bollingen next Monday or Tuesday, or whether you will still be in Zürich after the 5th of Oct. and would rather come to Küsnacht or see me in town then? I also am looking forward to seeing you and hope you are feeling better now. We have had a fine holyday in the Wallis.

With kind regards,

Yours sincerely,

Emma Jung

Only late in the autumn did Katy's thoughts turn again to Zürich. Ascona had been the place *par excellence* for a recuperative escape, and now she could begin to resume life again. She writes to Jung:

Casa Eranos

Ascona-Moscia

Tessin

November 23rd, 1942

Dear Onkel,

Due to the fact that the Zürich hotels are not being heated, I decided to stay on here, until December 1st. I come to the Waldhaus on December 1st (Tuesday) until the 6th, when I go to visit my cousin[1] in Bern, who is at the American Legation there and wants to have some parties, so that Janey can meet some of the 120 single men who are now there. My cousin seems to feel it would be too bad if Janey married a "foreigner"!!!? Since de Trafford died, I have been through so much that I can hardly believe, today, that I am the same person, whom he knew all those years. But whatever has happened to me, this I can say, that I am no more inhuman or unnatural, nor the "bad sausage done up as a pheasant" – perhaps a "bad sausage," but without the "pheasant" camouflage, nor do I anymore go to infinite pains to make a bad

---

[1] Gardner Richardson, the diplomat mentioned above, was a cousin of Katy's mother by marriage.

impression. I may make it, but only being as I am, not by trying to
"impress." I just tell you these things because they are a load off my
back and it is you who helped me get out of all that nonsense.

I am getting up a small book (on the order of what Toni did for
her mother) in memory of de Trafford. Barbara Hannah (my old
vendetta) is translating the *Grabrede* [the speech given at the grave]
and I wanted to ask you, if you would write something for it – if
you will do so, I will then ask a few other people, who knew and
admired de Trafford, to do so – it would mean *so much* to me if *you*
would write something about him, for you knew him better than
anyone, besides myself and I feel so strongly, that his family should
have an appreciation of his splendid and unique personality. I
know you have so much to do, but for you, it would not be difficult,
as you are so intelligent.

May I also ask for an appointment with you between the 1st and
6th December?

I will be in the Waldhaus on December 1st. I do hope you and
Mrs. Jung are very well. Here, the weather is marvelous.

With kind regards,
Yours affectionately,
Catharine Cabot

Jung replies:

> Mrs. Cabot
> Casa Eranos
> Ascona-Moscia

Dear Mrs. Cabot,
Unfortunately I shall be away in the second part of that week
from December 1st to 6th. I have to deliver a lecture in Basel and
have to leave on Thursday. The only time I have would be Tuesday
at 12 o'clock, but I assume that you wouldn't be here by that time.

I will try to write something about Major de Trafford hoping
that it is not urgent, since I am unusually busy these days.

I also think like your cousin that it wouldn't be suitable for
Janey to marry that *dolce far niente* [sweet, 'do-nothing'] person,
who is only good to play with but for the seriousness of marriage
hardly suitable.

Yours cordially,
C.G. Jung

Whether Jung actually did write something to honor Tommy de Trafford is not recorded; I never saw the "small book" my mother intended to put together. But after the War, she commissioned a memorial stained-glass window for the de Trafford Family Chapel at Haselour Hall in Staffordshire. As for the man I had been seeing, Jung was perfectly right. Even I realized that he was quite unsuitable, charming but no worker, and I knew that I had led a *dolce far niente* life in Ascona with people much older than myself. Clews and Leni acted to some degree as surrogate parents during my mother's absence, and although both were decent people *au fond* [basically], their excessive drinking hardly made them suitable for that role. So when we left Ascona for Bern, I was only mildly upset, certainly not heartbroken – as when my Zürich boyfriend had left for New York. But the Ticinese was persistent, following us on our way. By 7 December 1942, we were in Bern, where my grandmother joined us, having been invited by Gardner Richardson (whose wife was her cousin).

I was glad to be there and to meet new people, and so felt rather awkward when the Ticinese, twice my age, came along uninvited to Bern. He joined us for lunch as often as possible when we were not otherwise engaged. It was only after we had returned briefly to Zürich and then come back for a final pre-Christmas party in Bern that he returned to the Ticino, to my great relief. On the evening after our first coming to Bern, we went to Gardner's official cocktail party where I met many unattached young men, as Gardner had promised my mother I would. Some were 2nd and 3rd secretaries at the American Legation who had been forced by the State Department to leave their girlfriends and even wives at home while *en poste* in wartime Europe. Gardner's wife was also in America. There were also some British officers who had recently escaped from the high-security officer's camp, Colditz Castle in Saxony. On Christmas Eve, as many of our new acquaintances were doing, we went to Wengen for the holidays, a resort unknown to us – a British favorite before the War, but in 1942-43, quite empty except at the holidays. Hardly a foreigner was there, and certainly no Greeks! There we met a young man, Pat Reid, who had been the "escape officer" at Colditz Castle. After organizing the escapes of many other officers, in October 1942 he had escaped himself with three others, and they traveled through Germany in two pairs, mostly by train. Getting into Switzerland itself safely was a particularly difficult enterprise; having been warned that people were often turned back by the Swiss frontier guards, they crossed after dark, but the configuration of the frontier east of Schaffhausen also makes it easy to walk into Switzerland and out again! They were successful, however, avoiding detection and walking to the nearest village before giving themselves up.[1]

Pat came up to Wengen from Montreux, where he had been looked after by kindly British people, and even supplied with secondhand clothes. He joined his fellow escapees – Billie Stephens, Ronnie Littledale and Hank Wardle[2] – in the process of learning how to ski. In the evenings, they drank and made merry in bars, being pretty wild after their ordeal, and in no time greatly increased my vocabulary with swear words I had never heard before. Pat made friends with my mother, his senior by sixteen years, who, flattered by his attention, began a mild flirtation. I was occupied elsewhere, or thought I was, but the young man I was beginning to fancy was not interested in a *jeune fille* [young girl], soon falling head-over-heels in love with a married woman whom he eventually did marry after the War. On the rebound, I began going out occasionally with Pat. A good time such as I had enjoyed in Ascona was all I had in view, since I was mentally much too young for marriage. But Pat had other ideas. Though he continued to be friendly with Katy, he began to give me more of his attention. ... After the holidays my mother returned to Zürich, but I stayed in Bern, taking a typing and shorthand course in preparation for a war job and glad to leave the *dolce far niente* crowd behind. I lived in the same hotel as our elderly cousin, who became my chaperone, and went off skiing on weekends. By late January the Colditz escapees had been transferred to Saanenmöser above Gstaad, a more remote resort than Wengen. The policy of the British Military Attaché in Bern, Colonel Henry Cartwright, was to keep these officers out of town and so out of trouble; Bern was riddled with Axis spies, and Cartwright allowed these officers to associate only with a very small group, to which I was allowed to belong. Several would-be girlfriends were banned because they or their families had German connections, either through business or lineage; the Allies kept a blacklist of Swiss friendly to the Axis.

---

[1] See P. R. Reid, *The Colditz Story* (Hodder & Stoughton, London, 1952).
[2] Lt. Commander William Stephens RN D.S.O., Major Ronald Littledale, and Flt. Lt. Howard Douglas Wardle.

My ambitious mother hoped that when I had finished my secretarial course that I would be given a job as typist by Allen Dulles, who had come to Bern in November 1942 from Washington to direct O.S.S. operations in Switzerland.[1] He was not keen to take on a green girl of nineteen, preferring a more experienced secretary and a more sophisticated woman. So, much to my mother's disappointment, he recruited a red-headed Irish woman recently arrived from Lyon. Soon, too, Mary Rüfenacht *née* Bancroft joined his ranks as a spy, continuing to live in Zürich but traveling frequently to Bern. In turn she tried to recruit my mother, but Katy refused, saying she was not cut out for such work. Mary Rüfenacht was not annoyed. She soon found a willing recruit in her friend Mary Briner. She continued to see Katy in Zürich and also sometimes in Bern when she came to report to Dulles at his residence in the Herrengasse. She wrote the following letter to Katy shortly after being recruited:

> Pestalozzistrasse 47
> Zürich
> Friday evening – December 11, 1942

Dear Katy,

That certainly was something we staged today and I arrived home more dead than alive and very grateful with no hard feelings – but nevertheless greatly baffled and confused, and EXHAUSTED. For it was *not* a simple performance and if you think it was, pardon me for disagreeing.

After I left you I went to the Schweizerhof [Bern] and telephoned my boss[2] who said, "What the hell have you been doing all day?" And I started on my role of THE HYPOCRITE said, "Sorry, I couldn't. I had to see a man about a dog." Then I made a couple more telephone calls and got nobody and then started upstairs to get myself a cognac to see if I could stop my headache and fluttering heart, for believe me, I had both. And at that point I met the gentleman from the Associated Press and his wife who are the people I should have seen and in fifteen minutes accomplished just

---

[1] Office of Strategic Services, later renamed the Central Intelligence Agency.
[2] Mary had been working for Gerry Mayer for some months, who was O.S.S. but had the cover title of American Press Attaché. She met her new boss, Allen Dulles, at the Baur-au-Lac Hotel early in December 1942, and was invited to his house in Bern a few days later: see *Autobiography of a Spy* (Morrow, New York, 1983), 129.

out of sheer exhaustion and the fact that I could no longer speak except in monosyllables what I had failed to accomplish since middle September. Then I staggered onto the train, feeling as if a Panzer Division had gone over me and not till Olten did I brighten up for then it suddenly occurred to me that at some point in the slaughter I had got myself compared to Dr. George Draper whom I have admired profoundly![1]

I have reread all those letters you wrote me with the intention of sending them back and seeing if I couldn't thereby hurt *your* feelings – but they are simply grand letters, Katy – really marvelous and I am not giving them up.

I also telephoned Mary [Briner][2] and asked if she could remember if I had told her who had told me that thing and she said she couldn't. She doesn't think I told her but is sure, as I am, that I had been told. I am dead certain that she is the only person I ever discussed the matter with and if other people who won't be quoted told you I said it – I think they are lying. Furthermore, I am sure it was nobody in 'psychological circles' who said it for I have never discussed you with 'psychological' people.

The "little one" certainly did run "the big one"[3] into a corner and "the big one" is still there – standing up, all frightened to death, in the corner, hoping God will turn her into a great, great, GREAT GENIUS so she can rush out and "BOO! BOO!" at the "little one." If I were Vincent van Gogh, I would cut out my tongue and send it to you but I still need it – to get myself into some more trouble with. And in the meantime, thanks for the truth. I live on it. Do you suppose the same is true of Dr. George Draper?

Give my love to Janey. Does she know she was the cheese in the mousetrap?[4] And as for your mother – well, I wish I could look like that when I am seventy-two. But there's not a chance, is there,

---

[1] Being compared to him was no compliment from Katy's point of view. She had been in love with him during her early days in Zürich; Toni Wolff thought he had treated her very badly (cf. earlier discussion on this subject).

[2] Mary Briner, an American married to a Swiss businessman who had helped found the Jungian Klinik am Zürichberg, was a member of the Jung group in Zürich and later became an analyst.

[3] These refer to Katy and Mary Rüfenacht.

[4] I was living in Bern. Katy was visiting me, hence her seeing Mary R. in Bern and not in Zürich.

Katy? "NOT UNLESS YOU WILL DO WHAT I TELL YOU AND TURN INTO A HYPOCRITE!" shrieked the little one. And that is that.

Yours,

Mary

And will you please stop saying I'm "clever." That is an abuse of the English language. Do you think it clever to let myself in for what I let myself in for today?

There is a second page to the letter, in longhand, with a drawing of a large, malevolent looking animal with a tiny female figure running, as if for shelter, beneath it.

Dear Katy,

This is the monster and this is ME – or rather that is how I *used* to run into its clutches – and believe me they were (& still are sometimes) mighty deathly clutches. Don't flatter me by thinking *I* drew this picture – I did not – I just saw it in a book of Thurber drawings – "Why, there's my friend the monster!" says I – delighted to see the beast immortalized & herewith I send the immortalization to you – since you are going to play St. George to this dragon and would greatly appreciate an objectivization of your prey! My fish is beautiful & now I know of what it reminds me, *mais ça c'est une autre histoire & pour une autre fois*! [but that is another story and for another time.] I had a lovely time today. Excuse scrawl! When one is mean to the Monster he *deflates*. See him deflated.

Love,

Mary

Mary Rüfenacht often traveled to Bern to report to Allen Dulles, but she did not move in Bern society. As a good spy should, she remained an *eminence grise* in the background; she and Dulles met frequently at his house on the Herrengasse, and soon they became lovers.[1] As for Dulles's Irish secretary, she soon became prominent in Bern. Before coming to Switzerland in 1942 she had worked several years, according to rumor, for the German Consul in Lyon. At one of the informal parties this lady was soon giving, the guests arrived to find dog messes of every shape, hue and size throughout the apartment but particularly on the sitting room floor. After careful inspec-

[1] See *Autobiography of a Spy*, 138.

tion they proved to be made of plaster. Though unconventional, these parties were highly successful, members of the British and American Legations flocking to them, and featuring also an American group of single men who lived together in a house dubbed the *Love Nest*. She married one of these men after the War.

The British Minister's wife, "Peter" Norton,[1] would have liked to have employed her, but our Irish secretary had a better-paying job with Dulles. The two women remained friends, however, Mrs. Norton calling her, as she did all the people she liked, "*chérie.*" When I landed a job with her she started calling me *chérie* also. I became her maid-of-all-work (more elegantly titled as "personal secretary"), running errands, typing letters, filing documents and even frequently faking Mrs. Norton's signature on letters she could not be bothered to sign herself. I also accompanied her on expeditions outside Bern. There were funerals of Allied airmen whose planes had crashed in Switzerland; wounded POWs being repatriated through Switzerland and needing succor, and the five thousand POWs who arrived on foot from Italy in 1944, many of them having crossed the Alps, over snow, ice and rock, some wearing only leather-soled street shoes. All these people were in great need of clothes and food when they arrived, and were also glad to have contact with people who spoke their own language. As there were too many to keep an eye on should they be billeted in hotels, like the earlier arrivals from Germany, they were placed by the Swiss in camps. The luckier ones managed to find administrative jobs at the British Legation in Bern. The camp group issued a full-size newspaper called *Marking Time*.

While I was busy adjusting to my new life, my mother went back to Zürich and then to Ascona. She was pretty lonely, but occupied herself with writing prose, and also poetry in French. Before returning to Zürich she received the following letter from Linda Fierz.

Bollingen, 4. January 1943

Dear Katy!

Thank you very much for your letter and good wishes. When on the evening of the Club-dinner you understood that it would be impossible for me to write a small article for the memory of Major de Trafford, you certainly didn't come to this conclusion from what I said. Your question was so unexpected for me that at the

---

[1] Her real name was Noel.

moment I didn't have a reaction at all. I had to think about it first and that was what I told you, didn't I?

Now when thinking about it, it isn't a question at all of whether or how much I liked Major de Trafford – or whether I knew or didn't know that. It would be a big error to believe such a thing. You mustn't forget that I didn't know Major de Trafford personally. I have seen him only with you and known him as a friend of yours. And it was as a friend of yours that I appreciated him most highly and most deplored his death. For me that was all that mattered, for *you* were – and are – the person I know well enough to feel with.

And therefore also now, I would love to do what I can for Major de Trafford's memory, if it were only to please you. I understand so very well how much the wish of giving your friend this last honor must lie at your heart. And I see myself how important it would be both humanly *and* socially that his memory should be carried back to England in the right way. Of course who else but you could have the gift to achieve that task? I understand too that you could never do all of it alone, and that the words of the priest at the burial would not be sufficient. If I grasp you right you will want also to show Major de Trafford's personality in his social surroundings over here, and the values he carried in this respect. And just to show this – if *I* were writing about him as you wished – I do feel that it wouldn't be quite it. It would seem to me not *entirely* correct from the social point of view, if a woman have a say on such a more or less 'official' occasion. You know, coming from Basel, about *social questions* I am hopelessly old fashioned and must stick to it. It simply is my upbringing.

So after long consideration I have thought of something else in order to help you. What would you think and how would you like it, if my husband would write the article you want? To be sure, before writing to you I have asked my husband already whether he would do it. We have talked things over and sort of fixed a general trend of thoughts, which later on might form a short article – not more than two typewritten pages, I suppose. On the condition of writing in German (as you already told me) my husband would be very willing to write the article for you, and of course I would stand in the background and do my best too. So please let me know what you think, and as soon as I would hear that you like the idea you would get an article signed by my husband.

It took me long to find out all this, as your question really demanded ripe reflection. Therefore it is only now I can write to you. The article itself wouldn't take an awful lot of time anymore, I suppose. Excuse my long silence, please, and the belatedness of all the good wishes I am sending you for 1943.

Affectionately yours,

Linda

Katy's replies to this and the following letters are not available. Being touchy, she may not have been happy with Linda's suggestion. Linda wrote a few days later:

18.1.43

Dear Katy!
Thank you very much for your last letter. I am very sorry that you don't feel at ease within yourself. It must be a terrible torment, just to keep going outwardly, and I only wish that a change for the better might soon come to you.

Although I hope we shall be able pretty soon to talk things over I do want to write once more about what you said of my attitude towards Major de Trafford. It troubles me that something seems to be wrong there and I have a vague feeling as if in all this you were underrating yourself quite a lot. You seem to forget what a part you played in my acquaintance with your friend, and that it was only through you that I could see him. When I was together with both of you I always had the impression that you were the container and he the contained one – indeed that a great deal of him was sort of your making. What I appreciated most in him was the exceeding *human* way in which he let himself be contained in you. But what he was by himself I know so little, that hadn't you been present I have no idea whether we should have had enough in common even for a single conversation about more than the weather etc. I was interested in this part of your life that seemed to me so important. And when he died I was really and truly sorry that this important part of your life had come to an end. I also feared, that this loss might bring you very great difficulties. When the contained one goes away, there must be a terrible hole in the container, I think. Without daring to say so – as I didn't want to hurt you after all you had gone through – it was out of this feeling that I wrote to you and approached you at the burial. And it would be out of this same feeling for you that I would write the article you want with my husband. If this gets falsified I don't know that I could write anything at all. I also fear that a wrong interpretation might make trouble between you and me. In the end it might look as if I had liked Major de Trafford more than you – but that really is by no means the case.

As I believe that by now you will have left Wengen I am again sending this letter to your Waldhaus [Dolder] address and hope that it will reach you.

With all my best wishes, affectionately,

Yours,

Linda

Several days later Linda wrote once again:

26.1.43

Dear Katy!

Thank you very much for your long letter. I am so glad, that this misunderstanding about my attitude towards you and Major de Trafford seems to be set aright. And really, Katy, it also seems to me that for once my intuition has been right, and that indeed you underrate yourself most terribly! Your idea, that all this time you were no more than an appendage has quite shocked me, and I do hope that at bottom you don't really think so, it's so wrong! Of course there can have been stupid people who didn't take you seriously, and God knows what intentions were behind it. There always will be such people, but how can you generalize their stupidity!

Well, I'll start at the beginning – that's to say about the 'container' and the 'contained one' – where I seem not to have been clear enough. You know the expression comes from Dr. Jung[1]. He has applied it when writing about marriage, meaning that of two married people always one is sort of the bigger personality, richer in activities, in life-force and a variety of gifts, while the other is simpler, not so active and therefore the one who rather follows the lead of the other. Dr. Jung thinks that is why two people need each other – the one for applying all his or her faculties in giving to the other and finding a sort of mirror for all the 'facets' of his or her being – and the other in being fascinated by all these 'facets' and in

---

[1] See *Collected Works* Vol. 17, "Marriage as a Psychological Relationship," Paragraphs 331c to 334 (Routledge edition pp. 194-197)

this way finding an amount of life he or she couldn't find alone. Dr. Jung's description in his article is excellent, and I think that in many ways it fits every kind of relationship between man and woman. So I didn't mean that you simply *swallowed* Major de Trafford, but rather that you were a *source of life* for him. At least it always looked to me so. Why – even if he was very intelligent and able to decide about difficult questions (what I certainly don't doubt) wasn't it very often you, who presented him the life he could think about? You also went to analysis and did the work he could take a part in. And I have an idea, that sometimes you also presented him with enough conflicts to make things interesting for him. You know what courage it needs to raise the necessary difficulties or to stick to necessities and to be what one is. It seemed to me that in all these ways you had a great deal of initiative and courage and vitality, which quite evidently he enjoyed enormously. If you hadn't been there spreading life around you, Major de Trafford wouldn't have had half as many interesting things to think about, I believe. That's the reason why I thought rather you were the one who contained him, I meant, within your *life*. And as I said, I always thought that a great deal of it was your making.

Dear Katy, when you say that now you have such difficulties in making decisions all by yourself, I understand so well what you mean, and I am sorry for you. It's perhaps the hardest thing for a woman to 'grow-up' in this way. I know that so well from myself. Women really have no talent and no wish to take responsibilities in matters of thinking or of the mind in general. It goes against one's female nature, I suppose, and one needs a man to put one on the right track. Or even more, one needs a man to make fusses about decisions until he shares the responsibility with one. I really think that it is so difficult to find the right way in these matters, that – having had a friend to mirror yourself in for so long – you perhaps shouldn't ask too much of yourself now all of a sudden – but how do I know, perhaps it simply is so for now, and you must find your way? It is terribly hard! Well, it's not that I think I *know*, but just because it might help you a little bit: You know I have sometimes found in such cases, that it was not the decision that was hard to make, but only the responsibility. I knew what was to be done all along, but there is a terrible strong instinct in woman to hide herself. It often seems to me that in the young generation that is a little different. The 'male' side in young women is better developed than it was before. But that has its drawbacks too.

I hope I am not making a nuisance of myself with all I write you. At bottom I just want to tell you how much I am feeling with you.

Affectionately yours,

Linda

Katy never mentioned to me her correspondence with Linda about Tommy's personality. Since she preferred always to imagine herself as very feminine, the picture Linda paints, of Katy as the dominant partner, would not have suited her at all. Her inferiority complex would have blocked the insight. Thanks to her intuition, Linda sees Katy more clearly than Toni Wolff ever did. Knowing that Katy sees herself as a "harmless" and boring kind of woman (see below), she hammers home her qualities using Jung's thesis of the container and the contained, and expressions such as "richer in activities," "bigger personality," "initiative, courage and vitality," "spreading life around," etc. Toni, seeing only Katy's infantile side, never realized her dominance in the relationship with Tommy. Katy herself never realized such dominance in most of her relationships, being so aware of her sensitivity and presuming it meant that she was weak. She also liked to see herself as the feeling type, even though Jung early in the analysis had said that she was *sensation* not *feeling*.

As for Tommy's personality, as I was too young to be able to gauge it accurately I simply remember his as easygoing though also repressed. He was kind and intelligent, but his mind was untrained; like many Englishmen of his generation and class, he had no higher education, joining the Army immediately after leaving school. He was compliant, allowing my mother to choose his clothes and letting her take, as it seemed to me, most of the important decisions in their lives together, although from the above letter it seems that Katy was unaware of her influence over him. Sometimes Tommy's good nature was eclipsed by an "anima mood," usually because his patience was exhausted by Katy's constant demands. These moods could last for several days, during which time he would withdraw into himself or become grumpy if spoken to; it was his way of gaining some distance from Katy.

My view of the helplessness which Katy says that she experienced after Tommy's death is that it was not helplessness but rather emptiness. She lacked someone for whom to take decisions. With

Tommy dead, me in Bern, and even her mother living independently in Geneva, Katy's energy no longer had an outlet. However, she would very soon find one. In early 1943, not long after the exchange of letters with Linda Fierz, Katy filled the void by taking on Henry Clews' blind Ticinese pianist, the *Poupon*. Not only did she instantly have him wearing tailor-made clothes, made by the tailor she discovered in Lugano, but more significantly she promoted and finally arranged an eye operation for him with the famous Geneva eye specialist, Professor Francischetti. Katy had known the Francischettis socially for several years; he was said to be the eye doctor frequented by Mussolini.[1] Blinded as a child with measles, the *Poupon* would be able to see again if the operation were successful. Pleased by the attention and full of bonhomie, he agreed to the operation which initially was a complete success. But he caught a nasty cold from one of his visitors and, as had happened with the measles, his newly operated eyes were unable to withstand the onslaught of the infection. He left the hospital as blind as he had entered it. It was a great disappointment for Katy, whose interest in medical science was intense, but the pianist appeared unperturbed, seeming almost relieved to continue with his life as before. Though this man could not replace Tommy as an outlet for Katy's tremendous vigor for organizing people, he was a useful stop-gap. Though she was shortly to become involved with yet another Swiss, it was five years before she fond a suitable replacement for Tommy. In the meantime, she used her energy to write, and also to organize my engagement and marriage in 1943.

Early in the year Katy received the following letter from Mrs. Jung:

Küsnacht-Zürich
Seestrasse 228
15.1.1943

Dear Mrs. Cabot!

I have been sending you affectionate New Years wishes in my own wireless style, that is in thought, but nevertheless feel somewhat guilty for not having put them down on paper at the right time. Please forgive me and believe that it is not because I had forgotten you; I had such a rush before Xmas, that I just couldn't make myself do anything in the week we spent in Locarno over New Year. Now, even if it is late, I want to express you my heartiest

---

[1] The rumor went around in 1944 that Mussolini had prevented Hitler from invading Switzerland because his eye specialist, Professor Francischetti, lived in Geneva.

wishes and to thank you for your letters, which I was greatly
pleased to read. I was particularly glad to hear about Janey, and so
was Onkel, it is splendid that she is taking that job at the Legation;
this will be excellent for her, I am sure, and help her to get a more
real standpoint in life, and to realize what she needs or what is
suitable for her or not. I hope also that you both enjoyed your
holydays at Wengen, and that it had a good effect!

It is a pity you cannot be here for the Club discussion; your
contribution is very valuable to me and I hope to be able to get it
into the discussion, for you have [come?] upon a very important
point.

We enjoyed our Locarno holydays very much, walking almost
every day from morning to evening (another reason for not having
written). The weather was nice though not so much sun as we
would have liked. Now we feel rested again and prepare ourselves
to start work next week.

I am looking forward to seeing you in February – in the
meantime my warmest greetings.

> Yours very sincerely,
> Emma Jung

Having been occupied with the eye surgery in Geneva, Katy had
missed the Psychological Club meeting. Zürich brought back memories of Tommy, so she spent very little time there after his death. In
another letter from Mrs. Jung in April, it becomes apparent that my
departure from the Tessin and settlement in the better atmosphere of
Bern brought a sense of relief all round. The job I had there with Mrs.
Norton I kept until the end of the War.

Mrs. Jung writes again in April:

> Küsnacht-Zürich
> Seestrasse 228
> Bollingen 20.4.43

Dear Mrs. Cabot!

Indeed, I often was wondering what had become of you, as you
did not turn up in Zürich as we had expected, so I was very pleased
indeed to hear from you now and to conclude from your letter that
you are doing well. So you are in Geneva now![1] Or perhaps this will
reach you already in Casa Eranos. Easter-time in this lovely spring
weather will be marvelous there. I do hope to see you in May and

---

[1] Officially visiting her mother and helping with her move to Lausanne.

hear more fully about how you spent the winter.

I was very interested to hear about Janey. It is splendid, I think, that she has this position in Bern. Does she like to be there? And how fortunate the Tessiner beau had got eclipsed, and lost its importance!

We have had a very good winter indeed and now are enjoying our holyday at Bollingen.

Yes, our discussion at the Club was interesting & considered a success. We had so much material that we could not even discuss it all and so are planning another evening in May or June. It would be nice if you could be present then. Somehow I could not get your thoughts into the discussion, as it took another line, where I could not fit it in, but maybe next time there will be an occasion, as we will discuss probably the collective aspect of relations. If you were present you could make your contribution yourself!

The X affair was rather exciting, I must tell you about it when I see you. The reason why he was excluded [from the Club] is really that through his continued money borrowing and making debts etc., he was considered to discredit the Club, which is true. As something happened just then, the *Vorstand* thought the moment had come to take this step. It was very *pénible* of course, one does not like to do such a thing and he is to be pitied in a way, but on the other hand it is true, that he never seems to learn anything and that it makes a very bad impression as he boasts with being a psychologist & a member of the Club.

I wish you a happy Eastertime and with affectionate greetings,

Yours,

Emma Jung

I have to add this post-scriptum to say: Did you hear of Prof. Zimmer's death?[1] And isn't it awfully sad? He died of pneumonia in New York, as we heard through a cable from Mrs. Mellon. It is

---

[1] The great Indologist Heinrich Zimmer (1890-1943) was a personal friend of Jung. Among his books were *Myths and Symbols in Indian Art and Civilization*, *The Art of Indian Asia: Its Mythology and Transformations*, *Philosophies of India*, and *The King and the Corpse* (all edited for the Bollingen Foundation by Joseph Campbell). He never actually visited India, his only chance for doing so having been thwarted by the outbreak of World War II. Jung alludes to this in his introduction to Zimmer's *Der Weg zum Selbst* (1940, in *CW* 11. Jung also pays tribute to Zimmer's role in confirming his hypotheses of the archetype and the collective unconscious, in a speech, article, and preface from 1948 and 1953 (see *CW* 18, pp. 472, 485, 529).

really a loss. He could have done such fine work and things that nobody else was able to. And for his family it means a terrible loss; I feel such pity for poor Mrs. Zimmer, who first lost her home and now her husband. It is comforting to think, though, that she has found such nice friends in America, who, I feel sure, will stand by her.

Another sad news we read today in the paper: Dr. [Kurt] Binswanger's only son was killed in a flying accident. This is terrible too. He was quite young and just starting as pilot in the army.

Poor Dr. Binswanger – this will be a terrible blow for him.

It is a pity not to know what thoughts my mother had, which Mrs. Jung failed to get into discussing at the Club, but most likely they were about relationships. My mother thought Club members deficient in this respect, as they themselves did also, and for that reason relationships were a perennial Club problem.[1] Since Mrs. Jung was a forceful Club member, whether on the committee or off, if she did not speak up on this occasion there must have been good reason for her not doing so.

About two weeks later Katy received a letter from Linda Fierz in reply to hers. Katy's mother Jane Rush, who had found the Geneva winters too bleak because of the *Bise*, a northeasterly wind that sweeps down the lake, was moving to Lausanne – it was no hardship, as she had friends in both places. Thanks to the move Katy had a useful excuse for being in Geneva.

Zürich, 6.V.43

Dear Katy!

Thank you very much for your letter and Easter wishes! I was very glad to hear from you as it is quite a while since I had your news. I would have answered your letter sooner, if I only had had time. But I spent my holidays traveling back and forth between Zürich and Bollingen, and therefore never had quite a rest anywhere. Just the same I enjoyed this wonderful springtime also in doing a little of an *Anbauschlacht* on our tiny potato field! The new

---

[1] This problem of relationships surfaced repeatedly. I take up this fact in a compact Club History which I wrote in German for the Jung Institute in 1998, a shorter English version of which was distributed by the Club at the Zürich IAAP Congress in 1995.

room at Bollingen is nearly finished, that's to say the workmen have left it and it waits now for its inner perfection.

I often wondered how things are for you at Lausanne and how you were feeling there. I can so well understand that you had to take your time to settle there for good and do it really. I am sure this will make all the difference of the world if you return to Lausanne after this summer. But what I admire most, dear Katy, is the way in which you have let go Janey her own way without a single word of complaint, although it cannot have been all too easy. Of course it must be fine for you to know that she had found an interesting and useful occupation in a nice milieu. I am glad to think that this is a fine solution for more than one problem. At the present time I think it is such a good thing for young people, if they can work and somewhere be a help.

Have you heard that Dr. Binswanger lost his only son in an airplane accident during military service? He was buried Thursday before Easter. It was unspeakably sad, and I am afraid that Dr. Binswanger, who is in military service just now himself, is having most terribly trying hours, without anybody being able to help him. It is an awful thing what he must be going through and to know that one can do just nothing.

As you think of coming to Zürich soon I do hope it will not be long before we see each other. I certainly would love to lunch or dine with you once. If you can only tell me a little beforehand, I shall do my best to arrange things.

Till then with best wishes,

Yours affectionately,

Linda

After Tommy's death and my departure for Bern, my mother no longer spent much time at the Waldhaus Dolder. Lausanne became her official (tax) residence, but she spent little time there either; she preferred Ascona, especially in the summer months. Lausanne could not hold her because, for one thing, she and her mother never could get on together for long, and for another because her official residence, as she did not wish to rent a flat, was the "Lausanne Palace," whose expense, along with her dislike of Palaces for long stays, kept her on the move.

Back in Ascona in May 1943, Katy writes the following letter to Jung:

Casa Eranos
Ascona-Moscia
Tessin
May 24th, 1943

Dear Onkel,

I am very glad indeed that I am going to see you on Monday June 7th at ten o'clock in the morning.

This is to tell you and Mrs. Jung that Janey has just become engaged to a British Captain Reid, assistant Military Attaché at the British Legation in Bern. I think he is Irish, but a very pleasant fellow and good fun. Whether it goes further, I really can't say? A certain amount of character and determination he must have, as he has been recently decorated by the British government [1] for his organization in helping many British to escape from Germany. He himself escaped.

As I spent all last year in trying to prevent Janey from marrying a good-for-nothing Tessiner, I really can't go on trying to save her from herself and though I should think that later she might get tired of this present fellow (but as you said, she will sink her teeth in many things) I feel definitely that it is best to let this go through, as they are both very definite that they wish to be married.

I am giving a large formal cocktail party for all the Ministers [2] and important people, diplomatically speaking, in Bern on June 8th also young people etc. ... to announce the engagement officially. I hope very much that you and Mrs. Jung will be able to come and I am sending you an invitation. At all events, if you can't come to this, Janey and I both hope that you will come to the wedding, which is to take place, sometime during the second half of August.

Well, did you ever? I never thought I'd be doing this so soon.

---

[1] With the Military Cross.
[2] Bern had only legations at that time. The French Embassy was the only exception.

Please give my kindest regards to Mrs. Jung and tell her that I
am so looking forward to seeing her at eleven o'clock on Monday
June 7th.

With love, affectionately yours,

Catharine Cabot

As I have said already, I never had intended to marry the Tessiner,
though he may have hoped to marry me, even though he never asked.
He had been an attractive, good companion while I was keen on
having a good time while living alone. Looking back it seems both
that he filled the bill as a father figure for me, and that he unconsciously sensed this, as he never tried to seduce me. I had no feelings
of guilt when I began going out with the young man I *was* to marry;
Pat Reid at thirty-two was a good ten years younger than the Tessiner,
whom I never saw again after going to Bern, save for one glimpse. In
mid May 1943, while sitting in the dining car with my fiancé on our
way to Zürich from Bern to choose an engagement ring, out of the
corner of my eye I spotted him at another table staring in our
direction.

Pat had been bolder than the Ticinese gentleman. After a few
months of going steady, albeit in a group, he asked me to marry him.
I did not know that he was about to become Assistant Military Attaché
at the British Legation, and would therefore not be repatriated, so I
replied that I did not wish to tie myself down to someone about to
leave Switzerland, which I had already done. Almost immediately Pat
told me that he was staying on in Bern, and repeated his request.
Obviously, at nineteen I was not mentally ripe for marriage, but I did
love a good time. When I hesitated, saying that I would have to think
about it, Pat replied that if I did not say yes, he would no longer go
out with me. So, fearing that a boring time lay ahead, and being fond
of Pat, without further thought I agreed! My employer Mrs. Norton
was thrilled at the prospect of an Anglo-American marriage in the
offing. The wedding preparations were great fun, and a teenager loves
to be the center of attention. It was a great lark and I never looked
back. Even younger than my years mentally, I had no qualms. All I
thought was that, married, I would not be left on my own out of the
group. I was far too infantile to reflect on the seriousness of marriage,
and that I had known my future husband only four months; so I was
shocked when my mother said to me, shortly before the wedding, that
if it didn't work I could get a divorce. I had not thought that far.

Jung replies to Katy's news:

May 27th, 1943

Mrs. C. Cabot
Casa Eranos
Ascona-Moscia

My dear Mrs. Cabot,

This is great news! My most cordial congratulations to yourself as well as to Janey. I hope that this start will turn out to be the right one. One only can be hopeful.

It is very nice of you to invite Mrs. Jung and myself to your cocktail-Party in Bern on June 9th. Unfortunately I have so much work here that I cannot possibly leave. But I will ask Mrs. Jung how she feels about the wedding, which I personally should like to attend. But we first must calculate how it fits into our [vacation] program. At all events I'm very grateful for your kind invitation. I suppose that you have already many guests and if you should feel in any way that there are too many, we shouldn't mind to be left out of the royal feast, since we would be complete outsiders in that show, so to say mere curiosities.

Well, we still can talk it over when I see you next.

With best regards to Janey,

Yours cordially,

C.G. Jung

Though the Jungs did not come to the engagement tea, they sent me beautiful flowers, and Dr. Jung wrote the following note:

Küsnacht-Zürich
Seestrasse 228
June 7th, 1943

Dear Janey,

The surprising news of your engagement have reached my attentive ears and I hasten to deposit my feelings in the form of flowers at your feet. Mrs. Jung joins me in muttering our most sincere congratulations and magic wishes for the permanency of happiness, good luck and general welfare.

Yours affectionately,

C.G. Jung

In 1943 my mother rented an apartment by the year in Frau Froebe's house *Casa Gabriella*, at Moscia outside Ascona, with the proviso that she vacate it during the Eranos Tagung to make it available for VIP visitors such as the Jungs. This arrangement was perfectly agreeable to Katy. In the summer of 1943 she was busy making the wedding arrangements and attending parties in Bern, so it was no hardship for her to have the Jungs take over the flat. Shortly before leaving for Ascona, Mrs. Jung writes:

Küsnacht-Zürich
Seestrasse 228
July 30th, 1943

Dear Mrs. Cabot!

Thank you very much for your nice long letter and quite particularly for all the friendly *'égards'* you are taking on our behalf. I feel sorry, that you have to leave your apartment because of us and I hope, that it does not mean too much of a disturbance for you. You really are most awfully kind! I am looking forward to seeing you and having a good talk with you. How strange that Frau Froebe seems to have changed so; I wonder what is behind it. You probably have the right idea about her, it is a pity if you have to adapt too much in your habits, this must be rather disagreeable!

Your plan for Janey's wedding sounds very fine and original, I am sure it will be much nicer than in the conventional Bern-atmosphere.

With best regards,
Yours cordially,
Emma Jung

P.S. I shall bring biscuits and tea! so please don't sacrifice your valuable coupons!

As it was to be a summer wedding it was decided to hold the church wedding and reception outside of Bern (our residence requiring the civil ceremony in the city on 27 August). The religious ceremony would be on the following afternoon in Thun, followed by a boat trip up the lake to Neuhaus near Interlaken for a reception and dinner party with dancing. Before leaving Ascona for the mountains Mrs. Jung writes:

[Undated]
Casa Eranos
Ascona-Moscia
Tessin

Dear Mrs. Cabot,

Besides this formal reply – I don't know whether it is correctly styled – I want to thank you also personally for the invitation to Janey's marriage and tell you, that we are looking forward to this event. Also I want to express to you our gratefulness for your kindness and generosity in having let us have your apartment with all the *Aufmerksamkeiten* [attentiveness] you thought of so kindly. We enjoyed it so and it made things much nicer and easier for Dr. Jung & myself.

With affectionate greetings,
Yours,

Emma Jung

Then from Saas-Fee:

Saas-Fee, 24.VIII.1943
Hotel Allalin

Dear Mrs. Cabot!

Thank you for your letter, which reached us here in Saas-Fee, which is an extraordinarily beautiful mountain-place, where we enjoy a very peaceful holyday. The weather had been fine almost the whole time and we are walking a lot.[1] It is a splendid counter-balance to Ascona!

I was glad to hear that you were well & that something is 'crystalizing' in you, as you say and I think it may become more tangible after this busy time is over and you have the necessary quietness for such inner things. I feel so glad for you that after this time of what you call "feeling *abrutie*" [stunned] new life announces itself!

We are looking forward to next Saturday and Uncle asks me to tell you, that he will say a few words as a sort of 'Grandfather' & according to your wish.

---

[1] Saas-Fee was accessible in those days only on foot or on the back of a mule.

I find it very nice and amusing that you want the wedding to be in Swiss Style, it's a very nice idea of yours, and I hope everybody will enjoy it.

Thank you also for letting me know about the silver; I am glad to know.

With affectionate greetings from both of us,

Yours,

Emma Jung

My silver list was at Wiskemann (now owned by Meister) on the Bahnhofstrasse in Zürich, and I received many pieces towards my flat silver service from diplomatic friends. The Jungs contributed handsomely, as did other friends from Zürich. Considering we had almost no family in Switzerland, and that relatives in the U.K. and U.S. could not send presents under wartime conditions, it was astonishing how many really good wedding presents we received. My cousin Gardner Richardson gave me away and also gave us a comfortable armchair, which later traveled world-wide and which I still have. He told us it cost Sfr. 700, a fortune in those days, and its quality has been well tested!

The civil marriage took place at the *Standesamt* in Bern on the 27th with my mother and Gardner Richardson as witnesses and a few close friends. After lunch with champagne at the Hotel Bellevue, we went by train to Thun to spend the night prior to the church ceremony. I stayed in one hotel with my mother, grandmother and my dog, the Scottie brought out from England by Tommy in 1940, while Pat booked into another with his best man Howard Douglas (Hank) Wardle and other escapee friends. As we walked through town to the church rehearsal we met the Jungs, "looking very fit after their holiday," my mother writes on 24 November to Frau Dr. Jacobi. She continues, "They were in wonderful form and we stopped and talked for a bit and had a few good laughs, such as one always has with them, for they are so jolly and good fun. They had on good sturdy boots with nails and had been doing a lot of climbing during their holiday" [in Saas-Fee]. The religious ceremony at the small Catholic church on the outskirts of Thun was brief as I was not a Catholic. I was disappointed that it took place in a foreign language, mostly Latin, and not much seemed to happen. Even at that tender age I noticed the priest's displeasure that I was outside the fold, so much so that I remember little else about the service which made me feel a pariah. But I did not dwell on these thoughts for long. I was thankful for the wedding march composed by the blind pianist and performed by him as we left the church, giving some warmth to an otherwise austere ceremony. Friends from Bern and other parts of Switzerland attended, as did some escapees including two New Zealand generals who had escaped from Italy early in 1943, more than a year before the Italians opened the prison gates and allowed all Allied prisoners to find their way, either south through German lines to the Allies in Calabria or north to Switzerland. As I said before, five thousand chose the northern route in spite of the high mountain passes.

We gathered outside for photographs, the weather being sunny and warm, then walked to the nearby harbor and boarded the steamer *Oberhofen*, hired for the occasion and flying both the Swiss flag and an approximation of the Red Ensign. Tea was served on board during the one-and-a-half-hour journey up the lake towards Interlaken. My mother, with her usual enthusiasm and energy, threw austerity to the winds and decided, on the excuse that I had requested a *real* wedding, to give a really good party. Food and drink would be plentiful, she promised, and it was Jack Gauer, proprietor of the *Schweizerhof* in Bern, who organized the party at his restaurant in an old Bernese farmhouse at Neuhaus. It would be a small wedding by Anglo-Saxon standards, only sixty-five people for a sit-down dinner in Swiss style. The only snag was that his restaurant was situated in the *réduit national* close to General Guisan's headquarters, so we had to obtain special permission from the Swiss Army High Command to have the party there. By summer 1943, because the War was beginning to turn in the Allies' favor, the Swiss felt less fearful of their German neighbor and somewhat relaxed their rigorous neutrality towards the Allies. The Americans had landed in Africa in late 1942, Sicily had been invaded in June 1943, and in August the Allies were poised to invade Italy. So the Swiss were willing that Allied diplomats and Military Attachés congregate in a forbidden zone, although having the party so close to Guisan's HQ was not easy to organize (the General himself probably would not have allowed a German wedding so close by). There were also Swiss and foreigners invited from elsewhere in Switzerland, some from Zürich, including Professor and Mrs. Jung, Toni Wolff and Mr. and Mrs. Carl Briner, and Dr. and Mrs. Heinrich

Mantel-Hess. The escaped prisoners of war included two of the four officers who escaped with Pat.[1]

My grandmother, looking very chic and pretty in a frilly black ensemble with a becoming hat, was also very much present. (At my engagement "tea" in June, where the champagne flowed, she had danced with abandonment.) Though Jack Gauer put on a wonderful dinner in spite of wartime restrictions, it was thanks to my grandmother that we were able to have a wedding cake. White flour, sugar, dried raisins and currants were either rationed or scarce at the time, but my grandmother managed with great difficulty to obtain these; she begged sugar from her cousin Gardner Richardson, who writes to her from the American Legation:

Sunday, August 7, 1943

Dear Cousin Jane: –

... I *have* taken over the question of sugar for Janey's wedding cake. I have already packed up and ready to mail 4 lbs of "Domino lump sugar" which according to the accepted mathematical calculations equals about 1.8 Kilos! Also enclose a coupon of 250 to round out the 2 Kilos ... Also in case the caterers do not accept the *lump* sugar (which I doubt) would you like me to endeavor to exchange it for crystal [sugar] in Bern?

My grandmother also searched Lausanne for a suitable *patissier*, and finally found a Mr. Baumgartner. Thanks to my grandmother's persistence he obtained with great difficulty the other ingredients for her recipe, and together with three assistants baked and decorated the cake exquisitely. It was a sensation, not only for its size and beauty but also because of everything that had been assembled to make it. A photo of the decorated cake was taken at the *patisserie* and later signed by all the *patissiers*.

---

[1] One officer, Ronnie Littledale, had already left by an underground route through France to the U.K. There were other Colditz escapees as well, and the two New Zealand Brigadier Generals I have mentioned, who had escaped from Italy, until 1944 a rare occurrence. Only one other R.A.F. officer had made it to Switzerland before them. Brigadier Reginald Miles D.S.O., M.C. was killed later in Spain while trying to reach England. Brigadier James Hargest D.S.O., M.C. reached the U.K., wrote a book about their escape, then went to France and was blown up in his jeep in Normandy shortly after D-Day. Two submarine E.R.A.s who had escaped from Germany, Tubby Lister and Wally Hammond, were also at our marriage.

Emma and C.G. Jung and Clifford Norton at the wedding

In obedience to prevailing wartime customs, dress for the wedding was informal. Men wore business suits, women (except for close family) wore short dresses with hats which were removed for dinner. Professor Jung looked festive in a black suit and a waistcoat edged in white. Though it was mainly a military wedding, the many officers of different nationalities present wore civilian dress, forbidden by diplomatic protocol to wear their uniforms. Professor and Mrs. Jung were neither the "curiosities" nor the "outsiders" they had suggested they might be. In the church they sat as surrogate family in the front row with my mother, grandmother, Gardner Richardson and the American Minister to Bern Leland Harrison. The British Minister and Mrs. Norton played the role of parents for Pat. During tea on the *Oberhofen* Clifford Norton, the British Minister, asked my mother if the Jungs were related to *the* Jung. When they were introduced he instantly embarked on a discussion with Jung that lasted the whole trip. Later while we were drinking champagne in the Gasthaus garden, my mother noticed, as she reported in her letter to Frau Dr. Jolande Jacobi, that "Professor Jung was in fine form and surrounded by at least twenty men, who were listening to him intently." She continued, "this time the men had certainly got in first and made a solid circle around him and the ladies would have had difficulty in approaching him, if they had wanted to!"

At the dinner Jung, the British Minister and the Dutch Minister von Rosenthal made speeches. Among the points raised by Jung in his speech was that he understood how difficult it must be for foreigners to be cooped up in such a small country for so long![1] After cutting the cake Toni Wolff also spoke a few words mainly about the tone of the wedding, which she liked for its "Swissness." This pleased my mother who disapproved heartily of the huge impersonal weddings Americans gave. After the speeches we danced to a band until 2:30 a.m., when a buffet supper was served. According to my mother, I ate nearly a whole *gigot* of lamb! Also according to her, Professor Jung also had an excellent appetite; in fact he and I were the big eaters.[2] Pat and I left the party rather reluctantly (it was still going strong), going by taxi at 3:30 a.m. with my dog Tipler to Spiez, before continuing on next day to Saas-Fee and Zermatt for a week's honeymoon. The Jungs left sometime afterwards for the Hotel du Lac in Interlaken; the last guests left the party at 5 a.m., "leaving behind only those who wished to make a complete night of it," my mother reported in her letter. "They celebrated through the night." My mother and grandmother finally went to bed at 7 a.m. Mrs. Rush, it seems removing only shoes and hat, "slipped between the sheets fully dressed!" When my mother scolded her saying she would ruin her outfit, she replied firmly that she would never wear it again, then fell fast asleep. There were still merrymakers below my mother's window; she finally rose and saw that some guests were sitting in their bathing suits eating eggs and bacon while others swam. The American Military Attaché General Legge apparently spent much of his time that morning sitting waist-deep in the cool lake water sobering up. My Mother reports to Frau Jacobi that twenty-five guests stayed at Neuhaus most of Sunday, "talking and relaxing, leaving for their various destinations only in the evening."

---

[1] My mother felt cooped up. Maybe that is why she remembered this particular point of the speech. I have mentioned her habit of taking pilgrimages to various Swiss frontiers and looking over the barriers! Once we even traveled in a "sealed train" to Schaffhausen; the line passes through a small section of Germany, and Katy thought it would be fun to take that route.

[2] We must have felt starved for meat! The ration was small in 1943, and even in hotels and restaurants there were, during the worst shortages, three meatless days per week.

By that time we had finally reached Saas-Fee via Kandersteg, the Lötschberg Tunnel and Brig, and were tired. The last section from Saas-Grund we walked, or "traveled" on mule-back as there was only a mountain track. The novelty of sitting on those mules soon wore off, so the animals carried our luggage only. After three days at Saas-Fee we moved to Zermatt; we had kept our honeymoon destinations secret, so were astonished to see Gardner Richardson sitting by himself in the hotel dining room our first evening there. He looked, we thought, rather sheepish as he greeted us. We wondered if he had discovered our itinerary and had come to Zermatt to be nosy, but decided it was coincidence as Zermatt was a favorite resort and not too far from Bern, and senior diplomats had to be within easy reach in the event of a crisis. Zermatt's only uphill transport at that time was the Gornergrat railway, so we walked a great deal, including the steep climb up to the Schwarzsee. Neither of us was in training, and our Scotty was exhausted as well by the long excursion. We returned to Bern at the end of the week and began married life staying with friends, Roger Frewen and his first wife (he was Press Secretary at the British Legation), who generously gave us the guestroom in their small flat. Foreigners were forbidden to rent flats in Bern unless they had diplomatic status, which Pat had yet to obtain; although already working at the Legation, he was still classified as an "escapee."

Among the many letters my mother received after the wedding were the following three which she kept:

September 1, 1943
Legation of the United States of America

Dear Katy,

I simply can't resist writing you a line to tell you what a perfectly wonderful wedding, which was *überhaupt* one of the best and nicest parties I've been to, certainly by far the nicest we've ever had in Bern!

Janey looked a darling; Mme. Tschannen [dressmaker in Zürich] deserves a great many compliments for the wedding-gown, and the coiffe was so original & not the usual useless meters & meters of tulle!

Your gown was beautiful too, and if that is a sample of what your dressmaker in Geneva can do, I'm all for her!

Needless to say Grand Mama Rush was enchanting as ever & my last vision of her at 4.30 a.m., she was sitting beside a very handsome member of the Swiss Army, looking about, & as fresh, as sweet sixteen (*she* was not the member of the Swiss Army!).

Sophie Reagan, Dale Maher, Mac Godly[1] & myself spent the night, or rather the early morning at Interlaken, & all would have been well had our rooms not been *directly* over the railroad station!

I shall never forget those *65 Poussins* (nor will Prof. Jung, I gather) and should the War go on much longer, I fear I shall suffer many inhibitions on their account! You must prescribe a cure! I suppose nothing would do except another round of *65 poussins*, but there is only one Janey so my hope is that we shall be able to celebrate your wedding!

I had a card from Gardner [Richardson] from Zermatt this morning: I think he made the best speech of all!

I hope you will come to Bern again soon!

Affectionate greetings,

Matilde (Tilly)[2]

Mary Briner wrote the following:

Wednesday [1.9.43]

My dearest Katy:

Soon now you will be back in the Tessin. I am sure, glad to rest after the excitement, but perhaps too there is a let-down. I do want to tell you how very much Carl [her husband] and I enjoyed the wedding – how dear of you to ask us – and how beautifully I thought everything went off. Really it could not have been nicer in every way. The tables looked so pretty. The food was so very good – and everybody had a good time – but best of all I thought Janey looked lovely and radiant. You my dear did everything to make it a perfect wedding – and I am sure you feel it was so too.

It was such a lovely day. The next day Carl and I were up for the ten-thirty train home about two. We found T.W. [Toni Wolff] in the [hotel] dining room – but she wanted to wait for the Jungs who were not yet up. They had to stop in Thun for their luggage & only arrived in Zürich after seven! A long day. And you dear – what did you do? and where are the bride and groom?

---

[1] All three were Americans working at the U.S. Legation.
[2] Matilde Sinclair was a senior official at the U. S. Legation.

When are you coming to Zürich? Do come and stay a while when the weather down there is getting bad so we can see something of you.

Again my warmest thanks to you and my dearest love. Greetings from Carl – and I hope it won't be too long until we see you again.

Yours with love,

Mary[1]

A letter from Mrs. Jung followed:

Bollingen, 3 Sept. 1943

Dear Mrs. Cabot!

I hope you had a good rest after the wonderful wedding party, which we enjoyed exceedingly. It was so nice and *gemütlich* and everyone enjoyed himself so, that surely you must have felt pleased too! For us it was very interesting to meet all those people and I want to tell you again how much I appreciated the invitation & to express you our thanks. Janey was such a lovely bride, I was quite impressed and we both find her husband such a nice and *sympathisch* man; I think you must feel pleased with your son-in-law too!

Would you be so kind as to send me the address of the young couple so that I could send them our marriage present?

We are here in Bollingen again for about a fortnight and send you affectionate greetings.

Yours,

Emma Jung

---

[1] Mary Briner and her husband Carl, among the guests who stayed overnight at the Du Lac in Interlaken, owned a period house at Kilchberg on the Lake of Zürich.

Chapter Ten

Katy's First Grandchild and Her Adventures,
Winter 1943-44 to Winter 1946

Though Katy traveled frequently to Zürich, Lausanne and also Bern to visit us, she was now based at Ascona, even out of season. A letter from Mrs. Jung reached her there in November:

Küsnacht-Zürich
Seestrasse 228
23 Nov. 1943

Dear Mrs. Cabot!

Thank you very much for your letter and your most kind offer to stay in your house in the New Year's vacation. It is indeed tempting, but for several reasons we cannot accept it. First of all, we are not yet decided whether we shall go to the Tessin at all and if we go, we shouldn't want to be in Ascona, especially as Frau Foebe has arranged or is planning to arrange a Seminar of Prof. Kerényi, and as we won't take part in it both of us needing a very quiet holyday without people nor lectures, so it wouldn't do to be so near. Moreover we used to stay in Locarno because it is more convenient for excursions to the Centovalli or Vallemaggia etc. while it is much more difficult to get to those places from Ascona. I hope you will understand and I want to tell you again how much we appreciate this kind and generous thought of yours. I was pleased to hear from you and am looking forward to February, when you will be in Zürich. Is it not a bit lonely down there now? Or do you see many and nice people?

We got an invitation the other day to a *Wohltätigkeits*-party in Bern; it was addressed by Janey & I could see in the Programme that she has taken an active part in it. I think she does this kind of thing extremely well!

I hope the winter won't bring too bad colds or other hardships. There is always much to do, of course; Onkel is writing on another alchemistic text and is quite immersed in it. I am following with great interest Kerényi's seminar about *Seele & Griechentum*. I like very much to hear him and find him very original and *anregend*. At the Club we had another discussion evening, which went off well.

With affectionate greetings,

Emma Jung

The Jungs finally did choose to spend the Christmas holidays in the Tessin. Mrs. Jung writes:

Locarno, 30.XII.43

Dear Mrs. Cabot!

We are sending you our heartiest wishes for the New Year, which I hope will be a happy one for you and bring us the long wanted peace. I hope you had a nice Xmas with your young couple and that you enjoy spending a holyday with them.

It was nice of you to come to our Club dinner; I appreciated it so much and was pleased to see you.

We are now here in Locarno and enjoy a "quiet time." The weather is marvelous though rather cold, but it is fine for walking which we do a great deal. Looking forward to seeing you soon in Zürich and with affectionate greetings from Onkel and myself,

Yours affectionately,

Emma Jung

Before our marriage, we had looked at apartments but all were in the process of being built. After our honeymoon we continued searching, finally finding a small one about to be completed on the Schlosshaldenstrasse. We tentatively booked it, while staying on with the Frewens at Ensingerstrasse 18, grateful for their hospitality but keen to have a flat of our own. So we were overjoyed when we were told that we could move in on 2 November, but the snag was that Pat still had not been granted diplomatic status by the Bernese authorities, who move slowly. We decided to take a chance and move in on the appointed day, hoping that we would have the permit by then. But it still had not come through when I received the few sticks of furniture on delivery at our flat, trembling that we would be evicted. I knew that Pat was grappling with the civil servants at the Ministry of Foreign Affairs, but as afternoon wore on and darkness fell, with no sign of Pat, I became more and more apprehensive. I was giving up all hope of a satisfactory outcome when Pat finally arrived triumphantly with the vital news that he had become a diplomat! The relief was immense, and our rudimentary flat, built to wartime specifications, felt to me (who had lived mostly in hotels) like a castle.

Soon after we moved in, I found I was pregnant, which did not astonish me, as being practical, I opted to begin a family while the War was still on and we were unable to travel.

Always ready to give advice, my mother insisted we should have a maid even though the flat was tiny. (Maids' rooms were available under the eaves on the top floor of the apartment block.) Maids were pretty rare, and the one sent to us by the agency was elderly – indeed, the typical rather grumpy old maid. As there was no choice we engaged her. It soon became obvious that the maid disliked taking orders from a girl of twenty! My mother, who had never laid eyes on the woman, wanted me to train her to be a lady's maid, insisting on the telephone that I instruct the maid, in making the beds, to iron the top sheet daily (the part folded over the blanket). Much to my mother's disgust, Pat and I shared a bedroom, but to pacify her we had bought twin beds instead of a double bed. The instructions I was to give the maid about ironing the sheets bothered me, but eventually, not daring to go against my mother's will, and trembling because I knew it was absurd to expect this rough woman to do such work, I instructed the maid to iron the sheets. After my timid request the maid gave a sinister cackle and a sideways glance of complete contempt, looking as if she would have liked to spit in my face. The sheets remained as rumpled as my relationship with the maid, who would hardly speak to me. The unpleasant atmosphere did not last long, for a few days later when I entered the kitchen one morning, the maid, who was peeling potatoes with a large knife, rose from her stool brandishing it and pursued me with curses to the door. I beat a hasty and ignominious retreat. Despite these domestic difficulties, we managed to invite my mother and Grandmother Rush to spend Christmas 1943 in Bern, with them staying at a hotel but eating their meals at our flat.

The quiet time that Mrs. Jung says she was enjoying in her letter of December 30 would be short-lived. On 11 February, Katy, who was due to see both Jungs, was with Mrs. Jung while Jung was still out walking. On his way home he slipped on a patch of ice and broke his ankle. Katy mentions the accident in a postcard of 12 February 1944 to her son-in-law:

> Dr. Jung slipped yesterday, on the ice near his house, while I was there and broke his ankle. He is now in hospital waiting for the swelling to go down, before being put in plaster. It is a plain break – no complications. He is suffering no pain. He asked after you & Janey. …

Jung was taken to the Klinik Hirslanden and put to bed with no prospect of getting up for a long time. Fortunately, the treatment was simple. Jung's simple fracture did not require weights to stretch the limb as was often the custom before the introduction of bone pinning. Nevertheless the bed rest, which was supposed to cure all ills in those days, did him no good; after several days he developed a blood clot in the lung with near-fatal consequences. Because of this he was kept in bed even longer than usual, only many weeks later sitting up, with bandaged legs, over the side of his bed. In Swiss hospitals this was the first stage of recovery: before the patient was allowed up, the legs were bandaged from ankle to knee – a form of treatment I encountered after giving birth in Bern, but never anywhere else.

Katy saw neither of the Jungs after his accident, its consequences turning out to be so serious. Her first authentic news of Jung's progress came in a letter from Mrs. Jung over three months later, while she was residing at the Klinik Hirslanden ministering to her husband (she had previously sent a note thanking my mother for flowers; both messages were written after Jung was on the road to recovery).

Klinik Hirslanden, 20.V.44.

Dear Mrs. Cabot!

I was very pleased to get your note and to hear how you are faring. You must have a strenuous time indeed, with your mother in hospital and no maid! What bad luck for Mrs. Rush, to have broken her arm; it must be particularly hard for her as she is so lively, and as you are saying she has to stay in hospital so long I am afraid it is quite a complicated thing. Is the high blood pressure in connection with it or something *à part*? I am awfully sorry for her and for yourself too and hope she will soon get better.

Of Uncle I can give you good news, fortunately, he is now out of bed the greater part of the day and begins to walk about a little. To-day he will even be able to go into the garden for the first time. We are still at Hirslanden and will stay on until he is still a little stronger and does not need the different treatments, as massage, lamps and so on, any longer.

He sends you his love with mine and we both hope that you stand all the strain that is put on you, well. Have you good news from Janey? I hope she is feeling well! It is strange to think that she will be a mother soon, and you a grandmother! You both seem so young!

We also got a new grandchild last week; our youngest daughter has a little boy, it's her third child. Fortunately it all went well and she went home yesterday, and *en passant* came in to show her son to his grand-father, which was a great joy to both of us.

Yours affectionately,

Emma Jung

Mrs. Jung need not have worried about Katy being under strain when her mother was ill; she was always in great form when she had illnesses to deal with. And in spite of her high blood pressure, my grandmother had no complications during her long hospital stay in Locarno, returning to carry on life as usual in Lausanne. Katy herself spent the second half of 1944 in Ascona writing, playing golf and seeing friends. Though she traveled to Zürich from time to time, there is no record of analytical hours with Jung, who spent most of that year recovering, or with anybody else (Katy had stopped analysis with Toni Wolff in 1941). Katy's travels took her most frequently to Lausanne and sometimes to visit us in Bern. She arrived for the birth of my first child at the Lindenhof Hospital in the early afternoon of 13 August 1944.

With thirty-six hours of labor behind me, I was still in the delivery room when my mother arrived – about to give birth, exhausted, distraught and yelling lustily! (Ante-natal relaxing exercises had not yet been invented, and the Swiss were against using anesthetics.) My mother, hearing the bellowing, was horrified, and turning to a midwife who was coming out of the labor room she exclaimed, "How can you allow my daughter to suffer so! In America, such a thing would not be tolerated." The nurse replied in acid tones, "The Americans are a puny race. The women are cowards and the men grow up weaklings. The Swiss are a strong race." Katy replied instantly and crisply, "It's the puny Americans, not the strong Swiss, who are at the gates of Paris!"[1] Though I felt fine immediately, despite the long labor, I stayed in hospital for two weeks because in those days, bed rest was considered essential.

The day following Michael's birth, Mrs. Jung wrote to me:

> Küsnacht-Zürich
> Seestrasse 228
> 14 August 1944

Dear Mrs. Reid!

We heard the news of the arrival of your son with great joy and send our heartfelt congratulations to you and your husband.

I hope that all has gone well and that you will soon be recovered and that also your little boy is in good health and thriving.

With warmest greetings from Dr. Jung and myself,

> Yours sincerely,

> Emma Jung

She also wrote to my mother on the same day:

Dear Mrs. Cabot!

Our very best congratulations for this happy event, the arrival of your grandson! I hope it will bring much joy and happiness also into your life; it is so nice to be in contact with new, young life through one's children and grandchildren! I am looking forward to seeing you, and to hearing how you feel about your new dignity. I do hope it was not too hard for Janey and that she will soon be well again.

With warmest greetings from Onkel and myself,

> Yours,

> Emma Jung

---

[1] The story is from Jane Cabot Reid, *Ten Lunar Months* (William Heinemann Medical Books, London, 1956). I was still in hospital on Friday, 25 August 1944, when Paris was liberated.

Mrs. Jung's New Year wish, "that the long wanted peace would come in 1944," was on the way to being fulfilled by August 1944, though it would take another nine months to be completed.

By January 1945, Katy – in the midst of her other intellectual pursuits – had written an article on the Swiss. She also decided to begin analysis "in the New Year [1945] with Dr. C.A. Meier," as she said "in order to develop my intellectual side and my thinking." She saw him for the first time on 16 January. But Katy had not stopped analyzing with Jung, who was seeing patients again and met with Katy five days after her first interview with Meier.[1]

Onkel – January 22, 1945

At long last, I seem to be able to write down Onkel's hours again. I became so utterly indifferent to things, after de Trafford's death, that I just followed the line of least resistance and just wasted two years. But perhaps they were not wasted? We will see later on!

As I walked into Onkel's study today, he was sitting and writing at the table in front of his window, wearing his fur-lined dressing-gown and skull cap. He looked rather like Erasmus, Faust, or some mediaeval alchemist. I had a decided mediaeval impression when I came in.

He asked me to wait a bit, so I began to finger a book, which I saw that Onkel had just recently acquired. It was called *Problèmes Français, Problèmes humains* by Gillouin. I asked Onkel if it was interesting – the way he explained these problems? Onkel said, "He doesn't get the grip, it escapes him like air." It seems that Professor Baudoin, a professor in Geneva, said to Onkel, *"Ah, si vous voulez vous compromettre avec un fasciste!"* ["If you wish to compromise yourself with a fascist!"] This Gillouin was private secretary or minister to Pétain. When Laval showed his hand, he quit in time. It seems he wrote a good letter to Onkel and is interested in the religious problems of our day, and particularly in Catholicism because he is French. He thought that through religion he would get at the religious problem which troubles us today. Onkel went

[1] Carl Alfred Meier (1905-1995), Dr. med., analyst, and Jung's successor in the chair of psychology at the Federal Polytechnic, as well as first president of the Jung Institute. Among Dr. Meier's many works available in English are his classic *Healing Dream and Ritual: Ancient Incubation and Modern Psychotherapy* (Daimon, Einsiedeln, 1989) and *Soul and Body: Essays on the Theories of C.G. Jung* (Lapis, Santa Monica, 1986).

Professor C.A. Meier

on to say that one could see what happens when people are no longer Christian. Today we have no authority anymore. Formerly, the Pope and Church were international law. In the Middle Ages, when someone was under the ban of the Pope, it meant something serious. A German Emperor, Henry IV, had to make a pilgrimage to the castle of Canossa, where he had to stand long hours barefoot in the snow, until the Pope, *daignait le recevoir* [deigned to receive him]. And he had to humbly ask to be readmitted to the Church.

Formerly, a Hitler, Göbbels or Göring would have had no show. In the Middle Ages such people, who were liars and cheats, would never have been followed. After the Reformation there was the great revolution of the peasants in Germany, and the Anabapatists (*Wiedertäufer*). The Anabaptists were those that held that baptism in childhood means nothing. (A Protestant movement, which favored adult baptism.) The peasant upheavals also started after the Reformation.

Our epoch started something: In Germany the Kings were put out of their palaces, removed from authority. Without anymore authority, and being a monarchic people, the Germans lost their tiller in the storm and fell prey to these gangsters.

Gillouin 'smellt' this thing, but he understood that nothing can be done. He wrote to Onkel, "*On nous donne des noix espérant qu'ils s'ouvrent eux-mêmes dans l'estomac!*" ['We are given nuts in the hope that they will open themselves in the stomach!"]

The Catholic Church gives you a dogma, but you do not understand what the Church is teaching. (A Frenchman who is no longer a practicing Catholic, is an atheist, whereas a Protestant usually joins a sect and doesn't become an atheist.)

In Catholicism you have to swallow so many nuts, that you can't digest them. If you ask a priest what is the Trinity, he does not know. You just *have* to believe it, but that is the nut with the shell. A practicing Catholic doesn't think and when he does start in 'thinking,' he just flies out of the Church, Onkel emphasized: "Believe it, they just don't *think*. I can't swallow nuts with the shell, for those damn things give me indigestion, for I have nothing in the stomach to break the nuts open." "This is the first time," Onkel went on, "that someone who was a Catholic has said that to me. He may have read something that I have written and that got under his skin." He went on to say that without analysis, Gillouin could never really grasp the problems of France nor the problems of humanity – they would just keep on eluding him. But he said that he was impressed by the fact that G. wrote him about the nuts and Onkel thought he must be very intelligent. However, so often clever people won't *think*!

I told him that Mary Rüfenacht told me she only went to him for 'world problems' and not for her personal stuff anymore. He said that Mary R. was an extravert, projecting [her own] problems out in the world. At the moment, he said, she was only 'busy,' but she will be tortured. I presume he means that M.R. is taken up now with her writing and it suffices her.[1] Later, her personal problems will come to the front. For the moment analysis has got into the background. The day may come when she feels that analysis becomes necessary, but as long as she is on top, you can't make her see something.

I told Onkel that I thought it wonderful that from his study he was directing things in the world. He said that he thought he had some influence, for the Swiss Catholic philosophical society had just met and the whole meeting was of a discussion of his psychol-

---

[1] She was doing war work for Allen Dulles. See Chapter Nine.

ogy. I told him I thought it was so touching that he was working so hard and had put so much of himself in the whole thing to work out all the problems for us poor people, and in a way, it was little people like myself who had profited by him. He said that where you don't put yourself into it, nothing comes out of it – one has to sweat for a thing, then it can develop. He said that he was becoming the *stumbling block* for many. He said that a theologian from Bern visited him here [in Küsnacht], and produced a manual of his [Jung's] psychology, which he had arranged for the clergy. Onkel said that he read it, corrected it, and gave him several tips. This theologian would have liked to publish it, but Onkel thinks his colleagues got behind him and told him not to disturb the old church idea. It's easier to run along in the same old rut!

I showed Onkel the picture of my old monk, or saint, or 'ancestor' as the Mantel's said.[1] Onkel said he must be a saint, or a sainted ancestor, because he has a halo and the staff of the hermit, and the rosary. He was surely a Chinese ancestor who was a holy man, on account of the halo and the rosary. He said the rosary, with a Chinaman, was decidedly *Buddhist*. Part of the cloak is orange-red, and in China is a Buddhistic mantle of the priests and the monks.

Then I told Onkel of my qualms of conscience, and wanting to write to the person from whom I had purchased the monk that it had been sold to me too cheap and that someone was willing to give 2000. frs. for it. I loved it and 'discovered it' and did not want to give it up. Onkel said, that if I bought it to keep, and not as a 'dealer' with the idea to make money off it, then I had the right to keep it at the price agreed upon, considering the person I had bought it from had had experts in to value it. I saw that he was saving me from rushing into nonsense, that usual 'generous' side of mine, being really silly at times. With today's financial situation, it would be "robbing Peter to pay Paul."

Onkel said, "Don't try and overreach yourself and be too noble. Later on you get a resentment. *One must spare one's nobility*, and not throw it away uselessly, because afterwards when one needs it then one gets a resistance. Supposing a case arises where your

---

[1] Heinrich Mantel-Hess from Zürich. He and his wife were friends of my mother, and were present at my wedding. He was a Sinologist and had lived in China.

nobility is really needed, and if you have thrown your nobility away uselessly before, you say, 'Damn it, I have been noble long enough.' So I would advise you to keep your picture and not try and spend money you have not got."

I then told Onkel the Poupon thing was over. He only lifted his eyebrows and said, "Well, it doesn't matter." He said not to cling to a thing when it was worn out, and that everything changes. I said the Poupon had said that too, and he laughed. I told him I just had to have the Poupon experience, something with a Latin man, even perhaps a frivolous relation. He said that one couldn't take things as one wanted to take them. One should take things as they present themselves, and when a thing presents itself as important and gives one a serious reason, or serious impression, take it *as* important. He said that certain things were very important and other things less so. There are things good to eat and other things not so good to eat. Some people like certain things and other people different things. *Nothing is important in itself!* If you had a valley full of diamonds and no one knew about it, it would not be so important.

I told him that I had laughed a lot recently over things my mother said, and over the Poupon and lots of other things. He said that I had evidently developed my sense of humor! I think I have, because I have really had a lot of good laughs!

I then embarked on the subject which was uppermost in my mind when I came to him and I told him that I didn't face death with equanimity. He said the following, which I will write down in his own words as I remember them:

"If you are in such a situation (death) all that you can say is, 'Now we are in for it.' When I didn't die I was awfully disappointed and I said to myself, 'Now I have to begin again the damn life.' The world was far beyond the horizon to me. There seemed to be a corner, somewhere, where people said: 'It is a world.' At the beginning of April, I sat on the edge of the bed and then the thing began to change, but up until then the world was a curtain made of paper and a view was painted on it.[1] There were holes in it. I couldn't read a paper because it was full of holes, I just couldn't see the world outside, it was non-existent. I was far out of it and very

---

[1] For another account of the course of Jung's illness, see Barbara Hannah, *Jung: His Life and Work* (Putnam, New York, 1976, and Michael Joseph, London, 1977).

reluctant to come back. My night nurse, who was very intuitive, said to me that she knew that I didn't want to come back and that I thought it was too difficult to come back. It gave me terrible depressions to get back into the body. There was a certain moment when things just snapped and I felt my body and extreme weakness."

"*In the nights* I didn't feel my body anymore, I was quite out of it. It was like suddenly falling asleep in the Universe. The room vanished, my body vanished, it was good that way and I liked it better. My night nurse thought I would die, but I knew I wouldn't die because I had a vision. The world interfered, I was needed by the world."

The Vision

"*I was out of the body and away in space and saw the world from 50 thousand kilometers. I saw the world in a blue light. It was lovely, iridescent and the continent looked blueish silver and the sea was deep blue. There were stars in space and a huge hollowed out rock and in the rock were hundreds of lights. In the hollowed out rock, amidst the hundreds of lights, sat a very dark Indian, on a bench. I felt grand as I knew I was going in there. Suddenly Dr. Haemerli[1] loomed up like a portrait, but the real Haemerli was as if behind it – a doctor of Greek times, 2400 years ago; one of the princely medical families of Cos. He came with a delegate from earth, an ambassador, and they said they couldn't allow my going away.*"

"*From this moment all I saw vanished, and I was again in my body. I had this vision when I was at my worst and was having oxygen. I had this vision at the critical moment.*"

"*In the nights I was in bliss and the nurse was convinced I was going to die, for when I was in a bad state, I was out of my body and I looked peculiar. It took me a long time to realize this world was real. Finally, when I came home, and was in my garden this summer, it was like heaven, it just didn't seem real. It was like a marvel-*

---

[1] There were two doctors Haemerli who looked after Jung at different times: Dr. Haemerli-Schindler and Dr. Haemerli-Steiner. The one mentioned above died suddenly during Jung's illness.

ous dream and I still have the impression that I am not completely 'back.'"

I asked him if he thought he would ever get 'back' as he called it. He said, "It is relative. If you suffer a bad disappointment, it may last for ever. Or when you have lost your confidence in somebody, how can it ever be completely restored? I am no longer in the things as I used to be. It's as if I had lost my belief in things. It's important for my work that I get a vista of the world now that I am no longer identified with it."

I told him this experience was to him a sort of analysis and had brought him on, there being no one in the world to bring him on, but himself, just as he had brought me on, all these years. He said that it was so.

The view of Earth Jung describes in his vision resembles the colored photographs we now have of Earth taken from space. Katy knew nothing of Jung's experiences during his severe illness when she embarked on the subject of death with him; despite the intervening years, Tommy's passing was still uppermost in her mind. She had been shattered by his death, or would never have gone into the *Poupon* relationship. Belonging to a generation of women who needed a man in tow, she did not realize that she could manage perfectly well on her own. She took on this unsuitable man only because she was then most of the time in the Tessin, and no one else was available. Born in 1908 and so much younger than Katy, he came from a different social milieu even though his family was an old one and owned a *Palazzo* in Locarno. He was not without intellect, and was also fun at a party as Henry Clews well knew, having discovered him playing the piano in a Locarno bar. At the time of my marriage the *"Poupon* thing," as it was called, was still going strong. So that he could be at the wedding Katy urged him to compose a wedding march – an extra one in addition to the classical one – and to hide the relationship still better she identified him to guests as "an old friend of Janey's." But by 1945, thanks to her frequent visits to Bern, Katy met a more sophisticated Swiss whose "analyst by correspondence" she was to become.

Katy returned frequently to the subject of Catholicism with Jung. It had fascinated her ever since her convent-school days. From Tommy she had obtained only negative vibes about it, and the *Poupon*, the "Latin man," was a Catholic in name only. It was only from Jung that she could obtain an unbiased opinion. Many years later when she married an Italian, she decided to join the Catholic Church out of expediency, not piety.

Katy's generous side was not simple. Some people she actually *wanted* to help, but with others she made herself popular through generosity, dinner parties, etc. And though she appeared generous to a fault, Katy had a stingy streak. She gave no money to organized charities because, as she reasoned, the money was spent on the organizers' salaries and expenses, and she preferred to give to needy friends. This she did. But whenever Katy *bought* objects from friends, she bought them as cheaply as possible! The "friend" in the case she mentions to Jung was an American schoolmate from Florence who, through several foolish marriages, had lost most of her money and was compelled to sell her fine North Korean furniture and other Eastern *objets d'art* at any price she could obtain. My mother bought quite a few pieces of furniture from her, and the picture she describes, at low prices, so her twinges of conscience were justified. Being artful, however, she omitted the background story to her latest purchase, so was able to obtain Jung's blessing! In Katy's defense, it must be remembered that she herself was short of money during the War. The U.S. government restricted the export of income to $500 per person per month, and at one moment Katy had been obliged to put her pride in her pocket to borrow money from Barbara Hannah.

February 9, 1945

Onkel said the important point in Swiss psychology was the smallness of the country. Anyone coming from a big country like America doesn't see what the world looks like to a fellow coming from a small country, wedged in between peoples of very definite national character.

These peoples' character is very uniform, despite the difference in the north and the south of such countries like France, Italy, Germany and Austria.

It is in between these four countries that Switzerland has had to maintain her national character, her peculiar character, otherwise she was lost!

Onkel said that if we [the Swiss] become French, then we *are* French and the same with the Germans. We are *opponents* to all these countries and we are not in sympathy with whatever comes along. We are critical and we are prejudiced.

He went on to say that when the German talks, we say, "It's a mouthful of words." When the French talk, we say, "Polite phrases." When the Italian talks, we say, 'Oh that's a cinque." Superficial, unreliable liars. (Cinque: a game, Morra, played with the hands.) With the Austrian we say, "A nice chap, but no good, lazy, irresponsible and all *Schlamperei* [slovenliness]."

He said that was the Swiss attitude, an attitude of self-defense, and that it makes the crust we have. We have to defend our national character for we are mistrustful of ourselves. We project onto people stuff we have in ourselves – things we would be capable of doing.

The Swiss won't admit that he is astonished or surprised. A magic behavior. Never show one is too much enjoying oneself with foreigners or that one is being influenced. It is the same with the English, the insular type. In that way they keep their national character. With the French and Spanish it is different, they get assimilated by blacks when they colonize, for they don't have that self-defense.

The Englishman won't learn other languages because he thinks everyone ought to speak English. The Americans have also no defense and even play football with the Germans[1] – they are impressed. And what will one day happen to the American if he goes on like that, one just wonders?

In Switzerland, a stranger is a stranger. Then Onkel told me his ma-in-law story, which he had told me once before in connection with Toni.

The Swiss crust is due to that self-defense against the psychological influence of the surrounding countries. We *mustn't* be impressed and if we don't think like that we lose our national character. If the British had not had that same characteristic of not being impressed, they would have lost their national character long ago – they would have gone under.

A Frenchman forgets that the English built an empire. The Americans don't defend themselves and they are now fraternizing with German soldiers. They will be eaten up. The English have more form and behave as if they were not impressed. The Ameri-

---

[1] After the War, Allied military personnel were forbidden to fraternize with the Germans. The Americans may have made an exception to that rule and played with P.O.W.s in sporting events.

cans are impressed with lots of foolish nonsense, and being representative of a big continent, they can't understand the psychology of a people who have had to defend themselves. The Dutch are very disagreeable! De Gaulle is the typical disputing Frenchman. You can live 20 years in France, but you never get anywhere with the people. The only person Onkel said he knew in France was a M. de Clermont, a half-wit, polite and spoke fine French.

When one wants to have a MENTAL contact with the French the CHURCH comes in between.

With the human contact it is not easy, because the French have no sense of humor. He then told the story of his daughter's husband who laughed when a Frenchman fell down and opened a door with his head. Suddenly he saw this head on the floor, coming into his office – pushing the door open, as it was, and he just roared with laughter. INSTEAD he should have rushed forwards and said, "*Mais j'espère que vous ne vous êtes pas fait mal.*" ["But I hope you have not hurt yourself."] I said that is what I would have done.

Onkel said that the Frenchman was hurt in his pride. In Switzerland, people would be glad to have people grin, that they had a sense of humor. The Frenchman wanted compassion.

Swiss

Onkel went on to say that when you were dealing with the Swiss, or representatives of a small country, you will notice edges and sharpness and coldness and coarseness. The French say, of a 'coldness,' '*peu agréable.*'

The Swiss will be all self-defense, but then later, if you go and get a drink together, you have a jolly evening. The Swiss has a sanguine type of character – a carnival spirit inside. He can get drunk as hell. The Zürichois love a good time.

The Swiss have a lively temperament which shows in their music. The folk music expresses the Swiss and they have a festive temperament. They like dancing, drinking, yodeling.

With the Swiss one must wait and stand still, as if you had to deal with animals. Just wait and they will thaw.

The Swiss are identical with their crusts. A Swiss can't afford to be the big fellow, he is too well known. Only in a big country, where you are not known, and the towns are far apart, can you afford to be big and get away with it. But where one is personally known, it is impossible, one does not impress. The big fellow lives a 100 miles away.

Katy was interested in having Jung's views on his countrymen as she had been busy writing a paper on the Swiss and was keen for information on the Swiss character. She was scheduled to give it as a lecture (which Toni Wolff called a *causerie*, an informal talk) at the Psychological Club, but alas, she caught a severe cold and was unable to do so; Professor Meier therefore read it to the members on 24 March 1945.[1]

Her so-called old enemy Mary Foote, who attended the lecture, wrote the following undated letter:

> My dear Katy Cabot,
> Everybody was laughing at your wit & lamenting your absence last night. And I – alas – could not understand much, as I am deafer than ever these days. So *please*, if you have an extra copy of the English original, let me have it to read! I shall be extremely careful of it & get it back to you at once. ...
> I had no idea that the article you told me of having written about Switzerland was so long & so wise & so thorough – Good for you!
> I am looking forward very much to reading it when you have the possibility of sending it.
>
> > Always affectionately yours,
> > Mary Foote

My mother obviously appreciated receiving Mary Foote's letter as she kept it in an album together with other important letters and newspaper articles.

Without a man in tow to consume her time and energy, Katy was able to write creatively. But as she was constantly in need of a companion her creative periods were short-lived. While she always threw herself whole-heartedly into any enterprise, she was not able to combine writing and having boyfriends, who were always more important, even when difficult, and consumed much of her time and energy. I suspect that she had a lifelong urge to find the "ideal" man

---

[1] The paper was translated into German by Toni Wolff as *"Die Schweizer, durch eine amerikanische Brille,"* and published in *Annabelle* in August 1945 (in both the German and French editions). I read my mother's paper at the Psychological Club on 11 November 1994 when it was again well received.

to make up for her less-than-ideal father. As I have written in earlier chapters, he was mostly absent during her childhood, had little time for her when at home, and was apt to be negative. Her mother, consequently, had to be both mother and father to Catharine for long stretches of time, so was forced to punish and scold her when she was naughty. One of Katy's stories of her early childhood, was that when she was about three she had gathered up all her father's shoes and floated them in a full bathtub. Most likely in her fantasy they became a fleet of ships, but to her Victorian parents, less romantic, they were expensive shoes transformed within minutes into soggy pieces of leather. Her punishment was swift: she was locked in a closet and put on bread and water. A very sensitive girl, Katy placed her mother on a pedestal while very young but eventually developed a negative mother complex. When Katy spoke of her mother to me, she blamed her for all the unpleasantness of her childhood; father was too remote and godlike to shoulder any blame. As William Rush in his last years of failing health became more mellow and more approachable, Katy drew closer to him. Though uncomplimentary about him in early sessions with Jung, she was prepared to do everything when he was seriously ill, as her letters to "Dads" testify.

Given her own childhood experience, Katy must have realized when she took me to Europe that she too would have to take on the dual role of mother-and-father. Yet she seems to have been oblivious to the difficulty of such a role. She liked to call herself, jokingly, *Mépère* (a contraction of Mother-father), a name I thought amusing – but unfortunately a mother's ranting animus is untenable, lacking the figure of masculine authority. I too developed a negative mother complex. My mother found me a handful as a young child, wondering why I could be so belligerent since she was doing an excellent job in her dual role; but her reprimands, however legitimate, instead of disciplining me, grated on me and made me rebellious.

By 1945 Katy and Toni Wolff were corresponding again. Toni was translating her article, and in the letter below encloses a newspaper clipping advertising a house in Porto Ronco, as my mother was looking for another flat, finding that moving out of Casa Gabriella during the Eranos week a nuisance.

> Freiestrasse 9
> Zürich 7
> Feb. 28th, 1945

Dear Katy,

This looks very nice, but I am afraid it is too far away. Anyhow I thought of you when I saw it in yesterday's evening paper [an advertisement for a house].

I love the two Swiss episodes, and was delighted to find you brought in Mrs. P. [the British Minister's wife].

I could work them in easily. I am soon finished and shall then send you your ms. and the translation, as I wish you would go through it and see if I got your meaning all right.

I think your letter to her[1] is very good and covers up the part that you were ill – at least it would to most people.

I do hope, Katy, that you consider 2 weeks in the Tessin – I am sure a change of air would be good, and Janey could begin her school a bit later. The weather seems fine – only occasionally a bit of wind.

I do hope you feel better every day.

> Love and good wishes,

> Toni

What Toni means about my "beginning school a bit later" is a mystery. It was a phrase she had used when I was a child, but by the end of February 1945 I had been married eighteen months and was a mother! Katy could only have told her that she was going to Bern to baby-sit while I was at Kreuzlingen with Mrs. Norton, Colonel Cartwright and other Legation Staff, together with the American Military Attaché Barney Legge and his assistant Howard Free, helping in the exchange of sick prisoners of war. It is possible that she may have wanted to make her Bern visit sound less domestic and glamorized it in some way, but even Katy would have had difficulty making me out as a school girl, especially as Toni had been at my marriage. We had an excellent trained nanny, but thought our absence at Kreuzlingen would give Michael the opportunity to get to know his granny. We were not sure how long our stay would be. Our British and American Legation groups, with Swiss top brass, remained at the border for almost a week awaiting the repatriation trains. The sick

---

[1] Probably a letter to Mrs. L. She was supposed to dislike people being ill!

German prisoners had already arrived for exchange, but had to wait for the Allied prisoners before they could be repatriated. The Swiss officers told us the German soldiers to whom they had spoken were in no hurry to return to war-torn Germany.

The Allied prisoners were being repatriated from a number of camps, mostly in eastern Germany, and their journey to the Swiss frontier was delayed by the almost constant bombing of German railroads by the Allies. So we sat patiently in the icy hotel at Kreuzlingen, whiling away the time playing cards and drinking *Schnapps*. The Swiss officers were kept busier: they crossed daily to Constance to liaise with the Germans. What they told us of conditions in that city made us shiver even more. Apparently the hospital at Constance specialized in skin grafts. The officers saw freshly operated patients walking about the streets practicing with musical instruments, to give their fellow soldiers a suitable reception at their homecoming. The instrument a man could play depended on which parts of him were giving and receiving the graft. Many of these patients had badly burnt faces, and needed a skin graft from a hand or arm; both face and hand remained attached until the graft "took." These particular patients could play wind instruments. The Swiss did not have to give us further details, our imaginations supplying the rest. And though we were rabidly anti-German, we nevertheless felt sorry both for these German patients and the returnees who would be greeted by such a gory spectacle.

Eventually after a week of waiting, playing cards and sitting about, the trains carrying the Allied prisoners began arriving. Suddenly we were very busy. All the trains stopped as soon as they had crossed the frontier at Kreuzlingen, so that prisoners could receive food, cigarettes and other "comforts" as well as any immediate medical treatment needed before continuing their journey to Geneva and on to the U.K. All the soldiers and officers to whom we spoke and gave parcels were very sick. Most of them were cheerful and looked forward to going home, but on some trains there were also locked carriages for mental patients which none of us women were permitted to enter. Pat saw some of them, and told me that a few were extremely violent and others suicidal. On the relatively short train journey through Switzerland, three prisoners died, and sadly, more died before reaching England. Many coaches transported TB patients, some severely ill; we spent a long time in these carriages talking to as many soldiers as possible and distributing gifts. Back in Bern, the Embassy helpers were advised to wait some weeks then to have a medical check-up. Along with others, Pat and I were X-rayed for TB, but none of us had been infected.

It was after her return from baby-sitting in Bern, where she also enjoyed a vigorous social life, that Katy fell ill and could not deliver her paper at the Psychological Club. Besides knowing many members of the diplomatic corps, Katy was also, unbeknownst to us, consolidating a new relationship which proved to be a strain. She received the following letter from Toni:

Das PRÄSIDIUM
Psychological Club, Zürich
Gemeindestrasse 25
Zürich 7
March 23rd, 1945

Dear Mrs. Cabot,

The Vorstand is heartbroken, that you have fallen ill and can't read that charming causerie of yours yourself. Your article of course stands in itself and loses none of its value when read by someone else. But all the charm of your personality and all the life of the evening, when the author herself holds the chair, will be absent. For your own sake we are equally sorry. We should have wished so much that you could have earned in person the fruits of your labour. We admire the keen observation and the great fervour you show in understanding the Swiss. We are, too, grateful for the critical and unflattering things you say about us, for it is a well known fact that no person and no nation is able to understand themselves without learning from others the impression they make. After due consideration we have however come to the conclusion to have the paper read by Dr. Q. First, not to disappoint the people who will come to hear your causerie, and second, because the article being published in May, it were impossible to arrange for another *Tee-Abend* or lecture before the publication, our annual meeting being due in May also. We are hoping that you will recover speedily from your grippe and that in spite of the general disappointment your illness is causing, you will hear a good deal of what this evening's audience feels about your paper.

With best wishes,

Very sincerely yours,

Toni Wolff

Katy's next journal entry for the analysis resumes several months later:

June 19, 1945

I saw Onkel and asked him about Aurelia and what he thought of it and, why he had Gérard de Nerval[1] to lecture on. I got no answer, really, and kept on wondering? However, I think I know why, but won't discuss it in this paper, as this is only a recording of my hour with him [Jung].

Onkel said that de Nerval had real talent, but would not accept the ANIMA (his soul) and so he killed himself. But first I told Onkel that I thought there were parts in the book, which though sad, as a whole, were laughable. He said he would call them more 'grotesque' than laughable. He said that all those fantasies of de Nerval were not really 'funny' but tragic; they happened against his will. He was in the clutches of the unconscious, and as one reads on, one feels it will find a terrible *dénouement* [end]. Onkel went on to tell me that de Nerval went a lot to Germany, and that he was an interesting intermediary between Germany and France. He translated Goethe's *Faust*. He also translated some Klopstock and Heine. Onkel went on to say that such people as de Nerval *are* grotesque and sometimes they are so comical that one forgets their insanity. Aurelia is an unknown actress. She played no particular role on the stage or off it and de Nerval was rather upset by the idea that *'une personne ordinaire de son siècle'* [an ordinary person of his century] would have the role of being the carrier of his ANIMA. One doesn't know why de Nerval thinks he committed a particular sin in caring for Aurelia. He hasn't recognized her as the Anima, and he took her for an ordinary person, and she was that type of woman who touched the souls of men and who particularly touched his soul. He mistook her for an ordinary everyday person and then suddenly, he realized that he had *missed his chance*. That

[1] Gérard de Nerval (1808-1855), the adopted name of Gérard Labrunie, a French man of letters born in Paris. His father was an army doctor; while Mme. Labrunie accompanied her husband on his campaigns, the child was left with an uncle in the country. The father returned in 1811, and taught his son Greek, Latin and modern languages. At 21 de Nerval conceived a violent passion for the actress Jennie Colon. He wrote and traveled a great deal, and later nearly married the daughter of a Druse sheikh. He had several bouts of insanity during his life and committed suicide by hanging.

is what happens to men who don't realize at the right moment such a thing of vital import.

De Nerval had such extraordinary experiences in those moments of madness and phantasy he had. Pulling off his clothes publicly meant that he was depositing his earthly body. One night, he was prowling around in Paris aimlessly and he came to a shop window where a mummy was displayed, then he came to a place where he hanged himself. It was called Rue de la Tuerie [Massacre Street]. The mummy suggested death already! If he had been analyzed he might have been saved, for if he could have talked to someone about the girl, someone might have opened his eyes to his Anima.

The Anima

Then Onkel went on to talk about the important thing that is the Anima. It means the WHOLE man, but first people must know what the unconscious is and that takes weeks to understand.

People have prejudices and they can't think at all and can't grasp it. It is as if you tried to explain to them the secrets of the atom. Onkel went on to say, that to doctors he explained the Animus and Anima, but even they had great difficulty in understanding *what* it is. It is very difficult to understand the whole import of the Anima. One must have the right conception of the unconscious and that is difficult. Onkel then went on to explain the unconscious, and started like this:

"If one strips the King of England and puts him in a workman's clothes, everyone will say that he is an ordinary workman. Nevertheless, the King of England means the whole might of the British Empire, like the President of the United States embodies all the power and might. *They are living figures who express that power!* If one didn't know who Stalin was one would think he was a coachman!"

The Anima is like living on a planet where no human ever appeared, then suddenly a figure appears (the Anima) and you are surprised!

In January, Katy had told Jung that her relationship with the *Poupon* was over. During the autumn months in Bern, while visiting us, she had met a more interesting Swiss, a high-ranking civil servant named Ernst Feisst.[1] This bachelor in his late forties had made his

[1] Ernst Feisst was born in 1897 in Riehen near Basel and died in 1968.

reputation during the War years for his diligent implementation of the Wahlen Plan.[1] Pat and I knew him well and introduced him to my mother at one of the diplomatic receptions. He liked good food and wine and was fun at a party, but also appeared relaxed with women, on a superficial level anyhow, which for a Swiss man is not self-evident. At parties in the 1940s, Swiss men tended to be stiff with the women they met, particularly foreigners, but Feisst was very different. He was on good terms with everyone in the diplomatic corps, regardless of sex, and was at most of their parties. The danger sign was that he was still a bachelor, which seemed strange as he was not known to be homosexual. He obviously had difficulty going beyond casual relationships, and this seemed to puzzle Katy, who had been caught up by his *bonhomie*. She turned to Toni for advice:

Freiestrasse 9
Zürich 7
July 8, 1945

Dear Katy,

I was *most* interested in your tale. And so glad you had some really perfect situations with that man. But when you ask for advice or information, I am at a loss. I can only say that Swiss men *are* slow. Therefore don't hurry them, or they get frightened or shy and withdraw. But to have a real judgement I ought to know him. It seems to me he is unconscious about something, otherwise you would not get those waves. But again, about what he is, I could not say.

To be quite frank, I don't quite understand either about what exactly you are puzzled or disappointed. What did you expect to be the next step? Is it a marriage proposition, or the complete sexual experience? But was the situation, and the relatively few times you had with him (and relatively short time you know him) already so that you can expect a further step? Or is the situation so that he just makes the best of what he can have at the moment, perhaps

---

[1] Friedrich Traugott Wahlen was Professor of Agriculture (*Pflanzenbau*) at the Polytechnic (E.T.H.) in Zürich. He conceived a plan for intensive agriculture during the War to reduce the impact of the double blockade (by both the Allies and the Germans) to which Switzerland was subjected. Crops such as potatoes were grown at altitudes unheard of before, and cereals, legumes and vegetables were grown everywhere – in domestic gardens, parks and other public green spaces, and even in swampy ground after it had been drained.

because he does have an obligation otherwise? Was that the meaning when he talked of *loyauté* – as you indeed supposed?

Perhaps, if you want to find out, it were a good thing if from now on you left the initiative more or less to him. Then he will have to do or say something, whereas when you create a situation, or at least suggest one, he does not have to do more than comply, nor will he have to think about what could be done, or invent a situation where things can be continued or become possible. If you want a person to realize his responsibility, or even where he stands, don't do anything yourself, but let him take the initiative.

I am afraid that is all I can say so far. I am so glad you are taking the dog [a Skye Terrier my mother took over from an American friend who was returning permanently to the U.S.]. You will feel much less lonely.

I shall be here for a few days at least round July 26th for Dr. C.'s birthday. I don't yet know where I am going afterwards, as I ought to go to Leukerbad, but they can take me only about August 25th. So I may not come to Eranos.

> With best of luck to you – you *do* deserve it.
> Affectionately,
>
> Toni

X. had no loyalty elsewhere, if by that Toni meant a long-term relationship. He was a workaholic, and too much of a *Puer* for real intimacy with the opposite sex. He liked to flirt with women but avoided involvement with them. Though intelligent, charming, and sophisticated, he could offer nothing long-term. Katy kept her feelings for X. to herself. If she had told Pat and me about them we could have warned her that X. was superficial. The trouble with Katy was that she had great confidence in her judgment when it came to curing illness or reforming people. The Sea Captain found it impossible to follow Toni's advice and leave the initiative to X.

Meanwhile her article on the Swiss was not published in May as Toni had expected; Katy was still gathering opinions from various people right into the summer, about both contents and translation. While this and her new boyfriend were occupying her, the destroyer named in memory of her father was being completed across the Atlantic, and was launched as the *U.S.S. William R. Rush* on 8 July 1945. Travel to America still had not been normalized, so Katy and her mother were unable to attend the ceremony, her young cousin

Catharine with "Dopey," ca. 1948

Dorothy Mary Flagg standing proxy for them. The *Rush* was commissioned on 21 September 1945 and immediately joined the Atlantic Fleet. Katy was very proud that a ship bore her father's name, and after her mother died she kept in touch with each successive captain of the *Rush* until her own death. When it came to the Mediterranean in the 1950s and 1960s, frequently anchoring off San Remo, Katy always invited the officers and crew to parties at her villa. I kept on corresponding with the *Rush* after my mother's death in 1976, until it was sold a few years later to the South Korean Navy.

Toni writes again on 24 and 26 July:

Freiestrasse 9

Zürich 7

July 24, 1945

Dearest Katy,

Many thanks for all your interesting letters etc. I would have written before, only I was so busy with that article, they ordered it with very short notice and I had to write it here in Bollingen right under Dr. C.'s nose. As I was through with it, Dr. and Mrs. Q. came to stay for a week, Dr. C. needs another man to go sailing. And so Dr. Q. could help me with his criticism. We are all going home tomorrow as there are too many people wanting to see Dr. C. to have them here. Dr. Q. and I are presenting the tapestry Thursday morning. It is wonderful. Don't go into too much money for it, say between 20 to 50 frs. would be right to my judgment.

I am glad you like the dog. Dr. C. will also get one from his son and daughters, a little Dackel [Dachshund]. But don't know when he arrives, so don't mention him in your birthday telegram.

I read your welcome pamphlet with interest and think it is very good. The only thing I would have suggested if consulted was a number of very good ciders and *Obstsäfte* for teetotalers.[1]

I am really happy that you get out of R's [clutches]. He was quite alright as a temporary *Ersatz*. But as you say, better to be alone than with an inferior man. The right one will come one day, if so is your fate, when [until then?] you can enjoy yourself by yourself.

It looks as if the Dr. S. relation is a rather unique one, something without purpose, just a beautiful thing in itself and for its own sake. It may continue sporadically when you are back in Bern. But with no definite plan and program other than what happens when you are together. That is a very rare thing, because few women could appreciate it like that.

Your dream can hardly be analysed. It seems to me you should just feel the atmosphere and personality of that man and then you will get an effect. As a commander, he is certainly a positive and leading animus, so let him just work from the unconscious.

I don't know yet if I am coming to Eranos, it is such a nuisance to have to live in the village, it is so far away. Dr. C. is really meaning to go.

[1] This refers to one of the articles Katy was writing on Switzerland for Mrs. Rüfenacht's publication. See below.

It is fine how you put yourself to work on these articles. By the way, what happened to the one about Switzerland in Annabelle. Did it ever appear?

It is rather hot here too, and worst must be in town which I shall endure presently.

All good wishes,

Affectionately,

Toni

As I said earlier, Katy could not very long live by Toni's maxim, "enjoy yourself by yourself," having to have a male companion. The dream Toni mentions is not available, but if Katy dreamed that S. was a "commander," it could well have been a *naval* commander, as at this time the launching of her father's ship was very much on her mind. Unfortunately, S. was also beginning to see Katy as a commanding figure.

The *Wandteppich* presented to Jung by the members of the Psychological Club on his seventieth birthday is indeed very beautiful and hangs now permanently at the Club. Jung wrote a detailed two-page comment on the tapestry, the last paragraph of which I give below, as it sums up his thoughts on the subject:

> *Der Teppich enthält eine große Anzahl von archetypischen Gestaltungen und Beziehungen, daß eine sehr starke Mitbeteiligung des kollektiven Unbewußten wahrscheinlich ist. Den archetypischen Einflüssen verdankt das Bild seine Architektonik sowohl wie seinen ahnungsvollen Bedeutungshintergrund. Die Zahlensymbole mit ihren Trinitäten und Quaternitäten scheinen in naher Beziehung zur hermetischen Philosophie zu stehen, obschon ein solcher Zusammenhang im Bewußtsein der Künstlerin nicht bestehen kann. Die im Teppich zum Ausdruck gelangenden Inhalte dürften nicht nur etwas von der bemerkenswerten Auswahl der Farben, sondern auch die Andacht und Geduld der Schöpferin des Werkes erklären: das Bild hat den Wert einer Offenbarung oder besser einer Neugestaltung traditioneller religiöser Vorstellungen in einer Form, die dem Wesen der mittelalterlichen Naturphilosophie und damit der Struktur des Unbewußten entspricht.*

[The wall-hanging contains a great number of archetypal figures and relationships which probably mean a very strong participation of the collective unconscious. The structure of the picture as well as its meaningful background is due to its archetypal influences. The symbols of numbers with their trinities and quaternities seem to be closely associated to Hermetic philosophy, even though such a connection cannot exist in the artist's consciousness. The contents which the carpet expresses are not only thanks to the remarkable choice of colors used, but also thanks to the devotion and patience of the creator: the picture has the value of revelation or better said is a renewal of traditional religious conceptions in a form which accords both with the spirit of natural philosophy of the Middle Ages and therefore corresponds with the structure of the unconscious.]

Freiestrassse 9
Zürich 7
July 26th, 1945

Dearest Katy,

I write in haste to return the manuscript, as I think Dr. S's suggestions excellent. I used most of them and I hope there is time for you to send the ms to Mrs. T.
in the present form. Otherwise, you ask for the proofs and put the corrections there.

I am glad that paper appears only in the August number, it is so appropriate now with the U.S. [military] visitors, much better than early in the spring. Dr. F.'s letter is most charming and warm. I think you misunderstood what I said, or I expressed it badly. I meant, there seems to be no practical planning or scheming in your relation, and this is of very positive value. The only purpose being the relation itself.

Thanks very much for both your letters. It is nice to see how you feel towards me and Dr. C., and I am glad you got real value out of analysis.

After many ups and downs, Dr. Q. and I presented the tapestry yesterday evening, as we were asked for the family dinner. We hung it in the library, and it was just enough light left to see it. Dr. C. was *most* impressed, in fact overcome, and repeated again and again how beautiful it was and how like things of the unconscious, only much more beautiful. It gave quite a Chinese effect. Also all people present said the same, particularly his son, the architect. He admired our choice as a present, chosen by so many people like a Club was as a rule something inferior.

Dr. C. got a simply charming Dackel whom he named Puck. He is 3 months and was not even frightened or nervous after the long trip. He comes from a kennel in Basel. I am glad you are happy with Dopey [my mother's Skye Terrier] and I shall look forward to meet him. I have to go to Leukerbad in August, got rooms for the 11th and don't know what I am doing before hand, as I have to close the house for the maid's holidays.

I suppose I shall come to Eranos. I meant the long way being so far away from Dr. C. whom I like to see occasionally at other times than the lecture hours.

Excuse this letter. I am a bit tired, because the party lasted until very late. We left at 1.30 a.m. and Dr. C. did not look then as he meant to go to bed.

> With love and good wishes,
>
> Toni

On 31 July, Katy received the following letter from Jung's secretary, Marie-Jeanne Schmid:

Dear Mrs. Cabot,

May I ask you a favour? Prof. Jung would like to send a ms. to America in the safest possible way. Now Dr. Meier told me that you know of a lady who was in charge of a special service for cultural relations (or some such thing) at the Embassy in Berne and he thinks that this special service would take care of the ms. Would you be so very kind as to let me know the name of the lady (or the exact name of the service) and the exact address in Berne, so that I could send the ms.? If you could just drop me a postcard as soon as possible I should be awfully grateful. Dr. and Mrs. Jung have gone off to Bollingen having got over the festivities very well indeed.

> With many thanks in advance,
>
> Yours,
>
> Marie-Jeanne Schmid

Katy replies:

La Pergola
Ascona Tessin
August 2nd, 1945

Dear Miss Schmid: –

I have just this moment got back from Lugano and find your letter about this ms. of Dr. Jung's and I hasten to tell you the service is the "Press Bureau" (I have also heard it called Cultural Relations) and the name of the woman in charge is "Mrs. Plunder."

However the head of this bureau is "Jerry Mayer"[1] whom Dr. Jung met at my daughter's wedding and with whom he talked a long time. Mrs. Plunder comes after Mr. Mayer. I think it best that I send the enclosed note to Mr. Mayer and then Dr. Jung can do the rest and write himself.

Let me know if I can do anything more and I am always at Dr. Jung's disposition.

> With kindest regards,
> Yours very sincerely,
> Catharine Cabot

P.S.

I wrote as I did to Mr. Mayer, for I thought, if one wants to get anything to America, one rather has to look as if one wanted to "consult" Mr. Mayer, as the article etc. … for that bureau is awfully sticky and only likes to *send* to America things *they* wish to publish or have published. They refused to have anything to do with my article on Switzerland, but Dr. Jung being a famous man, I am quite sure they will take quite another attitude.

CRC

Katy enclosed a carbon of her letter to Mayer:

Gerald Mayer Esq.
Press Dept.
Legation of the united States of America
Bern

Dear Mr. Mayer: –

This morning I received a communication from Professor Jung in which he expressed the desire to get in touch with you, as to a

---

[1] Actually he was Gerry Mayer.

certain M.S. he wishes to have published in America. I have sent him your address and he will communicate with you direct himself as to the nature of the article and what he hopes to have done with it. I trust that you are very well. It was so nice seeing you at Mrs. de Cholley's party that night. Since then, I have been stewing in this impossibly hot Tessin! With my kindest regards to you and Mrs. Mayer and looking forward to seeing you, the next time I come to Bern,

I am,

very sincerely yours,

Catharine R. Cabot

The war had been over for barely three months. Travel between Europe and America was not yet possible for private individuals, though the wives of diplomats stationed in Switzerland were finally allowed to go to Europe, on troop ships designated by the State Department. The postal services in 1945 could not yet be relied upon either.[1] The exact name of the "Service" which Frl. Schmid was so keen to know would not have been divulged at that time to anybody. The office my mother mentions had various cover names, but in reality the so-called "Press Office" was part of the O.S.S. over which Allen Dulles then presided, later to be known as the C.I.A. Gerry Mayer[2] was his assistant. Gathering intelligence was the main business; sending mail would have been a favor.

In August, Toni is still hopeful that Katy's new relationship will work out. She writes:

Leukerbad

Aug. 15th, 1945

Dear Katy,

Many thanks for your express letter of 10th Aug. I thought

---

[1] In May 1945, we received two letters from an aunt in the United States which had been written and posted in *May 1940*.

[2] Gerry Mayer is described by Leonard Mosely (*in Dulles* [Daily Press/James Wade, New York, 1978]) as an American of German Jewish extraction, and a skeptical type. Pat and I knew him well and liked him a lot. He kept a lower profile than Dulles, so at that time we were not sure what his job was though we suspected he was secret service. My mother was ignorant of his clandestine activities. After the War he bought land in Gstaad, built a very nice chalet and lived there for the rest of his life.

something important was happening as you did not write. Katy I am so glad you are getting to the bottom of things. I think it is just wonderful how you penetrate right into a personality. It is the result of all your previous experiences of seeing through people. It can be a wonderful thing for Dr. F. too if he can take it. It is the supreme test for him. Either he is a real human being and can build up on what you tell him – and then he is really exceptional. Or he is only a function and a persona – and then he can't. But maybe the fact that he comes from solid stock enables him to get through the shell. It would mean a really great achievement, for a man that has risen so high socially the problem of accepting his real human side would include to get back somehow to where he came from. But naturally that would mean a real salvation. From what you told me about him it seems likely that he can do it.

I think it is wonderful too that you don't let him down and that you understand when he's a bit weak – as with that party. *I really do think Katy that you understand Dr. C.'s teaching far better and deeper than almost anyone else.* [Emphasis added.]

I am looking forward to seeing you here. You will find my previous letter with all the details. I think you're putting up at the *Hotel des Alpes* by far the best solution. I went there again and they promised me a room for certain for the 23rd (6-7 frs.). (They could not tell me which room would be free.) The hotel is really nice and what's most important here, has a very nice hall to sit in. In the village, there is only one locality to sit in at evenings, and that's not very nice. The food at the *des Alpes* is said to be very good. But you can tell me when you are here which way you prefer it. It's really quite good here too, particularly on meatless days.[1] Do take a rain-coat and skirt along, because you might like to come with me to the so-called foot bath, an open place where you sit on stones and bathe your feet and hands at a spring of 50 degrees [centigrade]. It is very good for the circulation. If you should like to take the baths, you could take one of two without going to the doctor. They have them at the *des Alpes*. You could not go to the swimming pool, but to the single cabins, for which you need no bathing suit.

---

[1] As I noted in the previous chapter about my wedding, for much of the War two meatless days were observed even in restaurants, but at one period, when importing food became very difficult, there were three meatless days.

If you should go back to the Tessin from here, you can do so by going back to Brigue, then take the *Furkabahn* to Göschenen and from there through the Gotthard. Tickets can be made out that way.

Do let me know when you arrive, I shall come to the train.

Au revoir then,

Affectionately,

Toni

Toni's remark, that Katy understood Jung's teaching far better and more deeply than almost anyone else, was no empty compliment. Toni was not the type to flatter. Katy *did* understand Jung's teaching remarkably well, but she found it difficult to impart it to people she was attached to. When they did not respond as she expected, she became impatient and applied pressure. This frightened her "analysand" who felt hobbled, and either rebelled (as did Mrs. Rüfenacht) or faded from the scene. Her Bern boyfriend had the latter reaction. The S. relationship came to nothing (despite Toni's encouragement) because Katy, in her zeal to consolidate it, began to analyze her beau in long earnest letters written in French which he eventually resented. She was unable to take Toni's advice and give *him* the initiative. The Sea Captain animus had to steer [the ship of] romance. Katy complained that S. compared her to the *Marschallin* in the *Rosenkavalier* (see p. 486). Though he and Katy were nearly the same age, he must have felt like the seventeen-year-old Octavian when in her company. The older *Marschallin* whom Katy resembled, also enjoyed delivering monologues.

Leukerbad's thermal waters are well known in Switzerland for the treatment of rheumatism. Toni's arthritis was already a great problem to her; Katy had also suffered from rheumatic knees in her youth, but thanks to analysis was quickly cured, she said. Her visit to Toni was therefore to be a social one. Though the War was over, it was still not possible for persons without some official status to leave Switzerland. So presumably it was for lack of other options that Katy was willing to join Toni at a place like Leukerbad, which normally she would never have wanted to visit. Just after the War, Leukerbad was a pretty, very quiet alpine village on the Valais side of the Gemmi Pass, at the foot of the Daubenhorn. The narrow trail which Victorians traveled on mules descends steeply from the pass to the village, which is blessed with hot springs of such great abundance that hot water flows not only into the bath establishment but also from certain village fountains. However attractive scenically, Leukerbad was more a place for introverts like Toni than for Katy, who liked night life; she would have much preferred the evening in the "village locality" than in a hotel lounge, however nice. If Katy went there, she must have been at loose ends, and my guess is that she did not go, or I would have heard the juicy details of the visit. Likely she gave a last-minute excuse for canceling. She was excellent at making excuses appear valid.

On 9 October, Miss Schmid wrote to Katy offering her hours on the 19th with both Jungs (as mentioned earlier, the arrangement was that first she had an hour with Mrs. Jung). But possibly she did not take up the offer, as there is no record of an hour with either of them. But Katy did see Jung in November:

November 12, 1945

As soon as I arrived, I told Onkel that I was sure analysis had done lots for me because for years I had to take calcium and had had colds etc. ... since 1936, when I was so ill and in bed almost a year. However, I told him that I was under Dr. Reist and that he was giving me hormones and that it could be that which had improved my general health. Onkel said he thought it was undoubtedly that, for the climactarium can produce a carence [lack] of metabolism and the hormones force the glands to produce chemical stuff that goes into the blood, and carried about helps the whole vitality [of the organism]. He said that scurvy is also a deficiency disease and that is why one has to take vitamins to cure scurvy. He said that the ovaries normally produce a lot of hormones, which is important for the metabolism of a woman. But, when the climacterium starts, the ovaries produce less hormones and need to be helped artificially. He said, that with me this glandular defect was deeply rooted in the body, and that in such a case analysis cannot help and he sends such people to the doctor.

Then I told Onkel that I had been to see Lothar [a cover name for Feisst] and that he had had a *fissura ani*. Onkel said that it was an uncomfortable spot. He explained that a fissure develops when the skin cracks, like the lips, and it gets painful, and worse and worse because the spot can't rest and it gets deeper and deeper – a most disgusting ailment because it poisons your life. All one can do

is to sew it together and hope that it will last. He said that it came
sometimes to people under pressure in work and they suffer
constipation, and if they work under strain and are concentrated
they forget about it [the constipation?] and then the thing develops. Working under strain is a condition which helps a fissure to
develop.

The I told Onkel about Lothar and how strange it was that he
should seek me out, because usually such people in Bern, never
worried about me. Onkel said that somewhere in Lothar there was
a soul behind the scene, and he 'smelt a rat,' and that it speaks in
favor of such a man. He said that probably Lothar was sensitive
and his anima had got a bit active and he had a certain feeling of
inferiority, and also a certain insight into his character which is
only half admitted. Onkel said, for instance, that people like Dulles,
who were not too split, the more they get powerful, the more the
Anima begins to stir for she gets short of love. Then they get a
peculiar uncertainty and develop an inferiority and a sensibility.
With Dulles there is a huge façade of nothing but power, and you
can go a long way and walk through corridors and corridors and
long buildings before you come to the Anima. With a Swiss, he
said, one gets behind the façade soon. If Lothar admires Dulles, it
is because he sees this wonderful front. But as Onkel said, with
Dulles it is as if he were living in such an enormous building and
the Anima living in a hut! He added that the Swiss unconscious
was much nearer to consciousness, for there is not that terrific
split which the American has. Dulles thinks he is pure gold. A
Swiss, Onkel said, has no time to build up such a tremendous
building in which to house himself, for, "We here in Switzerland
can never be an English lord, nor President of the United States,
nor president of an American bank, nor a big man on Wall Street
or Washington." He continued that the American way of life is to
work all day and then have an exciting evening, and to live as a
'success' and earn lots of money. The Americans are so busy doing
that that they find no moment when they can come to themselves.
One is *forced up against oneself* when one lives in Switzerland. In
America, there is no peace, or being alone. They [the Americans]
go in crowds on their holidays. Then Onkel told of going to a camp
in the Adirondacks with Dr. Putnam and fifty members of Dr.
Putnam's family. When Dr. Putnam was *alone* he was with his wife
and five or six people!!!

I told Onkel that I was using 'Dulles' to discuss with his admirer Lothar, because it served my purpose to get things over to Lothar. Onkel said that he often did that with his patients, and all the time one was discussing the patient's shadow. Dulles is Lothar's shadow – his power shadow – but with anyone who is not too far away from his unconscious like the Swiss, it can't last. I told him [Lothar] about our Secretary of State Hull, who was photographed with his family, while in office, the family being poor whites in the Virginia mountains, and just the simplest of simple people, sitting outside their miserable cabins smoking corn pipes. I told Onkel that I had written that to Lothar and also not to lose *'le fil' qui vous relie au petit garçon que j'ai vu en quittant l'hôpital* [the thread that links you to the little boy whom I saw while leaving the hospital].

Then I told Onkel about Toni and how she had asked me to consult the Monsters on her behalf.[1] He looked *bouche béante* [open-mouthed], his heavenly sense of humor came to the front, and he roared with laughter and said, "What was her idea?" I said that it was to develop and better herself, but that of course I could never tell her what the Monsters would say, and he said, "What would they say?" I answered, "They would first tell her to get rid of her bad tempers and generally become a 'regular' person, before embarking in the realm of the super-person!" He shook his head solemnly and said, "That is just it, those bad tempers are impossible and she won't see anything. I went into things deeply with her and it made no impression." He said that he had told her three times, and, as she hadn't taken it in, he could do nothing about it.

Then I told Onkel what I had done to Mrs. Briner and asked him if I had done right. He said *absolutely*. I was so relieved because I *felt* reproaches all over her! And Toni had reproached me twice, and had unspoken reproach written all over her. Onkel said that one can often 'right' things by kicking a person and that was evidently what Mrs. Briner needed. He said that he couldn't do much for her in her daily life, as he didn't see her in it; they only talked deep things when she came to see him. I asked him if it wasn't better to 'right' the obvious things, before going down into deep layers? He said one can talk about, and even understand, many deep things before one realizes what one ought to do.

---

[1] Who the Monsters were is unknown to me.

In November 1945, while moving from La Pergola, a temporary address, to her new abode, Casa Britannia, Katy found time to write to Lothar again, in excellent French. The letter, however, is long-winded and schoolmarmish, hardly conducive to increasing a lover's ardor. In it she protests astonishment that he compares her to the *Marschallin* in the *Rosenkavalier*. She says (my translation): "I must say before ending this letter that I was, at first, painfully surprised that I gave the impression of the *Marschallin* in the *Rosenkavalier*. I could not understand it, because knowing myself to be weak inside, and not at all what the *Marschallin* represents, I could not understand at first what you meant. But on thinking it over, I see that it is certain qualities of my character which made you think this. Also I see that I grew a *Marschallin* 'defense' without realizing it to compensate for my fundamental weakness." She goes on to say that people think she is strong because she appears independent and lives her life with unconstraint and philosophically, not falling any more into human stupidities. But deep down, she says, she is timid, unsure and sensitive, with all the faults and qualities of a woman. Feisst had told her apparently that he had a "heart of granite"; she replies that because she is weak she saw him as "all granite." He was obviously not impressed by her profession of weakness, because of course it did not fit her. She herself was unaware of her vigorous animus which Feisst, not being an expert on Jung's psychology, interpreted in female guise as the *Marschallin*. The relationship was made worse by the long letter she wrote. Urgently needing more advice, Katy writes:

> La Pergola
> Ascona
> Tessin
> November 27th, 1945

Dear Onkel,

I shall be in Zürich again on December 16th for a week. May I have *one* appointment with you, that week if possible on Tuesday the 18th or Thursday the 20th. Certain rather important things are shaping themselves in my life and I should so like to talk over everything with you, for you have brought me *so far*, that in the last analysis, it is only you and your opinion which really count in decisive moments. Perhaps Miss Schmid would send me a card, with the appointment, if it is possible.

With my best love,

Yours very affectionately,

Catharine Cabot

No record of an interview in December 1945 exists, nor is there any reply extant from Frl. Schmid, so it is not possible to know if Katy saw Jung. Preoccupied with her Bern beau and fearful that the relationship could break up, she saw that "important things were shaping" only out of wishful thinking, as the relationship was at its last gasp. The next recorded hour with Jung takes place in February 1946, in which Jung explains Feisst's psychology; the difficulties she had encountered in her relationship were then still very much in her mind. But in December, probably because she could not see Jung immediately, Katy must have asked for an analytical hour with Toni Wolff, with whom she was on better terms again. In January, she received the following reply from Toni:

> Freiestrasse 9
> Zürich 7
> Jan. 24th, 1946

Dear Katy,

Many thanks for your letter. I am sorry the X. thing is definitely ended, but I am sure you know best. By the way, if it is ended, will you please ask him to return my Huxley manuscript, no matter whether he has finished it or not. He will not learn from it anyhow.

Is 'Casa Britannia' now the name of your house? It is only for sending Club mail.

I think you are right to come here and work with Dr. Q. And I shall keep time for you once a week. I definitely prefer it to be at my house. My rheumatism is so bad, despite the stay at the mountains, that I don't like to go out in the evening more than I can help it. Besides, rationing is so much better that economy in this respect is unnecessary. Also, I work much better in my own room, if it comes to real work. I do hope we shall be able to find the way to your own style. I simply felt that so far you were on your way, but have not quite managed to find your individual way. But naturally this cannot be done at the very beginning.

Affectionately,

Toni

Toni's mention of rations being better, implying that there is less need to go out to eat, makes me suppose that Katy was suggesting an analytical dinner *à deux* in a restaurant! Whether they met at Toni's house, or Katy pushed through her invitation (she could be very insistent), is unknown. But some incident must have occurred between 24 January and 14 February because Toni, when she writes again, asks Katy to retrieve her ms. from X.; she is obviously very upset as her English deteriorates:

Freiestrasse 9
Zürich
Feb. 14th, 1946

Dear Katy,

I find, after all, that I cannot accept your standpoint about my Huxley manuscript.[1] Naturally I understand your standpoint, but it does not agree with me. Mostly I feel that I cannot lose trust in you which I would if nothing were done about it. You remember you reassured me time and again that I would get the ms. back. I know that the situation has changed for you more or less, but that does not help me.

Second, I cannot have a manuscript of mine in the hands of a person I don't know and who moreover is a reliable person and surely does not want anybody to be let down.

And third, I find it absurd, that another 45 Frs. have to be spent, when it was already paid and when you have no money for such extravagances. So I am sure that a way can be found, not at the moment perhaps, but with due consideration. An indirect way perhaps. Maybe Janey could drop a word or your friend Mrs. L. or maybe you will see X. yourself. There is no hurry, but I had to tell you.

I hope you are better. Maybe you are not so interested in the lecture which takes place instead of Mrs. V's.

Affectionately,

Toni

Katy's longhand note on this letter reads, "What does such a sentence mean? Surely it is *just* in such hands one would want one's

---

[1] Toni Wolff, "Aus Aldous Huxleys *Die Graue Eminenz*: Eine Untersuchung über Religion und Politik," given as a lecture at the Psychological Club on 8 and 10 March 1945.

ms." The second paragraph does read rather strangely until the unwritten part comes to mind, namely that the "reliable person" was perhaps wanting to send back the manuscript but had no address. I cannot remember having to retrieve it myself, so perhaps a special messenger did.

February 21, 1946

I told Onkel the whole show [about Lothar] starting in with Dr. Meier's discoveries *et tout ce qui s'en suit* [and all that follows from them].... He didn't seem much interested that I had jumped from the frying pan into the fire, by taking on another mother, but he said that he thought that *my instinct* should have told me that one can't go at people and then try to bring out their nice sides. They naturally have resistances against that. People who have not been analysed naturally cannot stand that sort of thing. I told him that I was trying to be interesting and have more exciting conversation, than just Bern gossip etc. etc. ... Onkel said that Psychology was not 'conversation' but 'hot stuff,' too much of a good thing. An obvious truth blows a person up. For instance, a man has a mother complex and you tell him so, or tell a girl she has a father complex, they *explode*! He went on to say that he could do it because that is what is expected of him. It is like going to the dentist: people take it 'professionally' and know that it is disagreeable, but they have to stand it. But if he or anyone said the same thing in the open, over a dinner table, you push them into the hottest conflict and get yourself burnt too.

Then he went on to tell me how, through the years, I have got used to that kind of talk, but that if I look backward, it took me a long, long time to grasp it, and that because now I was a psychologist, there was no reason to think that others were too! I told him that Feisst said he liked that talk and even asked me to go on writing those letters on his troubles etc. ... Onkel said that it was decent of him to acknowledge what I had told him as being true and that it may appeal to a person for a while, but that *à la longue* it gets on a person's nerves. His complexes get the upper hand and he ceased to like that talk. At first, he no doubt admired me and thought I was original and a genius in my line, but he started slowly gathering 'resistances' and though at first he thought I was a clever person, he finally got to hate it and me. If people tell someone too many truths, you get a resistance, get negative and feel a revolution going on inside you. I played the *enfant terrible* and it is astounding that I didn't have more 'feeling' from such a man. Every word I said to him was a kick and though it may be 'original' to meet someone like that, at first, who doesn't seem to be impressed by position, in the end one gets sick of the kicks! It is too strong and too spiced and one just gets fed up. Onkel went on to say that he had seen it often and he had to be exceedingly careful when with people, for he could easily play the *enfant terrible*, by being witty and gay. One never knows what an inadvertent remark may mean to people, for one can even set something on fire, by saying something quite reasonable. He told of how he talked to a clergyman once about a certain parable of Christ, and his wife was listening to him and her clergyman husband's conversation. His remarks excited her and she said to him, "It wasn't so much what you said, but the way you said it." Onkel had pricked the bubble, though he never talked to her, nor addressed a word to her. She had a compartment psychology where she harbored a mountain of resistances against her husband because he was a clergyman. On the surface, his [Jung's] conversation was inoffensive, but she sensed underneath another point of view.

Onkel reiterated that the mere fact that he knows something about psychology makes him a queer bird. "If I nod in a place which is unexpected, then everyone thinks it is 'something.' Everyone has some skeleton in a cupboard. People think I know something about *them*. They think that I have a sort of 'clairvoyance' and look into the recesses of their minds or into their secret drawers." He said that when his children were young, they were supposed to have his knowledge, and then later, and even now, they have to assure people that they know nothing of psychology. I told Onkel how it was with me, when I went to a party in Bern and people would come forward saying, "Oh, Dr. Jung!" To which I would answer, "But I am not Dr. Jung, and I hope that I don't look like him!" He laughed and went on that people project all their things onto him as it gives them an aura. People who are not analysed, Onkel said, were like raw eggs: vulnerable and sensitive. If one gives anyone a "Father Joseph" paper (to a friend) one must confess one's ignorance of the question. Onkel went on to say that he could not even shake hands with a person without that person thinking that a deep truth or secret purpose lies behind the gesture. Psychology is explosive. Lothar is a boy from a modest family, and

I know Psychology, so when I talk, it makes more of an impression than things that are said by people who don't know it. If I say to him, "You are an adorable man, why don't you use your good qualities?" He thinks, "Here's a woman I love and who loves me and thinks that of me, so what do other people think?" He thinks he is *depreciated* and feels that it all falls on his head and gives him a sleepless night. I told Onkel that he said he didn't sleep and that I only said that it was 'overwork' and at that time did not mention psychological causes! Onkel then told me of a play in New York, where a person had to tell the truth for twenty-four hours and when he finished, he was in the most hellish muddle. Terribly amusing!

He also said that it was a mistake to say that one wasn't a *grande dame*; one should never disturb men's illusions about a woman. It was his [Feisst's] greatest ambition to have a *grande dame* on his knees and that is what he *wants*. When she says she isn't one, he says to himself: "What bad taste!" Onkel went on to say that if he had a lady on his knees and said to her, "'My dear angel, you are the most admirable thing' and then she takes off her shoes and stockings and trousers ...!" A complete disenchantment! He wants above all a *grande dame*. Being from such a family is his one black spot: no Swiss girl of good family would want to marry him. It would be difficult for him to appear in an old Swiss family. A European hasn't the same standpoint as has the American, about marrying. Probably a Bostonian would not want to marry out of his milieu, as it is embarrassing to have the queer relatives turn up. And Onkel added humorously:

"His plan was to have a *grande dame* on his knees,

Even if she was in her chemise!"

If a Bostonian of low descent wants to come up [in the world], the woman he loves and wants to marry must be a society woman and when she sits on his knees, she must not remind him that she is an ordinary woman, for then he is cheated of the great experience of holding a *grande dame* on his knees. Then Onkel went on to say, "If I had an English duchess on my knees," (he added, evidently underestimating my understanding and sense of humor?) "but God forbid that I should ever have, then I have *something* on my knees! Lothar is socially ambitious (*Streber*) and when she proves not to be a duchess, *er ist einfach blamiert*! [he is simply exposed to ridicule!] He wishes to be thought of as 'made of

granite' for he is afraid he might have a human weakness somewhere." Then I told Onkel of sending Lothar the *briquet* [cigarette
lighter] which is a souvenir of the latest destroyer [launched]
named after my father.[1] Onkel said that made him feel good, for
the *grande dame* now has a father whose name has been used for a
big ship. It is 'prestige' psychology!! (How I laughed. Onkel is
unique in his humor!)

I was working on the human line, but can only use 'prestige
psychology' in such an enterprise. He puts up a stone wall of
granite to give me an idea of his unshakableness in the *grande
dame* idea. If I am a *grande dame*, then he is like butter. He
wouldn't have reacted like that if he had been human. In a way, he
appreciates me from the human point of view, but "up comes his
ambition!"

He does not want to be reminded that he is an ordinary man, he
likes to think he's a great man! He is already living his biography!
These power men live for an imaginary day of great fame which
will come. If it does come, there is no human side left to enjoy it!
He went after me because he found me an accessible *grande dame*
when his countrywomen weren't, and I had some human quality
which he liked. However, he is ridden by his ambition, and such a
man would not be a suitable husband, and I'd be left out in the
cold. Also, it was a very inferior feeling kissing me on a sofa in front
of Phyllis and Pat.[2]

I asked Onkel how to go on, as I was terribly lonely. Onkel said
to just drift along, and try to see people and accept things as they
come along, and keep one's eyes open to what comes along and do
the best one can. One also hopes that something turns up, that
things will come to one. [The things that will come to me, which I
am, for no one escapes his own fate.] He said that I was something
quite nice, though I have my other sides as well, and though I don't
know who I am and can be taken by surprise myself. The inferior
function has one on a string. It is a most powerful thing, a big
daemon, for it has the whole collective unconscious behind it.

The inferior function is one with the collective which is the law
of nature and the law of our life. It is so big we can't see it, but we

---

[1] The *U.S.S. William R. Rush* (DD-714), keel laid 19 October 1944, and
launched 8 July 1945.
[2] Phyllis Legge (wife of the American Military Attaché) and Pat Reid (Katy's
son-in-law).

imagine we can see it. It is only small to our conscious. Lothar's inferior function is all over the place.

I am the sensation type and that type is irrational and the auxiliary function is feeling. My inferior functions are intuition and intellect. While I am apparently following my sensation and feeling and making them the main source of what I do, *in reality* I am driven to things by my inferior function, such as *wrong* opinions, nasty *negative* intuitions, which influence me very much.

A typical intellectual rules his life by intellect, but stumbles over his feelings: wrong impressions, bad relations with people. He is influenced by his inferior feeling everywhere and that decides his fate. His unconscious feeling influences his marriage, his children, his relation to his wife. That *invisible something* will always enter and decide his fate.

In my case *intellect* and *intuition* are the great powers of evil. The more I build up my mind, the more I decrease the fatal influence of these factors, as I get them under control!!!!!

To an intellectual man my looks are O.K., but I get nowhere due to his damned inferior feeling.

A feeling type clings to people cos he thinks they are nice and they turn out to be the damndest people under the sun. He says, "I thought …!" One never thought at all. These people one thinks nice are rotten people and if one had *thought* one would have seen behind the fine surface! One should try and *use one's inferior function and make up one's mind!* If I think over such a man, *the key note is ambition.* One can't take off one's stockings until one knows whom one has to deal with! I follow my feeling without *thinking.* I think I will appeal to his better qualities, and such intuitions are no good. He doesn't want to sacrifice one inch to his ambition. You are a *grande dame* and you promise so much 'capital' for that 'business'!

Onkel said that I was in the inferior function over my ears. Just *think* of our Dr. Lothar. What do you think about people? I must play the *enfant terrible* to myself. I shall, in the beginning, think worse of people than Onkel, cos my negative intuitions will give me a worse judgement than Onkel. Only by constant use of my inferior function can I develop it. Onkel went on to say, "People can flood me with positive feeling, and I think: 'This is too much,' then I find the truth is somewhere in between the two points." And that, Onkel said, was what I would do. I would *think* too positively or too

negatively about people at first. Lothar is a *Streber* [arriviste], and
it was a stroke of fate that he should become acquainted with a
woman who was not interested in 'POSITION.'

The last sentence seems strange in view of Jung's earlier view that
Katy *was* interested in position, as her Débutante side made plain.
Perhaps he now declares the opposite because he sensed that the anti-
society Sea-Captain side was in the ascendant, eclipsed from Katy's
consciousness because she loved to imagine herself a timid, feminine
flower. Timid she certainly was not, though highly sensitive. When
she pleaded timidity, "with all the faults and qualities of woman," she
was claiming that phony womanly role which Linda Fierz saw
through (see above) and which failed to impress Lothar either, as he
needed a strong but feminine woman, not a weak one to play opposite
his youthful "Octavian." Though he may not have realized it, Lothar
was looking for a mature, motherly woman, and Katy certainly was
not that. When with the passing of years, she fell less into the *jeune
fille* role, the next stage was not female maturity, because Katy
identified too much with her father. Lothar already sensed this
masculine vigor and projected the *Marschallin* onto her. Jung is
wrong, however, about Katy's being disinterested in social position,
as we shall see when she meets her next beau.

Pat and I knew Lothar well and liked him very much, but we never
saw him as emotionally mature enough to become a husband. To us
he was a confirmed bachelor, with whom we had many jolly evenings
together. When we went on a wine-tasting weekend to the Valais with
him and Dulles's secretary, we noticed that he liked to flirt with her
but also that the flirtation was entirely superficial. Of Lothar's
relationship with Katy we knew very little, and certainly had no idea
that Katy hoped to marry him. From our evaluation, he was as
unsuited to Katy as the *Poupon* was. But it seems that Katy took the
relationship quite seriously. From his side, at first Lothar obviously
liked the attention from a foreign woman, but then became frightened by Katy's know-all and possessive sides. Though she seems never
to have realized it, she liked to run the show with men; because of the
pressure she put upon Lothar to change himself and his way of life,
he beat a hasty retreat. Valuing his freedom and being ambitious, he
had no intention of changing his life-style to suit Katy. Feisst did keep
his freedom but never reached the top echelons in the Federal
Administration. After the War, in recognition of his efficient work

organizing wartime food distribution, he was appointed Swiss Ambassador to Hungary for three years. Pat and I kept in touch with him, and in 1949, we asked him to be Godfather to our third child, Christopher, which he gladly accepted. We saw Feisst from time to time and exchanged Christmas cards for many years; he sent us beautiful Swiss scenes, which I had framed. We then lost touch with him and [finally] heard that he had died. By that time Katy had found a more constant companion and, loneliness no longer a problem, lost her urge to be a writer, for men occupied her totally.

Toni's next letter has a more friendly ring to it. With her dynamic temperament, it must have been very difficult at times to control herself, especially with Katy, who was so much her opposite in character.

> Freiestrasse 9
> Zürich 7
> March 5th, 1946

Dear Katy,

I had hoped to be able to thank you for your letter last Saturday and was sorry to hear you were in bed. I do hope it is not the flu after all. I am sure there will be a way to recover my manuscript. Thanks for the trouble.

Janey must have had a most thrilling time with W. I do not see, however, how X. got into it too? Marvelous how he manages to be in everything.

I do hope you are better and can go to Basel for the Fastnacht with the Lüttichaus.

> Affectionately,
>
> Toni

Because he was a senior government official, Feisst was invited to most diplomatic functions in Bern, and, as I have already said, was popular with members of the diplomatic corps, particularly the Americans and British. Field Marshal Montgomery's visit to Switzerland was official, carefully planned in advance by the Swiss government and military authorities to meet the General's wishes. At his request, the first part of the visit was to be spent in the mountains (he had been a skier before the War). On his return to Bern from the *Berner Oberland*, among the many receptions for him, the British Legation gave a big party to which Feisst was naturally invited.

Pat and I, however, together with the British Military Attaché Herbert Fryer and his wife Penelope, were involved with Montgomery before the official part of his visit. Monty had arrived from Germany in Hitler's former train, but did not intend showing himself until after his mountain holiday. Colonel Fryer was informed by the Swiss High Command that Monty's train would arrive at Zweisimmen in the *Oberland* at 7:30 a.m., and that the reception committee must be there well beforehand as Monty was very punctual. The British Military Attaché, the Assistant Military Attaché, their wives, and two Swiss officials, Colonel Bracher and the *chef de protocole* Jean-Pierre Weber, were to form an official reception party for the General at the station. Montgomery, an early riser, spent the night traveling from Germany to Switzerland. Pat and I, and some of Montgomery's young aides, went to a ball that night at the Château de Gümlingen outside Bern, owned by the Aloys de Tscharners. We left early, but even so had only a couple of hours of sleep, interrupted by a phone call telling us that Monty's train would be delayed by forty minutes. Nonetheless, we rose very early to drive on the icy, rutted roads eighty kilometers in the dark to Zweisimmen. When we reached the Simmental, we also had to contend with even worse road conditions on the winding road up the valley, which made us skid all over the place. After mounting chains with difficulty in the darkness, we managed to reach Zweisimmen in Katy's 1939 Packard with its British plates, just ahead of Monty's train which came in at 8:30 a.m.

All but one of Monty's *aides de camp* traveled with him on his official train (more about the train in a moment). The stray sheep was an officer who stayed longer at the ball than we did, Carol Mather,[1] who planned to join the train as it went past Gümlingen in the early hours. When he was told the train would be late, he found a cosy signal-box in which there was a convenient stretcher to sleep on; a friendly railway worker told him where the train would slow down enough so that he could jump aboard. But Carol's sleep was cut short by exploding flashbulbs from a photographer who had tracked him to his lair. Monty, a strict disciplinarian, had vetted his aide's absence on this occasion, but some days later at Gstaad, two ADCs were

---

[1] Lt. Col. Carol Mather was liaison officer to Montgomery during much of the War (the two had met skiing in Gstaad/Saanenmöser when Mather was a boy). A former Member of Parliament, he has written several books including *Aftermath of War* (1992) and *When the Grass Stops Growing* (1997).

caught by him as they returned late one night to the chalet Gifferhorn lent to the General by the Guinesses. Entering tipsily, the ADCs tripped over a cable; a lamp crashed to the floor, and Montgomery, a nemesis in nightshirt, descended the chalet stairs and instantly meted out a 10 p.m. curfew to the officers for the duration of their stay in Gstaad. As we had been having many jolly evenings with these aides, Pat and I felt that our own wings had been clipped as well.

Just as Montgomery's train was arriving at Zweisimmen, where he was due to change trains for Saanenmöser for a two-day stay before going on to Gstaad, the *chef de protocole* told us that Monty disliked meeting women early in the morning because he was in a mess kit. We women did not appreciate this sudden change of plan. Penelope Fryer, no longer young, had made a special effort to accompany her husband on the precarious expedition from Bern in their old red Citroen called *Bloody Mary*. She looked forward to being part of the reception committee and was very disappointed to be left out. I was young and less vulnerable to the cavalier treatment, but still annoyed. Soon I realized it was an excuse, as Monty always wore battle dress. While the male members of the party went forward to greet Monty as he jumped out into their arms, because the steps failed to come down, we females stood at some distance in the half-light, watching with a few villagers who happened to be passing by. Though Monty's arrival had been kept secret, a couple of reporters arrived as he was changing trains. This change was required as only the narrow-gauge mountain trains could negotiate the upper valley. The M.O.B. (*Montreux Oberland Bernois*) had one carriage, whose amazingly ornate character dated it to the Edwardian era, and in which Montgomery was ensconced. Pat and I and the Fryers slithered on up the narrow winding road to Saanenmöser in our cars.

After a three-night visit to Saanenmöser, a hamlet at the top of the pass between Zweisimmen and Saanen, Monty went on to Gstaad where he spent several more days being entertained by the local authorities and watching army maneuvers and ski jumping on the Eggli. There he was lent a magnificent very long white lambskin coat, a type used at that time exclusively for mountain maneuvers by senior Swiss officers. He was so enchanted with it that, much to the Army's consternation, he refused to return it after his visit.[1] Monty did not

---

[1] He wore this coat to Russia immediately afterwards. There he was given a similar coat, grey and of lesser quality, which out of courtesy he wore while in Russia; but after leaving, he was back in the Swiss coat.

use Hitler's train for the return journey to Bern. After depositing him in Zweisimmen, it immediately returned to a siding at Bern station. We left our car in Gstaad to be retrieved later and accompanied the General by train with Colonel Bracher (the Fryers had long since returned), making the first stretch in the afternoon from Gstaad to Zweisimmen with Monty in the ornate carriage. Hitler's train, though not ornate in this way, had comfortable accommodations for him and his staff, with a luxurious yellow-tiled bathroom which I thought had been for Göring but which I learned later had been built into the *Gauleiter*'s compartment by Montgomery.[1] The second train that we boarded in Zweisimmen had three carriages with diesel engines at both ends. It had just been put into service between Zweisimmen and Spiez; though the engines were technically advanced the carriages, second and third class only, were comfortable but plain. Monty was intrigued by this new type of train, and so insisted on sitting up front with the engine driver who spoke excellent English. Pat and I joined him in the cabin, which was larger than usual and had several comfortable seats. Montgomery asked many technical questions and was allowed to take the controls for a while, as the train more or less ran itself. But I noticed that even so, with Monty at the controls, the engine driver became very alert; and this was comforting. As he had not been in the early morning at Zweisimmen, Monty grew talkative, even with me the only woman present. The train stopped at one station down the Simmental for the school children of the valley, who had been given the day off to see the General. They greeted him in droves, waving flags and bearing gifts, one of which was a five-kilo tin of honey. Monty encouraged them to sing English songs, but apart from attempting a faint *Tipperary*, which they knew only in part, they responded with loud yodels. Montgomery, who seemed to love the attention, stood at the open window waving and gathering his gifts. At Spiez, on the Lake of Thun, we did not make the customary change of trains, but continued with ours by heading in the other direction. Monty, who wanted to continue sitting up front, was forced to move to the other end and the second diesel engine. The Swiss officers accompanying him, with some extras who had materialized in Spiez,

[1] Pat and I visited the train twice both in Zweisimmen and in Bern, sitting in the carriage where Hitler had received Pétain for the signing of the armistice in 1940. One of Monty's aides took a photo of Pat impersonating Hitler, in which I pretended to be Eva Braun, and Colonel Bracher, of the Swiss General Staff, aped a Hitler aide!

tried to dissuade him from moving, but he insisted, so we marched the whole length of the train; the Swiss officers were visibly embarrassed, as they knew the carriages at the other end were third class, with wooden slatted benches. (Officers traveled second class, with officers of high rank going first class when it was available.) The second engine driver's section was identical to the first except for these seats, but Monty was not put off by wood. Again he sat next to the driver and handled the controls on the Bern stretch. The train stopped outside the capital at Ostermündigen, where official cars and Colonel Fryer met our party to whisk us away with Monty in a motorcade.

Chapter Eleven

Voyages, Transitions, Closures

While Pat and I were involved with Montgomery's visit, Katy had taken part in the first postwar *Fastnacht* or *Carneval* in Basel. Toni writes:

Freiestrasse 9
Zürich
March 18th, 1946

Dear Katy,

Many thanks for your letter. I am glad you enjoyed the Fastnacht, because I heard that it was awful on account of the incredible crowds. No certainly I was not there. I had been once when it was still the real thing for Basel people only.

Did you mean to write a causerie for the Club? I am not sure this would be possible. There is only one Club evening before the spring vacations, Y's Tea Evening March 30th. And later in the summer the Stimmung for Fastnacht (never say 'carneval' in Basel!) is no more quite *à propos*. 2. Quite a number of Club people know it of course, some real Basel people, others have been there. I believe we went once a party of Club people. So if you meant it for the Club, I am rather uncertain. I ought to discuss it with Dr. Q. too, the Club president is really the one to give the final word about the programme. We are having a committee meeting tomorrow Tuesday at 6 p.m. where we discuss the programme for the summer term. If you like to talk to me about it please ring me up tomorrow between 1 and 2 o'clock, if you are back by then. Or at the latest between 4 and 5 p.m. Afterwards I have to dress and leave before 6. But do write it by all means and you may be able to publish the article in some American magazine.

I wonder how and why the Fastnacht made such a big change in your life.

I am sorry about the Huxley ms. business.

Affectionately,

Toni

P.S. If you say nothing to the contrary, I take it that your address for this year is Villa Britannia, Ascona. It is for the Club report.

over! [On the reverse of the page Toni continues:]

I kept the letter as I thought you would only be here tomorrow and so will answer your second [letter]. The description of the ball's grand and you certainly can write an article about the Basler Fastnacht! I see now too why it made such an impression on you.

Am glad you enjoyed the P. fare-well dinner ball, and about X., I wonder how you felt in seeing him and how he felt?

Would Dr. C. perhaps like to read the Fastnacht letter? He would certainly understand.

Affectionately,

Toni

The undated letter which Toni mentions Katy wrote to Margaret Lüttichau, approximately a week after the Basler Fastnacht. It appears that the older Lüttichaus did not go to Basel but that their daughter Vita did. In it Katy writes that she went with a group of friends from Bern, who deserted her early in the evening because they had gone only to see the processions, bringing no costumes with them and so not interested in staying for the ball. Katy, however, had a costume and booking at the *Hotel Trois Rois*, determined to stay on even alone. Luckily for her, the U.S. Military Attaché in Bern, General Barnwell Legge, had alerted a couple of American officers living in Basel, as well as an Admiral's daughter, that Katy would be there. The officers phoned Katy at her hotel as she was dressing for the ball, so she invited everyone for cocktails at the hotel bar. Everybody was in fancy dress, and Katy appeared in a beautiful black and white satin Pierrot. Her new friends told her that in Basel people were not fond of Pierrots, but Katy remained impervious to this piece of intelligence. Normally she was not so thick-skinned, but on this occasion she was not going to allow her evening to be spoiled by negative talk. After the drinks, she and her companions went first to the Casino which had "sumptuous marble halls." Katy writes:

As I looked around, I could see only men in *Frack* [white tie and tails] and dozens and dozens of my 'grandmother's great aunts,' all dancing decorously with the men in *Frack* or together. Funny to see so many women dancing together. I had a feeling that I was at a *bal masqué* of the [18]50s, the sort of old fashioned thing that my great grandmother Rush used to go to. ... The whole was extremely distingué and decorous ... and earnest, terribly earnest, just like the *Umzüge* [processions]. Again, I had that feeling that I was not, and could never be a participant in that ball. I was just again witnessing *une manifestation mystique*. As I saw the thing to be *très collet monté*, [stuck up] even behind masks. I put on the grand manner and glanced around to take in these old girls!

These old girls or 'great aunts' ... were beautifully and very expensively got up in yard upon yard of moiré, satin, taffeta – hats dripping with feathers, flowers, old lace. ... It repelled me so many hideous women yet it fascinated me. Suddenly, as I stood there feeling small and insignificant in front of so many 'Aunts,' a huge Aunt bore down on me. ... I backed towards the wall. She was splendiferous – a battleship woman, strong, big, rich, secure, dressed in pale lavender moiré, a huge hat of the same material, dripping with lovely ostrich feathers in the same tone caught up with exquisite roses. Her jewelry was equal to the *époque* and the dress very beautiful of its kind. ... Imagine my surprise, as we whirled around the floor, to be dancing with a beautiful dancer and held in strong, muscular arms! Then, and only then, I realized that half of these 'Aunts' were men!

Katy continues her letter to Margaret telling her that she learned a great deal about herself that night. "All the evening I played the 'visiting' French lady and 'the grande dame' which was the keynote of the evening. And suddenly I felt terribly light and airy amidst those solid people, those 'worthies.' I felt I was treading on a cloud, for I had found out I did not belong there, wasn't wanted there, was only tolerated and was not in my 'world.' It was a rather startling revelation."

Later that evening Katy returned to the *Hotel Trois Rois* as did some of her companions, and they "shook up some more cocktails in

the Admiral's private suite." The Admiral's daughter told Katy that the
hotel director, who had seen her in the hall, thought she was the
"young countess [Vita] Lüttichau," and said that he was longing to
dance with her. She was urged to go downstairs again. "Is your
mother now safely tucked away in bed?" the director asked. Katy
Nodded. They danced and danced.[1] Katy, her mask firmly on, drank
champagne through a straw. She writes, "Finally, as I was longing to
extricate myself from his love-making, down comes the General and
says, 'Oh, here you are Mrs. Cabot.' The director, like a man of wax to
whom one puts a torch, just fell to pieces at my feet, muttering and
murmuring apologies. ..."

A few days after Toni's letter, Linda Fierz also wrote. At first she
broaches other subjects but then she too requests first-hand information about Katy's *carneval* experiences. She came originally from
Basel but had not lived there for many years, so the first postwar
Fastnacht was of particular interest to her, a fact which she managed
to admit only at the very end of her letter.

26.III.46

Dear Katy!
  It was ever so nice of you to write me and send these amusing
  poems. Thank you so much – first of all for your letter and
  sympathy, which certainly helped my recovery, as it made me feel
  well that you were thinking of me a little! Your poems are very nice
  and they made me laugh. Then I began thinking about it all. And it
  seemed to me that with the way man and woman have changed –
  or developed? – recently, what would be needed, wouldn't be a
  going back to the past but something brand new. I always feel that
  women are much more awake just now than men in general. Even
  if men put up thousands of sham activities they sleep somewhere
  under a big night-cap. So perhaps what is needed wouldn't be a
  new kind of *Don Juan*, but something like a *Donna Juanna* – ha ha
  – but that would be a very, very subtle thing. Women of course like
  rough-handling, and therefore the old *Don Juan* could well just
  jump in and out of windows. But men underneath are something
  like spinsters – infinitely prudish – and so the *Donna Juanna* would
  have to learn to creep completely unnoticed through the back door
  with a perfect poker-face.

---

[1] Katy was an excellent dancer.

Well, in one of the last numbers of the *Reader's Digest* somebody found another solution, stating that every woman really ought to have three husbands: The Business husband, like the one you had in mind, then the handy husband, who does all the mending and tinkering in the house and is something like a glorified butler, and the lover-husband, who has nice ties and pyjamas and makes nothing but love. It wouldn't be a solution to my taste though, as I am afraid the last item might have a tendency to be a bore.

Sir Clifford Norton's poem interested me really, it's quite a *document humain*. I congratulate you for having got it, apparently there you have made an *Eroberung*! [conquest] Of course it's sad, but then one knows the dreadful kind of life these diplomats have to lead, ever unstable and so much surrounded by that scum of humanity that deals in international business and politics. No wonder the poor man is so impressed by the two extremes of snobs and cads and misses the common human beings in between. Perhaps he has noticed the human being that you are though, and that's at least a comfort. I am feeling much better and if everything goes right shall leave here for Bollingen beginning of next week and be away till about end of April. I am eager to hear from your *Fastnachts Erlebnis* [carneval experience]. You must tell me all you can, it interests me no end!

> Affectionately,
> Yours,
>
> Linda

IF [a parody on Kipling's poem "If," by Clifford Norton]:

> If you can keep your job while all about you
> Are losing theirs and rightly blaming you,
> If Big Men trust you, though friends all doubt you
> And yet you keep in with the doubters too:
>
> If you can lunch with Labour politicians
> But sup with Tories nightly at the Ritz,
> Hiding your own, while flatt'ring their ambitions,
> And not behave too badly in the Blitz:
>
> If you are the first to spread the latest rumour
> So that "They" think you're always in the know
> And get a name for 'such a sense of humour'

By pladgerizing other men's bon mots:

If you dine out on words unwisely spoken
In those off hours to which the great are prone,
And see unmoved a lifelong friendship broken
Through confidences meant for you alone:

If you can turn out platitudes for Master
Sandwiched between large slabs of holy Wit,
And grandly brush aside each new disaster
By saying that we'd long discounted it:

If you can write the same dull routine "minute"
On office jackets fifty times a day,
Whoever else may lose the War, you'll win it:
And what is more, you'll end up with a "K."

Clifford Norton's poem was written in 1940 at the Foreign Office in London (whether it has been published is not certain). Not only did he play a part in helping the Allies win the War, but also, in recognition for his services to his country, when he left Switzerland in 1946 for his next posting as Ambassador to Greece, he actually ended up "with a 'K.'"(a knighthood).

In July 1946 Katy met her old friend Dorothy Thayer Smith again, from Charleston, West Virginia. They had not seen each other since 1931, when Katy went to Charleston to decide what to do with her furniture still stored in a warehouse. Dot Smith had been able to obtain a passage to Europe to visit her daughter who had married Robert Marjolin, an up-and-coming young French economist who was working for the French government at Brussels. After Dot Smith's visit to Paris and Bruxelles, she joined Katy in Switzerland. In 1946, traveling outside Switzerland was still an adventure, but the two women were determined to visit Italy. On their trip – Katy's first beyond the Swiss frontier for six years – they visited Milan, Venice and San Remo. No Italian trains ran regularly yet, so they mainly took long-distance buses. Dot Smith and Katy were the first bona fide tourists after the War! Italy was occupied by the Allies and only military personnel were traveling; hotels, commandeered by the military, were overcrowded, and public transport in the towns was limited. The only people able to travel relatively comfortably were those on official missions who had private transport. Trams overflowed with passengers, and finding no accommodations inside, people hung on outside wherever they could find a hold, and even clambered onto the roof! Packed trains and crowded trams were a new experience for Dot and Katy. As we ourselves had the year before, Katy paid a brief visit to her parents' villa in San Remo, from which they had fled in June 1940, wanting to see for herself what damage there was and to report back to her mother.

During Katy's Italian journey in the summer of 1946 Winston Churchill was invited to Switzerland with his wife Clementine and youngest daughter Mary, for an official visit. But first they spent three weeks resting in a private house at Bursinell on Lake Geneva. Out of office, Churchill had plenty of time to indulge his hobby of painting, while Mary, accompanied by her mother in a motor boat, water-skied. Unfortunately, shortly before the official visit began Mrs. Churchill, when the boat made an abrupt turn to pick up Mary in the water, was hit hard by the rudder, and was so badly concussed that she could not attend the various state functions. So Mary stood in for her. All three Churchills stayed at the Lohn near Bern, the Swiss government's official guest residence. Father and daughter arrived in a train as near to the house as possible, descending onto a wooden platform erected in a field[1] then continuing on to the house by horse and carriage. Mrs. Churchill arrived later discreetly in a motor car.

I had met Mary Churchill at the Geneva horse show three weeks earlier.[2] On that occasion the wife of the British Military Attaché joined the loo queue where Mary Churchill and I were already standing, and began shouting repeatedly to the other women, "Miss Churchill is tired of waiting, make way for her!" Thoroughly embarrassed, Mary blushed and pleaded for her to stop, but to no avail. This same woman also attended the small reception for the Churchills at the Lohn. When Mary, trying to be helpful, offered her a glass of champagne, she made a fuss again repeating several times, "Oh Miss Churchill you must have it."[3] We were all standing around a table with a large chocolate cake, a huge cigar adorning its center, while

---

[1] The field happened to belong to a Swiss who was blacklisted by the Allies. A wire was drawn across the field at a good distance from the wooden platform to keep the owner at a distance, but she was inquisitive, so came right up to the wire to catch a glimpse of Churchill.

[2] The Psychological Club has an excellent photo of Jung talking with Mary at the horse show.

[3] The champagne was Pol Roger 1934.

Prof. Jung with Mary Churchill

ringing it were the colorful flags of the United nations in sugar. The British Minister Thomas Snow was present with four other members of the British Legation, and the President of the Swiss Confederation with only a few other Swiss, including the *Chef de Protocole* Mr. Cutat, who made the introductions. When my turn came his attention was taken, so Churchill and I remained hand in hand for what seemed to me an age. I felt embarrassed, and finally we withdrew our hands. When Cutat turned around again, Churchill said, "Will you please introduce me to this lady," so we shook hands again.

For the official celebrations there was a luncheon in Churchill's honor at the very beautiful *Schloss Oberhofen*, about seven miles outside Bern. President Kobelt attended with other prominent members of the government, and Professor Jung came over from Zürich for the occasion. After lunch, Mary rode through the streets of Bern with her father in a carriage-and-four, whose coachman and footmen wore colorful 17th-century costumes. Then the Churchills attended a number of receptions, with finally a late one at the British Legation to which Jung was also invited. All official Bern was there. The guests were so numerous that the party took place on two floors, the prominent guests taking turns talking with Churchill on the first floor where they could sit down with him. Fortunately on the following day Jung was able to meet Churchill to talk with him in a privately-owned

Schloss seven kilometers outside Bern. Years later, when he was well over a hundred years old but still very alert, the British Minister Thomas Snow told me how he and Churchill had similarly dined together in September 1946 at a Château near Bern. Churchill told Snow that he had two lectures in mind to give at the University of Zürich, and wondered which one should he give – the one on youth or the one on a United Europe? Snow opted for Europe, and so it was that on 19 September 1946 Churchill delivered his famous speech. The preceding day, the French Embassy[1] hosted a luncheon for Churchill, a small affair with only seventeen guests, Pat and I being the most junior people by far. All the others were at least a generation older and held senior positions, such as British Minister Snow. On one side of me at table sat General Guisan, Commander in Chief of the Swiss Army; on the other side was Bundesrat Petitpierre, younger than his fellow Bundesrats and known to be pro-Ally. Churchill spoke much of the time, sketching what he proposed saying in Zürich the following day and asking everyone for their opinions. I was so attentive to the conversation that I remember only the first course, a salmon aspic served with green mayonnaise, which I had never seen before; the rest passed me by! When we rose from table I noticed Churchill's custom-made black shoes with zippers instead of laces, which fascinated me.

In the autumn of 1946 Pat was offered the post of Assistant Commercial Attaché at Ankara, which he accepted. We were expected to arrive in Turkey well before Christmas, and in connection with our imminent departure my mother writes the following note to Miss Schmid from Ascona:

> Casa Britannia
> Ascona, Tessin
> Le 12 novembre 1946

Mademoiselle: –

J'envoie aujourd'hui au Professeur Jung deux photos – une que j'ai acheté pour ma fille et l'autre pour moi-même.

Accompagnant les photos, sous couverture séparée, j'ai adressé un petit mot au Professeur en lui demandant de les signer. Voudriez-

---

[1] The French had the only embassy in Bern at that time. All the other countries had legations with a minister.

*vous avoir la gentillesse de le lui rappeler, car je sais qu'il est très
occupé.*

*Aussi ai-je demandé un rendez-vous pour le 9 Décembre, si
possible, mais si non, je viendrai de Berne le 2 Décembre. Peut-être
pourriez-vous m'aviser si l'une ou l'autre de ces dates sont possible?*

Veuillez agréer mes salutations

les meilleurs,

Catharine Cabot

*P.S. Je voudrais faire encadrer les photos, avant le départ de ma
fille le 7 Décembre en Turquie, et c'est pour cette raison que je vous
prierai de demander au Professeur qu'il les signe.*

[I am sending Professor Jung two photos today, one which I
bought for my daughter and the other for myself. Accompanying
the photos, under separate cover, I have addressed a short note to
the Professor asking him to sign them. I have also asked for an
appointment on December 9, if possible. If that is not possible I
could come from Bern on December 2. Could you kindly let me
know which of these dates would be possible.]

[P.S. I want to have the photos framed before my daughter's
departure on December 7, to Turkey, and it is for this reason that
I would beg you to ask the Professor to sign them. CRC]

She received the following reply:

le 10 novembre 1946

*Mrs. Catharine C. Cabot
Casa Britannia
Ascona-Moscia*

Chère Madame,

*Malheureusement je dois vous dire que le Professeur Jung est
tombé malade et que depuis hier son état est très grave. Je suis donc
obligé de vous renvoyer les photos car il ne pourra en tous cas pas les
signer à temps.*

En toute hâte,

M-J S.

[Unfortunately I must inform you that Professor Jung has fallen
ill, and since yesterday his condition is very serious. Therefore I
must return your photos because in any case he would not be able
to sign them in time. In haste, M-J S.]

Though we did not know it at the time, Jung had had another heart attack. As for inscribed photos of him, I already had a prewar one taken in Ascona by Frau Fellerer on which he had written, *"Rerum omnium satietas vitae facit satietatem. C.G. Jung. The Uncle."* [Enough life makes one fed up with everything.] My mother also had a photo with the inscription, *"Fluctuat nec mergitur bonis tamen submisis vinis."*[1] I suppose my mother's ardor for obtaining another signed photo for me before I left Switzerland grew out of her feeling that I was going to a spiritual jungle in which I would need a talisman.

Pat and I, with our two-year-old son Michael and a new Swiss nanny, were to leave for Ankara from Geneva on 10 December by air because Pat was required in Ankara in a hurry. The Foreign Office considered the six-day trip by train and ship from Bern, via Genoa, too slow, so we booked our flight with SAS and on day one traveled by train to Geneva. At Bern Station our first nanny, whose father had fallen seriously ill, bid us a sad farewell; luckily we found a replacement. In Geneva we spent two nights instead of one awaiting the SAS plane overdue from Copenhagen, and a one-night stop in Rome followed. On day three, which began at Rome Airport at 5 a.m., the next leg of the journey to Athens was delayed by several hours, and when we finally got there our flight on to Istanbul was canceled. Our friends, now Sir Clifford and Lady Norton (he was the British Ambassador to Greece), had invited us to stay should we have to stop over in Athens, so we phoned them and did so. On the morning of day four we said good-bye to the Nortons and left for the airport, where we waited all morning to resume our flight, with Michael running about the empty hall. The weather deteriorated once more and finally at 1 p.m. the flight was canceled. The Nortons took us back, and the same scenario replayed itself twice more: our stopover at Athens for refueling was prolonged to *four nights*, the Embassy staff daily remaking our beds, with their supply running out at eight sheets per day. In the afternoons the long-suffering Nortons arranged sightseeing trips, both in Athens and the countryside. It was our first trip to Greece and extremely interesting. Unfortunately, the roads around Athens were still full of potholes from the War. As I was six months pregnant, my pleasure in touring was dampened; every time I hit the

---

[1] The first part is the motto of Paris – "He is beaten by the waves but does not go under" – while the second part says, "If it happens submerge yourself in good wine."

roof as we bumped along, I grimly thought of a premature birth. Eventually on 15 December we reached Istanbul, but there again remained grounded for twenty-four hours because of bad weather. There were rumors that we would be put on the night sleeper to Ankara, but in the end we spent an extra night at Istanbul. Eventually the Swedish pilot refused to fly to Ankara, saying that not only was his knowledge of the airport limited and the visibility poor, but also that he should have been back in Stockholm days ago! So we were transferred to a *Devlet Hava Yolari* (Turkish Airways) plane, leaving on 7 December. The Turkish pilot was skilled but discipline was casual, the stewardess chatting with the pilots, and the door between the crews' quarters and the passenger cabin remaining open, banging maddeningly all the way. The two-hour flight was unnerving. After crossing the Bosporus we hedge-hopped over countless peaks on the Asian side. Mercifully, the updrafts were more powerful than the downdrafts, so that each time we were moments away from being impaled on a peak we soared again. When the clouds broke the scenery was dramatic, but we hated every moment of the flight. We were to experience a much worse flight, however, only three months later, after my daughter's birth. We finally arrived in Ankara nine days after leaving Bern. As I have said, travel time by boat and rail would have been six days.[1]

As the hospital in Ankara lacked nurses because Turkish women considered nursing a menial job, and as patients also had to provide their own food, I decided to have my baby at the American Hospital in Istanbul. Early in April we traveled there by sleeper and, because Diana was eleven days late, the nanny, Michael and I stayed two weeks in a hotel, Pat coming to visit us at weekends. This time the birth was far quicker and less unpleasant. The American Hospital was staffed by Christian nurses, mostly Armenians who did not think nursing to be below their dignity, so the care was good. My gynecologist was a skilled Turkish obstetrician with very modern ideas. I was out of bed in no time, and only four days after giving birth was walking along the Istanbul streets alone to the doctor's office. However, he recommended my staying on a few days longer in Istanbul before returning to Ankara. During that wait, Pat and the nanny went down with sandfly fever while I remained healthy. Because of their

[1] See Jane Cabot Reid, *Ten Lunar Months* (William Heinemann Medical Books, Ltd., London, 1956).

illness we did not return to Ankara by sleeper, deciding it would be more comfortable to fly. We also thought it would be quicker and more convenient with a tiny baby than the train journey. At that time of year, the end of April, delays because of bad weather were rare. Yet though the weather was thought good enough to fly in on the day we left, the flight soon became a nightmare. Again we dropped like a stone towards peaks in our path, so frequently and rapidly this time that my daughter was levitating in her carry-cot! It was terrifying. Again and again, just as the plane approached a knife-sharp peak at great speed on a powerful downdraft, there came a strong and merciful updraft and we sailed over the ridge like a kite. Pat and the nurse felt so awful that they kept their eyes tight shut, but I could not take my eyes off the fast-approaching rocky needles and anticipating a terrible crash. Guilt gripped me, that I had consented to this mode of travel with a week-old baby.

To my relief, in Ankara I was out of my mother's orbit. She had a way, even after my marriage, of constantly offering me unsolicited advice – either *viva voce* when she came to visit us in Bern, or by letter. She was careful, however, to be on the best of terms with her son-in-law, and even took advice from him which was flattering. All the same, I was fond of my mother, so I looked forward to her visit to Turkey after the birth of my second child, which she planned for the late spring of 1947.

In the meantime, as Katy was able to travel once more she found new outlets for he energy; for example she began putting to rights the villa in San Remo. Fortunately for Katy, my grandmother, because of her age and the still prevailing chaotic conditions in Italy, did not feel up to visiting San Remo. My mother therefore had free rein in the house to make the changes she saw fit. She omitted to restore it to what she considered was its previous bourgeois style; instead, with the help of the English artist Daniel Cobb, who had decorated the bathrooms prewar with painted fish and aquatic plants, she turned the main house into a Pompeian villa with frescos, a fountain, and Pompeian furniture made to order by a talented local cabinetmaker and then painted by the artist. These renovations would take several years. Katy was happy to have an excuse to travel to Italy again. By 1947 the Allied Military Government had given back much authority to the Italians, so Katy had to obtain an Italian visa, which she did with some difficulty. She left by train for San Remo in the winter of

1947, and writes to a Mrs. Montgomery in Geneva (a friend of my grandmother's) about conditions there:

Villa Aloha, San Remo, February 6th, 1947

When I walked into the two houses in September there was not *one* thing left of the beautiful rugs, furniture and silver of which both houses had once been full. The Fascists then the French Gestapo[1] and finally the German Gestapo took all. There was not even a nail left! *Literally!* nails [brass hooks] which I had on the bathroom doors to hang one's dressing gown on were taken as well as the bathroom mirrors, W.C. seats, soap dishes, as well as all bathroom fixtures (except the tubs that were built in & which they didn't have time to get out) were unscrewed and taken!

Naturally all lighting fixtures went too and all the windows, and built in windows were in pieces due to the air pressure from the exploding bombs and shells. ...

The catalogue of disaster continues. But Katy says she is having repairs done to a ceiling which had fallen in, with the hope of getting the place in "semi-shape" for camping out in the summer. And then she adds:

I can't say much when I see the damage done to other Allied property. Most people can't even take their property back, as there is nothing to 'take back,' for San Remo lost 150 villas, which is a lot for such a small place. Some Britishers have recently come to take back their houses, but either they have ceased to exist or the repairs are so enormous that they naturally don't want to undertake them. Everyone here thinks I am awfully lucky to have got off so well.

The garden was virgin forest, she writes. Pat and I had noticed this when we went to San Remo in October 1945. (Both of us were in uniform, mine a phony one; Mrs. Fryer insisted that the wives of Military Attachés wear uniform when traveling outside of Switzerland, as at that time the Allied Military were in control everywhere, and access to hotel accommodations was possible only for uniformed personnel). Before the War the garden had been watered daily throughout the summer; after the War broke out, there was no watering at all for five years, yet the rare plants brought by a German

---

[1] Actually the Italian secret police.

botanist from all over the world – Chile, Peru, Africa and Australia – survived and even flourished. My mother tells her friend that conditions were difficult in San Remo that winter (1945-1946) especially for the upper classes, whose assets had dwindled during the War or had been confiscated by Allied governments. But the black market was flourishing, and beggars and others in financial straits before the War had found postwar Italy lucrative, becoming the new rich. Food prices on the black market were high because some foods were normally unobtainable while others were scarce and the official ration paltry. Electricity was available for limited periods only; Katy says in her letter that she yearns for the oil lamps her mother used in Paris in 1903. After living through the War in Switzerland with only minor hardships, spending a few weeks in San Remo brought home to her what the surrounding countries had endured during those five years of war.

In the same letter, Katy mentions that her mother suddenly wants to go to America. She "has sprung it on me and I who have to go to Turkey in May.[1] I don't know really how my strength will hold out. I don't think I can go for both physical and financial reasons. My mother is so strong and never tires, and so doesn't realize that I am a 'delicate flower' or I should say 'an aging flower!'" My mother confused delicacy with depression, bouts of which she had from time to time (she explained depressions to me when I was five) but which she never associated with her occasional lack of energy.

Back in Switzerland, Katy was soon at her typewriter composing letters, this time to Mary Rüfenacht (two within three days!). In both letters, written from the Waldhaus Dolder, her mother's forthcoming trip to America serves as introduction to the important subject: the problems of their recent collaboration on a book about Switzerland. Both women had written separate chapters on the Swiss cantons, and Mary Bancroft also edited the book (Mary had reverted to her maiden name, using it as her *nom de plume*).

Waldhaus Dolder
Zürich
April 27, 1947

Dear Mary: –

I am simply swamped with things to do for my mother while she is here and 'getting off' to America on May 8th. I never realized

---

[1] To meet her second grandchild.

before how much an 'old lady' even of Madame Roche's [nickname for her mother] strong caliber, needed the help of a younger person. It is pathetic to me to see how much she depends on me and I almost preferred her in the old days when she 'horsed around'! As I don't hide behind bushes, I told her so and to make matters worse, she broke down and wept on my shoulder, a thing which is always hard to have happen, when one sees that it's sincere.

Well, in spite of this work, I am taking off an hour to write you as I think your letter needs an answer, as well as my attitude at the [Baur au Lac] Coiffeurs.

My attitude at the Coiffeurs would have been quite different had I not been so tired. In the first place, I have had a lot of work in doing over the Italian property and at the end lots of things came up (such as the Italian Bank who were in charge of it [the property] not wanting to give my silver back) which necessitated my staying over in Genoa with the American Consul (who incidentally is a dear) and leaping at the last minute on a train to get to Milan in time to take the Swiss train to Switzerland, on the day my reentry into Switzerland expired. If you have ever traveled on an Italian train these days, you will realize what a trip I had! I landed in the Coiffeurs absolutely all in and all I wanted was to see *nobody*, but just relax and have my hair and toes done. I told them so, but they insisted on telling you, as you were such a friend. Well, I just wanted to see no one, and so when you came in all bouncing with life and vigor, I, who was completely wilted from my trip, hadn't the desire, or even the energy to react and also become bouncing and vigorous. Also, at that moment, came up certain thoughts about my not finding the books when I had stopped over a few hours in the Tessin. I had hoped they were well away, as I had planned it all so well, and had Madame Roche and my new flat etc. … on my hands, and in my tired state knew that once back, I would have to tie them up and get them off, instead of the maid, who I thought had done it all.

Now you say you also had a lot to do. That I am sure of, but when I left, you had offered to do each one [book] separately and send them off to all those nice Swiss people with libraries who had been so helpful and kind during the work. I had said vigorously 'no' to your most kind suggestion, for I knew I would have to write a line and you even said you would write the line! I remember saying that I would think of putting such a huge piece of work on to you, and you said you wouldn't mind doing it at all. Which I must say surprised me very much. On the 26th of March you wrote me that you had the books and I thought that of course you wouldn't have minded shoving in the whole bunch into a post office, as you had offered to do up each one separately and send them off with a note!

At the Coiffeurs all that went through my tired head, and when you said you had too much to do to send them to my maid in bulk, I got out of patience and out of sorts.

Now, of course one should never get out of sorts or impatient, but I did and then my major *'ressentiment'* came up and as always is the case, when one is in a negative mood, and the barriers are down, the *'ressentiment'* which I had harbored ever since last spring, was called forth by a letter you wrote me, lambasting me for having told you that I was working hard to get things right and was peeking into libraries of kind friends. It made you feel that you should do something for these people etc. All I had meant, was to make you feel at peace that your 'amateur' writer friend was doing her best. This letter went on to say that I was not to call you up and 'explain' and went on about God knows what. But it was a very uncalled-for letter and disagreeable.

At the time I received it, I had taken off a few moments and was sitting sipping a coffee in the Bellevue bar [in Bern] with a great friend, a diplomat, who a few months ago was chosen through his cleverness, to be a delegate to the UN. Calling you only "the person whom I am working for," I handed over your letter and asked him what he thought of it. He advised me to write a good one back and let you and the work go to hell. I did neither, though, when I found that to stay back from Italy and do the work didn't suit me, I didn't do it [stay]. But had you not written me that letter, I would have stayed and finished the *Gastronomies* for you, with the same pleasure, that I always wrote you, I had doing the work.

I do not claim to be a writer at all, but I do know something about Psychology, which makes me realize that my mistake was in harboring a *'ressentiment.'* When I met you at the Coiffeurs, in my tired state, my *'ressentiment'* had grown to be a nice little monster and came right out from under my chair and spat fire at you. Your part in the show does not concern me a little bit, but my part does concern me very much. One should tell people immediately when one considers they have not been fair with one. However, as I had already done that often and found people getting mad, I was too much of a coward to do it again, it's so much easier to be a coward and let things ride – but in the end no decent friendship can develop if one lets people run roughshod over one and does not try to stop it.

I have absolutely no hard feeling left now that you have met my little 'Adolf' [Hitler]. But I have learnt my lesson. It's a far reaching lesson.

I don't know how and where your life will lead you, but I can say this, that one only gets ahead to a certain point, *"si on flanque des injures aux gens"* [if one throws insults at people]. In the end it gets one nowhere to do that, or to always play a superior role. We are all just *"des pauvres gens"* [wretched people] who are doing their best to get along in this awful 'fix' in which we find ourselves as inhabitants of this difficult world. And those who find themselves in a position of temporary power, 'horse around' their subordinates, they get much less out of them. Everyone reacts sympathetically to the 'human touch' and to decent feeling. If one isn't nice to people out of sheer decency, it's wise to be nice to them anyhow, as one can never tell if the underdog of one day, may not be the top dog of another day. The latter is of course a purely worldly philosophy.

Well, I must run now and I am glad that you know the truth. Once I decide, I never beat around the bush, and think it's best to come out with the truth. This is the way I have felt, and no *contre-argument* can make me feel that things were otherwise, for me, things were that way. The world looks differently to each one of us.

> The best luck on your trip to America,

> As ever,

> Katy

Mary Rüfenacht replies, and Katy speedily writes her second letter:

> Waldhaus Dolder
> Zürich
> April 30th, 1947

Dear Mary: –

I am still here and still busy with Madame Roche whom I am now helping with clothes and who is going to look very chic in America, when she gets finished with hats and dresses. She heard there was nothing chic to be bought over there and so she is stocking up here. We now don't go until Sunday. I must say she looks awfully pretty in her things and as old ladies are greatly admired over here, if they are well and good looking, she is getting her last bit of admiration (though she doesn't know it!) before she steps into the country where only youth holds sway!

Your very nice letter reached me this morning and because I don't think there is any time to be lost, I am answering it immediately. Your letter couldn't be nicer, but it is so *humble*. It reminds me of our American weather – such a difference in temperature from this letter and the one you wrote me, which awoke all my *ressentiments*! And there we have got hold of something really valuable. You should never really have to put yourself in either position. However, the humble position came quite naturally out of the ruthless position and so therefore, as long as there is a ruthless attitude there well be by all the laws of gravity an equally powerful humble attitude. Neither are healthy and I am sure cause one of the barriers to getting the best out of yourself. That 'self' which you *have* got to get quite crystal clear with in order to do your best work.

I have no idea where your letter is, as I have traveled so much and I think I destroyed it – in a fury – one day when I ran across the damn thing. I am sure you were sincere when you wrote it. It sounded very definitely so and as if you meant every word you said. But now the thing is to *find out* why it upset you to the point of feeling that someone was spraying the firehose on you, for a green-horn writer, to reassure you that he was doing his best and had found some kind friends who had been willing to put their libraries at his disposal. My reaction to such a reassuring bit of news would have been the following: "Well, thank God that green-horn has got access to some decent books and though she may not write as well as I would like, she may pull out some interesting bits here and there about the different cantons, which will fit in very nicely in my book. I am certainly glad she had the common sense to get in touch with some people who had certain unusual books which are now out of print, but which may well contain some valuable information, helpful to my work."

Now, the interesting thing in all this is how you could have felt that poking into a few private libraries, was terribly out of place and would "make talk and trouble." In the first place anyone who

writes historical stuff like, let's say, Aldous Huxley, or even Linda
Fierz in her *Poliphilo* not only gets access to books but even
publishes the source from where they took their information, if
they quote it word for word.

I did not quote word for word, but just 'read up' in historical
books and got a birds-eye view of the lay of the land. Not one of the
nice people who loaned me books, thought it at all out of the way.
On the contrary they seemed to think it was the most natural thing
in the world. After I had read up on the historical places, they took
me around to show me the places and, by both reading and seeing,
I was able to put down in my own way what I thought. I do not
claim that I did very well, but in the case of Geneva, I really never
quite understood what you wanted except that it should be very
short and I am evidently not good enough yet to condense such a
remarkable proposition as Geneva in a short resume. In Basel, I
did not understand that there would be room enough to describe
the Fastnacht. But now I am getting on to my own stuff and it's
beyond the point.

The important thing, I am sure for you is to *find out why* this
perfectly natural thing irritated you to such a tremendous extent,
that you were willing practically to kick me out, rather than have
me go on. Such an *intense feeling of anger* (which one felt in your
letter) was out of all proportion to the crime I was supposed to
have committed. I don't know whether you are doing analysis with
someone now, but if you are, I would strongly advise you to take it
up and get to the bottom of it. Such powerful reactions usually
hold a *gold mine* in them, if one has the courage to go into it. Only
it takes a hell of a lot of courage and may destroy some pet ideal
that one has of oneself. It's just *awful* to have to do it and all I can
say is, that I don't blame you if you are unwilling to get to the
bottom of it.

If you are not doing analysis with anyone, there is a system,
which works, and that is to take a paper and pencil and sit in front
of it quietly and say, "Why did I react so strongly to Katy going so
conscientiously into those libraries?" Then you write down the
first answer that comes into your head. Then you say: "What next?"
And write that down, and you go on saying "What next," until at
last you say: "Ah, so that's it!" And then you *know!* Of course then
you are furious and deny it, but that doesn't matter, you *know!* And
what's more you have hacked out the golden nugget! It looks like a

pretty moldy nugget at first, but slowly it emerges into pure gold and you are surprised yourself how it shines.

I am sure that if you get to the bottom of whatever that THING is that makes you so *ruthless*, you will never again be humble. Neither are a healthy state and there is no reason for an attractive and clever woman like you to be either. You say to me in your letter that you felt '*menaced*' by my writing you that I was conscientiously plodding along in those libraries. Well, I am sure that you felt 'menaced' and you *were* and are menaced by that THING. If it stays in it will eat you up and ruin your life, if it comes out it will be of utmost value.

You will never get 'atomized' (as you mention as possibly happening in America) if you get the THING *out*. It is probably the ROTTEN MUSHROOM we have tracked to its lair! I have felt it there a long time. Your whole trip depends on getting it into the open and looking at it. And what's important is that if you can't get it out alone, you take Dr. Meier or Frau Jacobi (but you know best which suits you) and have them just drain the abscess. You wouldn't be going to America with a badly abscessed tooth, it would be too dangerous and you would have to get it fixed. Well, you can't go trotting off like that into 'Indian country.' You know what primitives do to the weak, old and sick. If you succeed in getting it out alone, go all the same to one of those two and *tell* them, for that will complete the catharsis.

Now, I have 'thought' enough and my mind is aching! One's inferior function usually aches when it is being used too much. One thing I must tell you before closing is, that by coming out at long last with my '*ressentiment*' I was able, when I sent off one of the nice books to Martinet[1] to say to him that it was due to Mrs. Bancroft that the book was so beautifully and artistically gotten up and that she should get all the credit for making it so nice. If I hadn't got that out of my system, I couldn't have said it. My idea was that I hoped that if I liked it, he would say a word about it in his column and mention you. That's why a *ressentiment* is a beastly thing to harbor, as it prevents one from doing the 'decent' and makes one small and really *la vie est trop courte pour être petit*! [life is too short to be small-minded].

---

[1] Martinet was a journalist living in Geneva who corrected Katy's French poetry.

Well, I am sure that now that *all* is out in the open, we know where we stand and there is no hard feeling on either side. I also hope that you don't mind my having written about getting that thing out, but HAVING BEEN THROUGH IT MANY TIMES MYSELF I know that is the only way, unless one wishes to be swamped by one's emotions and remain *stagnant*! And – one has to be terribly careful when in primitive company – awfully conscious!

I *am* interested in your trip to America and just hope that it will be a great enlightenment in every way. I imagine that you will understand many things after the trip.

Really, I wish you the best possible time and should love to hear from you – if you ever get time – which I very much doubt, in all that rush. I am off to Turkey sometime and now Jack Cabot, [her brother-in-law] who is our Counselor at our Embassy in Belgrade, has written me that he has a plane at his disposal and will fetch me in Istanbul and bring me to Belgrade, which sounds awfully nice. But I want to go by boat to Istanbul, as I want to sail up the Bosporus and see a bit of Greece en route and 'experience' slowly all the '*Bysance*.' I am sure it is going to be a funny trip and probably very different from what I think.

Good-bye and good luck,

Yours affectionately,

Katy

P.S. Just one thing more. To feel embarrassed about my saying I was your *Putzfrau* [cleaning woman] certainly shows a *pompös* [pompous] attitude and a lack of humour! Only a person sure of themselves would say it. However, you took me at my word!! Now, that is also meant to be 'funny.'

When writing these letters, Katy seems to have been in her vigorous mode. Her "analysand" Lothar had vamoosed and her daughter was in Asia Minor. The energy often devoted to writing epistles to Lothar or to me was now directed fully at Mary. Katy must have also put a fair amount of energy into fitting out her mother for her trip to America, as dressing people was a job she thoroughly enjoyed. Both I in my youth and then my daughters were dressed by Katy. But in the case of her mother her efforts to make her look presentable for the trip would be in vain. There were to be no more journeys for Mrs. Rush, and Katy would be prevented from traveling anywhere overseas in 1947.

Mrs. Rush had intended to take her husband's ashes to America for interment at Arlington National Cemetery in Washington, D.C., but suddenly fell ill early in May on the day of her vaccination for smallpox. As she did not immediately recover she canceled her flight for 8 May. In her first letter to Mary Rüfenacht my mother mentions the change, saying "It is pathetic ... to see how she depends on me." Most likely it was just too much for my grandmother to contemplate making such a long journey alone so soon after the War had ended, and having to deal with red tape when she arrived. Knowing my grandmother, I assume she found the clothes were fun to buy, and even a little wicked, but the vaccination meant business and may well have been a trigger both physical and mental which set her already precarious health (due to high blood pressure) into rapid decline. Katy had not yet booked passage to Turkey though she was unaware, even after the vaccination, that her mother's health was faltering. Before returning to Ascona she writes to Frl. Schmid asking for an appointment with Jung. The reply on 7 May says that Professor Jung cannot see her before she leaves for Ascona but that she should write again for an appointment in a few weeks' time.

In the meantime Linda Fierz, to whom Katy had sent a copy of the book on Switzerland, writes:

27.V.47

Dear Katy!

I write only now because you said in your letter you would be back by 22nd only. For *Switzerland* [1] I thank you *most heartily*. It is a delightful book, so nicely done, full of humour and yet so instructive that it contains lots we don't know. Also for Swiss people it is a treasure of interesting details about our own country and besides that quite a mirror! Of course I searched first of all for your articles, reading about Basel and admiring your intimate knowledge, which is also displayed in the other parts you have done. What a work you have achieved, dear Katy! But what I

---

[1] *Switzerland*, ed. Doré Ogrizek and J. G. Rüfenacht (B.O.R. Zürich, 1947) ("Adapted and Translated by Mary Bancroft"). Catharine Rush Cabot was one of thirteen contributors, writing three chapters: "Basel and Northwest Switzerland," "Lake Leman," and "Tessin." Eighteen people illustrated the text, most of the pictures in color.

admire most is the graceful way in which you have adapted yourself to the general character of the whole book. It must be enormously difficult to follow a lead in their [the other contributors] way without losing one's own stand (and good humour). Especially if the leading angels aren't pure sources of wisdom, as the change from 'spiritual' into 'physical' shows. They probably don't know what passion is *at all*. But although *for you* such an uninvited change is most disagreeable, I do believe that it's not obvious to the general reader. Anyhow I am delighted to have the book. I love it and think of you whenever I look at it. Isn't it great that there are people like you who do something about the country they live in, study it really and express their feelings about it all! Nowadays, it seems to be quite rare.

Why, by the way, do you think that I put my light under a bushel? I didn't know I was guilty of such a horrid crime. In the contrary I was always rather anxious not to play the blue stocking, which, as I think, is much more horrid.

I do hope that in the meantime you have been able to prepare a nice little nest in Ascona for yourself. You mustn't forget to give me your address, please.

Just now I have rung up the Waldhaus and heard that you come only next week. So this letter must still wait. But if ever you have time, you know I would be delighted to see you!

Yours,

Linda

N.B. On the 28th this letter made an Odysee with a bunch of flowers up to the Waldhaus, and came back – flowers and all – to the shop with the news that you aren't coming for an indefinite time. So I send the old letter to an address I got from Toni, with the greatest regret that owing to circumstances my thanks for the Switzerland-book is coming so shamingly late and also that the opportunity to see you has dwindled away like today's summer clouds.

Katy had not returned to Zürich because she had been called to her mother's bedside in Lausanne. By early June, word of this reached Zürich and Katy received the following letters:

Küsnacht, June 5th, 1947

Dear Mrs. Cabot!

Thank you very much for the book and your letter and please excuse me for not writing sooner: we have been staying at Bollingen for a week and when coming home found that Miss Schmid was ill with a sort of intestinal grippe, so that I have to take on more or less her job and am exceedingly busy of course.

I was awfully sorry to hear about your mother's illness and can figure what it must be for you. It is certainly an enormous comfort for her that you are at her side at such a crucial time and for you too it will be a great satisfaction. I am only afraid, it will be too strenuous for you if she needs much care and I am hoping, that if this should be the case, you would find a good nurse who would also please your Mother.

It seems so strange, that after having prepared everything for going to America, she should be prevented from going and that now this should happen. It would have been so much more sad for both of you if it had happened while she was over there. I am so glad that you now can see her in such a positive light, against which past difficulties become unimportant, and I am convinced this attitude of yours will be of great help, whatever destiny will decide!

I am hoping for the best and thinking of you in deep sympathy.

Please remember me to your mother, if that is at all possible and transmit her my best wishes.

With affectionate greetings, from Onkel as well,
Yours very sincerely,
Emma Jung

Mrs. Jung seems worried once again that Katy may have difficulty coping with her mother's illness. That illness was not strenuous for Katy physically, but during its course she began to feel guilty about her negative attitude to her mother. Even so, her tremendous reserves of energy surfaced, as always when illness loomed. The next letter is from Toni Wolff, who writes:

Freiestrasse 9
Zürich 7
June 7th, 1947

Dear Katy,

I am sorry indeed to hear about your predicament with you

mother and am certain there ought to be a way out, as that is no life neither for you nor for her. The best thing would be to pack her off to America with a rained nurse. I am glad you are firm and don't let her make you change your plans. Sometime this summer you want to go to Janey, and you just do.

I am not feeling very well, my knee is very stiff and won't get better, it is too far gone. I have made no plans for the summer, though I ought to, because everywhere seems very full. But I am terribly busy, there is a whole English invasion here. For a change, there is one awfully nice American, Mrs. Z., who has been here before. I hope you got the announcement for her lecture and following seminar. There was no address of yours to be had, so the Club things are sent to Ascona. I suppose I shall have to make a cure sometime and somewhere, but I have really lost faith. It were nice to have you near, only it would have to be the right kind of thermal water for you too. If you really have arthritis you ought to look after it, as it tends to spread and get worse.

I have not seen your book nor known that it is out. I thought you said you were going to send it to me after publication.

If X. was really a Jew, that would explain his erotic talents as well as his resistance to commit himself. Well, he is now in a hell of a situation in Hungary.

All good wishes,
Affectionately,

Toni

Katy may have told Toni that the doctor suspected her mother was putting on an act to gain attention. As for X. being Jewish, there was never any talk of that in Bern, but possibly this was among Dr. Meier's "discoveries" (see above). When I asked him in 1992 what he had found out about X., he could not recall.

Finally, Barbara Hannah writes:

Hornweg 2
Küsnacht-Zürich
June 8th 47

Dear Katy,

Thank you ever so much for your nice letter. I was awfully sorry to hear that your mother was so seriously ill & can well understand how awful it is to see someone so vital & energetic so ill. I think I only saw her the one time at Sprüngli's with Toni after Major de Trafford's funeral but was greatly struck by her 'Lebenslust' and independence, and both Toni and I agreed that as an individual she was unusual & most satisfactory. This feeling was strengthened by Dr. Jung's account of her at Janey's wedding. He said, "She is somebody." Of course the relation between parent and child is necessarily difficult or one would just remain *'fille à mama'* all one's life. One must kick free, but it doesn't prevent one from seeing the individual value and loving it. You will have heard that Dr. Meier's father was also taken ill about the same time. As it was quite hopeless, it was fortunate that it did not drag on. As Dr. M. is president, the whole committee [of the Psychological Club] went to the funeral. It was in the most beautiful cemetery I have ever seen. Thank you a lot about the 60 dollars. I would awfully like to have it *here* in Swiss francs as for the first time I have been having difficulty in getting money from England.

Don't forget to ring me up directly you come to Zürich, so that we may be sure to be able to arrange your visit here!

Hoping very much that your mother is going on as well as possible & that you are not over-tiring yourself.

Affectionately,

Barbara

(With the War over, restrictions on money from the U.S. were lifted, so Katy was able to pay back her debt.)

Katy tries once again to make an appointment with Jung, but Miss Schmid replies on 7 July that Jung is unable to see her because he is already at Bollingen, and will be going to Hurden only briefly without stopping at Küsnacht. Mrs. Jung writes a more positive letter from Bollingen, and a meeting is arranged.

Bollingen, 10.7.47

Dear Mrs. Cabot!

The last fortnight has been so crowded with work and all kinds of things to do, that I could not answer your letter, for which I must apologize. And the first days in Bollingen both of us were quite exhausted and did nothing but rest. To-day your letter to C.G. has arrived and I hasten to send you a word, at least to express you my sympathy and understanding for the difficult situation you find yourself in. How strange that your mother should fall ill just before leaving for U.S.A. and that now it all turns out as a neurotic attempt to put pressure on you! I fully realize, what a dilemma you are in now, and only hope you will be able to lead your own life in spite of everything.

C.G. says that perhaps you might talk to him about it at Hurden. I am looking forward to seeing you there.

In the meantime affectionate greetings,
Yours,
Emma Jung

Katy did not see Jung at Hurden as Mrs. Jung suggests might be possible, but did see him at Bollingen three days later.

July 13, 1947 Bollingen

The following two hour talk took place with Onkel on a gorgeous summer's day, in deck chairs, stretched out at the edge of the Zürich lake, the water gently lapping against the walls of Onkel's mediaeval castle.

***

Bollingen in Winter

"I never saw anything so beautiful," I said to Onkel, as I stretched myself lazily in the comfortable chair. "Do you know that it was only after I had worked with you for four years, that I saw color." "When people get in touch with their feeling, they see color," answered Onkel.

I went on to tell Onkel that I had had two dreams in which I had been with him, and later wept over him because he was so nice. They had been very vivid. He said that he thought those dreams were repeating my first feeling realization, which had taken place in 1934, and now, for some reason, I was reminded of those days. In those dreams, I am spending a week-end with the Jungs. Onkel said, It was in a way as if I didn't realize the way in which I belong to the big family of human beings! He added, "In analysis there is that 'transference' business to the analyst (the positive or negative feeling the patient has to his analyst) and people think the transference is awkward – that it shouldn't be, and that one should make people independent, for some people cling to the analyst instead of trying to establish relations to people. Some patients are just too auto-erotic and egotistical and they just cling! They should be admonished not to cling and to try their best to establish relations to other people. Some people seemed forced to cling, against their reason." He went on: "To be related to someone is *usual* but to be related to your analyst, that is a particular thing which belongs to the question of becoming *oneself* and that becoming oneself can't be accomplished *if one is related to people who aren't themselves*! Therefore it is a good idea to see with what people one goes about with, for if one is related to stupid people, gossips, uncouth people, one has no earthly chance of acquiring those qualities, which bring one to the Self. For instance, what does one learn – if one wants to learn – in being related to people with no education? I am constantly dealing with people who are not themselves," he added, "and I need friends who have a certain degree of ripeness. You are able to establish relations to people rather easily. In fact, I should think that if you wanted to you could establish a relation to anyone easily, so why do you, as your dreams show, establish a relation with me? It's because you have set yourself that task of becoming individuated and you are therefore in need of someone more individuated than yourself! You call me Onkel and its not a joke, for you really are a relative of mine. But just to belong to an ordinary family, doesn't do the trick, you have to belong to an *unconscious* family, and your unconscious family is me!"

Onkel then went on to say: "The first human society was formed by little groups of natives clinging together for vital reasons such as protection from common enemies. You see, two are more than one, so these natives established a communistic life and equally divided the catch. In such a group the children belonged to every woman, and often were breast fed by women who were not their mother. That was usual in all such tribes, and also with the Eskimos, the women even took the dogs (who were most vital to their way of life) to their breast. And it didn't matter to them which child they took to their breast – they were all one group. Slowly other groups would form, from the relatives of the original group, so there would be more groups! Eventually there would be rivalry between groups. In prehistoric time the groups established *exogamous* laws (*outside* as opposed to *endogamous*, inside). For instance, a group consists of two families. Your mother's brother lives in Rapperswil, and you have a daughter for whom you seek a husband. There is no one in your group to whom she can be married, so she marries her maternal uncle's son – a cross cousin marriage. The maternal uncle is the most important person, so your daughter and son marry their *maternal* uncle's children, they marry cousins! The *paternal* uncle's children don't enter the picture for you. If your grandmother has a son or daughter and they have children, you marry the cousins of the second degree. The main person is the *maternal* grand uncle. If you have a daughter to marry, you apply to the grand uncle's family – they are farther away still than the maternal uncle. As the grandmother is much bigger than the mother (the great grandmother is doubly grand) her group is even more important. The great grandmother's dignity is raised to high degree. There is enormous dignity in a primitive society and under the surface, there's a hell of a lot to the fact that you are a grandmother. You ask about the father?" Onkel inquired. "In the next stage of social development, the father enters the game. In our civilization, the more it developed, the mother's importance lessened and she assumed an equal position with the father. In the beginning of society there were brother and sister marriages. Then their groups would be increased by marrying cousins, and soon Bollingen and Rapperswil became allies! Finally, a group where people were not related, became a country.

Primitive desire is to maintain the family relation. The *endoga-mous* libido is not satisfied and is seeking application, that secret dissatisfaction is always trying to establish the original family relationship."

Onkel went on to speak of the middle-ages. How the convents attempted to establish the original family relation on a spiritual level. (Frater – brotherhood. Nun – sisterhood.) "It proved to be a great satisfaction for a time," he said, "as long as people really loved each other. As long as they did that it LIVED." He said that in the middle-ages people really did love each other, things weren't as they are now! This original family which they established was a great satisfaction for a time, and these 'families' were the carriers of civilization. But, he said, it petered out just as the idea of Christian love did. "The whole of the mediaeval love is incredible to us," Onkel continued, "and we can't make it work, so we have a neurosis because the endogamous libido is not satisfied."

"So, in treating a neurosis," Onkel said, "the analyst becomes the maternal Uncle, and instinctively the primitive clan is estab-lished on a spiritual level. The patient and analyst are also *the carriers of civilization* because they establish the big family of primitives in which all are relatives. The psychological transfer-ence shows itself in my being called, '*Mon très cher père*' by a French woman, '*Mon père*' by a Russian woman. You see they belong to the family. For a woman over seventy, I am the brother. It is a most mysterious thing and the most primitive, original emotion. That is the external form it takes." He continued, "How-ever, there is a mystery in it which people don't understand. You see, you reach the *Self* not just through your ego (the person you know) but the Self includes the *unconscious*. You are the uncon-scious and how far does that unconscious go? (That 'Self' in the unconscious?) Perhaps you are in my unconscious?"

The Self is a collective idea, which the Hindus call 'conglomer-ate soul,' consisting of many souls – built out of many souls as it were, both masculine and feminine ones."

Onkel emphasized that relationship between individuals is due to the Self, not only to the ego. There is a 'something,' an indefin-able sympathy, a 'peculiar' kind of relationship between this 'primitive family' which is unique because of its *illimitableness*. He said, "I represent all men and you represent all women – *one* man and *one* woman! Each one of us is a potential criminal or assassin, for the same forces and emotions are alive in each individual. It is only due to favorable circumstances that we don't become murderers. Of course we condemn such things, and lying and cheating also. We have all those things in ourselves, and we must condemn them in ourselves, *and not be charitable with ourselves.* We must say to ourselves, 'You reckless devil or egotistical criminal!' Onkel went on, 'In such matters, there must be no charity to ourselves or others. Inasmuch as you represent womanhood and I represent manhood *'We are related to each other through the Self*, and the relationship is *unique* – all such relationships are. Your animus perhaps says, 'To how many people is Onkel related like that?'" "Yes," I interposed, "I don't like other people being related to you like that, you are *my* Onkel!" Onkel laughed. "It reminds me of a story," he said. "In an insane asylum, of which I was the head, a clergyman once came to give a talk to the inmates. He spoke a lot about 'our Jesus.' After a while a woman got up, and said, 'I will not have you speak of him as "our" Jesus, he's *my* Jesus!' We both laughed. Onkel's sense of humor is unique – just like the relationship!

Onkel repeated that each relationship of that kind was unique – no two were alike – for *individual* relationships cannot be conventional. If it is conventional, then it is not an individual relationship!

I went on to tell Onkel how fed up I was with never getting anywhere; just plodding away working on myself and studying, and looking after my mother for years now, and never seeming to 'get anywhere.' He said that was just the way things were. "Now for *years*," he added, "for *thirty* years, my patients were only British and American spinsters! I never seemed to have an interesting patient, some scientific mind, some man of quality who had achieved something at least. Just the eternal line of spinsters, they arrived in droves; it never seemed to end. I used to ask myself, 'Why am I cursed'? But I plodded along looking after them, the best I could, and doing my research work on the side. An analyst must have extra work, for if he doesn't, he puts all his energies into the patients and gives the patients too much food for the Animus. (It can produce an inflation in the patients.) But I kept saying to myself, 'You are an intelligent man, but you seem to be getting nowhere.' Everybody and everything was against me for thirty years. It was a dog's life but it was lived *sincerely*! I decided that I must stand it and make the best of it. In those early days I analysed a schizophrenic patient who was a spinster and not at all good looking, in fact horribly ugly. I worked with her long and hard and learned a lot from that case. Finally, I submitted my work to Freud; he was delighted with it. He asked to meet the patient. I introduced her to him. Afterwards he said to me, 'I admire the work you have done very much indeed, but what I admire more than your deductions is the fact that you could have done this work with such an *ugly* woman!' I was overwhelmed by these ugly spinsters; it got to be almost too much and I'd say to myself, 'Am I going to spend my whole life laboring for these impossible creatures?'" Onkel went on, "It is a great thing to stand a situation in life that comes to you. Then and only then do you get to where you belong. I finally got to where I belonged. If you have to scrub your floor then do it *well*."

I told Onkel about a very flattering letter I received from Dr. [C.A.] Meier. I told him that I felt so elated about it that I went around for a few days feeling intensely superior, then I got nervous over this feeling and realized that it was all *wrong*. I said to myself, "Such a letter is dangerous, if it's producing this effect on me." Onkel said, "You *suffered* a success!" He added, "*Nichts ist schwerer zu ertragen als eine Reihe von guten Tagen*." (Nothing is more difficult to bear than a series of good days.) You get *sloppy*. That is the way people are, if one says things that are too nice to them. You must remember that man is a swine – man is a helluva swine." Onkel dwelt fairly at length on man's swinishness, and I felt he wanted to impress me with it. He went on, "The letter 'got' you. You have to gain merit through simple things done in a careful way. If you do anything you have to do it in a humble spirit. If you get an inflation from such a letter, you won't go on in a humble spirit. I admit the letter is most agreeable, and you '*lapped it up*'! A dog laps a bowl of milk. And he feels agreeable and all is O.K. It would be wrong if he behaved otherwise, and he would be a sophisticated dog if he said, 'What a fine moral dog I am to get this bowl of milk!' Fortunately, he does not conclude that he is a specially fine dog or a moral dog. 'I can "lap it up" but it is better if I don't draw conclusions as to my values," Onkel said. "For if you draw conclusions," Onkel went on, "They will be sophisticated conclusions, which mean, 'I'm a helluva feller.'" It is the fellow who *gave* me the bowl of milk who is the top dog! Then Onkel went on very forcibly to tell me *never to forget* that we human beings are *animals* and that we should pattern ourselves on them for they lead a far more natural life than we do. We should be *humble*, take things naturally – animals are like that they don't draw conclusions. "In your case," he said, "the Animus got hold of that letter and began to *chew it up!*" Onkel went on emphasizing two things: the first, that man was a swine capable of anything, and the second thing, was that one should pattern oneself on animals.

Onkel then resumed: "If you carry through something with self sacrifice, and care, then your deeds are *proven*! To *receive* flattery proves *nothing*! Flattery proves something for the flatterer only! I must be able honestly to give recognition to myself. FACTS are the only valid reason, for giving myself compliments. One must give oneself the necessary recognition and if you can't honestly do that, then you must *do* something first which gives you that possibility, and which proves to *yourself* what you are capable of."

We only spoke of my mother for a minute. Onkel did not seem very interested, but said: "I understand that she was always a difficult person." I answered that it was so, but somehow, I could not bring myself to waste those precious moments on that problem, as I felt that getting into 'bigger' questions, I would automatically get 'something' with which to deal with my mother-problem. I asked him if he thought I should leave her and go to Turkey. He didn't say much, only, "If she is all right (?) then I don't see why not." I spoke of the fact that she never liked Europe and had been forced by my father's desire for 'retirement' to live in such a quiet place as San Remo. Onkel said the following: 'These British and Americans are uprooted, when they settle down here, as grown people. The British less, they seem more able to adapt. But their own society is too severe, too oppressive, so they feel that they have to get away. There is much likeness between the British and American society and Basel. *One* must do such and such a thing or one mustn't do such and such a thing. It's done, or it's not done and so it goes on interminably with taboos. That is why I quit Basel, it was too narrow.

Again, I spoke of my mother and how I had a real 'resistance' to her and had had for years as she was so difficult, overpowering and crushing. Onkel said that my feeling towards my mother was a *'moral defeat'* and one must not heap up defeats, for then one gets *morally discouraged*.

He went on: "The devil comes and tries to break me asunder in this thing with my mother. When one gets resistances to someone, one shouldn't go further – one must be careful. People like my mother should learn to stand themselves." (I confess to being a little nebulous on that mother-problem, or how he meant best to work it out.)

Onkel went on to say the following: "It is important to do everything one can before one dies. If, before one dies, one can tell oneself 'I have scrubbed that floor well and with the utmost sincerity,' then one can die! But if you say, 'I haven't scrubbed that floor in a decent way,' then you are in for it. *Everything drops off of you when you die, but those things which you have really accomplished don't drop off.* When you die, you are on a par with a scrubwoman, then it's of no importance, whether you have done one book or ten books, *but have you done that which you had to do, as well as you could?* The judge in you gives it to you. If you have, then it's *in* you! If you can tell yourself: 'It's been a wonderful performance,' but the judge in you says NO, then it was all no good, but if the inner judgement is in favor, it's O.K. If it's a *'fact'* it is O.K. But it must be a *fact* that you have scrubbed in a decent way."

"In the case of your mother, you may 'think' you have done your duty, and if it is *so*, no one can take it from you. When it is *really* there no one can shake it!! Don't *ask* yourself if you have done your duty, you ought to *know*! If you *have*, nothing, nor anything anyone says, ought to put you in doubt, you've done your duty, it's a fact and that is that. But why are you in doubt? Is it a fact? Have you done your duty? The judge in you *knows!*"

Onkel added, just before we stopped our conversation: "During my illness, when I was almost dead, I saw what *stands and what doesn't stand!*" "YOUR REAL PERFORMANCE IS AN UNSHAKABLE FACT and if it was GOOD and a thousand people assure you to the contrary, it nevertheless remains what it WAS!" "THAT is what you carry away with you, WHAT YOU HAVE DONE! And that no one can ever take from you!"

***

I forgot to add, that when I first sat down, I spoke of having lunch in Linda's beautiful *Kloster* [convent]. Onkel said he liked the *Kreuzgang* [cloister] part of her house, but thought the rest impossible. I said, I was much impressed by that room of hers, without windows and the light coming through slits at the top. I said it seemed to me to be very old – pre Egyptian. Onkel laughed and said: "That room is a tomb!" "But what period?" I asked. He answered laughingly, "MINOAN!" He was so humorous, I had to laugh.

On the same evening after Katy's session with Jung at Bollingen, a group postcard was written to me in Ankara:

13.7.47
"Cordial greetings from maternal Grand-uncle C.G. Jung."

"We enjoy the visit of your mother and are having a very gay time with her here in Bollingen. With best greetings, Emma Jung."

"Us der Schwyz, vieli Grüss. Leider han ich Sie nie känne g'lehrnt. Franz Jung" [From Switzerland many wishes. Unfortunately I have never met you.]

"Herzliche Grüsse, L. Fierz"

Katy writes the address, but there is no room for her to add any message. The card comforted me as it meant that my mother was having a *gemütlich* interval in a very trying time. After her interview with Jung, she shelved all her ideas of traveling to Turkey, and instead returned to do her duty towards her mother at *Clinique Cécile* in Lausanne.

For in fact my grandmother was very ill. Mis-diagnosed by her G.P., she was not putting on a neurotic act to pressure my mother, as Katy had reported to Mrs. Jung and Toni. Only Jung seems to have had an open mind about Mrs. Rush's condition when Katy told him the doctor's diagnosis. His words at Bollingen must have sunk in because Katy spent most of the time after her visit to Bollingen at Lausanne, using a flat lent to her by a friend away on her summer vacation, Odette Roy. From the *Clinique* where my grandmother spent her last weeks, she writes to two old friends in America:

Clinique Cécile
Lausanne
6. August. 1947

Precious friends ...

Excuse my crotchets and quavers, but I am still so weak & in bed. Still with nurse and daily Drs. visits. I know you would be sorry for your old, old friend. I am gotten out of bed now every p.m. & with shoes & stockings, leaning on my nurses arm walk for a few turns in the corridor. It all came like a bolt from the blue. I was vaccinated in the a.m. & the p.m. had what I thought was a stroke. High blood pressure & I was bled of almost a litre of blood. My suffering has been intense & so hard to eat. I am a skeleton. Catharine has been Heaven-sent, her kindness & devotion beautiful. Since two weeks have been able to give up the night nurse, so I am said to be improving. I wonder if I will ever see your dear faces & hear your voices again. It is hard to get my strength & try to again "*avoir courage.*"

Catharine assures me I will be nice & strong again. I wonder. Thank you my dears for such understanding letters and cables. I can never forget you ever.

Always your devoted,

Janey

My mother adds a note: "Great grandmother Rush's last letter. / Perhaps keep for Michael. It's such a sad little note." It was in fact not her last letter, for she wrote to us in Turkey in an even shakier, barely decipherable hand on the following day, on both sides of thin airmail writing paper.

Cecile, Lausanne – le 7 Août '47

Darling Janey, dear Pat, Precious Michael with precious Diana in his arms,

I have been too ill to hold a pen. The lovely one from you & dear Pat gave me. Dear Mother is so optimistic. If I improve a little she tells everyone I am well. I am allowed no visitors, it tires one but I am now out of danger. Altho' I longed to go Home[1]. I have no fear. I love precious Dianne & have left her my onyx earrings with diamonds. The snap shots I keep near & look at them so many times a day., I love them so much. Precious Michael holding sister is too sweet & he playing in his tub with you present ... all are so interesting. I will love also having Michael near my portrait pointing his finger and saying "nonna." [I must have promised her this photo.] That precious child brought something into my life, I

---

[1] Home in this context meant dying. My grandmother often spoke of 'going to her long home.'

thought, I could never have again. God bless him. I have left him my Grand (great) Mother's cameo brooch for him to give to his wife. It may be very modish then. [Katy thought it very un-modish!] Also my gold watch for Diana & my thimble (Gold ... I have ... JPH) [Jane Pomroy Hare] and given by my teacher [?] for being *first* in my class ... gave me the silver box to keep it safe. It was for you. I was always stitching, my dear mother being like you a great sewer. When I do get well, I will send a present to Baby Diana & her silver too. I long to see her & all of you.

Your letters are so interesting ... thank you darling Janey, devoted Mme. Roche. Mother comes every day for 15 minutes. I want her to go to Ankara & see you. I have a splendid nurse, but [am] thin & weak. I can't eat.

Forgive this doleful letter – will hope when stronger to do better. But this is my first letter. I am sorry you missed English Fleet. Michael must be an admiral.

I must rest now –

Affect. your devoted,

Mme. Roche

Don't let dear Pat work too hard. Nonna.[1]

That was her last written message. My mother writes to me three weeks later:

Clinique Cécile
Lausanne
August 20th, 1947

Dearest Janey: –

I am sitting by Nonna's bedside and she is speaking of dear little Michael and she says: "Dear little Michael, he brought something into my life, I never had after Daddy left. I loved him so much & they were so good as to bring him over to Lucerne on a long drive." She went on to say, "after they left, I went upstairs in my room & I cried, as I was afraid I might never see them again. He was so blessed. Those lovely little smiles & curls. He is going to amount to something." We are sitting here looking at pictures. And Nonna is so charmed with the little suit you made Michael. She wants you

---

[1] Living as they did in Italy, my grandparents liked me to call them *Nonna* and *Nonno*, Italian for granny and grandpa.

to have her gold thimble, for she thinks it's lovely, you made his pretty little clothes. She suddenly fell asleep (due to Morphia) and said as she fell off, "The day he came over to Lucerne, he had the sweetest little red and blue smocking." He'd come in & *serré la main si gentiment* ..." She thus talks of him, all the time and I sit here and weep, Janey, cos its so sad to hear her, as she loves him so. She says, "His little manners were so sweet." She tells me to tell Pat, that "Daddy [W.R.R.] would have taught him to put his little legs together & make the salute." Janey, she just talks of him all the time. I'm afraid she will soon be unconscious, but I wanted to get her words about Michael *as he is the whole topic of conversation.*

Later:

The doctor has just come in & gone & he tells me that she is nearing the end. Her heart does not react anymore to all the well known heart remedies & injections. It's a tired, old & worn out heart, he tells me. He says that all *desperately* sick people talk a lot about their past life at the end. He says that her *"Malaise,"* this thing she has talked about *so long* comes from the *heart* & is well known as the *Malaise or Angoisse Cardiaque.* [Cardiac anguish?] I still fume when I think of the 'other' doctor telling me that she had 'Angoisse nerveuse.' Had we known in the beginning, all we know now, we should have gone to Dr. Fingerhuth for heart last autumn, it could have all been prevented. Her life sheltered & no such excitements allowed as planning trips to America. Poor Nonna – she has had a long life, but *no one* is ready to go *at any age,* and when we are all 76 (if we live that long), we won't be ready either. She is so courageous. The only *conscious* person I've ever been with who talks calmly about dying & seems to *face* it. Poor darling. I'll never be so brave when my time comes. It's *terrible* to think that the Técoz doctor treated her for nerves when it was her heart which should have had treatment. What a strange thing this life is? that we all have to follow this hard road. Love darling from Ma.

Turkey was a long way in those days, even by air, as we discovered on the outward journey. I felt pretty badly about not going to Switzerland to be with my mother during my grandmother's last illness, but I had a new baby daughter whom I was nursing. My son had developed serious eczema at three months from being on formula at that age, when I could not breast-feed him. After that harrowing experience I was determined to breast-feed Diana as long as possible. I felt torn between my duty to my daughter and my filial duty to my mother; in the end, the easier one won out and I remained in Turkey. My grandmother went to her "long home," as she liked to say, on the 28th of August 1947. She was 77 years old. The funeral took place on the 30th at the *Église St. François* in Lausanne; the following year Katy took both her parents' ashes to America for burial at Arlington National Cemetery. A few days after the funeral, when my mother had left Lausanne and her friend Odette Roy was back in her flat, the front door bell rang. A young man stood there holding an enormous wreath, saying it had been ordered for Mrs. Rush's funeral by friends in America, and inquiring where and at what time the funeral would be taking place. Odette was embarrassed by the boy's pertinent questions, because she knew it had already taken place, and that the remains were not buried but reposing in an urn at a depository. As she did not reply immediately, the boy asked impatiently, "What shall I do with the wreath?" Odette pulled herself together and replied with authority, "Take it to the nearest cemetery and put it on any grave you fancy!"

The first letter of condolence arrived from Mrs. Jung:

Küsnacht, Aug. 31st, 1947

Dear Mrs. Cabot,

Through my daughter, I heard of the passing of your mother, as I had not seen the paper with the *faire-part* I am sorry to be late in expressing you our deepest sympathy. I thought of you often, while in Ascona, and particularly when we got your letter telling us that your mother was going to die and I felt deeply with you all the time. What a sad and deep reaching experience it was and is for you, I know, particularly, as you have been alone with nobody near you to give you support! What a good thing, at least, you came to Bollingen and had that talk with C.G., which I hope, was of some help to you in these difficult days or weeks.

I have great admiration for the way you dealt with the problem of your relationship to your mother during these past months and I think your positive attitude and your love and devotion made the last of her life very beautiful and peaceful, and I think it must also be very satisfactory for yourself.

I wonder whether you will be coming to Zürich soon? C.G. has gone to Bollingen again, to get a rest after the extraverted and rather strenuous Eranos week; I am staying at home until the end of the week, then shall also go to Bollingen for a couple of days.

In case I can do anything for you, please tell me, I would be glad if I could be of any help.

With love and sympathy,

Yours,

Emma Jung

Jung writes a handwritten note the following day from Bollingen:

Bollingen. Sept. 1st, 1947

Dear Mrs. Cabot,

I just heard that your mother died – it is good when old people can die. Only for the surviving there is cause for pain and lamentations as it is they who experience a loss. For the dead it must be, if anything, a gain after the hardships and worries of earthly life.

For you it is the loss of a mother and the realization that there is nobody ahead of you anymore. This letter may convey all my feelings of sympathy.

Yours affectionately,

C.G. Jung

Linda Fierz writes on 1 September on her return from Lausanne where she had visited Katy at the time of he mother's death and funeral.

1. Sept. '47

Dear Katy!

First of all let me thank you again for all your kindness in Lausanne and all your careful thinking about my smallest need (in the midst of all your troubles!) which made my stay there such a lovable experience. I was happy indeed to be allowed so generously to accompany you for a tiny bit on the strange way of life.

Curiously enough I cannot yet take away my mind and feeling from the many things we talked of together. On my way home and today I am sort of talking on and on with you, and I think I must take the risk to tell you what I am mumbling into my beard. If you feel I am intruding you must say so.

I am preoccupied with two things mostly – first this idea you had of your 'harmlessness' and being a bore, and then your question at the train of what you could actually do to show your throwing off the 'Cinderella' business. It was such an important question, it seemed to me, that I got overwhelmed. And you are so right in thinking that a change means just nothing at all, if it isn't realized in practical everyday life. But I was unable to give you a real reaction right away at the station. I should have said so or nothing at all, and my silly remark about your mother's fan was really worse than wrong.[1] I am sorry!

It still makes me a little sad to think that with this 'harmlessness' idea you had, for I don't know how long, you have thought meanly about yourself. Even if your son-in-law is perfectly right in saying that you are the sweetest and kindest of person *to others*, yet your kindness is very imperfect and must fail, if you leave out *yourself*. It is as if you had looked at yourself with very unloving hard and oversharp eyes, and that is simply dangerous. It's a curious thing, but Dr. Jung stated it often enough: that if you don't love yourself, nobody else will love you. He also said often, that it is quite a difficult thing to love oneself rightly and be nice with oneself (something unchristian and nothing for the old vicar). As long as you think meanly about yourself, that certainly is neither nice nor loving.

Yet, on the other hand, if you are so very sure that you are 'harmless' there must be something in it. It must be taken seriously too, as such strong inward conviction cannot be just a senseless thing. But one would have to find out what it *means*. First of all: if I understood you right, you mostly meant that from a society point of view you are 'harmless' – or to say it with a bang, that for Hollywood standards you would be no vamp. But there are also other standards and other points of view, and I really don't see the necessity of your judging yourself in an important respect from an extremely worldly view point. If you judge yourself from such a view point, everybody else will do so too (that's the same as said above about loving oneself – *you*, by your own judgement, which shows in your attitude, bring about the judgement of others).

In order to understand your 'harmlessness' right, I think one would have to interpret or translate the expression with more love and care than just by the 'placards' of the sandwich-man (that's

---

[1] Mrs. Rush had a valuable collection of fans.

Monsieur Animus). But this is a difficult job! The language of the unconscious is never a platitude, but it is so cryptic!

The only material I can contribute is a very vivid impression I got yesterday, when we sat together in the afternoon: and that is you in your apron. I have never seen you nicer and more convincing. Now please read without saying anything and don't misunderstand me. I know the apron was of the cheapest kind, but you in it were everything else than cheap. Sitting there you had a harmonious simplicity, which made me feel marvelously at ease and all natural with you. From a society point of view one *could* (with the inherent short-sightedness) call such simplicity 'harmless.' But from such a point of view one can belittle everything human. What it made *me* feel I can best describe to you by comparing it with Bollingen. All that's contained as within a nutshell in what you represented in your apron. It is as if, that where I needed a whole house and a garden and God knows what, you needed only an apron for a few francs to reach something representing indeed a very high value. Of course it would be no value you could show directly to anybody, just as little as you could walk about in your blue apron. You are a *'femme du monde'* and must dress and appear accordingly – in spite of Dr. Mantel![1] He was of course quite foolish to want to correct your strategical apparel. But after having seen you yesterday I would suggest that perhaps in *one* way just the same he wasn't quite wrong, at least at bottom. I rather have the idea that somehow he did feel that your appearance doesn't express you sufficiently, because it leaves out an important part. The part you until now have only seen negatively and judged in a belittling way – I mean charming simplicity, which I felt as so *'wohltuend'* [beneficial]. If the *'femme du monde'* and the inborn simplicity which as opposites are both within you, get too far apart, if you adapt more or differently to the world than is true to your essential being, that is as if I had built Bollingen let's say near Paris or somewhere in the Balkans. Then there is a split in you, and a man who is fond of you may well sense that and try and say something, as Dr. Mantel did. Of course, as such an unconscious man cannot express his feelings adequately, he distorts them by

---

[1] Dr. Heinrich Mantel-Hess, the Sinologist (see p. 458). My mother had met him and his wife playing golf at Ascona. Though he was good-looking, he was never a boyfriend of Katy.

narrow-minded thinking and blunders. But that's not terrible. It's woman's job anyhow to see through that and to distinguish between such male 'thoughts' and the real underlying feeling.

What I write you here may make you quite mad, I am afraid. Perhaps I have put my foot into it again like yesterday with the vicar and the signs of the zodiac. (I'll never again speak of the signs of the zodiac!) But nevertheless I suggest that a practical program would be for you to try to unite the *femme du monde* more closely with the *'femme au tablier,'* whose valuable contents seem yet excitingly unknown. What I felt about her with my best Sunday tentacles is: that she is neither cook nor any subordinate being, nor a bore, nor harmless, nor stupid etc. I have even sort of an idea, dear Katy, that she might be the woman who would *not* think about who loves her, but could decide the much more important question of whom *she* loves (and that would bust Cinderella for good). Furthermore I have also an idea that the *femme au tablier* is somehow the author of your poems. But the poems don't express her but hazily, she must *live* ...

> With all good wishes to both of you and love,
>
> Yours,
>
> Linda

Linda is pretty astute in the way she spots the two sides of Katy's personality and feels that the *femme au tablier* and the *femme du monde* "should unite more closely." She says that the *femme au tablier* represents the human side which gets things done and yet is subordinate to no one! For the same opposites in Katy I have used different symbols, the Sea-Captain animus and the débutante. But both sets of terms express the same characteristics: one has leader qualities, while the other is socially minded but meek. These opposites in Katy intrigue Linda, who suspects, as I do, that Katy was never really a *femme du monde*, but adopted that role because social position was so important in her youth. Playing that role and neglecting the other qualities of course misfired, as we have seen. Katy became depressive and was forced to seek an analyst – but not just any analyst, as a meek maiden might have done. Steered by the Sea-Captain animus, she homed in on Jung, despite the fact that in 1920s America she was light years away from what Jung stood for. Katy was at her best after her mother's funeral, says Linda, and obviously, after such a traumatic event, Katy was in no mood for her usual play-acting with Linda and was just herself, showing the "harmonious simplicity" Linda observed, whereas Katy sees herself as "harmless" (to her "boring"). Though the other, more mature personality pressed for recognition as Katy grew older, she kept disregarding it, failing to see through her own disguise as a *femme du monde*. Not only Linda did perceive her best side, but so did Dr. Mantel-Hess, who had no connection with psychology[1] but was intelligent. Perhaps Katy remained benighted in this respect because simplicity seemed to her "unglamorous," reminding her of her ancestors' undistinguished arrival in America. While Katy was proud of what the Rush family had accomplished later, she spoke only rarely and apologetically of her backwoods descent, never mentioning that they had been Quakers when they arrived in Pennsylvania.

All her life, Katy was in search of her other side, and that quest may have been the reason for her frequenting different analysts. Unfortunately, she never really knew what she was after, though she may have hoped that one of them would identify the elusive other personality. She was totally unaware of her similarity to her father, and would have been horrified had she been told that she had masculine traits. As is evident from her letter to Feisst, she saw herself as very feminine, period. Often women are much closer to their fathers temperamentally than they consciously realize. Some show their similarity in concrete form, by walking, sitting and gesturing like Father.[2] Katy's likeness to Father was mainly mental: her inner man was a leader who could lay down the law, exhibit a temper, show courage, and when in a jovial mood drink heartily and tell ribald jokes.

Soon after Mrs. Rush's death the Club wrote Katy an official letter of condolence:

Psychologischer Club
Zürich
September 3rd, 1947

Dear Mrs. Cabot,
    We have heard with great regret of the death of your Mother, Mrs. Rush, and should like to express our warmest sympathy to

---

[1] The psychological jargon used by everybody today, though only partially understood, was unknown in Dr. Mantel's time.
[2] At the Klinik am Zürichberg I noted this interesting fact.

you in the name of the Club. It seems very hard that you should have to face this new, and worse separation so soon after your daughter has left Switzerland, and we hope that the Club may be able to prove that it is a kind of family, even if of a quite different kind.

Assuring you of our sincere participation in your trouble and with our best wishes to you,

> Yours very sincerely,
> > The Committee:
> > C. A. Meier
> > Hch. Steiger
> > Marie-Jeanne Schmid
> > Barbara Hannah
> > Kurt Binswanger

Katy writes a note to me beneath the above letter: "Please return with Mrs. Jung's condolence letter. Throw all others away. Ma." In mid September Katy received another letter about her mother from Mrs. Jung:

> Küsnacht-Zürich
> Seestrasse 228
> Sept. 19ᵗʰ, 1947

Dear Mrs. Cabot!

Thank you very much for your nice letter & the picture of your mother's funeral. It must have been very beautiful & very impressive, as I had already heard from L. Fierz, and I am sure Janey will be pleased to have this (how shall I call it?) last sign of her grandmother.

I was glad to hear, that Linda had gone to the funeral and to be a support to you, who certainly needed it in such a situation!

How I do understand that you feel the loss so deeply now, but also, how very glad you must feel, that you lived those weeks of illness so devotedly with your mother.

I hope you will have a good rest at Ragaz, the sort of introversion and finding back to oneself which one needs after such an experience. And I think in time your plans will become more definite and you will know, what the best thing for you to do is. I am looking forward to seeing you in the beginning of October; we shall both be in Küsnacht then. With affectionate greetings

> Yours,
> > Emma Jung

My mother writes the following to me in a corner of Mrs. Jung's letter: "Such a nice letter in answer to mine thanking her for hers of condolence. Thought you might enjoy reading it. Love, Ma."

In November Katy requested an hour with Jung. Frl. Schmid replies:

le 10 novembre 1947

Madame C. Cabot,
Casa Abbondio,
Ascona

Chère Madame,
Le Professeur Jung me charge de vous écrire – et je le fais à regret, car il vous fait dire qu'il ne peut malheureusement pas vous voir vendredi. Il n'est pas réellement malade, mais il se sent très fatigué et va partir à la fin de la semaine pour le Rigi où il espère se reposer et se remettre tout a fait. Il vous fait dire son regret et de vous transmettre his kind regards.

   Très sincèrement navrée,

   votre

   Marie-Jeanne Schmid

[Professor Jung asks me to write to you – and I do so with regret – because he asks me to tell you that unfortunately he cannot see you Friday. He is not really ill, but he feels very tired and is leaving at the end of the week for the Rigi where he hopes to rest and recover completely. He asks me to express his regrets and to transmit his kind regards.

   Very sincerely sorry,

   Your,

   M-J. S.]

Katy was now ensconced in a new home at Ascona, renting a flat directly on the road leading out of the village towards Brissago. She kept the flat for the rest of her life, despite the increased traffic after the War; on two occasions trucks passing too close to the building took off part of her balcony! When the War was over Katy began to spend more time in San Remo and less in Switzerland. Ascona became her stopping-off place between San Remo and Zürich, but also gave her a more permanent contact with Switzerland, which she loved. Hotels could not give her that. An American citizen by birth, and later an Italian citizen by marriage, at the end of her life Katy also became a Swiss citizen,[1] a *bourgeoise de la ville de Lausanne* thanks to her being a permanent resident at the Lausanne Palace! (She could have chosen Zürich, but though she was good at languages she never mastered Swiss German, which a foreigner must be able to speak when taking citizenship in a Swiss-German canton.) Though speaking excellent Italian and having the flat in Ascona, she did not try for her papers in the Tessin, as she knew the Italian style of procrastination and wanting tips and feared the Ticinese might be of that ilk. Her first-class French made a Swiss-French canton the natural choice. Her French-Swiss examiner, André Chevallaz (later a Conseil Federal/ Bundesrat), was kindly inclined towards an old lady – whom he treated, however, more like an old gentleman – and so asked his examinee many questions on Swiss wines, omitting the awkward questions on government and Swiss history, which relieved and delighted Katy.

Pat and I, with our two children – Diana newly arrived in April 1947 – had been living a year in Ankara by December, and had been touch with my mother only by letter. Where she spent Christmas 1947 I have no idea, but it must have been a dreary one for her wherever she was, as she had neither family nor boyfriend to keep her company. Luckily, however, her energies were occupied writing both prose in English and poetry in French. She was also continuing with the work of putting her parents' villa in San Remo in order, which she had begun to do the previous year.

---

[1] She was a citizen of all three countries when she died.

Chapter Twelve

Our Return to Europe, and Pat's Illness

In the spring of 1948, Katy began planning a trip to the U.S. to take her parents' ashes to be interred at the Arlington National Cemetery, Washington, D.C., and to visit friends she had not seen for twenty years. The following letter from Mrs. Jung refers to her forthcoming journey:

Bollingen, April 9th, 1948

Dear Mrs. Cabot!

Thank you for your letter from which I see that you must be in Zürich by now. Could you come to Bollingen next Wednesday, April 14th? You might see Linda at the same time, as she is here too and Toni as well who is staying with us. It is nice that you will take the trouble to come to say good-bye before you leave, and we are interested to hear how things are in Italy. Your letter sounds as if people were pretty excited!

Looking forward to your visit and with affectionate greetings, also from Onkel,

Emma Jung

Katy left Zürich on 30 April, traveling by train to Rome then on to Naples by bus. Between Rome and Naples she saw much war damage; on the Riviera she had seen damage as well, but it was less serious – mostly buildings pitted by shrapnel. She sailed from Naples on the *Vulcania* on 5 May and arrived in New York ten days later. After depositing her parents' ashes at Arlington National Cemetery, she visited Philadelphia, West Virginia and Boston. She also went to

Newport in early July, where her father had been stationed when she was a small child, and where she had returned as a young married woman to escape the West Virginia summer heat. The newly launched destroyer *U.S.S. William R. Rush* was in port, and she was invited by Captain Chenault to visit the ship and have lunch on board. Before returning to Europe she visited friends in the Blue Grass country of Kentucky. Back in New York by mid-July, she embarked again for Europe on the *Vulcania*.

Katy kept a record of her visit and wrote up her impressions, composing them in French in the hope of having her *memoir* published in Geneva; the journalist who corrected her poems written French was also a publisher there. But French proved to be an unsuitable language for a report written by an American about her own country, and Katy must have sensed this because the text was stilted, as if the author had misgivings about writing in a foreign language. It would have needed much revision, but Katy was already planning her next trip, so she shelved her book until a later date and almost immediately set off by sea to visit us in Turkey. She arrived in Ankara in mid-August via Istanbul, where we went to meet her. Shortly after Katy's arrival, we decided mutually to go on a diet. Katy had put on weight in America; I had never recovered my figure after two pregnancies, and Pat noticed that the rich Turkish food, given his sedentary way of life, was thickening his girth. A magazine that I subscribed to wrote that with the *diète Antoine* you were guaranteed to lose three kilos in a week, so we followed it to the letter: milk days, egg days, vegetable days, and fruit days, the last day of all being fruit only. It was hard going! To make the diet less tedious we decided to offer a prize to the one who lost the most weight, and Katy won the competition with ease, receiving a tiny silver cup from Pat and myself for her pains. I was relieved that my mother's visit had started harmoniously, for I had been apprehensive about her stay because she liked to dominate the scene. But this time she seemed easy-going, and the diet had been quite fun *à trois*. Unfortunately, a few days after we had completed it, I began feeling out of sorts then rapidly became extremely ill. I could keep no food down; when I had languished in bed for some time without recovering my appetite, my mother diagnosed my illness as psychological. She was convinced that a really tasty meal would put me right, so she asked the cook to roast a quail! (There were plenty of game birds in the vicinity of Ankara; we went at weekends to a nearby lake where duck, geese and quail were bountiful.) She served the quail to me in bed. I was horrified when she appeared proudly bearing a tray with a plate on which was perched a small bird on a thick, greasy crouton! Not to offend her, I forced the whole lot down, but in less than no time it was up again. Though I failed to turn yellow I was eventually diagnosed as having jaundice, a disease prevalent in Ankara at that time. (Badly washed fruit or salad were considered the culprits.) I lost ten kilos in the following weeks and hardly had the strength to rise for my daily session on the sitting room sofa prescribed by the doctor. Some weeks later I realized I was pregnant. By then it must have been the end of September and I continued to lose weight.

While I was confined to bed, Katy took my place at all the diplomatic functions with Pat. She was in her element! I was far too sick to care about missing parties. And I loved it when Pat and my mother were out of the house in the evenings. What I could not bear was when they stayed in. Jaundice had made me hypersensitive to noise, and my bedroom stood next to a room where we had a small wooden bar brought with us from Switzerland. On the evenings that Katy and Pat had no engagements they repaired to the bar at about 7 p.m. and began mixing cocktails. Gradually, as they imbibed, their voices rose and their laughter became extremely loud, so that by 9 p.m., when dinner was finally served, I could bear the noise no longer. With head buried in the pillows, however, I held my tongue, and sighed with relief when they moved to the dining room. It would have been useless to complain because the two Scorpios[1] were by that time too tipsy to have any feeling for my distress.

A Scottish trained nurse from Edinburgh, Jean Wilkie, married to a British soldier stationed in Ankara, came to me daily for a couple of hours. She was very understanding of my plight and a great comfort, helping me wash, making the bed and serving me a light repast. The first solid food I was able to keep down was a lightly boiled egg. She seemed to be the only person who understood that I was really ill and not malingering. My doctor Celal Kent,[2] having tried a number of remedies to no avail, eventually prescribed injections of vitamins B and C which Mrs. Wilkie administered daily. By this time it was mid-November and my mother's return journey was booked. Seeing that I

---

[1] Both Katy and Pat were born in the first half of November sixteen years apart. In many ways their characters were similar.
[2] I dedicated my book *Ten Lunar Months* (1956) to him.

was getting no worse, she left as scheduled. Three days after her departure the vitamin injections began to take effect, and I rose from bed and rapidly regained my strength. Despite my pregnancy I soon felt very well and really enjoyed Christmas dinner with Pat and the children.

Back in Europe again, Katy began putting the finishing touches to the manuscript about her American experiences. In that connection she writes to Onkel from Geneva in the early spring:

March 28th, 1949
Hotel de la Paix
Quai de Mont Blanc
Geneve

Dear Onkel,

My book on America, *Une Américaine Redécouvre son Pays*, is three quarters finished and those pages are already in the hands of M. Martinet, who is writing the preface and who intends publishing them. There remains the last quarter (the most important!) to write and I return to the Tessin through Zürich, to finish that last quarter. I cannot finish the book completely unless I see you once! I have said so much about America, but there must be something important I have forgotten and somehow I feel desperately in need of your spirit to bring the book to a fitting end. So far, the only way I have been able to commune with you is through your books, in which I feel your humor and lightness of touch, even in the most serious parts.

May I see you now? April 5th or 6th? Or will you see me once April 30th when I return to Geneva, to go over the last quarter with M. Martinet? I would appreciate it no end, for now I feel 'cut off' – as you are near and not in Timbuctoo – cut off from, *"cette source"* which has given me so much all these years. I arrive at the Waldhaus Dolder, Zürich, on April 4th.

Could Miss Schmid drop me a line, if an interview were possible?

With affectionate greetings,
Catharine Cabot

If I don't hear in Zürich, I shall hope for a line in the Tessin –
Casa Abbondio
Ascona, Tessin
until April 30th

Miss Schmid replies:

April 1st 1949

Chère Madame,
Le "Patron" me charge de vous faire savoir qu'il quitte Küsnacht
lundi matin pour Bollingen, mais que si cela vous ennuie pas trop de
l'y rejoindre là-haut, il pourrait vous y voir mardi après-midi (5
avril). Vous seriez gentille de me donner un coup de téléphone lundi
matin pour confirmer le rendez-vous d'une part et de l'autre.

Cordialement votre

Marie-Jeanne Schmidt

[The 'Boss' asks me to let you know that he is leaving Küsnacht
Monday morning for Bollingen, but if it does not bother you too
much to join him up there, he could see you there Tuesday
afternoon (5. April) Kindly give me a telephone call Monday
morning to confirm the appointment one way or another.]

There is no record of this interview at Bollingen, but Katy, being
en route to Geneva, may not have written it up. She was also
preoccupied with her book. Mr. Martinet did not publish it, and she
never told me what happened. However, as remarked earlier, I believe
it should not have been written in French; she was more at ease
writing in English, and it somehow rang false that an American
woman would use French to write about her American journey. As I
have already remarked, the heavy style perhaps indicates Katy's own
discomfort. Then, too, much of the book was written as a travelogue
for foreigners, like the Swiss book on which she had collaborated
with Mary Rüfenacht. While some passages are interesting and well-
written, much revision would have been needed; the ms. is heavily
marked with suggestions by the publisher for cuts and other changes.

In late August 1949 I drove from Le Vésinet near Paris with my
three children to visit my mother for a month's holiday in San Remo,
accompanied by the English nanny who had been with us in Turkey.
Pat, I and the children had returned to Europe from Turkey in April
1949; on 27 May my son Christopher was born at the British hospital
in Paris. After a harrowing two-week session with a new baby in a
small hotel on the Faubourg St. Honoré, we found a house in Le
Vésinet with a large garden and settled down there in June. Pat, now

working at the O.E.E.C. (later O.E.C.D.)[1] was due to join us a couple
of weeks later. During the time Pat was alone in Paris he worked very
hard learning his new job, so he was looking forward to a fortnight's
holiday at San Remo. He arrived in early September seeming tired
but cheerful. On arrival he mentioned briefly that he felt a "burning
line" across the center of his head (along the line joining the two lobes
of the brain); otherwise, he said, he felt fine! Every morning we went
to the beach with the children, built sand castles and swam. About a
week later Mountbatten's flagship anchored off San Remo for an
official visit, and my mother, Pat and I were among many local
residents invited to meet Mountbatten[2] at a reception on board. By
the time we arrived many people stood about on deck with drinks
talking; we went our separate ways and mingled with the other
guests. After about an hour an acquaintance came up to me, interrupted my conversation, and whispered that Pat was unwell. I was
alarmed, for he had been perfectly well when we arrived. When I went
over to him, he was standing and at first glance looked normal. But
my relief was short-lived; Pat told me that after a couple of drinks he
had suddenly developed tunnel vision, which he described as seeing
through the wrong end of a telescope. Pat said he suspected bad
alcohol; he gave a sober impression as he spoke, but was having
difficulty walking. I hoped he was right about the alcohol, and
comforted myself remembering that I had heard hooch was being
sold in some San Remo liquor stores. As he was keen to leave the
party, I drove him home and put him to bed, where he sank into a half
sleep which persisted the following day. So Katy called her G.P., who
could not make out what Pat was suffering from; he suspected sun
stroke and prescribed bed rest with laxatives and enemas to reduce
pressure on the brain, and the constant application of ice packs to the
head. After three days Pat's condition improved, but bright light still
bothered him. He managed, however, to make an appearance downstairs and even joined us for lunch when some cousins from Boston
arrived. The following morning Pat felt much better and insisted on
spending the morning at the beach with the children. He swam and
built sand castles, and was still in fine form as we drove home, and on
returning to the villa before lunch he went up to his room to deposit

[1] The Organization for European Economic Cooperation, later the Organization for European Cooperation and Development.
[2] Earl Mountbatten of Burma, last Viceroy of India.

his bathing kit. I was on the terrace, where lunch was about to be served, when I heard loud screams coming from our bedroom. I rushed upstairs. Pat was very agitated; I managed with difficulty to put him into bed where eventually he sank into a restless twilight sleep. That afternoon the doctor prescribed the same treatment as before, but this time there was no improvement. Pat lay in a half conscious state for several weeks, complaining of numbness and "cold spots" on his torso and down one leg. His tunnel vision had given way to impaired peripheral vision, with blind spots on the left side of his visual field. When he attempted to go to the bathroom he was unsteady on his legs.

I was numbed by seeing Pat in such a condition and being incapable of helping him. But my mother, seeing no improvement, became active. She said a specialist must be called, and eventually a "famous" *Professore* recommended by the G.P. arrived from Genoa. A pompous individual, he hardly looked at Pat; after a bit of reflection he pronounced him to be suffering from juvenile senility, for which he regretfully announced there was no treatment. As Pat was only thirty-nine years old, Katy thought the diagnosis ridiculous and so phoned C.A. Meier in Zürich, quite an undertaking in those days as there was no direct dialing and the lines were constantly engaged; sometimes you had to queue three hours to make a call. When she finally got through she asked Meier for the name of a first-class Swiss neurologist; Meier replied that the best man was not in Switzerland but in Leeds.

By now it was early November. Pat was no longer bed-ridden but remained very weak. He had difficulty concentrating, became easily tired and could be in a strange, distant mood. My mother decided we should all three leave immediately for England. With the help of hormones I rapidly weaned my baby son, now five months old, and reluctantly abandoned him to the nanny, but as she was a trained nurse I thought he should be in good hands. And in fact she was thoroughly competent and managed to travel back to France with all three children. We then traveled by *Wagons Lits* from Nice to Calais, and on to London were we arrived some twenty-four hours later, spending the night at the Grosvenor Hotel, Victoria Station. Pat had withstood the journey better than expected, but was very tired and desperately cold. We put him to bed and piled blankets over him; the maid brought several hot water bottles. Admittedly the hotel was ill-heated, but Katy and I did not feel the cold to that extent. After Italy, the austerity in England was a shock; London was black with soot from the Blitz, and the food was terrible. These hardships did not bother Katy, however, who was in her element when succoring the sick. The following day we entrained for Leeds, where Pat was admitted to the Brotherton Ward of the Leeds General Hospital while my mother and I stayed at a hotel. While it had no central heating, it did have effective coal fires in the public rooms which gave off much-needed warmth. We liked the hotel, which my mother thought "very English," but to our dismay could spend only two nights there. Pat's session was to last a week, so with difficulty we found rooms in the so-called smartest hotel, which my mother loathed immediately. It seemed to her pretentious, and instead of the cosy coal fires in the lounge, this hotel boasted air conditioning in the public rooms which blasted cold air down the napes of our necks wherever we sat. Leeds was crowded and even grimier than London, and the lighting was poor both in and out of doors, which in November made the place very gloomy. But funnily enough Katy was in the best form. She liked Leeds, and I was relieved that Pat was at last in good hands. After a week of tests in the well-appointed hospital, he was diagnosed as having encephalitis. As it was a virus infection, similar to polio, there were no miracle injections to cure it, the doctor said. Fortunately I did not know then that it is a virus that remains for life, albeit dormant. None of the doctors who saw Pat told him that he should give up alcohol.

Back in Paris, a French neurologist, pooh-poohing his English colleague's diagnosis, prescribed a series of injections. Enormous quantities of some mysterious fluid were pumped into Pat's veins every other day. Having joined the O.E.E.C. only in May 1949, Pat was now on six-months leave. Gradually his powers of concentration returned, though sometimes at night he walked around the bedroom murmuring strangely, which terrified me. Eventually that stage passed, and he appeared pretty normal again, even working for awhile at his former job. But eventually, for reasons I never knew, he was pronounced redundant.

In 1952, we bought a house in the south of England and took up farming. Pat's mind recovered, but emotionally he had changed. Gradually it became apparent that he would never be his old self again. The fun-loving puer became a rather severe senex. Pat's doctors never told him to give up alcohol, so he went on drinking as before, which I heard much later is harmful for people with encephalitis. I soon noticed that when Pat drank more than usual at a party, he acted strangely the following day. One day, after a party the previous evening, I was driving Pat to a luncheon party organized by the Wine and Food Society at Brighton. Though sober, he was suddenly in a very restless state similar to his restlessness during the acute stage of the illness. Though not screaming he was very strange, and so, fearing that he might interfere with my driving, I pushed him over into the back seat. Mercifully there were no head-rests in those days, so I was able to shove him over, with his cooperation, and he slithered onto the back seat. We were not quite half way to Brighton; seeing that Pat was in no state to attend a luncheon party, I turned back and drove him to our local hospital at Uckfield instead, where he remained under observation for twenty-four hours. With the crisis over, and presumably the alcohol out of his system, he was allowed home.

Despite such episodes, Pat was able to write two best-sellers[1] about his war experiences, and later other books. But as the years passed his energy waned markedly. His jovial temperament disappeared completely and he fluctuated between being stiff, judgmental, or irascible; at other times he was simply distant. His judgment became poor. Dr. Meier had told my mother that encephalitis changed a person's personality, and, though I hated to admit it to myself, Pat was no longer the man I had married. His change of personality was difficult to live with, but worse still there was no maturing of his personality. He became mentally rigid and psychologically static. As the years passed I matured, becoming more self-assured and independent, a development which Pat disliked. He himself became a forbidding father and would lay down the law at meal times in an uncharacteristic way. After being treated as a naughty child for a while, I began to realize that a relationship was no longer possible. At about that time Jung's autobiography, *Memories, Dreams, Reflections*, was published. In it I came upon a passage which helped me overcome feelings of guilt and gave me the courage to end my twenty-three-year marriage.

[1] *The Colditz Story* (Hodder & Stoughton, London, 1952) and *The Latter Days* (Hodder again, 1953), published as *Men of Colditz* in the U.S.A. Both books were translated into many languages, and *The Colditz Story* was also made into a film by Ivan Foxwell.

Liliane Frey-Rohn, C.G. Jung and Aniela Jaffé

Chapter Thirteen

Meeting Cencio, and Toni's Death, 1950-1953

At the crucial period when the ms. describing her visit to America should have been reworked, Katy met a man with whom she fell madly in love. A fifty-nine-year-old San Remo fisherman of a special sort, his name was Vincenzo Visconti-Prasca. During the War he had been a high-ranking officer in the Italian Army; now, with the War over and his assets much reduced (his property in France had been confiscated), he was forced to earn his living. The army was no longer a possible profession for him after the War, so, as he liked fishing, he acquired a boat and began fishing off San Remo. The Mediterranean had not yet been polluted, so he caught an abundance of fish and sold it at the San Remo market. He and his wife were separated; she lived in Rome while he lived most of the year in a modest flat on the west side of San Remo. When Cencio was not fishing he was going out in San Remo society, and was very popular with hostesses, for not only did he provide them with very fresh fish, but also he was a genuine Count,[1] which despite the abolition of the monarchy in 1946 still carried weight in postwar Italy. Katy was introduced to Cencio through friends in 1949, and by 1950 the friendship had blossomed into a permanent attachment.

After Katy met Cencio Visconti she became so involved with her new life that she spent more time in Italy and less in Switzerland, eventually losing contact for a while with her Zürich friends. There is

---

[1] He was the eldest son of a deceased count. All the sons of Italian counts like to call themselves "Count," but only the eldest can print "Count" on his visiting cards.

no correspondence between Katy and them from April 1949 to December 1950, and none in 1951. But Katy did not lose touch completely with the Jungs. Mrs. Jung writes:

Bollingen, 29.XII.1950

Dear Mrs. Cabot,

Thank you very much also in Onkel's name for the lovely and most appreciated Xmas greetings. The shawl [scarf?] is marvelous & C.G. is enormously pleased with it. He never had such a beautiful one. And the Foie Gras is quite delicious.

We enjoy it here at Bollingen, where we spend most quiet and restful days after the rather strenuous time before Xmas.

I am looking forward to seeing you soon & to hear all the interesting things you are going to tell me.

With best wishes for the New Year & cordial greetings,

Yours,

Emma Jung

The "interesting things" were most likely about her new boyfriend.

Katy did not spend Christmas with us at Paris in 1950, for she got a bee in her bonnet during our annual visit to San Remo in September about our children's nurse, convinced that she had tried to seduce her new boyfriend. Cencio, at fifty-nine, was an attractive man, tall but with a slight stoop and plenty of gray hair across his brow and parted to the side. A scar ran down the left cheek of his rugged face. He gave a medieval impression and would have looked well in a suit of armor, but I doubted that his type would attract a girl in her twenties. The nurse retaliated by maintaining that it was *he* who had acted, by tapping on her window one night. What she actually saw from her window she never revealed. Presuming that she saw nothing, the tapping noise was explained away as palm rats throwing nuts about high in the palm trees near her bedroom and striking the window-panes. This theory pacified the nurse. The incident seemed closed and relegated to history, but Katy refused to accept the explanation, maintaining that the nurse was a seductress and insisting that we give her notice. Pat and I thought it quite absurd. Unfortunately, Pat then also got a bee in *his* bonnet, judging that Cencio – being Italian – might well have been hoping to seduce the nurse. He kept the story alive for the remainder of our stay by ostentatiously patrolling the garden paths before retiring to bed, walking slowly and banging noisily with a heavy cane on the pavement. I felt embarrassed by this strange behavior but concluded it had to do with his illness of the previous year. When Katy found out that we did not fire the nurse on our return to France, she ordered me to get rid of her and threatened, if I did not, never to come near our house again while "that girl" was under our roof. Mercifully, early in 1951 the nanny, who was a trained nurse and wanted to return to hospital work gave notice, and left when we were able to find a replacement. Though my mother and I were reconciled, Katy kept bringing up the nurse story for years, for she could never drop such a thing entirely.

As we discovered, Cencio did not spend all his time in his San Remo abode. When he was not there for the fishing, or over the summers, he returned to his Rome apartment where his wife was ensconced. This was hard on Katy, but she soon worked out a way of spending time in Rome as well. She had despised charity work in her youth, but suddenly took an interest in good works for the American Episcopal Church in Rome, St. Paul's within the Walls. She was immediately on good terms with the American Rector, Canon Shreve, who rented her a *pied à terre* in his Rectory on Via Napoli 58. She began work there, describing it in a letter of 30 January 1956 to her brother-in-law Ralph Bradley:

> I have been working for the American Church in Rome, living in the organist's flat of 1860, when the church was built, for the present day organist has a sumptuous flat on Via S. Teodoro. I have enjoyed the work, mostly typing and also 'seeing' people who feel lost in Europe & need some guidance, which my years over here have made me competent to give. ... Canon Shreve [is] a most efficient & delightful person to work for.
>
> I received some amusing books as Xmas presents, amongst them was 'Sincerely, Willis Wade' by Marquand.[1] Have you read it? It took me right back into New England and to America as it is so extraordinarily *vivid*! I can relive my first years in Boston & the feelings I had in 1915 when I first got there! It always seems a pity that one never *understands* things when one is young, and it is strange, how one always comes back to one's beginnings! One makes a complete circle and eventually finds oneself exactly where one started! One's 'early years,' first as a child & then as a

[1] J. P. Marquand, *Sincerely, Willis Wade* (Little, Brown & Co., Boston/Toronto, 1955).

'teenager,' seems like a magnet, pulling one around the world in forty years and landing me at the *point de depart*!

Divorce had been abolished in Italy soon after the War, so Cencio could not become legally free. Katy badgered him to obtain an annulment, but he moved slowly, and said it would be impossibly expensive. In his case he had been married a long time and had had a child who unfortunately died in infancy of dehydration. Though it was Cencio's *mother* who had chosen his wife, he may still have felt some loyalty to the woman he had married. From the Anglo-Saxon point of view his position might have appeared hypocritical, but in Latin countries it was the custom to stay married while having girlfriends on the side. In San Remo Cencio had quite a reputation with women, but was more or less unattached when Katy came on the scene. She soon saw to it that all his previous flirts faded away and that she became the sole person in his life. Katy was different from the Italian society women of that period who had little else in their heads but gossip; the years working in Zürich had made her interesting to talk with, and she was also good fun, had a great sense of humor, and entertained very well. Liking her style immediately, Cencio found it no hardship to give up his previous women friends, but Katy had to suffer their loathing for usurping their position. Though Cencio enjoyed being at the villa, he continued to live in his own flat outside San Remo.

Like most Italians, Cencio loved children. One day at lunch he told me that he had been broken-hearted when his baby died of dehydration. I commiserated with him. He seemed astonished, then told me how hurt he was when Katy was unsympathetic about his loss. Katy always found it difficult to be objective, and to put herself into another person's shoes. Even though no marriage appeared forthcoming, Pat and I integrated Cencio into the family. This was easy as he loved children and our children therefore liked him immediately, soon calling him *Zio* (Uncle) Cencio. When my youngest daughter Christina was to be christened in August 1952, we asked him to be Godfather. In fact, since the *contretemps* in 1950 when we first met Cencio, we did all we could to counteract the unfortunate nurse incident; though my mother had a long memory Cencio did not, so we succeeded fairly well.

When the first flush of love for Cencio had passed, Katy began corresponding again with Zürich friends, especially the Jungs. Mrs.

Jung writes from the Tessin at Easter 1952:

Locarno, 15.IV.1952

Dear Mrs. Cabot,

You have really spoilt us with lovely flowers! Thank you so much for your charming Easter-Greeting, which brings a delightful touch of colour and perfume to our room.

Uncle sends you warmest greetings and apologizes for not having come to see you [in Ascona]. He felt such a need for a rest & introversion, that we had to remain quietly by ourselves. I hope you will understand. Now we both feel really rested & are returning home to-morrow.

Thanking you again for your kindness,
Cordially yours,

Emma Jung

In the autumn of the same year, Mrs. Jung writes:

Küsnacht-Zürich
Seestrasse 228
Nov. 22nd, 1952

Dear Mrs. Cabot,

What a lovely greeting you sent us! The beautiful carnations – I never saw the like of them – give us the greatest pleasure. Thank you very very much!

It was so nice of you to think of us! You know, Uncle has been ill for the last six weeks, he again had heart trouble, the same as six years ago, a too high pulse frequency; and has spent practically the whole time in bed. Now thank God, he is getting better again and can get up for meals and spend part of the day in the library. We really had a bad autumn; I was not well during September & when I felt better C.G. fell ill. We had both been overstrained; it is so difficult to adapt the demands of life with the physical strength of old age! And having been so well, we didn't realise, that we would have needed a far more restful holyday than we actually had. Ascona was so to speak the last straw, I had to go to bed right after our return.

And how are you? I hope you are quite recovered by now. With warmest greetings from both of us.

Yours sincerely,

Emma Jung

San Remo's most profitable industry was carnations! These were grown in greenhouses on the terraced hills behind the town where previously olive trees had been. Both wholesalers and retailers bought directly from the growers at the San Remo flower market. Each weekday morning a bell rang at 7 a.m. and the flowers, lying covered on stands in the enormous market hall, were uncovered all at once. The sudden sight of dazzling color was impressive. The sales began at a brisk pace; the carnations were sold mostly wholesale, many to foreign buyers who shipped them off in wicker hampers. Private persons who wanted only a few carnations were less welcome, and if you wanted good quality flowers you had to arrive early. The main carnation season was in winter and early spring.

Katy was now out in the world "living," as Jung urged his patients to do, but she never forgot the Jungs. The more she "lived" the more frequent were her floral tributes to them. It was a means of keeping in touch with people whom she was very fond of and admired, and to whom she also felt grateful. Katy spent little time in Zürich at this period – only for doctors' visits and occasionally to see C.A. Meier. But she went to Ascona off and on when she needed a rest from San Remo society with its gossip and intrigues. Katy's giving of flowers and presents was not entirely one-sided; Mrs. Jung reciprocated at Christmas time with books.[1]

> Küsnacht-Zürich
> Seestrasse 228
> 16.III.53

Dear Mrs. Cabot,

How very kind of you to send us such lovely carnations; they are of such beautiful colouring and arrived absolutely fresh. Thank you very much for them and also for your good wishes to our Golden wedding.

How on earth did you know about it? For we had told nobody, except of course the family and a few very close friends, so that we were greatly surprised when your telegram arrived. As it seemed to come from Rome & I didn't know your address, I am thanking you only now. We were indeed quite touched by your affectionate thought.

---

[1] A book Katy received from Mrs. Jung at Christmas 1945 was *Psychologische Betrachtungen* by Jolande Jacobi.

Since the last weeks we have now finally some sunshine after a really awfully cold & sunless winter, and C.G. enjoys it quite particularly. He is getting on very well now, fortunately. I am well too, and just recovered from a light grippe, which I rather welcomed, as it gave me the opportunity to have a good rest, which I needed badly.

I always thought of old age as a quiet & restful way of living, but with me, there seems to be more & more work & demands from all sides. The [Jung] Institute is partly responsible for this; on the whole I rather like it, though, for it keeps one alive.

But now we are all looking forward to the spring holyday, which begins next week. I don't know yet, whether we shall go away, it all depends on how "Uncle" feels – so far he didn't think it would be a good idea, as he still felt so uncertain, as it [the weather] was still so very changeable.

We both are sending you our warmest greetings & hope you are being well too!

Very sincerely yours,

Emma Jung

Less than a week after Mrs. Jung wrote the above letter, Toni Wolff died unexpectedly of a stroke on 21 March at the age of sixty-four. Though she had suffered from severe arthritis for many years, she still had been very active. Toni's death was a shock to the psychological group in Zürich, as no one had anticipated it. A year previously, after serving on the committee of the Psychological Club for twenty years as President, she had been made Honorary President; six days before her death she presided at the Club in that capacity for the first and only time. When the news reached Katy in San Remo she wrote the following to Jung:

March 28th, 1953
Villa Aloha
San Remo

Dear Onkel: –

It was a great shock to me to get the news of Toni's death and I know that it must have been the same for you and also a great loss, for she was not only a wonderful person, but a magnificent collaborator in your work. How well I remember those first years, before you took me on, when she "led me by the hand" and taught me to walk! It makes me very sad to think that I shall never see her again, for I do owe her *so* much. Please accept my deepest sympathy, and if you feel like it, *do* come down here, for a visit with me after Easter, for a rest.

Very affectionately yours,

Catharine Cabot

Katy generously issued several invitations to the Jungs to visit San Remo. Villa Aloha in its tropical garden was a beautiful and restful place in those days as there was little traffic on the surrounding roads. But to reach San Remo from Switzerland was still a very long journey by train via Milan. We sometimes took the route via Turin before the War, but it no longer existed, the bridges on that mountainous line having been destroyed by the French. Flying from Geneva to Nice eventually became an alternative, but even then the road or rail journey from Nice to San Remo was long due to heavy tourist traffic, and the *Autoroute* was not yet built. The Jungs were too old to make such trips, but the younger C.A. Meiers were visitors at the Villa. Jung replied:

March 31, 1953

Mrs. Catharine Cabot
Villa Aloha
San Remo

Dear Mrs. Cabot,

Thank you very much for your kind letter of sympathy, it was good of you to write. Toni's death has been a terrible shock to me and to us all, especially as it was so sudden and entirely unexpected. There are many people who will feel as you do over her loss which is quite irreparable in many ways.

It is very kind of you to ask me to come down to you for a rest after Easter, but I have not yet been away from the house since my long illness began last autumn, and now this fresh shock has set me back again. I do not think therefore that it is possible for me to accept, though I very much appreciate the invitation and your kind thought.

Cordially yours,

C.G. Jung

In June Mrs. Jung replies to a letter from Katy who asks to see her:

Küsnacht-Zürich
Seestrasse 228
June 15ᵗʰ, 1953

Dear Mrs. Cabot,

I am sorry, but July 7ᵗʰ I shall be in Schaffhausen, as it is my sister's 70ᵗʰ birthday. If you let me know in time, I could arrange another day, but I have only little time left, as the examinations of the Institute take place during the first 2 weeks of July.

With cordial greetings

Yours sincerely,

Emma Jung

Katy seems in need of advice. I can only guess that after the first flush of the romance with Cencio Visconti, things were not going the way she had hoped. As I said, divorce was not then possible in Italy, and Cencio was slow in seeking an annulment.[1] While very fond of Katy, he knew that an annulment would be difficult to obtain and that there would be publicity. Just like Tommy his prospects for freedom were remote, and just like Tommy he lacked the energy to work for it.

My mother's letters to Mrs. Jung were not kept, but it appears that she was again regularly in touch with Zürich people.

Bollingen, 29.7.53

Dear Mrs. Cabot,

Thank you for your letter; I was very sorry too not to have seen you, when you were in Zürich, but I was so busy with the examinations at the Institute, which it was not possible to miss or to change, that I couldn't help it. Now again, on the 4ᵗʰ of August, it won't be possible either, as we are away for our holyday. I am going to Baden, as I need a good rest without responsibilities and C.G. is staying here with our son & his family. (or part of it.)

Thank you also for your most kind invitation to come to San Remo, I am afraid we cannot accept it, as it would be too long a journey for C.G.

---

[1] He began annulment proceedings, he said in 1949, but obviously he never kept the pressure up, as there was no progress, despite the help he got from a Monsignor who had been his army chaplain when he served in Africa pre-war.

We are not going to Ascona either, as it would be much too strenuous. C.G. although fairly well now, has to be very careful & quiet.

Hoping that you will feel all right again & recovered from your egg-cure, with affectionate greetings from both of us,

Yours very sincerely,

Emma Jung

I hope that there will be a chance of seeing you on your later visits.

The following letter from Mrs. Jung is undated but was most probably written in September 1953.

Küsnacht-Zürich
Seestrasse 228

Dear Mrs. Cabot!

Thank you for your letters and your invitation to have lunch with you, when you will be in Zürich. It reached me with some delay as we were in Bollingen for the vacation, which we even prolonged. From that you see, that Uncle is rather well, although he still has to be careful & to limit his work as much as possible.

I hope very much to see you, when you are here but should prefer you to come to Küsnacht as I have so much to do just now & hardly could manage to come to town, for I also [have] got to be careful about myself.

As you say, Toni's departure was a terrible blow and we miss her very much; it still seems not quite true.

I hope that your cure is not too strenuous & will be successful; it would be a good thing for me too!

With warmest greetings,

Yours very sincerely,

Emma Jung

I have no idea which cure Mrs. Jung is referring to. My mother, who was inclined to be a *bon viveur*, periodically did diets or cures to lose weight. As she grew older, these measures unfortunately were not able to counteract the bad effects which her indulgence in good food and drink over the years had on her health. Gradually she began to develop a heart problem to which she would not admit, preferring to call it *grippe*. But in the nineteen fifties she was still pretty well though good living also began to affect her liver. She would do fruit days, and every morning she drank a large quantity of a special water for the liver and then lie for thirty minutes on her right side. That remedy was pretty harmless, but unfortunately she also took all sorts of pills. I remember particularly those that accelerated her digestion, because she was always hungry and willing to eat a further meal even when younger members of the family were still replete, after large Christmas dinners at 3 p.m. Since meeting Cencio her weight was difficult to control because she was going out regularly wining and dining with him, while he, a heavy smoker, remained thin.

Katy went to Zürich for very short visits, and rarely spoke of her Zürich friends to me at that time. I had lost contact with everybody in Zürich myself when I moved to Bern in 1942, and only saw Jung again at my marriage in 1943 and at the British Legation during Churchill's visit to Bern in 1946. But in spite of my travels to Turkey, France, and England when I eventually settled there, the benign influence he had exerted upon me in my youth never deserted me. Though I was continuing to read his new books as they were published, I was doing what he advocated for young people – getting on with living!

Though she spent much time in San Remo and Ascona, Katy stayed in touch with Zürich and felt a certain nostalgia, though it is obvious from the next letter that she was also following Jung's precepts. She writes:

Villa Aloha
San Remo
October 30th, 1953

Dear Onkel: –

Princess Hohenzollern is now here for a visit and we have naturally been thinking a great deal of you and those wonderful 'old days' in Zürich, when we saw you so often and lived under the rays of your wonderful *Geist*!

Just yesterday, we were talking of those Pfauen lunches with you and the fun and wit at those reunions, which flowed so easily and gaily, like the Pfauen wine! It was rare privilege to be so closely associated with you, for so many years, unforgettable years, which leave memories never to be erased. It is really awful to be cut off from you, but I realize that you were right to send one out into the world to 'live.' However one misses you always, that can't be helped and I suppose will go on as long as one lives. The main thing is to be worthy of you and your teachings, for you certainly left no stone unturned to put one 'ship-shape' back into the world again.

These and many other thoughts have come into our conversations, during the quiet, peaceful days which Princess Hohenzollern is spending here in the sun and it has somehow given one a certain sense of nostalgia and a desire to recapture the 'spirit' of those days. The 'modern' Zürich is so different maybe more 'efficient' but to older people like myself, far less human. But then, you are *so far* in the background and it was YOU who were *everything*.

I must now leave some space for the Princess and so will close with my most affectionate regards to you and Mrs. Jung.

Catharine Cabot

Jung replied on his headed stationery:

Prof. Dr. C.G. Jung
Küsnacht-Zürich
Seestrasse 228
Nov. 6, 1953

Mrs. Catharine Cabot
Villa Aloha
San Remo

My dear Niece Catharine,

I have received you letter with much pleasure, and I only regret that I cannot join your party and *faire revivre les temps passés* [relive past times]. At all events, it was very nice of you to remember our joyous repasts and the good wine we had together.

It was an additional pleasure to have the letter of our dear Princess at the same time. Will you give her my best regards and tell her that the letter to you must do for both since dictating letters takes time, and my time is short! Please raise your glass to my health. I recently discovered a 45 year old Bordeaux in my cellar, and this evening I shall drink a glass in memory of an old vanishing world.

My best wishes to you both,

Yours fidelissimo,

Uncle

C.G. Jung

What made the relationship between Jung and his "niece" Catharine a unique one, outside of analysis, was that she appealed to his *bon viveur* side. Many of his contemporaries saw Jung only as a famous man – a great intellectual. They failed to recognize his human side: his love of fun and appreciation of good food and drink. Jung had a great capacity for relaxation when he was in *Stimmung*, and Katy's "Old Sea Captain" met Jung on this convivial level, a plane on which they were soul mates.

Chapter Fourteen

A Sixtieth Birthday, and Two Partings

Katy was not always being "peaceful" in San Remo or doing good works in Rome. She and Cencio also traveled frequently together, as the following letter from Linda Fierz indicates:

8. Dec. 53

Dear Katy,
I thank you a thousand times for your long letter and your 3 postcards from your memorable trips through – what looks like a "country of the Gods." I especially love the photographs from Chiusi where all sorts of birds are pleasantly sitting on the lid of a stone sarcophagus. It must be the soul-birds having a tea-party or something celebrating a new arrival. I'd envy you for seeing all these marvels, and in such good company – only I cannot, because I am not well enough yet. But I *am* better, and very slowly I am coming back to life a bit. It's curious how all during this time I am so suddenly grateful for the friends I have – for you f.i. [for instance?] even if I don't see you. It is so very helpful – to tell you the truth, much more so than my family. They are a different generation, which doesn't matter in general, but in the really serious events of life it makes sort of a gap that cannot be bridged over. I remember that Prof. Kerényi once, when he spoke of the classical mystery cults, said that each generation fundamentally is a mystery for the following one, who can never understand that people had secrets at all before *they* were born. I think this is really true, and probably it is just right, that it is so.

I appreciate it highly that you are "great friends with the memory of my husband," dear Katy. I am sure though, that he didn't think of you as a *précieuse ridicule*,[1] not at all. On the contrary he liked you, but quite in general he had almost no contact with women – except me. Just as there are "one-man-dogs," he was a "one-woman-man" thoroughly and entirely. He couldn't help it, and I could[n't?] help it and actually, honestly and truly it is only very recently that I have begun to understand what it all meant.

I am having a course at the Institute just now, where I have started on a big adventure – speaking about the symbolical pictures of the *Villa dei Misteri* in Pompeii. It is an adventure that for *me* is thrilling, but I don't know how it will turn out. People will perhaps think that I have a megalomania. But I have decided that since I have got to lead this hateful existence all alone in this house, I'll at least do some things that interest me.

It's *weeks* now that we are sitting buried in a thick, bleak grey fog, smelling and feeling like an ice-box. I do wish you won't have any of that, if you go to England. But perhaps, if you eat enough of your young couple's turkeys, they'll keep you nicely warm from inside. It would be fine, if you'd send your son-in-law's books to the Club, I think. I would certainly read them! Would you send them to me? I am in the library-Commission.

Give my love to your dear grandchildren and all my love to you, dear Katy and a thousand good wishes.

> Yours,
>
> Old Linda (megalomaniac)

By this time Pat, I and the four children had settled in Sussex, buying a Jacobean house with a farm of a hundred and sixty acres. We inherited a Jersey herd from the former owners, and also kept pigs. I took up turkey farming, which in England in the early fifties was profitable even in small numbers. I started with fifty turkeys the first year and had fifty-three to sell at Christmas-time, thanks to spares given me by the hatchery. Emboldened by my beginner's luck, I decided the next year to double my order of day-old birds. The turkey poults arrived looking the same as before, but about three days later began to die, first singly then in larger numbers. At first I

---

[1] *Précieuse ridicule*: a woman of affected literary tastes.

thought they had been trampling each other, but then became suspicious. Eventually the farmer who sold me the birds told me his eggs had been infected by Salmonella, and agreed to replace my poults free of charge a month later. The next lot were fine but lacked time to grow to full size before Christmas. Though smaller, however, they were tender and tasty; Linda could rest assured my mother was being well fed against the cold. Unfortunately, like most English houses, ours was badly heated. The temperature never rose much above 60 Fahrenheit (15 centigrade), and parts of the house were permanently damp. But I cannot remember my mother complaining of the cold.

After the New Year Linda wrote again:

Küsnacht, Jan. 10, 54

My dear Katy,

After all I felt I could not stick it out here alone during the Xmas holidays, so when the Institute closed I fled and stayed away till a few days ago. Your dear long letter I got just before leaving and read it with great interest. Thank you dear Katy! I am so glad that with nice relatives[1] you can follow your inclination for classical art, that seems to form such a living part of your being, and since such a long time. Or if it didn't, you surely would never have achieved all you did in your house at San Remo. Don't you think so? Therefore it must be wonderful indeed for you now to be able to drink the whole of that sparkling cup. Sicily is something I have often dreamt about and hoped to see once. But I never got as far as that, and now I can't even dream of traveling as long as my health isn't a good deal better.

Katy's love of art was not a pose; insatiable, it was almost a vocation. If she had only had a chance to develop her interest professionally the psychological problems might never have developed. Her energies needed a constructive venue, but neither parent ever suggested a career; the conventions of her day won out. Catharine never thought of launching into a career in defiance of her mother's expectation about a good marriage, and her father, staying in the background, was too busy to interfere with his wife's plans for

---

[1] "The nice relatives" were Robert Cabot (my first cousin) and his wife Charlotte (Charlie) and their children. They had newly arrived in Rome from Thailand where Robert had held a diplomatic post. He had given this up and decided to write. His wife was greatly interested in art.

his daughter. But as is often the case with "absent fathers," he played
an active role in his daughter's unconscious. When Catharine lived in
Europe and rarely saw her father, her complex had fertile terrain for
taking root. (As her memories of him were unpleasant, the more
conscious part of the complex was negative.) What took shape, as I
have shown chiefly through her analysis with Jung, was the Sea
Captain figure; and as I have said, she *identified* with her father, as
daughters will when they are unable to *relate* to them. Even when
Katy married she remained daddy's little girl – quite unripe for
marriage – yet had the Sea Captain energy. Though mature femininity
eluded Catharine all her life, with Jung's help she matured into the far
less timid Captain personality. Though the Captain remained completely unconscious to Katy, he influenced her life profoundly.
Though Katy thought she did not like being on her own, in fact the
Captain personality made her independent. She could remain unmarried in an era when it was *mal vu* for a woman to be on her own.
Women on their own were the ideal hook on which to hang all sorts
of negative projections. Katy was a widow for thirty-four years; the
self-confidence given her by the Captain made it possible for her not
to rush into a new marriage. Her friends noticed that she became
more self-confident as she grew older, yet *she* continued to see herself
as a timid Cinderella who needed a man's protection.

Linda Fierz continues:

And thank you especially for what you wrote about your life and
plans for the future. I actually often did wonder what was happening to you and the Count, and whether everything was developing
to your satisfaction. So now I am happy to know that fundamentally things are alright. It is funny – the older one gets the more one
needs to do things *right* and therefore stops hurrying. I often
remember how Dr. Jung told me once, long ago: You must live as
if you had at least a *thousand* years before you. It is so true – the
more one is impatient and hurries the more one loses.

In coming home I also found the London parcel from you with
two books of your son-in-law. I shall hand them over to the library
as soon as the Club is re-opened. In the meantime I am very
pleased to have them for myself. I have already sniffed at the first
volume yesterday and shall certainly read it. But the 'official'
manifestation of gratefulness is due to you from the Club and will
come in time. Literature, which shows the reaction of people to

war and war-experiences always interests me very much. It is most curious to see *how* differently the different nations react, and it seems to me so typical for each of them. The whiff I had of your son-in-law's first book already seemed to me entirely British, with that peculiar matter-of-factness and enjoyment they have even in approaching the most heartbreaking sufferings. Well, I shall see, when I go on.

Of my course about the *Villa dei Misteri*[1] I cannot tell you much at the moment, as I am going at it somewhat like a blind goose – always only groping for the next step. One thing I am nearly certain of though is, that this – I mean the series of wall-paintings – didn't mean *only* a marriage ceremony. As far as I can see, when the Villa was discovered in 1910, the learned beards were most terribly puzzled and not a little shocked about it all. They tried this and that explanation – they did hope it would not be all too meaningful, because that would have been horrid – probably ending in a loss of beard for them. But *thank God* to the delight of the learned beards a German woman suddenly popped up, whose name was *Bieber* and who, being German, knew it all. It was she who fixed on the solution of the paintings meaning a marriage ceremony. The whole chorus of the learned beards fervently agreed. You see, what marriage is even learned beards do know. They probably at once thought of all their faithful wives, thinking, maybe, in the depth of their hearts, how excellent it was and would be also now-a-days, if those faithful wives would get a good thrashing at least once in their lives. Having no beard (at least not to speak of), being not learned *and* not German I do not trust that whole theory. The very first scene of the painting speaks against it. There, under the supervision of a priestess a naked boy reads a sacred text to the listening initiand. Do you think that at the beginning of the ceremony the young fiancées got a lecture in a classical kind of Freudianism by that boy? It seems improbable. Shall tell you more about it later on though.

It did me no end of good to go away from here at least for a short time. I feel at least mentally refreshed, it was so extremely good to be among *healthy* people again for the first time in I don't know how long.

---

[1] Linda Fierz wrote a book translated into English as *Women's Dionysian Initiation: The Villa of Mysteries in Pompei* (Spring, Dallas, 1988).

Dear Katy, I wish you every kind of good things – a fine journey and a happy return to San Remo, where you may find my letter only, when it is completely *altbacken*. I *am* sorry I couldn't write as long as you were in England and I had your beautifully written address.

With much love,

Yours as ever,

Linda

Unfortunately Katy's timid side had not taken Jung's advice; she *was* in a hurry to marry and was becoming impatient that Cencio was doing nothing to accelerate legal procedures for an annulment. Linda writes again on the subject of the *Villa dei Misteri*:

Küsnacht, 7.III.54

My dear Katy,

Thank you very much for your postcard from Pompeji – it was nice that you thought of me in the *Villa dei Misteri*. I have finished my lectures about these paintings now, at least as far as I could do it. It is of course a material one ought to discuss in a fat book, as it contains a whole revelation about the psychology of women. I have never seen anything like it and really didn't know in what deep waters I was diving, when I started. In a way the cultured women of the Roman empire were the actual predecessors of modern women. Medieval Christianity being so murderously patriarchal, European women from the Renaissance to our day, in waking up couldn't fall back on any other model but the Roman one. So they did it as hard as they could and got on with it stubbornly at least on the worldly side. But of the kind of *Delikatessen* on the spiritual plane, that are depicted in the Villa, we know only very little as yet. There exists: a very nice essay, by the way, about Roman women by the historian Giuglielmo Ferrero, *The Wives of the Caesars*, which you might find perhaps in Italian, and which would certainly interest you. You'd see there the germs of that kind of Solomonic feminine *rightness* that f.i. modern women's associations now stand for especially in the U.S.A., in figures like the empress Livia, and the scapegoat of the 'right' women, in figures like the two Julias, who were Livia's step-daughter and grand-daughter. In the mystery-cult at the Villa in Pompeji apparently both these kinds of women were nicely tamed and sent on their own ways by some shrewd Roman predecessor of 'Uncle.' I wonder, if the women also did such an enormous amount of huddling around him, as is the custom here.

Well, I am happy I haven't got to do anything 'spiritual' for the time being – at least for about a fortnight. Then that awful mill begins again with preparing for next term.

I do hope you are well. According to your postcard you will be back at San Remo by now. I wonder if it is still cold in Italy. Here we are still having winter, and even if the sun shines there is no warmth. When I read in the news-papers about all that snow and the storms in Italy I often thought of you and *how* you must have shivered. In your own beautiful house at San Remo you will at least have decent heating, if you need it, so keep nicely swarm and well and write soon.

Yours very affectionately,

Linda

In actual fact the San Remo villa could be very cold and damp in the winter, as the central heating was inadequate. When we arrived for Easter the beds often felt so damp that we had to wear our coats for the first night and dry them out with our own body heat! Though Linda appears very interested in her *Villa dei Misteri* project, warmth is an underlying theme in her letters since her husband's death the previous August. She must have been missing the Warm relationship she had with him. I do not remember her husband, though I met him at the Club. But I remember Linda as a tallish, slim figure, almost angular and rather austere. She herself did not exude much warmth, so without her sheltering husband she must have felt very vulnerable underneath her self-assured persona. She survived her husband by only a year and a half.

Katy sent flowers again to the Jungs for Easter. Though her life in San Remo with Cencio was happy enough, it was not entirely satisfying, and she continued to feel nostalgia for Zürich.

Mrs. Jung writes:

Küsnacht-Zürich
Seestrasse 228
15.IV.1954

Dear Mrs. Cabot,

The flowers you sent us are simply enchanting; I enjoy so looking at their lovely colours and their fragrance is marvelous too,

Thank you very much for your kind thought of sending us this Easter-greetings!

We are spending our holyday in our beloved Bollingen, but unfortunately the weather is not very good; so far we had only a few sunny days. Nevertheless we enjoy the quietness & restfulness of the place. C.G. is well, fortunately & I just had a little grippe, but am better again now.

We had a good winter on the whole, but a very busy one. How are you? It is such a long time since I saw you. I hope at your next visit to Zürich this will be possible.

Since a couple of weeks Mrs. H. has been doing some work with me; I think you will have heard from her directly. She told me that you advised her long ago to have an analysis *a propos* of a dream she told you. You were certainly right then!

With cordial greetings from both of us,

Yours sincerely,

Emma Jung

The sands were running out for Mrs. Jung, whose "little grippe" may have been something more serious. Her next letter would be written after a long session at the Klinik Hirslanden.

My mother not only liked to give flowers, and presents, but also to give dinner parties for her friends when in Zürich. Her relationship with the (C.A.) Meiers, for instance, developed from an analytical one with him to a social one with both him and his wife Joan. She entertained Katy with delicious lunches and dinners at her flat; Katy reciprocated by inviting the Meiers to good restaurants. Flowers and parties were a way of bridging the self-imposed distance from her Zürich friends. Sending postcards was another method she used for keeping contact with friends when Katy was traveling, as she did with Linda and also with the Meiers. Dr. Meier replies from Zürich:

20.5.54

My dear Katy,

Many thanks for your postcard from S. Gimignano. It looks as if we had been in Rome simultaneously. What a shame we should not have seen each other. We left on Good Friday and had called the Hotel majestic to find out whether Cencio was there. But they said they had not seen him for a long time. We are leaving here again for Lipari on the 1st June and shan't be back before the 13th again. I very much hope you can manage to be here after our return. I am looking very much forward to seeing you again after such a long time.

Our best love to you and Cencio,

Yours ever,

Fredy

Of all her analysts, however, Katy was most fond of Jung. On returning to San Remo she writes to him for an appointment:

May 25th, 1954
Villa Aloha
San Remo

Dear Onkel: –
I am coming into Switzerland, after Whitsuntide, June 10th & will be there for a month. Could I possibly see you again? It is so many years, since I have been able to talk with you and I just *long* to see you. Would there be any chance of seeing you during the week of June 14th to June 26th? I can arrange to come to Zürich [from Ascona] at any time however convenient to you. I feel dreadfully out of touch with essential things, though I am not allowing myself to be 'side-tracked' too much, yet I badly need you!

I trust you are very well and send my most affectionate regards,

Catharine Cabot

She was seeking a guideline from Jung, whose advice she trusted implicitly, on the subject of Cencio. Mrs. Grautschy, a temporary secretary, replies:

June 5, 1954

Mrs. Catharine Cabot
Villa Aloha
San Remo

Dear Mrs. Cabot,
Prof. Jung has just left for a 10 days' holiday, but he is ready to see you later. I have reserved for you June 23rd, 5 p.m., which I

should like you to confirm just to know this letter has safely reached you.

Yours sincerely,

(D. Grautschy, Secretary)

Katy replies the following day from San Remo:

June 6th, 1954
Villa Aloha San Remo

Madam B. Gautschy
c/o Prof. C.G. Jung
Küsnacht-Zürich

Dear Madam Grautschy: –
Thank you for your note with the appointment with Professor Jung for June 23rd at 5 p.m. Will you kindly tell Professor Jung that I shall be there, without fail, unless I hear from you to the contrary.

By June 17th I shall be in my flat in Ascona, Tessin (Casa Abbondio – Tel. Ascona 740-62) so please phone me, should anything come up to prevent my seeing Professor Jung on June 23rd – as I shall leave by the early train for Zürich on that day.

With kind regards,
Yours very sincerely,

Catharine Cabot

This hour never took place though nothing came up from Jung's side to prevent it. As mentioned, Katy wanted to discuss the problems she was having with yet another *puer* boyfriend. She was becoming more and more preoccupied about Cencio's lack of action to end his marriage. Katy was nearly sixty and was not keen on living (as Linda quoted Jung as saying) "as if you had a thousand years before you." Katy was still in a hurry despite her age, for after all, in 1954, she had been a widow for twenty-four years. Cencio was not really a lightweight, but with respect to his marriage he was very much like Tommy, making little effort if any to end it. Otherwise he had a Latin temperament and so differed from Tommy in many respects. For instance, he refused to let Katy "dress" him, wearing what he wanted despite her remonstrances. He was also much more independent, never getting tied to Katy's apron strings. But he had heavy smoking in common with Tommy (though he drank less), and as with Tommy unfortunately, smoking would be his downfall. It is strange that after being so keen to see Jung, Katy was prevented from doing so by illness. It was surely not an excuse, covering for cold feet about reporting yet another difficulty with a boyfriend. She would not have used that old expedient with Jung, whom she could tell nearly anything. The illness was likely from overeating, or possibly the beginning of a heart problem, a condition she had for a long time before she admitted to it. Already at this period she often had what she called *grippe*; it seemed strange to me that flu could hit her out of season. Katy was inclined both to overdo and to overindulge with food and drink. The good living with Cencio and the added strain of a stationary relationship were probably responsible for the deterioration in her health, but her overeating cannot be blamed exclusively on the relationship, for she had developed the habit early with her parents, who were great trenchmen. Already during her Christmas visit with us in 1951 she went down with "flu," sneezing a lot and ailing in bed. Our French doctor, an expert on the symptoms of overeating, dismissed "flu" and instead diagnosed an enlarged liver. To Katy's consternation he told her that if she went on indulging she would be able to tie it around her waist in a bow!

Two days after the appointment should have taken place, Jung writes:

Prof. Dr. C.G. Jung
Küsnacht-Zürich
Seestrasse 228
June 25, 1954

Mrs. K. Cabot
Casa Abbondio
Ascona

Dear Katy,

This is really a sad stroke of fate for you to be laid up with a chill. I try to get away from here in the course of next week to Bollingen to have a much needed rest. I have been perfectly besieged in the last weeks; work is always heaping up like mad before vacations. I only return for my birthday party on July 25, otherwise I am invisible if the Lord permits it.

Wishing you a speedy recovery
I remain,
Yours Cordially,
C.G. Jung

Though Katy missed seeing Jung in June, she would see him again at a later date to discuss Cencio. Jung writes again in October on the occasion of Katy's forthcoming sixtieth birthday:

Prof. Dr. C.G. Jung
Küsnacht-Zürich
Seestrasse 228
Oct. 14, 1954

Mrs. Katie Cabot
Casa Abbondio
Ascona

My dear Niece Katie,

This is indeed a momentous time approaching the 60th birthday. I should like very much to be near you at the celebration, but unfortunately I am detained in Küsnacht by my work, and my wife being in hospital is a further obligation. It will be now the 6th week that she is in Hirslanden on account of a discus trouble in the vertebra, but she is now much better and expecting to leave in a week's time or so.

Please accept my best wishes and congratulations. I hope you will be able to enjoy your birthday feast to which I shall be a silent and invisible attendant. If you come to Zürich, let me know about a week ahead so that I can arrange to see you; I am as usually much too busy and time is scarce.

My best regards to Janie.

Yours cordially,

C.G. Jung

Katy's birthday was on 2 November, but she decided to have her party in October when the Tessin was still agreeably warm.

Pat and I, feeling the pinch financially because of our unprofitable farming operations, traveled out to Switzerland for the celebration by train. Coming not by sleeper or even *couchette*, we sat up all night in a compartment with what appeared to be second-generation Italians resident in England, speaking both Italian and English and telling us that they were to visit relatives in Italy. On our return journey we traveled with Italian immigrants to the U.K. of an entirely different breed, with loud voices, uncouth manners and – worst of all – eating oranges throughout the night.

To Jung's letter Katy replies:

October 25th, 1954
Casa Abbondio
Ascona
Tessin

Dear Onkel:

Your birthday wishes meant a *lot* to me, thank you so much for sending them. Janey and her husband came out from England and have just gone back. It was all very nice, this celebration. I was so sorry to hear of Mrs. Jung's illness, as I had heard nothing whatsoever about it. I have written her.

I shall be coming to Zürich on November 1st. Is there any chance of seeing you on the afternoon of the 1st or on the 2nd, 3rd or 4th?

I trust you are well & send my most affectionate greetings.

Catharine Cabot

Janey sends you much love.

Across the top of the card in an unknown hand is written, "Appointment *keine ganze Stunde*." Katy kept no record of this half hour with Jung.

She does not mention in her letter to him how disappointed she was with our birthday present. Remembering her intellectual days when she had written both articles and poetry, Pat and I bought her a recently published, coffee-table-size facsimile of a medieval Bible, with fine leather binding, superbly reproduced illuminations, and numbering in a limited edition. We were proud of our purchase and were sure my mother would be pleased, but Katy, rather than being impressed by the Bible, was rather annoyed with it. She showed no *noblesse oblige*; the gift fell very flat indeed. What she had really been hoping for, she said, was a single pearl to enhance her pearl necklace[1] – a modest request, it seemed, until it transpired that the pearl she had in mind should be the largest in the string, the centerpiece, and *real* not cultured. We should have realized that Katy, after meeting Cencio, had entered a new phase, more social than intellectual, in which an upgraded pearl necklace was of more value to her than a Bible!

[1] For her seventieth birthday she requested *two* pearls!

While there is no record of Katy's November appointment with
Jung, she may have seen Mrs. Jung in Küsnacht after she left hospital,
for Mrs. Jung writes on 27 October:

> Küsnacht-Zürich
> Seestrasse 228
> Oct. 27ᵗʰ, 1954

Dear Mrs. Cabot,

Thank you for your kind note and your intention to come and
see me at the Hirslanden. This is to tell you that I am at home again
and feeling much better. I am looking forward to your visit, which
you might combine with that to Onkel. It would be best to ring me
up, when you are in Zürich, so that we can arrange for a day next
week.

> With cordial greetings,
>
> Yours sincerely,
>
> Emma Jung

Linda, still very much involved in her *Villa dei Misteri*, writes:

> 20 Nov. 54

Dear Katy,

after having written to you yesterday night, this morning I
received the coloured photograph. I hasten to thank you for your
speedy help which of course is *invaluable*. Now for once I have
something substantial to show in my course. And you don't know
how much easier it makes things for me, as up to now I always was
so uncertain, whether I could convey a sufficient impression or
not. You will let us know about the costs as soon as you can, please.
The Institute will pay for it. And if you come upon something
more, my dear, you will know that I am always hungry for real
good things.

> Your grateful,
>
> Linda
>
> in a hurry

The above message was written on a card; the letter written the day
before which it mentions, if sent, was not kept. Linda wrote again in
the New Year:

Küsnacht, 29.I.55

My dear Katy,

it is, I am afraid, an endless long time, since you heard from me. Already before middle of last December I fell seriously ill, had an awful Xmas time and New Year and was in no condition to write letters. Now I do feel better again, but I am still pretty weak and in bed part of the day. It has been a trying experience – the less one says about it the better.

So I have not thanked you yet for all you did for me about the new edition of the *Villa dei Misteri*. Just the same you will know, dear Katy, how grateful I am for the trouble you took. I also thank you for your Xmas wishes and little calendar. Even if I couldn't write I was thinking of you and glad to follow your journeys over Europe with the help of your addresses. I do hope you had a nice stay in England with children, grandchildren, and turkeys – especially with the grandchildren, I suppose, as it must be ever so nice for you to watch their development.

If you haven't changed your plans, this letter may come at the right moment to greet you back at San Remo. And perhaps you'll find already the first signs of spring there, which must be wonderful. Here we are still deep in winter and darkness, so that I actually don't mind it much not to be able to go about.

It's a real blessing that this little house of mine is so cosy and comfortable. I have never enjoyed it more than just now. Perhaps, if you come to Zürich again, you'll visit the 'old invalid,' which sounds awful, but as a matter of a fact I have not lost my good humour completely and would love to have a good laugh with you again.

With all my love,
Yours as always,
Linda

By the way I have also now written to the *Libreria dello Stato* and sent lots of Lira to Rome, so I hope the treasure in white and gold will reach me soon.

This was Linda's last letter to my mother. She was terminally ill with cancer, and died peacefully on 6 May 1955 at the age of sixty-four, only thirty months after her husband. The Psychological Club's obituary states that she endured her long, severe illness with great courage. I am not sure whether Katy knew how seriously ill Linda was. She never spoke to me of her in the period before Linda's death, though she had said plenty about Linda earlier! Linda's attendance at my grandmother's funeral may have improved my mother's relationship with her; on the other hand she was probably not happy about Linda's seeing through her disguise on that occasion and writing to her about it. Because Katy could not pull the wool over Linda's eyes, she may have felt vulnerable in her presence. All the same, I heard no more about Linda after the War. Often with Katy, "no news was good news."

After spending Christmas 1954 with us in England, Katy, who sometimes joined us in the mountains, must have returned directly to San Remo, as the following letter from C.A. Meier suggests:

C.A. Meier, Ph.D. Dr. Med.
Steinwiesstr. 37
Zürich 7
18.1.55

My dear Katy,

I hope you have had a very pleasant time with your family in England and this letter will find you in the best of health when you arrive in San Remo. Your kind letter with all the valuable information about America reached me when I arrived in New York. The whole trip was very interesting, but even more tiring. I am still labouring with the exhaustion. I hadn't been aware so much of the strain when I was over there, but in retrospect I must say that the Americans have still got a good deal of their slave driving in their blood. You would not believe it, but I thought Boston was the nicest of all the American towns I have seen. I stayed there 3 days in Prof. Harry Murray's house. The town struck me exactly as any of the English *Kleinstädte* [small towns]. However I don't think I could live there if it was not for Harvard, which is really an extremely fine place. I think America as a whole is in a terrific spiritual confusion and I think it's mainly this fact that exhausted me so much. However I can't tell you more than this in a letter and hope we will have a chance of seeing each other here, where I could give you a lot more details and show you the many color photographs I took.

Much love from Joan and myself to you and Cencio
Yours ever,
Fredy

A month later he writes again:

C.A. Meier
Ph.D. Dr. med.
Steinwiesstr. 37
Zürich 7
15.2.55

Dear Katy,

Many thanks for your letter and postcards. It is always such a pleasure to accompany you on your archaeological discoveries and to be reminded of so many beautiful things we once saw in Italy. However, I have never been in the bowels of St. Peter and as we shall probably be in Rome in April, I should like to ask you what has to be done in order to get permission to visit those excavations. I am growing more disgusted of this world and am looking forward to the vacations and to the final realisation of my old plan to retire somewhere in Southern Italy i.e. somewhere near Paestum. Did you ever get my letter sent to the Majestic? How is San Remo, how are you and how is Cencio, to whom we are both sending our love.

Hoping to see you before long,

much love,

Fredy

Shortly after receiving Fredy's letter Katy received one from Mrs. Jung, who writes:

Küsnacht-Zürich
Seestrasse 228
8.VI.1955

Dear Mrs. Cabot,

It was such bad luck to miss seeing you, but as you stayed only such a short time, it was not possible. When I tried to ring you up your hotel said you had already left. It was very kind of you to send me the lovely azalea; thank you most heartily. It is still wonderfully blooming and the flowers as well as the colours are so delicate and nearly spring like. I hope you have a nice time with your family. Onkel has gone to Bollingen, I am not allowed because of my sciatica (which is better however).

With best wishes for Easter and cordial greetings,

Yours,

Emma Jung

An important event in 1955 was to be Jung's eightieth birthday celebrations. Both the Jung Institute and the Psychological Club were already preparing for the event in the late spring. The Club's Committee sent out a notice on 25 June telling the members that they had found a fine pair of Louis XVI silver candlesticks which cost Sfr 1200. Hardly had they decided to buy them for Jung than a message came from his office that he would be very pleased to receive a dictaphone; it would be of great assistance in his work. The Committee reports that they discussed the matter with a number of members and finally decided to give him both the candlesticks and the dictaphone (which would cost Sfr 1000). In the same letter they remind members that they are expected at the Grand Hotel Dolder on 2 July, when there will be a lecture by Frau Dr. Rivkah Kluger-Schärf. The Committee adds that the subject is a surprise.[1] On 5 July a smaller party was organized for Jung at the Psychological Club. The following day Dr. Jung wrote formally to the Club thanking members for the presents "that rained" upon him! He says he is profoundly thankful, and is especially pleased to have the dictaphone and the candlesticks, and adds that his thank you letter "is written with the assistance of this wonder box which represents the ideal 'secretary!'" The Jung Institute also arranged a reception for Jung at the Grand Hotel Dolder on 25 July at 10:30 a.m., and a second gathering on the following day – a boat trip on the Lake of Zürich, departing from the Bürkliplatz at 4 p.m. and returning at 9:30 p.m., with dinner served on board.

Katy was obviously planning to take part in some of these festivities. She receives the following letter from Joan Meier:

Zürich, 19th of July 1955

Dear Katy,

Many thanks for your kind letter of July 17th. Things look pretty difficult as Fredy is having an official dinner at the 25th and there is the boat trip which lasts till 9.30 p.m. Fredy is in charge of all the official meetings and there will be many colleagues he has to see and will like to see. We have two guests in our house to the 29th which also makes it difficult but not impossible to see Prinzessin Hohenzollern and you. Fredy is working the 27th so that the only possibility I can see would be the 27th or 28th for lunch or dinner. We do not know yet how those very busy days will be shaped under the given circumstances.

---

[1] *Die Königin von Saba* [The Queen of Sheba].

If you arrange something with Klaus and Heinrich Fierz[1] we might join and turn up for a while. As I read from your letter you both will be here the 25ᵗʰ and 26ᵗʰ which makes it very difficult for Fredy.

I think the best would be for you to arrange something and for us to join you if possible.

I am terribly sorry we will be so busy those days and it is a shame not to have the leisure to meet you both with ease. I was very sorry not to have seen more of you the day we had the Club birthday-party. We had to leave sooner for an other party and I did not even have the chance to talk to you.

So please let us know what decisions you make and what sort of an arrangement so that we can join if possible.

We will see you anyhow the 25ᵗʰ at the Dolder Grand.

> With my very best regards,
>
> Yours very sincerely,
>
> Joan

Another letter had been sent by the Committee of the Psychological Club on 18 July to the members, informing them that Frau E. Naeff-Wolff (Toni Wolff's sister) was giving the Club a two-volume work by Maiuri on the *Villa dei Misteri* for the library, in memory of Linda Fierz whose last lectures at the Institute were on that subject. The books are folio-size, the first volume devoted to both the text and black-and-white photographs, and the second to fine color reproductions of the frescoes of the Dionysos mysteries.

Katy drafted the following birthday telegram to Jung:

> Dear Onkel,
>
> You taught me that Life is made up of many things, even thistles.
>
> This brings to you my deep affection and regard on your birthday and many happy returns.
>
> Affectionately Catharine

I knew nothing of the Zürich festivities for Jung in July 1955, nor did I receive a letter on the subject from my mother. Katy had arranged to attend the anniversary in the company of Marie-Alix Hohenzollern; as far as I can ascertain, she went to some of the

---

[1] Two of Linda Fierz's grown-up sons.

parties though not to all. She felt herself to be an outsider in Zürich by the mid-fifties. The prewar and wartime period that she had known so well had vanished forever. For her, postwar Zürich *was a very different place*, as she had written Jung from San Remo in October 1953.

Unfortunately, "thistles" were on the way for Jung after his eightieth birthday celebrations in the summer. In the late autumn, when Katy was back at work in Rome helping the American padre with his charitable activities, she received the following telegram from Joan Meier on 29 November 1955:

> *E morta la Signora Jung funerale mercoledi ore undici*
> Johanna Meier

[Mrs. Jung has died funeral Wednesday at eleven]

The Psychological Club obituary in the *Jahrbuch* states that Mrs. Jung died in her 73rd year after a short but serious illness on 27 November 1955. But in a letter to the Club members the Committee reports that Mrs. Jung had died in the morning of 27 November unexpectedly after a patiently born affliction [*nach geduldig ertragenem Leiden*]. In fact Mrs. Jung had been ill for a long time, and like Linda had kept her illness quiet. After seeing her husband through his eightieth birthday celebrations she quietly left the scene. Emma Jung was the first President of the Psychological Club, and after retiring from the presidency she remained an active member, both serving on the committee and lecturing. She was the unofficial leader of the Jungian group in Zürich, not because she was Jung's wife but because of her own strong and serene personality. Of all the women who surrounded Jung, she was the only one who had not been a patient. My mother, who had difficulty relating to the other psychological women in Zürich, never had any problems with Mrs. Jung, of whom she was very fond. She had been jealous of Mrs. Jung's intellectual ability in her early days in Zürich (her learning Greek and Latin)[1], but that soon gave way to admiration and respect. When I was in my teens she always held Mrs. Jung before me as a rounded personality that we should try to emulate.

---

[1] Her youngest daughter, Mrs. Hoerni, told me that Mrs. Jung began her studies when she was still a small child, and that her studies had also included mathematics. Mrs. Hoerni also remarked that her mother was a great help with homework (information 9.11.97).

After receiving Joan's telegram, Katy replied directly to Jung. The following is the draft of a telegram she sent:

> Professor Carl Jung
> Küsnacht Zurigo
> Svizzera
>
> Stunned and terribly grieved over irreparable loss of Mrs. Jung deepest sympathy dear Onkel
>
> from Catharine Cabot

She also sent Mrs. Jung a last floral tribute but did not attend the funeral, although she returned to Zürich shortly afterward; it was her habit to be in Zürich in December to do her Christmas shopping. Because of Mrs. Jung's death, the Psychological Club decided to cancel the Club's Christmas party which normally took place in a private room at a Zürich restaurant. The Committee proposed instead that the members meet at the Club on 17 December at 7 p.m. for a small Christmas celebration and a modest meal, an occasion for which Katy was present. Before leaving Switzerland again, she received the following undated latter from Carol Baumann. It must have been written early December 1955, shortly after Mrs. Jung's funeral, and in it she writes:

> Dear Katy: –
> Possibly this will catch you before you go to England or the Riviera? It was pleasant to have your good letter, last Xmas & to catch a glimpse of you at Jung's birthday celebration. ... I think you did speak to Peggy [her daughter] at the Jung celebrations? I have 4 grandchildren too now – ... Unfortunately I have not seen the last two!
> We were all so overwhelmed in losing Mrs. Jung – such a huge gap in our ranks. But she had a beautiful death, & it is such a blessing that she could go without a long lingering illness. The night before she died, she said good-bye to each member of family & the next day slipped away in her sleep. I went to see her lying-in-state – like a medieval Queen – so *beautiful* & serene in the solemn majesty of Death ... Dr. Jung is getting on remarkably well, in his deep sorrow. Ruth Bailey has come to keep house for him – you know she was friends of both, & has often visited here & in

Bollingen, & knows all the ropes. She just lost (in Oct.) her last living brother – so everything fits together well.

Let me know when you pass through Zürich again & come to see my house!

Every wish for Christmas & the coming year!

Most sincerely,

Carol Baumann

By year's end a gaping hole had opened in the ranks of the Jungian group in Zürich. Toni had died in 1953, followed by Linda Fierz and then Emma Jung in 1955. It was depressing for Katy to lose these people who had become friends and had been part of her life in Zürich for the past twenty-five years. Though Jung was still alive, with their passing much of the cohesion of the early Jungians was lost. Jung himself was growing older and so was less able to lead the ever expanding Jungian group. Katy herself felt less and less the need to be in Zürich, though occasionally she had an analytical hour with Fredy Meier or was forced to Zürich for medical reasons.

Chapter Fifteen

1956-1960

Katy spent Christmas 1955 in Rome rather than in England, as we were leaving with the children for a skiing holiday in Switzerland on 26 December 1955. As it happened, she was struck down right after Christmas with an affliction which her Italian doctor could not diagnose; having no faith in Italian doctors (particularly after Pat's mis-diagnosis), she immediately left for Zürich on 27 December. On the 28th she was ensconced at the Klinik Hirslanden where she stayed several weeks. The doctor diagnosed a serious intestinal infection, but also said that she must lose weight, so she was put on a severe diet and lost ten kilos while at the clinic. In a letter to her brother-in-law Ralph Bradley she says the diet "was awfully hard to stick to, but I feel light & healthy, so it was worth it!" As I have mentioned previously, Katy was a *bon viveur* who could not eat moderately and who, as she grew older, had to take time off to lose weight, either by doing "fruit days" or following a strict diet in a clinic.

When she was not working for Canon Shreve or traveling, Katy was in correspondence with friends and relatives, chiefly about health. Her father-in-law Godfrey Cabot had had his ninety-fifth birthday in February 1956, and Katy was determined he must live to be a hundred. She wrote on 28 March 1956 to Ralph Bradley:

> I was interested in what you wrote about Grandpa Cabot & how difficult it was for you all to prevent him doing foolish things as to his health. Can't you represent to him, how *he owes it to all of us* to stay well and reach his hundredth birthday and that he should look after himself for *our* sakes, if not his own. It would mean a lot to

his children to celebrate with him *such* an outstanding birthday, and he should *not* rob them of that *pleasure!* He should have vitamin injections & a good doctor to look after him who doesn't mind him being irritable, for at that age one has to be understanding. ... He should also perhaps have 'hormones' as they are very strengthening, but they of course have to be gone into with a specialist, as I really don't know how they would affect a man of ninety-five.

Hormone treatment was in its infancy, but Katy, consulting a modern gynecologist in Zürich, was already very much into hormones for herself. Her letter crossed one from her brother-in-law, who writes that he is glad that she is well again and back at work in Rome, and then says:

> Why do you continue to try to give advice as to what to do with Mr. Cabot and how to keep him from catching cold and getting chills, etc. etc.!! How completely you misunderstand the situation.
> The Old Gentleman does just what he God damn pleases to do. He goes out in the snow – at least he did yesterday; kept himself from falling by catching his balance against the piles of snow that are 6' high. He wore no galoshes. ...

A month later Ralph writes:

> I cannot refrain from smiling at your continued desire to give advice as to what to do with Mr. Cabot. It would be wonderful if you could give advice as to how to make him do any of these things that you recommend other than by binding his hands behind his back with handcuffs, and choking him so that he has got to swallow willy-nilly. However your efforts are not completely wasted as I shall take unto myself the hormones, vitamins etc.

Godfrey never took any of the medicines Katy suggested, but the "Old Gentleman" managed to keep alive and celebrate his hundredth birthday with most of his family. I flew to Boston for the celebrations; Pat stayed at home as did the children who were at school. My mother, after repeatedly saying she wanted to be at the party, declined to travel to Boston. She gave no reason, but knowing her, I imagine that the thought of meeting all the family again *en masse* deterred her. Grandpa enjoyed his party and was pleased to receive birthday greetings from President Eisenhower and a visit from the

Mayor of Boston – as well as congratulations from a female admirer who had chatted with him when he still strode through the Boston Common in his nineties en route to his office. Godfrey lived another thirty months and died on 2 November 1962 (Katy's birthday) at the age of one hundred and one years and three quarters.

On 1 September 1956 Pat and I with our eldest son Michael, aged twelve, met my mother at Venice to embark on an archaeological tour to Greece and Turkey and the Lebanon. We traveled on the *S.S. Proleterka*, a Jugoslav ship which after the War had been sliced in two, enlarged, then rejoined! This information was not very comforting; the "experts" among the passengers who revealed it said that the ship could break apart in a storm. But, they added philosophically, we were traveling at the best time of year. In fact we had perfect weather the whole way there and back. Every evening we had lectures on the sites we would visit the following day. All this archaeology and art, the intellectual atmosphere, and the friendly British passengers kept my mother in a serene mood. To my relief the trip was a success. We parted in Venice, we three returning to England with the other passengers by *Wagons-lits* and my mother staying on in Venice for the *Biennale*, where she took to bed with one of her "awful colds." Katy felt out of sorts from this, and abandoned by us, I suppose, though Cencio reappeared very promptly while she was there. But after the serenity of the trip I was due for a string of reproaches. Writing from Ascona, before telling me about Venice she began with a long harangue, reproaching me for not giving her the results of a medical intervention I had undergone on my return to England. She had had a dream, she said, which she took seriously as she always had premonitions via dreams.[1] She writes: "This dream was particularly disagreeable. ... It said quite distinctly: 'It is more than a curetage!' Then all my serenity fell off me like a cloak and I rolled up my sleeves and got busy." First she enquired about my health from her friend Odette Roy in Lausanne, who had recently been in touch with me, and who assured Katy that I was well. Then my mother reproached me for not writing (though in fact I had, my letter not being immediately forwarded). But that did not finish the matter. Now in possession of a few details, Katy began to diagnose the doctor's

---

[1] This dream was wrong; it was nothing more than a curetage, an alternative method to hormones for curing severe menstrual bleeding. But on other occasions she *did* have dream premonitions which came true. One still haunts us, which she had a few months before her death in 1976.

diagnosis in depth, making a big thing of something very minor. I did
not let myself get scared by her wrath; I was familiar with these
harangues, though it made me feel uncomfortable to have her still
meddling, which even only on paper by now was loathsome all the
same, for it expressed her continuing desire to dominate me. In
medical matters my mother always knew better and constantly gave
advice, so I avoided giving her details of illnesses or even reporting
them.[1]

When Katy had finally finished on the subject of my health, the
letter became interesting. She described her chance meeting in a
pharmacy with the Italian artist Giorgio de Chirico,[2] whom she knew
already. When she rose from her sickbed she went out to buy
medicines and found de Chirico stocking up with medications himself.

> From that moment on I began to enjoy Venice more and more.
> … De Chirico asked me to go again to the Bienale with him and it
> was just too much fun! First we visited his own 'room' (a large
> room chuck full of his work and which he had arranged in May)
> and then we visited many other pavilions (each nation has its own
> pavilion) and he explained so much and we laughed so much over
> the awful moderns where you can make [neither] head nor tail of
> anything, and in general it was most instructive, as well as a most
> hilarious visit, because de Chirico is just full of fun and humor and
> wit. He then invited me to lunch and there I met his wife, who is
> Russian and *most* attractive. After that we went to the Delacroix
> exhibition on piazza San Marco, which is also part of the *Bienale,*
> that was a great treat. I really don't know Delacroix well at all, but
> with de Chirico I got to know him much better. He is fabulous and
> what struck me with Delacroix (and also with de Chirico) such
> artists are *incapable* of bad taste. Even a dead man or wounded
> man is so beautifully done, that you don't get a 'disagreeable'
> feeling. (I remember this spring in Spain the same impression with

---

[1] On the Hellenic cruise my mother and I had almost formed a relationship,
but the reproaches in the first half of her letter killed it. In later years she
sometimes asked me how it was possible for me to have a good relationship
with my own daughters. The question perplexed her because from early
childhood I had instinctively fought my mother to avoid her smothering
my personality.

[2] Giorgio de Chirico was born at Volos near Athens in 1888, and died in
Rome in 1978.

Goya's paintings of gruesome firing-squads, but they weren't grue-some, one just had the feeling they were magnificent *that is art*.) I don't mean I don't like 'Modern Art,' I just don't care about these abstractions, zig-zags in color and one has to guess what the artist means, for the titles of these pictures are: 'Solitude,' 'Happiness,' Thoughts on a May Morning,' 'Adolescence' etc. *ad infinitum*. De Chirico was pointing out the worst ones (those awful collages) and saying: *"Questo sarebbe bello per la vostra living-room!"* [That would be lovely for your living-room.]

For some time I had been asking my mother to sit for a portrait. But she was not keen on the conventional English portrait painters, even when they were R.A.s, and I, who was paying for the painting, was not keen on their enormous prices; so we got no further. Most likely it was on the day Katy spent with de Chirico at the *Bienale* that they hatched the plot that he would paint her portrait. There was no suggestion of this in the letter, but soon after her meeting with de Chirico, when the sittings were almost over, she casually told me that he was painting her portrait and charging a much reduced fee. This of course attracted me at first, until I remembered de Chirico's style of painting. Though he may have said to Katy that he didn't like modern painting, to me his work was very "modern," and so I became apprehensive, but I could do nothing before a *fait accompli*. Sooner than I expected a large crate was delivered at our front door at Blackboys in Sussex. When I opened it and began removing the wrapping, I saw the framed portrait of an unknown woman. The frame was nice, even conventional, but when I realized that the picture was supposed to portray my mother, I was shocked. The face that gazed up at me was that of a *nouveau riche* mid-western housewife; it was too round, the aquiline "Rush nose" was squashed and snub, the upper lip was thick, the skin on the neck and arms was greyish, the hair was a hard battleship grey and the eyes were also grey instead of light blue, but they had her determined *"Oison"* expression![1] What was visible of the dress was hideous. The pearl necklace was the only thing that came out well – the pearls were luminous – but the double row of large fake pearls the artist had created was thoroughly vulgar. (As we had been so stingy for her 60th birthday, she hinted, she could not wear her own *real* pearls for the portrait as they would have looked too forlorn!) I was shocked at the

---

[1] The bird caricature I drew of my mother in my youth had a lively eye.

poor likeness as well as the style of painting, and told my mother so, but she insisted that it was a *conventional* portrait. After all, she had an attractive hair-do, was wearing a dress, jewelry and make-up! In a previous full-length portrait by the French artist Verna,[1] who lived near Ascona (Katy had sat for her several years earlier), Katy was painted lounging in a chair wearing slacks and holding a cigarette holder and cigarette; she wore a band in her hair and bright red lipstick, looking like an ancient version of a rebellious teenager or hippie. Even Katy must have had second thoughts about offering me that awful picture, though she liked its unconventional style. The de Chirico was conventional compared to the Verna, but far from the classical portrait I had commissioned. However, making a fuss about the de Chirico portrait was a waste of time; I was doomed to keep it. That I was supposed to be grateful that such a famous painter had done it was obvious.

When my Uncle Ralph and Aunt Eleanor (my father's sister) came to visit us in Sussex in 1957, I had already been the proud possessor of the portrait for several months. As Ralph Bradley was himself an artist, I showed it to him and my aunt immediately, being particularly keen to have his professional opinion. I knew that unlike myself he would be unprejudiced. With some trepidation I produced the portrait, but I need not have worried that he would approve of it. After one glance it was obvious that both my aunt and uncle were shocked at such a picture. Knowing the Bradleys were due to visit me in England, Katy had attempted to prepare Ralph for the portrait by

---

[1] Germaine Verna, born in 1908, was a French post-Impressionist who had settled in a farmhouse on a hill above Ascona with her husband. Though I disliked her portrait, I found her landscapes and Ascona scenes well-painted. One of these hangs in the *Musée National d'Art Moderne* in Paris (see Maximilien Gautier, *Verna* [Edition les Gemeaux, Paris, 1953]). Apart from painting, the Vernas' mutual hobby was taking in stray dogs. There seemed to be at least twenty or more when we visited them at feeding time one evening. The smell of the food was revolting. But my mother and I had no time to ponder on what they were feeding because a fire was fast approaching the property, conveyed by dry grass. Immediately we were given buckets and told to help put out the flames. In the meantime the Vernas used a hose then beat the flames with sticks when the water pressure became too low. At the crucial moment, as the flames were licking the grass beyond the fence, the wind subsided enough for the ineffective hose to keep the fire at bay.

commenting on it in a long letter written from Klinik Hirslanden where once more she was undergoing a slimming cure.

Janey insisted she wished to have a portrait of me. (I almost fell over when she wrote me of her desire.) She left the choice of artist to me though she is footing the bill! I chose a friend of mine, an Italian artist of about seventy odd years, who was very famous in his youth and worked in Paris[1] with the Impressionist School, becoming one of them. He painted me as he saw me and which to me seems to be, *as I am!* When Janey received it, she had an awful shock. I think she expected a "British Duchess"; and instead received, as she said, a "midwestern American woman"; who surely must have as a *pendantif* [appendage] a husband smoking a huge cigar, wearing a ten Gallon hat!! I explained to her, that having had an ancestor who drove a herd of cattle from East to West, that probably I 'inherited' something from him and the artist *lifted the veil*!! Certainly, it is a *vivid* (the colors are *brilliant*. He mixes his own!) *living*, thing, which would be hard to live with unless you could have a curtain to draw over it at times for it has brought out many inner characteristics and looks as if it might jump out of the frame & speak to you! Janey had it photographed, by an excellent portrait photographer in London and I'll send you a photo of it when I get one made. It will interest you from the artist's point of view. Maybe she showed it to you when you were at Possingworth? She keeps it in her boudoir.

In spite of Katy's enthusiastic letter, Ralph replied succinctly, "We saw the portrait. The artist must have had some ulterior motive for showing you as he does. I shall continue to think of you as a lovely person."

Everybody to whom I showed the portrait, and who knew Katy, agreed it was dreadful. I puzzled for a long time on the reason why Katy was so attached to it. Eventually I came to the conclusion that it was her *enfant terrible* side which liked it. Not only did it give her a *biricchina* expression (the English "mischievous" does not quite convey the meaning), but I felt also that she took a certain pleasure in annoying me by singing its praises! My own favorite portrait of my mother was painted by my Great Aunt Lilla Cabot Perry in the nineteen twenties. Katy snubbed it because it was done by a relative.

---

[1] Where Germaine Verna met him.

Aunt Lilla (Godfrey Cabot's elder sister) and her husband spent many years in France and were close friends of Monet. She studied painting with Monet at Giverny and became famous; her pictures hang in several American museums, and four of her portraits hang at the *Musée d'Art Américain* at Giverny near Paris. The museum advertised its 1997 exhibition with a poster of *The Green Hat*, a portrait by Lilla Cabot Perry of her daughter.

Less than a month after our return from the cruise, the Suez Crisis and the Hungarian Uprising took place. Europeans suddenly realized how unstable was the peace which they had been enjoying since 1945. American tourists and even permanent residents began buying tickets to return home. To preserve supplies of gasoline, the Swiss government restricted the use of private cars on weekends. Katy began using her wartime bicycle again. In England there were no restrictions, but in Italy a black market in coal and sugar soon began to flourish. By Christmas 1956 the political situation had grown quiet, and Katy spent the holiday with us in England. But her mail went to her permanent address in San Remo. Jung writes to her there:

December 29th, 1956

Mrs. Katy Cabot
Villa Aloha
San Remo

My dear Katy,
thank you for your nice Christmas-card. It is awfully good of you to invite me to your enviable San Remo-place with all its delights. Unfortunately I cannot avail myself of your kindness since I am afraid of the long trip and the inevitable effort involved. I have to live quietly and more or less withdrawn from the adventures of the world. Though my state of health gives me no cause for serious complaints.
Many thanks for your kind and generous intentions.

Hoping you will have a good New Year, I remain,

Yours cordially

C.G. Jung

There is no correspondence extant between Katy and Zürich Jungians in 1957, but sometime during 1958 Katy saw Jung again. She did not write up the hour meticulously as she used to. By chance, however, I found notes of this session tucked away in a book, written on thin blue sheets of airmail paper, in a mixture of shorthand and longhand. When I discovered this document I realized that it was by using this combination that she had been able to take down Jung's words as he spoke, for Katy also wrote longhand very fast. Years later, when I gave C.A. Meier my mother's Jung diaries to read, I checked with him how it was possible for her to retain so much detail of her analytical hours. He explained that during sessions with him Katy scribbled notes at high speed as he spoke,[1] and he guessed she had done the same with Jung. While the following notes are undated, Jung's age is given as eighty-three, and so they must have been written in 1958. The subject is the *puer* or Don Juan type man. Eight years had passed since Katy had met Cencio, yet they were still not married. She must have been wondering why there was such a deadlock in their relationship. The notes are difficult to read and rather dis-jointed, but it is possible to gather that first Jung explains the temperament of Don Juan type men and then illustrates his thinking with examples of well-known puers of the period. Though Katy must have felt the need to have the Don Juan temperament explained to her by Jung, she does not seem particularly unhappy. In fact she appears to have reached the degree of inner serenity which Linda Fierz told her came as one grew older. Katy writes the following notes in a mixture of shorthand and longhand:

Told Onkel how happy I was in old age. He said that I owed a lot to my naturalness. The standardized people, the monkey takes them from behind. Onkel prevented my getting standardized and keeps me liquid; that's the trick my outlook *is as it was* (when young). I'm flowing along with people I'm not stiff, I'm not *figée* [stiff] – that keeps one's sense of humor. Schopenhauer said it's the only divine quality of man. Those *stiff* standardized people are apt to get *silly & senile*. I stuck *to main things love never ceases* when it comes along in a natural way. Don Juan men, they have an immortal mother complex & by *nature* a good flair, they are too Catholic & then their creative fantasies are caught in the form of church – mostly paralyzing. It doesn't matter if they are pious or not. The Church is the biggest building in the village. It's uncon-scious, a form of life about which they don't reflect. One just *lives*

---

[1] She wrote up in detail some sessions with Meier.

"church" without reflection. A *Kollege*, of Onkel, says: I don't see why Jung bothers about psychology, Rome answers all. *Keep fluid*!

Italian women are expressed by the madonna. Their mental life is in ecclesiastical forms. In France in their blood, too, but *they rationalize it*. The Italians just *live* it. You never find a Frenchman who is *in* or *out* of the church – [if out of the Church] then he is an atheist. (Anglo Saxon & Swiss are in Sects.) [They do not become atheists.] The typical Atheist is in France & in Italy. *French like a rational explanation*; for out of their Catholic Christianity, a certain rationalization has developed. Descartes, *Diderot* [1] developed that French rationalism. A French Hugenot is terribly rationalistic & his imagination is in the church & they [Hugenots] are most disagreeable. *Pederastes*: their sexuality is caught by the mother – when her feelings are too sophisticated. I constellate the mother complex for Jerome.[2] The eternal Don Juan, unable to stick to one woman, cos she isn't the mother.

Worst complex of mother:

1st *boys*

2nd *Don Juanism*

or a terrible kind of marriage (married a woman who was the contrary of the mother – an evil woman.)

They [Don Juans] are looking for that steady value, which they themselves don't possess. In relation to a woman, they don't find it. The unconscious settles on a woman & [then] it emigrates – it's always another woman – as long as they themselves don't change. That's for homos also.

Don Juans: In oncoming age, they steady & have loss of sexuality.

[such] people don't develop & are afraid of what might happen to them. If they develop, they must take up something new & dark and it could cause difficulties. (A man who avoids 'difficulties' gets nowhere. He doesn't gain life by avoiding it.) They are prejudiced against life. Monty[3] on bad terms with many people. Churchill is a bully, in his personal life – most difficult. Monty wasn't agreeable with his colleagues, he likes to be with 'detractors.' Such *big* people are great for what they *do*, but for other things, they haven't

---

[1] René Descartes (1596-1650), French philosopher and man of science, and Denis Diderot (1713-1784), French man of letters and encyclopedist.

[2] Pseudonym for Cencio. He had been a Don Juan until he met Katy!

[3] Field-Marshal Viscount Sir Bernard Montgomery.

enough *resistance*. People of extra intelligence have an inferior feeling. Successful men, a miserable family life. Churchill wonderful humor – a terrible bully in personal relations. Monty can't stand someone beside him. So many people dislike him – a disagreeable *ton*. Monty rebuffed, and had to fight for his career. (Onkel was punished for having written a good thesis.) It means for a young boy, who comes from nowhere, discouragement in his best efforts. Monty made bitter experiences. (People told Onkel he hadn't written his own books.) Monty depended on old boys, conservative and lazy, to think further. It makes these [clever] people bitter and sarcastic [to have to rely on lesser brains?]. When you feel that Auchinlek[1] must have felt terribly – the way Monty takes hold of a situation – he did it with *ressentiment* & did it in a sharp & reckless way – *C'est le ton qui fait la musique*. Monty received people in ridiculous garments – a thought out simplicity or matter of factness. 'I don't respect you. I don't dress to see you.' Monty received the German Generals in that kit.[2] [If] one dines out with people in short sleeves & apron one does not feel 'received.' It's impolite. Monty has a resentment, an unmistakable sign & symptom of one who had an inferiority complex – had to fight his way against *unjust* prejudices. De Gaulle wrote a good book about mechanized war[fare] & he got a terrible *ressentiment* [because it was not appreciated?]. De Gaulle and Monty have conscious resentments. They couldn't do a *thing* because 'old brass hats' were against them. Onkel is sarcastic to a great professor, "Well this academical idiocy. ..." A sarcastic remarks hits the nail on the head. A professor says, "most interesting" (but dangerous) & then Onkel says: "Who doesn't risk something ... one must 'risk' it."

To push through all those stuffed shirts & tin soldiers! and old brass hats! gets nowhere.

P.S. Onkel said he's not interested in Procaine, as he'd get *too energetic* & would undertake more work & he feels *now* he'd like to take things *easy* – that he's done enough work. He says that [doctor] Haemerli[3] being twenty years younger & looking after so

---

[1] Field-Marshal Sir Claude Auchinlek was appointed Supreme Commander over the three services (Navy, Army, Air) in 1942.

[2] When Germany capitulated in 1945.

[3] A brother of the Dr. Haemerli who looked after Jung in 1944, and who died shortly afterwards.

many patients *should* take it, but that he feels that at eighty-three he'd best not engender all that energy!!!

Katy should have been a doctor, for her enthusiasm for treating people was insatiable, and she was always alert to new treatments, believing that pills could cure all ills and living by that belief herself. As for the main theme in the session, Katy rarely discussed the Cencio problem with me. She told me that he was against trying to obtain an annulment, thinking it would be a waste of money and bring no result. Katy liked to appear "modern," and so pretended that it was all right to have a boyfriend, but in reality she was old fashioned and loathed not being able to legalize her union with Cencio. By 1958 she had been a widow for twenty-eight years. Both men she had been really fond of lacked the energy to make a really serious effort to free themselves from their failed marriages. In this last recorded hour with Jung, he explains fully the Don Juan type to Katy, the type she always fell for, the type opposite to her father. She herself was always stable in her relationships, never wanting to change partners when she was in love. Whenever I was in their company, both Cencio and Katy gave a serene impression.

Fortunately for Katy, four years after her last interview with Jung an unexpected event played into her hand. Late in 1962 Cencio's wife suddenly died. She had been ailing for years, but her death had not been considered imminent. After a three-month period of mourning, Cencio and Katy were married on 25 April 1963 in London at the Jesuit Church, St. Mary's, Farm Street. A bishop, the Rev. Alistair Russell and the Rev. Cyril Plummer from Uckfield, Sussex officiated. Cencio's sister and nephew came from Italy, and a number of relatives and friends from both families attended. But so many psychological friends from her Zürich days had died by the time Katy and Cencio were finally married that the only people from the "old days" who came to London were Princess Marie-Alix and her husband, Prince Franz-Joseph Hohenzollern. Among the guests from other parts of Switzerland were Erich Maria Remarque and his wife Paulette Goddard whom Katy knew from Ascona. After the ceremony Pat and I gave a luncheon party at Claridge's for about thirty-five guests.

Katy continued to send flowers to Jung after Mrs. Jung's death. Despite his great age, he was always punctilious in thanking Katy. Late in 1958 he writes:

Prof. Dr. C.G. Jung
Küsnacht-Zürich
Seestrasse 228
5 December 1958

Dear Mrs. Cabot,

thank you ever so much for the beautiful flowers you have sent me from the Riviera. It was a miraculous contrast to the cold and misty week we are passing through. This is just to send you my greeting and my best Christmas wishes and also for the New Year, towards which we are just rolling on.

I am sorry to hear that you undergo a severe cure. I hope it is nothing really serious.

It was nice to hear of you again.

Cordially,

C.G. Jung

In her later years, Katy was forced to do more frequent "severe cures" because she was still eating and drinking far too much. This affected not only her heart and liver but eventually also her circulation. Thanks to her strong constitution, and despite all the remedies she swallowed, in 1958 she was still pretty fit.

The last message Katy was to receive from Jung was written on a "thank you" form printed in English and dated July 1960, for the flowers, telegrams and letters on the occasion of his 85th birthday. He writes in his own hand:

Sorry to have missed you at the feast! These celebrations *have* been exhausting. I am just coming up for air. No visitors for me for now and for a long time!

It has almost wrecked me.

I had no idea, you were in Zürich and for such a regrettable purpose. I am glad to hear that Dr. Haemerli has read me *twice*.

My best wishes and thanks. Yours cordially,

C.G. Jung

Dr. Haemerli-Steiner was the brother of Dr. Haemerli-Schindler who was Jung's doctor during his severe illness in 1944, and who died suddenly while Jung was still in hospital. He was a specialist in internal medicine, and treated my mother for her digestion which was often strained because of her love for rich food. The regrettable purpose Jung mentions is yet another stay at the Klinik Hirslanden to rest her liver and lose weight. Not only did Katy enter clinics to lose weight, but she needed time to be by herself as she found it difficult to introvert at home. Luckily clinics were less sought after in those days, so it was possible to stay on as long as one wanted. By that time Katy was enjoying her American old-age insurance which helped pay her medical expenses.

I have found no further communications between Onkel and his "Niece" after the occasion of Jung's birthday in 1960.

Epilogue

Jung died the following year, on June 6, 1961. The funeral took place on 9 June at the Reformed Church at Küsnacht. With Jung's death an era ended. The small group which he had founded had expanded more and more rapidly as the years passed, especially after the creation of the Jung Institute in 1947. The whole style of Jungian analysis evolved, becoming more professional. Friendships between analyst and analysands were discouraged, and professional secrecy became all-important. Gossiping between patient and analyst became strictly taboo, though the older analysts found it difficult to stop the habit. The same ethics as those of medical doctors were prescribed, though not always adopted, for non-medical as well as medical psychologists. The analyst was no longer supposed to adapt his treatment to suit a particular patient. The more regimented Freudian school began to influence Jungians, and rules for treating mental illnesses were devised. Therapists had fewer neurotic patients willing to pay for treatment and took on more borderline and psychotic cases. So seeing patients socially, as had been the practice in the 1930s and 1940s, went out of favor. When contact was restricted to the office, however, much useful information was lost to the therapist.

The last of the first-generation analysts[1] who worked with Jung in Zürich was Professor C.A. Meier, who died in November 1995 at the age of ninety. He was my mother's analyst from 1945 until her death

---

[1] Marie-Louise von Franz died in 1998 – she was much younger than the other "first-generation" Jungians.

in 1976, and my own analyst from 1976 to 1986. My mother's work with him was intermittent as she spent less and less time in Zürich. In the early 1980s Fredy Meier read the "Diary" of my mother's analysis with Jung, made some corrections and suggestions, and encouraged me to publish it. But the time was not yet ripe for publication. A well-known older American analyst to whom I sent the manuscript for his opinion, a pupil of Jung, said categorically that it should not be published, his reason being that it was uncomplimentary to Jung. He returned my ms. with a very cool note, but obviously thought it had value because he kept a copy for himself. I took his advice and put the document on ice.

Ten years later a younger analyst, a friend of the older one, was helping him move house when by chance my ms. came to light in his effects. He read it, and was of a very different opinion. He did not think it would be damaging to Jung; in fact he was so enthusiastic about the recorded sessions of the analysis that he requested permission from me to discuss them with a group of professionals in his area. I gave him permission but requested a tape of the discussion, and also asked to have my original ms. returned. He sent me the tape but refused to return the ms., saying that it meant a lot to him and so he was keeping it. When I told Fredy Meier of the incident he was shocked. But as he was getting older, I did not feel I should ask him to intervene in retrieving my document. By then it had also been suggested to me that the record of my mother's analysis with Jung would be more interesting if I wove into it her family history, including not only her relationship with her parents but also the tale of our own relationship during my childhood, adolescence and married life. This task in fact partly brought one of my mother's aims into being, for, realizing that she had lived through a very interesting period, she had kept letters to and from friends, relatives, and also analysts and other members of the Zürich Jung group, intending to write her memoirs. In mid October 1972, three and one-half years before her death, Katy wrote to her son-in-law Pat Reid from San Remo about her intention to write an account of her thirty years in analysis with Jung. She said, "I must 'get down' to my Jung memoires, after November 15th in Ascona as here it is impossible to get down to *anything*." Katy never did get down to writing her memories, but she had kept a great number of valuable documents which have been a great help to me.

Also of great help to me was Fredy Meier, who in 1992 gave me his valuable time and answered questions, offering information about people mentioned in the diary of whom I knew little, or had met only fleetingly as a child, or had never met at all. Fredy Meier would have been the ideal person to write an introduction to this record, because not only did he know my mother well but also he lived through the whole period she records and was himself a close collaborator of Jung's. Sadly, however, he died before the editing was completed.

My mother's diaries are a personal record, yet a forceful voice among those witnesses to Jung's life and works. She understood Jung better than many. This Captain's daughter and this Uncle's niece was always more her own woman than she ever realized herself to be. With my contribution to the book, I hope to have emphasized her qualities.

List of Illustrations

(The copyright remains with the photographer / source, to the extent this could be determined. Heartfelt thanks to all who supplied material.)

Bibliography

Helena G. Allen, *The Betrayal of Liliuokalani, Last Queen of Hawaii 1838-1917*. Mutual Publishing, Honolulu, 1982

E. Digby Baltzell, *Puritan Boston and Quaker Philadelphia*. Transaction, New Brunswick & London, 1996.

Mary Bancroft, *Autobiography of a Spy*. William Morrow & Co., New York, 1983. [Mary Bancroft Rüfenacht.]

Carol Baumann, "Tierpsyche und menschliche Psyche. Referat und Kommentar und Vergleichsmaterial über die *Seele der Weissen Ameisen*, von Eugène Marais." Lecture, the Psychological Club of Zürich, November 1940.

E. A. Bennett, *Meetings with Jung*. Daimon, Zürch, 1985.

Eleanor Cabot Bradley, *Stories from My Life*. Memoirs Unlimited, Beverly, Mass., 1998.

John M. Bradley, *Everything was an Adventure*. Memoirs Unlimited, Beverly, Mass., 1992.

Webster Bull, *My Father, My Brother*. Memoirs Unlimited, Beverly, MA, 1996.

Catharine Rush Cabot, "Basel and Northwest Switzerland," "Lake Leman," "Tessin." In *Switzerland*, eds. Dore Ogrizek and J. G. Rüfenacht. B.O.R. Zürich, 1947.

——, "Die Schweizer durch eine amerikanische Brille." Tr. Toni Wolff. *Annabelle*, August 1945.

John S. D. Eisenhower, *Intervention! The United States and the Mexican Revolution, 1913-1917*. W. W. Norton, New York & London, 1993.

Linda Fierz, *Der Liebestraum des Poliphilo*. Rhein Verlag, Zürich, 1947. Tr. Mary Hottinger, *The Dream of Poliphilo: The Soul in Love*. Pantheon, New York, 1950; reprint, Spring Publications, Dallas, 1987.

——, *Psychologische Betrachtungen zu der Freskenfolge der Villa dei Misteri in Pompei: Ein Versuch.* The Psychological Club of Zürich [mimeograph], 1957. Tr. Gladys Phelan, *Women's Dionysian Initiation: The Villa of Mysteries in Pompei.* Spring Publications, Dallas, 1988.

Maximilien Gautier, *Verna.* Edition les Gemeaux, Paris, 1953.

Doris Kearns Goodwin, *No Ordinary Time.* Simon & Schuster, New York, 1994.

John Guenther, *Inside Europe.* Hamish Hamilton, London, 1938.

Barbara Hannah, *Jung: His Life and Work.* Putnam, New York, 1976, and Michael Joseph, London, 1977.

Leon Harris, *Only to God.* Atheneum, New York, 1967.

Hawaii's Story by Hawaii's Queen. Charles Tuttle, Rutland & Tokyo, 1964. C.G. Jung, *The Collected Works.* Princeton University Press/The Bollingen Foundation (Bollingen Series XX), Princeton, 20 vols.

Memories, Dreams, Reflections by C.G. Jung. Compiled and edited by Aniela Jaffe, Pantheon, New York, 1962.

Collected Works of C.G. Jung. Princeton University Press, Princeton (1953-1976).

S. Levenkron, *Treating and Overcoming Anorexia Nervosa.* Charles Scribner's Sons, New York, 1982.

Magnus Ljunggren, *The Russian Mephisto.* Stockholm, 1994.

J. P. Marquand, *Sincerely, Willis Wade.* Little, Brown & Co., Boston/Toronto, 1955.

Paul Mellon, *Reflections in a Silver Spoon.* William Morrow & Co., New York, 1992.

Leonard Mosely, *Dulles.* Dial Press/James Wade, New York, 1978.

Doré Ogrizek and J. G. Rüfenacht, eds., *Switzerland.* B.O.R. Zürich, 1947.

Jane Cabot Reid, "A History of the Psychological Club in Zürich." 1995. Die Geschichte des Psychologischen Clubs, Zürich, 1997.

——, "Der Gang zum Brunnen des Lebens: Geschichte einer Regression." *Analytische Psychologie* 21 (1990), 81-97.

——, "Der lebenswichtige Vater." *Analytische Psychologie* 17 (1986), 38-56.

——, *Ten Lunar Months.* William Heinemann Medical Books, London, 1956.

P. R. Reid, *The Colditz Story.* Hodder & Stoughton, London, 1952.

——, *The Latter Days.* Hodder & Stoughton, London, 1953.

Gitta Sereny, *Albert Speer: His Battle with Truth.* Macmillan, London, 1995.

Toni Wolff, "Aus Aldous Huxleys *Die Graue Eminenz*: Eine Untersuchung über Religion und Politik." Lecture, the Psychological Club of Zürich, March 1945.

Index

Regina Abt, Irmgard Bosch, Vivienne MacKrell
Dream Child

Creation and New Life in Dreams of Pregnant Women

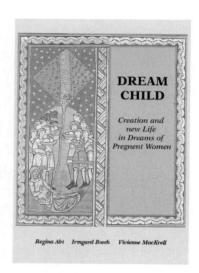

The spiritual dimension of pregnancy has been overshadowed in recent times by the dramatic developments in scientific and medical realms. The sense of wonder and mystery at the creation of new human life is ever more ignored in the wake of so many innovative technical developments.

Once-awesome religious rites and traditions that accompanied the dangerous and significant transitions of life – such as birth, puberty, marriage, illness and death, as well as pregnancy – are hardly to be found in much of today's world. A pregnant woman often feels spiritually isolated and at odds with herself.

This book consists of a rich selection of contemporary dreams from many lands, chosen from a collection of some 700 dreams. They are psychologically interpreted and can offer orientation and stimulation not only for pregnant women, but for all who are concerned with the great questions of pregnancy, birth and life's transitions.

As … the foetus repeats the biological evolution, so is the creation of the universe psychically repeated in the birth of each human being; for, the universe only exists for us to the extent that it exists in our consciousness. This is what Jung calls the cosmogonic meaning of human consciousness.

– Marie-Louise von Franz, from the Foreword

hardcover, 480 pages, richly illustrated, ISBN 3-85630-592-0

E.A. Bennet
Meetings with Jung

In this collection of diary entries made by British psychiatrist E.A. Bennet during his visits with the Swiss analyst C.G. Jung over a 15-year period, Bennet's colorfully spontaneous accounts reveal Jung's down-to-earth personality and his extraordinary mind, at ease in his daily surroundings. Meetings with Jung serves as an ideal introduction to Jungian psychology while providing a rare, intimate perspective into Jung's life and work for those already familiar with the more scholarly literature.

125 pages, ISBN 3-85630-501-7

The Rock Rabbit
and
The Rainbow

Laurens van der Post
among Friends

The Rock Rabbit and The Rainbow
Laurens van der Post among Friends

Sir Laurens van der Post, author, filmmaker, storyteller of worldwide renown, soldier, prisoner of war, political advisor to heads of state, humanitarian, explorer, conservationist ... the list goes on and on. His extraordinary curiosity, his love for the small and the great, and his tremendous feeling and concern for his surroundings and all that they included, set him traveling the lands and the waters of the world, a messenger in search of meaning. He touched and inspired many along the way, some of whom are to be found in the pages of this book.

A true man of his time, Sir Laurens was born in 1906 in the interior of South Africa, served in the British forces during World War II, including three-and-a-half years in Japanese captivity, and lived and worked since that time in London, where he died just after celebrating his 90th birthday in December, 1996.

The Rock Rabbit and The Rainbow was originally conceived as a *Festschrift*, or gift collection of writings, for Sir Laurens by several of his friends and then evolved into its present form, which includes numerous original contributions by Sir Laurens himself.

hardcover, 400 pages, illustrated, ISBN 3-85630-512-2

Alan McGlashan
The Savage and Beautiful Country

Alan McGlashan presents a sensitive view of the modern world and of time, of our memories and forgetfulness, joys and sorrows. He takes the reader on a safari into regions that are strange and yet familiar – into the savage and beautiful country of the mind. No "cures" are offered, but we are provoked to reflect on our roles and attitudes in the contemporary world jungle.

Alan McGlashan conveys a poetic vision which has more to do with life as it can be lived than all the experiments of the laboratory psychologist or the dialectic of the professional philosopher.
            – The Times Literary Supplement

A highly provocative work, filled with astonishing and exciting insights about the less rational aspects of man, but communicated to the intelligent layman in an engagingly informal manner. – Library Journal

228 pages, ISBN 3-85630-517-3

ENGLISH PUBLICATIONS BY **DAIMON**

ENGLISH PUBLICATIONS BY **DAIMON**